Lecture Notes in Computer Science　　10804

Commenced Publication in 1973
Founding and Former Series Editors:
Gerhard Goos, Juris Hartmanis, and Jan van Leeuwen

Advanced Research in Computing and Software Science
Subline of Lecture Notes in Computer Science

More information about this series at http://www.springer.com/series/7410

Lujo Bauer · Ralf Küsters (Eds.)

Principles of Security and Trust

7th International Conference, POST 2018
Held as Part of the European Joint Conferences
on Theory and Practice of Software, ETAPS 2018
Thessaloniki, Greece, April 14–20, 2018
Proceedings

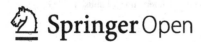

Editors
Lujo Bauer
Carnegie Mellon University
Pittsburgh, PA
USA

Ralf Küsters
University of Stuttgart
Stuttgart
Germany

ISSN 0302-9743   ISSN 1611-3349   (electronic)
Lecture Notes in Computer Science
ISBN 978-3-319-89721-9   ISBN 978-3-319-89722-6   (eBook)
https://doi.org/10.1007/978-3-319-89722-6

Library of Congress Control Number: 2018939619

LNCS Sublibrary: SL4 – Security and Cryptology

Printed on acid-free paper

This Springer imprint is published by the registered company Springer International Publishing AG
part of Springer Nature
The registered company address is: Gewerbestrasse 11, 6330 Cham, Switzerland

ETAPS Foreword

Welcome to the proceedings of ETAPS 2018! After a somewhat coldish ETAPS 2017 in Uppsala in the north, ETAPS this year took place in Thessaloniki, Greece. I am happy to announce that this is the first ETAPS with gold open access proceedings. This means that all papers are accessible by anyone for free.

ETAPS 2018 was the 21st instance of the European Joint Conferences on Theory and Practice of Software. ETAPS is an annual federated conference established in 1998, and consists of five conferences: ESOP, FASE, FoSSaCS, TACAS, and POST. Each conference has its own Program Committee (PC) and its own Steering Committee. The conferences cover various aspects of software systems, ranging from theoretical computer science to foundations to programming language developments, analysis tools, formal approaches to software engineering, and security. Organizing these conferences in a coherent, highly synchronized conference program facilitates participation in an exciting event, offering attendees the possibility to meet many researchers working in different directions in the field, and to easily attend talks of different conferences. Before and after the main conference, numerous satellite workshops take place and attract many researchers from all over the globe.

ETAPS 2018 received 479 submissions in total, 144 of which were accepted, yielding an overall acceptance rate of 30%. I thank all the authors for their interest in ETAPS, all the reviewers for their peer reviewing efforts, the PC members for their contributions, and in particular the PC (co-)chairs for their hard work in running this entire intensive process. Last but not least, my congratulations to all authors of the accepted papers!

ETAPS 2018 was enriched by the unifying invited speaker Martin Abadi (Google Brain, USA) and the conference-specific invited speakers (FASE) Pamela Zave (AT & T Labs, USA), (POST) Benjamin C. Pierce (University of Pennsylvania, USA), and (ESOP) Derek Dreyer (Max Planck Institute for Software Systems, Germany). Invited tutorials were provided by Armin Biere (Johannes Kepler University, Linz, Austria) on modern SAT solving and Fabio Somenzi (University of Colorado, Boulder, USA) on hardware verification. My sincere thanks to all these speakers for their inspiring and interesting talks!

ETAPS 2018 took place in Thessaloniki, Greece, and was organised by the Department of Informatics of the Aristotle University of Thessaloniki. The university was founded in 1925 and currently has around 75,000 students; it is the largest university in Greece. ETAPS 2018 was further supported by the following associations and societies: ETAPS e.V., EATCS (European Association for Theoretical Computer Science), EAPLS (European Association for Programming Languages and Systems), and EASST (European Association of Software Science and Technology). The local organization team consisted of Panagiotis Katsaros (general chair), Ioannis Stamelos,

Lefteris Angelis, George Rahonis, Nick Bassiliades, Alexander Chatzigeorgiou, Ezio Bartocci, Simon Bliudze, Emmanouela Stachtiari, Kyriakos Georgiadis, and Petros Stratis (EasyConferences).

The overall planning for ETAPS is the main responsibility of the Steering Committee, and in particular of its Executive Board. The ETAPS Steering Committee consists of an Executive Board and representatives of the individual ETAPS conferences, as well as representatives of EATCS, EAPLS, and EASST. The Executive Board consists of Gilles Barthe (Madrid), Holger Hermanns (Saarbrücken), Joost-Pieter Katoen (chair, Aachen and Twente), Gerald Lüttgen (Bamberg), Vladimiro Sassone (Southampton), Tarmo Uustalu (Tallinn), and Lenore Zuck (Chicago). Other members of the Steering Committee are: Wil van der Aalst (Aachen), Parosh Abdulla (Uppsala), Amal Ahmed (Boston), Christel Baier (Dresden), Lujo Bauer (Pittsburgh), Dirk Beyer (Munich), Mikolaj Bojanczyk (Warsaw), Luis Caires (Lisbon), Jurriaan Hage (Utrecht), Rainer Hähnle (Darmstadt), Reiko Heckel (Leicester), Marieke Huisman (Twente), Panagiotis Katsaros (Thessaloniki), Ralf Küsters (Stuttgart), Ugo Dal Lago (Bologna), Kim G. Larsen (Aalborg), Matteo Maffei (Vienna), Tiziana Margaria (Limerick), Flemming Nielson (Copenhagen), Catuscia Palamidessi (Palaiseau), Andrew M. Pitts (Cambridge), Alessandra Russo (London), Dave Sands (Göteborg), Don Sannella (Edinburgh), Andy Schürr (Darmstadt), Alex Simpson (Ljubljana), Gabriele Taentzer (Marburg), Peter Thiemann (Freiburg), Jan Vitek (Prague), Tomas Vojnar (Brno), and Lijun Zhang (Beijing).

I would like to take this opportunity to thank all speakers, attendees, organizers of the satellite workshops, and Springer for their support. I hope you all enjoy the proceedings of ETAPS 2018. Finally, a big thanks to Panagiotis and his local organization team for all their enormous efforts that led to a fantastic ETAPS in Thessaloniki!

February 2018   Joost-Pieter Katoen

Preface

This volume contains the papers presented at POST 2018, the 7th Conference on Principles of Security and Trust, held April 16–17, 2018, in Thessaloniki, Greece, as part of ETAPS. Principles of Security and Trust is a broad forum related to all theoretical and foundational aspects of security and trust, and thus welcomes papers of many kinds: new theoretical results, practical applications of existing foundational ideas, and innovative approaches stimulated by pressing practical problems; as well as systemization-of-knowledge papers, papers describing tools, and position papers. POST was created in 2012 to combine and replace a number of successful and long-standing workshops in this area: Automated Reasoning and Security Protocol Analysis (ARSPA), Formal Aspects of Security and Trust (FAST), Security in Concurrency (SecCo), and the Workshop on Issues in the Theory of Security (WITS). A subset of these events met jointly as an event affiliated with ETAPS 2011 under the name "Theory of Security and Applications" (TOSCA).

There were 45 submissions to POST 2018. Each submission was reviewed by at least three Program Committee members, who in some cases solicited the help of outside experts to review the papers. We employed a double-blind reviewing process with a rebuttal phase. Electronic discussion was used to decide which papers to select for the program. The committee decided to accept 14 papers, including one SoK paper and one tool demonstration paper.

We would like to thank the members of the Program Committee, the additional reviewers, the POST Steering Committee, the ETAPS Steering Committee, and the local Organizing Committee, who all contributed to the success of POST 2018. We also thank all authors of submitted papers for their interest in POST and congratulate the authors of accepted papers.

March 2018

Lujo Bauer
Ralf Küsters

Organization

Program Committee

Lujo Bauer	Carnegie Mellon University, USA
Karthikeyan Bhargavan	Inria, France
Nataliia Bielova	Inria, France
Stephen Chong	Harvard University, USA
Veronique Cortier	CNRS, Loria, France
Stephanie Delaune	IRISA, France
Cormac Flanagan	U. C. Santa Cruz, USA
Riccardo Focardi	Università Ca' Foscari, Venezia, Italy
Michael Hicks	University of Maryland, USA
Ralf Küsters	University of Stuttgart, Germany
Anja Lehmann	IBM Research – Zurich, Switzerland
Jay Ligatti	University of South Florida, USA
Sergio Maffeis	Imperial College London,UK
Heiko Mantel	TU Darmstadt, Germany
Catherine Meadows	NRL
Frank Piessens	Katholieke Universiteit Leuven, Belgium
Tamara Rezk	Inria, France
Andrei Sabelfeld	Chalmers University of Technology, Sweden
Gregor Snelting	Karlsruhe Institute of Technology, Germany
Cynthia Sturton	The University of North Carolina at Chapel Hill, USA
Vanessa Teague	The University of Melbourne, Australia
Luca Viganò	King's College London, UK

Additional Reviewers

Calzavara, Stefano	Ngo, Minh
De Maria, Elisabetta	Ochoa, Martin
Kiesel, Sebastian	Rafnsson, Willard
Kremer, Steve	Vassena, Marco
Mardziel, Piotr	

The Science of Deep Specification
(Abstract of Invited Talk)

Benjamin C. Pierce[ID]

University of Pennsylvania

Formal specifications significantly improve the security and robustness of critical, low-level software and hardware, especially when deeply integrated into the processes of system engineering and design [4]. Such "deep specifications" can also be challenging to work with, since they must be simultaneously *rich* (describing complex component behaviors in detail), *two-sided* (connected to both implementations and clients), and *live* (connected directly to the source code of implementations via machine-checkable proofs and/or automated testing).

The DeepSpec project [1] is a multi-institution effort to develop experience with building and using serious specifications at many architectural levels—hardware instruction-set architectures (MIT), hypervisor kernels (Yale), C semantics (Princeton, Yale), compilers for both C (Penn, Princeton, Yale) and functional languages (Penn, Princeton), cryptographic operations (Princeton, MIT), and web infrastructure (Penn)—and to create new tools for machine-assisted formal verification [2, 3, 5] and specification-based testing [6], all within the Coq ecosystem.

To exercise several of these specifications together, we are building a formally specified, tested, and verified web server. Our goal is a "single Q.E.D." spanning all levels of the system—from an executable specification of correct server behavior in terms of valid sequences of HTTP requests and responses, all the way down to an RTL description of a RISC-V chip and the binary code for a hypervisor running on that chip.

References

1. deepspec.org
2. Appel, A.W.: Verified software toolchain. In: G. Barthe (ed.) ESOP 2011. LNCS, vol. 6602, pp. 1–17. Springer, Heidelberg (2011)
3. Choi, J., Vijayaraghavan, M., Sherman, B., Chlipala, A., Arvind: Kami: a platform for high-level parametric hardware specification and its modular verification. In: Proceedings of the 22nd ACM SIGPLAN International Conference on Functional Programming, ICFP 2017 (2017). http://adam.chlipala.net/papers/KamiICFP17/
4. Fisher, K., Launchbury, J., Richards, R.: The HACMS program: using formal methods to eliminate exploitable bugs. Phil. Trans. R. Soc. A **375**(2104), 20150401 (2017)

5. Gu, R., Shao, Z., Chen, H., Wu, X.N., Kim, J., Sjöberg, V., Costanzo, D.: CertiKOS: an extensible architecture for building certified concurrent OS kernels. In: 12th USENIX Symposium on Operating Systems Design and Implementation, OSDI 2016, pp. 653–669. USENIX Association, GA (2016)
6. Paraskevopoulou, Z., Hriţcu, C., Dénès, M., Lampropoulos, L., Pierce, B.C.: Foundational property-based testing. In: International Conference on Interactive Theorem Proving, ITP 2015 (2015)

Contents

XIV   Contents

Information Flow and Non-intereference

What's the Over/Under? Probabilistic Bounds on Information Leakage

Ian Sweet[1], José Manuel Calderón Trilla[2], Chad Scherrer[2], Michael Hicks[1], and Stephen Magill[2(✉)]

[1] University of Maryland, College Park, USA
[2] Galois Inc., Portland, USA
stephen@galois.com

Abstract. Quantitative information flow (QIF) is concerned with measuring how much of a secret is leaked to an adversary who observes the result of a computation that uses it. Prior work has shown that QIF techniques based on *abstract interpretation* with *probabilistic polyhedra* can be used to analyze the worst-case leakage of a query, on-line, to determine whether that query can be safely answered. While this approach can provide precise estimates, it does not scale well. This paper shows how to solve the scalability problem by augmenting the baseline technique with *sampling* and *symbolic execution*. We prove that our approach never underestimates a query's leakage (it is sound), and detailed experimental results show that we can match the precision of the baseline technique but with orders of magnitude better performance.

1 Introduction

As more sensitive data is created, collected, and analyzed, we face the problem of how to productively use this data while preserving privacy. One approach to this problem is to analyze a query f in order to *quantify* how much information about secret input s is leaked by the output $f(s)$. More precisely, we can consider a querier to have some *prior belief* of the secret's possible values. The belief can be modeled as a probability distribution [10], i.e., a function δ from each possible value of s to its probability. When a querier observes output $o = f(s)$, he *revises* his belief, using Bayesian inference, to produce a *posterior* distribution δ'. If the posterior could reveal too much about the secret, then the query should be rejected. One common definition of "too much" is *Bayes Vulnerability*, which is the probability of the adversary guessing the secret in one try [41]. Formally,

$$V(\delta) \stackrel{\text{def}}{=} \max_i \delta(i)$$

Various works [6,19,24,25] propose rejecting f if there exists an output that makes the vulnerability of the posterior exceed a fixed threshold K. In particular, for all possible values i of s (i.e., $\delta(i) > 0$), if the output $o = f(i)$ could induce a posterior δ' with $V(\delta') > K$, then the query is rejected.

© The Author(s) 2018
L. Bauer and R. Küsters (Eds.): POST 2018, LNCS 10804, pp. 3–27, 2018.
https://doi.org/10.1007/978-3-319-89722-6_1

One way to implement this approach is to estimate $f(\delta)$—the distribution of f's outputs when the inputs are distributed according to δ—by viewing f as a program in a *probabilistic programming language* (PPL) [18]. Unfortunately, as discussed in Sect. 9, most PPLs are approximate in a manner that could easily result in *underestimating* the vulnerability, leading to an unsafe security decision. Techniques designed specifically to quantify information leakage often assume only uniform priors, cannot compute vulnerability (favoring, for example, Shannon entropy), and/or cannot maintain assumed knowledge between queries.

Mardziel et al. [25] propose a *sound* analysis technique based on abstract interpretation [12]. In particular, they estimate a program's probability distribution using an abstract domain called a *probabilistic polyhedron* (PP), which pairs a standard numeric abstract domain, such as *convex polyhedra* [13], with some additional *ornaments*, which include lower and upper bounds on the size of the support of the distribution, and bounds on the probability of each possible secret value. Using PP can yield a precise, yet safe, estimate of the vulnerability, and allows the posterior PP (which is not necessarily uniform) to be used as a prior for the next query. Unfortunately, PPs can be very inefficient. Defining *intervals* [11] as the PP's numeric domain can dramatically improve performance, but only with an unacceptable loss of precision.

In this paper we present a new approach that ensures a better balance of both precision and performance in vulnerability computation, augmenting PP with two new techniques. In both cases we begin by analyzing a query using the fast interval-based analysis. Our first technique is then to use *sampling* to augment the result. In particular, we execute the query using possible secret values i sampled from the posterior δ' derived from a particular output o_i. If the analysis were perfectly accurate, executing $f(i)$ would produce o_i. But since intervals are overapproximate, sometimes it will not. With many sampled outcomes, we can construct a Beta distribution to estimate the size of the support of the posterior, up to some level of confidence. We can use this estimate to boost the lower bound of the abstraction, and thus improve the precision of the estimated vulnerability.

Our second technique is of a similar flavor, but uses symbolic reasoning to magnify the impact of a successful sample. In particular, we execute a query result-consistent sample *concolically* [39], thus maintaining a symbolic formula (called the *path condition*) that characterizes the set of variable valuations that would cause execution to follow the observed path. We then count the number of possible solutions and use the count to boost the lower bound of the support (with 100% confidence).

Sampling and concolic execution can be combined for even greater precision.

We have formalized and proved our techniques are sound (Sects. 3–6) and implemented and evaluated them (Sects. 7 and 8). Using a privacy-sensitive ship planning scenario (Sect. 2) we find that our techniques provide similar precision to convex polyhedra while providing orders-of-magnitude better performance. More experiments are needed to see if the approach provides such benefits more generally. Our implementation freely available at https://github.com/GaloisInc/TAMBA.

Field	Type	Range	Private?
ShipID	Integer	1–10	No
NationID	Integer	1–20	No
Capacity	Integer	0–1000	Yes
Latitude	Integer	-900,000–900,000	Yes
Longitude	Integer	-1,800,000–1,800,000	Yes

Fig. 1. The data model used in the evacuation scenario.

2 Overview

To provide an overview of our approach, we will describe the application of our techniques to a scenario that involves a coalition of ships from various nations operating in a shared region. Suppose a natural disaster has impacted some islands in the region. Some number of individuals need to be evacuated from the islands, and it falls to a regional disaster response coordinator to determine how to accomplish this. While the coalition wants to collaborate to achieve these humanitarian aims, we assume that each nation also wants to protect their sensitive data—namely ship locations and capacity.

More formally, we assume the use of the data model shown in Fig. 1, which considers a set of ships, their coalition affiliation, the evacuation capacity of the ship, and its position, given in terms of latitude and longitude.[1] We sometimes refer to the latter two as a location L, with $L.x$ as the longitude and $L.y$ as the latitude. We will often index properties by ship ID, writing Capacity(z) for the capacity associated with ship ID z, or Location(z) for the location.

The **evacuation problem** is defined as follows

Given a target location L and number of people to evacuate N, compute a set of nearby ships S such that $\sum_{z \in S} \text{Capacity}(z) \geq N$.

Our goal is to solve this problem in a way that minimizes the vulnerability to the coordinator of private information, i.e., the ship locations and their exact capacity. We assume that this coordinator initially has no knowledge of the positions or capabilities of the ships other than that they fall within certain expected ranges.

If all members of the coalition share all of their data with the coordinator, then a solution is easy to compute, but it affords no privacy. Figure 2 gives an algorithm the response coordinator can follow that does not require each member to share all of their data. Instead, it iteratively performs queries *AtLeast* and *Nearby*. These queries do not reveal precise values about ship locations or capacity, but rather admit ranges of possibilities. The algorithm works by maintaining upper and lower bounds on the capacity of each ship i in the array berths. Each ship's bounds are updated based on the results of queries about its

---

[1] We give latitude and longitude values as integer representations of *decimal degrees* fixed to four decimal places; e.g., 14.3579 decimal degrees is encoded as 143579.

capacity and location. These queries aim to be privacy preserving, doing a sort of binary search to narrow in on the capacity of each ship in the operating area. The procedure completes once is_solution determines the minimum required capacity is reached.

```
(* S = #ships; N = #evacuees; L = island loc.;  D = min. proximity to L *)
    let  berths  = Array.make S (0,1000)
    let  is_solution  () = sum (Array.map fst berths) ≥ N
    let  mid (x,y) = (x + y) / 2
    let  AtLeast(z,b) = Capacity(z) ≥ b
    let  Nearby(z,l,d) = |Loc(z).x − l.x| + |Loc(z).y − l.y| ≤ d
    while true do
      for  i = 0 to S do
        let  ask = mid berths[i]
        let  ok = AtLeast(i,ask) && Nearby(i,L,D)
        if  ok then    berths[i] ← (ask, snd berths[i])
        else           berths[i] ← (fst berths[i], ask)
        if  is_solution () then return berths
      done
    done
```

Fig. 2. Algorithm to solve the evacuation problem for a single island.

2.1   Computing Vulnerability with Abstract Interpretation

Using this procedure, what is revealed about the private variables (location and capacity)? Consider a single $Nearby(z, l, d)$ query. At the start, the coordinator is assumed to know only that z is somewhere within the operating region. If the query returns true, the coordinator now knows that s is within d units of l (using Manhattan distance). This makes $Location(z)$ more vulnerable because the adversary has less uncertainty about it.

Mardziel et al. [25] proposed a static analysis for analyzing queries such as $Nearby(z, l, d)$ to estimate the worst-case vulnerability of private data. If the worst-case vulnerability is too great, the query can be rejected. A key element of their approach is to perform abstract interpretation over the query using an abstract domain called a *probabilistic polyhedron*. An element P of this domain represents the set of possible distributions over the query's state. This state includes both the hidden secrets and the visible query results. The abstract interpretation is sound in the sense that the true distribution δ is contained in the set of distributions represented by the computed probabilistic polyhedron P.

A probabilistic polyhedron P is a tuple comprising a *shape* and three *ornaments*. The shape C is an element of a standard numeric domain—e.g., intervals [11], octagons [29], or convex polyhedra [13]—which overapproximates the set of possible values in the support of the distribution. The ornaments $p \in [0, 1]$, $m \in \mathbb{R}$, and $s \in \mathbb{Z}$ are pairs which store upper and lower bounds on the probability per point, the total mass, and number of support points in the distribution, respectively. (Distributions represented by P are not necessarily normalized, so the mass m is not always 1.)

Figure 3(a) gives an example probabilistic polyhedron that represents the posterior of a *Nearby* query that returns true. In particular, if *Nearby(z,L$_1$,D)* is true then Location(z) is somewhere within the depicted diamond around L_1. Using convex polyhedra or octagons for the shape domain would permit representing this diamond exactly; using intervals would overapproximate it as the depicted 9×9 bounding box. The ornaments would be the same in any case: the size s of the support is 41 possible (x,y) points, the probability p per point is 0.01, and the total mass is 0.41, i.e., $p \cdot s$. In general, each ornament is a pair of a lower and upper bound (e.g., s_{min} and s_{max}), and m might be a more accurate estimate than $p \cdot s$. In this case shown in the figure, the bounds are tight.

Mardziel et al's procedure works by computing the posterior P for each possible query output o, and from that posterior determining the vulnerability. This is easy to do. The upper bound p_{max} of p maximizes the probability of any given point. Dividing this by the *lower bound* m_{min} of the probability mass m normalizes this probability for the worst case. For P shown in Fig. 3(a), the bounds of p and m are tight, so the vulnerability is simply $0.01/0.41 = 0.024$.

2.2   Improving Precision with Sampling and Concolic Execution

In Fig. 3(a), the parameters s, p, and m are precise. However, as additional operations are performed, these quantities can accumulate imprecision. For example, suppose we are using intervals for the shape domain, and we wish to analyze the query $Nearby(z, L_1, 4) \vee Nearby(z, L_2, 4)$ (for some nearby point L_2). The result is produced by analyzing the two queries separately and then combining them with an *abstract join*; this is shown in the top row of Fig. 3(b). Unfortunately, the result is very imprecise. The bottom row of Fig. 3(b) illustrates the result we would get by using convex polyhedra as our shape domain. When using intervals (top row), the vulnerability is estimated as 0.036, whereas the precise answer (bottom row) is actually 0.026. Unfortunately, obtaining this precise answer is far more expensive than obtaining the imprecise one.

This paper presents two techniques that can allow us to use the less precise interval domain but then *recover* lost precision in a relatively cheap post-processing step. The effect of our techniques is shown in the middle-right of Fig. 3(b). Both techniques aim to obtain better lower bounds for s. This allows us to update lower bounds on the probability mass m since m_{min} is at least $s_{min} \cdot p_{min}$ (each point has at least probability p_{min} and there are at least s_{min} of them). A larger m means a smaller vulnerability.

The first technique we explore is *sampling*, depicted to the right of the arrow in Fig. 3(b). Sampling chooses random points and evaluates the query on them to determine whether they are in the support of the posterior distribution for a particular query result. By tracking the ratio of points that produce the expected output, we can produce an estimate of s, whose confidence increases as we include more samples. This approach is depicted in the figure, where we conclude that $s \in [72, 81]$ and $m \in [0.72, 1.62]$ with 90% confidence after taking 1000 samples, improving our vulnerability estimate to $V \leq \frac{0.02}{0.72} = 0.028$.

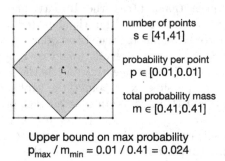

(a) Probabilistic polyhedra

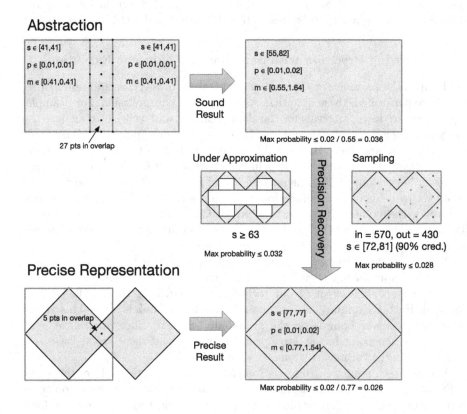

(b) Improving precision with sampling and underapproximation (concolic execution)

Fig. 3. Computing vulnerability (max probability) using abstract interpretation

Variables	x	$\in$ **Var**
Integers	n	$\in$ $\mathbb{Z}$
Rationals	q	$\in$ $\mathbb{Q}$
States	σ	$\in$ **State** $\stackrel{\text{def}}{=}$ **Var** $\rightharpoonup$ $\mathbb{Z}$
Distributions	δ	$\in$ **Dist** $\stackrel{\text{def}}{=}$ **State** $\to$ $\mathbb{R}+_0$
Arith.ops	aop	$::= +\ \vert\ \times\ \vert\ -$
Rel.ops	$relop$	$::= \leq\ \vert\ <\ \vert\ =\ \vert\ \neq\ \vert\ \cdots$
Arith.exps	E	$::= x\ \vert\ n\ \vert\ E_1\ aop\ E_2$
Bool.exps	B	$::= E_1\ relop\ E_2\ \vert\ B_1 \wedge B_2\ \vert\ B_1 \vee B_2\ \vert\ \neg B$
Statements	S	$::= \mathsf{skip}\ \vert\ x := E\ \vert\ S_1\ ;\ S_2\ \vert\ \mathsf{while}\ B\ \mathsf{do}\ S\ \vert$
		$\mathsf{if}\ B\ \mathsf{then}\ S_1\ \mathsf{else}\ S_2\ \vert\ \mathsf{pif}\ q\ \mathsf{then}\ S_1\ \mathsf{else}\ S_2$

Fig. 4. Core language syntax

The second technique we explore is the use of *concolic execution* to derive a *path condition*, which is a formula over secret values that is consistent with a query result. By performing *model counting* to estimate the number of solutions to this formula, which are an underapproximation of the true size of the distribution, we can safely boost the lower bound of s. This approach is depicted to the left of the arrow in Fig. 3(b). The depicted shapes represent discovered path condition's disjuncts, whose size sums to 63. This is a better lower bound on s and improves the vulnerability estimate to 0.032.

These techniques can be used together to further increase precision. In particular, we can first perform concolic execution, and then sample from the area not covered by this underapproximation. Importantly, Sect. 8 shows that using our techniques with the interval-based analysis yields an orders of magnitude performance improvement over using polyhedra-based analysis alone, while achieving similar levels of precision, with high confidence.

3   Preliminaries: Syntax and Semantics

This section presents the core language—syntax and semantics—in which we formalize our approach to computing vulnerability. We also review *probabilistic polyhedra* [25], which is the baseline analysis technique that we augment.

3.1   Core Language and Semantics

The programming language we use for queries is given in Fig. 4. The language is essentially standard, apart from $\mathsf{pif}\ q\ \mathsf{then}\ S_1\ \mathsf{else}\ S_2$, which implements probabilistic choice: S_1 is executed with probability q, and S_2 with probability $1 - q$. We limit the form of expressions E so that they can be approximated by standard numeric abstract domains such as convex polyhedra [13]. Such domains require linear forms; e.g., there is no division operator and multiplication of two variables is disallowed.[2]

---

[2] Relaxing such limitations is possible—e.g., polynominal inequalities can be approximated using convex polyhedra [5]—but doing so precisely and scalably is a challenge.

We define the semantics of a program in terms of its effect on (discrete) distributions of states. States σ are partial maps from variables to integers; we write $domain(\sigma)$ for the set of variables over which σ is defined. Distributions δ are maps from states to nonnegative real numbers, interpreted as probabilities (in range $[0, 1]$). The denotational semantics considers a program as a relation between distributions. In particular, the semantics of statement S, written $[\![S]\!]$, is a function of the form $\textbf{Dist} \rightarrow \textbf{Dist}$; we write $[\![S]\!]\delta = \delta'$ to say that the semantics of S maps input distribution δ to output distribution δ'. Distributions are not necessarily normalized; we write $\|\delta\|$ as the probability mass of δ (which is between 0 and 1). We write $\dot{\sigma}$ to denote the point distribution that gives σ probability 1, and all other states 0.

The semantics is standard and not crucial in order to understand our techniques. In Appendix B we provide the semantics in full. See Clarkson et al. [10] or Mardziel et al. [25] for detailed explanations.

3.2 Probabilistic Polyhedra

To compute vulnerability for a program S we must compute (an approximation of) its output distribution. One way to do that would be to use sampling: Choose states σ at random from the input distribution δ, "run" the program using that input state, and collect the frequencies of output states σ' into a distribution δ'. While using sampling in this manner is simple and appealing, it could be both expensive and imprecise. In particular, depending on the size of the input and output space, it may take many samples to arrive at a proper approximation of the output distribution.

Probabilistic polyhedra [25] can address both problems. This abstract domain combines a standard domain C for representing numeric program states with additional *ornaments* that all together can safely represent S's output distribution.

Probabilistic polyhedra work for any numeric domain; in this paper we use both convex polyhedra [13] and intervals [11]. For concreteness, we present the definition using convex polyhedra. We use the meta-variables β, β_1, β_2, etc. to denote linear inequalities.

Definition 1. *A convex polyhedron $C = (B, V)$ is a set of linear inequalities $B = \{\beta_1, \ldots, \beta_m\}$, interpreted conjunctively, over variables V. We write $\mathbb{C}$ for the set of all convex polyhedra. A polyhedron C represents a set of states, denoted $\gamma_{\mathbb{C}}(C)$, as follows, where $\sigma \models \beta$ indicates that the state σ satisfies the inequality β.*

$$\gamma_{\mathbb{C}}((B, V)) \stackrel{\text{def}}{=} \{\sigma \ : \ domain(\sigma) = V, \ \forall \beta \in B. \ \sigma \models \beta\}$$

Naturally we require that $domain(\{\beta_1, \ldots, \beta_n\}) \subseteq V$; i.e., V mentions all variables in the inequalities. Let $domain((B, V)) = V$.

Probabilistic polyhedra extend this standard representation of sets of program states to sets of *distributions* over program states.

Definition 2. *A probabilistic polyhedron P is a tuple $(C, \mathrm{s}^{\min}, \mathrm{s}^{\max}, \mathrm{p}^{\min}, \mathrm{p}^{\max}, \mathrm{m}^{\min}, \mathrm{m}^{\max})$. We write $\mathbb{P}$ for the set of probabilistic polyhedra. The quantities $\mathrm{s}^{\min}$ and $\mathrm{s}^{\max}$ are lower and upper bounds on the number of support points in the concrete distribution(s) P represents. A support point of a distribution is one which has non-zero probability. The quantities $\mathrm{p}^{\min}$ and $\mathrm{p}^{\max}$ are lower and upper bounds on the probability mass per support point. The $\mathrm{m}^{\min}$ and $\mathrm{m}^{\max}$ components give bounds on the total probability mass (i.e., the sum of the probabilities of all support points). Thus P represents the set of distributions $\gamma_{\mathbb{P}}(P)$ defined below.*

$$\gamma_{\mathbb{P}}(P) \overset{\text{def}}{=} \{\delta \ : \ support(\delta) \subseteq \gamma_{\mathbb{C}}(C) \ \wedge$$
$$\mathrm{s}^{\min} \leq |support(\delta)| \leq \mathrm{s}^{\max} \ \wedge$$
$$\mathrm{m}^{\min} \leq \|\delta\| \leq \mathrm{m}^{\max} \wedge$$
$$\forall \sigma \in support(\delta). \ \mathrm{p}^{\min} \leq \delta(\sigma) \leq \mathrm{p}^{\max}\}$$

We will write $domain(P) \overset{\text{def}}{=} domain(C)$ to denote the set of variables used in the probabilistic polyhedron.

Note the set $\gamma_{\mathbb{P}}(P)$ is a singleton exactly when $\mathrm{s}^{\min} = \mathrm{s}^{\max} = \#(C)$ and $\mathrm{p}^{\min} = \mathrm{p}^{\max}$, and $\mathrm{m}^{\min} = \mathrm{m}^{\max}$, where $\#(C)$ denotes the number of discrete points in convex polyhedron C. In such a case $\gamma_{\mathbb{P}}(P)$ contains only the uniform distribution where each state in $\gamma_{\mathbb{C}}(C)$ has probability $\mathrm{p}^{\min}$. In general, however, the concretization of a probabilistic polyhedron will have an infinite number of distributions, with per-point probabilities varied somewhere in the range $\mathrm{p}^{\min}$ and $\mathrm{p}^{\max}$. Distributions represented by a probabilistic polyhedron are not necessarily normalized. In general, there is a relationship between $\mathrm{p}^{\min}, \mathrm{s}^{\min}$, and $\mathrm{m}^{\min}$, in that $\mathrm{m}^{\min} \geq \mathrm{p}^{\min} \cdot \mathrm{s}^{\min}$ (and $\mathrm{m}^{\max} \leq \mathrm{p}^{\max} \cdot \mathrm{s}^{\max}$), and the combination of the three can yield more information than any two in isolation.

The *abstract semantics* of S is written $\langle\!\langle S \rangle\!\rangle \, P = P'$, and indicates that abstractly interpreting S where the distribution of input states are approximated by P will produce P', which approximates the distribution of output states. Following standard abstract interpretation terminology, $\wp\mathbf{Dist}$ (sets of distributions) is the *concrete domain*, $\mathbb{P}$ is the *abstract domain*, and $\gamma_{\mathbb{P}} : \mathbb{P} \to \wp\mathbf{Dist}$ is the *concretization function* for $\mathbb{P}$. We do not present the abstract semantics here; details can be found in Mardziel et al. [25]. Importantly, this abstract semantics is sound:

Theorem 1 (Soundness). *For all $S, P_1, P_2, \delta_1, \delta_2$, if $\delta_1 \in \gamma_{\mathbb{P}}(P_1)$ and $\langle\!\langle S \rangle\!\rangle \, P_1 = P_2$, then $[\![S]\!]\delta_1 = \delta_2$ with $\delta_2 \in \gamma_{\mathbb{P}}(P_2)$.*

Proof. See Theorem 6 in Mardziel et al. [25].

Consider the example from Sect. 2.2. We assume the adversary has no prior information about the location of ship s. So, δ_1 above is simply the uniform distribution over all possible locations. The statement S is the query issued by the adversary, $Nearby(z, L_1, 4) \vee Nearby(z, L_2, 4)$.[3] If we assume that the result of the

---

[3] Appendix A shows the code, which computes Manhattan distance between s and L_1 and L_2 and then sets an output variable if either distance is within four units.

query is $|\mathsf{true}|$ then the adversary learns that the location of s is within (Manhattan) distance 4 of L_1 or L_2. This posterior belief (δ_2) is represented by the overlapping diamonds on the bottom-right of Fig. 3(b). The abstract interpretation produces a sound (interval) overapproximation (P_2) of the posterior belief. This is modeled by the rectangle which surrounds the overlapping diamonds. This rectangle is the "join" of two overlapping boxes, which each correspond to one of the *Nearby* calls in the disjuncts of S.

4   Computing Vulnerability: Basic Procedure

The key goal of this paper is to quantify the risk to secret information of running a query over that information. This section explains the basic approach by which we can use probabilistic polyhedra to compute *vulnerability*, i.e., the probability of the most probable point of the posterior distribution. Improvements on this basic approach are given in the next two sections.

Our convention will be to use C_1, $s_1^{\min}$, $s_1^{\max}$, etc. for the components associated with probabilistic polyhedron P_1. In the program S of interest, we assume that secret variables are in the set T, so input states are written σ_T, and we assume there is a single output variable r. We assume that the adversary's initial uncertainty about the possible values of the secrets T is captured by the probabilistic polyhedron P_0 (such that $domain(P_0) \supseteq T$).

Computing vulnerability occurs according to the following procedure.

1. Perform abstract interpretation: $\langle\!\langle S \rangle\!\rangle P_0 = P$
2. Given a concrete output value of interest, o, perform abstract conditioning to define $P_{r=o} \overset{\text{def}}{=} (P \wedge r = o)$.[4]

The vulnerability V is the probability of the most likely state(s). When a probabilistic polyhedron represents one or more true distributions (i.e., the probabilities all sum to 1), the most probable state's probability is bounded by $\mathrm{p}^{\max}$. However, the abstract semantics does not always normalize the probabilistic polyhedron as it computes, so we need to scale $\mathrm{p}^{\max}$ according to the total probability mass. To ensure that our estimate is on the safe side, we scale $\mathrm{p}^{\max}$ using the *minimum* probability mass: $V = \frac{\mathrm{p}^{\max}}{\mathrm{m}^{\min}}$. In Fig. 3(b), the sound approximation in the top-right has $V \leq \frac{0.02}{0.55} = 0.036$ and the most precise approximation in the bottom-right has $V \leq \frac{0.02}{0.77} = 0.026$.

5   Improving Precision with Sampling

We can improve the precision of the basic procedure using sampling. First we introduce some notational convenience:

$$P_T \overset{\text{def}}{=} P \wedge (r = o) \downarrow T$$
$$P_{T+} \overset{\text{def}}{=} P_T \text{ revised polyhedron with confidence } \omega$$

---

[4] We write $P \wedge B$ and not $P \mid B$ because P need not be normalized.

P_T is equivalent to step 2, above, but projected onto the set of secret variables T. P_{T+} is the improved (via sampling) polyhedron.

After computing P_T with the basic procedure from the previous section we take the following additional steps:

1. Set counters α and β to zero.
2. Do the following N times (for some N, see below):
   (a) Randomly select an input state $\sigma_T \in \gamma_C(C_T)$.
   (b) "Run" the program by computing $[\![S]\!]\acute{\sigma}_T = \delta$. If there exists $\sigma \in$ $support(\delta)$ with $\sigma(r) = o$ then increment α, else increment β.
3. We can interpret α and β as the parameters of a Beta distribution of the likelihood that an arbitrary state in $\gamma_C(C_T)$ is in the support of the true distribution. From these parameters we can compute the *credible interval* $[p_L, p_U]$ within which is contained the true likelihood, with confidence ω (where $0 \le \omega \le 1$). A credible interval is essentially a Bayesian analogue of a confidence interval and can be computed from the cumulative distribution function (CDF) of the Beta distribution (the 99% credible interval is the interval $[a, b]$ such that the CDF at a has value 0.005 and the CDF at b has value 0.995). In general, obtaining a higher confidence or a narrower interval will require a higher N. Let result $P_{T+} = P_T$ except that $s_{T+}^{min} = p_L \cdot \#(C_T)$ and $s_{T+}^{max} = p_U \cdot \#(C_T)$ (assuming these improve on s_T^{min} and s_T^{max}). We can then propagate these improvements to m^{min} and m^{max} by defining $m_{T+}^{min} = p_T^{min} \cdot s_{T+}^{min}$ and $m_{T+}^{max} = p_T^{max} \cdot s_{T+}^{max}$. Note that if $m_T^{min} > m_{T+}^{min}$ we leave it unchanged, and do likewise if $m_T^{max} < m_{T+}^{max}$.

At this point we can compute the vulnerability as in the basic procedure, but using P_{T+} instead of P_T.

Consider the example of Sect. 2.2. In Fig. 3(b), we draw samples from the rectangle in the top-right. This rectangle overapproximates the set of locations where s might be, given that the query returned true. We sample locations from this rectangle and run the query on each sample. The green (red) dots indicate true (false) results, which are added to α (β). After sampling $N = 1000$ locations, we have $\alpha = 570$ and $\beta = 430$. Choosing $\omega = .9$ (90%), we compute the credible interval $[0.53, 0.60]$. With $\#(C_T) = 135$, we compute $[s_{T+}^{min}, s_{T+}^{max}]$ as $[0.53 \cdot 135, 0.60 \cdot 135] = [72, 81]$.

There are several things to notice about this procedure. First, observe that in step 2b we "run" the program using the point distribution $\acute{\sigma}$ as an input; in the case that S is deterministic (has no pif statements) the output distribution will also be a point distribution. However, for programs with pif statements there are multiple possible outputs depending on which branch is taken by a pif. We consider all of these outputs so that we can confidently determine whether the input state σ could ever cause S to produce result o. If so, then σ should be considered part of P_{T+}. If not, then we can safely rule it out (i.e., it is part of the overapproximation).

Second, we only update the size parameters of P_{T+}; we make no changes to p_{T+}^{min} and p_{T+}^{max}. This is because our sampling procedure only determines whether it is *possible* for an input state to produce the expected output. The probability that an input state produces an output state is already captured (soundly) by p_T so we do not change that. This is useful because the approximation of p_T does not degrade with the use of the interval domain in the way the approximation of the size degrades (as illustrated in Fig. 3(b)). Using sampling is an attempt to regain the precision lost on the size component (only).

Finally, the confidence we have that sampling has accurately assessed which input states are in the support is orthogonal to the probability of any given state. In particular, P_T is an abstraction of a distribution δ_T, which is a mathematical object. Confidence ω is a measure of how likely it is that our abstraction (or, at least, the size part of it) is accurate.

We prove (in our extended report [43]) that our sampling procedure is sound:

Theorem 2 (Sampling is Sound). *If $\delta_0 \in \gamma_{\mathbb{P}}(P_0)$, $\langle\!\langle S \rangle\!\rangle P_0 = P$, and $[\![S]\!]\delta_0 = \delta$ then $\delta_T \in \gamma_{\mathbb{P}}(P_{T+})$ with confidence ω where*

$$\delta_T \overset{\text{def}}{=} \delta \wedge (r = o) \restriction T$$
$$P_T \overset{\text{def}}{=} P \wedge (r = o) \restriction T$$
$$P_{T+} \overset{\text{def}}{=} P_T \text{ sampling revised with confidence } \omega.$$

6 Improving Precision with Concolic Execution

Another approach to improving the precision of a probabilistic polyhedron P is to use concolic execution. The idea here is to "magnify" the impact of a single sample to soundly increase $s^{\min}$ by considering its execution *symbolically*. More precisely, we concretely execute a program using a particular secret value, but maintain symbolic constraints about how that value is used. This is referred to as *concolic* execution [39]. We use the collected constraints to identify all points that would induce the same execution path, which we can include as part of $s^{\min}$.

We begin by defining the semantics of concolic execution, and then show how it can be used to increase $s^{\min}$ soundly.

6.1 (Probabilistic) Concolic Execution

Concolic execution is expressed as rewrite rules defining a judgment $\langle \Pi, S \rangle \longrightarrow^p_\pi \langle \Pi', S' \rangle$. Here, Π is pair consisting of a concrete state σ and symbolic state ζ. The latter maps variables $x \in \mathbf{Var}$ to *symbolic expressions* $\mathcal{E}$ which extend expressions E with *symbolic variables* α. This judgment indicates that under input state Π the statement S reduces to statement S' and output state Π' with probability p, with *path condition* π. The path condition is a conjunction of boolean symbolic expressions $\mathcal{B}$ (which are just boolean expressions B but altered to use symbolic expressions $\mathcal{E}$ instead of expressions E) that record which branch is taken during execution. For brevity, we omit π in a rule when it is true.

The rules for the concolic semantics are given in Fig. 5. Most of these are standard, and deterministic (the probability annotation p is 1). Path conditions are recorded for if and while, depending on the branch taken. The semantics of

$$\langle(\sigma,\zeta),x := E\rangle \longrightarrow^1 \langle(\sigma[x \mapsto \sigma(E)], \zeta[x \mapsto \zeta(E)]), \mathsf{skip}\rangle$$

$$\langle(\sigma,\zeta), \mathsf{if}\ B\ \mathsf{then}\ S_1\ \mathsf{else}\ S_2\rangle \longrightarrow^1_{\zeta(B)} \langle(\sigma,\zeta), S_1\rangle \quad \mathsf{if}\ \sigma(B)$$

$$\langle(\sigma,\zeta), \mathsf{if}\ B\ \mathsf{then}\ S_1\ \mathsf{else}\ S_2\rangle \longrightarrow^1_{\zeta(\neg B)} \langle(\sigma,\zeta), S_2\rangle\ \mathsf{if}\ \sigma(\neg B)$$

$$\langle\Pi, \mathsf{pif}\ q\ \mathsf{then}\ S_1\ \mathsf{else}\ S_2\rangle \longrightarrow^q \langle\Pi, S_1\rangle$$

$$\langle\Pi, \mathsf{pif}\ q\ \mathsf{then}\ S_1\ \mathsf{else}\ S_2\rangle \longrightarrow^{1-q} \langle\Pi, S_2\rangle$$

$$\langle\Pi, S_1\ ;\ S_2\rangle \longrightarrow^1_\pi \langle\Pi', S_1'\ ;\ S_2\rangle \quad \mathsf{if}\ \langle\Pi, S_1\rangle \longrightarrow^1_\pi \langle\Pi', S_1'\rangle$$

$$\langle\Pi, \mathsf{skip}\ ;\ S\rangle \longrightarrow^1 \langle\Pi, S\rangle$$

$$\langle\Pi, \mathsf{while}\ B\ \mathsf{do}\ S\rangle \longrightarrow^1_{\zeta(B)} \langle\Pi, S\ ;\ \mathsf{while}\ B\ \mathsf{do}\ S\rangle \quad \mathsf{if}\ \sigma(B)$$

$$\langle\Pi, \mathsf{while}\ B\ \mathsf{do}\ S\rangle \longrightarrow^1_{\zeta(\neg B)} \langle\Pi, \mathsf{skip}\rangle \quad \mathsf{if}\ \sigma(\neg B)$$

Fig. 5. Concolic semantics

pif q then S_1 else S_2 is non-deterministic: the result is that of S_1 with probability q, and S_2 with probability $1 - q$. We write $\zeta(B)$ to substitute free variables $x \in B$ with their mapped-to values $\zeta(x)$ and then simplify the result as much as possible. For example, if $\zeta(x) = \alpha$ and $\zeta(y) = 2$, then $\zeta(x > y + 3) = \alpha > 5$. The same goes for $\zeta(E)$.

We define a *complete run* of the concolic semantics with the judgment $\langle\Pi, S\rangle \Downarrow^p_\pi \Pi'$, which has two rules:

$$\langle\Pi, \mathsf{skip}\rangle \Downarrow^1_{\mathsf{true}} \Pi$$

$$\frac{\langle\Pi, S\rangle \longrightarrow^p_\pi \langle\Pi', S'\rangle \quad \langle\Pi', S'\rangle \Downarrow^q_{\pi'} \Pi''}{\langle\Pi, S\rangle \Downarrow^{p \cdot q}_{\pi \wedge \pi'} \Pi''}$$

A complete run's probability is thus the product of the probability of each individual step taken. The run's path condition is the conjunction of the conditions of each step.

The path condition π for a complete run is a conjunction of the (symbolic) boolean guards evaluated during an execution. π can be converted to disjunctive normal form (DNF), and given the restrictions of the language the result is essentially a set of convex polyhedra over symbolic variables α.

6.2 Improving Precision

Using concolic execution, we can improve our estimate of the size of a probabilistic polyhedron as follows:

1. Randomly select an input state $\sigma_T \in \gamma_{\mathbb{C}}(C_T)$ (recall that C_T is the polyhedron describing the possible valuations of secrets T).
2. Set $\Pi = (\sigma_T, \zeta_T)$ where ζ_T maps each variable $x \in T$ to a fresh symbolic variable α_x. Perform a complete concolic run $\langle\Pi, S\rangle \Downarrow^p_\pi (\sigma', \zeta')$. Make sure that $\sigma'(r) = o$, i.e., the expected output. If not, select a new σ_T and retry. Give up after some number of failures N. For our example shown in Fig. 3(b), we might obtain a path condition $|Loc(z).x - L_1.x| + |Loc(z).y - L_1.y| \leq 4$ that captures the left diamond of the disjunctive query.

3. After a successful concolic run, convert path condition π to DNF, where each conjunctive clause is a polyhedron C_i. Also convert uses of disequality ($\leq$ and $\geq$) to be strict ($<$ and $>$).
4. Let $C = C_T \sqcap (\bigsqcup_i C_i)$; that is, it is the join of each of the polyhedra in $DNF(\pi)$ "intersected" with the original constraints. This captures all of the points that could possibly lead to the observed outcome along the concolically executed path. Compute $n = \#(C)$. Let $P_{T+} = P_T$ except define $s_{T+}^{\min} = n$ if $s_T^{\min} < n$ and $m_{T+}^{\min} = p_T^{\min} \cdot n$ if $m_T^{\min} < p_T^{\min} \cdot n$. (Leave them as is, otherwise.) For our example, $n = 41$, the size of the left diamond. We do not update $s_T^{\min}$ since $41 < 55$, the probabilistic polyhedron's lower bound (but see below).

Theorem 3 (Concolic Execution is Sound). *If $\delta_0 \in \gamma_{\mathbb{P}}(P_0)$, $\langle\langle S \rangle\rangle P_0 = P$, and $[\![S]\!]\delta_0 = \delta$ then $\delta_T \in \gamma_{\mathbb{P}}(P_{T+})$ where*

$$\delta_T \overset{\text{def}}{=} \delta \wedge (r = o) \restriction T$$
$$P_T \overset{\text{def}}{=} P \wedge (r = o) \restriction T$$
$$P_{T+} \overset{\text{def}}{=} P_T \text{ concolically revised.}$$

The proof is in the extended technical report [43].

6.3   Combining Sampling with Concolic Execution

Sampling can be used to further augment the results of concolic execution. The key insight is that the presence of a sound under-approximation generated by the concolic execution means that it is unnecessary to sample from the under-approximating region. Here is the algorithm:

1. Let $C = C_0 \sqcap (\bigsqcup_i C_i)$ be the under-approximating region.
2. Perform sampling per the algorithm in Sect. 5, but with two changes:
   - if a sampled state $\sigma_T \in \gamma_{\mathbb{C}}(C)$, ignore it
   - When done sampling, compute $s_{T+}^{\min} = p_L \cdot (\#(C_T) - \#(C)) + \#(C)$ and $s_{T+}^{\max} = p_U \cdot (\#(C_T) - \#(C)) + \#(C)$. This differs from Sect. 5 in not including the count from concolic region C in the computation. This is because, since we ignored samples $\sigma_T \in \gamma_{\mathbb{C}}(C)$, the credible interval $[p_L, p_U]$ bounds the likelihood that any given point in $C_T \setminus C$ is in the support of the true distribution.

For our example, concolic execution indicated there are at least 41 points that satisfy the query. With this in hand, and using the same samples as shown in Sect. 5, we can refine $s \in [74, 80]$ and $m \in [0.74, 0.160]$ (the credible interval is formed over only those samples which satisfy the query but fall outside the under-approximation returned by concolic execution). We improve the vulnerability estimate to $V \leq \frac{0.02}{0.0.74} = 0.027$. These bounds (and vulnerability estimate) are better than those of sampling alone ($s \in [72, 81]$ with $V \leq 0.028$).

The statement of soundness and its proof can be found in the extended technical report [43].

7   Implementation

We have implemented our approach as an extension of Mardziel et al. [25], which is written in OCaml. This baseline implements numeric domains C via an OCaml interface to the Parma Polyhedra Library [4]. The counting procedure $\#(C)$ is implemented by LattE [15]. Support for arbitrary precision and exact arithmetic (e.g., for manipulating m^{min}, p^{min}, etc.) is provided by the mlgmp OCaml interface to the GNU Multi Precision Arithmetic library. Rather than maintaining a single probabilistic polyhedron P, the implementation maintains a *powerset* of polyhedra [3], i.e., a finite disjunction. Doing so results in a more precise handling of join points in the control flow, at a somewhat higher performance cost.

We have implemented our extensions to this baseline for the case that domain C is the interval numeric domain [11]. Of course, the theory fully applies to any numeric abstract domain. We use Gibbs sampling, which we implemented ourselves. We delegate the calculation of the beta distribution and its corresponding credible interval to the ocephes OCaml library, which in turn uses the GNU Scientific Library. It is straightforward to lift the various operations we have described to the powerset domain. All of our code is available at https://github. com/GaloisInc/TAMBA.

8   Experiments

To evaluate the benefits of our techniques, we applied them to queries based on the evacuation problem outlined in Sect. 2. We found that while the baseline technique can yield precise answers when computing vulnerability, our new techniques can achieve close to the same level of precision far more efficiently.

8.1   Experimental Setup

For our experiments we analyzed queries similar to $Nearby(s, l, d)$ from Fig. 2. We generalize the $Nearby$ query to accept a set of locations L—the query returns true if s is within d units of any one of the islands having location $l \in L$. In our experiments we fix $d = 100$. We consider the secrecy of the location of s, $Location(s)$. We also analyze the execution of the resource allocation algorithm of Fig. 2 directly; we discuss this in Sect. 8.3.

We measure the time it takes to compute the *vulnerability* (i.e., the probability of the most probable point) following each query. In our experiments, we consider a single ship s and set its coordinates so that it is always in range of some island in L, so that the concrete query result returns true (i.e. $Nearby(s, L, 100) = true$). We measure the vulnerability following this query result starting from a prior belief that the coordinates of s are uniformly distributed with $0 \leq Location(s).x \leq 1000$ and $0 \leq Location(s).y \leq 1000$.

In our experiments, we varied several experimental parameters: *analysis method* (either P, I, CE, S, or CE+S), *query complexity* c; *AI precision level* p; and *number of samples* n. We describe each in turn.

Analysis Method. We compared five techniques for computing vulnerability:

P: Abstract interpretation (AI) with convex polyhedra for domain C (Sect. 4),
I: AI with intervals for C (Sect. 4),
S: AI with intervals augmented with sampling (Sect. 5),
CE: AI with intervals augmented with concolic execution (Sect. 6), and
CE+S: AI with intervals augmented with both techniques (Sect. 6.3)

The first two techniques are due to Mardziel et al. [25], where the former uses convex polyhedra and the latter uses intervals (aka boxes) for the underlying polygons. In our experiments we tend to focus on P since I's precision is unacceptably poor (e.g., often vulnerability $= 1$).

Query Complexity. We consider queries with different L; we say we are increasing the *complexity* of the query as L gets larger. Let $c = |L|$; we consider $1 \leq c \leq 5$, where larger L include the same locations as smaller ones. We set each location to be at least $2 \cdot d$ Manhattan distance units away from any other island (so diamonds like those in Fig. 3(a) never overlap).

Precision. The precision parameter p bounds the size of the powerset abstract domain at all points during abstract interpretation. This has the effect of forcing joins when the powerset grows larger than the specified precision. As p grows larger, the results of abstract interpretation are likely to become more precise (i.e. vulnerability gets closer to the true value). We considered p values of 1, 2, 4, 8, 16, 32, and 64.

Samples Taken. For the latter three analysis methods, we varied the number of samples taken n. For analysis CE, n is interpreted as the number of samples to try per polyhedron before giving up trying to find a "valid sample."[5] For analysis S, n is the number of samples, distributed proportionally across all the polyhedra in the powerset. For analysis CE+S, n is the combination of the two. We considered sample size values of $1,000 - 50,000$ in increments of $1,000$. We always compute an interval with $\omega = 99.9\%$ confidence (which will be wider when fewer samples are used).

System Description. We ran experiments varying all possible parameters. For each run, we measured the total execution time (wall clock) in seconds to analyze the query and compute vulnerability. All experiments were carried out on a MacBook Air with OSX version 10.11.6, a 1.7 GHz Intel Core i7, and 8 GB of RAM. We ran a single trial for each configuration of parameters. Only wall-clock time varies across trials; informally, we observed time variations to be small.

8.2   Results

Figure 6(a)–(c) measure vulnerability (y-axis) as a function of time (x-axis) for each analysis.[6] These three figures characterize three interesting "zones" in the

---

[5] This is the N parameter from Sect. 6.
[6] These are best viewed on a color display.

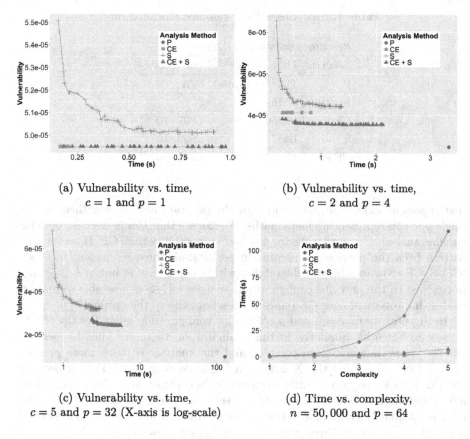

(a) Vulnerability vs. time,
$c = 1$ and $p = 1$

(b) Vulnerability vs. time,
$c = 2$ and $p = 4$

(c) Vulnerability vs. time,
$c = 5$ and $p = 32$ (X-axis is log-scale)

(d) Time vs. complexity,
$n = 50,000$ and $p = 64$

Fig. 6. Experimental results

space of complexity and precision. The results for method I are not shown in any of the figures. This is because I always produces a vulnerability of 1. The refinement methods (CE, S, and CE+S) are all over the interval domain, and should be considered as "improving" the vulnerability of I.

In Fig. 6(a) we fix $c = 1$ and $p = 1$. In this configuration, baseline analysis P can compute the true vulnerability in $\sim 0.95\,$s. Analysis CE is also able to compute the true vulnerability, but in $\sim 0.19\,$s. Analysis S is able to compute a vulnerability to within $\sim 5 \cdot e^{-6}$ of optimal in $\sim 0.15\,$s. These data points support two key observations. First, even a very modest number of samples improves vulnerability significantly over just analyzing with intervals. Second, concolic execution is only slightly slower and can achieve the optimal vulnerability. Of course, concolic execution is not a panacea. As we will see, a feature of this configuration is that no joins take place during abstract interpretation. This is critical to the precision of the concolic execution.

In Fig. 6(b) we fix $c = 2$ and $p = 4$. In contrast to the configuration of Fig. 6(a), the values for c and p in this configuration are not sufficient to prevent all joins during abstract interpretation. This has the effect of taking polygons

Table 1. Analyzing a 3-ship resource allocation run

Resource allocation (3 ships)		
Analysis	Time (s)	Vulnerability
P	Timeout (5 min)	N/A
I	0.516	1
CE	16.650	$1.997 \cdot 10^{-24}$
S	1.487	$1.962 \cdot 10^{-24}$
CE+S	17.452	$1.037 \cdot 10^{-24}$

that represent individual paths through the program and joining them into a single polygon representing many paths. We can see that this is the case because baseline analysis P is now achieving a better vulnerability than CE. However, one pattern from the previous configuration persists: all three refinement methods (CE, S, CE+S) can achieve vulnerability within $\sim 1 \cdot e^{-5}$ of P, but in $\frac{1}{4}$ the time. In contrast to the previous configuration, analysis CE+S is now able to make a modest improvement over CE (since it does not achieve the optimal).

In Fig. 6(c) we fix $c = 5$ and $p = 32$. This configuration magnifies the effects we saw in Fig. 6(b). Similarly, in this configuration there are joins happening, but the query is much more complex and the analysis is much more precise. In this figure, we label the X axis as a log scale over time. This is because analysis P took over two minutes to complete, in contrast to the longest-running refinement method, which took less than 6 seconds. The relationship between the refinement analyses is similar to the previous configuration. The key observation here is that, again, all three refinement analyses achieve within $\sim 3 \cdot e^{-5}$ of P, but this time in 4% of the time (as opposed to $\frac{1}{4}$ in the previous configuration).

Figure 6(d) makes more explicit the relationship between refinements (CE, S, CE+S) and P. We fix $n = 50,000$ (the maximum) here, and $p = 64$ (the maximum). We can see that as query complexity goes up, P gets exponentially slower, while CE, S, and CE+S slow at a much lower rate, while retaining (per the previous graphs) similar precision.

8.3   Evacuation Problem

We conclude this section by briefly discussing an analysis of an execution of the resource allocation algorithm of Fig. 2. In our experiment, we set the number of ships to be three, where two were in range $d = 300$ of the evacuation site, and their sum-total berths (500) were sufficient to satisfy demand at the site (also 500). For our analysis refinements we set $n = 1000$. Running the algorithm, a total of seven pairs of *Nearby* and *Capacity* queries were issued. In the end, the algorithm selects two ships to handle the evacuation.

Table 1 shows the time to execute the algorithm using the different analysis methods, along with the computed vulnerability—this latter number represents the coordinator's view of the most likely nine-tuple of the private data of the three ships involved (x coordinate, y coordinate, and capacity for each). We can see that, as expected, our refinement analyses are far more efficient than baseline P, and far more precise than baseline I. The CE methods are precise but slower than S. This is because of the need to count the number of points in the DNF of the concolic path conditions, which is expensive.

Discussion. The queries considered in Fig. 6 have two features that contribute to the effectiveness of our refinement methods. First, they are defined over large domains, but return true for only a small subset of those values. For larger subsets of values, the benefits of sampling may degrade, though concolic execution should still provide an improvement. Further experiments are needed to explore such scenarios. Second, the example in Fig. 6 contains short but complex queries. A result of this query structure is that abstract interpretation with polyhedra is expensive but sampling can be performed efficiently. The evacuation problem results in Table 1 provide some evidence that the benefits of our techniques also apply to longer queries. However it may still be possible to construct queries where the gap in runtime between polyhedral analysis and sampling is smaller, in which case sampling would provide less improvement.

9 Related Work

Quantifying Information Flow. There is a rich research literature on techniques that aim to *quantify* information that a program may release, or has released, and then use that quantification as a basis for policy. One question is what measure of information release should be used. Past work largely considers information theoretic measures, including *Bayes vulnerability* [41] and *Bayes risk* [8], *Shannon entropy* [40], and *guessing entropy* [26]. The *g-vulnerability* framework [1] was recently introduced to express measures having richer operational interpretations, and subsumes other measures.

Our work focuses on Bayes Vulnerability, which is related to min-entropy. Vulnerability is appealing operationally: As Smith [41] explains, it estimates the risk of the secret being guessed in one try. While challenging to compute, this approach provides meaningful results for non-uniform priors. Work that has focused on other, easier-to-compute metrics, such as Shannon entropy and channel capacity, require deterministic programs and priors that conform to uniform distributions [2,22,23,27,32]. The work of Klebanov [20] supports computation of both Shannon entropy and min-entropy over deterministic programs with non-uniform priors. The work takes a symbolic execution and program specification approach to QIF. Our use of concolic execution for counting polyhedral constraints is similar to that of Klebanov. However, our language supports probabilistic choice and in addition to concolic execution we also provide a sampling technique and a sound composition. Like Mardziel et al. [25], we are able to compute the worst-case vulnerability, i.e., due to a particular output, rather than a *static* estimate, i.e., as an expectation over all possible outputs. Köpf and Basin [21] originally proposed this idea, and Mardziel et al. were the first to implement it, followed by several others [6,19,24].

Köpf and Rybalchenko [22] (KR) also use sampling and concolic execution to statically quantify information leakage. But their approach is quite different from ours. KR uses sampling of a query's inputs in lieu of considering (as we do) all possible outputs, and uses concolic execution with each sample to ultimately compute Shannon entropy, by underapproximation, within a confidence interval. This approach benefits from not having to enumerate outputs, but also requires expensive model counting *for each sample*. By contrast, we use sampling and concolic execution *from the posterior* computed by abstract interpretation, using the results to boost the lower bound on the size/probability mass of the abstraction. Our use of sampling is especially efficient, and the use of concolic execution is completely sound (i.e., it retains 100% confidence in the result). As with the above work, KR requires deterministic programs and uniform priors.

Probabilistic Programming Langauges. A probabilistic program is essentially a lifting of a normal program operating on single values to a program operating on distributions of values. As a result, the program represents a joint distribution over its variables [18]. As discussed in this paper, quantifying the information released by a query can be done by writing the query in a probabilistic programming language (PPL) and representing the uncertain secret inputs as distributions. Quantifying release generally corresponds to either the maximum likelihood estimation (MLE) problem or the maximum a-posteriori probability (MAP) problem. Not all PPLs support computation of MLE and MAP, but several do.

PPLs based on partial sampling [17,34] or full enumeration [37] of the state space are unsuitable in our setting: they are either too inefficient or too imprecise. PPLs based on algebraic decision diagrams [9], graphical models [28], and factor graphs [7,30,36] translate programs into convenient structures and take advantage of efficient algorithms for their manipulation or inference, in some cases supporting MAP or MLE queries (e.g. [33,35]). PSI [16] supports exact inference via computation of precise symbolic representations of posterior distributions, and has been used for dynamic policy enforcement [24]. Guarnieri et al. [19] use probabilistic logic programming as the basis for inference; it scales well but only for a class of queries with certain structural limits, and which do not involve numeric relationships.

Our implementation for probabilistic computation and inference differs from the above work in two main ways. Firstly, we are capable of *sound* approximation and hence can trade off precision for performance, while maintaining soundness in terms of a strong security policy. Even when using sampling, we are able to provide precise confidence measures. The second difference is our *compositional* representation of probability distributions, which is based on numerical abstractions: intervals [11], octagons [29], and polyhedra [13]. The posterior can be easily used as the prior for the next query, whereas prior work would have to repeatedly analyze the composition of past queries.

A few other works have also focused on abstract interpretation, or related techniques, for reasoning about probabilistic programs. Monniaux [31] defines an abstract domain for distributions. Smith [42] describes probabilistic abstract interpretation for verification of quantitative program properties. Cousot [14] unifies these and other probabilistic program analysis tools. However, these do not deal with sound distribution conditioning, which is crucial for belief-based information flow analysis. Work by Sankaranarayanan et al. [38] uses a combination of techniques from program analysis to reason about distributions (including abstract interpretation), but the representation does not support efficient retrieval of the maximal probability, needed to compute vulnerability.

10   Conclusions

Quantitative information flow is concerned with measuring the knowledge about secret data that is gained by observing the answer to a query. This paper has presented a combination of static analysis using probabilistic abstract interpretation, sampling, and underapproximation via concolic execution to compute high-confidence upper bounds on information flow. Preliminary experimental results are promising and suggest that this approach can operate more precisely and efficiently than abstract interpretation alone. As next steps, we plan to evaluate the technique more rigorously – including on programs with probabilistic choice. We also plan to integrate static analysis and sampling more closely so as to avoid precision loss at decision points in programs. We also look to extend programs to be able to store random choices in variables, to thereby implement more advanced probabilistic structures.

A   Query Code

The following is the query code of the example developed in Sect. 2.2. Here, s_x and s_y represent a ship's secret location. The variables l1_x, l1_y, l2_x, l2_y, and d are inputs to the query. The first pair represents position L_1, the second pair represents the position L_2, and the last is the distance threshold, set to 4. We assume for the example that L_1 and L_2 have the same y coordinate, and their x coordinates differ by 6 units.

We express the query in the language of Fig. 4 basically as follows:

```
d_l1 := |s_x - l1_x| + |s_y - l1_y|;
d_l2 := |s_x - l2_x| + |s_y - l2_y|;
if (d_l1 <= d || d_l2 <= d) then
  out := true // assume this result
else
  out := false
```

The variable out is the result of the query. We simplify the code by assuming the absolute value function is built-in; we can implement this with a simple conditional. We run this query probabilistically under the assumption that s_x and s_y are uniformly distributed within the range given in Fig. 1. We then condition the output on the assumption that out = true. When using intervals as the baseline of probabilistic polyhedra, this produces the result given in the upper right of Fig. 3(b); when using convex polyhedra, the result is shown in the lower right of the figure. The use of sampling and concolic execution to augment the former is shown via arrows between the two.

B   Formal Semantics

Here we defined the probabilistic semantics for the programming language given in Fig. 4. The semantics of statement S, written $[\![S]\!]$, is a function of the form **Dist** $\rightarrow$ **Dist**, i.e., it is a function from distributions of states to distributions of states. We write $[\![S]\!]\delta = \delta'$ to say that the semantics of S maps input distribution δ to output distribution δ'.

Figure 7 gives this denotational semantics along with definitions of relevant auxiliary operations. We write $[\![E]\!]\sigma$ to denote the (integer) result of evaluating expression E in σ, and $[\![B]\!]\sigma$ to denote the truth or falsehood of B in σ. The variables of a state σ, written $domain(\sigma)$, is defined by $domain(\sigma)$; sometimes we will refer to this set as just the $domain$ of σ. We will also use the this notation for distributions; $domain(\delta) \stackrel{\text{def}}{=} domain(domain(\delta))$. We write lfp as the least fixed-point operator. The notation $\sum_{x\,:\,\phi}\rho$ can be read ρ *is the sum over all x such that formula ϕ is satisfied* (where x is bound in ρ and ϕ).

This semantics is standard. See Clarkson et al. [10] or Mardziel et al. [25] for detailed explanations.

$$[\![skip]\!]\delta = \delta$$
$$[\![x := E]\!]\delta = \delta\,[x \rightarrow E]$$
$$[\![if\ B\ then\ S_1\ else\ S_2]\!]\delta = [\![S_1]\!](\delta \wedge B) + [\![S_2]\!](\delta \wedge \neg B)$$
$$[\![pif\ q\ then\ S_1\ else\ S_2]\!]\delta = [\![S_1]\!](q \cdot \delta) + [\![S_2]\!]((1-q) \cdot \delta)$$
$$[\![S_1\ ;\ S_2]\!]\delta = [\![S_2]\!]([\![S_1]\!]\delta)$$
$$[\![while\ B\ do\ S]\!] = \text{lfp}\,[\lambda f : \textbf{Dist} \rightarrow \textbf{Dist}.\ \lambda\delta.$$
$$f\,([\![S]\!](\delta \wedge B)) + (\delta \wedge \neg B)]$$

where

$$\delta\,[x \rightarrow E] \stackrel{\text{def}}{=} \lambda\sigma.\ \sum\nolimits_{\tau\,:\,\tau[x \rightarrow [\![E]\!]\tau] = \sigma} \delta(\tau)$$
$$\delta_1 + \delta_2 \stackrel{\text{def}}{=} \lambda\sigma.\ \delta_1(\sigma) + \delta_2(\sigma)$$
$$\delta \wedge B \stackrel{\text{def}}{=} \lambda\sigma.\ \textbf{if } [\![B]\!]\sigma \textbf{ then } \delta(\sigma) \textbf{ else } 0$$
$$p \cdot \delta \stackrel{\text{def}}{=} \lambda\sigma.\ p \cdot \delta(\sigma)$$
$$\|\delta\| \stackrel{\text{def}}{=} \sum\nolimits_\sigma \delta(\sigma)$$
$$\text{normal}(\delta) \stackrel{\text{def}}{=} \frac{1}{\|\delta\|} \cdot \delta$$
$$\delta|B \stackrel{\text{def}}{=} \text{normal}(\delta \wedge B)$$
$$\delta_1 \times \delta_2 \stackrel{\text{def}}{=} \lambda(\sigma_1, \sigma_2).\ \delta_1(\sigma_1) \cdot \delta_2(\sigma_2)$$
$$\dot{\sigma} \stackrel{\text{def}}{=} \lambda\sigma_0.\ \textbf{if } \sigma = \sigma_0 \textbf{ then } 1 \textbf{ else } 0$$
$$\sigma \downarrow V \stackrel{\text{def}}{=} \lambda x \in \textbf{Var}_V.\ \sigma(x)$$
$$\delta \downarrow V \stackrel{\text{def}}{=} \lambda\sigma_V \in \textbf{State}_V.\ \sum\nolimits_{\tau\,:\,\tau\downarrow V = \sigma_V} \delta(\tau)$$
$$f_x(\delta) \stackrel{\text{def}}{=} \delta \downarrow (domain(\delta) - \{x\})$$
$$support(\delta) \stackrel{\text{def}}{=} \{\sigma\ :\ \delta(\sigma) > 0\}$$

Fig. 7. Distribution semantics

References

1. Alvim, M.S., Chatzikokolakis, K., Palamidessi, C., Smith, G.: Measuring information leakage using generalized gain functions. In: Proceedings of the IEEE Computer Security Foundations Symposium (CSF) (2012)
2. Backes, M., Köpf, B., Rybalchenko, A.: Automatic discovery and quantification of information leaks. In: Proceedings of the IEEE Symposium on Security and Privacy (S&P) (2009)
3. Bagnara, R., Hill, P.M., Zaffanella, E.: Widening operators for powerset domains. Int. J. Softw. Tools Tech. Transf. **8**(4), 449–466 (2006)
4. Bagnara, R., Hill, P.M., Zaffanella, E.: The Parma polyhedra library: toward a complete set of numerical abstractions for the analysis and verification of hardware and software systems. Sci. Comput. Program. **72**, 3–21 (2008)
5. Bagnara, R., Rodríguez-Carbonell, E., Zaffanella, E.: Generation of basic semi-algebraic invariants using convex polyhedra. In: Hankin, C., Siveroni, I. (eds.) SAS 2005. LNCS, vol. 3672, pp. 19–34. Springer, Heidelberg (2005). https://doi.org/10.1007/11547662_4
6. Besson, F., Bielova, N., Jensen, T.: Browser randomisation against fingerprinting: a quantitative information flow approach. In: Bernsmed, K., Fischer-Hübner, S. (eds.) NordSec 2014. LNCS, vol. 8788, pp. 181–196. Springer, Cham (2014). https://doi.org/10.1007/978-3-319-11599-3_11
7. Borgström, J., Gordon, A.D., Greenberg, M., Margetson, J., Van Gael, J.: Measure transformer semantics for Bayesian machine learning. In: Barthe, G. (ed.) ESOP 2011. LNCS, vol. 6602, pp. 77–96. Springer, Heidelberg (2011). https://doi.org/10.1007/978-3-642-19718-5_5
8. Chatzikokolakis, K., Palamidessi, C., Panangaden, P.: On the Bayes risk in information-hiding protocols. J. Comput. Secur. **16**(5), 531–571 (2008)
9. Claret, G., Rajamani, S.K., Nori, A.V., Gordon, A.D., Borgstroem, J.: Bayesian inference for probabilistic programs via symbolic execution. Technical report MSR-TR-2012-86. Microsoft Research (2012)
10. Clarkson, M.R., Myers, A.C., Schneider, F.B.: Quantifying information flow with beliefs. J. Comput. Secur. **17**(5), 655–701 (2009)
11. Cousot, P., Cousot, R.: Static determination of dynamic properties of programs. In: Proceedings of the Second International Symposium on Programming (1976)
12. Cousot, P., Cousot, R.: Abstract interpretation: a unified lattice model for static analysis of programs by construction or approximation of fixpoints. In: Proceedings of the ACM SIGPLAN Conference on Principles of Programming Languages (POPL) (1977)
13. Cousot, P., Halbwachs, N.: Automatic discovery of linear restraints among variables of a program. In: POPL (1978)
14. Cousot, P., Monerau, M.: Probabilistic abstract interpretation. In: Seidl, H. (ed.) ESOP 2012. LNCS, vol. 7211, pp. 169–193. Springer, Heidelberg (2012). https://doi.org/10.1007/978-3-642-28869-2_9
15. De Loera, J.A., Haws, D., Hemmecke, R., Huggins, P., Tauzer, J., Yoshida, R.: LattE (2008). https://www.math.ucdavis.edu/~latte/
16. Gehr, T., Misailovic, S., Vechev, M.: PSI: exact symbolic inference for probabilistic programs. In: Chaudhuri, S., Farzan, A. (eds.) CAV 2016. LNCS, vol. 9779, pp. 62–83. Springer, Cham (2016). https://doi.org/10.1007/978-3-319-41528-4_4
17. Goodman, N.D., Mansinghka, V.K., Roy, D.M., Bonawitz, K., Tenenbaum, J.B.: Church: a language for generative models. In: Proceedings of the Conference on Uncertainty in Artificial Intelligence (UAI) (2008)

18. Gordon, A.D., Henzinger, T.A., Nori, A.V., Rajamani, S.K.: Probabilistic programming. In: Conference on the Future of Software Engineering, FOSE 2014, pp. 167–181. ACM, New York (2014)
19. Guarnieri, M., Marinovic, S., Basin, D.: Securing databases from probabilistic inference. In: Proceedings of IEEE Computer Security Foundations Symposium (CSF) (2017)
20. Klebanov, V.: Precise quantitative information flow analysis—a symbolic approach. Theor. Comput. Sci. **538**, 124–139 (2014)
21. Köpf, B., Basin, D.: An information-theoretic model for adaptive side-channel attacks. In: Proceedings of the ACM Conference on Computer and Communications Security (CCS) (2007)
22. Köpf, B., Rybalchenko, A.: Approximation and randomization for quantitative information-flow analysis. In: Proceedings of the IEEE Computer Security Foundations Symposium (CSF) (2010)
23. Köpf, B., Rybalchenko, A.: Automation of quantitative information-flow analysis. In: Bernardo, M., de Vink, E., Di Pierro, A., Wiklicky, H. (eds.) SFM 2013. LNCS, vol. 7938, pp. 1–28. Springer, Heidelberg (2013). https://doi.org/10.1007/978-3-642-38874-3_1
24. Kučera, M., Tsankov, P., Gehr, T., Guarnieri, M., Vechev, M.: Synthesis of probabilistic privacy enforcement. In: Proceedings of the ACM Conference on Computer and Communications Security (CCS) (2017)
25. Mardziel, P., Magill, S., Hicks, M., Srivatsa, M.: Dynamic enforcement of knowledge-based security policies using probabilistic abstract interpretation. J. Comput. Secur. **21**, 463–532 (2013)
26. Massey, J.L.: Guessing and entropy. In: Proceedings of IEEE International Symposium on Information Theory (ISIT) (1994)
27. McCamant, S., Ernst, M.D.: Quantitative information flow as network flow capacity. In: Proceedings of the ACM SIGPLAN Conference on Programming Language Design and Implementation (PLDI) (2008)
28. Milch, B., Marthi, B., Russell, S., Sontag, D., Ong, D.L., Kolobov, A.: Blog: probabilistic models with unknown objects. In: Proceedings of the International Joint Conference on Artificial Intelligence (IJCAI) (2005)
29. Miné, A.: The octagon abstract domain. In: Proceedings of the Working Conference on Reverse Engineering (WCRE) (2001)
30. Minka, T., Winn, J., Guiver, J., Webster, S., Zaykov, Y., Yangel, B., Spengler, A., Bronskill, J.: Infer.NET 2.6. Microsoft Research, Cambridge (2014). http://research.microsoft.com/infernet
31. Monniaux, D.: Analyse de programmes probabilistes par interprétation abstraite. Thése de doctorat, Université Paris IX Dauphine (2001)
32. Mu, C., Clark, D.: An interval-based abstraction for quantifying information flow. Electron. Notes Theor. Comput. Sci. **253**(3), 119–141 (2009)
33. Narayanan, P., Carette, J., Romano, W., Shan, C., Zinkov, R.: Probabilistic inference by program transformation in Hakaru (system description). In: Kiselyov, O., King, A. (eds.) FLOPS 2016. LNCS, vol. 9613, pp. 62–79. Springer, Cham (2016). https://doi.org/10.1007/978-3-319-29604-3_5
34. Park, S., Pfenning, F., Thrun, S.: A probabilistic language based on sampling functions. ACM Trans. Program. Lang. Syst. (TOPLAS) **31**(1), 4:1–4:46 (2008)
35. Pfeffer, A.: Figaro: an object-oriented probabilistic programming language. Technical report. Charles River Analytics (2000)

36. Pfeffer, A.: The design and implementation of IBAL: a general-purpose probabilistic language. In: Getoor, L., Taskar, B. (eds.) Statistical Relational Learning. MIT Press, Cambridge (2007)

37. Radul, A.: Report on the probabilistic language scheme. In: Proceedings of the Dynamic Languages Symposium (DLS) (2007)

38. Sankaranarayanan, S., Chakarov, A., Gulwani, S.: Static analysis for probabilistic programs: inferring whole program properties from finitely many paths. In: Conference on Programming Language Design and Implementation, PLDI (2013)

39. Sen, K., Marinov, D., Agha, G.: CUTE: a concolic unit testing engine for C. In: ESEC/FSE (2005)

40. Shannon, C.: A mathematical theory of communication. Bell Syst. Tech. J. **27**, 379–423 (1948)

41. Smith, G.: On the foundations of quantitative information flow. In: de Alfaro, L. (ed.) FoSSaCS 2009. LNCS, vol. 5504, pp. 288–302. Springer, Heidelberg (2009). https://doi.org/10.1007/978-3-642-00596-1_21

42. Smith, M.J.A.: Probabilistic abstract interpretation of imperative programs using truncated normal distributions. Electron. Notes Theor. Comput. Sci. **220**, 43–59 (2008)

43. Sweet, I., Trilla, J.M.C., Scherrer, C., Hicks, M., Magill, S.: What's the over/under? probabilistic bounds on information leakage. CoRR abs/1802.08234, February 2018. https://arxiv.org/abs/1802.08234

Secure Information Release
in Timed Automata

Panagiotis Vasilikos$^{(\boxtimes)}$ ⓘ, Flemming Nielson ⓘ, and Hanne Riis Nielson ⓘ

Department of Applied Mathematics and Computer Science,
Technical University of Denmark, Kongens Lyngby, Denmark
{panva,fnie,hrni}@dtu.dk

Abstract. One of the key demands of cyberphysical systems is that they meet their safety goals. *Timed automata* has established itself as a formalism for modeling and analyzing the real-time safety aspects of cyberphysical systems. Increasingly it is also demanded that cyberphysical systems meet a number of security goals for confidentiality and integrity. Notions of security based on *Information flow control*, such as non-interference, provide strong guarantees that no information is leaked; however, many cyberphysical systems leak intentionally some information in order to achieve their purposes.

In this paper, we develop a formal approach of information flow for timed automata that allows intentional information leaks. The security of a timed automaton is then defined using a bisimulation relation that takes account of the non-determinism and the clocks of timed automata. Finally, we define an algorithm that traverses a timed automaton and imposes information flow constraints on it and we prove that our algorithm is sound with respect to our security notion.

1   Introduction

Motivation. Embedded systems are key components of cyberphysical systems and are often subject to stringent safety goals. Among the current approaches to the modeling and analysis of timed systems, the approach of *timed automata* [5] stands out as being a very successful approach with well-developed tool support – in particular the *UPPAAL* suite [28] of tools. As cyberphysical systems become increasingly distributed and interconnected through wireless communication links it becomes even more important to ensure that they meet suitable security goals.

In this paper, we are motivated by an example of a smart power grid system. In its very basic form, a smart grid system consists of a meter that measures the electricity consumption in a customer's (C) house and then sends this data to the utility company (UC). The detailed measurements of the meter provide more accurate billings for UC, while C receives energy management plans that optimize his energy consumption. Although this setting seems to be beneficial for both UC and C, it has been shown that high-frequent monitoring of the power flow poses a major threat to the privacy of C [14,23,27]. To deal with

© The Author(s) 2018
L. Bauer and R. Küsters (Eds.): POST 2018, LNCS 10804, pp. 28–52, 2018.
https://doi.org/10.1007/978-3-319-89722-6_2

this problem many smart grid systems introduce a trusted third-party (TTP), on which both UC and C agree [27]. The data of the meter now is collected by the TTP and by the end of each month the TTP charges C depending on the tariff prices defined by UC. In this protocol, UC trusts TTP for the accurate billing of C, while C trusts TTP with its sensitive data. However, in some cases, C may desire an energy management plan by UC, and consequently he makes a clear statement to TTP that allows the latter to release the private data of C to UC. Therefore, it is challenging to formally prove that our trusted smart grid system leaks information only under $C's$ decision.

Information Flow Control. [10, 26, 29] is a key approach to ensuring that software systems maintain the confidentiality and/or integrity of their data. Policies for secure information flow are usually formalized as non-interference [29] properties and systems that adhere to the stated policy are guaranteed to admit no flow of information that violates it. However, in many applications information is leaked by intention as in our smart grid example. To deal with such systems, information flow control approaches are usually extended with mechanisms that permit controlled information leakage. The major difficulty imposed by this extension is to formalize notions of security that are able to differentiate between the intentional and the unintentional information leakages in a system.

Contribution. It is therefore natural to extend the enforcement of safety properties of *timed automata* with the enforcement of appropriate Information Flow policies. It is immediate that the treatment of *clocks*, the *non-determinism*, and the *unstructured control flow* inherent in automata will pose a challenge. More fundamentally there is the challenge that *timed automata* is an automata-based formalism whereas most approaches to Information Flow take a language-based approach by developing type systems for programming languages with structured control flow or process calculi.

We start by giving the semantics of timed automata (Sect. 2) based on the ones used in UPPAAL [28]. Next, we formalize the security of a timed automaton using a bisimulation relation (Sect. 3). This notion describes the observations of a *passive attacker* and formally describes where an observation is allowed to leak information and where it is not. To deal with implicit flows we define a general notion of the post-dominator relation [18] (Sect. 4). We then develop a sound algorithm (Sect. 5) that imposes information flow constraints on the clocks and the variables of a timed automaton. We finish with our conclusions (Sect. 6) and the proofs of our main results (Appendix).

Related Work. There are other papers dealing with Information Flow using language based techniques for programs with a notion of time [2, 9, 16, 22] or programs that leak information intentionally [6, 13, 19–21, 24]. Our contribution focuses on the challenges of continuous time and the guarded actions of timed automata.

The work of [7, 8] define a notion of non-interference for timed automata with high-level (secret) and low-level (public) actions. Their notion of security is expressed as a non-interference property and it depends on a natural number m, representing a minimum delay between high-level actions such that the low-level behaviors are not affected by the high-level ones. The authors of [17] define a notion of timed non-interference based on bisimulations for probabilistic timed automata which again have high-level (secret) and low-level (public) actions. A somewhat different approach is taken in [12] that studies the synthesis of controllers. None of those approaches considers timed automata that have data variables, nor is their notion of security able to accommodate systems that leak information intentionally.

The authors of [25] take a language-based approach and they define a type-system for programs written in the language Timed Commands. A program in their language gives rise to a timed automaton, and type-checked programs adhere to a non-interference like security property. However, their approach is limited only to automata that can be described by their language and they do not consider information release.

2 Timed Automata

A *timed automaton* [1,5] $\mathsf{TA} = (\mathsf{Q}, \mathsf{E}, \mathsf{I}, q_\circ)$ consists of a set of nodes Q, a set of annotated edges E, and a labelling function I on nodes. A node $q_\circ \in \mathsf{Q}$ will be the initial node and the mapping I maps each node in Q to a condition (to be introduced below) that will be imposed as an invariant at the node.

The edges are annotated with actions and take the form $(q_s, g \to \boldsymbol{x} := \boldsymbol{a} \colon \boldsymbol{r}, q_t)$ where $q_s \in \mathsf{Q}$ is the source node and $q_t \in \mathsf{Q}$ is the target node. The action $g \to \boldsymbol{x} := \boldsymbol{a} \colon \boldsymbol{r}$ consists of a guard g that has to be satisfied in order for the multiple assignments $\boldsymbol{x} := \boldsymbol{a}$ to be performed and the clock variables $\boldsymbol{r}$ to be reset. We shall assume that the sequences $\boldsymbol{x}$ and $\boldsymbol{a}$ of program variables and expressions, respectively, have the same length and that $\boldsymbol{x}$ does not contain any repetitions. To cater for special cases we shall allow to write skip for the assignments of $g \to \boldsymbol{x} := \boldsymbol{a} \colon \boldsymbol{r}$ when $\boldsymbol{x}$ (and hence $\boldsymbol{a}$) is empty; also we shall allow to omit the guard g when it equals tt and to omit the clock resets when $\boldsymbol{r}$ is empty.

It has already emerged that we distinguish between (program) variables x and clock variables (or simply clocks) r. The arithmetic expressions a, guards g and conditions c are defined as follows using boolean tests b:

$$
\begin{aligned}
a &::= a_1 \, \mathsf{op}_a \, a_2 \mid x \mid n \\
b &::= \mathsf{tt} \mid \mathsf{ff} \mid a_1 \, \mathsf{op}_r \, a_2 \mid \neg b \mid b_1 \wedge b_2 \\
g &::= b \mid r \, \mathsf{op}_c \, n \mid (r_1 - r_2) \, \mathsf{op}_c \, n \mid g_1 \wedge g_2 \\
c &::= b \mid r \, \mathsf{op}_d \, n \mid (r_1 - r_2) \, \mathsf{op}_d \, n \mid c_1 \wedge c_2
\end{aligned}
$$

The arithmetic operators op_a and the relational operators op_r are as usual. For comparisons of clocks we use the operators $\mathsf{op}_c \in \{<, \leq, =, \geq, >\}$ in guards and the less permissive set of operators $\mathsf{op}_d \in \{<, \leq, =\}$ in conditions.

To specify the semantics of timed automata let σ be a state mapping variables to values (which we take to be integers) and let δ be a clock assignment mapping clocks to non-negative reals. We then have total semantic functions $[\![\cdot]\!]$ for evaluating the arithmetic expressions, boolean tests, guards and conditions;

the values of the arithmetic expressions and boolean expressions only depend on the states whereas that of guards and conditions also depend on the clock assignments.

The configurations of the timed automata have the form $\langle q, \sigma, \delta \rangle \in \mathbf{Config}$ where $[\![I(q)]\!](\sigma, \delta)$ is true, and the transitions are described by an initial delay (possibly none) that increases the values of all the clocks followed by an action. Therefore, whenever $(q_s, g \to \boldsymbol{x} := \boldsymbol{a} \colon \boldsymbol{r}, q_t)$ is in E we have the rule:

$$\langle q_s, \sigma, \delta \rangle \xrightarrow{d} \langle q_t, \sigma', \delta' \rangle \begin{cases} d \geq 0 \\ [\![I(q_s)]\!](\sigma, \delta + d) = \mathsf{tt}, \\ [\![g]\!](\sigma, \delta + d) = \mathsf{tt}, \\ \sigma' = \sigma[\boldsymbol{x} \mapsto [\![\boldsymbol{a}]\!]\sigma], \delta' = (\delta + d)[\boldsymbol{r} \mapsto \boldsymbol{0}], \\ [\![I(q_t)]\!](\sigma', \delta') = \mathsf{tt} \end{cases}$$

where d corresponds to the initial delay. The rule ensures that after the initial delay the invariant and the guard are satisfied in the starting configuration and updates the mappings σ and δ where $\delta + d$ abbreviates $\lambda r. \delta(r) + d$. Finally, it ensures that the invariant is satisfied in the resulting configuration. Initial configurations assume that all clocks are initialized to 0 and have the form $\langle q_0, \sigma, \lambda r.0 \rangle$.

Traces. We define a *trace* from $\langle q_s, \sigma, \delta \rangle$ to q_t in a timed automaton TA to have one of three forms. It may be a finite "successful" sequence

$$\langle q_s, \sigma, \delta \rangle = \langle q_0', \sigma_0', \delta_0' \rangle \xrightarrow{d_1} \cdots \xrightarrow{d_n} \langle q_n', \sigma_n', \delta_n' \rangle \quad (n > 0)$$
$$\text{such that } \{n\} = \{i \mid q_i' = q_t \wedge 0 < i \leq n\}.$$

in which case at least one step is performed. It may be a finite "unsuccessful" sequence

$$\langle q_s, \sigma, \delta \rangle = \langle q_0', \sigma_0', \delta_0' \rangle \xrightarrow{d_1} \cdots \xrightarrow{d_n} \langle q_n', \sigma_n', \delta_n' \rangle \quad (n \geq 0)$$
$$\text{such that } \langle q_n', \sigma_n', \delta_n' \rangle \text{ is stuck and } q_t \notin \{q_1', \cdots, q_n'\}$$

where $\langle q_n', \sigma_n', \delta_n' \rangle$ is stuck when there is no action starting from $\langle q_n', \sigma_n', \delta_n' \rangle$. Finally, it may be an infinite "unsuccessful" sequence

$$\langle q_s, \sigma, \delta \rangle = \langle q_0', \sigma_0', \delta_0' \rangle \xrightarrow{d_1} \cdots \xrightarrow{d_n} \langle q_n', \sigma_n', \delta_n' \rangle \xrightarrow{d_{n+1}} \cdots$$
$$\text{such that } q_t \notin \{q_1', \cdots, q_n', \cdots\}.$$

We shall write $[\![\mathrm{TA} : q_s \mapsto q_t]\!](\sigma, \delta)$ for the set of traces from $\langle q_s, \sigma, \delta \rangle$ to q_t. We then have the following proposition

Proposition 1 [15]. *For a pair (σ, δ) whenever $[\![\mathrm{TA} : q_s \mapsto q_t]\!](\sigma, \delta)$ contains only successful traces, then there exists a trace $t \in [\![\mathrm{TA} : q_s \mapsto q_t]\!](\sigma, \delta)$ with maximal length.*

We also define the *delay* of a trace t from $\langle q_s, \sigma, \delta \rangle$ to q_t and we have that if t is a successful trace

$$\langle q_s, \sigma, \delta \rangle = \langle q_0', \sigma_0', \delta_0' \rangle \xrightarrow{d_1} \cdots \xrightarrow{d_n} \langle q_n', \sigma_n', \delta_n' \rangle = \langle q_t, \sigma', \delta' \rangle$$

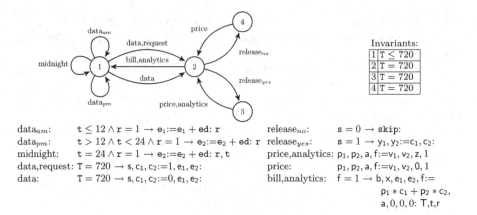

Fig. 1. The timed automaton SG (and the abbreviations used).

then

$$\Delta(t) = \sum_{i=1}^{n} d_i$$

In the case of t being an unsuccessful (finite or infinite) trace we have that

$$\Delta(t) = \infty$$

Finally for (σ_1, δ_1), (σ_2, δ_2) whenever for all $t_1 \in [\![TA : q_s \mapsto q_t]\!](\sigma_1, \delta_1)$ and $t_2 \in [\![TA : q_s \mapsto q_t]\!](\sigma_2, \delta_2)$ we have that $\Delta(t_1) = \Delta(t_2)$, we will say that (σ_1, δ_1) and (σ_2, δ_2) have the same *termination behaviour* with respect to q_s and q_t. Note that it is not necessarily the case that a pair (σ, δ) has the same termination behaviour as itself.

Example 1. To illustrate our development we shall consider an example automaton of a smart grid system as the one described in Sect. 1. The timed automaton SG is given in Fig. 1 and it uses the clocks t and T to model the time elapse of a day and a month respectively. Between midnight and noon, the electricity data ed is aggregated in the variable e_1, while from noon to midnight the measurements are saved in the variable e_2. The clock r is used to regulate the frequency of the measurements, by allowing one measurement every full hour. At the end of a day (midnight) the last measurement is calculated and the clock t is being reset to 0 indicating the start of a new day. At the end of each month ($T = 720$) the trusted party TTP collects the data e_1 and e_2 of the meter and stores it in the collectors c_1 and c_2 respectively. At the same time, the customer C sends a service request s to TTP in case he desires to get some analytics regarding his energy consumption. The TTP then requests from the UC the prices p_1, p_2 of the electricity tariffs for the two time periods of interest and in case that C has made a request for his data to be analysed ($s = 1$ otherwise $s = 0$), TTP also reveals the collected data c_1 and c_2 to the UC where the latter stores them in the variables y_1 and y_2 respectively. The UC then responds back to the TTP by sending the values v_1 and v_2 of the electricity tariffs and also the result z of C's data analytics in case C made a request for that, otherwise it sends the value 0.

Once the TTP receives everything ($f = 1$) he calculates the bill b for C, sends it to him together with the analysis result a (C stores it in x), the clocks and the variables of the meter are being reset to 0 and a new month starts. For simplicity here we assume that all the calculations done by the TTP and the UC by the end of the month are being completed in zero time.

3 Information Flow

We envisage that there is a security lattice expressing the permissible flows [10]. Formally this is a complete lattice and the permitted flows go in the direction of the partial order. In our development, it will contain just two elements, L (for low) and H (for high), and we set $L \sqsubseteq H$ so that only the flow from H to L is disallowed. For confidentiality, one would take L to mean public and H to mean private and for integrity one would take L to mean trusted and H to mean dubious.

A *security policy* is then expressed by a mapping $\mathcal{L}$ that assigns an element of the security lattice to each program variable and clock variable. An entity is called *high* if it is mapped to H by $\mathcal{L}$, and it is said to be *low* if it is mapped to L by $\mathcal{L}$. To express adherence to the security policy we use the binary operation $\rightsquigarrow$ defined on sets χ and χ' (of variables and clocks):

$$\chi \rightsquigarrow \chi' \Leftrightarrow \forall u \in \chi : \forall u' \in \chi' : \mathcal{L}(u) \sqsubseteq \mathcal{L}(u')$$

This expresses that all the entities of χ may flow into those of χ'; note that if one of the entities of χ has a high security level then it must be the case that all the entities of χ' have high security level.

Example 2. Returning to Example 1 of our smart grid system, we have that $\mathcal{L}$ maps the program variable ed of the electricity data, the variables e_1, e_2 that store this data, the collectors c_1, c_2 and the bill b to the security level H, while the rest of the program variables and clocks are mapped to L.

Information flow control enforces a security policy by imposing constraints of the form $\{y\} \rightsquigarrow \{x\}$ whenever the value of y may somehow influence (or flow into) that of x. Traditionally we distinguish between *explicit* and *implicit* flows as explained below. As an example of an *explicit* flow consider a simple assignment of the form $x:=a$. This gives rise to a condition $\mathsf{fv}(a) \rightsquigarrow \{x\}$ so as to indicate that the *explicit* flow from the variables of a to the variable x must adhere to the security policy: if a contains a variable with high security level then x also must have high security level. For an example of an *implicit* flow consider a conditional assignment $g \rightarrow x:=0$ where x is assigned the constant value 0 in case g evaluates to true. This gives rise to a condition $\mathsf{fv}(g) \rightsquigarrow \{x\}$ so as to indicate that the *implicit* flow from the variables of g to the variable x must adhere to the security policy: if g contains a variable with high security level then x also must have high security level.

As has already been explained, many applications as our smart grid example inevitably leak some information. In this paper we develop an approach to ensure that the security policy is adhered to by the timed automaton of interest, however in certain conditions it can be bypassed. Thus, for a timed automaton $\mathsf{TA} = (\mathsf{Q}, \mathsf{E}, \mathsf{I}, q_o)$, we shall assume that there exists a set of *observable nodes* $Y \subseteq \mathsf{Q}$, that are the nodes where the values of program variables and clocks with low security are observable by an attacker. The observable nodes will be described by the union of two *disjoint* sets Y_s and Y_w, where a node q in Y_s (Y_w resp.) will be called *strongly observable* (*weakly observable* resp.). The key idea is to ensure that $\{x\} \leadsto \{y\}$ whenever there is an *explicit* flow of information from x to y (as illustrated above) or an *implicit* flow from x to y in computations that lead to strongly observable nodes, while computations that lead to weakly observable nodes are allowed to bypass the security policy $\mathcal{L}$.

To overcome the vagueness of this explanation we need to define a semantic condition that encompasses our notion of permissible information flow, where information leakage occurs only at specific places in our automaton.

Observable Steps. Since the values of low program variables and clocks are only observable at the nodes in Y, we collapse the transitions of the automaton that lead to non-observable nodes into one. Thus we have an *observable successful step*

$$\langle q_s, \sigma, \delta \rangle \overset{D}{\Longrightarrow}_Y \langle q_t, \sigma', \delta' \rangle$$

whenever there exists a successful trace t

$$\langle q_s, \sigma, \delta \rangle = \langle q_0, \sigma_0, \delta_0 \rangle \overset{d_1}{\longrightarrow} \cdots \overset{d_n}{\longrightarrow} \langle q_n, \sigma_n, \delta_n \rangle = \langle q_t, \sigma', \delta' \rangle \quad (n > 0)$$

from $\langle q_s, \sigma, \delta \rangle$ to q_t in TA and $q_t \in Y$, $D = \Delta(t)$ and $\forall i \in \{1, ..., n-1\} : q_i \notin Y$.

And we have an *observable unsuccessful trace*

$$\langle q_s, \sigma, \delta \rangle \overset{\infty}{\Longrightarrow}_Y \bot$$

whenever there exists an unsuccessful finite trace

$$\langle q_s, \sigma, \delta \rangle = \langle q_0, \sigma_0, \delta_0 \rangle \overset{d_1}{\longrightarrow} \cdots \overset{d_n}{\longrightarrow} \langle q_n, \sigma_n, \delta_n \rangle \quad (n \geq 0)$$

or an unsuccessful infinite trace

$$\langle q_s, \sigma, \delta \rangle = \langle q_0, \sigma_0, \delta_0 \rangle \overset{d_1}{\longrightarrow} \cdots \overset{d_n}{\longrightarrow} \langle q_n, \sigma_n, \delta_n \rangle \overset{d_{n+1}}{\longrightarrow} \cdots$$

from $\langle q_s, \sigma, \delta \rangle$ to any of the nodes in Y and $\forall i > 0 : q_i \notin Y$. From now on it should be clear that a configuration γ will range over $\mathbf{Config} \cup \{\bot\}$.

We write $(\sigma, \delta) \equiv (\sigma', \delta')$ to indicate that the two pairs are equal on low variables and low clocks:

$$(\sigma, \delta) \equiv (\sigma', \delta') \quad \text{iff} \quad \forall x : \mathcal{L}(x) = L \Rightarrow \sigma(x) = \sigma'(x) \wedge \\ \forall r : \mathcal{L}(r) = L \Rightarrow \delta(r) = \delta'(r)$$

It is immediate that this definition of $\equiv$ gives rise to an equivalence relation. Intuitively $\equiv$ represents the view of a *passive attacker* as defined in [24], a principal that is able to observe the computations of a timed automaton and deduce information.

We will now define our security notion with the use of a bisimulation relation. Our notion shares some ideas from [19,21], where a bisimulation-based security is defined for a programming language with threads. In their approach, the bypassing of the security policy is localized on the actions, and that is because their attacker model is able to observe the low variables of a program at any of its computation steps (e.g. in a timed-automaton all of the nodes would have been observable). In contrast to [19,21], we localize bypassing of policies at the level of the nodes, while we also define a more flexible notion of security with respect to the attacker's observability.

Definition 1 *(Y−Bisimulation). For a timed automaton* $\mathsf{TA} = (Q, E, I, q_o)$ *and a set of nodes* $Y = Y_s \cup Y_w$, *a relation* $\simeq_Y \subseteq (\boldsymbol{Config} \cup \{\bot\}) \times (\boldsymbol{Config} \cup \{\bot\})$ *will be called a* Y−*bisimulation relation if* $\simeq_Y$ *is symmetric and we have that if* $\gamma_1 = \langle q_1, \sigma_1, \delta_1 \rangle \simeq_Y \langle q_2, \sigma_2, \delta_2 \rangle = \gamma_2$ *then*

$$(\sigma_1, \delta_1) \equiv (\sigma_2, \delta_2) \Rightarrow \textit{if } \gamma_1 \overset{D_1}{\Longrightarrow}_Y \gamma_1' \textit{ then } \exists \gamma_2', D_2 :$$
$$\gamma_2 \overset{D_2}{\Longrightarrow}_Y \gamma_2' \wedge \gamma_1' \simeq_Y \gamma_2' \wedge$$
$$(\gamma_1' \neq \bot \wedge \gamma_2' \neq \bot) \Rightarrow ((node(\gamma_1') \in Y_w \wedge node(\gamma_2') \in Y_w) \vee$$
$$pair(\gamma_1') \equiv pair(\gamma_2'))$$

where $node(\langle q, \sigma, \delta \rangle) = q$, $pair(\langle q, \sigma, \delta \rangle) = (\sigma, \delta)$, *and if* $\gamma_1 \simeq_Y \gamma_2$ *then*

$$(\gamma_1 = \bot \Leftrightarrow \gamma_2 = \bot)$$

We write $\sim_Y$ for the union of all the Y−bisimulations and it is immediate that this definition of $\sim_Y$ is both a Y−bisimulation and an equivalence relation. Intuitively, when two configurations are related in $\sim_Y$, and they are low equivalent then they produce distinguishable pairs of states only at the weakly observable nodes. Otherwise, observations made at strongly observable nodes should be still indistinguishable. In both cases, the resulting configurations of two Y−bisimilar configurations should also be Y−bisimilar. We are now ready to define our security notion.

Definition 2 *(Security of Timed Automata). For a timed automaton* $\mathsf{TA} = (Q, E, I, q_o)$ *and a set* $Y = Y_s \cup Y_w$ *of observable nodes, we will say that* TA *satisfies the* information security policy $\mathcal{L}$ *whenever:*

$$\forall q \in \{q_o\} \cup Y : \forall (\sigma, \delta), (\sigma', \delta') :$$
$$(\llbracket I(q) \rrbracket (\sigma, \delta) \wedge \llbracket I(q) \rrbracket (\sigma', \delta')) \Rightarrow \langle q, \sigma, \delta \rangle \sim_Y \langle q, \sigma', \delta' \rangle$$

Whenever $Y_w = \emptyset$ our notion of security coincides with standard definitions of non-interference [29], where an automaton that satisfies the information security policy $\mathcal{L}$ does not leak any information about its high variables.

Example 3. For the smart grid automaton SG of the Example 1, we have the set of observable nodes $Y = \{2, 3, 4\}$, where the strongly observable ones are the nodes 2 and 4 ($Y_s = \{2, 4\}$), and the weakly one is the node 3 ($Y_w = \{3\}$), where the TTP is allowed to release the secret information of C.

4 Post-dominators

For the implicit flows arising from conditions, we are interested in finding their end points (nodes) that are the points where the control flow is not dependent on the conditions anymore. For that, we define a generalized version of the post-dominator relation and the immediate post-dominator relation [18].

Paths. A *path* π in a timed automaton $\mathsf{TA} = (\mathsf{Q}, \mathsf{E}, \mathsf{I}, q_\circ)$ is a finite $\pi = q_0 act_1 q_1 ... q_{n-1} act_n q_n$ ($n \geq 0$) or infinite $\pi = q_0 act_1 q_1 ... q_{n-1} act_n q_n ...$ sequence of nodes and actions such that $\forall i > 0 : (q_{i-1}, act_i, q_i) \in \mathsf{E}$. We say that a path is *trivial* if $\pi = q_0$ and we say that a node q belongs to the path π, or π contains q, and we will write $q \in \pi$, if there exists some i such that $q_i = q$. For a finite path $\pi = q_0 act_1 q_1 ... q_{n-1} act_n q_n$ we write $\pi(i) = q_i act_{i+1} q_{i+1} ... q_{n-1} act_n q_n$ ($i \leq n$) for the suffix of π that starts at the i-th position and we usually refer to it as the i-th suffix of π. Finally, for a node q and a set of nodes $Y \subseteq \mathsf{Q}$ we write

$$\Pi_{(q,Y)} = \{\pi \mid \pi = q_0 act_1 q_1 ... q_{n-1} act_n q_n : n > 0 \wedge q_0 = q \wedge q_n \in Y \wedge$$
$$\forall i \in \{1, ..., n-1\} : q_i \notin Y\}$$

for the set of all the non-trivial finite paths that start at q, end at a node y in Y and all the intermediate nodes of the path do not belong in Y.

Definition 3 *(Post-dominators). For a node q and a set of nodes $Y \subseteq \mathsf{Q}$ we define the set*

$$pdom_Y(q) = \{q' \mid \forall \pi \in \Pi_{(q,Y)} : q' \in \pi(1)\}$$

and whenever $q' \in pdom_Y(q)$, we will say that q' is a Y post-dominator of q.

Intuitively whenever a node q' is a Y post-dominator of a node q it means that every non-trivial path that starts at q has to visit q' before it visits one of the nodes in Y. We write $pdom_y(q)$ whenever $Y = \{y\}$ is a singleton and we have the following facts

Fact 1. *For a set of nodes $Y \subseteq \mathsf{Q}$ and for a node q we have that*

$$pdom_Y(q) = \bigcap_{y \in Y} pdom_y(q)$$

Fact 2. *The post-dominator set for a singleton set $\{y\}$ can be computed by finding the greatest solution of the following data-flow equations:*

$$\begin{array}{ll} pdom_y(q) = \mathsf{Q} & \text{if } \Pi_{(q,\{y\})} = \emptyset \\ pdom_y(q) = \{y\} & \text{if } y \in succ(q) \\ pdom_y(q) = \bigcap_{q' \in succ(q)} (\{q'\} \cup pdom_y(q')) & \text{otherwise} \end{array}$$

For a node q, we are interested in finding the Y post-dominator "closest" to it.

Definition 4. *For a node q and a set of nodes Y we definite the set*

$$ipdom_Y(q) = \{q' \in pdom_Y(q) \mid pdom_Y(q) = \{q'\} \vee$$
$$q' \notin Y \wedge (\forall q'' \in pdom_Y(q) : q'' \neq q' \Rightarrow$$
$$q'' \in pdom_Y(q'))\}$$

and a node $q' \in ipdom_Y(q)$ will be called an immediate Y post-dominator *of q.*

The following fact gives us a unique immediate Y post-dominator for the nodes that can reach Y $(\Pi_{(q,Y)} \neq \emptyset)$. Intuitively this unique immediate Y post-dominator of a node q is the node that is the "closest" Y post-dominator of q, meaning that in any non-trivial path starting from q and ending in Y, the Y immediate post-dominator of q will always be visited first before any other Y post-dominator of q.

Fact 3. *For a set of nodes Y and a node q, whenever $\Pi_{(q,Y)} \neq \emptyset$ and pdom$_Y(q) \neq \emptyset$ then there exists node q' such that ipdom$_Y(q) = \{q'\}$.*

For simplicity, whenever a node q' is the unique immediate Y post-dominator of a node q and $\Pi_{(q,Y)} \neq \emptyset$ we shall write ipd$_Y(q)$ for q' and we will say that *the unique immediate Y post-dominator of q is defined.* For any other case where q can either not reach Y $(\Pi_{(q,Y)} = \emptyset)$ or pdom$_Y(q) = \emptyset$ we will say that *the unique immediate post-dominator of q is not defined.*

Example 4. For the timed automaton SG and for the set of observable nodes $Y = \{2, 3, 4\}$, we have that pdom$_Y(q) = $ ipd$_Y(q) = \{2\}$ for q being 1, 3 and 4 while pdom$_Y(2) = $ ipd$_Y(2) = \emptyset$. Therefore for the nodes 1,3 and 4 their unique immediate Y post-dominator is defined and it is the node 2, while the unique immediate Y post-dominator of the node 2 is not defined.

5   Algorithm for Secure Information Flow

We develop an algorithm (Fig. 2) that traverses the graph of a timed automaton TA $= (Q, E, I, q_o)$ and imposes information flow constraints on the program variables and clocks of the automaton with respect to a security policy $\mathcal{L}$ and a Y post-dominator relation, where $Y = Y_s \cup Y_w$ is the set of observable nodes. Before we explain the algorithm we start by defining some auxiliary operators.

Auxiliary Operators. For an edge $(q_s, g \rightarrow \boldsymbol{x} := \boldsymbol{a}: \boldsymbol{r}, q_t) \in $ E we define the auxiliary operator ass$(.)$, expr$(.)$ and con$(.)$ as

$$\text{ass}((q_s, g \rightarrow \boldsymbol{x} := \boldsymbol{a}: \boldsymbol{r}, q_t)) = \{\boldsymbol{x}, \boldsymbol{r}\}$$
$$\text{expr}((q_s, g \rightarrow \boldsymbol{x} := \boldsymbol{a}: \boldsymbol{r}, q_t)) = \{\boldsymbol{a}\}$$
$$\text{con}((q_s, g \rightarrow \boldsymbol{x} := \boldsymbol{a}: \boldsymbol{r}, q_t)) = \mathsf{I}(q_s) \wedge g \wedge \mathsf{I}(q_t)[\boldsymbol{a}/\boldsymbol{x}][0/\boldsymbol{r}]$$

where ass$(.)$ gives the modified variables and clocks of the assignment performed by TA using that edge, expr$(.)$ gives the expressions used for the assignment, and the operator con$(.)$ returns the condition that has to hold in order for the assignment to be performed. We finally lift the ass$(.)$ operator to finite paths and thus for a finite path $\pi = q_0 act_1 q_1 ... q_{n-1} act_n q_n$ we define the auxiliary operators Ass$(.)$ as

$$\text{Ass}(q_0 act_1 q_1 ... q_{n-1} act_n q_n) = \bigcup_{i=1}^{n} \text{ass}((q_{i-1}, act_i, q_i))$$

We write

$$Q_{\leadsto \mathsf{w}} = \{q \mid \forall \pi = q..q' \in \Pi_{(q,Y)} : q' \in Y_w\}$$

C1. For all $q \in Q_{\leadsto w}$:

(a) $\quad \bigwedge_{e \in E_q} \forall y \in \mathsf{fv}(\mathsf{con}(e)) : \mathcal{L}(y) = L \wedge (\Psi_e \vee A_e)$

C2. For all $q \in Q^c_{\leadsto w}$ such that their unique immediate Y post-dominator is defined :

(a) $\quad \bigwedge_{e \in E_q} \bigcup_{\pi \in \Pi_{(e,\{ipd_Y(q)\})}} \mathsf{fv}(\mathsf{con}(e)) \leadsto \mathsf{Ass}(\pi) \wedge A_e$

(b) $\quad \bigwedge_{e \neq e' : e \in E_q, \ e' \in E_q, \ \underline{sat}(\mathsf{con}(e) \wedge \mathsf{con}(e'))} \mathsf{fv}(\mathsf{con}(e)) \leadsto \bigcup_{\pi \in \Pi_{(e',\{ipd_Y(q)\})}} \mathsf{Ass}(\pi)$

(c) $\quad \Phi_q \Rightarrow \bigwedge_{e \in E_q} \forall y \in \mathsf{fv}(\mathsf{con}(e)) : \mathcal{L}(y) = L$

C3. For all $q \in Q^c_{\leadsto w}$ such that their unique immediate Y post-dominator is not defined :

(a) $\quad \bigwedge_{e \in E_q} \forall y \in \mathsf{fv}(\mathsf{con}(e)) : \mathcal{L}(y) = L \wedge$

(b) $\quad ((e \leadsto w \wedge \Psi_e) \vee A_e)$

Fig. 2. Security of $\mathsf{TA} = (\mathsf{Q}, \mathsf{E}, \mathsf{I}, q_o)$ with respect to $\mathcal{L}$ and the Y post-dominator relation

for the set of nodes, where whenever the automaton performs a successful observable step starting from a node $q \in Q_{\leadsto w}$ and ending in an observable node $q' \in Y$, then it is always the case that q' is weakly observable.

Condition **C1**. We start by looking at the nodes in $Q_{\leadsto w}$. According to our security notion (Definition 2), for two low equivalent configurations at a node q, whenever the first one performs a successful (or unsuccessful) observable step that ends at a weakly observable node, then also the second should be able to perform an observable step that ends at a weakly observable node (or an unsuccessful one resp.). For that, the condition **C1** (a) first requires that the conditions of the outgoing edges in E_q where $\mathsf{E}_q = \{(q, act, q') \mid (q, act, q') \in \mathsf{E}\}$ contain only low variables. However, this is not enough.

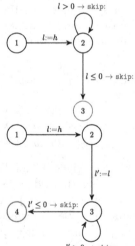

Fig. 3. Example automata **(a)** (top) and **(b)** (bottom)

To explain the rest of the constraints imposed by the condition **C1** (a) consider the automaton **(a)** of Fig. 3, where the node 3 is weakly observable, h and l is a high and a low variable respectively, and all the invariants of the nodes are set to tt. This automaton is not secure with respect to Definition 2. To see this, we have $([l \mapsto 0, h \mapsto 1], \delta) \equiv ([l \mapsto 0, h \mapsto 0], \delta)$ (for some clock state δ) but the pair $([l \mapsto 0, h \mapsto 1], \delta)$ always produces $\perp$ since we will have an infinite loop at the node 2, while $([l \mapsto 0, h \mapsto 0], \delta)$ always terminates at the node 3. That is because even if both edges of the node 2 contain only the low variable l in their condition, the assignment l:=h bypasses the policy $\mathcal{L}$ and thus, right after it, the two pairs stop being low equivalent.

As another example, consider the automaton **(b)** of Fig. 3. Here the node 4 is weakly observable, h is a high variable, l, l' are two low variables and all the invariants of nodes are set to tt again. We have $([l \mapsto 0, l' \mapsto 0, h \mapsto 1], \delta) \equiv ([l \mapsto 0, l' \mapsto 0, h \mapsto 0], \delta)$ (for some clock state δ)

and again the first pair produces $\bot$ by looping at the node 3, whereas the second pair always terminates. Here even if the variable l is not used in any condition after the assignment l:=h, it influences the value of l' and consequently, since l' appears on the condition of the edges of the node 3 we get this behavior.

To cater for such cases, for an edge $e = (q_s, g \rightarrow \boldsymbol{x} := \boldsymbol{a}\colon \boldsymbol{r}, q_t)$ we first define the predicate

$$A_e = \bigwedge_i \mathsf{fv}(a_i) \rightsquigarrow \{x_i\}$$

that takes care of the explicit flows arising from the assignments. We then define

$$\Pi_{(e,Y)} = \{\pi \mid e = (q_0, act_1, q_1) : \pi = q_0 act_1 q_1 ... q_{n-1} act_n q_n \in \Pi_{(q_0, Y)}\}$$

to be set of paths (the ones defined in Sect. 4) that start with e and end in Y, and all the intermediate nodes do not belong to Y. Finally, whenever an assignment bypasses the security policy $\mathcal{L}$ due to an explicit flow and thus A_e is false, we then impose the predicate

$$\Psi_e = \forall \pi \in \Pi_{(e,Y)} : \forall q' \in \pi(1) :$$
$$q' \notin Y \Rightarrow (\forall e' \in E_{q'} : (\mathsf{ass}(e) \setminus R) \cap (\mathsf{fv}(\mathsf{con}(e')) \cup \mathsf{fv}(\mathsf{expr}(e'))) = \emptyset)$$

The predicate Ψ_e demands that the assigned program variables of $e = (q_s, act, q_t)$ cannot be used in any expression or condition that appears in a path that starts with q_t and goes to an observable node. Note here that even if Ψ_e quantifies over a possibly infinite set of paths ($\Pi_{(e,Y)}$), it can be computed in *finite time* by only looking at the paths where each cycle occurs at most once.

We will now look at the nodes where the automaton may perform a successful observable step that ends in a strongly observable node. Those nodes are described by the set $Q^c_{\rightsquigarrow w} = Q \setminus Q_{\rightsquigarrow w}$, that is the complement of $Q_{\rightsquigarrow w}$.

Condition **C2**. For a node q in $Q^c_{\rightsquigarrow w}$, whose immediate Y post-dominator is defined, condition **C2** (a) takes care of the explicit and the implicit flows generated by the assignment and the control dependencies respectively, arising from the edges of q. Note here that we do not propagate the implicit flows any further after $\mathsf{ipd}_Y(q)$. This is because $\mathsf{ipd}_Y(q)$ is the point where all the branches of q are joining and any further computation is not control-dependent on them anymore. Those constraints are along the line of Denning's approach [10] of the so-called *block-labels*.

To understand condition **C2** (b) consider the automaton (c) of Fig. 4, where h and l is a high and a low variable respectively, the node 2 is strongly observable, and both nodes 1 and 2 have their invariant set to tt. Next take $([l \mapsto 0, h \mapsto 1], \delta) \equiv ([l \mapsto 0, h \mapsto 0], \delta)$ (for some clock state δ) and note that the first pair can result in a configuration in 2 with $([l \mapsto 0, h \mapsto 1], \delta)$ (taking the top branch) while the second pair always ends in 2 with $[l \mapsto 1, h \mapsto 0]$. Therefore this automaton is not secure with respect to our Definition 2.

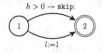

Fig. 4. Example automaton (c)

To take care of such behaviours we write $\underline{sat}(\cdots)$ to express the satisfiability of the $\cdots$ formula. Whenever there are two branches (induced by the edges e and e' both leaving q) that are not mutually exclusive (that is, where $\underline{sat}(\mathrm{con}(e) \wedge \mathrm{con}(e'))$) we make sure to record the information flow arising from *bypassing* the branch that would otherwise perform an assignment. This is essential for dealing with *non-determinism*.

Fact 4. *For a timed automaton* $\mathsf{TA} = (\mathsf{Q}, \mathsf{E}, \mathsf{I}, q_0)$, *we have that if*

$$\langle q, \sigma, \delta \rangle \overset{D}{\Longrightarrow}_{\{q'\}} \langle q', \sigma', \delta' \rangle$$

then

$$\{x \mid \sigma(x) \neq \sigma'(x)\} \cup \{r \mid \delta'(r) \neq \delta(r) + D\} \subseteq \bigcup_{\pi \in \Pi_{(e,\{q'\})}} \mathsf{Ass}(\pi)$$

where e corresponds to the initial edge of this observable step.

Condition **C2** (c) takes care of cases where a *timing/termination* side channel [2] could have occurred.

As an example of such a case consider the automaton **(d)** of Fig. 5, where h and t is a high program variable and a low clock respectively, node 2 is strongly observable and both 1 and 2 have their invariant set to tt. Next, for $([h \mapsto 1], [t \mapsto 0]) \equiv ([h \mapsto 0], [t \mapsto 0])$ we have that the first pair always delays at least 30 units and ends in 2 with a clock state that has $t > 30$, whereas the second pair can go to 2, taking the

$h > 0 \wedge t > 30 \rightarrow \mathrm{skip}:$

$h \leq 0 \rightarrow \mathrm{skip}:$

Fig. 5. Example automaton **(d)**

lower branch immediately without any delay, and thus the resulting pairs will not be low equivalent. To take care of such behaviours, we stipulate a predicate Φ_q such that

$$\exists t_1, t_2 \in \bigcup_{(\sigma,\delta):[\![\mathsf{I}(q)]\!](\sigma,\delta)} [\![\mathsf{TA} : q \mapsto \mathrm{ipd}_Y(q)]\!](\sigma, \delta) : \Delta(t_1) \neq \Delta(t_2)$$
$$\Downarrow$$
$$\Phi_q$$

Using this predicate we demand that whenever the TA does not have a "constant" *termination behavior* from the node q to the node $\mathrm{ipd}_Y(q)$, then variables that influence the termination behavior should not be of high security level.

Condition **C3**. We are now left with the nodes in $\mathsf{Q}^c_{\leadsto w}$, whose immediate Y post-dominator is not defined. Since for such a node q, we cannot find a point (the unique immediate Y post-dominator) where the control dependencies from the branches of q end, condition **C3** (a) requires that the conditions of the edges of q should not be dependent on high security variables.

Condition **C3** (b) caters for the explicit flows, of an edge e using the predicate A_e. However we are allowed to dispense A_e, whenever further computations after taking the edge e may lead only to weakly observable nodes and Ψ_e holds. To express this for an edge $e = (q_s, g \to \boldsymbol{x} := \boldsymbol{a}\colon \boldsymbol{r}, q_t)$ we write

$$e \leadsto w$$

whenever $q_t \in Y_w$ or $q_t \in \mathsf{Q}_{\leadsto w}$.

Example 5. Consider now the automaton SG of Example 1, and the Y post-dominator relation of Example 4.

We have that the nodes 1, 3 and 4 are in $Q^c_{\leadsto w}$ and also that their immediate unique Y post-dominator is defined. Condition **C2** (a) and **C2** (b) impose the following constraints

$$\{T, t, r\} \leadsto \{ed, e_i, c_i, s, t, r\}, \{ed, e_i\} \leadsto \{e_i\}, \{e_i\} \leadsto \{c_i\}, \{v_i\} \leadsto \{p_i\} \quad (i = 1, 2)$$
$$\{T\} \leadsto \{p_1, p_2, a, f\}, \{z\} \leadsto \{a\}, \{\} \leadsto \{s, f, a\}$$

Finally, for the node 1, because Φ_1 (**C2** (c)) all the clocks need to be of low security level.

Next, the node 2 is in $Q^c_{\leadsto w}$ and since its unique immediate Y post-dominator is not defined, condition **C3** (b) impose the constraints

$$\{p_1, p_2, c_1, c_2\} \leadsto \{b\}, \{a\} \leadsto \{x\}, \{\} \leadsto \{e_1, e_2, f\}$$

and condition **C3** (a) imposes that T, s and f should be of low security level. Notice here that since for the edge $e = (2, s = 1 \rightarrow y_1, y_2 := c_1, c_2: , 3)$ that releases the sensitive information of C we have that $e \leadsto w$, we are not imposing the constraint $\{c_i\} \leadsto \{y_i\}$ $(i = (1, 2))$. Those constraints are easy to verify for the security assignment of Example 2.

Now if we were to change the node 3 from being a weakly observable to a strongly observable node, the automaton SG will not be secure with respect to Definition 2. In that case our algorithm will reject it, since for the edge e we would have that $e \not\leadsto w$ and the predicate A_e would have resulted in false.

Finally, we shall write $sec_{Y,\mathcal{L}}(\mathsf{TA})$ whenever the constraints arising from our algorithm (Fig. 2) are satisfied and thus we have the following lemmas

Lemma 1. *For a timed automaton* $\mathsf{TA} = (Q, E, I, q_o)$, *if* $sec_{Y,\mathcal{L}}(\mathsf{TA})$ *then for* $(\sigma_1, \delta_1), (\sigma_2, \delta_2)$ *such that* $[\![I(q)]\!](\sigma_1, \delta_1)$ *and* $[\![I(q)]\!](\sigma_2, \delta_2)$ *and* $(\sigma_1, \delta_1) \equiv (\sigma_2, \delta_2)$ *we have that*

$$if \langle q, \sigma_1, \delta_1 \rangle \overset{D_1}{\Longrightarrow}_Y \langle q', \sigma'_1, \delta'_1 \rangle \; then \; \exists(\sigma'_2, \delta'_2), D_2 : \langle q, \sigma_2, \delta_2 \rangle \overset{D_2}{\Longrightarrow}_Y \langle q', \sigma'_2, \delta'_2 \rangle \wedge$$
$$(q' \in Y_w \vee (\sigma'_1, \delta'_1) \equiv (\sigma'_2, \delta'_2))$$

Lemma 2. *For a timed automaton* $\mathsf{TA} = (Q, E, I, q_o)$, *if* $sec_{Y,\mathcal{L}}(\mathsf{TA})$ *then for* $(\sigma_1, \delta_1), (\sigma_2, \delta_2)$ *such that* $[\![I(q)]\!](\sigma_1, \delta_1)$ *and* $[\![I(q)]\!](\sigma_2, \delta_2)$ *and* $(\sigma_1, \delta_1) \equiv (\sigma_2, \delta_2)$ *we have that*

$$if \langle q, \sigma_1, \delta_1 \rangle \overset{\infty}{\Longrightarrow}_Y \bot \; then \; also \; \langle q, \sigma_2, \delta_2 \rangle \overset{\infty}{\Longrightarrow}_Y \bot$$

The following theorem concludes the two lemmas from above to establish the soundness of our algorithm with respect to the notion of security of Definition 2.

Theorem 1. *For a timed automaton* $\mathsf{TA} = (Q, E, I, q_o)$, *if* $sec_{Y,\mathcal{L}}(\mathsf{TA})$ *then* TA *satisfies the information security policy* $\mathcal{L}$.

6   Conclusion

We have shown how to successfully enforce *Information Flow Control* policies
on timed automata. This has facilitated developing an algorithm that prevents
unnecessary *label creep* and that deals with *non-determinism, non-termination,*
and *continuous real-time*. The algorithm has been proved sound by means of a
bisimulation result, that allows controlled information leakage.

We are exploring how to automate the analysis and in particular how to
implement (a sound approximation of) the Φ_q predicate. There has been a lot of
research [3,4] done for determining the maximum (max_t) or minimum (min_t)
execution time that an automaton needs to move from a location q_s to a location
q_t. One possibility is to make use of this work [3,4] and thus the predicate Φ_q
would amount to checking if the execution time between the two nodes of interest
(q and $ipd_Y(q)$) is constant (e.g. $max_t = min_t$).

A longer-term goal is to allow policies to simultaneously deal with safety and
security properties of cyberphysical systems.

Appendix

Proposition 1

Assume that all the traces in $[\![TA : q_s \mapsto q_t]\!](\sigma, \delta)$ are successful and we want to
show that there exists $t \in [\![TA : q_s \mapsto q_t]\!](\sigma, \delta)$ with a maximal length m.

We use results from model-checking for timed automata [15]. As in [15] we
first transform our automaton to an equivalent diagonal-free automaton, that
is an automaton where clocks appearing in its guards and invariants can be
compared only to integers (e.g. $r_1 - r_2 \leq 5$ is not allowed). We then define the
region graph $RG(TA)$ of TA, that is a finite graph where nodes of the region graph
are of the form (q, reg) where reg is a clock region, that is an equivalence class
defined on the clock states (for details we refer to [15]). Configurations of $RG(TA)$
are of the form $\langle (q, reg), \sigma \rangle$ and we have that $\langle (q, reg), \sigma \rangle \Longrightarrow \langle (q', reg'), \sigma' \rangle$ if
there are $\delta \in reg$, $\delta' \in reg'$, $d \geq 0$, σ' such that the automaton TA performs the
transition $\langle q, \sigma, \delta \rangle \xrightarrow{d} \langle q', \sigma', \delta' \rangle$. Lemma 1 of [15] then states that each abstract
run (finite or infinite) in the region graph $RG(TA)$ can be instantiated by a run
(finite or infinite resp.) in TA and vice verca. This is based on the property of
the region graph of being *pre-stable* that is that $\langle (q, reg), \sigma \rangle \Longrightarrow \langle (q', reg'), \sigma' \rangle$ if
$\forall \delta \in reg$ there are $\delta' \in reg'$, $d \geq 0$, σ' such that $\langle q, \sigma, \delta \rangle \xrightarrow{d} \langle q', \sigma', \delta' \rangle$. Therefore
the computation tree T of $\langle q, \sigma, \delta \rangle$ in TA has the same depth as the computation
tree T' of $\langle (q, [\delta]), \sigma \rangle$ in $RG(TA)$ where $[\delta]$ is the region that contains all the
clock states that are equivalent to δ. We then recall König's infinity lemma as it
applies to trees – that every tree who has infinitely-many vertices but is locally
finite (each vertex has finitely-many successor vertices), has at least one infinite
path [11]. It is immediate that T' is a locally finite tree. Now if T' is infinite
then by König's infinity lemma we have that T' has an infinite path and thus
using Lemma 1 of [15] we have also that T has an infinite path that corresponds

to a trace $\langle q, \sigma, \delta \rangle$ in TA which contradicts our assumptions that all the traces of $\langle q, \sigma, \delta \rangle$ are finite. Therefore we can conclude that T' has a finite depth and therefore also T and that they are equal to the number m.

Proof of Fact 2

Proof. The first equation is straightforward by the definition of the post-dominator relation. For the second one, that is when y is a successor (an immediate one) of q then the only post-dominators of q is the node y, since there exists a non-trivial path $\pi = q\, act\, y \in \Pi_{(q,y)}$ (for some action act) such that the trivial path $\pi(1) = y$ contains only y, and therefore for any other path $\pi' \in \Pi_{(q,y)}$ in which a node q' different from y is contained in $\pi'(1)$, q' can not be a post-dominator of q since it is not contained in the trivial path $\pi(1)$. To understand the last equation notice that if a node q'' post-dominates all of the successors of q or it is a successor of q that post-dominates all the other successors of q then all the non-trivial paths from q to y will always visit q'' and thus $q'' \in \mathrm{pdom}_y(q)$; similarly if $q'' \notin \bigcap_{q' \in \mathrm{succ}(q)} (\{q'\} \cup \mathrm{pdom}_y(q'))$ then there exists a successor of q, $q' \neq q''$ such that q'' does not post-dominate q' and thus we can find a non-trivial path $\pi \in \Pi_{(q,Y)}$ that starts with $q\, act\, q'$ (for some action act) and does not contain q'' and thus q'' is not a post-dominator of q.

Proof of Fact 3

Proof. To prove that $\mathrm{ipdom}_Y(q)$ is singleton we consider two cases. In the case that $\mathrm{pdom}_Y(q) = \{q'\}$ then the proof is trivial.

Assume now that $\mathrm{pdom}_Y(q) = \{q_1, ..., q_n\}$ $(n \geq 2)$ and take an arbitrary non-trivial path $\pi \in \Pi_{(q,Y)}$ and find the closest to q (the one that appears first in the path) Y post-dominator $q_j \in \mathrm{pdom}_Y(q)$ in that path. Next note that $q_j \notin Y$ since if $q_j \in Y$, we could shorten that path to the point that we meet q_j for the first time and thus we have found a non trivial path $\pi' \in \Pi_{(q,Y)}$ (since $q_j \in Y$) in which $\forall i \neq j : q_i \notin \pi'(1)$ and thus $\forall i \neq j : q_i \notin \mathrm{pdom}_Y(q)$ which contradicts our assumption. Next to prove that $\forall i \neq j : q_i \in \mathrm{pdom}_Y(q_j)$ assume that this is not the case and thus we can find $q_l \neq q_j : q_l \notin \mathrm{pdom}_Y(q_j)$. Therefore we can find a path $\pi'' \in \Pi_{(q_j,Y)}$ such that $q_l \notin \pi''(1)$, but this means that if we concatenate the paths π' and π'' we have a path in $\Pi_{(q,Y)}$ in which q_l does not belong to it and thus q_l does not belong in its 1-suffix either and therefore $q_l \notin \mathrm{pdom}_Y(q)$, which again contradicts our assumption.

Finally to prove that $\mathrm{ipdom}_Y(q)$ is singleton assume that there exists another Y post-dominator of q, q_l such that $q_l \neq q_j$ and $q_l \notin Y$ and $q_j \in \mathrm{pdom}(q_l)$. Then this means that q_j belongs in all the 1-suffixes of the paths in the set $\Pi_{(q_l,Y)}$. Therefore take $\pi = q_l...q_j...y \in \Pi_{(q_l,Y)}$ (for some $y \in Y$) such that π contains no cycles (e.g. each node occurs exactly once in the path) but then there exists a path $\pi' = q_j...y$ (the suffix of the path π) such that $q_l \notin \pi'$ and thus $q_l \notin \mathrm{pdom}_Y(q_j)$ which contradicts our assumption. Therefore we have proved that q_j is the unique immediate Y post-dominator of q.

Proof of Lemma 1

Proof. Assume that $\langle q, \sigma_1, \delta_1 \rangle \overset{D_1}{\Longrightarrow}_Y \langle q', \sigma_1', \delta_1' \rangle$ because of the trace

$$\langle q, \sigma_1, \delta_1 \rangle = \langle q, \sigma_{01}, \delta_{01} \rangle \xrightarrow{d_1} \ ... \ \xrightarrow{d_k} \langle q_{k1}, \sigma_{k1}, \delta_{k1} \rangle = \langle q', \sigma_1', \delta_1' \rangle \quad (*)$$

where $k > 0$ and $\forall i \in \{1, .., k-1\} : q_{i1} \notin Y$ and $D_1 = \sum_{j=1}^{k} d_j$ and the first transition of the trace has happened because of the edge $e \in E_q$.

We shall consider two main cases. The one where q is in $Q_{\leadsto w}$ and one where it is not.

Main Case 1: q is in $Q_{\leadsto w}$. In that case $q' \in Y_w$ and thus we only have to prove that (σ_2, δ_2) can reach q'. We start by proving a small fact.

First for a set of variables and clocks $\mathcal{Z}$, and two pairs (σ, δ), (σ', δ') we write

$$(\sigma, \delta) \equiv^{\mathcal{Z}} (\sigma', \delta') \quad \text{iff} \quad \begin{aligned} &\forall x : (x \in \mathcal{Z} \wedge \mathcal{L}(x) = L) \Rightarrow \sigma(x) = \sigma'(x) \wedge \\ &\forall r : (r \in \mathcal{Z} \wedge \mathcal{L}(r) = L) \Rightarrow \delta(r) = \delta'(r) \end{aligned}$$

Next, for a finite path $\pi = q_0 act_1 q_1 ... q_{n-1} act_n q_n$ we define the auxiliary operator $\mathcal{Z}(.)$ as $\mathcal{Z}(\pi) = \bigcup_{i=0}^{n-1} (\bigcup_{e' \in E_{q_i}} \mathsf{fv}(\mathsf{con}(e')) \cup \mathsf{fv}(\mathsf{expr}(e')))$.

Now we will prove that for a path $\pi = q'_{01} act'_1 q'_{11} ... q'_{(n-1)1} act'_n q'_n \in \Pi_{(e,Y)}$, if

$$\langle q, \sigma_1, \delta_1 \rangle = \langle q'_{01}, \sigma'_{01}, \delta'_{01} \rangle \xrightarrow{d'_1} \ ... \ \xrightarrow{d'_l} \langle q'_{l1}, \sigma'_{l1}, \delta'_{l1} \rangle \quad (l \leq n) \tag{1}$$

using the edges $(q'_{01}, act'_1, q'_{11}), ..., (q'_{(l-1)1}, act'_l, q'_l)$ and $(\sigma_1, \delta_1) \equiv^{\mathcal{Z}(\pi)} (\sigma_2, \delta_2)$ then $\exists (\sigma'_{l2}, \delta'_{l2})$:

$$\langle q, \sigma_2, \delta_2 \rangle = \langle q'_{01}, \sigma'_{02}, \delta'_{02} \rangle \xrightarrow{d'_1} \ ... \ \xrightarrow{d'_l} \langle q'_{l1}, \sigma'_{l2}, \delta'_{l2} \rangle \quad (a)$$

and

$$l < n \Rightarrow (\sigma'_{l1}, \delta'_{l1}) \equiv^{\mathcal{Z}(\pi(l))} (\sigma'_{l2}, \delta'_{l2}) \tag{b}$$

where recall that $\pi(l)$ is the l-suffix of π. The proof proceeds by induction on l.

Base Case $l = 1$. To prove (a), let $e = (q'_{01}, g \to x := a: r, q'_{11})$ and note that because $(\sigma_1, \delta_1) \equiv^{\mathcal{Z}(\pi)} (\sigma_2, \delta_2)$ and $\mathsf{con}(e)$ contains only low variables (since $q'_{01} = q \in Q_{\leadsto w}$ and **C1** (a)) it is immediate that there exists $\sigma'_{12} = \sigma_2[x \mapsto [\![a]\!]\sigma_2]$, $\delta'_{12} = (\delta_2 + d'_1)[r \mapsto 0]$ such that $[\![l(q'_{01})]\!](\sigma_2, \delta_2 + d'_1) = \mathsf{tt}$ and $[\![l(q'_{11})]\!](\sigma'_{12}, \delta'_{12}) = \mathsf{tt}$, and $\langle q'_{01}, \sigma_2, \delta_2 \rangle \xrightarrow{d'_1} \langle q'_{11}, \sigma'_{12}, \delta'_{12} \rangle$.

Now if $l < n$, to prove (b) we consider two cases. One where A_e is true and one where it is false. If A_e is true we note that $(\sigma'_{11}, \delta'_{11}) \equiv^{\mathcal{Z}(\pi)} (\sigma'_{12}, \delta'_{12})$, and then it is immediate that also $(\sigma'_{11}, \delta'_{11}) \equiv^{\mathcal{Z}(\pi(1))} (\sigma'_{12}, \delta'_{12})$ as required. Otherwise, if A_e is false then Ψ_e is true and thus $(\sigma'_{11}, \delta'_{11}) \equiv^{\mathcal{Z}(\pi(1))} (\sigma'_{12}, \delta'_{12})$, because the two pairs are still low equivalent for the variables that are not used in the assignment of e, while the ones used in the assignment of e they do not appear in any condition (or expression) of an edge of a node q that belongs in $\pi(1)$.

Inductive Case $l = l_0 + 1$ $(l_0 > 0)$. Because of the trace in (1) we have that $t_1 = \langle q'_{01}, \sigma'_{01}, \delta'_{01} \rangle \xrightarrow{d'_1} \langle q'_{11}, \sigma'_{11}, \delta'_{11} \rangle$ and $t_2 = \langle q'_{11}, \sigma'_{11}, \delta'_{11} \rangle \xrightarrow{d'_2} \ ... \ \xrightarrow{d'_l} \langle q'_{l1}, \sigma'_{l1}, \delta'_{l1} \rangle$.

Using our induction hypothesis on t_1 we have that there exists $(\sigma'_{12}, \delta'_{12})$ such that $\langle q'_{01}, \sigma_2, \delta_2 \rangle \xrightarrow{d'_1} \langle q'_{11}, \sigma'_{12}, \delta'_{12} \rangle$ and $(\sigma'_{11}, \delta'_{11}) \equiv^{\mathcal{Z}(\pi(1))} (\sigma'_{12}, \delta'_{12})$ and the proof is completed using our induction hypothesis on t_2. The proof of *Main Case 1* follows by the result (a) of the fact from above, taking the path π that corresponds to the trace $(*)$ and using that $(\sigma_1, \delta_1) \equiv^{\mathcal{Z}(\pi)} (\sigma_2, \delta_2)$ (since $(\sigma_1, \delta_1) \equiv (\sigma_2, \delta_2)$ and all the nodes in π except q_{k1} have edges whose conditions contain only low variables). Therefore, since (σ_1, δ_1) creates the trace $(*)$ we also have that $\exists (\sigma'_2, \delta'_2)$:

$$\langle q, \sigma_2, \delta_2 \rangle = \langle q_{01}, \sigma_{02}, \delta_{02} \rangle \xrightarrow{d_1} \cdots \xrightarrow{d_k} \langle q_{k1}, \sigma_{k2}, \delta_{k2} \rangle = \langle q', \sigma'_2, \delta'_2 \rangle$$

and thus for $D_2 = d_1 + \ldots + d_k$ we have that

$$\langle q, \sigma_2, \delta_2 \rangle \xRightarrow{D_2}_Y \langle q', \sigma'_2, \delta'_2 \rangle$$

where $q' \in Y_w$ and this completes the proof for this case.

Main Case 2: When q is not in $Q_{\rightsquigarrow w}$. The proof proceeds by induction on the length k of the trace $(*)$.

Base Case (k = 1). We have that

$$\langle q, \sigma_1, \delta_1 \rangle \xrightarrow{d_1} \langle q', \sigma'_1, \delta'_1 \rangle$$

and let $e = (q, g \to \boldsymbol{x} := \boldsymbol{a} \colon \boldsymbol{r}, q')$, then it is immediate that $D_1 = d_1$, $\sigma'_1 = \sigma_1[\boldsymbol{x} \mapsto [\![\boldsymbol{a}]\!]\sigma_1]$, $\delta'_1 = (\delta_1 + d_1)[\boldsymbol{r} \mapsto \boldsymbol{0}]$ and $[\![l(q)]\!](\sigma_1, \delta_1 + d_1) = \text{tt}$ and $[\![l(q')]\!](\sigma'_1, \delta'_1) = \text{tt}$.

We shall consider two subcases one where the unique immediate Y post-dominator of q is defined and one where it is not.

Subcase 1: When the unique immediate Y post-dominator $\text{ipd}_Y(q)$ is defined. It has to be the case then that $q' = \text{ipd}_Y(q)$ since $q' \in Y$ and in particular, we have that $q' \in Y_s$. We will proceed by considering two other subcases of the *Subcase 1*, one where the condition Φ_q is *true* and one which it is *false*.

Subcase 1(a): When Φ_q is true. Then it is the case that all the variables of the condition $\text{con}(e)$ are low and thus it is immediate that there exists $d_2 = d_1$ and $\sigma'_2 = \sigma_2[\boldsymbol{x} \mapsto [\![\boldsymbol{a}]\!]\sigma_2]$, $\delta'_2 = (\delta_2 + d_2)[\boldsymbol{r} \mapsto \boldsymbol{0}]$ and $[\![l(q)]\!](\sigma_2, \delta_2 + d_2) = \text{tt}$ and $[\![l(q')]\!](\sigma'_2, \delta'_2) = \text{tt}$ such that $\langle q, \sigma_2, \delta_2 \rangle \xrightarrow{d_2} \langle q', \sigma'_2, \delta'_2 \rangle$ which implies that for $D_2 = d_2$

$$\langle q, \sigma_2, \delta_2 \rangle \xRightarrow{D_2}_Y \langle q', \sigma'_2, \delta'_2 \rangle$$

Finally, because $\text{sec}_{Y, \mathcal{L}}(\text{TA})$, condition **C2** (a) gives us that A_e is true, and thus all the *explicit flows* arising from the assignments $\boldsymbol{x} := \boldsymbol{a}$ are permissible and thus $(\sigma'_1, \delta'_1) \equiv (\sigma'_2, \delta'_2)$ as required.

Subcase 1(b): When Φ_q is false. If it is the case that all the variables in the condition $\text{con}(e)$ are low then the proof proceeds as in *Subcase 1(a)*.

For the case now that at least one variable in the condition $con(e)$ is high then because $sec_{Y,\mathcal{L}}(\mathsf{TA})$, condition **C2** (a) and Fact 4 ensure that $\forall x : \mathcal{L}(x) = L \Rightarrow \sigma_1'(x) = \sigma_1(x)$ and $\forall r : \mathcal{L}(r) = L \Rightarrow \delta_1'(r) = \delta_1(r) + d_1$. Since Φ_q is false (σ_1, δ_1) and (σ_2, δ_2) have the same *termination behaviour* and thus there exists $d_2 = d_1$ and (σ_2', δ_2') such that $\langle q, \sigma_2, \delta_2 \rangle \xrightarrow{d_2} \langle q', \sigma_2', \delta_2' \rangle$ and therefore for $D_2 = d_2$ we have that

$$\langle q, \sigma_2, \delta_2 \rangle \overset{D_2}{\Longrightarrow}_Y \langle q', \sigma_2', \delta_2' \rangle$$

We just showed that $(\sigma_1', \delta_1') \equiv (\sigma_1, \delta_1 + d_1) \equiv (\sigma_2, \delta_2 + d_2)$ and we will now show that $(\sigma_2', \delta_2') \equiv (\sigma_2, \delta_2 + d_2)$.

Now if

$$\langle q, \sigma_2, \delta_2 \rangle \xrightarrow{d_2} \langle q', \sigma_2', \delta_2' \rangle$$

using the edge e or an edge $e' \neq e$ such that $con(e')$ contains a high variable, since $sec_{Y,\mathcal{L}}(\mathsf{TA})$, condition **C2** (a) and Fact 4 gives that $\forall x : \mathcal{L}(x) = L \Rightarrow \sigma_2'(x) = \sigma_2(x)$ and $\forall r : \mathcal{L}(r) = L \Rightarrow \delta_2'(r) = \delta_2(r) + d_2$ and therefore $(\sigma_2', \delta_2') \equiv (\sigma_2, \delta_2 + d_2)$ as required. If now $con(e')$ contains only low variables, (σ_1, δ_1) is a witness of $sat(con(e) \wedge con(e'))$ and therefore because $sec_{Y,\mathcal{L}}(\mathsf{TA})$, using the condition **C2** (b) and Fact 4 we work as before and we obtain that $(\sigma_2', \delta_2') \equiv (\sigma_2, \delta_2 + d_2)$.

Subcase 2: When the unique immediate Y post-dominator of q is not defined. In that case, all the variables in $con(e)$ are low. If q' is in Y_w we have that $e \rightsquigarrow w$ and we proceed as in *Main Case 1*. Otherwise, we proceed as in *Subcase 1(a)*.

This completes the case for $k = 1$.

Inductive Case $(k = k_0 + 1)$. We have that

$$\langle q, \sigma_1, \delta_1 \rangle = \langle q, \sigma_{01}, \delta_{01} \rangle \xrightarrow{d_1} \dots \xrightarrow{d_k} \langle q_{k1}, \sigma_{k1}, \delta_{k1} \rangle = \langle q', \sigma_1', \delta_1' \rangle$$

and recall that the first transition happened because of the edge e and that q is not in $Q_{\rightsquigarrow w}$.

We shall consider two cases again, one where the unique immediate Y post-dominator of q is defined and one where it is not.

Subcase 1: When the unique immediate-post dominator $ipd_Y(q)$ is defined. We will proceed by considering two subcases of *Subcase 1*, one where Φ_q is *true* and one where Φ_q is *false*.

Subcase 1(a): When Φ_q is true. Since Φ_q is true we have that all the variables in $con(e)$ are low and thus $\exists d_1' = d_1$ and $(\sigma_{12}, \delta_{12}) \equiv (\sigma_{11}, \delta_{11})$ (this is ensured by our assumptions that $sec_{Y,\mathcal{L}}(\mathsf{TA})$ and the predicate A_e of the condition **C2** (a) that takes care of the *explicit flows* arising from the assignment in the edge e) such that

$$\langle q, \sigma_2, \delta_2 \rangle = \langle q_{01}, \sigma_{02}, \delta_{02} \rangle \xrightarrow{d_1'} \langle q_{11}, \sigma_{12}, \delta_{12} \rangle \tag{1}$$

Since q is not in $Q_{\rightsquigarrow w}$, note that it is also the case that q_{11} is not in $Q_{\rightsquigarrow w}$ and thus using that $(\sigma_{12}, \delta_{12}) \equiv (\sigma_{11}, \delta_{11})$ and our induction hypothesis on the trace

$$\langle q_{11}, \sigma_{11}, \delta_{11} \rangle \xrightarrow{d_2} \dots \xrightarrow{d_k} \langle q_{k1}, \sigma_{k1}, \delta_{k1} \rangle$$

we have that $\exists(\sigma_2', \delta_2')$ and D_2' such that

$$\langle q_{11}, \sigma_{12}, \delta_{12}\rangle \overset{D_2'}{\Longrightarrow}_Y \langle q', \sigma_2', \delta_2'\rangle \qquad (2)$$

and therefore by (1) and (2) and for $D_2 = d_1' + D_2'$ we have that

$$\langle q, \sigma_2, \delta_2\rangle \overset{D_2}{\Longrightarrow}_Y \langle q', \sigma_2', \delta_2'\rangle$$

and $(\sigma_1', \delta_1') \equiv (\sigma_2', \delta_2') \vee q' \in Y_w$ as required.

Subcase 1(b): When Φ_q is false. In the case that all the variables in con(e) are low then the proof proceeds as in Subcase 1(a).

Assume now that at least one variable in con(e) is high. Since $\mathrm{ipd}_Y(q)$ is defined then there exists $j \in \{1, ..., k\}$ such that $q_{j1} = \mathrm{ipd}_Y(q)$ and $\forall i \in \{1, .., j-1\} : q_{i1} \neq \mathrm{ipd}_Y(q)$. Therefore we have that

$$\langle q_{01}, \sigma_{01}, \delta_{01}\rangle \xrightarrow{d_1} ... \xrightarrow{d_j} \langle q_{j1}, \sigma_{j1}, \delta_{j1}\rangle \xrightarrow{d_{j+1}} ... \xrightarrow{d_k} \langle q_{k1}, \sigma_{k1}, \delta_{k1}\rangle$$

Next, using that $\mathrm{sec}_{Y,\mathcal{L}}(\mathsf{TA})$, condition **C2** (a) and Fact 4 gives us that $\forall x : \mathcal{L}(x) = L \Rightarrow \sigma_{j1}(x) = \sigma_{01}(x)$ and $\forall r : \mathcal{L}(r) = L \Rightarrow \delta_{j1}(r) = \delta_{01}(r) + d_1 + ... + d_j$. Since Φ_q is false, (σ_1, δ_1) and (σ_2, δ_2) have the same *termination behaviour* and thus there exists trace $t' \in [\![\mathsf{TA} : q \mapsto \mathrm{ipd}_Y(q)]\!](\sigma_2, \delta_2)$ and $d_1', ..., d_l'$ such that $d_1 + ... + d_j = d_1' + ... + d_l'$ and $(\sigma_{l2}, \delta_{l2})$ such that t' is

$$\langle q, \sigma_2, \delta_2\rangle = \langle q, \sigma_{02}, \delta_{02}\rangle \xrightarrow{d_1'} ... \xrightarrow{d_l'} \langle q_{l2}, \sigma_{l2}, \delta_{l2}\rangle \qquad (3)$$

and $q_{l2} = \mathrm{ipd}_Y(q)$.

It is immediate that $\forall x : \mathcal{L}(x) = L \Rightarrow \sigma_{l2}(x) = \sigma_{02}(x)$ and $\forall r : \mathcal{L}(r) = L \Rightarrow \delta_{l2}(r) = \delta_{02}(r) + d_1' + ... + d_l'$. To see how we obtain this result, we have that if t' has started using the edge e or an edge $e' \neq e$, where con(e') contains at least one high variable, then this result follows by our assumptions that $\mathrm{sec}_{Y,\mathcal{L}}(\mathsf{TA})$, condition **C2** (a) and Fact 4. Now if the t' has started using an edge $e' \neq e$ and con(e') contains only low variables then (σ_1, δ_1) is a witness of $\underline{\mathrm{sat}}(\mathrm{con}(e) \wedge \mathrm{con}(e'))$ and the result follows by our assumptions that $\mathrm{sec}_{Y,\mathcal{L}}(\mathsf{TA})$, condition **C2** (b) and Fact 4. Therefore in any case $(\sigma_{j1}, \delta_{j1}) \equiv (\sigma_{l2}, \delta_{l2})$.

Now if $\mathrm{ipd}_Y(q) = q_{k1}$ the proof has been completed. Otherwise we have that $\mathrm{ipd}_Y(q)$ is not in $Q_{\rightsquigarrow w}$ and the proof follows by an induction on the trace

$$\langle q_{j1}, \sigma_{j1}, \delta_{j1}\rangle \xrightarrow{d_j} ... \xrightarrow{d_k} \langle q_{k1}, \sigma_{k1}, \delta_{k1}\rangle$$

using that $(\sigma_{j1}, \delta_{j1}) \equiv (\sigma_{l2}, \delta_{l2})$

Subcase 2: When the unique immediate Y post-dominator of q is not defined. In that case, all the variables in con(e) are low. Therefore, if $e \rightsquigarrow w$ we proceed similar to *Main Case 1*, otherwise we proceed as in Subcase 1(a).

This completes our proof.

Proof of Lemma 2

Proof. Assume that $\langle q, \sigma_1, \delta_1 \rangle \overset{\infty}{\Longrightarrow}_Y \bot$ and thus either there exists a finite unsuccessful trace t

$$\langle q, \sigma_1, \delta_1 \rangle = \langle q_{01}, \sigma_{01}, \delta_{01} \rangle \xrightarrow{d_1} \dots \xrightarrow{d_n} \langle q_{n1}, \sigma_{n1}, \delta_{n1} \rangle \quad (n \geq 0)$$

such that $\forall i \in \{1, \dots, n\} : q_{i1} \notin Y$ and $\langle q_{n1}, \sigma_{n1}, \delta_{n1} \rangle$ is stuck, or there exists an infinite unsuccessful trace t

$$\langle q, \sigma_1, \delta_1 \rangle = \langle q_{01}, \sigma_{01}, \delta_{01} \rangle \xrightarrow{d_1} \dots \xrightarrow{d_n} \langle q_{n1}, \sigma_{n1}, \delta_{n1} \rangle \xrightarrow{d_{n+1}} \dots$$

such that $\forall i > 0 : q_{i1} \notin Y$.

Assume now that all the traces from $\langle q, \sigma_2, \delta_2 \rangle$ to a node $q' \in Y$ are successful, which means that $\langle q, \sigma_2, \delta_2 \rangle \overset{\infty}{\nRightarrow}_Y \bot$ and thus by Proposition 1 the set

$$\{k \mid \langle q'_0, \sigma'_0, \delta'_0 \rangle \xrightarrow{d'_1} \dots \xrightarrow{d'_k} \langle q'_k, \sigma'_k, \delta'_k \rangle : \langle q'_0, \sigma'_0, \delta'_0 \rangle = \langle q, \sigma_2, \delta_2 \rangle \wedge q'_k \in Y \wedge \\ \forall i \in \{1, \dots, k-1\} : q'_i \notin Y\}$$

has a maximum m.

The proof proceeds by contradiction where we show that we can either construct an unsuccessful trace of $\langle q, \sigma_2, \delta_2 \rangle$ or a "long" trace t'

$$\langle q, \sigma_2, \delta_2 \rangle = \langle q_{02}, \sigma_{02}, \delta_{02} \rangle \xrightarrow{d'_1} \dots \xrightarrow{d'_l} \langle q_{l2}, \sigma_{l2}, \delta_{l2} \rangle \quad (l > 0)$$

where $\forall i \in \{1, \dots, l\} : q_{i2} \notin Y$ and $m \leq l$ and that would mean that this trace will either terminate later (at a node in Y) and thus it will have a length greater than m, or it will result into an unsuccessful trace.

We consider two main cases one where q is in $Q_{\leadsto w}$ and one where it isn't.

Main Case 1: When q is in $Q_{\leadsto w}$. If the trace t of $\langle q, \sigma_1, \delta_1 \rangle$ visits only nodes that can reach Y ($\forall i : \Pi_{q_{i1}} \neq \emptyset$) then we proceed similar to the proof of Main Case 1 of Lemma 1, using the result (a) and (b) of the fact proven there. Therefore if t is infinite we can show that (σ_2, δ_2) can simulate the first m steps of (σ_1, δ_1) and this give us the desired trace t'. Similarly, in case of t being a finite unsuccessful trace that stops at the node q_{n1}, and $\langle q_{n1}, \sigma_{n1}, \delta_{n1} \rangle$ is a stuck, we can also show that (σ_2, δ_2) can reach the node q_{n1} (using the result (a)) and the resulting configuration will be stuck (using the result (b)).

Now if the first $j > 0$ nodes $q_{01} \dots q_{j1}$ (visited by t) can reach Y and then for the node $q_{(j+1)1}$ we have that $\Pi_{(q_{(j+1)1}, Y)} = \emptyset$, we can show similarly as before that (σ_2, δ_2) can reach the node $q_{(j+1)1}$ (using the results (a) and (b)), and thus any further computation will lead to an unsuccessful trace since $\Pi_{(q_{(j+1)1}, Y)} = \emptyset$.

Finally if t visits only nodes that cannot reach Y ($\forall i : \Pi_{q_{i1}} = \emptyset$) and thus also q cannot reach Y, the proof is trivial since all the traces of $\langle q, \sigma_2, \delta_2 \rangle$ will be unsuccessful with respect to Y. This completes the proof of Main Case 1.

Main Case 2: When q is not in $Q_{\leadsto w}$. We will now present a finite construction strategy for the desired trace t'.

Construction. We start by looking at the configurations $\langle q, \sigma_1, \delta_1 \rangle$, $\langle q, \sigma_2, \delta_2 \rangle$ the unsuccessful trace t of (σ_1, δ_1), and we remember that so far we have created a trace $t' = \langle q, \sigma_2, \delta_2 \rangle$ of length $l = 0$. We proceed according to the following cases:

Case 1: When the unique immediate Y post-dominator $\mathrm{ipd}_Y(q)$ of q is defined. We then consider two subcases, one where Φ_q is *false* and one where Φ_q is *true*.

Subcase (a): Φ_q is false. Now if the trace t does *not* visit $\mathrm{ipd}_Y(q)$, we have that (σ_1, δ_1) and (σ_2, δ_2) have the same *termination behaviour* (using that Φ_q is false) and thus there exists a trace t' of (σ_2, δ_2) that never visits $\mathrm{ipd}_Y(q)$. However, then we would have the case that t' is an unsuccessful trace with respect to q and the set Y which contradicts our assumptions.

If the trace t does visit $\mathrm{ipd}_Y(q)$, then it has to be the case that $\mathrm{ipd}_Y(q)$ is not in Y. Assume now that t starts with an edge $e \in \mathsf{E}_q$. If $\mathrm{con}(e)$ contains only low variables then $\exists d_1' = d_1$ and $(\sigma_{12}, \delta_{12}) \equiv (\sigma_{11}, \delta_{11})$ (this is ensured by our assumptions that $\mathrm{sec}_{Y,\mathcal{L}}(\mathsf{TA})$ and the predicate A_e of condition **C2** (a) that takes care of the *explicit flows* arising from the assignment in the edge e) such that

$$\langle q, \sigma_2, \delta_2 \rangle = \langle q_{02}, \sigma_{02}, \delta_{02} \rangle \xrightarrow{d_1'} \langle q_{12}, \sigma_{12}, \delta_{12} \rangle$$

where $q_{12} = q_{11}$. If now $m \le l+1$ then we have our desired trace t' and we stop.

Otherwise, notice that also q_{11} is not in $\mathsf{Q}_{\rightsquigarrow \mathsf{w}}$ and we repeat the *Construction* by looking at the configurations $\langle q_{11}, \sigma_{11}, \delta_{11} \rangle$, $\langle q_{11}, \sigma_{12}, \delta_{12} \rangle$, the suffix of t that starts with $\langle q_{11}, \sigma_{11}, \delta_{11} \rangle$ and we remember that so far we have created the trace

$$t' = \langle q_{02}, \sigma_{02}, \delta_{02} \rangle \xrightarrow{d_1'} \langle q_{12}, \sigma_{12}, \delta_{12} \rangle \quad (\langle q, \sigma_2, \delta_2 \rangle = \langle q_{02}, \sigma_{02}, \delta_{02} \rangle)$$

that has length equal to $l+1$.

Now if $\mathrm{con}(e)$ contains at least one high variable then we look at the first occurrence of $\mathrm{ipd}_Y(q)$ in t and let that to be the configuration $\langle q_{h1}, \sigma_{h1}, \delta_{h1} \rangle$ for some $h > 0$. Therefore, since $\mathrm{sec}_{Y,\mathcal{L}}(\mathsf{TA})$, using the condition **C2** (a) and Fact 4 we have that $\forall x : \mathcal{L}(x) = L \Rightarrow \sigma_{h1}(x) = \sigma_{01}(x)$ and $\forall r : \mathcal{L}(r) = L \Rightarrow \delta_{h1}(r) = \delta_{01}(r) + d_1 + \ldots + d_h$. Since Φ_q is false (σ_1, δ_1) and (σ_2, δ_2) have the same *termination behaviour* and thus there exists trace $t' \in [\![\mathsf{TA} : q \mapsto \mathrm{ipd}_Y(q)]\!](\sigma_2, \delta_2)$ and $d_1', \ldots, d_j'$ such that $d_1 + \ldots + d_h = d_1' + \ldots + d_j'$ and $(\sigma_{j2}, \delta_{j2})$ such that t' is

$$\langle q, \sigma_2, \delta_2 \rangle = \langle q_{02}, \sigma_{02}, \delta_{02} \rangle \xrightarrow{d_1'} \ldots \xrightarrow{d_j'} \langle q_{j2}, \sigma_{j2}, \delta_{j2} \rangle$$

where $q_{j2} = \mathrm{ipd}_Y(q)$.

Now if $j + l \ge m$ we have constructed the required trace t'.

Otherwise, we have that $\forall x : \mathcal{L}(x) = L \Rightarrow \sigma_{j2}(x) = \sigma_{02}(x)$ and $\forall r : \mathcal{L}(r) = L \Rightarrow \delta_{j2}(r) = \delta_{02}(r) + d_1' + \ldots + d_j'$. To see how we obtain this result, we have that if t' has started using the edge e or an edge $e' \ne e$, where $\mathrm{con}(e')$ contains at least one high variable, then this result follows by our assumptions that $\mathrm{sec}_{Y,\mathcal{L}}(\mathsf{TA})$, condition **C2** (a) and Fact 4. Now if the t' has started using an edge $e' \ne e$ and $\mathrm{con}(e')$ has only low variables then (σ_1, δ_1) is a witness of $\underline{\mathrm{sat}}(\mathrm{con}(e) \wedge \mathrm{con}(e'))$ and the result follows again by our assumptions that $\mathrm{sec}_{Y,\mathcal{L}}(\mathsf{TA})$, condition **C2**

(b) and Fact 4. Therefore in any case $(\sigma_{h1}, \delta_{h1}) \equiv (\sigma_{j2}, \delta_{j2})$ and thus we repeat the *Construction* by looking at the configurations $\langle q_{h1}, \sigma_{h1}, \delta_{h1} \rangle$, $\langle q_{j2}, \sigma_{j2}, \delta_{j2} \rangle$ the suffix of t that starts with $\langle q_{h1}, \sigma_{h1}, \delta_{h1} \rangle$ and we remember that so far we have created the trace t'

$$\langle q, \sigma_2, \delta_2 \rangle = \langle q_{02}, \sigma_{02}, \delta_{02} \rangle \xrightarrow{d'_1} \ldots \xrightarrow{d'_j} \langle q_{j2}, \sigma_{j2}, \delta_{j2} \rangle$$

of length equal to $l + j$.

Subcase (b): Φ_q is true. Then if t starts with the edge e, because $sec_{Y,\mathcal{L}}(\mathsf{TA})$, con($e$) contains only low variables and we proceed as in Subcase (a).

Case 2: When the unique immediate Y post-dominator $ipd_Y(q)$ of q is not defined. In this case, if t starts with the edge e, because $sec_{Y,\mathcal{L}}(\mathsf{TA})$ we have that con(e) contains only low variables. Now if $e \rightsquigarrow w$ working as in Main Case 1 we can get an unsuccessful trace t', otherwise we proceed as in Subcase (a).

Proof of Theorem 1

Proof. Let

$$Z = \{(\langle q, \sigma, \delta \rangle, \langle q, \sigma', \delta' \rangle) \mid [\![\mathsf{I}(q)]\!](\sigma, \delta) \wedge [\![\mathsf{I}(q)]\!](\sigma', \delta')\}$$
$$\cup \{(\bot, \bot)\}$$

It is immediate by Lemmas 1 and 2 that Z is a Y−bisimulation and that

$$\forall q \in \{q_0\} \cup Y : \forall (\sigma, \delta), (\sigma', \delta') : [\![\mathsf{I}(q)]\!](\sigma, \delta) \wedge [\![\mathsf{I}(q)]\!](\sigma', \delta')$$
$$\Downarrow$$
$$(\langle q, \sigma, \delta \rangle, \langle q, \sigma', \delta' \rangle) \in Z$$

Therefore since $\sim_Y$ is the largest Y−bisimulation we have that $Z \subseteq \sim_Y$ and thus TA satisfies the information security policy $\mathcal{L}$.

References

1. Aceto, L., Ingolfsdottir, A., Larsen, K.G., Srba, J.: Reactive Systems: Modelling, Specification and Verification. Cambridge University Press, Cambridge (2007)
2. Agat, J.: Transforming out timing leaks. In: Proceedings of the POPL, pp. 40–53 (2000)
3. Al-Bataineh, O.I., Reynolds, M., French, T.: Finding minimum and maximum termination time of timed automata models with cyclic behaviour. CoRR, abs/1610.09795 (2016)
4. Al-Bataineh, O.I., Reynolds, M., French, T.: Finding minimum and maximum termination time of timed automata models with cyclic behaviour. Theor. Comput. Sci. **665**, 87–104 (2017)
5. Alur, R., Dill, D.L.: A theory of timed automata. Theor. Comput. Sci. **126**(2), 183–235 (1994)

6. Askarov, A., Sabelfeld, A.: Localized delimited release: combining the what and where dimensions of information release. In: Proceedings of the 2007 Workshop on Programming Languages and Analysis for Security, PLAS 2007, San Diego, California, USA, 14 June 2007, pp. 53–60 (2007)
7. Barbuti, R., De Francesco, N., Santone, A., Tesei, L.: A notion of non-interference for timed automata. Fundam. Inform. **51**(1–2), 1–11 (2002)
8. Barbuti, R., Tesei, L.: A decidable notion of timed non-interference. Fundam. Inform. **54**(2–3), 137–150 (2003)
9. Barthe, G., Rezk, T., Warnier, M.: Preventing timing leaks through transactional branching instructions. Electron Notes Theor. Comput. Sci. **153**(2), 33–55 (2006)
10. Denning, D.E., Denning, P.J.: Certification of programs for secure information flow. Commun. ACM **20**(7), 504–513 (1977)
11. Franchella, M.: On the origins of Dénes König's infinity lemma. Arch. Hist. Exact Sci. **51**, 3–27 (1997)
12. Gardey, G., Mullins, J., Roux, O.H.: Non-interference control synthesis for security timed automata. Electron Notes Theor. Comput. Sci. **180**(1), 35–53 (2007)
13. Grewe, S., Lux, A., Mantel, H., Sauer, J.: A formalization of declassification with what-and-where-security. Archive of Formal Proofs (2014)
14. Gupta, B.B., Akhtar, T.: A survey on smart power grid: frameworks, tools, security issues, and solutions. Annales des Télécommunications **72**(9–10), 517–549 (2017)
15. Herbreteau, F., Srivathsan, B., Walukiewicz, I.: Efficient emptiness check for timed büchi automata. Form. Methods Syst. Des. **40**(2), 122–146 (2012)
16. Kashyap, V., Wiedermann, B., Hardekopf, B.: Timing- and termination-sensitive secure information flow: exploring a new approach. In: 32nd IEEE Symposium on Security and Privacy, S&P 2011, 22–25 May 2011, Berkeley, California, USA, pp. 413–428 (2011)
17. Lanotte, R., Maggiolo-Schettini, A., Troina, A.: Time and probability-based information flow analysis. IEEE Trans. Softw. Eng. **36**(5), 719–734 (2010)
18. Lengauer, T., Tarjan, R.E.: A fast algorithm for finding dominators in a flowgraph. ACM Trans. Program. Lang. Syst. **1**(1), 121–141 (1979)
19. Lux, A., Mantel, H., Perner, M.: Scheduler-independent declassification. In: Gibbons, J., Nogueira, P. (eds.) MPC 2012. LNCS, vol. 7342, pp. 25–47. Springer, Heidelberg (2012)
20. Magazinius, J., Askarov, A., Sabelfeld, A.: Decentralized delimited release. In: Yang, H. (ed.) APLAS 2011. LNCS, vol. 7078, pp. 220–237. Springer, Heidelberg (2011)
21. Mantel, H., Sands, D.: Controlled declassification based on intransitive noninterference. In: Chin, W.-N. (ed.) APLAS 2004. LNCS, vol. 3302, pp. 129–145. Springer, Heidelberg (2004)
22. Mantel, H., Starostin, A.: Transforming out timing leaks, more or less. In: Pernul, G., Ryan, P.Y.A., Weippl, E. (eds.) ESORICS 2015. LNCS, vol. 9326, pp. 447–467. Springer, Cham (2015)
23. McMillin, B.M., Roth, T.P.: Cyber-Physical Security and Privacy in the Electric Smart Grid. Synthesis Lectures on Information Security, Privacy, and Trust. Morgan & Claypool Publishers, San Rafael (2017)
24. Myers, A.C., Sabelfeld, A., Zdancewic, S.: Enforcing robust declassification and qualified robustness. J. Comput. Secur. **14**(2), 157–196 (2006)
25. Nielson, F., Nielson, H.R., Vasilikos, P.: Information flow for timed automata. In: Aceto, L., Bacci, G., Bacci, G., Ingólfsdóttir, A., Legay, A., Mardare, R. (eds.) Models, Algorithms, Logics and Tools. LNCS, vol. 10460, pp. 3–21. Springer, Cham (2017). https://doi.org/10.1007/978-3-319-63121-9_1

26. Sabelfeld, A., Myers, A.C.: Language-based information-flow security. IEEE J. Sel. Areas Commun. **21**(1), 5–19 (2003)
27. Baumgart, I., Finster, S.: Privacy-aware smart metering: a survey. IEEE Commun. Surv. Tutor. **17**(2), 1088–1101 (2015)
28. UPPAAL. http://www.uppaal.com/index.php?sida=200&rubrik=95
29. Volpano, D.M., Smith, G., Irvine, C.E.: A sound type system for secure flow analysis. J. Comput. Secur. **4**(2/3), 167–188 (1996)

Compositional Non-interference for Concurrent Programs via Separation and Framing

Aleksandr Karbyshev[1]([✉]), Kasper Svendsen[2], Aslan Askarov[1], and Lars Birkedal[1]

[1] Aarhus University, Aarhus, Denmark
karbyshev@mailbox.org
[2] University of Cambridge, Cambridge, UK

Abstract. Reasoning about information flow in a concurrent setting is notoriously difficult due in part to timing channels that may leak sensitive information. In this paper, we present a compositional and flexible type-and-effect system that guarantees non-interference by disallowing potentially insecure races that can be exploited through internal timing attacks. In contrast to many previous approaches, which disallow all races on public variables, we use an explicit scheduler model to give a more permissive security definition and type system, which allows benign races on public variables. To achieve compositionality, we use the idea of resources from separation logic, both to locally specify and reason about whether accesses may be racy and to bound the security level of data that may be learned through scheduling.

1 Introduction

Non-interference [15] is an important security property. Informally, a program satisfies non-interference if its publicly observable (*low*) outputs are independent of its private (*high*) inputs. In spite of the vast body of research on non-interference, reasoning about information flow control and enforcing non-interference for imperative concurrent programs remains a difficult problem. One of the main problems is prevention of information flows that originate from interaction of the scheduler with individual threads, also known as *internal timing leaks*.

Example 1. Consider the following program [44][1].

    fork(delay(50); $l := 1$);   // *Thread 1*

    fork(if h then skip else delay(100); $l := 2$);   // *Thread 2*

---

[1] delay(n) is used as an abbreviation for skip; ...; skip n times, i.e., it models a computation that takes n reduction steps.

L. Bauer and R. Küsters (Eds.): POST 2018, LNCS 10804, pp. 53–78, 2018.
https://doi.org/10.1007/978-3-319-89722-6_3

In this program, h is a high variable and l is intended to be a low variable. But the order of the two assignments to l depends on the branch that is picked by Thread 2. As a result, under many schedulers, the resulting value of $l = 1$ reveals the value of h being true to a low observer.

It may appear that the problem in the above example is that Thread 2 races to the low assignment after branching on a secret. The situation is actually worse. Without explicit assumptions on the scheduling of threads, a mere *presence* of a high branching in the pool of concurrently running threads is problematic.

Example 2. Consider the following program, which forks three threads.

fork(delay(50); $l := 1$);   // *Thread 1*
fork(if h then skip else delay(100));   // *Thread 2*
fork($l := 2$)   // *Thread 3*

In this program, every individual thread is secure, in the sense that it does not leak information about high variables to a low observer. Additionally, pairwise parallel composition of any of the threads is secure, too, including a benign race fork($l := 1$); fork($l := 2$). Even if we assume that the attacker fully controls the scheduler, the final value of l will be determined only by the scheduler of his choice. However, for the parallel execution of all the three threads, if the attacker can influence the scheduler, it can leak the secret value of h through public l.

In this paper, we present a compositional and flexible type-and-effect system that supports compositional reasoning about information flow in concurrent programs, with minimal assumptions on the scheduler. Our type system is based on ideas from separation logic; in particular, we track ownership of variables. An assignment to an exclusively-owned low variable is allowed as long as it does not create a thread-local information flow violation, regardless of the parallel context. Additionally, we introduce a notion of a *labeled scheduler resource*, which allows us to distinguish and accept benign races as secure.[2] A racy low assignment is allowed as long as the thread's scheduler resource is low; the latter, in its turn, prevents parallel composition of the assignment with high threads, avoiding potential scheduler leaks. This flexibility allows our type system to accept pairwise parallel compositions of threads from Example 2, while rightfully rejecting the composition of all three threads.

Following the idea of ownership transfer from separation logic, our type system allows static transfer of resource ownership along synchronization primitives. This enables typing of programs that use synchronization primitives to avoid races, as illustrated in the following example.

---

[2] One could argue that programs should not have any races on assignments at all; but in general we will want to allow races on some shareable resources (e.g., I/O) and that is why we study a setup in which we do try to accommodate benign races to assignments.

Example 3. Consider the following modification of Example 2.

fork(delay(50); $l := 1$; send(c));   *// Thread 1*
fork(if h then skip else delay(100)); *// Thread 2*
recv(c);   *// recover exclusive ownership of variable l*
fork($l := 2$)   *// Thread 3*

In this program, Thread 1 sends a message on channel c. Since the main program synchronizes on the c channel (by receiving on channel c), Thread 3 is not forked until after the assignment $l := 1$ in Thread 1 has happened. Hence, the synchronization ensures that there is no race on l and the program is therefore secure, even in the presence of the high branching in the concurrent Thread 2.

Note that unconstrained transfer of resources creates an additional covert channel that needs to be controlled. Section 3 describes how our type system prevents implicit flows via resource transfer.

One might expect that synchronization can also be used to allow races after high threads are removed from the scheduler. That is, however, problematic, as illustrated by the following example.

Example 4. Consider the following program.

fork(if h then s_1 else s_2; send(c));   *// Thread 1*
recv(c);
fork($l := 1$);   *// Thread 2*
fork($l := 2$)   *// Thread 3*

The program forks off three threads and uses send(c) and recv(c) on a channel c to postpone forking of Thread 2 and 3 until after Thread 1 has finished. Here it is possible for the high thread (Thread 1) to taint the scheduler and thus affect its choice of scheduling between Threads 2 and 3 after Thread 1 has finished. This could, e.g., happen if we have an adaptive scheduler and s_1 and s_2 have different workloads. Then the scheduler will be adapted differently depending on whether h is true or false and therefore the final value of l may reveal the value of h.

To remedy this issue, we introduce a special *rescheduling* operation that resets the scheduler state, effectively removing all possible taint from past high threads.

Example 5. Consider the following variation of Example 4:

fork(if h then s_1 else s_2; send(c));   *// Thread 1*
recv(c);
reschedule;   *// reset the scheduler state*
fork($l := 1$);   *// Thread 2*
fork($l := 2$)   *// Thread 3*

The reschedule operation resets the scheduler state and therefore no information about the high variable h is leaked from the high thread and this program is thus secure.

The above example illustrates that reschedule allows us to remove scheduler taint from high threads and thus accept programs with benign races as secure after high threads have finished executing.

Contributions. This paper proposes a new *compositional* model for enforcing information flow security in imperative concurrent programs. The key components of the model are:

- A fine-grained compositional[3] type-and-effect system that prevents internal timing leaks by tracking when races may occur and whether the scheduler state could be tainted with confidential information. The type-and-effect system allows us to verify programs with benign races as secure.
- A novel programming construct for resetting the scheduler state.
- A proof technique for termination-insensitive notion of security under possible low nondeterminism.

We emphasize that our model is independent of the choice of scheduler; the only restriction on the runtime system is that it should implement the reschedule operation for resetting the scheduler state. This is a very mild restriction. Compared to other earlier work that also allows for scheduler independence and benign low races, our type-and-effect system is, to the best of our knowledge, much more expressive in the sense that it allows to verify more programs as secure.

The choice of termination-insensitive security condition as the target condition is deliberate for we only consider batch-style executions. We believe that our results can be extended to progress-insensitive security [2] using standard techniques. Despite that termination-insensitive security conditions leak arbitrary information [3], these leaks occur only via unary encoding of the secret in the trace and are relatively slow, especially when the secret space is large, compared to fast internal timing channels that we aim to close. We do not consider termination (or progress)-sensitivity because it is generally difficult to close all possible termination and crashing channels that may be exploited by the adversary, including resource exhaustion, without appealing to system-level mechanisms that also mitigate external timing channels. We discuss this more in detail in Sect. 5. Finally, note that in this paper we only address leaks through interactions with the scheduler (i.e., the *internal* timing leaks). Preventing *external* leaks is an active area of research and is out of scope of the paper.

Outline. The remainder of this paper is organized as follows. In Sect. 2, we formally define the concurrent language and our security model. In Sect. 3, we

---

[3] We use a standard notion of compositionality for separation-style type systems, see comments to Theorem 1.

present the type system for establishing security of concurrent programs. For reasons of space, an overview of the soundness proof and the detailed proof can be found in the accompanying appendix. We discuss related work in Sect. 5. Finally, in Sect. 6, we conclude and discuss future work.

2   Language and Security Model

We begin by formally defining the syntax and operational semantics of a core concurrent imperative language. The syntax is defined by the grammar below and includes the usual imperative constructs, loops, conditionals and fork. Thread synchronization is achieved using channels which support a non-blocking send primitive and a blocking receive. In addition, the syntax also includes our novel reschedule construct for resetting the scheduler.

$$
\begin{aligned}
v \in Val &::= () \mid n \mid \mathsf{tt} \mid \mathsf{ff} \\
e \in Exp &::= x \mid v \mid e_1 = e_2 \mid e_1 + e_2 \\
s \in Stm &::= \mathsf{skip} \mid s_1; s_2 \mid x := e \mid \mathsf{if}\ e\ \mathsf{then}\ s_1\ \mathsf{else}\ s_2 \mid \mathsf{while}\ e\ \mathsf{do}\ s \\
&\quad\ \mid\ \mathsf{fork}(s) \mid \mathsf{send}(ch) \mid \mathsf{recv}(ch) \mid \mathsf{reschedule} \\
K \in ECtx &::= \bullet \mid K; s
\end{aligned}
$$

Here x and ch range over finite and disjoint sets of variable and channel identifiers, respectively. The sets are denoted by Var and $Chan$, respectively.

The operational semantics is defined as a small-step reduction relation over configurations of the form sf, S, T, M, ρ consisting of a scheduling function sf, a scheduler state S, a thread pool T, a message pool M and a heap ρ. A scheduling function sf takes a scheduler state, a thread pool, a message pool and a heap as arguments and returns a new scheduler state and a thread identifier of the next thread to be scheduled [30,33]. A thread pool T is a partial function from thread identifiers to sequences of statements, a message pool is a function from channel names to natural numbers, each representing a number of signals available on the respective channel, and a heap is a function from variables to values. We model a thread as a stack of statements, pushing whenever we encounter a branch and popping upon termination of branches. The semantic domains are defined formally in Fig. 1.

$$T \in TPool \overset{def}{=} TId \overset{fin}{\rightharpoonup} seq\ Stm \qquad sf \in Schd \overset{def}{=} S \times TPool \times MPool \times Heap \to S \times TId$$

$$M \in MPool \overset{def}{=} Chan \to \mathbb{N} \qquad \Psi \in ReSchd \overset{def}{=} Schd \times MPool \times Heap \to Schd \times S \times TId$$

$$\rho \in Heap \overset{def}{=} Var \to Val$$

Fig. 1. Semantic domains.

The reduction relation is split into a *local* reduction relation that reduces a given thread and a *global* reduction relation that picks the next thread to be

$$\frac{T, M, \rho \to^{t,a} T', M', \rho' \qquad sf(S, T, M, \rho) = (S', t) \qquad a \neq \mathbf{rs}(\cdot)}{sf, S, T, M, \rho \longrightarrow_\Psi sf, S', T', M', \rho'}$$

$$\frac{T, M, \rho \to^{t,a} T', M', \rho' \qquad \Psi(sf, M, \rho) = (sf', S', t') \qquad a = \mathbf{rs}(t')}{sf, S, T, M, \rho \longrightarrow_\Psi sf', S', T', M', \rho'}$$

Fig. 2. Global reduction relation.

scheduled. The global reduction relation is defined in terms of the local reduction relation, written $T, M, \rho \to^{t,a} T', M', \rho'$, which reduces the thread t in thread pool T, emitting action a during the reduction. The global reduction relation only distinguishes between reschedule actions and non-reschedule actions. To reduce reschedule actions, the global reduction relation refers to a rescheduling function Ψ, which computes the next scheduler and scheduler state. The global reduction relation, written $sf, S, T, M, \rho \longrightarrow_\Psi sf', S', T', M', \rho'$, is indexed by a rescheduling function Ψ, which takes as argument the current scheduling function, message pool and heap and returns a new scheduling function and scheduler state. The global reduction relation is defined formally in Fig. 2.

$$\frac{T(t) = K[s] :: stk \qquad s, \rho \to_a s'}{T, M, \rho \to^{t,a} [\![a]\!]_A(T[t \mapsto K[s'] :: stk], M, \rho, t)} \qquad \frac{T(t) = \mathsf{skip} :: stk}{T, M, \rho \to^{t,\epsilon} T[t \mapsto stk], M, \rho}$$

Fig. 3. Local reduction relation.

The local reduction relation is defined over configurations consisting of a thread pool, a message pool and a heap (Fig. 3). It is defined in terms of a statement reduction relation, $s, h \to_a s'$ that reduces a statement s to s' and emits an action a describing the behavior of the statement on the state. We use evaluation contexts, K, to refer to the primitive statement that appears in a reducible position inside a larger statement. We use $K[s]$ to denote the substitution of statement s in evaluation context K. Actions include a no-op action, ϵ, a branch action, $\mathbf{b}(e, s)$, an assignment action, $\mathbf{a}(x, v)$, a fork action, $\mathbf{f}(s)$, send and receive actions, $\mathbf{s}(ch)$, $\mathbf{r}(ch)$, a wait action for blocking on a receive $\mathbf{w}(ch)$, a reschedule action, $\mathbf{rs}(t)$, and a wait action for blocking on a reschedule, $\mathbf{wa}$. Formally,

$$a \in Act ::= \epsilon \mid \mathbf{b}(e, s) \mid \mathbf{a}(x, v) \mid \mathbf{f}(s) \mid \mathbf{s}(ch) \mid \mathbf{r}(ch) \mid \mathbf{w}(ch) \mid \mathbf{wa} \mid \mathbf{rs}(t)$$

The behavior of an action a on the state is given by the function $[\![a]\!]_A$ defined in Fig. 4. The function $tgen$ is used to generate a fresh thread identifier for newly forked threads. It thus satisfies the specification $tgen(T) \notin dom(T)$. We assume $tgen$ is a fixed global function, but it is possible to generalize the semantics and allow the rescheduling function to also pick a new thread identifier generator. $active(T)$ denotes the set of active threads in T, i.e., $active(T) = \{t \in dom(T) \mid T(t) \neq \varepsilon\}$. The statement reduction relation is defined in Fig. 5.

$$[\![\epsilon]\!]_A(T, M, \rho, t) = (T, M, \rho)$$
$$[\![\mathbf{b}(e, s)]\!]_A(T, M, \rho, t) = (T[t \mapsto s :: T(t)], M, \rho)$$
$$[\![\mathbf{a}(x, v)]\!]_A(T, M, \rho, t) = (T, M, \rho[x \mapsto v])$$
$$[\![\mathbf{f}(s)]\!]_A(T, M, \rho, t) = (T[tgen(T) \mapsto s], M, \rho)$$
$$[\![\mathbf{s}(ch)]\!]_A(T, M, \rho, t) = (T, M[ch \mapsto M(ch) + 1], \rho)$$
$$[\![\mathbf{r}(ch)]\!]_A(T, M, \rho, t) = \text{if } M(ch) > 0 \text{ then } (T, M[ch \mapsto M(ch) - 1], \rho) \text{ else } \bot$$
$$[\![\mathbf{w}(ch)]\!]_A(T, M, \rho, t) = \text{if } M(ch) = 0 \text{ then } (T, M, \rho) \text{ else } \bot$$
$$[\![\mathbf{rs}(t')]\!]_A(T, M, \rho, t) = \text{if } |active(T)| = 1 \text{ then } ([t' \mapsto T(t)], M, \rho) \text{ else } \bot$$
$$[\![\mathbf{wa}]\!]_A(T, M, \rho, t) = \text{if } |active(T)| > 1 \text{ then } (T, M, \rho) \text{ else } \bot$$

Fig. 4. Semantics of actions.

Note that semantics of events is deterministic. For example, $\mathbf{r}(ch)$-transition can only be executed if $M(ch) > 0$, while $\mathbf{w}(ch)$ can only be emitted if $M(ch) > 0$ (symbol $\bot$ in the definition means "undefined"). Note that reschedule only reduces globally once all other threads in the thread pool have reduced fully and that it further removes all other threads from the thread pool upon reducing and assigns a new thread identifier to the only active thread. This requirement ensures that once reschedule reduces and resets the scheduler state then other threads that exist prior to the reduction of reschedule cannot immediately taint the scheduler state again. The reschedule reduction step is deterministic: the value of t is bound in the respective rule in Fig. 2 by function Ψ.

Example 6. To illustrate the issue, consider the following code snippet. This program branches on a confidential (high) variable h and then spawns one of two threads with the sole purpose of tainting the scheduler with the state of h. It also contains a race on a public (low) variable l, which occurs after the rescheduling.

```
if h > 0 then fork(skip) else fork(skip; skip);
reschedule;
fork(l := 0); l := 1
```

If reschedule could reduce and reset the scheduler state before the forked thread had reduced, then the forked thread could reduce between reschedule and the assignment and therefore affect which of the two racy assignments to l would win the race. Our operational semantics therefore only reduces reschedule once all other threads have terminated, which for the above example ensures that the forked thread has already fully reduced, and cannot taint the scheduler state after reschedule has reset it.

$$\text{while } e \text{ do } s, \rho \to_e \text{ if } e \text{ then } (s; \text{while } e \text{ do } s) \text{ else skip}$$

if e then s_1 else $s_2, \rho \to_{\mathbf{b}(e,s_1)}$ skip	if $[\![e]\!](\rho) = \mathsf{tt}$
if e then s_1 else $s_2, \rho \to_{\mathbf{b}(e,s_2)}$ skip	if $[\![e]\!](\rho) = \mathsf{ff}$
$x := e, \rho \to_{\mathbf{a}(x,v)}$ skip	where $v = [\![e]\!](\rho)$

skip; $s, \rho \to_\epsilon s$	$\mathrm{recv}(ch), \rho \to_{\mathbf{w}(ch)} \mathrm{recv}(ch)$
$\mathrm{fork}(s), \rho \to_{\mathbf{f}(s)}$ skip	$\mathrm{recv}(ch), \rho \to_{\mathbf{r}(ch)}$ skip
$\mathrm{send}(ch), \rho \to_{\mathbf{s}(ch)}$ skip	reschedule, $\rho \to_{\mathbf{wa}}$ reschedule
	reschedule, $\rho \to_{\mathbf{rs}(t)}$ skip

Fig. 5. Statement reduction.

2.1 Security Model

In this section we introduce our formal security model for confidentiality. This is formalized as a non-interference property, requiring that attackers cannot learn anything about confidential inputs from observing public outputs.

To express this formally, we assume a bounded $\sqcup$-semilattice $\mathcal{L}$ of security levels for classifying the confidentiality levels of inputs and outputs. We say that level ℓ_1 *flows into* ℓ_2 if $\ell_1 \sqsubseteq \ell_2$. In examples we typically assume $\mathcal{L}$ is a bounded lattice with distinguished top and bottom elements, denoted H and L, and referred to as high and low, respectively. Given a security typing Γ that assigns security levels to all program variables and channel identifiers, we consider two heaps ρ_1 and ρ_2 indistinguishable at attacker level ℓ_A if the two heaps agree for all variables with a security level below or equal to the attacker security level:

$$\rho_1 \sim_\Gamma^{\ell_A} \rho_2 \stackrel{def}{=} \forall x \in Var.\, \Gamma(x) \sqsubseteq \ell_A \Rightarrow h_1(x) = h_2(x)$$

Likewise, we consider two message pools M_1 and M_2 indistinguishable at attacker level ℓ_A if they agree on all channels with security level below or equal to the attackers security level:

$$M_1 \sim_\Gamma^{\ell_A} M_2 \stackrel{def}{=} \forall ch \in Chan.\, \Gamma(ch) \sqsubseteq \ell_A \Rightarrow M_1(ch) = M_2(ch)$$

Non-interference expresses that attackers cannot learn confidential information by requiring that executions from attacker indistinguishable initial message pools and heaps should produce attacker indistinguishable terminal message pools and heaps, when executed from the same initial scheduler state and scheduling function. Since scheduling and rescheduling functions have complete access to the machine state, including confidential variables and channels, we restrict attention to schedulers and reschedulers that only access attacker-observable variables and channels. We say that a scheduler sf is an ℓ-scheduler iff it does not distinguish message pools and heaps that are ℓ-indistinguishable:

$$\ell\text{-}level(sf) \Leftrightarrow \forall S, T, M_1, M_2, \rho_1, \rho_2.$$

$$M_1 \sim_\Gamma^\ell M_2 \wedge \rho_1 \sim_\Gamma^\ell \rho_2 \Rightarrow sf(S, T, M_1, \rho_1) = sf(S, T, M_2, \rho_2)$$

Likewise, a rescheduling function is an ℓ-rescheduler iff it does not distinguish message pools and heaps that are ℓ-indistinguishable and only returns ℓ-schedulers:

$$\ell\text{-}level(\Psi) \Leftrightarrow \forall sf, M_1, M_2, \rho_1, \rho_2. \ell\text{-}level(\pi_1(\Psi(sf, M_1, \rho_1))) \wedge$$
$$(M_1 \sim^\ell_\Gamma M_2 \wedge \rho_1 \sim^\ell_\Gamma \rho_2 \Rightarrow \Psi(sf, M_1, \rho_1) = \Psi(sf, M_2, \rho_2))$$

where π_1 is a projection to the first component of the triple.

Definition 1 (Security). *A thread pool T satisfies non-interference at attacker level ℓ_A and security typing Γ iff all fully-reduced executions from ℓ_A-related initial heaps (starting with empty message pools) reduce to ℓ_A-related terminal heaps, for all ℓ_A-level schedulers sf and reschedulers Ψ:*

$$\forall \rho_1, \rho_2, \rho_1', \rho_2' \in Heap. \forall M_1', M_2' \in MPool. \forall S, S_1', S_2' \in \mathcal{S}. \forall T_1', T_2'. \forall sf, sf_1', sf_2'.$$
$$\ell_A\text{-}level(sf) \wedge \ell_A\text{-}level(\Psi) \wedge \rho_1 \sim^{\ell_A}_\Gamma \rho_2 \wedge final(T_1') \wedge final(T_2') \wedge$$
$$sf, S, T, \lambda ch.0, \rho_1 \longrightarrow^*_\Psi sf_1', S_1', T_1', M_1', \rho_1' \wedge$$
$$sf, S, T, \lambda ch.0, \rho_2 \longrightarrow^*_\Psi sf_2', S_2', T_2', M_2', \rho_2' \Rightarrow M_1' \sim^{\ell_A}_\Gamma M_2' \wedge \rho_1' \sim^{\ell_A}_\Gamma \rho_2'$$

where $final(T) \stackrel{def}{=} \forall t \in dom(T). T(t) = \varepsilon$.

This non-interference property can be specialized in the obvious way from thread pools to programs by considering a thread pool with only the given program.

In our security model, we focus on standard end-to-end security, i.e., the attacker is allowed to observe low parts of the initial and final heaps. The security definition quantifies over all possible schedulers, which in particular means that the attacker is allowed to choose any scheduler.

To develop some intuition about our security model, let's consider a few basic examples. The program fork($x := 1$); $x := 2$ is *secure* for any attacker level ℓ_A, because in any two executions from the same initial scheduler state and ℓ_A-equivalent initial message pools and heaps, the scheduler must schedule the assignments in the same order. This follows from the assumption that the scheduler cannot distinguish ℓ_A-equivalent message pools and heaps.

If prior to a race on a low variable a thread branches on confidential information, then we can construct a scheduler that leaks this information. To illustrate, consider the following variant of Example 1 from the Introduction:

fork(if h then skip else (skip; skip))	// *Thread 1*
fork($l := 1$);	// *Thread 2*
fork($l := 2$)	// *Thread 3*

If we take the scheduler state to be a natural number corresponding to the number of statements reduced so far, then we can construct a scheduler that first reduces Thread 1 and then schedules Thread 2 if Thread 1 was fully reduced in two steps and Thread 3 if Thread 1 was fully reduced in three steps. Therefore, this program is *not* secure.

3   Type System

In this section we present a type-and-effect system for establishing non-interference. The type-and-effect system is inspired by separation logic [36] and uses ideas of ownership and resources to track whether accesses to variables and channels may be racy and to bound the security level of the data that may be learned through observing how threads are scheduled. Statements are typed relative to a pre- and postcondition, where the precondition describes the resources necessary to run the statement and the postcondition the resources owned after executing the statement. The statement typing judgment has the following form:

$$\Gamma \mid \Delta \mid pc \vdash \{P\}\ s\ \{Q\}$$

Here P and Q are resources and pc is an upper bound on the security level of the data that can be learned through knowing the control of the program up to this point. Context Γ defines security levels for all program variables and channel identifiers and Δ defines a static resource specification for every channel identifier. We will return to these contexts later. Expressions are typed relative to a precondition and the expression typing judgment has the following form: $\Gamma \vdash \{P\}\ e : \ell$. Here ℓ is an upper bound on the security level of the data computed by e. Resources are described by the following grammar:

$$P, Q ::= emp \mid P * Q \mid x_\pi \mid ch_\pi \mid schd_\pi(\ell) \mid \lceil P \rceil^\ell$$

where $\pi \in \mathbb{Q} \cap (0, 1]$. The emp assertion describes the empty resource that does not assert ownership of anything. The $P * Q$ assertion describes a resource that can be split into two disjoint resources, P and Q, respectively. This assertion is inspired by separation logic and is used to reason about separation of resources.

Variable resources, written x_π, express fractional ownership of variable x with fraction $\pi \in \mathbb{Q} \cap (0, 1]$. We use these to reason locally about whether accesses to a given variable might cause a race. Ownership of the full fraction $\pi = 1$ expresses that we own the variable exclusively and can therefore access the variable without fears of causing a race. Any fraction less than 1 only expresses partial ownership and accessing the given variable could therefore cause a race. These variable resources can be split and recombined using the fraction. We express this using the resource entailment judgment, written $\Gamma \vdash P \Rightarrow Q$, which asserts that resource P can be converted into resource Q. We write $\Gamma \vdash P \Leftrightarrow Q$ when resource P can be converted into Q and Q can be converted into P. Splitting and recombination of variable resources comply with the rule: If $\pi_1 + \pi_2 \leq 1$ then $\Gamma \vdash x_{\pi_1 + \pi_2} \Leftrightarrow x_{\pi_1} * x_{\pi_2}$. This can for instance be used to split an exclusive permission into two partial permissions that can be passed to two different threads and later recombined back into the exclusive permission.

The other kind of crucial resources, $schd_\pi(\ell)$, where $\pi \in \mathbb{Q} \cap (0, 1]$, allows us to track the scheduler level (also called the scheduler taint). A *labeled scheduler resource*, $schd_\pi(\ell)$, expresses that the scheduler level currently cannot go above ℓ. This is both a guarantee we give to the environment and something we can rely on the environment to follow. This guarantee ensures that level of information that can be learned by observing how threads are scheduled is bounded by the scheduler level. Again, we use fractional permissions to split the scheduler resource between multiple threads: If $\pi_1 + \pi_2 \leq 1$ then $\Gamma \vdash schd_{\pi_1+\pi_2}(\ell) \Leftrightarrow schd_{\pi_1}(\ell) * schd_{\pi_2}(\ell)$. If we own the scheduler resource exclusively, then no one else is relying on the scheduler level staying below a given security level and we can thus change the scheduler rely-guarantee level to a higher security level: If $\ell_1 \sqsubseteq \ell_2$ then $\Gamma \vdash schd_1(\ell_1) \Rightarrow schd_1(\ell_2)$. In general it is not secure to lower the upper bound on the scheduler level in this way, even if we own the scheduler resource exclusively. Instead, we must use reschedule to lower the scheduler level. We will return to this issue in a subsequent section.

$$\frac{}{\Gamma \mid \Delta \mid pc \vdash \{P\} \text{ skip } \{P\}} \text{ T-Skip}$$

$$\frac{\Gamma \mid \Delta \mid pc \vdash \{P\}\, s_1\, \{R\} \qquad \Gamma \mid \Delta \mid pc \vdash \{R\}\, s_2\, \{Q\}}{\Gamma \mid \Delta \mid pc \vdash \{P\}\, s_1; s_2\, \{Q\}} \text{ T-Seq}$$

$$\frac{\begin{array}{c} \Gamma \vdash \{P\}\, e : \ell \\ P \equiv R * schd_\pi(\ell_s) \qquad \ell \sqsubseteq \ell_s \qquad \Gamma \mid \Delta \mid pc \sqcup \ell \vdash \{P\}\, s_i\, \{Q\} \quad for\ i \in \{1,2\} \end{array}}{\Gamma \mid \Delta \mid pc \vdash \{P\} \text{ if } e \text{ then } s_1 \text{ else } s_2\, \{Q\}} \text{ T-If}$$

$$\frac{\begin{array}{c} \Gamma \vdash \{P\}\, e : \ell \\ P \equiv R * schd_\pi(\ell_s) \qquad \ell \sqsubseteq \ell_s \qquad \Gamma \mid \Delta \mid pc \sqcup \ell \vdash \{P\}\, s\, \{P\} \end{array}}{\Gamma \mid \Delta \mid pc \vdash \{P\} \text{ while } e \text{ do } s\, \{P\}} \text{ T-While}$$

$$\frac{\Gamma \vdash \{P\}\, e : \ell \qquad \Gamma \vdash P \Rightarrow x_1 \qquad pc \sqcup \ell \sqsubseteq \Gamma(x)}{\Gamma \mid \Delta \mid pc \vdash \{P\}\, x := e\, \{P\}} \text{ T-Asgn-Excl}$$

$$\frac{\Gamma \vdash \{P\}\, e : \ell \qquad P \equiv R * schd_{\pi_s}(\ell_s) \qquad \Gamma \vdash P \Rightarrow x_\pi \qquad pc \sqcup \ell \sqcup \ell_s \sqsubseteq \Gamma(x)}{\Gamma \mid \Delta \mid pc \vdash \{P\}\, x := e\, \{P\}} \text{ T-Asgn-Racy}$$

Fig. 6. Typing rules for assignments and control flow statements.

State and Control Flow. Before introducing the remaining resources, let's look at the typing rules for assignments and control flow primitives, to illustrate how we use these variable and scheduler resources. The type-and-effect system features two assignment rules, one for non-racy assignments and one for potentially racy assignments (T-Asgn-Excl and T-Asgn-Racy, respectively, in Fig. 6). If we own a variable resource exclusively, then we can use the typing rule for non-racy assignments and we do not have to worry about leaking information through scheduling. However, if we only own a partial variable resource for a given variable, then any access to the variable could potentially introduce a race and we have to ensure information learned from scheduling is allowed to flow into the given variable. The typing rule for potentially racy assignments (T-Asgn-Racy) thus requires that we own a scheduler resource, $schd_\pi(\ell_s)$, that bounds the information that can be learned through scheduling, and requires that ℓ_s may flow into $\Gamma(x)$. Both assignment rules naturally also require that the security level of the assigned expression and the current pc-level is allowed to flow into the assigned variable. The assigned expression is typed using the expression typing judgment, $\Gamma \vdash \{P\}\ e : \ell$, using the rules from Fig. 7. This judgment computes an upper-bound ℓ on the security-level of the data computed by the expression and ensures that P asserts at least partial ownership of any variables accessed by e. Hence, exclusive ownership of a given variable x ensures both the absence of write-write races to the given variable, but also read-write races, which can also be exploited to leak confidential information through scheduling.

$$
\frac{\text{T-SUB}}{\Gamma \vdash \{P\}\ e : \ell_1 \quad \ell_1 \sqsubseteq \ell_2}{\Gamma \vdash \{P\}\ e : \ell_2} \qquad \frac{\text{T-CONST}}{\Gamma \vdash \{P\}\ v : \ell} \qquad \frac{\text{T-VAR}}{\Gamma \vdash P \Rightarrow x_\pi}{\Gamma \vdash \{P\}\ x : \Gamma(x)}
$$

$$
\frac{\Gamma \vdash \{P\}\ e_1 : \ell \quad \Gamma \vdash \{P\}\ e_2 : \ell}{\Gamma \vdash \{P\}\ e_1 + e_2 : \ell}\ \text{T-ADD} \qquad \frac{\Gamma \vdash \{P\}\ e_1 : \ell \quad \Gamma \vdash \{P\}\ e_2 : \ell}{\Gamma \vdash \{P\}\ e_1 = e_2 : \ell}\ \text{T-EQ}
$$

Fig. 7. Typing rules for expressions.

$$
\frac{\Gamma \mid \Delta \mid pc \vdash \{P\}\ s\ \{Q\}}{\Gamma \mid \Delta \mid pc \vdash \{P * R\}\ s\ \{Q * R\}}\ \text{T-FRAME}
$$

$$
\frac{\Gamma \vdash P_1 \Rightarrow P_2 \quad \Gamma \mid \Delta \mid pc_2 \vdash \{P_2\}\ s\ \{Q_2\} \quad \Gamma \vdash Q_2 \Rightarrow Q_1 \quad pc_1 \sqsubseteq pc_2}{\Gamma \mid \Delta \mid pc_1 \vdash \{P_1\}\ s\ \{Q_1\}}\ \text{T-CONSEQ}
$$

Fig. 8. Structural typing rules.

The typing rules for conditionals and loops (T-IF and T-WHILE) both require ownership of a scheduler resource with a scheduler level ℓ_s and this scheduler level must be an upper bound on the security level of the branching expression. The structural rule of consequence (T-CONSEQ in Fig. 8) allows to strengthen preconditions and weaken postconditions. In particular, in conjunction with resource implication rules Fig. 9, it allows to raise the level of scheduler resource, which is necessary to type branching on high-security data.

Spawning Threads. When spawning a new thread, the spawning thread is able to transfer some of its resources to the newly created thread. This is captured by the T-FORK rule given below, which transfers the resources described by P from the spawning thread to the spawned thread.

$$
\frac{\Gamma \mid \Delta \mid pc \vdash \{P\}\ s\ \{Q\}}{\Gamma \mid \Delta \mid pc \vdash \{P\}\ \mathsf{fork}(s)\ \{emp\}}\ \text{T-FORK}
$$

Naturally, the newly spawned thread inherits the pc-level of the spawning thread. Upon termination of the spawned thread, the resources still owned by the spawned thread are lost. To transfer resources back to the spawning thread or other threads requires synchronization using channels.

$$\overline{\Gamma \vdash P \Rightarrow P * emp} \qquad \overline{\Gamma \vdash P * Q \Rightarrow Q * P} \qquad \overline{\Gamma \vdash (P * Q) * R \Leftrightarrow P * (Q * R)}$$

$$\frac{}{\Gamma \vdash P * Q \Rightarrow P} \qquad \frac{\Gamma \vdash P \Rightarrow Q \quad \Gamma \vdash Q \Rightarrow R}{\Gamma \vdash P \Rightarrow R} \qquad \frac{\Gamma \vdash P \Rightarrow Q}{\Gamma \vdash P * R \Rightarrow Q * R}$$

$$\frac{\pi_1 + \pi_2 \le 1}{\Gamma \vdash x_{\pi_1} * x_{\pi_2} \Leftrightarrow x_{\pi_1 + \pi_2}} \qquad \frac{\pi_1 + \pi_2 \le 1}{\Gamma \vdash schd_{\pi_1}(\ell) * schd_{\pi_2}(\ell) \Leftrightarrow schd_{\pi_1 + \pi_2}(\ell)}$$

$$\frac{\ell_1 \sqsubseteq \ell_2}{\Gamma \vdash schd_1(\ell_1) \Rightarrow schd_1(\ell_2)}$$

Fig. 9. Resource implication rules.

Synchronization. From the point of view of resources, synchronization is about transferring ownership of resources between threads. When sending a message on a channel, we relinquish ownership of some of our resources, which become associated with the message until it is read. Conversely, when reading from a channel the reader may take ownership of a part of the resource associated with the message it reads. The Δ context defines a static specification for every channel identifier that describes the resources we wish to associate with messages on the given channel. If $\Delta(ch) = P$, then we must transfer resource P when sending a message on channel ch. However, when receiving a message from channel ch, we might only be able to acquire part of P, depending on whether our receive may race with other receives to acquire the resources and how our pc-level relates to the pc-level of the sender of the message and to the potential scheduler taint.

To capture this formally, our type-and-effect system contains channel resources, written ch_π, erased resources, written $\lceil P \rceil^\ell$, and channel security levels, $\Gamma(ch)$. Like variable resources, channel resources allow us to track whether a given receive operation on a channel might race with another receive on the same channel using a fraction π. To receive on a channel ch requires fractional ownership of the corresponding channel resource. The channel resource can be split and recombined freely: $\Gamma \vdash ch_{\pi_1 + \pi_2} \Leftrightarrow ch_{\pi_1} * ch_{\pi_2}$, with the full fraction, $\pi = 1$, indicating an exclusive right to receive on the given channel. The erased resource, $\lceil P \rceil^\ell$, is used to erase variable and channel resources in P with security levels that are not greater than or equal to the security level ℓ. To illustrate how we use these features to type send and receive commands, let us start by considering an example that is *not* secure, and that should therefore *not* be typeable.

We start with the simpler case of non-racy receives. In the case of non-racy receives, we have to prevent ownership transfer of low variables from a high security context to a lower security context. This is illustrated by the program

```
fork(if h then send(a) else send(b));
fork(recv(a); l := 1; send(b));
fork(recv(b); l := 2; send(a))
```

This code snippet spawns a thread which sends a message on either channel a or b depending on the value of the confidential variable h. Then the program spawns two other threads that wait until there is an available message on their channel, before they write to l and message the other thread that it may proceed. This code snippet is insecure, because if h is initially true, then the public variable l will contain the value 2 upon termination and if h is initially false, then l will contain the value 1.

$$\frac{pc \sqsubseteq \Gamma(ch)}{\Gamma \mid \Delta \mid pc \vdash \{\Delta(ch)\} \text{ send}(ch) \{emp\}} \text{ T-SEND}$$

$$\frac{P \equiv R * schd_{\pi_s}(\ell_s) \qquad pc \sqsubseteq \Gamma(ch) \sqsubseteq \ell_s \qquad \Gamma \vdash P \Rightarrow ch_1}{\Gamma \mid \Delta \mid pc \vdash \{P\} \text{ recv}(ch) \{P * \lceil \Delta(ch) \rceil^{\Gamma(ch)}\}} \text{ T-RECV-EXCL}$$

$$\frac{P \equiv R * schd_{\pi_s}(\ell_s) \qquad pc \sqsubseteq \Gamma(ch) = \ell_s \qquad \Gamma \vdash P \Rightarrow ch_\pi}{\Gamma \mid \Delta \mid pc \vdash \{P\} \text{ recv}(ch) \{P * \lceil \Delta(ch) \rceil^{\Gamma(ch)}\}} \text{ T-RECV-RACY}$$

Fig. 10. Typing rules for synchronization primitives.

To type this program, the idea would be to transfer exclusive ownership of the public variable l along channels a and b. However, our type system prevents this by erasing the resources received along channels a and b at the high security level, because the first thread may send messages on a and b in a high security context (i.e., with a high pc-level).

Formally, the typing rules for send and for exclusive receives are given by T-SEND and T-RECV-EXCL in Fig. 10. The send rule requires that the security level of the channel is greater than or equal to the sender's pc-level and the exclusive receive rule erases the resources received from the channel using the security-level of the channel. This means that the second and third threads do not get exclusive ownership of the l variable and that we therefore cannot type the subsequent assignments. The exclusive receive rule also requires fractional ownership of the scheduler resource and that the bound on the taint on the scheduler level is greater than or equal to the channel security level when receiving on a channel. This condition is related to the use of reschedule and we will return to this condition later.

Example 7. To illustrate how to use these rules for ownership transfer, consider the following variant of the examples from the introduction.

$$ex_7 \stackrel{def}{=} \text{fork(if } h \text{ then } s_1 \text{ else } s_2); \text{ /* high computation */}$$
$$\text{fork}(l := 1; \text{ send}(c));$$
$$\text{recv}(c); l := 2$$

It forks off a thread that does a high computation and potentially taints the scheduler with confidential information. The main thread also forks off a new thread that performs a write to public variable l, before itself writing to l. However, a communication through channel c in between these two assignments ensure that they are not racy and therefore do not leak private information for any chosen scheduling. We can, for instance, type this example as follows:

$$\Gamma \mid \Delta \mid L \vdash \{c_1 * l_1 * h_1 * schd_1(L)\} \; ex_7 \; \{c_1 * l_1 * schd_{\frac{1}{2}}(H)\}$$

where Γ and Δ are defined as follows: $\Gamma(l) = \Gamma(c) = L$, $\Gamma(h) = H$, and $\Delta(c) = l_1$.

This typing requires the main thread to pass exclusive ownership of l to the second thread upon forking, which is then passed back on channel c. Since we only send and receive on channel c in a low context, we can take the channel security level to be low for c. When the main thread receives a message on c it thus takes ownership of $\lceil l_1 \rceil^{\Gamma(c)}$ and since $\Gamma(c) = L$, it follows that $\Gamma \vdash \lceil l_1 \rceil^{\Gamma(c)} \Rightarrow l_1$. The main thread thus owns the variable resource for l exclusively when typing the second assignment.

We use the resource implication rules in Fig. 11 to reason about erased resources, by pulling resources out of the erasure. For instance, if the security level of a variable x is greater than or equal to the erasure security level, then we can pull it out of the erasure: if $\ell \sqsubseteq \Gamma(x)$ then $\Gamma \vdash \lceil x_\pi \rceil^\ell \Rightarrow x_\pi$; and likewise for channel resources: if $\ell \sqsubseteq \Gamma(ch)$ then $\Gamma \vdash \lceil ch_\pi \rceil^\ell \Rightarrow ch_\pi$. Resources that cannot be pulled out of the erasure cannot be used for anything; owning $\lceil x_\pi \rceil^\ell$ where $\Gamma(x) \not\sqsubseteq \ell$ is thus equivalent to owning emp. The full set of erasure implication rules is given in Fig. 11. Notice that scheduler resources never get erased: $\Gamma \vdash \lceil schd_\pi(\ell_s) \rceil^\ell \Rightarrow schd_\pi(\ell_s)$. Moreover, the resource erasure is idempotent and distributes over the star operator.

$$\frac{\ell \sqsubseteq \Gamma(x)}{\Gamma \vdash \lceil x_\pi \rceil^\ell \Rightarrow x_\pi} \qquad \frac{\ell \sqsubseteq \Gamma(ch)}{\Gamma \vdash \lceil ch_\pi \rceil^\ell \Rightarrow ch_\pi} \qquad \frac{}{\Gamma \vdash \lceil schd_\pi(\ell_s) \rceil^\ell \Rightarrow schd_\pi(\ell_s)}$$

$$\frac{}{\Gamma \vdash \lceil \lceil P \rceil^\ell \rceil^\ell \Rightarrow \lceil P \rceil^\ell} \qquad \frac{}{\Gamma \vdash \lceil P_1 * P_2 \rceil^\ell \Rightarrow \lceil P_1 \rceil^\ell * \lceil P_2 \rceil^\ell}$$

Fig. 11. Erasure implication rules

Racy Synchronization. In the case of racy receives, where we have multiple threads racing to take ownership of a message on the same channel, we have to restrict which resources the receivers can take ownership of even further. This is best illustrated with another example of an insecure program. The following is a variant of the earlier insecure program, but instead of sending a message on a channel in a high context it sends a message on a channel in a low context after the scheduler has been tainted and the scheduler level has been raised to high.

```
if h then skip else (skip; skip);
send(c);
fork(recv(c); l := 1; send(c));
recv(c); l := 2; send(c)
```

With a suitably chosen scheduler, the initial value of the confidential variable h could decide which of the two racy receives will receive the initial message on c and thereby leak the initial value of h through the public variable l. We thus have to ensure that this program is *not* typeable. Our type system ensures that this is the case by requiring the scheduler level to equal the channel security level when performing a potentially racy receive. In the case of the example above, the scheduler level gets high after the high branching and is still high when we type check the two receives; since they are racy we are forced to set the security level of channel c to high—see the typing rule T-RECV-RACY for racy receives in Fig. 10—which ensures we cannot transfer ownership of the public variable l on c. This in turn ensures that we cannot type the assignments to l as exclusive assignments and therefore that the example is not typeable.

Reschedule. Recall that if we own the scheduler resource exclusively, then we can freely raise the upper bound on the security level of the scheduler, since no other threads are relying on any upper bound. In general, it is not sound to lower this upper bound, unless we can guarantee that the current scheduler level is less than or equal to the new upper bound. This is exactly what the reschedule statement ensures. The typing rule for reschedule (T-RESCHED given below) thus requires exclusive ownership of the scheduler resource and allows us to change this upper bound to any security level we wish. To ensure soundness, we only allow reschedule to be used when the pc-level is $\perp_{\mathcal{L}}$, the bottom security level of the semilattice of security elements.

$$\frac{}{\Gamma \mid \Delta \mid \perp_{\mathcal{L}} \vdash \{schd_1(\ell_1)\} \text{ reschedule } \{schd_1(\ell_2)\}} \text{ T-RESCHED}$$

Example 8. To illustrate how the typing rule for reschedule is used, consider the following code snippet from the introduction section:

$$ex_8 \overset{def}{=} \text{ if } h \text{ then skip else (skip; skip);}$$
$$\text{reschedule;}$$
$$\text{fork}(l := 0); l := 1$$

Recall that this snippet is secure, since reschedule resets the scheduler state before the race on l. We can, for instance, type this example as follows:

$$\Gamma \mid \Delta \mid L \vdash \{l_1 * h_1 * schd_1(L)\} \ ex_8 \ \{l_{\frac{1}{2}} * schd_{\frac{1}{2}}(L)\}$$

with $\Gamma(l) = L$ and $\Gamma(h) = H$.

To type this example we first raise the upper bound on the scheduler level from low to high, so that we can branch on confidential h. Then we use T-RESCHED to reset it back to low after reschedule. At this point we split both the scheduler and variable resource for variable l into two, keep one part of each for the main thread and give away one part of each to the newly spawned thread. The two assignments to l are now typed by T-ASGN-RACY rule.

Example 9. To illustrate why we only allow reschedule to be used at pc-level $\perp_\mathcal{L}$, consider the following example, which branches on the confidential variable h before executing reschedule in both branches.

fork(if h then (reschedule; skip) else (reschedule; skip; skip));
fork($l := 0$); $l := 1$

Despite doing a reschedule in both branches, the subsequent statements in the two branches immediately taint the scheduler with information about h again, after the scheduler has been reset. This example is thus not safe.

In the full version of the paper, the reader will find several more intricate examples justifying the constraints of the rules.

Precision of the Type System. Notice that mere racy reading or writing from/to variables does not taint the scheduler. For example, programs

fork($l := 1$); fork($m := l$); fork($h := 0$); $h := 1$
fork($l := 0$); $h := h + 1$; $l := 1$
if l then $h := 0$ else $h := 1$; (fork($l := 0$); $l := 1$)

where l, m are low variables and h is a high variable, are all secure in the sense of Definition 1 and are typable. Indeed, there is no way to exploit scheduling to leak the secret value h in either of these programs. The scheduler may get tainted only if a high branch or receiving from a high channel is encountered, since the number of computation steps for the remaining computation (and hence its scheduling) may depend on a secret value as, for example, in the program while h do $h := h - 1$; (fork($l := 0$); $l := 1$). This example is rejected by our type system. To re-enable low races in the last example, rescheduling must be used:

while h do $h := h - 1$; reschedule; (fork($l := 0$); $l := 1$)

The last example is secure and accepted by the type system.

Limitations of our type system include imprecisions such as when both branches of a secret-dependent if-statement take the same number of steps, e.g., if h then skip else skip; (fork($l := 0$); $l := 1$), and standard imprecisions of flow-insensitive type-based approaches to information flow that reject programs such as in if h then $l := 0$ else $l := 0$ or in (if h then $l := 0$ else $l := 1$); $l := 42$.

Language Extensions. We believe that the ideas of this section can be extended to richer languages using standard techniques [17,32,51]. In particular, to handle a language with procedures we would use a separate environment to record types for procedures, similarly to what is done in, e.g., [34]. (In loc. cit. they did not cover concurrency; however, we take inspiration from [12] which presents a concurrent separation logic for a language with procedures and mutable stack variables.) Specifications for procedures would involve quantification over variables and security levels.

4   Soundness

Let T be a thread pool and let $\overline{P}$, $\overline{Q}$ map every thread identifier to $t \in dom(T)$ to a resource. We write $\Gamma \mid \Delta \vdash \{\overline{P}\}\ T\ \{\overline{Q}\}$ if $\overline{P}(t)$ and $\overline{Q}(t)$ are typing resources for every thread $T(t)$ with respect to Γ and Δ. We say that resource R is *compatible* if implication $\Gamma \vdash \circledast_{x \in Var} x_1 * \circledast_{ch \in Chan} ch_1 * schd_1(L) \Rightarrow R$ is provable.

Theorem 1 (Soundness). *Let $\Gamma \mid \Delta \vdash \{\overline{P}\}\ T\ \{\overline{Q}\}$ such that the composition of all the resources in $\overline{P}$ is compatible, then T satisfies non-interference for all attacker levels ℓ_A.*

Notice that the theorem quantifies universally over all attacker levels ℓ_A, hence, one typing is sufficient to guarantee security against all possible adversaries.

As a direct corollary from the theorem, we obtain a *compositionality* property for our type-and-effect system: Given two programs s_1, s_2 typable with preconditions P_1 and P_2, respectively, if $P_1 * P_2$ is compatible then the parallel composition of the two programs is typable with precondition $P_1 * P_2$.

Our soundness proof is inspired by previous non-interference results proved using a combination of erasure and confluence[4] for erased programs, but requires a number of novel techniques related to our reschedule construct, scheduler resources and support for benign races. A proof of Theorem 1 can be found in the full version of the paper.

5   Related Work

The problem of securing information flow in concurrent programs has received widespread attention. We review the relevant literature along the following three dimensions:

(1) *Scheduler-(in)dependence.* Sabelfeld and Sands [41] argue for importance of scheduler independence because in practice it may be difficult to accommodate for precise scheduler behavior under all circumstances, and attackers aware of the scheduler specifics can use that knowledge to their advantage,

---

[4] A property which guarantees that a given program can be reduced in different orders but yields the same result (up to a suitable equivalence relation).

also known as refinement attacks. However, designing a scheduler independent enforcement technique that is also practical comes at a price of additional restrictions. To this extent, a number of approaches gain permissiveness via scheduler support. This is manifested either as an assumption on a particular scheduling algorithm, i.e., round-robin, or scheduler awareness of security levels of the individual threads.

(2) *Permissiveness w.r.t. low races.* We are interested in seeing which of the approaches support benign low non-determinism and permit low races. We believe this is an important factor from a practical perspective, because an approach capable of handling low races has the potential of scaling to practical settings where parallel access, without extra synchronization overhead, to a single attacker-observable resource, such as network I/O, is desirable.

(3) *Termination-(in)sensitivity.* In sequential programs, ignoring leaks via program divergence is often a pragmatic choice, because the attacker is limited in how much information can be learned via the termination channel [3]. Can this pragmatic argument be carried over to a concurrent setting? On the one hand, malicious code with privileges to spawn threads may efficiently leak an N-bit secret by creating N threads and assigning every thread to leak a specific secret bit via the thread's termination behavior [48]. Motivated by this, many approaches reject programs that may potentially diverge depending on a secret. On the other hand, while it is possible to use techniques from literature on program termination to improve precision of the enforcement [29], a pragmatic attacker can instead use provably-terminating programs that take as much time as it is necessary for them to make their observations. So, for malicious code, one really needs to focus on the timing. But controlling timing behavior is difficult already in sequential programs, because many runtime aspects that have no source-level representation are in play, including hardware caches [50], memory management [35], or lazy evaluation [11].

Another reason for our attention on termination-(in)sensitivity is that it is our experience that technical restrictions that impose termination (or timing)-sensitivity often simplify soundness proofs. Without such restrictions, proving soundness for a (weaker) termination-insensitive definition can be more laborious.

	Scheduler-dependent or restricted to particular scheduler classes	Scheduler-independent
Low races allowed	**TI:** [30] **TS:** [9, 38, 25, 39, 7, 24, 45, 4, 10]	**TI:** [14] (whole-program), ⋆ **TS:** [41] (+timing-sensitive)
Low races forbidden	-	**TI:** [49, 16, 46] **TS:** [16, 26]

Fig. 12. Summary of the related work w.r.t. permissiveness of the language-based enforcement and scheduler dependence. **TI** stands for *termination-insensitive*; **TS** stands for *termination-sensitive*.

Figure 12 presents a high-level summary of the related work. The figure is by no means exhaustive and lists only a few representative works; we discuss the other related papers below. Observe how the literature is divided across two diametric quadrants. Approaches that prioritize scheduler independence are conservative in their treatment of low races. Approaches that do permit low races require specific scheduler support are confined to particular classes of schedulers. We discuss these quadrants in detail, followed by the discussion of rely-guarantee style reasoning for concurrent information flow and rescheduling.

5.1   Scheduler-Independent Approaches

Observational Determinism. The approach of preventing races to individual locations is initiated in the work on observational determinism by Zdancewic and Myers [49] (which itself draws upon the ideas of McLean [27] and Roscoe [37]). Subsequent efforts on observational determinism include the work by Huisman et al. [16] and by Terauchi [46]. Here, Huisman et al. [16] identify an issue in the Zdancewic and Myers' [49] definition of security—they construct a leaky program within the intended attacker model, i.e., not exploiting termination or timing, that is accepted by the definition (though it is ruled out by the type system). They also propose a modified definition and show how to enforce that using self-composition [8]. Terauchi's [46] paper presents a capability system with an inference algorithm for enforcing a restricted version of the Zdancewic and Myers' [49] definition.

Out of these, the work by Terauchi [46] is the closest to ours because of the use of fractional permissions, but there are important differences in the treatment of the low races and the underlying semantic condition. Terauchi's [46] type system is motivated by the design goal to reject racy programs of the form $l := 0 \parallel l := 1$. This is done through tracking fractional permissions on so-called abstract locations that represent a set of locations whose identity cannot be separated statically. Our type system uses fractional permissions in a similar spirit, but has additional expressivity, (even without the scheduler resource), because Terauchi's [46] typing also rules out programs such as $l_1 := 0 \parallel l_2 := 1$, even when l_1 and l_2 are statically known to be non-aliasing. This is because the type system has a restriction that groups *all low variables* into a single abstract location. While this restriction is a necessity if the attacker is assumed to observe the order of individual low assignments, this effectively forces synchronization of all low-updating threads, regardless of whether the updates are potentially racy or not. We do not have such a restriction in our model.

We suspect that lifting this restriction in the Terauchi's [46] system to accommodate a more permissive attacker model such as ours may be difficult without further changes to the type system, because their semantic security condition, being a variant of the one by Zdancewic and Myers [49], requires trace equivalence up to prefixing (and stuttering) for all locations in the set of the abstract low location. Without the typing restriction, the definition would appear to have the same semantic issue discovered by Huisman et al. [16]; the issue does not manifest itself with the restriction.

Note that adapting the security condition proposed by Huisman et al. [16] into a language-based setting also appears tricky. The paper [16] presents both termination-insensitive and termination-sensitive variants of their take on observational determinism. The key changes are the use of infinite traces instead of finite ones and requiring trace equivalence instead of prefix-equivalence (up to stuttering). Terauchi [46] expresses their concerns w.r.t. applicability of this definition ([46], Appendix A). We think there is an additional concern w.r.t. termination-insensitivity. Because the TI-definition requires equivalence of infinite low traces it rejects a program such as

$$l := 1; \text{ while } secret = 1 \text{ do skip}; l := 2; \text{ while } secret = 2 \text{ do skip}$$

This single-threaded program is a variant of a brute-force attack that is usually accepted by termination-insensitive definitions [3] and language-based techniques for information flow. We, thus, agree with the Terauchi's [46] conclusion [46] that enforcing such a condition via a type-based method without being overly conservative may prove difficult.

By contrast, our approach builds upon the technique of explicit refiners [30, 33], which allows non-determinism as long as it is not influenced by secrets, and does not exhibit the aforementioned semantic pitfalls.

Whole program analysis can be used to enforce concurrent non-interference with a high precision. Giffhorn and Snelting [14] use a PDG-based whole program analysis to enforce relaxed low-security observational determinism (RLSOD) in Java programs. RLSOD is similar to our security condition in that it allows low-nondeterminism as long as it does not depend on secrets.

Strong Security. Sabelfeld and Sands [41] present a definition of *strong security* that is a compositional semantic condition for a natural class of schedulers. The compositionality is attained by placing timing-sensitivity constraints on individual threads. This condition serves as a foundation for a number of works [13,19,22]. To establish timing sensitivity, these approaches often rely on program transformation [1,6,19,28]. A common limitation of the transformation-based techniques is that they do not apply to programs with high loops. Another concern is their general applicability, given the complexity of modern runtimes. A recent empirical study by Mantel and Starostin [23] investigates performance and security implications of these techniques, but as an initial step in this direction the paper [23] has a number of simplifying assumptions, such as disabled JIT optimizations and non-malicious code.

5.2   Scheduler-Dependent Approaches

Scheduler-dependent approaches vary in their assumptions on the underlying scheduler. Boudol and Castellani [9] study system and threads model where the scheduler code is explicit in the program source; a typing discipline regulates the secure interaction of the scheduler with the rest of the program [5].

Security-aware schedulers [7,38] track security levels of the program counters of each thread, and provide the interface that timing of high computations is not revealed to the low ones; this interface is realized by suspending all low threads when there is an alive high thread.

A number of approaches assume a particular scheduling strategy, typically round-robin [30,39,45]. Mantel and Sudbrock [24] define a class of *robust* schedulers as the schedulers where "the scheduling order of low threads does not depend on the high threads in a thread pool" [24]. The class of robust schedulers appears to be large enough to include a number of practical schedulers, including round-robin. Other works rely on nondeterministic [4,8,21,25,40,44] or probabilistically uniform [10,43,47] behavior.

5.3   Rely-Guarantee Style Reasoning for Concurrent Information Flow and Rescheduling

Rely-Guarantee Style Reasoning. Mantel et al. [26] develops a different rely-guarantee style compositional approach for concurrent non-interference in flow-sensitive settings. In this approach, permissions to read or write variables are expressed using special *data access modes*; a thread can obtain an exclusive read access or an exclusive write access via the specific mode. Note that the modes are different from fractional permissions, because, e.g., an exclusive write access to a variable does not automatically grant the exclusive read access. The modes also do not have a moral equivalent of the scheduler resource. Instead, the paper [26] suggests using an external may-happen-in-parallel global analysis to track their global consistency. Askarov et al. [4] give modes a runtime representation, and use a hybrid information flow monitor to establish concurrent non-interference. Li et al. [20] use rely-guarantee style reasoning to reason about information flows in a message-passing distributed settings, where scheduler cannot be controlled. Murray et al. [31] use mode-based reasoning in a flow-sensitive dependent type system to enforce timing-sensitive value-dependent non-interference for shared memory concurrent programs.

Rescheduling. The idea of barrier synchronization to recover permissiveness of language-based enforcement appears in papers with possibilistic scheduling [4, 25]. The rescheduling however does more than simple barrier synchronization— it also explicitly resets the scheduler state, which is crucial to avoid refinement attacks. The reason that simple barrier synchronization is insufficient is that despite synchronization at the barrier point, the scheduler state could be tainted by what happens before threads reach the barrier. For example, if the scheduler is implemented so that, after the barrier, the threads are scheduled to run in the order they have arrived to the barrier then there is little to be gained from the barrier synchronization.

Operationally, the reschedule is implementable in a straightforward manner, which is much simpler than security-aware schedulers [7,38]. We note that rescheduling allows programmers to explore the space of performance/expressivity without losing security. A program that type checks without reschedule, because there are no dangerous race conditions, does not need to suffer from the performance overhead of the rescheduling. Programmers only need to add the reschedule instruction if they wish to re-enable low races after the scheduler was tainted. In that light, rescheduling is no less practical than the earlier mentioned barrier synchronization [4].

While on one hand the need to reschedule appears heavy-handed, we are not aware of other techniques that re-enable low races when the scheduler can be tainted. How exactly the scheduler gets tainted depends on the scheduler implementation/model. Presently, we assume that any local control flow that depends on secrets may taint the scheduler. This conservative assumption can naturally be relaxed for more precise/realistic scheduler models. Future research efforts will focus on refining scheduler models to reduce the need for rescheduling and/or automatic placement of rescheduling to lessen the burden on programmers. The latter can utilize techniques from the literature on the automatic placement of declassifications [18].

5.4   This Work in the Context of Fig. 12

Developing a sound compositional technique for concurrent information flow that is scheduler-independent, low-nondeterministic, and termination-insensitive at the same time—a point marked by the star symbol in Fig. 12—is a tall order, but we believe we come close. Our only non-standard operation is reschedule that we argue has a simple operational implementation and can be introduced to many existing runtimes.

6   Conclusion and Future Work

In the paper, we have presented a new compositional model for enforcing information flow security against internal timing leaks for concurrent imperative programs. The model includes a compositional fine-grained type-and-effect system and a novel programming construct for resetting a scheduler state. The type system is agnostic in the level of adversary, which means that one typing judgment is sufficient to ensure security for all possible attacker level. We formulate and prove the soundness result for the type system.

In future work, we wish to support I/O; our proof technique appears to have all the necessary ingredients for that. Moreover, we wish to investigate a generalization of our concurrency model to an X10-like [30,42] setting where instead of one scheduler, we have several coarse-grained scheduling partitions.

Acknowledgments. Thanks are due to Andrei Sabelfeld, Deepak Garg and the anonymous reviewers for their comments on this paper. This research was supported in part by the ModuRes Sapere Aude Advanced Grant, DFF projects no. 4181-00273 and no. 6108-00363 from The Danish Council for Independent Research for the Natural Sciences (FNU), and in part by Aarhus University Research Foundation.

References

1. Agat, J.: Transforming out timing leaks. In: POPL (2000)
2. Askarov, A., Sabelfeld, A.: Tight enforcement of information-release policies for dynamic languages. In: CSF (2009)
3. Askarov, A., Hunt, S., Sabelfeld, A., Sands, D.: Termination-insensitive noninterference leaks more than just a bit. In: Jajodia, S., Lopez, J. (eds.) ESORICS 2008. LNCS, vol. 5283, pp. 333–348. Springer, Heidelberg (2008). https://doi.org/10.1007/978-3-540-88313-5_22
4. Askarov, A., Chong, S., Mantel, H.: Hybrid monitors for concurrent noninterference. In: CSF (2015)
5. Barthe, G., Nieto, L.P.: Formally verifying information flow type systems for concurrent and thread systems. In: FMSE (2004)
6. Barthe, G., Rezk, T., Warnier, M.: Preventing timing leaks through transactional branching instructions. Electron. Notes Theor. Comput. Sci. **153**(2), 33–55 (2006)
7. Barthe, G., Rezk, T., Russo, A., Sabelfeld, A.: Security of multithreaded programs by compilation. ACM Trans. Inf. Syst. Secur. **13**(3), 21 (2010)
8. Barthe, G., D'Argenio, P.R., Rezk, T.: Secure information flow by self-composition. Math. Struct. Comput. Sci. **21**(6), 1207–1252 (2011)
9. Boudol, G., Castellani, I.: Noninterference for concurrent programs and thread systems. Theor. Comput. Sci. **281**(1–2), 109–130 (2002)
10. Breitner, J., Graf, J., Hecker, M., Mohr, M., Snelting, G.: On improvements of low-deterministic security. In: Piessens, F., Viganò, L. (eds.) POST 2016. LNCS, vol. 9635, pp. 68–88. Springer, Heidelberg (2016). https://doi.org/10.1007/978-3-662-49635-0_4
11. Buiras, P., Russo, A.: Lazy programs leak secrets. In: Riis Nielson, H., Gollmann, D. (eds.) NordSec 2013. LNCS, vol. 8208, pp. 116–122. Springer, Heidelberg (2013). https://doi.org/10.1007/978-3-642-41488-6_8
12. Dinsdale-Young, T., da Rocha Pinto, P., Andersen, K.J., Birkedal, L.: CAPER: automatic verification for fine-grained concurrency. In: Yang, H. (ed.) ESOP 2017. LNCS, vol. 10201, pp. 420–447. Springer, Heidelberg (2017). https://doi.org/10.1007/978-3-662-54434-1_16
13. Focardi, R., Rossi, S., Sabelfeld, A.: Bridging language-based and process calculi security. In: Sassone, V. (ed.) FoSSaCS 2005. LNCS, vol. 3441, pp. 299–315. Springer, Heidelberg (2005). https://doi.org/10.1007/978-3-540-31982-5_19
14. Giffhorn, D., Snelting, G.: A new algorithm for low-deterministic security. Int. J. Inf. Secur. **14**(3), 263–287 (2015)
15. Goguen, J.A., Meseguer, J.: Security policies and security models: In: Security and Privacy (1982)
16. Huisman, M., Worah, P., Sunesen, K.: A temporal logic characterisation of observational determinism. In: CSFW (2006)
17. Hunt, S., Sands, D.: On flow-sensitive security types. In: POPL (2006)
18. King, D., Jha, S., Muthukumaran, D., Jaeger, T., Jha, S., Seshia, S.A.: Automating security mediation placement. In: Gordon, A.D. (ed.) ESOP 2010. LNCS, vol. 6012, pp. 327–344. Springer, Heidelberg (2010). https://doi.org/10.1007/978-3-642-11957-6_18
19. Köpf, B., Mantel, H.: Transformational typing and unification for automatically correcting insecure programs. Int. J. Inf. Secur. **6**(2–3), 107–131 (2007)

20. Li, X., Mantel, H., Tasch, M.: Taming message-passing communication in compositional reasoning about confidentiality. In: Chang, B.-Y.E. (ed.) APLAS 2017. LNCS, vol. 10695, pp. 45–66. Springer, Cham (2017). https://doi.org/10.1007/978-3-319-71237-6_3
21. Mantel, H., Reinhard, A.: Controlling the what and where of declassification in language-based security. In: De Nicola, R. (ed.) ESOP 2007. LNCS, vol. 4421, pp. 141–156. Springer, Heidelberg (2007). https://doi.org/10.1007/978-3-540-71316-6_11
22. Mantel, H., Sabelfeld, A.: A unifying approach to the security of distributed and multi-threaded programs. J. Comput. Secur. 11(4), 615–676 (2003)
23. Mantel, H., Starostin, A.: Transforming out timing leaks, more or less. In: Pernul, G., Ryan, P.Y.A., Weippl, E. (eds.) ESORICS 2015. LNCS, vol. 9326, pp. 447–467. Springer, Cham (2015). https://doi.org/10.1007/978-3-319-24174-6_23
24. Mantel, H., Sudbrock, H.: Flexible scheduler-independent security. In: Gritzalis, D., Preneel, B., Theoharidou, M. (eds.) ESORICS 2010. LNCS, vol. 6345, pp. 116–133. Springer, Heidelberg (2010). https://doi.org/10.1007/978-3-642-15497-3_8
25. Mantel, H., Sudbrock, H., Krauße, T.: Combining different proof techniques for verifying information flow security. In: Puebla, G. (ed.) LOPSTR 2006. LNCS, vol. 4407, pp. 94–110. Springer, Heidelberg (2007). https://doi.org/10.1007/978-3-540-71410-1_8
26. Mantel, H., Sands, D., Sudbrock, H.: Assumptions and guarantees for compositional noninterference. In: CSF (2011)
27. McLean, J.: Proving noninterference and functional correctness using traces. J. Comput. Secur. 1(1), 37–57 (1992)
28. Molnar, D., Piotrowski, M., Schultz, D., Wagner, D.: The program counter security model: automatic detection and removal of control-flow side channel attacks. In: Won, D.H., Kim, S. (eds.) ICISC 2005. LNCS, vol. 3935, pp. 156–168. Springer, Heidelberg (2006). https://doi.org/10.1007/11734727_14
29. Moore, S., Askarov, A., Chong, S.: Precise enforcement of progress-sensitive security. In: CCS (2012)
30. Muller, S., Chong, S.: Towards a practical secure concurrent language. In: OOPSLA (2012)
31. Murray, T.C., Sison, R., Pierzchalski, E., Rizkallah, C.: Compositional verification and refinement of concurrent value-dependent noninterference. In: CSF (2016)
32. Myers, A.C.: JFlow: practical mostly-static information flow control. In: POPL (1999)
33. O'Neill, K.R., Clarkson, M.R., Chong, S.: Information-flow security for interactive programs. In: CSFW (2006)
34. Parkinson, M.J., Bierman, G.M.: Separation logic and abstraction. In: POPL (2005)
35. Pedersen, M.V., Askarov, A.: From trash to treasure: timing-sensitive garbage collection. In: Security and Privacy (2017)
36. Reynolds, J.C.: Separation logic: a logic for shared mutable data structures. In: LICS (2002)
37. Roscoe, A.W.: CSP and determinism in security modelling. In: Security and Privacy (1995)
38. Russo, A., Sabelfeld, A.: Securing interaction between threads and the scheduler. In: CSFW (2006)

39. Russo, A., Hughes, J., Naumann, D., Sabelfeld, A.: Closing internal timing channels by transformation. In: Okada, M., Satoh, I. (eds.) ASIAN 2006. LNCS, vol. 4435, pp. 120–135. Springer, Heidelberg (2007). https://doi.org/10.1007/978-3-540-77505-8_10

40. Sabelfeld, A.: The impact of synchronisation on secure information flow in concurrent programs. In: Bjørner, D., Broy, M., Zamulin, A.V. (eds.) PSI 2001. LNCS, vol. 2244, pp. 225–239. Springer, Heidelberg (2001). https://doi.org/10.1007/3-540-45575-2_22

41. Sabelfeld, A., Sands, D.: Probabilistic noninterference for multi-threaded programs. In: CSFW (2000)

42. Saraswat, V., Bloom, B., Peshansky, I., Tardieu, O., Grove, D.: X10 language specification. Technical report, IBM, January 2012

43. Smith, G.: Probabilistic noninterference through weak probabilistic bisimulation. In: CSFW (2003)

44. Smith, G., Volpano, D.M.: Secure information flow in a multi-threaded imperative language. In: POPL (1998)

45. Stefan, D., Russo, A., Buiras, P., Levy, A., Mitchell, J.C., Mazières, D.: Addressing covert termination and timing channels in concurrent information flow systems. In: ICFP (2012)

46. Terauchi, T.: A type system for observational determinism. In: CSF (2008)

47. Volpano, D.M., Smith, G.: Probabilistic noninterference in a concurrent language. J. Comput. Secur. 7(1), 231–253 (1999)

48. Volpano, D.M., Smith, G.: Verifying secrets and relative secrecy, In: POPL (2000)

49. Zdancewic, S., Myers, A.C.: Observational determinism for concurrent program security. In: CSFW (2003)

50. Zhang, D., Askarov, A., Myers, A.C.: Language-based control and mitigation of timing channels. In: PLDI (2012)

51. Zheng, L., Myers, A.C.: Dynamic security labels and noninterference (extended abstract). In: Dimitrakos, T., Martinelli, F. (eds.) Formal Aspects in Security and Trust. IIFIP, vol. 173, pp. 27–40. Springer, Boston, MA (2005). https://doi.org/10.1007/0-387-24098-5_3

The Meaning of Memory Safety

Arthur Azevedo de Amorim[1]([✉]), Cătălin Hrițcu[2], and Benjamin C. Pierce[3]

[1] Carnegie Mellon University, Pittsburgh, USA
arthur.aa@gmail.com
[2] Inria, Paris, France
[3] University of Pennsylvania, Philadelphia, USA

Abstract. We give a rigorous characterization of what it means for a programming language to be *memory safe*, capturing the intuition that memory safety supports *local reasoning about state*. We formalize this principle in two ways. First, we show how a small memory-safe language validates a *noninterference* property: a program can neither affect nor be affected by unreachable parts of the state. Second, we extend separation logic, a proof system for heap-manipulating programs, with a "memory-safe variant" of its *frame rule*. The new rule is stronger because it applies even when parts of the program are buggy or malicious, but also weaker because it demands a stricter form of separation between parts of the program state. We also consider a number of pragmatically motivated variations on memory safety and the reasoning principles they support. As an application of our characterization, we evaluate the security of a previously proposed dynamic monitor for memory safety of heap-allocated data.

1 Introduction

Memory safety, and the vulnerabilities that follow from its absence [43], are common concerns. So what is it, exactly? Intuitions abound, but translating them into satisfying formal definitions is surprisingly difficult [20].

In large part, this difficulty stems from the prominent role that informal, everyday intuition assigns, in discussions of memory safety, to a range of errors related to memory *misuse*—buffer overruns, double frees, etc. Characterizing memory safety in terms of the absence of these errors is tempting, but this falls short for two reasons. First, there is often disagreement on which behaviors qualify as errors. For example, many real-world C programs intentionally rely on unrestricted pointer arithmetic [28], though it may yield undefined behavior according to the language standard [21, Sect. 6.5.6]. Second, from the perspective of security, the critical issue is not the errors themselves, but rather the fact that, when they occur in unsafe languages like C, the program's ensuing behavior is determined by obscure, low-level factors such as the compiler's choice of run-time memory layout, often leading to exploitable vulnerabilities. By contrast, in memory-safe languages like Java, programs can attempt to access arrays out of bounds, but such mistakes lead to sensible, predictable outcomes.

L. Bauer and R. Küsters (Eds.): POST 2018, LNCS 10804, pp. 79–105, 2018.
https://doi.org/10.1007/978-3-319-89722-6_4

Rather than attempting a definition in terms of bad things that cannot happen, we aim to formalize memory safety in terms of *reasoning principles* that programmers can soundly apply in its presence (or conversely, principles that programmers should *not* naively apply in unsafe settings, because doing so can lead to serious bugs and vulnerabilities). Specifically, to give an account of *memory* safety, as opposed to more inclusive terms such as "type safety," we focus on reasoning principles that are common to a wide range of stateful abstractions, such as records, tagged or untagged unions, local variables, closures, arrays, call stacks, objects, compartments, and address spaces.

What sort of reasoning principles? Our inspiration comes from *separation logic* [36], a variant of Hoare logic designed to verify complex heap-manipulating programs. The power of separation logic stems from *local reasoning* about state: to prove the correctness of a program component, we must argue that its memory accesses are confined to a *footprint*, a precise region demarcated by the specification. This discipline allows proofs to ignore regions outside of the footprint, while ensuring that arbitrary invariants for these regions are preserved during execution.

The locality of separation logic is deeply linked to memory safety. Consider a hypothetical jpeg decoding procedure that manipulates image buffers. We might expect its execution not to interfere with the integrity of an unrelated window object in the program. We can formalize this requirement in separation logic by proving a specification that includes only the image buffers, but not the window, in the decoder's footprint. Showing that the footprint is respected would amount to checking the bounds of individual buffer accesses, thus enforcing memory safety; conversely, if the decoder is not memory safe, a simple buffer overflow might suffice to tamper with the window object, thus violating locality and potentially paving the way to an attack.

Our aim is to extend this line of reasoning beyond conventional separation logic, encompassing settings such as ML, Java, or Lisp that enforce memory safety automatically without requiring complete correctness proofs—which can be prohibitively expensive for large code bases, especially in the presence of third-party libraries or plugins over which we have little control. The key observation is that memory safety forces code to respect a natural footprint: the set of its reachable memory locations (reachable with respect to the variables it mentions). Suppose that the jpeg decoder above is written in Java. Though we may not know much about its input-output behavior, we can still assert that it cannot have any effect on the window object simply by replacing the detailed reasoning demanded by separation logic by a simple inaccessibility check.

Our *first contribution* is to formalize local reasoning principles supported by an ideal notion of memory safety, using a simple language (Sect. 2) to ground our discussion. We show three results (Theorems 1, 3 and 4) that explain how the execution of a piece of code is affected by extending its initial heap. These results lead to a *noninterference* property (Corollary 1), ensuring that code cannot affect or be affected by unreachable memory. In Sect. 3.3, we show how these results yield a variant of the frame rule of separation logic (Theorem 6), which embodies its local reasoning capabilities. The two variants have complementary strengths and weaknesses: while the original rule applies to unsafe settings like C, but requires comprehensively verifying individual memory accesses, our variant does not require proving that every access is correct, but demands a stronger notion of separation between memory regions. These results have been verified with the Coq proof assistant.[1]

Our *second contribution* (Sect. 4) is to evaluate pragmatically motivated relaxations of the ideal notion above, exploring various trade-offs between safety, performance, flexibility, and backwards compatibility. These variants can be broadly classified into two groups according to reasoning principles they support. The stronger group gives up on some secrecy guarantees, but still ensures that pieces of code cannot modify the contents of unreachable parts of the heap. The weaker group, on the other hand, leaves gaps that completely invalidate reachability-based reasoning.

Our *third contribution* (Sect. 5) is to demonstrate how our characterization applies to more realistic settings, by analyzing a heap-safety monitor for machine code [5, 15]. We prove that the abstract machine that it implements also satisfies a noninterference property, which can be transferred to the monitor via refinement, modulo memory exhaustion issues discussed in Sect. 4. These proofs are also done in Coq.[2]

We discuss related work on memory safety and stronger reasoning principles in Sect. 6, and conclude in Sect. 7. While memory safety has seen prior formal investigation (e.g. [31,41]), our characterization is the first phrased in terms of reasoning principles that are valid when memory safety is enforced automatically. We hope that these principles can serve as good criteria for formally evaluating such enforcement mechanisms in practice. Moreover, our definition is self-contained and does not rely on additional features such as full-blown capabilities, objects, module systems, etc. Since these features tend to depend on some form of memory safety anyway, we could see our characterization as a common core of reasoning principles that underpin all of them.

2 An Idealized Memory-Safe Language

Our discussion begins with a concrete case study: a simple imperative language with manual memory management. It features several mechanisms for controlling the effects of memory misuse, ranging from the most conventional, such as bounds checking for spatial safety, to more uncommon ones, such as assigning unique identifiers to every allocated block for ensuring temporal safety.

Choosing a language with manual memory management may seem odd, since safety is often associated with garbage collection. We made this choice for two reasons. First, most discussions on memory safety are motivated by its absence from languages like C that also rely on manual memory management. There is

---

[1] The proofs are available at: https://github.com/arthuraa/memory-safe-language.
[2] Available at https://github.com/micro-policies/micro-policies-coq/tree/master/memory_safety.

Command	Description
$x \leftarrow e$	Local assignment
$x \leftarrow [e]$	Read from heap
$[e_1] \leftarrow e_2$	Heap assignment
$x \leftarrow \mathsf{alloc}(e_{size})$	Allocation
$\mathsf{free}(e)$	Deallocation
skip	Do nothing
if e then c_1 else c_2	Conditional
while e do c end	Loop
$c_1 ; c_2$	Sequencing

$$s \in \mathcal{S} \triangleq \mathcal{L} \times \mathcal{M} \qquad \text{(states)}$$

$$l \in \mathcal{L} \triangleq \mathsf{var} \rightharpoonup_{\mathsf{fin}} \mathcal{V} \qquad \text{(local stores)}$$

$$m \in \mathcal{M} \triangleq \mathbb{I} \times \mathbb{Z} \rightharpoonup_{\mathsf{fin}} \mathcal{V} \qquad \text{(heaps)}$$

$$v \in \mathcal{V} \triangleq \mathbb{Z} \uplus \mathbb{B} \uplus \{\mathsf{nil}\} \uplus \mathbb{I} \times \mathbb{Z} \text{ (values)}$$

$$\mathcal{O} \triangleq \mathcal{S} \uplus \{\mathsf{error}\} \qquad \text{(outcomes)}$$

$$\mathbb{I} \triangleq \text{a countably infinite set}$$

$$X \rightharpoonup_{\mathsf{fin}} Y \triangleq \text{finite partial functions } X \rightharpoonup Y$$

Fig. 1. Syntax, states and values

a vast body of research that tries to make such languages safer, and we would like our account to apply to it. Second, we wanted to stress that our characterization does not depend fundamentally on the mechanisms used to enforce memory safety, especially because they might have complementary advantages and shortcomings. For example, manual memory management can lead to more memory leaks; garbage collectors can degrade performance; and specialized type systems for managing memory [37,41] are more complex. After a brief overview of the language, we explore its reasoning principles in Sect. 3.

Figure 1 summarizes the language syntax and other basic definitions. Expressions e include variables $x \in \mathsf{var}$, numbers $n \in \mathbb{Z}$, booleans $b \in \mathbb{B}$, an invalid pointer nil, and various operations, both binary (arithmetic, logic, etc.) and unary (extracting the offset of a pointer). We write $[e]$ for dereferencing the pointer denoted by e.

Programs operate on states consisting of two components: a *local store*, which maps variables to values, and a *heap*, which maps pointers to values. Pointers are not bare integers, but rather pairs (i, n) of a *block identifier* $i \in \mathbb{I}$ and an offset $n \in \mathbb{Z}$. The offset is relative to the corresponding block, and the identifier i need not bear any direct relation to the physical address that might be used in a concrete implementation on a conventional machine. (That is, we can equivalently think of the heap as mapping each identifier to a separate array of heap cells.) Similar structured memory models are widely used in the literature, as in the CompCert verified C compiler [26] and other models of the C language [23], for instance.

We write $[\![c]\!](s)$ to denote the outcome of running a program c in an initial state s, which can be either a successful final state s' or a fatal run-time error. Note that $[\![c]\!]$ is partial, to account for non-termination. Similarly, $[\![e]\!](s)$ denotes the result of evaluating the expression e on the state s (expression evaluation is total and has no side effects). The formal definition of these functions is left to the Appendix; we just single out a few aspects that have a crucial effect on the security properties discussed later.

Illegal Memory Accesses Lead to Errors. The language controls the effect of memory misuse by raising errors that stop execution immediately. This contrasts with typical C implementations, where such errors lead to unpredictable *undefined behavior*. The main errors are caused by reads, writes, and frees to the current memory m using *invalid pointers*—that is, pointers p such that $m(p)$ is undefined. Such pointers typically arise by offsetting an existing pointer out of bounds or by freeing a structure on the heap (which turns all other pointers to that block in the program state into dangling ones). In common parlance, this discipline ensures both *spatial* and *temporal* memory safety.

Block Identifiers are Capabilities. Pointers can only be used to access memory corresponding to their identifiers, which effectively act as capabilities. Identifiers are set at allocation time, where they are chosen to be fresh with respect to the entire current state (i.e., the new identifier is not associated with any pointers defined in the current memory, stored in local variables, or stored on the heap). Once assigned, identifiers are immutable, making it impossible to fabricate a pointer to an allocated block out of thin air. This can be seen, for instance, in the semantics of addition, which allows pointer arithmetic but does not affect identifiers:

$$[\![e_1 + e_2]\!](s) \triangleq \begin{cases} n_1 + n_2 & \text{if } [\![e_i]\!](s) = n_i \\ (i, n_1 + n_2) & \text{if } [\![e_1]\!](s) = (i, n_1) \text{ and } [\![e_2]\!](s) = n_2 \\ \text{nil} & \text{otherwise} \end{cases}$$

For simplicity, nonsensical combinations such as adding two pointers simply result in the nil value. A real implementation might represent identifiers with hardware tags and use an increasing counter to generate identifiers for new blocks (as done by Dhawan *et al.* [15]; see Sect. 5.1); if enough tags are available, every identifier will be fresh.

Block Identifiers Cannot be Observed. Because of the freshness condition above, identifiers can reveal information about the entire program state. For example, if they are chosen according to an increasing counter, knowing what identifier was assigned to a new block tells us how many allocations have been performed. A concrete implementation would face similar issues related to the choice of physical addresses for new allocations. (Such issues are commonplace in systems that combine dynamic allocation and information-flow control [12].) For this reason, our language keeps identifiers opaque and inaccessible to programs; they can only be used to reference values in memory, and nothing else. We discuss a more permissive approach in Sect. 4.2.

Note that hiding identifiers doesn't mean we have to hide *everything* associated with a pointer: besides using pointers to access memory, programs can also safely extract their offsets and test if two pointers are equal (which means equality for both offsets and identifiers). Our Coq development also shows that it is sound to compute the size of a memory block via a valid pointer.

New Memory is Always Initialized. Whenever a memory block is allocated, all of its contents are initialized to 0. (The exact value does not matter, as long it is some constant that is not a previously allocated pointer.) This is important for ensuring that allocation does not leak secrets present in previously freed blocks; we return to this point in Sect. 4.3.

3   Reasoning with Memory Safety

Having presented our language, we now turn to the reasoning principles that it supports. Intuitively, these principles allow us to analyze the effect of a piece of code by restricting our attention to a smaller portion of the program state. A first set of *frame theorems* (1, 3, and 4) describes how the execution of a piece of code is affected by extending the initial state on which it runs. These in turn imply a noninterference property, Corollary 1, guaranteeing that program execution is independent of inaccessible memory regions—that is, those that correspond to block identifiers that a piece of code does not possess. Finally, in Sect. 3.3, we discuss how the frame theorems can be recast in the language of separation logic, leading to a new variant of its frame rule (Theorem 6).

$$(l_1, m_1) \cup (l_2, m_2) \triangleq (l_1 \cup l_2, m_1 \cup m_2) \qquad \text{(state union)}$$

$$(f \cup g)(x) \triangleq \begin{cases} f(x) & \text{if } x \in \text{dom}(f) \\ g(x) & \text{otherwise} \end{cases} \qquad \text{(partial function union)}$$

$$\text{blocks}(l, m) \triangleq \{i \in \mathbb{I} \mid \exists n, (i, n) \in \text{dom}(m)\} \qquad \text{(identifiers of live blocks)}$$

$$\text{ids}(l, m) \triangleq \text{blocks}(l, m) \qquad \text{(all identifiers in state)}$$
$$\cup \{i \mid \exists x, n, l(x) = (i, n)\}$$
$$\cup \{i \mid \exists p, n, m(p) = (i, n)\}$$

$$\text{vars}(l, m) \triangleq \text{dom}(l) \qquad \text{(defined local variables)}$$

$$\text{vars}(c) \triangleq \text{local variables of program } c$$

$$X \,\#\, Y \triangleq (X \cap Y = \emptyset) \qquad \text{(disjoint sets)}$$

$$\pi \cdot s \triangleq \text{rename identifiers with permutation } \pi$$

Fig. 2. Basic notation

3.1   Basic Properties of Memory Safety

Figure 2 summarizes basic notation used in our results. By *permutation*, we mean a function $\pi : \mathbb{I} \to \mathbb{I}$ that has a two-sided inverse π^{-1}; that is, $\pi \circ \pi^{-1} = \pi^{-1} \circ \pi = \text{id}_{\mathbb{I}}$. Some of these operations are standard and omitted for brevity.[3]

---

[3] The renaming operation $\pi \cdot s$, in particular, can be derived formally by viewing $\mathcal{S}$ as a nominal set over $\mathbb{I}$ [34] obtained by combining products, disjoint unions, and partial functions.

The first frame theorem states that, if a program terminates successfully, then we can extend its initial state almost without affecting execution.

Theorem 1 (Frame OK). *Let c be a command, and s_1, s_1', and s_2 be states. Suppose that $[\![c]\!](s_1) = s_1'$, $\mathsf{vars}(c) \subseteq \mathsf{vars}(s_1)$, and $\mathsf{blocks}(s_1) \mathbin{\#} \mathsf{blocks}(s_2)$. Then there exists a permutation π such that $[\![c]\!](s_1 \cup s_2) = \pi \cdot s_1' \cup s_2$ and $\mathsf{blocks}(\pi \cdot s_1') \mathbin{\#} \mathsf{blocks}(s_2)$.*

The second premise, $\mathsf{vars}(c) \subseteq \mathsf{vars}(s_1)$, guarantees that all the variables needed to run c are already defined in s_1, implying that their values do not change once we extend that initial state with s_2. The third premise, $\mathsf{blocks}(s_1) \mathbin{\#} \mathsf{blocks}(s_2)$, means that the memories of s_1 and s_2 store disjoint regions. Finally, the conclusion of the theorem states that (1) the execution of c does not affect the extra state s_2 and (2) the rest of the result is almost the same as s_1', except for a permutation of block identifiers.

Permutations are needed to avoid clashes between identifiers in s_2 and those assigned to regions allocated by c when running on s_1. For instance, suppose that the execution of c on s_1 allocated a new block, and that this block was assigned some identifier $i \in \mathbb{I}$. If the memory of s_2 already had a block corresponding to i, c would have to choose a different identifier i' for allocating that block when running on $s_1 \cup s_2$. This change requires replacing all occurrences of i by i' in the result of the first execution, which can be achieved with a permutation that swaps these two identifiers.

The proof of Theorem 1 relies crucially on the facts that programs cannot inspect identifiers, that memory can grow indefinitely (a common assumption in formal models of memory), and that memory operations fail on invalid pointers. Because of the permutations, we also need to show that permuting the initial state s of a command c with any permutation π yields the same outcome, up to some additional permutation π' that again accounts for different choices of fresh identifiers.

Theorem 2 (Renaming states). *Let s be a state, c a command, and π a permutation. There exists π' such that:*

$$[\![c]\!](\pi \cdot s) = \begin{cases} \mathsf{error} & \text{if } [\![c]\!](s) = \mathsf{error} \\ \bot & \text{if } [\![c]\!](s) = \bot \\ \pi' \cdot \pi \cdot s' & \text{if } [\![c]\!](s) = s' \end{cases}$$

A similar line of reasoning yields a second frame theorem, which says that we cannot make a program terminate just by extending its initial state.

Theorem 3 (Frame Loop). *Let c be a command, and s_1 and s_2 be states. If $[\![c]\!](s_1) = \bot$, $\mathsf{vars}(c) \subseteq \mathsf{vars}(s_1)$, and $\mathsf{blocks}(s_1) \mathbin{\#} \mathsf{blocks}(s_2)$, then $[\![c]\!](s_1 \cup s_2) = \bot$.*

The third frame theorem shows that extending the initial state also preserves erroneous executions. Its statement is similar to the previous ones, but with a subtle twist. In general, by extending the state of a program with a block, we might turn an erroneous execution into a successful one—if the error was caused by accessing a pointer whose identifier matches that new block. To avoid this, we need a different premise ($ids(s_1) \# blocks(s_2)$) preventing any pointers in the original state s_1 from referencing the new blocks in s_2—which is only useful because our language prevents programs from forging pointers to existing regions. Since $blocks(s) \subseteq ids(s)$, this premise is stronger than the analogous ones in the preceding results.

Theorem 4 (Frame Error). *Let c be a command, and s_1 and s_2 be states. If $[\![c]\!](s_1) = \text{error}$, $vars(c) \subseteq vars(s_1)$, and $ids(s_1) \# blocks(s_2)$, then $[\![c]\!](s_1 \cup s_2) = \text{error}$.*

3.2 Memory Safety and Noninterference

The consequences of memory safety analyzed so far are intimately tied to the notion of *noninterference* [19]. In its most widely understood sense, noninterference is a *secrecy* guarantee: varying secret inputs has no effect on public outputs. Sometimes, however, it is also used to describe *integrity* guarantees: low-integrity inputs have no effect on high-integrity outputs. In fact, both guarantees apply to unreachable memory in our language, since they do not affect code execution; that is, execution (1) cannot modify these inaccessible regions (preserving their integrity), and (2) cannot learn anything meaningful about them, not even their presence (preserving their secrecy).

Corollary 1 (Noninterference). *Let s_1, s_{21}, and s_{22} be states and c be a command. Suppose that $vars(c) \subseteq vars(s_1)$, that $ids(s_1) \# blocks(s_{21})$ and that $ids(s_1) \# blocks(s_{22})$. When running c on the extended states $s_1 \cup s_{21}$ and $s_1 \cup s_{22}$, only one of the following three possibilities holds: (1) both executions loop ($[\![c]\!](s_1 \cup s_{21}) = [\![c]\!](s_1 \cup s_{22}) = \bot$); (2) both executions terminate with an error ($[\![c]\!](s_1 \cup s_{21}) = [\![c]\!](s_1 \cup s_{22}) = \text{error}$); or (3) both executions successfully terminate without interfering with the inaccessible portions s_{21} and s_{22} (formally, there exists a state s_1' and permutations π_1 and π_2 such that $[\![c]\!](s_1 \cup s_{2i}) = \pi_i \cdot s_1' \cup s_{2i}$ and $ids(\pi_i \cdot s_1') \# blocks(s_{2i})$, for $i = 1, 2$).*

Noninterference is often formulated using an *indistinguishability relation* on states, which expresses that one state can be obtained from the other by varying its secrets. We could have equivalently phrased the above result in a similar way. Recall that the hypothesis $ids(s_1) \# blocks(s_2)$ means that memory regions stored in s_2 are unreachable via s_1. Then, we could call two states "indistinguishable" if the reachable portions are the same (except for a possible permutation). In Sect. 4, the connection with noninterference will provide a good benchmark for comparing different flavors of memory safety.

3.3 Memory Safety and Separation Logic

We now explore the relation between the principles identified above, especially regarding integrity, and the local reasoning facilities of separation logic.

Separation logic targets specifications of the form $\{p\}\ c\ \{q\}$, where p and q are predicates over program states (subsets of $\mathcal{S}$). For our language, this could roughly mean

$$\forall s \in p, \mathsf{vars}(c) \subseteq \mathsf{vars}(s) \Rightarrow [\![c]\!](s) \in q \cup \{\bot\}.$$

That is, if we run c in a state satisfying p, it will either diverge or terminate in a state that satisfies q, but it will not trigger an error. Part of the motivation for precluding errors is that in unsafe settings like C they yield undefined behavior, destroying all hope of verification.

Local reasoning in separation logic is embodied by the *frame rule*, a consequence of Theorems 1 and 3. Roughly, it says that a verified program can only affect a well-defined portion of the state, with all other memory regions left untouched.[4]

Theorem 5. *Let p, q, and r be predicates over states and c be a command. The rule*

$$\frac{\mathsf{independent}(r, \mathsf{modvars}(c)) \qquad \{p\}\ c\ \{q\}}{\{p * r\}\ c\ \{q * r\}}\ \text{FRAME}$$

is sound, where $\mathsf{modvars}(c)$ is the set of local variables modified by c, $\mathsf{independent}(r, V)$ means that the assertion r does not depend on the set of local variables V

$$\forall l_1\, l_2\, m, (\forall x \notin V,\ l_1(x) = l_2(x)) \Rightarrow (l_1, m) \in r \Rightarrow (l_2, m) \in r,$$

and $p * r$ denotes the separating conjunction *of p and r:*

$$\{(l, m_1 \cup m_2) \mid (l, m_1) \in p, (l, m_2) \in r, \mathsf{blocks}(l, m_1)\ \#\ \mathsf{blocks}(l, m_2)\}.$$

As useful as it is, precluding errors during execution makes it difficult to use separation logic for *partial verification*: proving *any* property, no matter how simple, of a nontrivial program requires detailed reasoning about its internals. Even the following vacuous rule is unsound in separation logic:

$$\frac{}{\{p\}\ c\ \{\mathsf{true}\}}\ \text{TAUT}$$

For a counterexample, take p to be true and c to be some arbitrary memory read $x \leftarrow [y]$. If we run c on an empty heap, which trivially satisfies the precondition, we obtain an error, contradicting the specification.

Fortunately, our memory-safe language—in which errors have a sensible, predictable semantics, as opposed to wild undefined behavior—supports a variant of separation logic that allows looser specifications of the form $\{p\}\ c\ \{q\}_e$, defined as

$$\forall s \in p, \mathsf{vars}(c) \subseteq \mathsf{vars}(s) \Rightarrow [\![c]\!](s) \in q \cup \{\bot, \mathsf{error}\}.$$

---

[4] Technically, the frame rule requires a slightly stronger notion of specification, accounting for permutations of allocated identifiers; our Coq development has a more precise statement.

These specifications are weaker than their conventional counterparts, leading to a subsumption rule:

$$\frac{\{p\}\ c\ \{q\}}{\{p\}\ c\ \{q\}_e}$$

Because errors are no longer prevented, the TAUT rule $\{p\}\ c\ \{\mathsf{true}\}_e$ becomes sound, since the true postcondition now means that any outcome whatsoever is acceptable. Unfortunately, there is a price to pay for allowing errors: they compromise the soundness of the frame rule. The reason, as hinted in the introduction, is that preventing run-time errors has an additional purpose in separation logic: it forces programs to act locally—that is, to access only the memory delimited their pre- and postconditions. To see why, consider the same program c as above, $x \leftarrow [y]$. This program clearly yields an error when run on an empty heap, implying that the triple $\{\mathsf{emp}\}\ c\ \{x = 0\}_e$ is valid, where the predicate emp holds of any state with an empty heap and $x = 0$ holds of states whose local store maps x to 0. Now consider what happens if we try to apply an analog of the frame rule to this triple using the frame predicate $y \mapsto 1$, which holds in states where y contains a pointer to the unique defined location on the heap, which stores the value 1. After some simplification, we arrive at the specification $\{y \mapsto 1\}\ c\ \{x = 0 \wedge y \mapsto 1\}_e$, which clearly does not hold, since executing c on a state satisfying the precondition leads to a successful final state mapping x to 1.

For the frame rule to be recovered, it needs to take errors into account. The solution lies on the reachability properties of memory safety: instead of enforcing locality by preventing errors, we can use the fact that memory operations in a safe language are automatically local—in particular, local to the identifiers that the program possesses.

Theorem 6. *Under the same assumptions as Theorem 5, the following rule is sound*

$$\frac{\mathsf{independent}(r, \mathsf{modvars}(c)) \qquad \{p\}\ c\ \{q\}_e}{\{p \triangleright r\}\ c\ \{q \triangleright r\}_e}\ \text{SAFEFRAME}$$

where $p \triangleright r$ denotes the isolating conjunction *of p and r, defined as*

$$\{(l, m_1 \cup m_2) \mid (l, m_1) \in p, (l, m_2) \in r, \mathsf{ids}(l, m_1) \mathrel{\#} \mathsf{blocks}(l, m_2)\}.$$

The proof is similar to the one for the original rule, but it relies additionally on Theorem 4. This explains why the isolating conjunction is needed, since it ensures that the fragment satisfying r is unreachable from the rest of the state.

3.4   Discussion

As hinted by their connection with the frame rule, the theorems of Sect. 3.1 are a form of local reasoning: to reason about a command, it suffices to consider its reachable state; *how* this state is used bears no effect on the unreachable portions. In a more realistic language, reachability might be inferred from additional information such as typing. But even here it can probably be accomplished by a simple check of the program text.

For example, consider the hypothetical jpeg decoder from Sect. 1. We would like to guarantee that the decoder cannot tamper with an unreachable object—a window object, a whitelist of trusted websites, etc. The frame theorems give us a means to do so, provided that we are able to show that the object is indeed unreachable; additionally, they imply that the jpeg decoder cannot directly extract any information from this unreachable object, such as passwords or private keys.

Many real-world attacks involve direct violations of these reasoning principles. For example, consider the infamous Heartbleed attack on OpenSSL, which used out-of-bounds reads from a buffer to leak data from completely unrelated parts of the program state and to steal sensitive information [16]. Given that the code fragment that enabled that attack was just manipulating an innocuous array, a programmer could easily be fooled into believing (as probably many have) that that snippet could not possibly access sensitive information, allowing that vulnerability to remain unnoticed for years.

Finally, our new frame rule only captures the fact that a command cannot influence the heap locations that it cannot reach, while our noninterference result (Corollary 1) captures not just this integrity aspect of memory safety, but also a secrecy aspect. We hope that future research will explore the connection between the secrecy aspect of memory safety and (relational) program logics.

4   Relaxing Memory Safety

So much for formalism. What about reality? Strictly speaking, the security properties we have identified do not hold of any real system. This is partly due to fundamental physical limitations—real systems run with finite memory, and interact with users in various ways that transcend inputs and outputs, notably through time and other side channels.[5] A more interesting reason is that real systems typically do not impose all the restrictions required for the proofs of these properties. Languages that aim for safety generally offer relatively benign glimpses of their implementation details (such accessing the contents of uninitialized memory, extract physical addresses from pointers or compare them for ordering) in return for significant flexibility or performance gains. In other systems, the concessions are more fundamental, to the extent that it is harder to clearly delimit what part of a program is unsafe: the SoftBound transformation [31], for example, adds bounds checks for C programs, but does not protect against memory-management bugs; a related transformation, CETS [32], is required for temporal safety.

---

[5] Though the attacker model considered in this paper does not try to address such side-channel attacks, one should be able to use the previous research on the subject to protect against them or limit the damage they can cause [6,39,40,49].

In this section, we enumerate common relaxed models of memory safety and evaluate how they affect the reasoning principles and security guarantees of Sect. 3. Some relaxations, such as allowing pointers to be forged out of thin air, completely give up on reachability-based reasoning. Others, however, retain strong guarantees for integrity while giving up on some secrecy, allowing aspects of the global state of a program to be observed. For example, a system with finite memory (Sect. 4.5) may leak some information about its memory consumption, and a system that allows pointer-to-integer casts (Sect. 4.2) may leak information about its memory layout. Naturally, the distinction between integrity and secrecy should be taken with a grain of salt, since the former often depends on the latter; for example, if a system grants privileges to access some component when given with the right password, a secrecy violation can escalate to an integrity violation!

4.1 Forging Pointers

Many real-world C programs use integers as pointers. If this idiom is allowed without restrictions, then local reasoning is compromised, as every memory region may be reached from anywhere in the program. It is not surprising that languages that strive for safety either forbid this kind of pointer forging or confine it to clear unsafe fragments.

More insidiously, and perhaps surprisingly, similar dangers lurk in the stateful abstractions of some systems that are widely regarded as "memory safe." JavaScript, for example, allows code to access *arbitrary* global variables by indexing an associative array with a string, a feature that enables many serious attacks [1,18,29,44]. One might argue that global variables in JavaScript are "memory unsafe" because they fail to validate local reasoning: even if part of a JavaScript program does not explicitly mention a given global variable, it might still change this variable or the objects it points to. Re-enabling local reasoning requires strong restrictions on the programming style [1,9,18].

4.2 Observing Pointers

The language of Sect. 2 maintains a complete separation between pointers and other values. In reality, this separation is often only enforced in one direction. For example, some tools for enforcing memory safety in C [13,31] allow pointer-to-integer casts [23] (a feature required by many low-level idioms [10,28]); and the default implementation of `hashCode()` in Java leaks address information. To model such features, we can extend the syntax of expressions with a form $\mathsf{cast}(e)$, the semantics of which are defined with some function $[\![\mathsf{cast}]\!] : \mathbb{I} \times \mathbb{Z} \to \mathbb{Z}$ for converting a pointer to an integer:

$$[\![\mathsf{cast}(e)]\!](s) = [\![\mathsf{cast}]\!]([\![e]\!](s)) \qquad \text{if } [\![e]\!](s) \in \mathbb{I} \times \mathbb{Z}$$

Note that the original language included an operator for extracting the offset of a pointer. Their definitions are similar, but have crucially different consequences: while offsets do not depend on the identifier, allocation order, or other low-level details of the language implementation (such as the choice of physical addresses when allocating a block), all of these could be relevant when defining the semantics of cast. The three frame theorems (1, 3, and 4) are thus lost, because the state of unreachable parts of the heap may influence integers observed by the program. An important consequence is that secrecy is weakened in this language: an attacker could exploit pointers as a side-channel to learn secrets about data it shouldn't access.

Nevertheless, *integrity* is not affected: if a block is unreachable, its contents will not change at the end of the execution. (This result was also proved in Coq.)

Theorem 7 (Integrity-only Noninterference). *Let s_1, s_2, and s' be states and c a command such that* vars$(c) \subseteq$ vars(s_1), ids(s_1) # blocks(s_2), *and* $[\![c]\!](s_1 \cup s_2) = s'$. *Then we can find $s_1' \in S$ such that $s' = s_1' \cup s_2$ and* ids(s_1') # blocks(s_2).

The stronger noninterference result of Corollary 1 showed that, if pointer-to-integer casts are prohibited, changing the contents of the unreachable portion s_2 has no effect on the reachable portion, s_1'. In contrast, Theorem 7 allows changes in s_2 to influence s_1' in arbitrary ways in the presence of these casts: not only can the contents of this final state change, but the execution can also loop forever or terminate in an error.

To see why, suppose that the jpeg decoder of Sect. 1 is part of a web browser, but that it does not have the required pointers to learn the address that the user is currently visiting. Suppose that there is some relation between the memory consumption of the program and that website, and that there is some correlation between the memory consumption and the identifier assigned to a new block. Then, by allocating a block and converting its pointer to a integer, the decoder might be able to infer useful information about the visited website [22]. Thus, if s_2 denoted the part of the state where that location is stored, changing its contents would have a nontrivial effect on s_1', the part of the state that the decoder does have access to. We could speculate that, in a reasonable system, this channel can only reveal information about the layout of unreachable regions, and not their contents. Indeed, we conjecture this for the language of this subsection.

Finally, it is worth noting that simply excluding casts might not suffice to prevent this sort of vulnerability. Recall that our language takes both offsets and identifiers into account for equality tests. For performance reasons, we could have chosen a different design that only compares physical addresses, completely discarding identifiers. If attackers know the address of a pointer in the program— which could happen, for instance, if they have access to the code of the program and of the allocator—they can use pointer arithmetic (which is generally harmless and allowed in our language) to find the address of other pointers. If x holds the pointer they control, they can run, for instance,

$$y \leftarrow \mathsf{alloc}(1); \mathsf{if}\ x + 1729 = y\ \mathsf{then}\ \ldots\ \mathsf{else}\ \ldots,$$

to learn the location assigned to y and draw conclusions about the global state.

4.3 Uninitialized Memory

Safe languages typically initialize new variables and objects. But this can degrade performance, leading to cases where this feature is dropped—including standard C implementations, safer alternatives [13,31], OCaml's `Bytes.create` primitive, or Node.js's `Buffer.allocUnsafe`, for example.

The problem with this concession is that the entire memory becomes relevant to execution, and local reasoning becomes much harder. By inspecting old values living in uninitialized memory, an attacker can learn about parts of the state they shouldn't access and violate secrecy. This issue would become even more severe in a system that allowed old pointers or other capabilities to occur in re-allocated memory in a way that the program can use, since they could yield access to restricted resources directly, leading to potential integrity violations as well. (The two examples given above—OCaml and Node.js—do not suffer from this issue, because any preexisting pointers in re-allocated memory are treated as bare bytes that cannot be used to access memory.)

4.4 Dangling Pointers and Freshness

Another crucial issue is the treatment of dangling pointers—references to previously freed objects. Dangling pointers are problematic because there is an inherent tension between giving them a sensible semantics (for instance, one that validates the properties of Sect. 3) and obtaining good performance and predictability. Languages with garbage collection avoid the issue by forbidding dangling pointers altogether—heap storage is freed only when it is unreachable. In the language of Sect. 2, besides giving a well-defined behavior to the use of dangling pointers (signaling an error), we imposed strong freshness requirements on allocation, mandating not only that the new identifier not correspond to any existing block, but also that it not be present *anywhere else* in the state.

To see how the results of Sect. 3 are affected by weakening freshness, suppose we run the program $x \leftarrow \mathsf{alloc}(1); z \leftarrow (y = x)$ on a state where y holds a dangling pointer. Depending on the allocator and the state of the memory, the pointer assigned to x could be equal to y. Since this outcome depends on the entire state of the system, not just the reachable memory, Theorems 1, 3 and 4 now fail. Furthermore, an attacker with detailed knowledge of the allocator could launder secret information by testing pointers for equality. Weakening freshness can also have integrity implications, since it becomes harder to ensure that blocks are properly isolated. For instance, a newly allocated block might be reachable through a dangling pointer controlled by an attacker, allowing them to access that block even if they were not supposed to.

Some practical solutions for memory safety use mechanisms similar to our language's, where each memory location is tagged with an identifier describing the region it belongs to [11,15]. Pointers are tagged similarly, and when a pointer is used to access memory, a violation is detected if its identifier does not match the location's. However, for performance reasons, the number of possible identifiers might be limited to a relatively small number, such as 2 or 4 [11] or

16 [46]. In addition to the problems above, since multiple live regions can share the same identifier in such schemes, it might be possible for buffer overflows to lead to violations of secrecy and integrity as well.

Although we framed our discussion in terms of identifiers, the issue of freshness can manifest itself in other ways. For example, many systems for spatial safety work by adding base and bounds information to pointers. In some of these [13,31], dangling pointers are treated as an orthogonal issue, and it is possible for the allocator to return a new memory region that overlaps with the range of a dangling pointer, in which case the new region will not be properly isolated from the rest of the state.

Finally, dangling pointers can have disastrous consequences for overall system security, independently of the freshness issues just described: freeing a pointer more than once can break allocator invariants, enabling attacks [43].

4.5 Infinite Memory

Our idealized language allows memory to grow indefinitely. But real languages run on finite memory, and allocation fails when programs run out of space. Besides enabling denial-of-service attacks, finite memory has consequences for secrecy. Corollary 1 does not hold in a real programming language as is, because an increase in memory consumption can cause a previously successful allocation to fail. By noticing this difference, a piece of code might learn something about the *entire* state of the program. How problematic this is in practice will depend on the particular system under consideration.

A potential solution is to force programs that run out of memory to terminate immediately. Though this choice might be bad from an availability standpoint, it is probably the most benign in terms of secrecy. We should be able to prove an *error-insensitive* variant of Corollary 1, where the only significant effect that unreachable memory can have is to turn a successful execution or infinite loop into an error. Similar issues arise for IFC mechanisms that often cannot prevent secrets from influencing program termination, leading to *termination-insensitive* notions of noninterference.

Unfortunately, even an error-insensitive result might be too strong for real systems, which often make it possible for attackers to extract multiple bits of information about the global state of the program—as previously noted in the IFC literature [4]. Java, for example, does not force termination when memory runs out, but triggers an exception that can be caught and handled by user code, which is then free to record the event and probe the allocator with a different test. And most languages do not operate in batch mode like ours does, merely producing a single answer at the end of execution; rather, their programs continuously interact with their environment through inputs and outputs, allowing them to communicate the exact amount of memory that caused an error.

This discussion suggests that, if size vulnerabilities are a real concern, they need to be treated with special care. One approach would be to limit the amount of memory an untrusted component can allocate [47], so that exhausting the memory allotted to that component doesn't reveal information about the state of the rest of the system (and so that also global denial-of-service attacks are prevented). A more speculative idea is to develop *quantitative* versions [6, 39] of the noninterference results discussed here that apply only if the total memory used by the program is below a certain limit.

5   Case Study: A Memory-Safety Monitor

To demonstrate the applicability of our characterization, we use it to analyze a tag-based monitor proposed by Dhawan *et al.* to enforce heap safety for low-level code [15]. In prior work [5], we and others showed that an idealized model of the monitor correctly implements a higher-level abstract machine with built-in memory safety—a bit more formally, every behavior of the monitor is also a behavior of the abstract machine. Building upon this work, we prove that this abstract machine satisfies a noninterference property similar to Corollary 1. We were also able to prove that a similar result holds for a lower-level machine that runs a so-called "symbolic" representation of the monitor—although we had to slightly weaken the result to account for memory exhaustion (cf. Sect. 4.5), since the machine that runs the monitor has finite memory, while the abstract machine has infinite memory. If we had a verified machine-code implementation of this monitor, it would be possible to prove a similar result for it as well.

5.1   Tag-Based Monitor

We content ourselves with a brief overview of Dhawan *et al.*'s monitor [5,15], since the formal statement of the reasoning principles it supports are more complex than the one for the abstract machine from Sect. 5.2, on which we will focus. Following a proposal by Clause *et al.* [11], Dhawan *et al.*'s monitor enforces memory safety for heap-allocated data by checking and propagating *metadata tags*. Every memory location receives a tag that uniquely identifies the allocated region to which that location belongs (akin to the identifiers in Sect. 2), and pointers receive the tag of the region they are allowed to reference. The monitor assigns these tags to new regions by storing a monotonic counter in protected memory that is bumped on every call to `malloc`; with a large number of possible tags, it is possible to avoid the freshness pitfalls discussed in Sect. 4.4. When a memory access occurs, the monitor checks whether the tag on the pointer matches the tag on the location. If they do, the operation is allowed; otherwise, execution halts. The monitor instruments the allocator to make set up tags correctly. Its implementation achieves good performance using the *PUMP*, a hardware extension accelerating such micro-policies for metadata tagging [15].

5.2   Abstract Machine

The memory-safe abstract machine [5] operates on two kinds of values: machine words w, or pointers (i, w), which are pairs of an identifier $i \in \mathbb{I}$ and an offset w. We use $\mathcal{W}$ to denote the set of machine words, and $\mathcal{V}$ to denote the set of values. Machine states are triples (m, rs, pc), where (1) $m \in \mathbb{I} \rightharpoonup_{\text{fin}} \mathcal{V}^*$ is a *memory* mapping identifiers to lists of values; (2) $rs \in \mathcal{R} \rightharpoonup_{\text{fin}} \mathcal{V}$ is a *register bank*, mapping register names to values; and (3) $pc \in \mathcal{V}$ is the *program counter*.

The execution of an instruction is specified by a step relation $s \rightarrow s'$. If there is no s' such that $s \rightarrow s'$, we say that s is stuck, which means that a fatal error occurred during execution. On each instruction, the machine checks if the current program counter is a pointer and, if so, tries to fetch the corresponding value in memory. The machine then ensures that this value is a word that correctly encodes an instruction and, if so, acts accordingly. The instructions of the machine, representative of typical RISC architectures, allow programs to perform binary and logical operations, move values to and from memory, and branch. The machine is in fact fairly similar to the language of Sect. 2. Some operations are overloaded to manipulate pointers; for example, adding a pointer to a word is allowed, and the result is obtained by adjusting the pointer's offset accordingly. Accessing memory causes the machine to halt when the corresponding position is undefined.

In addition to these basic instructions, the machine possesses a set of special *monitor services* that can be invoked as regular functions, using registers to pass in arguments and return values. There are two services alloc and free for managing memory, and one service eq for testing whether two values are equal. The reason for using separate monitor services instead of special instructions is to keep its semantics closer to the more concrete machine that implements it. While instructions include an equality test, it cannot replace the eq service, since it only takes physical addresses into account. As argued in Sect. 4.2, such comparisons can be turned into a side channel. To prevent this, testing two pointers for equality directly using the corresponding machine instruction results in an error if the pointers have different block identifiers.

5.3 Verifying Memory Safety

The proof of memory safety for this abstract machine mimics the one carried for the language in Sect. 3. We use similar notations as before: $\pi \cdot s$ means renaming every identifier that appears in s according to the permutation π, and $\text{ids}(s)$ is the finite set of all identifiers that appear in the state s. A simple case analysis on the possible instructions yields analogs of Theorems 1, 2 and 4 (we don't include an analog of Theorem 3 because we consider individual execution steps, where loops cannot occur).

Theorem 8. *Let π be a permutation, and s and s' be two machine states such that $s \rightarrow s'$. There exists another permutation π' such that $\pi \cdot s \rightarrow \pi' \cdot s'$.*

Theorem 9. *Let (m_1, rs, pc) be a state of the abstract machine, and m_2 a memory. Suppose that $\text{ids}(m_1, rs, pc) \;\#\; \text{dom}(m_2)$, and that $(m_1, rs, pc) \rightarrow (m', rs', pc')$. Then, there exists a permutation π such that $\text{ids}(\pi \cdot m', \pi \cdot rs, \pi \cdot pc) \;\#\; \text{dom}(m_2)$ and $(m_2 \cup m_1, rs, pc) \rightarrow (m_2 \cup \pi \cdot m', \pi \cdot rs', \pi \cdot pc')$.*

Theorem 10. *Let (m_1, rs, pc) be a machine state, and m_2 a memory. If* $\mathsf{ids}(m_1, rs, pc) \mathrel{\#} \mathsf{dom}(m_2)$, *and* (m_1, rs, pc) *is stuck, then* $(m_2 \cup m_1, rs, pc)$ *is also stuck.*

Once again, we can combine these properties to obtain a proof of noninterference. Our Coq development includes a complete statement.

5.4   Discussion

The reasoning principles supported by the memory-safety monitor have an important difference compared to the ones of Sect. 3. In the memory-safe language, reachability is relative to a program's local variables. If we want to argue that part of the state is isolated from some code fragment, we just have to consider that fragment's local variables—other parts of the program are still allowed to access the region. The memory-safety monitor, on the other hand, does not have an analogous notion: an unreachable memory region is useless, since it remains unreachable by all components forever.

It seems that, from the standpoint of noninterference, heap memory safety *taken in isolation* is much weaker than the guarantees it provides in the presence of other language features, such as local variables. Nevertheless, the properties studied above suggest several avenues for strengthening the mechanism and making its guarantees more useful. The most obvious one would be to use the mechanism as the target of a compiler for a programming language that provides other (safe) stateful abstractions, such as variables and a stack for procedure calls. A more modest approach would be to add other state abstractions to the mechanism itself. Besides variables and call stacks, if the mechanism made code immutable and separate from data, a simple check would suffice to tell whether a code segment stored in memory references a given privileged register. If the register is the only means of reaching a memory region, we should be able to soundly infer that that code segment is independent of that region.

On a last note, although the abstract machine we verified is fairly close to our original language, the dynamic monitor that implements it using tags is quite different (Sect. 5.1). In particular, the monitor works on a machine that has a flat memory model, and keeps track of free and allocated memory using a protected data structure that stores block metadata. It was claimed that reasoning about this base and bounds information was the most challenging part of the proof that the monitor implements the abstract machine [5]. For this reason, we believe that this proof can be adapted to other enforcement mechanisms that rely solely on base and bounds information—for example, fat pointers [13,25] or SoftBound [31]—while keeping a similar abstract machine as their specification, and thus satisfying a similar noninterference property. This gives us confidence that our memory safety characterization generalizes to other settings.

6   Related Work

The present work lies at the intersection of two areas of previous research: one on formal characterizations of memory safety, the other on reasoning principles for programs. We review the most closely related work in these areas.

Characterizing Memory Safety. Many formal characterizations of memory safety originated in attempts to reconcile its benefits with low-level code. Generally, these works claim that a mechanism is safe by showing that it prevents or catches typical temporal and spatial violations. Examples in the literature include: Cyclone [41], a language with a type system for safe manual memory management; CCured [33], a program transformation that adds temporal safety to C by refining its pointer type with various degrees of safety; Ivory [17] an embedding of a similar "safe-C variant" into Haskell; SoftBound [31], an instrumentation technique for C programs for spatial safety, including the detection of bounds violations within an object; CETS [32], a compiler pass for preventing temporal safety violations in C programs, including accessing dangling pointers into freed heap regions and stale stack frames; the memory-safety monitor for the PUMP [5,15], which formed the basis of our case study in Sect. 5; and languages like Mezzo [35] and Rust [45], whose guarantees extend to preventing data races [7]. Similar models appear in formalizations of C [24,26], which need to rigorously characterize its sources of undefined behavior—in particular, instances of memory misuse.

Either explicitly or implicitly, these works define memory errors as attempts to use a pointer to access a location that it was not meant to access—for example, an out-of-bounds or free one. This was noted by Hicks [20], who, inspired by SoftBound, proposed to define memory safety as an execution model that tracks what part of memory each pointer can access. Our characterization is complementary to these accounts, in that it is *extensional*: its data isolation properties allow us to reason directly about the observable behavior of the program. Furthermore, as demonstrated by our application to the monitor of Sect. 5 and the discussions on Sect. 4, it can be adapted to various enforcement mechanisms and variations of memory safety.

Reasoning Principles. Separation logic [36,48] has been an important source of inspiration for our work. The logic's frame rule enables its local reasoning capabilities and imposes restrictions that are similar to those mandated by memory-safe programming guidelines. As discussed in Sect. 3.3, our reasoning principles are reminiscent of the frame rule, but use reachability to guarantee locality in settings where memory safety is enforced automatically. In separation logic, by contrast, locality needs to be guaranteed for each program individually by comprehensive proofs.

Several works have investigated similar reasoning principles for a variety of program analyses, including static, dynamic, manual, or a mixture of those. Some of these are formulated as expressive logical relations, guaranteeing that programs are compatible with the framing of state invariants; representative works include: L^3 [3], a linear calculus featuring strong updates and aliasing control; the work of Benton and Tabereau [8] on a compiler for a higher-order language; and the work of Devriese *et al.* [14] on object capabilities for a JavaScript-like language. Other developments are based on proof systems reminiscent of separation logic; these include Yarra [38], an extension of C that allows programmers to protect the integrity of data structures marked as *critical*; the work of Agten *et al.* [2], which allows mixing unverified and verified components by instrumenting the program to check that required assertions hold at interfaces; and the logic of Swasey *et al.* [42] for reasoning about object capabilities.

Unlike our work, these developments do not propose reachability-based isolation as a general *definition* of memory safety, nor do they attempt to analyze how their reasoning principles are affected by common variants of memory safety. Furthermore, many of these other works—especially the logical relations—rely on encapsulation mechanisms such as closures, objects, or modules that go beyond plain memory safety. Memory safety alone can only provide complete isolation, while encapsulation provides finer control, allowing some interaction between components, while guaranteeing the preservation of certain state invariants. In this sense, one can see memory-safety reasoning as a special case of encapsulation reasoning. Nevertheless, it is a practically relevant special case that is interesting on its own, since when reasoning about an encapsulated component, one must argue explicitly that the invariants of interest are preserved by the private operations of that component; memory safety, on the other hand, guarantees that *any* invariant on unreachable parts of the memory is automatically preserved.

Perhaps closer to our work, Maffeis *et al.* [27] show that their notion of "authority safety" guarantees isolation, in the sense that a component's actions cannot influence the actions of another component with disjoint authority. Their notion of authority behaves similarly to the set of block identifiers accessible by a program in our language; however, they do not attempt to connect their notion of isolation to the frame rule, noninterference, or traditional notions of memory safety.

Morrisett *et al.* [30] state a correctness criterion for garbage collection based on program equivalence. Some of the properties they study are similar to the frame rule, describing the behavior of code running in an extended heap. However, they use this analysis to justify the validity of deallocating objects, rather than studying the possible interactions between the extra state and the program in terms of integrity and secrecy.

7   Conclusions and Future Work

We have explored the consequences of memory safety for reasoning about programs, formalizing intuitive principles that, we argue, capture the essential distinction between memory-safe systems and memory-unsafe ones. We showed how the reasoning principles we identified apply to a recent dynamic monitor for heap memory safety.

The systems studied in this paper have a simple storage model: the language of Sect. 2 has just global variables and flat, heap-allocated arrays, while the monitor of Sect. 5 doesn't even have variables or immutable code. Realistic programming platforms, of course, offer much richer stateful abstractions, including, for example, procedures with stack-allocated local variables as well as structured objects with contiguously allocated sub-objects. In terms of memory safety, these systems have a richer vocabulary for describing resources that programs can access, and programmers could benefit from isolation-based local reasoning involving these resources.

For example, in typical safe languages with procedures, the behavior of a procedure should depend only on its arguments, the global variables it uses, and the portions of the state that are reachable from these values; if the caller of that procedure has a private object that is not passed as an argument, it should not affect or be affected by the call. Additionally, languages such as C allow for objects consisting of contiguously allocated sub-objects for improved performance. Some systems for spatial safety [13,31] allow *capability downgrading*—that is, narrowing the range of a pointer so that it can't access outside of a sub-object's bounds. It would be interesting to refine our model to take these features into account. In the case of the monitor of Sect. 5, such considerations could lead to improved designs or to the integration of the monitor inside a secure compiler. Conversely, it would be interesting to derive finer security properties for relaxations like the ones discussed in Sect. 4. Some inspiration could come from the IFC literature, where quantitative noninterference results provide bounds on the probability that some secret is leaked, the rate at which it is leaked, how many bits are leaked, etc. [6,39].

The main goal of this work was to understand, formally, the benefits of memory safety for informal and partial reasoning, and to evaluate a variety of weakened forms of memory safety in terms of which reasoning principles they preserve. However, our approach may also suggest ways to improve program verification. One promising idea is to leverage the guarantees of memory safety to obtain proofs of program correctness modulo unverified code that could have errors, in contexts where complete verification is too expensive or not possible (e.g., for programs with a plugin mechanism).

Acknowledgments. We are grateful to Antal Spector-Zabusky, Greg Morrisett, Justin Hsu, Michael Hicks, Nick Benton, Yannis Juglaret, William Mansky, and Andrew Tolmach for useful suggestions on earlier drafts. This work is supported by NSF grants Micro-Policies (1513854) and DeepSpec (1521523), DARPA SSITH/HOPE, and ERC Starting Grant SECOMP (715753).

Appendix

This appendix defines the language of Sect. 2 more formally. Figure 3 summarizes the syntax of programs and repeats the definition of program states. The syntax is standard for a simple imperative language with pointers.

Figure 4 defines expression evaluation, $[\![e]\!] : S \to V$. Variables are looked up in the local-variable part of the state (for simplicity, heap cells cannot be dereferenced in expressions; the command $x \leftarrow [e]$ puts the value of a heap cell in a local variable). Constants (booleans, numbers, and the special value nil used to simplify error propagation) evaluate to themselves. Addition and subtraction can be applied both to numbers and to combinations of numbers and pointers (for pointer arithmetic); multiplication only works on numbers. Equality is allowed both on pointers and on numbers. Pointer equality compares both the block identifier and its offset, and while this is harder to implement in practice than just comparing physical addresses, this is needed for not leaking

$$\oplus ::= + \mid \times \mid - \mid = \mid \leq \mid \text{and} \mid \text{or} \quad \text{(operators)}$$
$$e ::= x \in \text{var} \mid b \in \mathbb{B} \mid n \in \mathbb{Z} \quad \text{(expressions)}$$
$$\mid e_1 \oplus e_2 \mid \text{not}\, e \mid \text{offset}\, e \mid \text{nil}$$
$$c ::= \text{skip} \mid c_1; c_2 \quad \text{(commands)}$$
$$\mid \text{if } e \text{ then } c_1 \text{ else } c_2$$
$$\mid \text{while } e \text{ do } c \text{ end}$$
$$\mid x \leftarrow e \mid x \leftarrow [e] \mid [e_1] \leftarrow e_2$$
$$\mid x \leftarrow \text{alloc}(e) \mid \text{free}(e)$$

$$s \in \mathcal{S} \triangleq \mathcal{L} \times \mathcal{M} \qquad\qquad \text{(states)}$$
$$l \in \mathcal{L} \triangleq \text{var} \rightharpoonup_{\text{fin}} \mathcal{V} \qquad\qquad \text{(local stores)}$$
$$m \in \mathcal{M} \triangleq \mathbb{I} \times \mathbb{Z} \rightharpoonup_{\text{fin}} \mathcal{V} \qquad\qquad \text{(heaps)}$$
$$v \in \mathcal{V} \triangleq \mathbb{Z} \uplus \mathbb{B} \uplus \{\text{nil}\} \uplus \mathbb{I} \times \mathbb{Z} \qquad\qquad \text{(values)}$$
$$\mathcal{O} \triangleq \mathcal{S} \uplus \{\text{error}\} \qquad\qquad \text{(outcomes)}$$

$$\mathbb{I} \triangleq \text{some countably infinite set}$$
$$X \rightharpoonup_{\text{fin}} Y \triangleq \text{partial functions } X \rightharpoonup Y \text{ with finite domain}$$

Fig. 3. Syntax and program states

information about pointers (see Sect. 4.2). The special expression offset extracts the offset component of a pointer; we introduce it to illustrate that for satisfying our memory characterization pointer offsets do not need to be hidden (as opposed to block identifiers). The less-than-or-equal operator only applies to numbers—in particular, pointers cannot be compared. However, since we can extract pointer offsets, we can compare those instead.

The definition of command evaluation employs an auxiliary partial function that computes the result of evaluating a program along with the set of block identifiers that were allocated during evaluation. Formally, $[\![c]\!]_+ : \mathcal{S} \rightharpoonup \mathcal{O}_+$, where $\mathcal{O}_+$ is an extended set of outcomes defined as $\mathcal{P}_{\text{fin}}(\mathbb{I}) \times \mathcal{S} \uplus \{\text{error}\}$. We then set

$$[\![c]\!](l, m) = \begin{cases} (l', m') & \text{if } [\![c]\!]_+(l, m) = (I, l', m') \\ \text{error} & \text{if } [\![c]\!]_+(l, m) = \text{error} \\ \bot & \text{if } [\![c]\!]_+(l, m) = \bot \end{cases}$$

$$\text{finalids}(l, m) = \begin{cases} \text{ids}(l, m) \setminus I & \text{if } [\![c]\!]_+(l, m) = (I, l', m') \\ \emptyset & \text{otherwise} \end{cases}$$

To define $[\![c]\!]_+$, we first endow the set $\mathcal{S} \rightharpoonup \mathcal{O}_+$ with the partial order of program approximation:

$$f \sqsubseteq g \triangleq \forall s, f(s) \neq \bot \Rightarrow f(x) = g(x)$$

$$[\![x]\!](l, m) \triangleq \begin{cases} l(x) & \text{if } x \in \text{dom}(l) \\ \text{nil} & \text{otherwise} \end{cases}$$

$$[\![b]\!](s) \triangleq b$$

$$[\![n]\!](s) \triangleq n$$

$$[\![\text{nil}]\!](s) \triangleq \text{nil}$$

$$[\![e_1 + e_2]\!](s) \triangleq \begin{cases} n_1 + n_2 & \text{if } [\![e_1]\!](s) = n_1 \text{ and } [\![e_2]\!](s) = n_2 \\ (i, n_1 + n_2) & \text{if } [\![e_1]\!](s) = (i, n_1) \text{ and } [\![e_2]\!](s) = n_2 \\ & \text{or } [\![e_1]\!](s) = n_1 \text{ and } [\![e_2]\!](s) = (i, n_2) \\ \text{nil} & \text{otherwise} \end{cases}$$

$$[\![e_1 - e_2]\!](s) \triangleq \begin{cases} n_1 - n_2 & \text{if } [\![e_1]\!](s) = n_1 \text{ and } [\![e_2]\!](s) = n_2 \\ (i, n_1 - n_2) & \text{if } [\![e_1]\!](s) = (i, n_1) \text{ and } [\![e_2]\!](s) = n_2 \\ \text{nil} & \text{otherwise} \end{cases}$$

$$[\![e_1 \times e_2]\!](s) \triangleq \begin{cases} n_1 \times n_2 & \text{if } [\![e_1]\!](s) = n_1 \text{ and } [\![e_2]\!](s) = n_2 \\ \text{nil} & \text{otherwise} \end{cases}$$

$$[\![e_1 = e_2]\!](s) \triangleq ([\![e_1]\!](s) = [\![e_2]\!](s))$$

$$[\![e_1 \leq e_2]\!](s) \triangleq \begin{cases} n_1 \leq n_2 & \text{if } [\![e_1]\!](s) = n_1 \text{ and } [\![e_2]\!](s) = n_2 \\ \text{nil} & \text{otherwise} \end{cases}$$

$$[\![e_1 \text{ and } e_2]\!](s) \triangleq \begin{cases} b_1 \wedge b_2 & \text{if } [\![e_1]\!](s) = b_1 \text{ and } [\![e_2]\!](s) = b_2 \\ \text{nil} & \text{otherwise} \end{cases}$$

$$[\![e_1 \text{ or } e_2]\!](s) \triangleq \begin{cases} b_1 \vee b_2 & \text{if } [\![e_1]\!](s) = b_1 \text{ and } [\![e_2]\!](s) = b_2 \\ \text{nil} & \text{otherwise} \end{cases}$$

$$[\![\text{not } e]\!](s) \triangleq \begin{cases} \neg b & \text{if } [\![e]\!](s) = b \\ \text{nil} & \text{otherwise} \end{cases}$$

$$[\![\text{offset } e]\!](s) \triangleq \begin{cases} n & \text{if } [\![e]\!](s) = (i, n) \\ \text{nil} & \text{otherwise} \end{cases}$$

Fig. 4. Expression evaluation

$$\text{bind}(f, \bot) \triangleq \bot$$

$$\text{bind}(f, \text{error}) \triangleq \text{error}$$

$$\text{bind}(f, (I, l, m)) \triangleq \begin{cases} (I \cup I', l', m') & \text{if } f(l, m) = (I', l', m') \\ \text{error} & \text{if } f(l, m) = \text{error} \\ \bot & \text{otherwise} \end{cases}$$

$$\text{if}(b, x, y) \triangleq \begin{cases} x & \text{if } b = \text{true} \\ y & \text{if } b = \text{false} \\ \text{error} & \text{otherwise} \end{cases}$$

Fig. 5. Auxiliary operators bind and if

$$[\![\mathsf{skip}]\!]_+(l,m) \triangleq (\emptyset,l,m) \qquad\qquad [\![c_1;c_2]\!]_+(l,m) \triangleq \mathsf{bind}([\![c_2]\!]_+,[\![c_1]\!]_+(l,m))$$

$$[\![\mathsf{if}\ e\ \mathsf{then}\ c_1\ \mathsf{else}\ c_2]\!]_+(l,m) \triangleq \mathsf{if}([\![e]\!](l,m),[\![c_1]\!]_+(l,m),[\![c_2]\!]_+(l,m))$$

$$[\![\mathsf{while}\ e\ \mathsf{do}\ c\ \mathsf{end}]\!]_+ \triangleq \mathsf{fix}(\lambda f\,(l,m).\ \mathsf{if}([\![e]\!](l,m),\mathsf{bind}([\![c]\!]_+,f(l,m)),(\emptyset,l,m)))$$

$$[\![x \leftarrow e]\!]_+(l,m) \triangleq (\emptyset,l[x \mapsto [\![e]\!](l,m)],m)$$

$$[\![x \leftarrow [e]]\!]_+(s) \triangleq \begin{cases} (\emptyset,l[x\mapsto v],m) & \text{if } [\![e]\!](s) = (i,n) \text{ and } m(i,n) = v \\ \mathsf{error} & \text{otherwise} \end{cases}$$

$$[\![[e_1] \leftarrow e_2]\!]_+(s) \triangleq \begin{cases} (\emptyset,l,m[(i,n) \mapsto [\![e_2]\!](l,m)]) & \text{if } [\![e_1]\!](s) = (i,n) \text{ and } m(i,n) \neq \bot \\ \mathsf{error} & \text{otherwise} \end{cases}$$

$$[\![x \leftarrow \mathsf{alloc}(e)]\!]_+(l,m) \triangleq$$

$$\begin{cases} (\{i\},l[x \mapsto (i,0)],m[(i,k) \mapsto 0 \mid 0 \le k < n]) & \text{if } [\![e]\!](l,m) = n \text{ and } i = \mathsf{fresh}(\mathsf{ids}(l,m)) \\ \mathsf{error} & \text{otherwise} \end{cases}$$

$$[\![\mathsf{free}(e)]\!]_+(l,m) \triangleq$$

$$\begin{cases} (\emptyset,l,m[(i,k) \mapsto \bot \mid k \in \mathbb{Z}]) & \text{if } [\![e]\!](l,m) = (i,0) \text{ and } m(i,n) \neq \bot \text{ for some } n \\ \mathsf{error} & \text{otherwise} \end{cases}$$

Fig. 6. Command evaluation with explicit allocation sets

This allows us to define the semantics of iteration (the rule for while e do c end) in a standard way using the Kleene fixed point operator fix.

The definition of $[\![c]\!]_+$ appears in Fig. 6, where several of the rules use a bind operator (Fig. 5) to manage the "plumbing" of the sets of allocated block ids between the evaluation of one subcommand and the next. The rules for if and while also use an auxiliary operator if (also defined in Fig. 5) that turns non-boolean guards into errors.

The evaluation rules for skip, sequencing, conditionals, while, and assignment are standard. The rule for heap lookup, $x \leftarrow [e]$, evaluates e to a pointer and then looks it up in the heap, yielding an error if e does not evaluate to a pointer or if it evaluates to a pointer that is invalid, either because its block id is not allocated or because its offset is out of bounds. Similarly, the heap mutation command, $[e_1] \leftarrow e_2$, requires that e_1 evaluate to a pointer that is valid in the current memory m (i.e., such that looking it up in m yields something other than $\bot$). The allocation command $x \leftarrow \mathsf{alloc}(e)$ first evaluates e to an integer n, then calculates the next free block id for the current machine state ($\mathsf{fresh}(\mathsf{ids}(l,m))$); it yields a new machine state where x points to the first cell in the new block and where a new block of n cells is added the heap, all initialized to 0. Finally, $\mathsf{free}(e)$ evaluates e to a pointer and yields a new heap where every cell sharing the same block id as this pointer is undefined.

References

1. Caja. Attack vectors for privilege escalation (2012). http://code.google.com/p/google-caja/wiki/AttackVectors
2. Agten, P., Jacobs, B., Piessens, F.: Sound modular verification of C code executing in an unverified context. In: POPL (2015). https://lirias.kuleuven.be/bitstream/123456789/471365/3/sound-verification.pdf
3. Ahmed, A., Fluet, M., Morrisett, G.: L^3: a linear language with locations. Fundam. Inform. **77**(4), 397–449 (2007). http://content.iospress.com/articles/fundamenta-informaticae/fi77-4-06
4. Askarov, A., Hunt, S., Sabelfeld, A., Sands, D.: Termination-insensitive noninterference leaks more than just a bit. In: ESORICS (2008). http://www.cse.chalmers.se/~andrei/esorics08.pdf
5. Azevedo de Amorim, A., Dénès, M., Giannarakis, N., Hriţcu, C., Pierce, B.C., Spector-Zabusky, A., Tolmach, A.: Micro-policies: formally verified, tag-based security monitors. In: S&P, Oakland (2015). http://prosecco.gforge.inria.fr/personal/hritcu/publications/micro-policies.pdf
6. Backes, M., Köpf, B., Rybalchenko, A.: Automatic discovery and quantification of information leaks. In: S&P, Oakland (2009). https://doi.org/10.1109/SP.2009.18
7. Balabonski, T., Pottier, F., Protzenko, J.: Type soundness and race freedom for Mezzo. In: Codish, M., Sumii, E. (eds.) FLOPS 2014. LNCS, vol. 8475, pp. 253–269. Springer, Cham (2014). https://doi.org/10.1007/978-3-319-07151-0_16
8. Benton, N., Tabareau, N.: Compiling functional types to relational specifications for low level imperative code. In: Kennedy, A., Ahmed, A. (eds.) TLDI (2009). http://dblp.uni-trier.de/db/conf/tldi/tldi2009.html#BentonT09
9. Bhargavan, K., Delignat-Lavaud, A., Maffeis, S.: Defensive JavaScript - building and verifying secure web components. In: FOSAD (2013). http://dx.doi.org/10.1007/978-3-319-10082-1_4
10. Chisnall, D., Rothwell, C., Watson, R.N.M., Woodruff, J., Vadera, M., Moore, S.W., Roe, M., Davis, B., Neumann, P.G.: Beyond the PDP-11: architectural support for a memory-safe C abstract machine. In: ASPLOS (2015). https://www.cl.cam.ac.uk/~dc552/papers/asplos15-memory-safe-c.pdf
11. Clause, J.A., Doudalis, I., Orso, A., Prvulovic, M.: Effective memory protection using dynamic tainting. In: ASE (2007). http://www.cc.gatech.edu/~orso/papers/clause.doudalis.orso.prvulovic.pdf
12. de Amorim, A.A., Collins, N., DeHon, A., Demange, D., Hritcu, C., Pichardie, D., Pierce, B.C., Pollack, R., Tolmach, A.: A verified information-flow architecture. J. Comput. Secur. **24**(6), 689–734 (2016). https://doi.org/10.3233/JCS-15784
13. Devietti, J., Blundell, C., Martin, M.M.K., Zdancewic, S.: HardBound: architectural support for spatial safety of the C programming language. In: ASPLOS (2008). http://acg.cis.upenn.edu/papers/asplos08_hardbound.pdf
14. Devriese, D., Piessens, F., Birkedal, L.: Reasoning about object capabilities with logical relations and effect parametricity. In: EuroS&P (2016). http://cs.au.dk/~birke/papers/object-capabilities-tr.pdf
15. Dhawan, U., Hriţcu, C., Rubin, R., Vasilakis, N., Chiricescu, S., Smith, J.M., Knight Jr., T.F., Pierce, B.C., DeHon, A.: Architectural support for software-defined metadata processing. In: ASPLOS (2015). http://ic.ese.upenn.edu/abstracts/sdmp_asplos2015.html
16. Durumeric, Z., Kasten, J., Adrian, D., Halderman, J.A., Bailey, M., Li, F., Weaver, N., Amann, J., Beekman, J., Payer, M., Paxson, V.: The matter of Heartbleed. In: IMC (2014). http://doi.acm.org/10.1145/2663716.2663755

17. Elliott, T., Pike, L., Winwood, S., Hickey, P.C., Bielman, J., Sharp, J., Seidel, E.L., Launchbury, J.: Guilt free Ivory. In: Haskell (2015). https://www.cs.indiana.edu/~lepike/pubs/ivory.pdf

18. Fournet, C., Swamy, N., Chen, J., Dagand, P.-É., Strub, P.-Y., Livshits, B.: Fully abstract compilation to JavaScript. In: POPL (2013). https://research.microsoft.com/pubs/176601/js-star.pdf

19. Goguen, J.A., Meseguer, J.: Security policies and security models. In: S&P (1982). http://spy.sci.univr.it/papers/Isa-orig/Sicurezza/NonInterferenza/noninter.pdf

20. Hicks, M.: What is memory safety? (2014). http://www.pl-enthusiast.net/2014/07/21/memory-safety/

21. ISO. ISO C standard 1999. Technical report. ISO/IEC 9899:1999 draft. ISO (1999). http://www.open-std.org/jtc1/sc22/wg14/www/docs/n1124.pdf

22. Jana, S., Shmatikov, V.: Memento: learning secrets from process footprints. In: S&P, Oakland (2012). https://doi.org/10.1109/SP.2012.19

23. Kang, J., Hur, C., Mansky, W., Garbuzov, D., Zdancewic, S., Vafeiadis, V.: A formal C memory model supporting integer-pointer casts. In: PLDI (2015). https://www.seas.upenn.edu/~wmansky/mcast.pdf

24. Krebbers, R.: The C standard formalized in Coq. Ph.D. thesis, Radboud University Nijmegen (2015). http://robbertkrebbers.nl/research/thesis.pdf

25. Kwon, A., Dhawan, U., Smith, J.M., Knight Jr., T.F., DeHon, A.: Low-fat pointers: compact encoding and efficient gate-level implementation of fat pointers for spatial safety and capability-based security. In: CCS (2013). http://www.crash-safe.org/node/27

26. Leroy, X., Blazy, S.: Formal verification of a C-like memory model and its uses for verifying program transformations. JAR **41**(1), 1–31 (2008). http://pauillac.inria.fr/~xleroy/publi/memory-model-journal.pdf

27. Maffeis, S., Mitchell, J.C., Taly, A.: Object capabilities and isolation of untrusted web applications. In: S&P, Oakland (2010). https://www.doc.ic.ac.uk/~maffeis/papers/oakland10.pdf

28. Memarian, K., Matthiesen, J., Lingard, J., Nienhuis, K., Chisnall, D., Watson, R.N.M., Sewell, P.: Into the depths of C: elaborating the de facto standards. In: PLDI (2016). http://doi.acm.org/10.1145/2908080.2908081

29. Meyerovich, L.A., Livshits, V.B.: Conscript: specifying and enforcing fine-grained security policies for JavaScript in the browser. In: S&P, Oakland (2010). http://dx.doi.org/10.1109/SP.2010.36

30. Morrisett, G., Felleisen, M., Harper, R.: Abstract models of memory management. In: FPCA (1995). http://doi.acm.org/10.1145/224164.224182

31. Nagarakatte, S., Zhao, J., Martin, M.M.K., Zdancewic, S.: SoftBound: highly compatible and complete spatial memory safety for C. In: PLDI (2009). http://repository.upenn.edu/cgi/viewcontent.cgi?article=1941&context=cis_reports

32. Nagarakatte, S., Zhao, J., Martin, M.M.K., Zdancewic, S.: CETS: compiler enforced temporal safety for C. In: ISMM (2010). http://acg.cis.upenn.edu/papers/ismm10_cets.pdf

33. Necula, G.C., Condit, J., Harren, M., McPeak, S., Weimer, W.: CCured: type-safe retrofitting of legacy software. TOPLAS **27**(3), 477–526 (2005). https://doi.org/10.1145/1065887.1065892

34. Pitts, A.M.: Nominal Sets: Names and Symmetry in Computer Science. Cambridge University Press, New York (2013)

35. Pottier, F., Protzenko, J.: Programming with permissions in Mezzo. In: ICFP (2013)

36. Reynolds, J.C.: Separation logic: a logic for shared mutable data structures. In: LICS (2002). http://dl.acm.org/citation.cfm?id=645683.664578
37. The Rust programming language (2017). http://www.rust-lang.org
38. Schlesinger, C., Pattabiraman, K., Swamy, N., Walker, D., Zorn, B.G.: Modular protections against non-control data attacks. JCS **22**(5), 699–742 (2014). https://doi.org/10.3233/JCS-140502
39. Smith, G.: On the foundations of quantitative information flow. In: FoSSaCS 2009. http://doi.org/10.1007/978-3-642-00596-1_21
40. Stefan, D., Buiras, P., Yang, E.Z., Levy, A., Terei, D., Russo, A., Mazières, D.: Eliminating cache-based timing attacks with instruction-based scheduling. In: Crampton, J., Jajodia, S., Mayes, K. (eds.) ESORICS 2013. LNCS, vol. 8134, pp. 718–735. Springer, Heidelberg (2013). https://doi.org/10.1007/978-3-642-40203-6_40
41. Swamy, N., Hicks, M.W., Morrisett, G., Grossman, D., Jim, T.: Safe manual memory management in Cyclone. SCP **62**(2), 122–144 (2006). http://www.cs.umd.edu/~mwh/papers/cyc-mm-scp.pdf
42. Swasey, D., Garg, D., Dreyer, D.: Robust and compositional verification of object capability patterns. In: OOPSLA (2017, to appear). https://people.mpi-sws.org/~swasey/papers/ocpl
43. Szekeres, L., Payer, M., Wei, T., Song, D.: SoK: eternal war in memory. In: IEEE S&P (2013). http://lenx.100871.net/papers/War-oakland-CR.pdf
44. Taly, A., Erlingsson, Ú., Mitchell, J.C., Miller, M.S., Nagra, J.: Automated analysis of security-critical JavaScript APIs. In: S&P, Oakland (2011). http://dx.doi.org/10.1109/SP.2011.39
45. Turon, A.: Rust: from POPL to practice (keynote). In: POPL (2017). http://dl.acm.org/citation.cfm?id=3011999
46. Williams, C.: Oracle's Larry Ellison claims his Sparc M7 chip is hacker-proof – errr... The Register (2015). http://www.theregister.co.uk/2015/10/28/oracle_sparc_m7/
47. Yang, E.Z., Mazières, D.: Dynamic space limits for Haskell. In: PLDI (2014). http://doi.acm.org/10.1145/2594291.2594341
48. Yang, H., O'Hearn, P.W.: A semantic basis for local reasoning. In: FoSSaCS (2002). http://dl.acm.org/citation.cfm?id=646794.704850
49. Zhang, D., Askarov, A., Myers, A.C.: Language-based control and mitigation of timing channels. In: PLDI (2012). http://doi.acm.org/10.1145/2254064.2254078

Leakage, Information Flow, and Protocols

Formal Verification
of Integrity-Preserving Countermeasures
Against Cache Storage Side-Channels

Hamed Nemati[1], Christoph Baumann[2(✉)], Roberto Guanciale[2],
and Mads Dam[2]

[1] CISPA, Saarland University, Saarbrücken, Germany
hnnemati@cispa.saarland
[2] KTH Royal Institute of Technology, Stockholm, Sweden
{cbaumann,robertog,mfd}@kth.se

Abstract. Formal verification of systems-level software such as hypervisors and operating systems can enhance system trustworthiness. However, without taking low level features like caches into account the verification may become unsound. While this is a well-known fact w.r.t. timing leaks, few works have addressed latent cache storage side-channels, whose effects are not limited to information leakage. We present a verification methodology to analyse soundness of countermeasures used to neutralise these channels. We apply the proposed methodology to existing countermeasures, showing that they allow to restore integrity of the system. We decompose the proof effort into verification conditions that allow for an easy adaption of our strategy to various software and hardware platforms. As case study, we extend the verification of an existing hypervisor whose integrity can be tampered using cache storage channels. We used the HOL4 theorem prover to validate our security analysis, applying the verification methodology to a generic hardware model.

1 Introduction

Formal verification of low-level software such as microkernels, hypervisors, and drivers has made big strides in recent years [3,4,17,21,22,33,37,38]. We appear to be approaching the point where the promise of provably secure, practical system software is becoming a reality. However, system verification is usually based on models that are far simpler than contemporary state-of-the-art hardware. Many features pose significant challenges: Memory models, pipelines, speculation, out-of-order execution, peripherals, and various coprocessors, for instance for system management. In a security context, caches are notorious. They have been known for years to give rise to timing side channels that are difficult to fully counteract [13,16,26,28,32,36]. Also, cache management is closely tied to memory management, which—since it governs memory mapping, access control, and cache configuration through page-tables residing in memory—is one of the most complex and security-critical components in the computer architecture flora.

© The Author(s) 2018
L. Bauer and R. Küsters (Eds.): POST 2018, LNCS 10804, pp. 109–133, 2018.
https://doi.org/10.1007/978-3-319-89722-6_5

Computer architects strive to hide this complexity from application programmers, but system software and device drivers need explicit control over features like cacheability attributes. In virtualization scenarios, for instance, it is critical for performance to be able to delegate cache management authority for pages belonging to a guest OS to the guest itself. With such a delegated authority a guest is free to configure its share of the memory system as it wishes, including configurations that may break conventions normally expected for a well-behaved OS. For instance, a guest OS will usually be able to create memory aliases and to set cacheability attributes as it wishes. Put together, these capabilities can, however, give rise to memory incoherence, since the same physical location can now be pointed to by two virtual addresses, one to cache and one to memory. This opens up for cache storage attacks on both confidentiality and integrity, as was shown in [20]. Analogous problems arise due to the presence of instruction-caches, that can contain binary code that differs from the one stored in memory. Differently from timing channels, which are external to models used for formal analysis and do not invalidate verification of integrity properties, storage channels make the cacheless models unsound: Using them for security analysis can lead to conclusions that are false.

This shows the need to develop verification frameworks for low-level system software that are able to adequately reflect the presence of caches. It is particularly desirable if this can be done in a manner that allows to reuse existing verification tools on simpler models that do not consider caches. This is the goal we set ourselves in this paper.

Our Contributions. We undertake the first rigorous analysis of integrity-preserving countermeasures against cache storage channel attacks. We propose a practical verification framework, which is independent of a specific hardware and the software executing on the platform, and can be used to analyse security of low-level software on models with enabled caches. Our framework accommodates both data and instruction caches and we have proved its soundness in the HOL4 theorem prover. Our strategy consists in introducing hardware and software proof obligations and demonstrating that they prevent attacks on integrity. The framework is used to verify soundness of two countermeasures for data-caches and two countermeasures for instruction-caches. This results in code verification conditions that can be analysed on cacheless models, so that existing tools [6,11,31] (mostly not available on cache-enabled models) can automate this task to a large extent. To demonstrate that our methodology can be applied to commodity hardware, we formally model a generic cache and demonstrate that extensions of existing cacheless architectural models with the generic cache model satisfy all requirements imposed by our methodology. The practicability of our approach is shown by applying it to repair the verification of an existing and vulnerable hypervisor [21], demonstrating that the modified design prevents cache-attacks.

2   Related Work

Cache Storage Channels. The existence of cache storage channels due to mismatched cacheability attributes was first pointed out in [20]. That paper also sketches how prior integrity and confidentiality proofs for a sequential memory model could be repaired, identifying that coherency of data-cache is a key requirement. However, the verification methodology is only sketched and provides merely an intuition about the proof strategy. The present paper develops these ideas in detail, providing several new contributions, including (i) a formal cache-aware hardware model, (ii) a revised and detailed proof strategy that allows to decompose verification into hardware-, software-, and countermeasure-dependent proof obligations, (iii) introduction and verification of instruction cache coherency, (iv) formal definitions of all proof obligations and invariants, (v) a detailed explanation of the proof and how the proof obligations can be discharged for given applications and countermeasures, and (vi) a complete mechanization in HOL4.

Formal Verification. Recent works on kernel and hypervisor verification [8,10, 17–19,21,24,25,33,34] all assume a sequential memory model and leave cache issues to be managed by model external means, while the CVM framework [4] treats caches only in the context of device management [23]. In [21], a cacheless model was used to prove security of the hypervisor used here as a case study. Due to absence of caches in the underlying hardware model, the verification result is unsound in presence of uncacheable aliases, as demonstrated in [20].

Timing Channels. Timing attacks and countermeasures have been formally verified to varying degrees of detail in the literature. Since their analysis generally ignores caches, verified kernels are susceptible to timing attacks. For instance, Cock et al. [13] examined the bandwidth of timing channels in seL4 and possible countermeasures including cache coloring. Other related work includes those adopting formal analysis to either check the rigour of countermeasures [5,7,9,15,20,35] or to examine bandwidth of side-channels [14,27].

There is no comparable formal treatment for cache storage channels. These channels carry information through memory and, additionally to permitting illicit information flows, can be used to compromise integrity. To the best of our knowledge we are the first to present a detailed security proof for countermeasures against cache storage channel attacks.

3   Threats, Countermeasures, and Verification Goal

Data-Caches and Aliases. Modern CPU architectures such as ARM, Power, and x64 permit to configure if a given virtual page is cacheable or not. This capability can result in a class of attacks called "alias-driven attacks". Suppose a victim reference monitor that (1) validates an input stored in a memory location against a security policy and (2) uses such input for implementing a critical functionality.

Assume an *incoherent* state for this memory location: the data-cache contains a value for this location that differs from the content of the memory but the cache is not dirty. If the cache line is evicted between (1) and (2), its content is not written into the memory, since it is not dirty. In this case, the victim can potentially evaluate the policy using the value fetched from the cache and later use the content stored in memory to implement the critical functionality, allowing untrusted inputs to bypass the policy. This behavior has been demonstrated for ARMv7 and ARMv8 CPUs [20] as well as for MIPS, where uncacheable aliases have been used to establish incoherency. This behavior clearly departs from the behavior of a system that has no cache. However, x64 processors that implement "self-snooping" appear to be immune to this phenomenon.

A system that (1) permits an attacker to configure cacheability of its virtual memory, (2) acquires ownership of that location from the attacker, and (3) uses the location to read security critical information can be target of this attack. An example is the hypervisor presented in Sect. 5.5. The runtime monitor presented in [12], which forbids the execution of unsigned code, can also be attacked using caches. The attacker can load a signed process in cache and a malware in memory. Similarly, remote attestation checks the integrity of a device by a trusted measuring function. If this function accesses stale data from the caches then the measurements can be inaccurate.

In this paper we analyse two countermeasures against alias-driven attacks: "always cacheability" consists in defining a fixed region of memory that is made always cacheable and ensuring that the trusted software rejects any input pointing outside this region; "selective eviction" consists in flushing from the cache every location that is accessed by the trusted software and that has been previously accessed by the attacker. A description and evaluation of other possible countermeasures against cache storage channels was provided in [20].

Instruction-Caches. In a similar vein, instruction-caches may be dangerous if the content of executable pages is changed without using cache management instructions to maintain memory coherency. Suppose that a software (1) executes instructions from a region of memory, thus filling the instruction-cache with the instructions of a program, (2) it updates the memory with the code of a new program without flushing the cache, and (3) it executes the new program. Since between (1) and (3) some lines of the instruction-cache are evicted and other not, the CPU can execute a mix of the code of the two programs, resulting in a behavior that is hard to predict.

The presence of instruction-caches affect systems whose security depends on dynamically loaded code. This includes the aforementioned runtime monitor, boot-loaders that load or relocate programs, systems that implement dynamic code randomization, and Software Fault Isolation [29] (SFI) sandboxes that inspect binary code to isolate loadable third party modules.

We analyse two countermeasures against attacks that use instruction-caches: "Constant program memory" ensures the trusted executable code is never modified; "Selective eviction" consists in selectively evicting lines of the instruction-cache and flushing lines of the data-cache for locations that are modified.

3.1   Verification Goals

In this work we consider a trusted system software (the "kernel") that shares the system with an untrusted user level software (the "application"): the application requests services from the kernel. The hardware execution mode used by the application is less privileged than the mode used by the kernel. The application is potentially malicious and takes the role of the attacker. The kernel dynamically manages memory ownership and can provide various services, for instance for secure ownership transfer. This enables the application to pass data to the kernel services, while avoiding expensive copy operations: The application prepares the input inside its own memory, the ownership of this memory is transferred to the kernel, and the corresponding kernel routine operates on the input in-place.

Intuitively for guaranteeing integrity we mean that it is not possible for the application to influence the kernel using cache features (except possibly for timing channels, which are not considered in this work). That is, if there is a possibility for the application to affect the kernel behavior (e.g. by providing parameters to a system call) in a system with caches, there must be the same possibility in an idealized system that has no caches. This goal is usually formalized by requiring that the cacheless system can simulate all possible executions of the system with caches (i.e. all executions of the real system are admitted by the specification, that in this case is represented by the cacheless system).

Unfortunately, ensuring this property for complete executions is not possible: since the application is untrusted we need to assume that its code is unknown and that it can exploit behaviors of caches that are not available in the cacheless system, making impossible to guarantee that the behavior of the application is the same in both systems. For this reason, we analyse executions of the application and of the kernel separately.

We first identify a set of memory resources called "critical". These are the resources for which integrity must be preserved and that affect the kernel behavior. For example, in an operating system the memory allocator uses a data structure to keep track of the ownership of allocated memory pages. Thus all pages not belonging to the untrusted process (the application) are considered critical. Since this classification depends on the content of the allocator data structure, this is also a critical resource. Similarly in [21] the page type data structure identifies critical resources.

Then we phrase integrity as two complementary properties: (1) direct or indirect modification of the critical resources is impossible while the application is executing on the system with caches; and (2) the kernel has the same behavior in the cacheless and the cache-aware system.

An alternative approach to phrase integrity might be to show the absence of information flow from application to kernel. There are a number of issues with such an approach in this context, however: First, attacks that do not involve information flow would not be covered; Second, it is not clear how an information flow oriented account would handle kernel invocations; these generally correspond to endorsement actions in a multi-level security lattice setting and are challenging to map to the present setting. On the other hand, our account of integrity permits any safety property that only depends on the critical resources and holds for the cacheless system to be transferred to the system with caches.

4 Formalisation

As basis for our study we define two models, a cacheless and a cache-aware model. The cacheless model represents a memory-coherent single-core system where all caches are disabled. The cache-aware model is the same system augmented by a single-level separated data- and instruction-cache.

4.1 Cacheless Model

The cacheless model is ARM-flavoured but general enough to apply to other architectures. A (cacheless) state $s = \langle reg, psreg, coreg, mem \rangle \in \mathbb{S}$ is a tuple of general-purpose registers reg (including program counter pc), program-status registers $psreg$, coprocessor registers $coreg$, and memory mem. The core executes either in non-privileged mode U or privileged mode P, $Mode(s) \in \{U, P\}$. Executions in privileged mode are necessarily trusted, since they are able to modify the system configuration, e.g., coprocessor registers, in arbitrary ways. The program-status registers $psreg$ encode the execution mode and other execution parameters such as the arithmetic flags. The coprocessor registers $coreg$ determine a range of system configuration parameters, including virtual memory mapping and memory protection. The word addressable memory is represented by $mem : \mathbb{PA} \rightarrow \mathbb{B}^w$, where $\mathbb{B} = \{0, 1\}$, $\mathbb{PA}$ is the set of physical addresses, and w is the word size.

Executions in non-privileged mode are unable to directly modify coprocessor registers as well as certain critical program-status registers. For instance, the execution mode can be switched to P only by raising an exception. Memory accesses are controlled by a Memory Management Unit (MMU), which also determines memory region attributes such as cacheability. Let $A = \{wt, rd, ex\}$ be the set of access permissions (for write, read, and execute respectively) and $M = \{U, P\}$ be the set of execution modes. The MMU model is the function $MMU(s, va) \in (2^{M \times A} \times \mathbb{PA} \times \mathbb{B})$ which yields for a virtual address $va \in \mathbb{VA}$ the set of granted access rights, the translation, and the cacheability attribute. Note that the same physical addresses can be accessed with different access rights and different cacheability settings using different virtual aliases. Hereafter, when it is clear from the context, we use $MMU(s, va)$ to represent the translation of va.

The behaviour of the system is defined as a labeled transition system using relation $\rightarrow_m \subseteq \mathbb{S} \times \mathbb{S}$, where $m \in M$ and if $s \rightarrow_m s'$ then $Mode(s) = m$. Each transition represents the execution of a single instruction. When needed, we let $s \rightarrow_m s'$ [ops] denote that the operations ops are performed on the memory subsystem, where ops is a list whose elements are either $wt(pa, c)$ (pa was written with cacheability attribute c), $rd(pa, c)$ (pa was read with cacheability attribute c), $fl_D(pa)$, or $fl_I(pa)$ (the data- or instruction-cache flush operation for pa, which have no effects in the cacheless model). We use $s_0 \rightsquigarrow s_n$ to represent the weak transition relation that holds if there is an execution $s_0 \to \cdots \to s_n$ such that $Mode(s_n) = U$ and $Mode(s_j) \neq U$ for $0 < j < n$, i.e. the weak transition hides states while the kernel is running.

4.2   Cache-Aware Model

We model a single-core processor with single-level separated instruction and data-caches, i.e., a modified Harvard architecture. In Sect. 7 we discuss variations and generalizations of this model.

A state $\bar{s} \in \bar{\mathbb{S}}$ in the cache-aware model has the components of the cacheless model together with a data-cache $d\text{-}cache$ and an instruction-cache $i\text{-}cache$, $\bar{s} = \langle reg, psreg, coreg, mem, d\text{-}cache, i\text{-}cache \rangle$. The function MMU and the transition relation $\to_m \subseteq \bar{\mathbb{S}} \times \bar{\mathbb{S}}$ are extended to take into account caches.

Other definitions of the previous subsection are extended trivially. We use $d\text{-}hit(\bar{s}, pa)$ to denote a data-cache hit for address pa, $d\text{-}dirty(\bar{s}, pa)$ to identify dirtiness of the address pa (i.e. if the value of pa has been modified in cache and differs from the memory content), and $d\text{-}cnt(\bar{s}, pa)$ to obtain the value for pa stored in the data-cache (respectively $i\text{-}hit(\bar{s}, pa)$, $i\text{-}dirty(\bar{s}, pa)$, and $i\text{-}cnt(\bar{s}, pa)$ for the instruction-cache).

Due to the use of the modified Harvard architecture and the presence of caches, there are three views of the memory subsystem: the *data-view Dv*, the *instruction-view Iv*, and the *memory-view Mv*:

$$Dv(\bar{s}, pa) = \text{if } d\text{-}hit(\bar{s}, pa) \text{ then } d\text{-}cnt(\bar{s}, pa) \text{ else } \bar{s}.mem(pa)$$

$$Iv(\bar{s}, pa) = \text{if } i\text{-}hit(\bar{s}, pa) \text{ then } i\text{-}cnt(\bar{s}, pa) \text{ else } \bar{s}.mem(pa)$$

$$Mv(\bar{s}, pa) = \text{if } d\text{-}dirty(\bar{s}, pa) \text{ then } d\text{-}cnt(\bar{s}, pa) \text{ else } \bar{s}.mem(pa)$$

We require that the kernel always uses cacheable virtual aliases. Therefore, kernel reads access the data-view and kernel instruction fetches access the instruction-view. Moreover, the MMU always consults first the data-cache when it fetches a page-table descriptor, as is the case for instance in ARM Cortex-A53 and ARM Cortex-A8. Therefore, the MMU model uses the data-view. Finally, the memory-view represents what can be observed from the data-view after non-dirty cache lines have been evicted.

4.3   Security Properties

As is common in designs of low-level software, we assume that the kernel uses a static region of virtual memory $\mathbf{K_{vm}} \subseteq \mathbb{VA}$ for its memory accesses and that the static region $\mathbf{K_{ex}} \subseteq \mathbf{K_{vm}}$ maps the kernel code.

We first identify the critical resources, i.e., those resources for which integrity must be preserved and on which kernel behavior depends. This set always includes the coprocessor registers, which the architecture protects from non-privileged modifications. The security type of memory locations, however, can dynamically change due to transfer of memory ownership, i.e., the criticality of resources depends on the state of the system. The function $CR : \bar{\mathbb{S}} \rightarrow 2^{\mathbb{PA}}$ retrieves the subset of memory resources that are critical. Function CR itself depends on a subset of resources, namely the internal kernel data-structures that determine the security type of memory resources (for the kernel being an operating system and the application being one of its user processes, imagine the internal state of the page allocator and the process descriptors). Similarly, the function $EX : \bar{\mathbb{S}} \rightarrow 2^{\mathbb{PA}}$ retrieves the subset of critical memory resources that contain trusted executable code. These definitions are naturally lifted to the cacheless model, by extending a cacheless state with empty caches. Two states $\bar{s}$ and $\bar{s}'$ have the same *data-view* (respectively *instruction-view*) of the critical memory, written $\bar{s} \equiv_D \bar{s}'$ (respectively $\bar{s} \equiv_I \bar{s}'$), if

$$\{(pa, Dv(\bar{s}, pa)) \mid pa \in CR(\bar{s})\} = \{(pa, Dv(\bar{s}', pa)) \mid pa \in CR(\bar{s}')\}$$

(respectively Iv and EX). Finally, two states $\bar{s}$ and $\bar{s}'$ have the same critical resources, and we write $\bar{s} \equiv_{CR} \bar{s}'$, iff $\bar{s} \equiv_D \bar{s}'$, $\bar{s} \equiv_I \bar{s}'$, and $\bar{s}.coreg = \bar{s}'.coreg$.

Our verification approach requires to introduce a system invariant $\bar{I}$ that is software dependent and defined per kernel. This invariant ensures that the kernel can work properly (e.g. stack pointer and its data structures are correctly configured) and its properties are detailed in Sect. 5. A corresponding invariant I for the cacheless model is derived from $\bar{I}$ by excluding properties that constrain caches. Our goal is to establish two theorems: an application integrity theorem showing that $\bar{I}$ correctly constrains application behaviour in the cache-aware model, and a kernel integrity theorem showing that kernel routines in the cache-aware model correctly refine the cacheless model.

As the application is able to break its memory coherency at will, the application integrity theorem is a statement about the processor hardware and its correct configuration. In particular, Theorem 1 shows that non-privileged execution in the cache-aware model preserves the required invariant, that the invariant is adequate to preserve the critical resources, and that entries into privileged level correctly follow the hardware mode switching convention. For the latter, we use predicate $ex\text{-}entry(\bar{s})$ to identify states of the system immediately after switching to the kernel, i.e., when an exception is triggered, the mode becomes privileged and the program counter points to an entry in the exception vector table.

Theorem 1 (Application Integrity). *For all $\bar{s}$, if $\bar{I}(\bar{s})$ and $\bar{s} \rightarrow_U \bar{s}'$ then $\bar{I}(\bar{s}')$, $\bar{s} \equiv_{CR} \bar{s}'$, and if $Mode(\bar{s}') \neq U$ then $ex\text{-}entry(\bar{s}')$.*

For the kernel we prove that the two models behave equivalently. We prove this using forward simulation, by defining a simulation relation $\mathcal{R}_{sim}$ guaranteeing equality of all registers and critical memory resources, and then showing that both the invariant and the relation are preserved by privileged transitions:

Theorem 2 (Kernel Integrity). *For all $\bar{s}_1$ and s_1 such that $\bar{I}(\bar{s}_1)$, $\bar{s}_1 \mathcal{R}_{sim}$ s_1, and $ex\text{-}entry(\bar{s}_1)$, if $\bar{s}_1 \leadsto \bar{s}_2$ then $\exists s_2. s_1 \leadsto s_2$, $\bar{s}_2 \mathcal{R}_{sim} s_2$ and $\bar{I}(\bar{s}_2)$.*

5   Proof Strategy

Theorems 1 and 2 are proved in five steps:

1. First we introduce crucial properties of the hardware, abstracting from the details of a specific hardware architecture. We obtain a set of proof obligations (i.e. **HW Obligation**) that must be discharged for any given hardware.
2. Next, we reduce application integrity, Theorem 1, to proof obligations (i.e. **SW-I Obligation**) on software-specific invariants of the cache-aware model.
3. The same approach applies for kernel integrity, Theorem 2, where we also derive proof obligations (i.e. **SW-C Obligation**) on the kernel code.
4. We then demonstrate correctness of the selected countermeasures of Sect. 3 by discharging the corresponding proof obligations.
5. The last step is kernel-specific: we sketch how our results allow standard cache-oblivious binary analysis tools to show that a kernel implements the countermeasures, establishing Theorems 1 and 2.

A fundamental notion for our proof is *coherency*, which captures memory resources whose content cannot be indirectly effected through cache eviction.

Definition 1 (Data-Coherency). *We say that a memory resource $pa \in \mathbb{PA}$ is data-coherent in $\bar{s}$, $D\text{-}Coh(\bar{s}, pa)$, iff $d\text{-}hit(\bar{s}, pa)$ and $d\text{-}cnt(\bar{s}, pa) \neq \bar{s}.mem(pa)$ implies $d\text{-}dirty(\bar{s}, pa)$. A set $R \subseteq \mathbb{PA}$ is data-coherent iff all $pa \in R$ are.*

In other words, a physical location pa is data-coherent if a non-dirty cache hit of pa in $\bar{s}$ implies that the cached value is equal to the value stored in memory. The general intuition is that, for an incoherent resource, the view can be changed indirectly without an explicit memory write by evicting a clean cache-line with different values in the cache and memory. For instance, consider an MMU that looks first into the caches when it fetches a descriptor. Then if the page-tables are coherent, a cache eviction cannot indirectly affect the behaviour of the MMU. This intuition also underpins the definition of instruction-coherency.

Definition 2 (Instruction-Coherency). *We say that a memory resource $pa \in \mathbb{PA}$ is instruction-coherent in $\bar{s}$, $I\text{-}Coh(\bar{s}, pa)$, iff the following statements hold:*

1. *pa is data-coherent,*
2. *if $i\text{-}hit(\bar{s}, pa)$ then $i\text{-}cnt(\bar{s}, pa) = \bar{s}.mem(pa)$, and*
3. *$\neg d\text{-}dirty(\bar{s}, pa)$*

Instruction-coherency requires the data-cache to be not dirty to ensure that eviction from the data-cache does not break part (2) of the definition.

The role of coherency is highlighted by the following Lemma. The memory-view differs from the data-view only in memory resources that are cached, clean, and have different values stored in the cache and memory, and data-view differs from instruction-view only for resources that are not instruction-coherent.

Lemma 1. *Let $pa \in \mathbb{PA}$ and $\bar{s} \in \bar{\mathbb{S}}$. Then:*

1. *$D\text{-}Coh(\bar{s}, \{pa\}) \Leftrightarrow (Dv(\bar{s}, pa) = Mv(\bar{s}, pa))$.*
2. *$I\text{-}Coh(\bar{s}, \{pa\}) \Rightarrow (Dv(\bar{s}, pa) = Iv(\bar{s}, pa))$.*

5.1   Hardware Abstraction Layer

ISA models are complex because they describe the behavior of hundreds of possible instructions. For this reason we introduce three key notions in order to isolate verification tasks that are architecture-dependent and that can be verified once and reused for multiple countermeasures and kernels. These notions are:

1. *MMU Domain*: This identifies the memory resources that affect the virtual memory translation.
2. *Derivability*: This provides an overapproximation of the effects over the memory and cache for instructions executed in non-privileged mode.
3. *Instruction Dependency*: This identifies the memory resources that affect the behavior of the current instruction.

Here we provide an intuitive definition of these notions and formalize the properties that must be verified for the specific hardware model to ensure that these abstractions are sound. Section 6 comments on the verification of these properties for a generic hardware model in HOL4.

   MMU domain is the function $MD(\bar{s}, V) \subseteq \mathbb{PA}$ that determines the memory resources (i.e., the current master page-table and the linked page-tables) that affect the translation of virtual addresses in $V \subseteq \mathbb{VA}$.

HW Obligation 1

1. *MD is monotone, i.e., $V' \subseteq V$ implies $MD(\bar{s}, V') \subseteq MD(\bar{s}, V)$.*
2. *For all $\bar{s}, \bar{s}'$ and $V \subseteq \mathbb{VA}$ if $Dv(\bar{s}, pa) = Dv(\bar{s}', pa)$ for all $pa \in MD(\bar{s}, V)$ and $\bar{s}.coreg = \bar{s}'.coreg$ then $MD(\bar{s}, V) = MD(\bar{s}', V)$ and for all $va \in V$, $MMU(\bar{s}, va) = MMU(\bar{s}', va)$.*

Definition 3 (Derivability). *We say $\bar{s}'$ is derivable from $\bar{s}$ in non-privileged mode (denoted as $\bar{s} \triangleright \bar{s}'$) if $\bar{s}.coreg = \bar{s}'.coreg$ and for every $pa \in \mathbb{PA}$ at least one of D_{acc} properties and at least one of I_{acc} hold:*

$D_\emptyset(\bar{s}, \bar{s}', pa)$: *Independently of the access rights for the address pa, a data-cache line can always change due to an eviction. An eviction of a dirty cache entry causes a write back; eviction of clean entries does not affect the memory.*

$D_{rd}(\bar{s}, \bar{s}', pa)$: *If non-privileged mode can read the address pa, the value of pa in the memory can be filled into its data-cache line, making it clean.*

$D_{wt}(\bar{s}, \bar{s}', pa)$: *If non-privileged mode can write the address pa, it can either write directly into the data-cache, potentially making it dirty, or bypass it, by using an uncacheable alias. Only writes can make a location in data-cache dirty.*

$I_\emptyset(\bar{s}, \bar{s}', pa)$: *Independently of the access rights for the address pa, the corresponding line can always be evicted, leaving memory unchanged.*

$I_{ex}(\bar{s}, \bar{s}', pa)$: *If non-privileged mode can execute the address pa, the instruction-cache state can change through a fill operation which updates the cache with the value of pa in the memory. Instruction-cache lines never become dirty.*

$D_\emptyset(\bar{s}, \bar{s}', pa) \stackrel{\text{def}}{=} (M'(pa) \neq M(pa) \Rightarrow (d\text{-}dirty(\bar{s}, pa) \wedge \neg d\text{-}hit(\bar{s}', pa) \wedge M'(pa) = d\text{-}cnt(\bar{s}, pa)))$
$\quad \wedge (d\text{-}W(\bar{s}', pa) \neq d\text{-}W(\bar{s}, pa) \Rightarrow (\neg d\text{-}hit(\bar{s}', pa) \wedge (d\text{-}dirty(\bar{s}, pa) \Rightarrow M'(pa) = d\text{-}cnt(\bar{s}, pa))))$

$D_{rd}(\bar{s}, \bar{s}', pa) \stackrel{\text{def}}{=} (MMU(\bar{s}, pa, U, rd, \_) \vee pa \in MD(\bar{s})) \wedge M'(pa) = M(pa)$
$\quad \wedge (d\text{-}W(\bar{s}', pa) \neq d\text{-}W(\bar{s}, pa) \Rightarrow \neg d\text{-}hit(\bar{s}, pa) \wedge d\text{-}hit(\bar{s}', pa) \wedge \neg d\text{-}dirty(\bar{s}', pa) \wedge d\text{-}cnt(\bar{s}', pa) = M(pa))$

$D_{wt}(\bar{s}, \bar{s}', pa) \stackrel{\text{def}}{=} MMU(\bar{s}, pa, U, wt, \_)$
$\quad \wedge (d\text{-}W(\bar{s}', pa) \neq d\text{-}W(\bar{s}, pa) \Rightarrow d\text{-}dirty(\bar{s}', pa) \vee M'(pa) = d\text{-}cnt(\bar{s}', pa))$
$\quad \wedge (M'(pa) \neq M(pa) \Rightarrow (\neg d\text{-}dirty(\bar{s}', pa) \Rightarrow MMU(\bar{s}, pa, U, wt, false)))$

$I_\emptyset(\bar{s}, \bar{s}', pa) \stackrel{\text{def}}{=} i\text{-}W(\bar{s}', pa) \neq i\text{-}W(\bar{s}, pa) \Rightarrow \neg i\text{-}hit(\bar{s}', pa)$

$I_{ex}(\bar{s}, \bar{s}', pa) \stackrel{\text{def}}{=} MMU(\bar{s}, pa, U, ex, \_)$
$\quad \wedge (i\text{-}W(\bar{s}', pa) \neq i\text{-}W(\bar{s}, pa) \Rightarrow \neg i\text{-}hit(\bar{s}, pa) \wedge i\text{-}hit(\bar{s}', pa) \wedge \neg i\text{-}dirty(\bar{s}', pa) \wedge i\text{-}cnt(\bar{s}', pa) = M(pa))$

Fig. 1. Derivability. Here $d\text{-}W(\bar{s}, pa) = \langle d\text{-}hit(\bar{s}, pa), d\text{-}dirty(\bar{s}, pa), d\text{-}cnt(\bar{s}, pa)\rangle$ and $i\text{-}W(\bar{s}, pa) = \langle i\text{-}hit(\bar{s}, pa), i\text{-}dirty(\bar{s}, pa), i\text{-}cnt(\bar{s}, pa)\rangle$ denote the cache-line contents corresponding to pa in $\bar{s}.d\text{-}cache$ and $\bar{s}.i\text{-}cache$, $M = \bar{s}.mem$, $M' = \bar{s}'.mem$, and $MMU(\bar{s}, pa, U, acc, c) = \exists va.MMU(\bar{s}, va, U, acc) = (pa, c)$.

Figure 1 reports the formal definition of these predicates for a cache operating in write-back mode, assuming cache line granularity is finer than page granularity, i.e., the same memory permissions hold for all entries of a given line.

Note that in a cache, one cache line contains several locations and that writing one such location marks the whole line of the data-cache dirty. However, due to our definition of *d-dirty* the locations in the written line are not considered dirty, if they have the same value in cache as in memory.

In practice, if $\bar{s} \triangleright \bar{s}'$ then for a given location *D-Coh* can be invalidated only if there exists a non-cacheable writable alias and *I-Coh* can be invalidated only if there exists a writable alias. The following obligation shows that derivability correctly overapproximates the hardware behavior:

HW Obligation 2. *For all $\bar{s}$ such that $D\text{-}Coh(\bar{s}, MD(\bar{s}, \mathbb{VA}))$ and $MD(\bar{s}, \mathbb{VA}) \cap \{pa \mid \exists va.\ MMU(\bar{s}, va) = (acc, pa, c)\ and\ (U, wt) \in acc\} = \emptyset$, if $\bar{s}'$ is reachable by a non-privileged transition, i.e. $\bar{s} \rightarrow_U \bar{s}'$, then*

1. $\bar{s} \triangleright \bar{s}'$, *i.e., $\bar{s}'$ is derivable from $\bar{s}$, and*
2. *if $Mode(\bar{s}') \neq U$ then ex-entry($\bar{s}'$), i.e., the mode can only change by entering an exception handler*

The precondition of the obligation requires the MMU domain to be data-coherent and to not overlap with the memory writable in non-privileged mode. This ensures that the MMU configuration is constant during the execution of instructions that update multiple memory locations. This requirement also ensures transitivity of derivability.

To complete the hardware abstraction we need sufficient conditions to ensure that the cache-aware model behaves like the cacheless one. We use the functions $p\text{-}deps(\bar{s}) \subseteq \mathbb{PA}$ and $v\text{-}deps(\bar{s}) \subseteq \mathbb{VA}$ to extract an overapproximation of the physical and virtual addresses that affect the next transition of $\bar{s}$. For instance, *v-deps* includes the program counter, the locations loaded and stored, while *p-deps(s)* includes the translation of the program counter, the translation of the virtual addresses read, and the addresses that affect the translation of *v-deps* (i.e. $MD(\bar{s}, v\text{-}deps(\bar{s}))$). As usual, these definitions are lifted to the cacheless model using empty caches. We say that $\bar{s}$ and s are *similar*, if $(\bar{s}.reg, \bar{s}.psreg, \bar{s}.coreg) = (s.reg, s.psreg, s.coreg)$, $Dv(\bar{s}, pa) = s.mem(pa)$ for all pa in $p\text{-}deps(s) \cap p\text{-}deps(\bar{s})$, and $Iv(\bar{s}, MMU(\bar{s}, \bar{s}.reg.pc)) = s.mem(MMU(s, s.reg.pc))$.

HW Obligation 3. *For all* similar $\bar{s}$ *and* s

1. $p\text{-}deps(\bar{s}) = p\text{-}deps(s)$ *and* $v\text{-}deps(\bar{s}) = v\text{-}deps(s)$
2. *if* $s \rightarrow_m s'$ $[ops_1]$, $\bar{s} \rightarrow_m \bar{s}'$ $[ops_2]$ *and all accesses in* ops_1 *are cacheable (i.e.* $wt(pa, c) \in ops_1$ *or* $rd(pa, c) \in ops_1$ *implies* c) *then*
   (a) $ops_2 = ops_1$
   (b) $(\bar{s}'.reg, \bar{s}'.psreg, \bar{s}'.coreg) = (s'.reg, s'.psreg, s'.coreg)$
   (c) *for every* pa *if* $wt(pa, c) \in ops_1$ *then* $Dv(\bar{s}', pa) = s'.mem(pa)$,
       otherwise $Mv(\bar{s}, pa) = Mv(\bar{s}', pa)$ *and* $s.mem(pa) = s'.mem(pa)$

The obligation, thus, is to show that if $\bar{s}$ and s are similar, then their instructions have the same dependencies; the same physical addresses are read, written, and flushed; registers are updated in the same way; addresses written have the same values; addresses that are not written preserve their memory view.

The last obligation describes cache effects of operations:

HW Obligation 4. *For every* $\bar{s}$ *if* $\bar{s} \rightarrow_m \bar{s}'$ $[ops]$ *and all accesses in* ops *are cacheable then*

1. *for every* pa *if* $wt(pa, c) \in ops$ *then* $D\text{-}Coh(\bar{s}', \{pa\})$,
   otherwise $D\text{-}Coh$, $I\text{-}Coh$ *and* $\neg d\text{-}dirty$ *of* pa *are preserved*
2. *if* $fl_D(pa) \in ops$ *then* $D\text{-}Coh(\bar{s}', \{pa\})$ *and* $\neg d\text{-}dirty(\bar{s}, pa)$
3. *if* $fl_I(pa) \in ops$, $D\text{-}Coh(\bar{s}, \{pa\})$, *and* $\neg d\text{-}dirty(\bar{s}, pa)$ *then* $I\text{-}Coh(\bar{s}', \{pa\})$

If the kernel only uses cacheable aliases then memory writes establish data-coherency; data- and instruction-coherency, as well as non-dirtyness are preserved for non-updated locations; data-cache flushes establish data-coherency and make locations non-dirty; instruction-cache flushes make data-coherent, non-dirty locations instruction-coherent.

5.2   Application Level: Theorem 1

To decompose the proof of Theorem 1, the invariant $\bar{I}$ is split in three parts: a functional part $\bar{I}_{fun}$ which only depends on the *data-view* of the critical resources, an invariant $\bar{I}_{coh}$ which only depends on data-coherency of the critical resources and instruction-coherency of executable resources, and an optional countermeasure-specific invariant $\bar{I}_{cm}$ which depends on coherency of non-critical memory resources such as resources in an always-cacheable region:

SW-I Obligation 1. *For all* $\bar{s}$, $\bar{I}(\bar{s}) = \bar{I}_{fun}(\bar{s}) \wedge \bar{I}_{coh}(\bar{s}) \wedge \bar{I}_{cm}(\bar{s})$ *and:*

1. *for all $\bar{s}'$ if $\bar{s} \equiv_{CR} \bar{s}'$ then $\bar{I}_{fun}(\bar{s}) = \bar{I}_{fun}(\bar{s}')$;*
2. *for all $\bar{s}'$ if $\bar{s} \equiv_{CR} \bar{s}'$, $D\text{-}Coh(\bar{s}, CR(\bar{s}))$, $D\text{-}Coh(\bar{s}', CR(\bar{s}'))$, $I\text{-}Coh(\bar{s}, EX(\bar{s}))$, and $I\text{-}Coh(\bar{s}', EX(\bar{s}'))$, then $\bar{I}_{coh}(\bar{s}) = \bar{I}_{coh}(\bar{s}')$;*
3. *for all $\bar{s}'$ if $\bar{I}(\bar{s})$ and $\bar{s} \rhd \bar{s}'$ then $\bar{I}_{cm}(\bar{s}')$.*

The invariants must prevent direct modification of the critical resources by the application, i.e., there is no address writable in non-privileged mode that points to a critical resource. Similarly, indirect modification, e.g., by line eviction, must be impossible. This is guaranteed if critical resources are data-coherent and executable resources are instruction-coherent.

SW-I Obligation 2. *For all $\bar{s}$:*

1. *If $\bar{I}_{fun}(\bar{s})$ and $pa \in CR(\bar{s})$ then there is no va such that $MMU(\bar{s}, va) = (acc, pa, c)$ and $(U, wt) \in acc$*
2. *If $\bar{I}_{fun}(\bar{s})$ and $\bar{I}_{coh}(\bar{s})$ then $D\text{-}Coh(\bar{s}, CR(\bar{s}))$ and $I\text{-}Coh(\bar{s}, EX(\bar{s}))$*

Also, the functions CR and EX must be correctly defined: resources needed to identify the set of critical kernel resources are critical themselves, as are resources affecting the MMU configuration (i.e., the page-tables).

SW-I Obligation 3. *For all $\bar{s}, \bar{s}'$:*

1. *If $\bar{I}_{fun}(\bar{s})$, $\bar{s} \equiv_D \bar{s}'$ and $\bar{s}.coreg = \bar{s}'.coreg$ then $CR(\bar{s}) = CR(\bar{s}')$, $EX(\bar{s}) = EX(\bar{s}')$, and $EX(\bar{s}) \subseteq CR(\bar{s})$*
2. *If $\bar{I}_{fun}(\bar{s})$ then $MD(\bar{s}, \mathbb{VA}) \subseteq CR(\bar{s})$*

The following lemmas assume HW Obligation 2 and SW-I Obligations 1–3. First, we show that the application cannot modify critical resources.

Lemma 2. *For all $\bar{s}, \bar{s}'$ such that $\bar{I}(\bar{s})$ if $\bar{s} \rhd \bar{s}'$ then $\bar{s} \equiv_{CR} \bar{s}'$.*

Proof. Since $\bar{I}(\bar{s})$ holds, the MMU prohibits writable accesses of the application to critical resources (SW-I Obligation 2.1). Also, derivability shows that the application can directly change only resources that are writable according to the MMU. Thus, the application cannot directly update $CR(\bar{s})$. Besides, the invariant guarantees data-coherency of critical resources and instruction-coherency of executable resources in $\bar{s}$ (SW-I Obligation 2.2). This prevents indirect modifications of these resources. Finally, SW-I Obligation 3.1 ensures that the kernel data-structures that identify what is critical cannot be altered. ■

To complete the proof of Theorem 1 we additionally need to show that coherency of critical resources (Lemma 3) and the functional invariant (Lemma 4) are preserved by non-privileged transitions.

Lemma 3. *For all $\bar{s}$ if $\bar{I}(\bar{s})$ and $\bar{s} \rhd \bar{s}'$ then $D\text{-}Coh(\bar{s}', CR(\bar{s}'))$, $I\text{-}Coh(\bar{s}', EX(\bar{s}'))$.*

Proof. From the previous lemma we get $CR(\bar{s}') = CR(\bar{s})$ and $EX(\bar{s}') = EX(\bar{s})$. Coherency of these resources in $\bar{s}$ is given by SW-I Obligation 2.2. From derivability we know that data-coherency can be invalidated only through non-cacheable writes; instruction-coherency can be invalidated only through writes to executable resources. SW-I Obligation 2.1 yields that there is no alias writable in non-privileged mode pointing to a critical resource, using SW-I Obligation 3.1 then also executable resources cannot be written.   ∎

Lemma 4. *For all $\bar{s}$ and $\bar{s}'$ if $\bar{I}(\bar{s})$ and $\bar{s} \rightarrow_U \bar{s}'$ then $\bar{I}_{fun}(\bar{s}')$.*

Proof. To show that non-privileged transitions preserve the invariant we use HW Obligation 2.1, Lemma 2, and SW-I Obligation 1.1.   ∎

We are now able to complete the proof of application integrity. The following Lemma directly proves Theorem 1 if the proof obligations are met.

Lemma 5 (Application Integrity). *For all $\bar{s}$, if $\bar{I}(\bar{s})$ and $\bar{s} \rightarrow_U \bar{s}'$ then $\bar{I}(\bar{s}')$, $\bar{s} \equiv_{CR} \bar{s}'$, and if $Mode(\bar{s}') \neq U$ then ex-entry($\bar{s}'$).*

Proof. By HW Obligation 2, $\bar{s} \rhd \bar{s}'$ and if $Mode(\bar{s}') \neq U$ then *ex-entry*($\bar{s}'$). By Lemma 2, $\bar{s} \equiv_{CR} \bar{s}'$. By Lemma 4, $\bar{I}_{fun}(\bar{s}')$. By Lemma 3, D-$Coh(\bar{s}',CR(\bar{s}'))$ and I-$Coh(\bar{s}',EX(\bar{s}'))$. By SW-I Obligation 2.2, D-$Coh(\bar{s},CR(\bar{s}))$ and I-$Coh(\bar{s},EX(\bar{s}))$. By SW-I Obligation 1.2 and $\bar{I}(\bar{s})$, $\bar{I}_{coh}(\bar{s}')$. Then by SW-I Obligation 1.3, $\bar{I}_{cm}(\bar{s}')$, thus $\bar{I}(\bar{s}') = \bar{I}_{fun}(\bar{s}') \wedge \bar{I}_{coh}(\bar{s}') \wedge \bar{I}_{cm}(\bar{s}')$ holds.   ∎

5.3   Kernel Level: Theorem 2

Our goal is to constrain kernel execution in such a way that it behaves identically in the cache-aware and the cacheless model. The challenge is to find suitable proof obligations for the kernel code that are stated on the cacheless model, so they can be verified using existing tools for binary analysis.

The first code verification obligation requires to show that the kernel preserves the invariant when there is no cache:

SW-C Obligation 1. *For all s,s' if $I(s)$, ex-entry(s), and $s \rightsquigarrow s'$, then $I(s')$.*

We impose two requirements on the kernel virtual memory: the addresses in $\mathbf{K_{vm}}$ must be cacheable (so that the kernel uses the data-view of memory resources) and $\mathbf{K_{ex}}$ must be mapped to a subset of the executable resources.

SW-I Obligation 4. *For all s such that $I(s)$:*

1. *For every $va \in \mathbf{K_{vm}}$ if $MMU(s,va) = (acc,pa,c)$ then c holds.*
2. *For every $va \in \mathbf{K_{ex}}$ if $MMU(s,va) = (acc,pa,c)$ then $pa \in EX(s)$.*

A common problem of verifying low-level software is to couple the invariant with every possible internal state of the kernel. This is a major concern here, since the set of critical resources changes dynamically and can be stale while the kernel is executing. We solve this problem by defining an *internal invariant* $II(s,s')$, which allows us to define properties of the state s' in relation with the initial state s of the kernel handler.

Definition 4. *The intermediate invariants $II(s, s')$ for the cacheless model and $\overline{II}(\bar{s}, \bar{s}')$ for the cache-aware model hold if:*

1. *$s'.reg.pc \in \mathbf{K_{ex}}$ and $\bar{s}'.reg.pc \in \mathbf{K_{ex}}$, respectively,*
2. *for all $pa \in \mathbb{PA}$: if $pa \in MD(s, \mathbf{K_{vm}})$ then $s.mem(pa) = s'.mem(pa)$ and if $pa \in MD(\bar{s}, \mathbf{K_{vm}})$ then $Dv(\bar{s}, pa) = Dv(\bar{s}', pa)$, respectively,*
3. *$v\text{-}deps(s') \subseteq \mathbf{K_{vm}}$ and $v\text{-}deps(\bar{s}') \subseteq \mathbf{K_{vm}}$, respectively,*
4. *$II_{cm}(s, s')$ and $\overline{II}_{cm}(\bar{s}, \bar{s}')$, respectively: additional countermeasure-specific requirements that will be instantiated in Sect. 5.4, and*
5. *only for the cache-aware model: $D\text{-}Coh(\bar{s}', CR(\bar{s}))$.*

Now we demand a proof that the intermediate invariant is preserved in the cacheless model during kernel execution, i.e., that (1) the kernel does not execute instructions outside its code region, (2) the kernel does not change page-table entries that map its virtual memory, (3) the kernel does not leave its virtual address space, and (4) the kernel implements the countermeasure correctly.

SW-C Obligation 2. *For all s,s' if $I(s)$, $ex\text{-}entry(s)$, and $s \rightarrow_P^* s'$, then $II(s, s')$.*

We require to demonstrate correctness of the countermeasure, by showing that it guarantees coherency of dependencies during kernel execution.

SW-I Obligation 5. *For all $\bar{s}, \bar{s}'$, if $\bar{I}(\bar{s})$, $\overline{II}_{cm}(\bar{s}, \bar{s}')$, and $\bar{s}'.reg.pc \in \mathbf{K_{ex}}$ then $D\text{-}Coh(\bar{s}', p\text{-}deps(\bar{s}'))$ and $I\text{-}Coh(\bar{s}', MMU(\bar{s}', \bar{s}'.reg.pc))$.*

We introduce the simulation relation between the two models: $\bar{s} \mathcal{R}_{sim} s$ iff $(\bar{s}.reg, \bar{s}.psreg, \bar{s}.coreg) = (s.reg, s.psreg, s.coreg)$ and for all pa, $Mv(\bar{s}, pa) = s.mem(pa)$. The intuition in using the memory-view is that it is equal to the data-view for coherent locations and is unchanged (as demonstrated by HW Obligation 3) for incoherent locations that are not directly accessed by the kernel.
    The following proof obligation connects the simulation relation, the invariants and the intermediate invariants: (1) the invariant of the cache-aware model can be transferred to the cacheless model via the simulation; (2) after the execution of a handler (i.e. $Mode(s') = U$) if the two intermediate invariants hold then the simulation allows to transfer the functional invariant of the cacheless model to the cache-aware model and guarantees coherency of critical resources; and (3) the cache-aware intermediate invariant ensures the countermeasure requirements.

SW-I Obligation 6. *For all $\bar{s}, s$ such that $\bar{s} \mathcal{R}_{sim} s$ and $\bar{I}(\bar{s})$*

1. *$I(s)$ holds and $II_{cm}(s, s)$ implies $\overline{II}_{cm}(\bar{s}, \bar{s})$,*
2. *for all $\bar{s}', s'$ such that $\bar{s}' \mathcal{R}_{sim} s'$ if $\overline{II}(\bar{s}, \bar{s}')$, $II(s, s')$, $I(s')$, and $Mode(s') = U$ then $\bar{I}_{fun}(\bar{s}')$ and $\bar{I}_{coh}(\bar{s}')$, and*
3. *for all $\bar{s}'$ if $\bar{I}_{fun}(\bar{s}')$, $\bar{I}_{coh}(\bar{s}')$, and $\overline{II}(\bar{s}, \bar{s}')$ then $\bar{I}_{cm}(\bar{s}')$.*

The following lemmas assume that the proof obligations hold. First we show that the intermediate invariant can be transferred from the cacheless to the cache-aware model.

Lemma 6. *Suppose that $\bar{s}_0 \; \mathcal{R}_{sim} \; s_0$, $\bar{s} \; \mathcal{R}_{sim} \; s$, $\bar{s} \rightarrow_P \bar{s}'[ops]$, $s \rightarrow_P s'[ops]$, and $\bar{s}' \; \mathcal{R}_{sim} \; s'$. If $\bar{I}(\bar{s}_0)$, $II(s_0, s)$, $II(s_0, s')$, and $\overline{II}(\bar{s}_0, \bar{s})$ then $\overline{II}(\bar{s}_0, \bar{s}')$.*

Proof. Transferring the property of Definition 4.1 from s' to $\bar{s}'$ is trivial, since $\mathcal{R}_{sim}$ guarantees equivalence of registers.

For Definition 4.5 we show that the kernel only performs cacheable accesses in *ops* from s (due to SW-I Obligation 4 and HW Obligation 1.2); these are the same accesses performed in $\bar{s}$; $CR(\bar{s}_0)$ is data-coherent in $\bar{s}$ due to $\overline{II}(\bar{s}_0, \bar{s})$; coherency is preserved from $\bar{s}$ to $\bar{s}'$ due to HW Obligation 4.

For Definition 4.2: Let $D = MD(s_0, \mathbf{K_{vm}})$; $II(s_0, s')$ ensures that the memory in D is the same in s_0, s, and s'; $\mathcal{R}_{sim}$ guarantees that the memory-view of D in $\bar{s}_0$ is the equal to the content of the memory in s_0; D is data-coherent in $\bar{s}_0$ by HW Obligation 1.1, SW-I Obligations 3.2 and 2.2, hence by Lemma 1 the data-view of D in $\bar{s}_0$ is equal to its memory content in s_0 and s'; also $D = MD(\bar{s}_0, \mathbf{K_{vm}})$ due to HW Obligation 1.2; similarly, $\mathcal{R}_{sim}$ guarantees that the memory-view of D in $\bar{s}'$ is equal to the memory content of D in s'; then locations D have the same data-view in $\bar{s}_0$ and $\bar{s}'$ via Lemma 1, if D is coherent in $\bar{s}'$. This follows from $D\text{-}Coh(\bar{s}', CR(\bar{s}_0))$ (shown above), HW Obligation 1.1, and SW-I Obligation 3.2.

For Definition 4.4 we rely on a further proof obligation that demonstrates correctness of the countermeasure: if the software implements the countermeasure in the cacheless model, then the additional coherency requirements on the cache-aware model are satisfied.

SW-I Obligation 7. *Assume $\bar{s}_0 \; \mathcal{R}_{sim} \; s_0$, $\bar{s} \; \mathcal{R}_{sim} \; s$, $\bar{s} \rightarrow_P \bar{s}'[ops]$, $s \rightarrow_P s'[ops]$, and $\bar{s}' \; \mathcal{R}_{sim} \; s'$. If $\bar{I}(\bar{s}_0)$, $II(s_0, s)$, $II(s_0, s')$, and $\overline{II}(\bar{s}_0, \bar{s})$ then $\overline{II}_{cm}(\bar{s}_0, \bar{s}')$.*

From this we also establish coherency of the dependencies of $\bar{s}'$ (due to SW-I Obligation 5), thus the data-view and the memory-view of the dependencies of $\bar{s}'$ are the same (Lemma 1). The dependencies of s' and $\bar{s}'$ have the same memory content via the simulation relation. Therefore s' and $\bar{s}'$ are *similar*; by HW Obligation 3.1, we transfer the property of Definition 4.3 from s' to $\bar{s}'$. ∎

The following lemma shows that the simulation relation and the intermediate invariant is preserved while the kernel is executing.

Lemma 7. *Suppose that $\bar{I}(\bar{s})$, ex-entry($\bar{s}$), and $\bar{s} \; \mathcal{R}_{sim} \; s$. If $\bar{s} \rightarrow_P^n \bar{s}'$ then $s \rightarrow_P^n s'$ for some s' such that $\bar{s}' \; \mathcal{R}_{sim} \; s'$, $\overline{II}(\bar{s}, \bar{s}')$, and $II(s, s')$.*

Proof. Internal invariant $II(s, s')$ is directly obtained from SW-C Obligation 2. We prove the remaining goals by induction on the execution length. Simulation in the base case is trivial, as no step is taken, and $\overline{II}(\bar{s}, \bar{s})$ follows from $II(\bar{s}, \bar{s})$, the coherency of critical resources in $\bar{s}$, SW-I Obligations 6.1 and 5, the simulation relation and Lemma 1, as well as HW Obligation 3.1.

For the inductive case we first show that the simulation relation is preserved. $\mathcal{R}_{sim}$ guarantees that s' and $\bar{s}'$ have the same registers, SW-I Obligation 5 ensures that the memory pointed by the program counter is instruction-coherent and the instruction dependencies are data-coherent. Therefore, by Lemma 1 and $\mathcal{R}_{sim}$ we

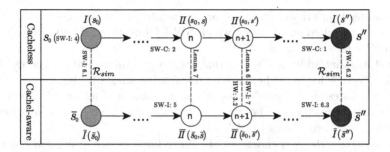

Fig. 2. Verification of kernel integrity; inductive simulation proof and invariant transfer

can ensure all preconditions of HW Obligation 3, which shows that the simulation is preserved. We use Lemma 6 to transfer the intermediate invariant. ■

Figure 2 indicates how the various proof obligations and lemmas of the section tie together. We are now able to complete the proof of kernel integrity. The following lemma directly proves Theorem 2 if the proof obligations are met.

Lemma 8 (Kernel Integrity). *For all $\bar{s}_1$ and s_1 such that $\bar{I}(\bar{s}_1)$, $\bar{s}_1\ \mathcal{R}_{sim}\ s_1$, and ex-entry($\bar{s}_1$), if $\bar{s}_1 \rightsquigarrow \bar{s}_2$ then $\exists s_2.\ s_1 \rightsquigarrow s_2,\ \bar{s}_2\ \mathcal{R}_{sim}\ s_2$ and $\bar{I}(\bar{s}_2)$.*

Proof. From $\bar{s}_1 \rightsquigarrow \bar{s}_2$. we have $\bar{s}_1 \rightarrow^n_P \bar{s}_2$ for some n; by Lemma 7 we find s_2 such that $s_1 \rightarrow^n_P s_2$, $\bar{s}_2\ \mathcal{R}_{sim}\ s_2$, $\overline{II}(\bar{s}_1,\bar{s}_2)$, and $II(s_1,s_2)$. Then $s_1 \rightsquigarrow s_2$ as s_2 and $\bar{s}_2$ are in the same mode. By SW-I Obligation 6.1 we obtain $I(s_1)$. Then by SW-C Obligation 1, $I(s_2)$. SW-I Obligation 6.2 yields $\bar{I}_{fun}(\bar{s}_2)$ and $\bar{I}_{coh}(\bar{s}_2)$, and by SW-I Obligation 6.3, $\bar{I}_{cm}(\bar{s}_2)$. It follows that $\bar{I}(\bar{s}_2)$ holds, as desired. ■

5.4 Correctness of Countermeasures

Verification of a countermeasure amounts to instantiating all invariants that are not software-specific and discharging the corresponding proof obligations. We verify combinations of always cacheablility or selective eviction of the data-cache, and constant program memory or selective eviction of the instruction-cache.

Always Cacheablility and Constant Program Memory. Let $M_{ac} \subseteq \mathbb{PA}$ be the region of physical memory that must always be accessed using cacheable aliases. The software needs to preserve two properties: (8.1) there are no uncacheable aliases to M_{ac}, (8.2) the kernel never allocates critical resources outside M_{ac}:

SW-I Obligation 8. *If $I(s)$ holds, then:*

1. For every va, if $MMU(s,va)=(acc,pa,c)$ and $pa \in M_{ac}$ then c.
2. $CR(s) \subseteq M_{ac}$.

For this countermeasure, the non-functional invariants are defined as follows

$\bar{I}_{coh}(\bar{s})$ states that critical resources are data-coherent and executable resources are instruction-coherent (from which SW-I Obligation 1.2 and SW-I Obligation 2.2 follow directly).

$\bar{I}_{cm}(\bar{s})$ states that addresses in M_{ac} that are not critical are data-coherent (SW-I Obligation 1.3 holds as there are no uncacheble aliases to M_{ac}).

$II_{cm}(s, s')$ states that dependencies of instructions in s' are in M_{ac}, no kernel write targets $EX(\bar{s})$ (i.e. there is no self-modifying code), and when the kernel handler completes $EX(\bar{s}') \subseteq EX(\bar{s})$.

$\overline{II}_{cm}(\bar{s}, \bar{s}')$ states that dependencies of instruction in $\bar{s}'$ are in M_{ac}, M_{ac} is data-coherent, and $EX(\bar{s})$ is instruction-coherent (SW-I Obligation 5 holds due to SW-I Obligation 4, i.e., the kernel fetches instructions from $EX(\bar{s})$ only).

The cache-aware functional invariant $\bar{I}_{fun}$ is defined equivalently to I using $Dv(\bar{s}, pa)$ in place of $s.mem(pa)$. This and the two intermediate invariants enable to transfer properties between the two models, establishing SW-I Obligation 6.

The proof of SW-I Obligation 7 (i.e. the cache-aware intermediate invariant $\overline{II}_{cm}$ is preserved) consists of three tasks: (1) data-coherency of M_{ac} is preserved, since SW-I Obligation 4 and II imply that the kernel only performs cacheble accesses, therefore, data-coherency cannot be invalidated; (2) instruction-coherency is guaranteed by the fact that there is no self-modifying code and HW Obligation 4; (3) the hypothesis of HW Obligation 3.1 (which shows that cacheless and cache-aware model have the same dependencies) is ensured by the fact that cacheless dependencies are in M_{ac} which is data-coherent.

Selective Eviction of Data-Cache and Constant Program Memory. Differently from always cacheability, selective eviction does not require to establish a functional property (i.e. SW-I Obligation 8). Instead, it is necessary to verify that resources acquired from the application are accessed by the kernel only after they are made coherent via cache flushing. For this purpose, we extend the two models with a history variable h that keeps track of all effects of instruction executed by the kernel (i.e. $s \to_m s'$ $[ops]$ then $(s, h) \to_m (s', h')$ $[ops]$ and $h' = h; ops$). Let $C(s, s')$ be the set of resources that were critical in s or that have been data-flushed in the history of s'. Hereafter we only describe the parts of the non-functional invariants that deal with the data-cache, since for the instruction-cache we use the same countermeasure as in the previous case.

$\bar{I}_{coh}(\bar{s})$ is the same as always cacheability, while $\bar{I}_{cm}(\bar{s}) = true$, since the countermeasure is not a state-based property.

$II_{cm}(s, s')$ (and $\overline{II}_{cm}(\bar{s}, \bar{s}')$) states that dependencies in s' are in $C(s, s')$ ($C(\bar{s}, \bar{s}')$, respectively) and that $CR(s') \subseteq CR(s) \cup C(s, s')$ if $Mode(s') = U$.

Again, the cache-aware functional invariant $\bar{I}_{fun}$ is defined equivalently to I using the data-view of memory resources.

The proofs of SW-I Obligation 6 and SW-I Obligation 7 are similar to the ones above. Instead of M_{ac} they rely on the data-coherency of $C(\bar{s}, \bar{s}')$ and the fact that data-cache flushes always establish coherency (HW Obligation 4).

Selective Eviction of Instruction-Cache. The two previous countermeasures for data-cache can be combined with selective eviction of instruction-cache to support dynamic code. The requirements that the kernel does not write into executable resources and that these are not extended are changed with the following property. Let $C'(s, s')$ be the set of executable resources in s that have not been written in the history of s', joined with the resources that have been data-flushed, instruction-flushed, and have not been overwritten after the flushes. The intermediate invariant $II_{cm}(s, s')$ (and analogously $\overline{II}_{cm}(\bar{s}, \bar{s}')$ for the cache-aware model) states that the translation of the program counter is in $C'(s, s')$, and when the kernel handler completes, $EX(s') \subseteq C'(s, s')$. Additionally, $\overline{II}_{cm}(\bar{s}, \bar{s}')$ states that $C'(\bar{s}, \bar{s}')$ is instruction-coherent. SW-I Obligation 5 holds because the kernel only fetches instructions from $C'(\bar{s}, \bar{s}')$.

The main change to the proof of SW-I Obligation 7 consists in showing instruction-coherency of $C'(\bar{s}, \bar{s}')$, which is ensured by the fact that data- and instruction-flushing a location makes it instruction-coherent (HW Obligation 4).

5.5   Verification of a Specific Software

Table 1 summarizes the proof obligations we identified. As the countermeasures are verified, three groups of proof obligations remain for a specific software: (1) SW-I Obligation 2.1, SW-I Obligation 3, and SW-C Obligation 1: these are requirements for a secure kernel independently of caches; (2) SW-I Obligation 4 (and SW-I Obligation 8 for always-cacheability): these only constrain the configuration of the MMU; (3) SW-C Obligation 2: during the execution the kernel (i) stays in its code region, (ii) does not change or leave its virtual memory,

Table 1. List of proof obligations

Type	#	Description
HW	1	Constraints on the MMU domain
HW	2	Derivability correctly overapproximates the hardware behavior
HW	3	Conditions ensuring that the cache-aware model behaves like the cacheless one
HW	4	Sufficient conditions for preserving coherency
SW-I	1	Decomposition of the invariant
SW-I	2	Invariant prevents direct and indirect modification of the critical resources
SW-I	3	Correct definition of CR and EX
SW-I	4	Kernel virtual memory is cacheable and its code is in the executable resources
		The following obligations were proved for the selected countermeasures
SW-I	5	Correctness of the countermeasure
SW-I	6	Transfer of the invariants from the cacheless model to the cache-aware one
SW-I	7	Transfer of the countermeasure properties
SW-C	1	Kernel preserves the invariant in the cacheless model
SW-C	2	Kernel preserves the intermediate invariant in the cacheless model

(iii) preserves the countermeasure specific intermediate invariant. These must be verified for intermediate states of the kernel, e.g., by inlining assertions that guarantee (i–iii). Notice that the two code verification tasks (SW-C Obligation 1 and SW-C Obligation 2) do not require the usage of the cache-aware model, enabling the usage of existing binary analysis tools.

Case Study. As a case study, we use a hypervisor capable of hosting a Linux guest that has been formally verified previously on a cacheless model [21] and its vulnerability to cache storage channel attacks is shown in [20]. The memory subsystem is virtualized through direct paging. To create a page-table, a guest prepares it in guest memory and requests its validation. If the validation succeeds the hypervisor can use the page-table to configure the MMU, without requiring memory copy operations. The validation ensures that the page-table does not allow writable accesses of the guest outside the guest's memory or to the page-tables. Other hypercalls allow to free and modify validated page-tables.

Using mismatched cacheability attributes, a guest can potentially violate memory isolation: it prepares a valid page-table in cache and a malicious page-table in memory; if the hypervisor validates stale data from the cache, after eviction, the MMU can be made to use the malicious page-table, enabling the guest to violate memory isolation. We fix this vulnerability by using always cacheability: The guest is forced to create page-tables only inside an always cacheable region of memory.

The general concepts of Sect. 4.1 are easily instantiated for the hypervisor. Since it uses a static region of physical memory HM, the critical resources consist of HM and every memory page that is allocated to store a page-table. Additionally to the properties described in [21], the invariant requires that all page-tables are allocated in M_{ac} and all aliases to M_{ac} are cacheable. To guarantee these properties the hypervisor code has been updated: validation of a page-table checks that the page resides in M_{ac} and that all new mapping to M_{ac} are cacheable; modification of a page-table forbids uncacheable aliases to M_{ac}.

6   Implementation

The complete proof strategy has been implemented [2] and machine-checked using the HOL4 interactive theorem prover [1]. The resulting application and kernel integrity theorems are parametric in the countermeasure-dependent proof obligations. These obligations have been discharged for the selected countermeasures yielding theorems that depend only on code verification conditions and properties of the functional kernel invariant. Hardware obligations have been verified on a single-core model consisting of a generic processor and memory interface. While the processor interface has not been instantiated yet, all assumptions on the memory system have been validated for an instantiation with single-level data- and instruction-caches using a rudimentary cache implementation. Instantiation with more realistic models is ongoing. The formal analysis took three person months and consists of roughly 10000 LoC for the hardware model specification and verification of its instantiation, 2500 LoC for the integrity proof, and 2000 LoC for the countermeasure verification.

For the case study we augmented the existing hypervisor with the always cacheability countermeasure. This entailed some engineering effort to adapt the memory allocator of the Linux kernel to allocate page-tables inside M_{ac}. The adaptation required changes to 45 LoC in the hypervisor and an addition of 35 LoC in the paravirtualized Linux kernel and imposes a negligible performance overhead ($\leq 1\%$ in micro- and macro-benchmarks [20]). The HOL4 model of the hypervisor design has been modified to include the additional checks performed by the hypervisor. Similarly, we extended the invariant with the new properties guaranteed by the adopted countermeasure. The model has been used to show that the new design preserves the invariant and that all proof obligations on the invariant hold, which required 2000 HOL4 LoC. Verification of the augmented hypervisor binary is left for future work. Even if binary verification can be automated to a large extent using binary analysis tools (e.g. [11,30]), it still requires a substantial engineering effort.

7 Conclusion

Modern hardware architectures are complex and can exhibit unforeseen vulnerabilities if low level details are not properly taken into account. The cache storage channels of [20], as well as the recent Meltdown [26] and Spectre [28] attacks are examples of this problem. They shows the importance of low-level system details and the need of sound and tractable strategies to reason about them in the verification of security-critical software.

Here we presented an approach to verify integrity-preserving countermeasures in the presence of cache storage side-channels. In particular, we identified conditions that must be met by a security mechanism to neutralise the attack vector and we verified correctness of some of the existing techniques to counter both (instruction- and data-cache) integrity attacks.

The countermeasures are formally modelled as new proof obligations that can be imposed on the cacheless model to ensure the absence of vulnerability due to cache storage channels. The result of this analysis are theorems in Sect. 4.3. They demonstrate that a software satisfying a set of proof obligations (i.e., correctly implementing the countermeasure) is not vulnerable because of cache storage channels.

Our analysis is based on an abstract hardware model that should fit a number of architectures. While here we only expose two execution modes, we can support multiple modes of executions, where the most privileged is used by the kernel and all other modes are considered to be used by the application. Also our MMU model is general enough to cover other hardware-based protection mechanisms, like Memory Protection Units or TrustZone memory controllers.

While this paper exemplifies the approach for first-level caches, our methodology can be extended to accommodate more complex scenarios and other hardware features too. For instance our approach can be used to counter storage channels due to TLBs, multi-level caches, and multi-core processing.

Translation Look-aside Buffers (TLBs) can be handled similarly to instruction-caches. Non-privileged instructions are unable to directly modify the

TLB and incoherent behaviours can arise only by the assistance of kernel modifying the page-tables. Incoherent behavior can be prevented using TLB cleans or demonstrating that the page-tables are not changed.

Multi-level caches can be handled iteratively in a straightforward fashion, starting from the cacheless model and adding CPU-closer levels of cache at each iteration. Iterative refinement has three benefits: Enabling the use of existing (cache unaware) analysis tools for verification, enabling transfer of results from Sects. 5.3 and 5.4 to the more complex models, and allowing to focus on each hardware feature independently, so at least partially counteracting the pressure towards ever larger and more complex global models.

In the same way the integrity proof can be repeated for the local caches in a multi-core system. For shared caches the proof strategy needs to be adapted to take into account interleaved privileged and non-privileged steps of different cores, depending on the chosen verification methodology for concurrent code.

It is also worth noting that our verification approach works for both preemptive and non-preemptive kernels, due to the use of the intermediate invariants II and $\overline{II}$ that do not depend on intermediate states of kernel data structures.

For non-privileged transitions the key tool is the derivability relation, which is abstract enough to fit a variety of memory systems. However, derivability has the underlying assumption that only uncacheable writes can bypass the cache and break coherency. If a given hardware allows the application to break coherency through other means, e.g., non-temporal store instructions or invalidate-only cache flushes, these cases need to be added to the derivability definition.

The security analysis requires trustworthy models of hardware, which are needed to verify platform-dependent proof obligations. Some of these properties require extensive tests to demonstrate that corner cases are correctly handled by models. For example, while the conventional wisdom is that flushing caches can close side-channels, a new study [16] showed flushing does not sanitize caches thoroughly and leaves some channels active, e.g. instruction-cache attack vectors.

There are several open questions concerning side-channels due to similar shared low-level hardware features such as branch prediction units, which undermine the soundness of formal verification. This is an unsatisfactory situation since formal proofs are costly and should pay off by giving reliable guarantees. Moreover, the complexity of contemporary hardware is such that a verification approach allowing reuse of models and proofs as new hardware features are added is essential for formal verification in this space to be economically sustainable. Our results represent a first step towards giving reliable guarantees and reusable proofs in the presence of low level storage channels.

Acknowledgments. This work was supported by the PROSPER project funded by the Swedish Foundation for Strategic Research, the KTH CERCES Center for Resilient Critical Infrastructures funded by the Swedish Civil Contingencies Agency, as well as the German Federal Ministry of Education and Research (BMBF) through funding for the CISPA-Stanford Center for Cybersecurity (FKZ: 13N1S0762).

References

1. HOL4. http://hol.sourceforge.net/. Accessed 13 Feb 2018
2. HOL4 implementation of proofs of this paper. https://github.com/rauhbein/cacheproofs. Accessed 13 Feb 2018
3. seL4 Project. http://sel4.systems/. Accessed 13 Feb 2018
4. Alkassar, E., Hillebrand, M.A., Leinenbach, D., Schirmer, N., Starostin, A., Tsyban, A.: Balancing the load. J. Autom. Reason. **42**(2–4), 389–454 (2009)
5. Almeida, J.B., Barbosa, M., Barthe, G., Dupressoir, F.: Verifiable side-channel security of cryptographic implementations: constant-time MEE-CBC. In: Peyrin, T. (ed.) FSE 2016. LNCS, vol. 9783, pp. 163–184. Springer, Heidelberg (2016). https://doi.org/10.1007/978-3-662-52993-5_9
6. Balliu, M., Dam, M., Guanciale, R.: Automating information flow analysis of low level code. In: Proceedings of CCS, pp. 1080–1091 (2014)
7. Barthe, G., Betarte, G., Campo, J.D., Chimento, J.M., Luna, C.: Formally verified implementation of an idealized model of virtualization. In: Proceedings of TYPES, pp. 45–63 (2013)
8. Barthe, G., Betarte, G., Campo, J.D., Luna, C.: Formally verifying isolation and availability in an idealized model of virtualization. In: Butler, M., Schulte, W. (eds.) FM 2011. LNCS, vol. 6664, pp. 231–245. Springer, Heidelberg (2011). https://doi.org/10.1007/978-3-642-21437-0_19
9. Barthe, G. Betarte, G., Campo, J.D., Luna, C.: Cache-leakage resilient OS isolation in an idealized model of virtualization. In: Proceedings of CSF, pp. 186–197 (2012)
10. Becker, H., Crespo, J.M., Galowicz, J., Hensel, U., Hirai, Y., Kunz, C., Nakata, K., Sacchini, J.L., Tews, H., Tuerk, T.: Combining mechanized proofs and model-based testing in the formal analysis of a hypervisor. In: Fitzgerald, J., Heitmeyer, C., Gnesi, S., Philippou, A. (eds.) FM 2016. LNCS, vol. 9995, pp. 69–84. Springer, Cham (2016). https://doi.org/10.1007/978-3-319-48989-6_5
11. Brumley, D., Jager, I., Avgerinos, T., Schwartz, E.J.: BAP: a binary analysis platform. In: Gopalakrishnan, G., Qadeer, S. (eds.) CAV 2011. LNCS, vol. 6806, pp. 463–469. Springer, Heidelberg (2011). https://doi.org/10.1007/978-3-642-22110-1_37
12. Chfouka, H., Nemati, H., Guanciale, R., Dam, M., Ekdahl, P.: Trustworthy prevention of code injection in linux on embedded devices. In: Pernul, G., Ryan, P.Y.A., Weippl, E. (eds.) ESORICS 2015. LNCS, vol. 9326, pp. 90–107. Springer, Cham (2015). https://doi.org/10.1007/978-3-319-24174-6_5
13. Cock, D., Ge, Q., Murray, T., Heiser, G.: The last mile: an empirical study of some timing channels on seL4. In: Proceedings of CCS, pp. 570–581 (2014)
14. Doychev, G., Feld, D., Köpf, B., Mauborgne, L., Reineke, J.: Cacheaudit: a tool for the static analysis of cache side channels. In: Proceedings SEC, pp. 431–446 (2013)
15. Doychev, G., Köpf, B.: Rigorous analysis of software countermeasures against cache attacks. CoRR, abs/1603.02187 (2016)
16. Ge, Q., Yarom, Y., Heiser, G.: Do Hardware Cache Flushing Operations Actually Meet Our Expectations? ArXiv e-prints, December 2016
17. Gu, L., Vaynberg, A., Ford, B., Shao, Z., Costanzo, D.: CertiKOS: a certified kernel for secure cloud computing. In: Proceedings of APSys, p. 3 (2011)
18. Gu, R., Koenig, J., Ramananandro, T., Shao, Z., Wu, X.N., Weng, S.-C., Zhang, H., Guo, Y.: Deep specifications and certified abstraction layers. In: SIGPLAN Notices, vol. 50, pp. 595–608. ACM (2015)

19. Gu, R., Shao, Z., Chen, H., Wu, X., Kim, J., Sjöberg, V., Costanzo, D.: Certikos: an extensible architecture for building certified concurrent OS kernels. In: Proceedings of OSDI, pp. 653–669 (2016)

20. Guanciale, R., Nemati, H., Baumann, C., Dam, M.: Cache storage channels: alias-driven attacks and verified countermeasures. In: SP, pp. 38–55 (2016)

21. Guanciale, R., Nemati, H., Dam, M., Baumann, C.: Provably secure memory isolation for Linux on ARM. J. Comput. Secur. **24**(6), 793–837 (2016)

22. Heitmeyer, C.L., Archer, M., Leonard, E.I., McLean, J.: Formal specification and verification of data separation in a separation kernel for an embedded system. In: CCS, pp. 346–355 (2006)

23. Hillebrand, M.A., der Rieden, T.I., Paul, W.J.: Dealing with I/O devices in the context of pervasive system verification. In: Proceedings of ICCD, pp. 309–316 (2005)

24. Klein, G., Andronick, J., Elphinstone, K., Murray, T.C., Sewell, T., Kolanski, R., Heiser, G.: Comprehensive formal verification of an OS microkernel. ACM Trans. Comput. Syst. **32**(1), 2 (2014)

25. Klein, G., Elphinstone, K., Heiser, G., Andronick, J., Cock, D., Derrin, P., Elkaduwe, D., Engelhardt, K., Kolanski, R., Norrish, M., Sewell, T., Tuch, H., Winwood, S.: seL4: formal verification of an OS kernel. In: Proceedings of SOSP, pp. 207–220 (2009)

26. Kocher, P., Genkin, D., Gruss, D., Haas, W., Hamburg, M., Lipp, M., Mangard, S., Prescher, T., Schwarz, M., Yarom, Y.: Spectre attacks: exploiting speculative execution. ArXiv e-prints, January 2018

27. Köpf, B., Mauborgne, L., Ochoa, M.: Automatic quantification of cache side-channels. In: Madhusudan, P., Seshia, S.A. (eds.) CAV 2012. LNCS, vol. 7358, pp. 564–580. Springer, Heidelberg (2012). https://doi.org/10.1007/978-3-642-31424-7_40

28. Lipp, M., Schwarz, M., Gruss, D., Prescher, T., Haas, W., Mangard, S., Kocher, P., Genkin, D., Yarom, Y., Hamburg, M.: Meltdown. ArXiv e-prints, January 2018

29. Morrisett, G., Tan, G., Tassarotti, J., Tristan, J.-B., Gan, E.: RockSalt: better, faster, stronger SFI for the x86. In: ACM SIGPLAN Notices, vol. 47, pp. 395–404 (2012)

30. Sewell, T.A.L., Myreen, M.O., Klein, G.: Translation validation for a verified OS kernel. In: Proceedings of PLDI, pp. 471–482 (2013)

31. Song, D., Brumley, D., Yin, H., Caballero, J., Jager, I., Kang, M.G., Liang, Z., Newsome, J., Poosankam, P., Saxena, P.: BitBlaze: a new approach to computer security via binary analysis. In: Sekar, R., Pujari, A.K. (eds.) ICISS 2008. LNCS, vol. 5352, pp. 1–25. Springer, Heidelberg (2008). https://doi.org/10.1007/978-3-540-89862-7_1

32. Stefan, D., Buiras, P., Yang, E.Z., Levy, A., Terei, D., Russo, A., Mazières, D.: Eliminating cache-based timing attacks with instruction-based scheduling. In: Crampton, J., Jajodia, S., Mayes, K. (eds.) ESORICS 2013. LNCS, vol. 8134, pp. 718–735. Springer, Heidelberg (2013). https://doi.org/10.1007/978-3-642-40203-6_40

33. Steinberg, U., Kauer, B.: NOVA: a microhypervisor-based secure virtualization architecture. In: Proceedings of EuroSys, pp. 209–222 (2010)

34. Tews, H., Völp, M., Weber, T.: Formal memory models for the verification of low-level operating-system code. J. Autom. Reason. **42**(2–4), 189–227 (2009)

35. Tiwari, M., Oberg, J.K., Li, X., Valamehr, J., Levin, T., Hardekopf, B., Kastner, R., Chong, F.T., Sherwood, T.: Crafting a usable microkernel, processor, and I/O system with strict and provable information flow security. In: Proceedings of ISCA, pp. 189–200 (2011)
36. Weiß, M., Heinz, B., Stumpf, F.: A cache timing attack on AES in virtualization environments. In: Keromytis, A.D. (ed.) FC 2012. LNCS, vol. 7397, pp. 314–328. Springer, Heidelberg (2012). https://doi.org/10.1007/978-3-642-32946-3_23
37. Wilding, M.M., Greve, D.A., Richards, R.J., Hardin, D.S.: Formal verification of partition management for the AAMP7G microprocessor. In: Hardin, D. (ed.) Design and Verification of Microprocessor Systems for High-Assurance Applications, pp. 175–191. Springer, Boston (2010). https://doi.org/10.1007/978-1-4419-1539-9_6
38. Zhao, L., Li, G., De Sutter, B., Regehr, J.: ARMor: fully verified software fault isolation. In: EMSOFT, pp. 289–298 (2011)

Leakage and Protocol Composition in a Game-Theoretic Perspective

Mário S. Alvim[1], Konstantinos Chatzikokolakis[2],

Yusuke Kawamoto[3]([✉]), and Catuscia Palamidessi[4]

[1] Universidade Federal de Minas Gerais, Belo Horizonte, Brazil
[2] CNRS and École Polytechnique, Palaiseau, France
[3] AIST, Tsukuba, Japan
yusuke.kawamoto.aist@gmail.com
[4] INRIA and École Polytechnique, Palaiseau, France

Abstract. In the inference attacks studied in Quantitative Information Flow (QIF), the adversary typically tries to interfere with the system in the attempt to increase its leakage of secret information. The defender, on the other hand, typically tries to decrease leakage by introducing some controlled noise. This noise introduction can be modeled as a type of protocol composition, i.e., a probabilistic choice among different protocols, and its effect on the amount of leakage depends heavily on whether or not this choice is visible to the adversary. In this work we consider operators for modeling visible and invisible choice in protocol composition, and we study their algebraic properties. We then formalize the interplay between defender and adversary in a game-theoretic framework adapted to the specific issues of QIF, where the payoff is information leakage. We consider various kinds of leakage games, depending on whether players act simultaneously or sequentially, and on whether or not the choices of the defender are visible to the adversary. Finally, we establish a hierarchy of these games in terms of their information leakage, and provide methods for finding optimal strategies (at the points of equilibrium) for both attacker and defender in the various cases.

1 Introduction

A fundamental problem in computer security is the leakage of sensitive information due to *correlation* of secret values with *observables*—i.e., any information accessible to the attacker, such as, for instance, the system's outputs or execution time. The typical defense consists in reducing this correlation, which can be done in, essentially, two ways. The first, applicable when the correspondence secret-observable is deterministic, consists in coarsening the equivalence classes of secrets that give rise to the same observables. This can be achieved with post-processing, i.e., sequentially composing the original system with a program that removes information from observables. For example, a typical attack on encrypted web traffic consists on the analysis of the packets' length, and a typical defense consists in padding extra bits so to diminish the length variety [28].

© The Author(s) 2018
L. Bauer and R. Küsters (Eds.): POST 2018, LNCS 10804, pp. 134–159, 2018.
https://doi.org/10.1007/978-3-319-89722-6_6

The second kind of defense, on which we focus in this work, consists in adding controlled noise to the observables produced by the system. This can be usually seen as a composition of different protocols via probabilistic choice.

Example 1 (Differential privacy). Consider a counting query f, namely a function that, applied to a dataset x, returns the number of individuals in x that satisfy a given property. A way to implement differential privacy [12] is to add geometrical noise to the result of f, so to obtain a probability distribution P on integers of the form $P(z) = c\,e^{|z-f(x)|}$, where c is a normalization factor. The resulting mechanism can be interpreted as a probabilistic choice on protocols of the form $f(x), f(x)+1, f(x)+2, \ldots, f(x)-1, f(x)-2, \ldots$, where the probability assigned to $f(x) + n$ and to $f(x) - n$ decreases exponentially with n.

Example 2 (Dining cryptographers). Consider two agents running the dining cryptographers protocol [11], which consists in tossing a fair binary coin and then declaring the exclusive or $\oplus$ of their secret value x and the result of the coin. The protocol can be thought as the fair probabilistic choice of two protocols, one consisting simply of declaring x, and the other declaring $x \oplus 1$.

Most of the work in the literature of quantitative information flow (QIF) considers passive attacks, in which the adversary only observes the system. Notable exceptions are the works [4,8,21], which consider attackers who interact with and influence the system, possibly in an adaptive way, with the purpose of maximizing the leakage of information.

Example 3 (CRIME attack). Compression Ratio Info-leak Made Easy (CRIME) [25] is a security exploit against secret web cookies over connections using the HTTPS and SPDY protocols and data compression. The idea is that the attacker can inject some content a in the communication of the secret x from the target site to the server. The server then compresses and encrypts the data, including both a and x, and sends back the result. By observing the length of the result, the attacker can then infer information about x. To mitigate the leakage, one possible defense would consist in transmitting, along with x, also an encryption method f selected randomly from a set F. Again, the resulting protocol can be seen as a composition, using probabilistic choice, of the protocols in the set F.

In all examples above the main use of the probabilistic choice is to obfuscate the relation between secrets and observables, thus reducing their correlation— and, hence, the information leakage. To achieve this goal, it is essential that the attacker never comes to know the result of the choice. In the CRIME example, however, if f and a are chosen independently, then (in general) it is still better to choose f probabilistically, even if the adversary will come to know, afterwards, the choice of f. In fact, this is true also for the attacker: his best strategies (in general) are to chose a according to some probability distribution. Indeed, suppose that $F = \{f_1, f_2\}$ are the defender's choices and $A = \{a_1, a_2\}$ are the attacker's, and that $f_1(\cdot, a_1)$ leaks more than $f_1(\cdot, a_2)$, while $f_2(\cdot, a_1)$ leaks less than $f_2(\cdot, a_2)$. This is a scenario like *the matching pennies* in game theory: if one player selects an action deterministically, the other player may exploit this choice and get an advantage. For each player the optimal strategy is to play probabilistically, using a distribution that maximizes his own gain for all possible actions of the adversary. In zero-sum games, in which the gain of one player coincides with the loss of the other, the optimal pair of distributions always exists, and it is called *saddle point*. It also coincides with the *Nash equilibrium*, which is defined as the point in which neither of the two players gets any advantage in changing unilaterally his strategy.

Motivated by these examples, this paper investigates the two kinds of choice, visible and hidden (to the attacker), in a game-theoretic setting. Looking at them as language operators, we study their algebraic properties, which will help reason about their behavior in games. We consider zero-sum games, in which the gain (for the attacker) is represented by the leakage. While for visible choice it is appropriate to use the "classic" game-theoretic framework, for hidden choice we need to adopt the more general framework of the *information leakage games* proposed in [4]. This happens because, in contrast with standard game theory, in games with hidden choice the utility of a mixed strategy is a convex function of the distribution on the defender's pure actions, rather than simply the expected value of their utilities. We will consider both simultaneous games—in which each player chooses independently—and sequential games—in which one player chooses his action first. We aim at comparing all these situations, and at identifying the precise advantage of the hidden choice over the visible one.

To measure leakage we use the well-known information-theoretic model. A central notion in this model is that of *entropy*, but here we use its converse, *vulnerability*, which represents the magnitude of the threat. In order to derive results as general as possible, we adopt the very comprehensive notion of vulnerability as any convex and continuous function, as used in [5,8]. This notion has been shown [5] to subsume most information measures, including *Bayes vulnerability* (aka minvulnerability, aka (the converse of) Bayes risk) [10,27], *Shannon entropy* [26], *guessing entropy* [22], and *g-vulnerability* [6].

The main contributions of this paper are:

- We present a general framework for reasoning about information leakage in a game-theoretic setting, extending the notion of information leakage games proposed in [4] to both simultaneous and sequential games, with either hidden or visible choice.
- We present a rigorous compositional way, using visible and hidden choice operators, for representing adversary and defender's actions in information leakage games. In particular, we study the algebraic properties of visible and hidden choice on channels, and compare the two kinds of choice with respect to the capability of reducing leakage, in presence of an adaptive attacker.
- We provide a taxonomy of the various scenarios (simultaneous and sequential) showing when randomization is necessary, for either attacker or defender, to achieve optimality. Although it is well-known in information flow that the defender's best strategy is usually randomized, only recently it has been

shown that when defender and adversary act simultaneously, the adversary's optimal strategy also requires randomization [4].

– We use our framework in a detailed case study of a password-checking protocol. The naive program, which checks the password bit by bit and stops when it finds a mismatch, is clearly very insecure, because it reveals at each attempt the maximum correct prefix. On the other hand, if we continue checking until the end of the string (time padding), the program becomes very inefficient. We show that, by using probabilistic choice instead, we can obtain a good trade-off between security and efficiency.

Plan of the Paper. The remaining of the paper is organized as follows. In Sect. 2 we review some basic notions of game theory and quantitative information flow. In Sect. 3 we introduce our running example. In Sect. 4 we define the visible and hidden choice operators and demonstrate their algebraic properties. In Sect. 5, the core of the paper, we examine various scenarios for leakage games. In Sect. 6 we show an application of our framework to a password checker. In Sect. 7 we discuss related work and, finally, in Sect. 8 we conclude.

2   Preliminaries

In this section we review some basic notions from game theory and quantitative information flow. We use the following notation: Given a set $\mathcal{I}$, we denote by $\mathbb{D}\mathcal{I}$ the *set of all probability distributions* over $\mathcal{I}$. Given $\mu \in \mathbb{D}\mathcal{I}$, its *support* $\mathsf{supp}(\mu) \stackrel{\text{def}}{=} \{i \in \mathcal{I} : \mu(i) > 0\}$ is the set of its elements with positive probability. We use $i \leftarrow \mu$ to indicate that a value $i \in \mathcal{I}$ is sampled from a distribution μ on $\mathcal{I}$.

2.1   Basic Concepts from Game Theory

Two-Player Games. *Two-player games* are a model for reasoning about the behavior of two players. In a game, each player has at its disposal a set of *actions* that he can perform, and he obtains some gain or loss depending on the actions chosen by both players. Gains and losses are defined using a real-valued *payoff function*. Each player is assumed to be *rational*, i.e., his choice is driven by the attempt to maximize his own expected payoff. We also assume that the set of possible actions and the payoff functions of both players are *common knowledge*.

In this paper we only consider *finite games*, in which the set of actions available to the players are finite. Next we introduce an important distinction between *simultaneous* and *sequential* games. In the following, we will call the two players *defender* and *attacker*.

Simultaneous Games. In a simultaneous game, each player chooses his action without knowing the action chosen by the other. The term "simultaneous" here does not mean that the players' actions are chosen at the same time, but only

that they are chosen independently. Formally, such a game is defined as a tuple[1]
$(\mathcal{D}, \mathcal{A}, u_{\mathsf{d}}, u_{\mathsf{a}})$, where $\mathcal{D}$ is a nonempty set of *defender's actions*, $\mathcal{A}$ is a nonempty
set of *attacker's actions*, $u_{\mathsf{d}} : \mathcal{D} \times \mathcal{A} \to \mathbb{R}$ is the *defender's payoff function*, and
$u_{\mathsf{a}} : \mathcal{D} \times \mathcal{A} \to \mathbb{R}$ is the *attacker's payoff function*.

Each player may choose an action deterministically or probabilistically. A
pure strategy of the defender (resp. attacker) is a deterministic choice of an
action, i.e., an element $d \in \mathcal{D}$ (resp. $a \in \mathcal{A}$). A pair (d, a) is called *pure strategy
profile*, and $u_{\mathsf{d}}(d, a)$, $u_{\mathsf{a}}(d, a)$ represent the defender's and the attacker's payoffs,
respectively. A *mixed strategy* of the defender (resp. attacker) is a probabilis-
tic choice of an action, defined as a probability distribution $\delta \in \mathbb{D}\mathcal{D}$ (resp.
$\alpha \in \mathbb{D}\mathcal{A}$). A pair (δ, α) is called *mixed strategy profile*. The defender's and
the attacker's *expected payoff functions* for mixed strategies are defined, respec-
tively, as: $U_{\mathsf{d}}(\delta, \alpha) \stackrel{\text{def}}{=} \mathbb{E}_{\substack{d \leftarrow \delta \\ a \leftarrow \alpha}} u_{\mathsf{d}}(d, a) = \sum_{\substack{d \in \mathcal{D} \\ a \in \mathcal{A}}} \delta(d)\alpha(a)u_{\mathsf{d}}(d, a)$ and $U_{\mathsf{a}}(\delta, \alpha) \stackrel{\text{def}}{=}$
$\mathbb{E}_{\substack{d \leftarrow \delta \\ a \leftarrow \alpha}} u_{\mathsf{a}}(d, a) = \sum_{\substack{d \in \mathcal{D} \\ a \in \mathcal{A}}} \delta(d)\alpha(a)u_{\mathsf{a}}(d, a)$.

A defender's mixed strategy $\delta \in \mathbb{D}\mathcal{D}$ is a *best response* to an attacker's mixed
strategy $\alpha \in \mathbb{D}\mathcal{A}$ if $U_{\mathsf{d}}(\delta, \alpha) = \max_{\delta' \in \mathbb{D}\mathcal{D}} U_{\mathsf{d}}(\delta', \alpha)$. Symmetrically, $\alpha \in \mathbb{D}\mathcal{A}$ is
a *best response* to $\delta \in \mathbb{D}\mathcal{D}$ if $U_{\mathsf{a}}(\delta, \alpha) = \max_{\alpha' \in \mathbb{D}\mathcal{A}} U_{\mathsf{d}}(\delta, \alpha')$. A *mixed-strategy
Nash equilibrium* is a profile (δ^*, α^*) such that δ^* is the best response to α^*
and vice versa. This means that in a Nash equilibrium, no unilateral deviation
by any single player provides better payoff to that player. If δ^* and α^* are
point distributions concentrated on some $d^* \in \mathcal{D}$ and $a^* \in \mathcal{A}$ respectively, then
(δ^*, α^*) is a *pure-strategy Nash equilibrium*, and will be denoted by (d^*, a^*).
While not all games have a pure strategy Nash equilibrium, every finite game
has a mixed strategy Nash equilibrium.

Sequential Games. In a sequential game players may take turns in choosing
their actions. In this paper, we only consider the case in which each player moves
only once, in such a way that one of the players (*the leader*) chooses his action
first, and commits to it, before the other player (*the follower*) makes his choice.
The follower may have total knowledge of the choice made by the leader, or
only partial. We refer to the two scenarios by the terms *perfect* and *imperfect
information*, respectively.

We now give the precise definitions assuming that the leader is the defender.
The case in which the leader is the attacker is similar.

A *defender-first sequential game with perfect information* is a tuple
$(\mathcal{D}, \mathcal{D} \to \mathcal{A}, u_{\mathsf{d}}, u_{\mathsf{a}})$ where $\mathcal{D}, \mathcal{A}, u_{\mathsf{d}}$ and u_{a} are defined as in simultaneous games.
Also the strategies of the defender (the leader) are defined as in simultane-
ous games: an action $d \in \mathcal{D}$ for the pure case, and a distribution $\delta \in \mathbb{D}\mathcal{D}$ for
the mixed one. On the other hand, a pure strategy for the attacker is a func-
tion $s_{\mathsf{a}} : \mathcal{D} \to \mathcal{A}$, which represents the fact that his choice of an action s_{a} in $\mathcal{A}$
depends on the defender's choice d. An attacker's mixed strategy is a probability

---

[1] Following the convention of *security games*, we set the first player to be the defender.

distribution $\sigma_a \in \mathbb{D}(\mathcal{D} \to \mathcal{A})$ over his pure strategies.[2] The defender's and the attacker's *expected payoff functions* for mixed strategies are defined, respectively, as $U_d(\delta, \sigma_a) \stackrel{\text{def}}{=} \mathbb{E}_{\substack{d \leftarrow \delta \\ s_a \leftarrow \sigma_a}} u_d(d, s_a(d)) = \sum_{\substack{d \in \mathcal{D} \\ s_a : \mathcal{D} \to \mathcal{A}}} \delta(d)\sigma_a(s_a)u_d(d, s_a(d))$ and

$U_a(\delta, \sigma_a) \stackrel{\text{def}}{=} \mathbb{E}_{\substack{d \leftarrow \delta \\ s_a \leftarrow \sigma_a}} u_a(d, s_a(d)) = \sum_{\substack{d \in \mathcal{D} \\ s_a : \mathcal{D} \to \mathcal{A}}} \delta(d)\sigma_a(s_a)u_a(d, s_a(d))$.

The case of imperfect information is typically formalized by assuming an *indistinguishability (equivalence) relation* over the actions chosen by the leader, representing a scenario in which the follower cannot distinguish between the actions belonging to the same equivalence class. The pure strategies of the followers, therefore, are functions from the set of the equivalence classes on the actions of the leader to his own actions. Formally, a *defender-first sequential game with imperfect information* is a tuple $(\mathcal{D}, K_a \to \mathcal{A}, u_d, u_a)$ where $\mathcal{D}, \mathcal{A}, u_d$ and u_a are defined as in simultaneous games, and K_a is a partition of $\mathcal{D}$. The *expected payoff functions* are defined as before, except that now the argument of s_a is the equivalence class of d. Note that in the case in which all defender's actions are indistinguishable from each other at the eyes of the attacker (*totally imperfect information*), we have $K_a = \{\mathcal{D}\}$ and the expected payoff functions coincide with those of the simultaneous games.

Zero-sum Games and Minimax Theorem. A game $(\mathcal{D}, \mathcal{A}, u_d, u_a)$ is *zero-sum* if for any $d \in \mathcal{D}$ and any $a \in \mathcal{A}$, the defender's loss is equivalent to the attacker's gain, i.e., $u_d(d, a) = -u_a(d, a)$. For brevity, in zero-sum games we denote by u the attacker's payoff function u_a, and by U the attacker's expected payoff U_a.[3] Consequently, the goal of the defender is to minimize U, and the goal of the attacker is to maximize it.

In simultaneous zero-sum games the Nash equilibrium corresponds to the solution of the *minimax* problem (or equivalently, the *maximin* problem), namely, the strategy profile (δ^*, α^*) such that $U(\delta^*, \alpha^*) = \min_\delta \max_\alpha U(\delta, \alpha)$. The von Neumann's minimax theorem, in fact, ensures that such solution (which always exists) is stable.

Theorem 1 (von Neumann's minimax theorem). *Let $\mathcal{X} \subset \mathbb{R}^m$ and $\mathcal{Y} \subset \mathbb{R}^n$ be compact convex sets, and $U : \mathcal{X} \times \mathcal{Y} \to \mathbb{R}$ be a continuous function such that $U(x, y)$ is a convex function in $x \in \mathcal{X}$ and a concave function in $y \in \mathcal{Y}$. Then $\min_{x \in \mathcal{X}} \max_{y \in \mathcal{Y}} U(x, y) = \max_{y \in \mathcal{Y}} \min_{x \in \mathcal{X}} U(x, y)$.*

---

[2] The definition of the mixed strategies as $\mathbb{D}(\mathcal{D} \to \mathcal{A})$ means that the attacker draws a function $s_a : \mathcal{D} \to \mathcal{A}$ *before* he knows the choice of the defender. In contrast, the so-called *behavioral strategies* are defined as functions $\mathcal{D} \to \mathbb{D}\mathcal{A}$, and formalize the idea that the draw is made after the attacker knows such choice. In our setting, these two definitions are equivalent, in the sense that they yield the same payoff.

[3] Conventionally in game theory the payoff u is set to be that of the first player, but we prefer to look at the payoff from the point of view of the attacker to be in line with the definition of payoff as vulnerability.

A related property is that, under the conditions of Theorem 1, there exists a *saddle point* (x^*, y^*) s.t., for all $x \in \mathcal{X}$ and $y \in \mathcal{Y}$: $U(x^*, y) \leq U(x^*, y^*) \leq U(x, y^*)$.

The solution of the minimax problem can be obtained by using convex optimization techniques. In case $U(x, y)$ is affine in x and in y, we can also use linear optimization.

In case $\mathcal{D}$ and $\mathcal{A}$ contain two elements each, there is a closed form for the solution. Let $\mathcal{D} = \{d_0, d_1\}$ and $\mathcal{A} = \{a_0, a_1\}$ respectively. Let u_{ij} be the utility of the defender on d_i, a_j. Then the Nash equilibrium (δ^*, α^*) is given by: $\delta^*(d_0) = {(u_{11}-u_{10})}/{(u_{00}-u_{01}-u_{10}+u_{11})}$ and $\alpha^*(a_0) = {(u_{11}-u_{01})}/{(u_{00}-u_{01}-u_{10}+u_{11})}$ if these values are in $[0, 1]$. Note that, since there are only two elements, the strategy δ^* is completely specified by its value in d_0, and analogously for α^*.

2.2 Quantitative Information Flow

Finally, we briefly review the standard framework of quantitative information flow, which is concerned with measuring the amount of information leakage in a (computational) system.

Secrets and Vulnerability. A *secret* is some piece of sensitive information the defender wants to protect, such as a user's password, social security number, or current location. The attacker usually only has some partial knowledge about the value of a secret, represented as a probability distribution on secrets called a *prior*. We denote by $\mathcal{X}$ the set of possible secrets, and we typically use π to denote a prior belonging to the set $\mathbb{D}\mathcal{X}$ of probability distributions over $\mathcal{X}$.

The *vulnerability* of a secret is a measure of the utility that it represents for the attacker. In this paper we consider a very general notion of vulnerability, following [5], and we define a vulnerability $\mathbb{V}$ to be any continuous and convex function of type $\mathbb{D}\mathcal{X} \rightarrow \mathbb{R}$. It has been shown in [5] that these functions coincide with the set of g-vulnerabilities, and are, in a precise sense, the most general information measures w.r.t. a set of basic axioms.[4]

Channels, Posterior Vulnerability, and Leakage. Computational systems can be modeled as information theoretic channels. A *channel* $C : \mathcal{X} \times \mathcal{Y} \rightarrow \mathbb{R}$ is a function in which $\mathcal{X}$ is a set of *input values*, $\mathcal{Y}$ is a set of *output values*, and $C(x, y)$ represents the conditional probability of the channel producing output $y \in \mathcal{Y}$ when input $x \in \mathcal{X}$ is provided. Every channel C satisfies $0 \leq C(x, y) \leq 1$ for all $x \in \mathcal{X}$ and $y \in \mathcal{Y}$, and $\sum_{y \in \mathcal{Y}} C(x, y) = 1$ for all $x \in \mathcal{X}$.

A distribution $\pi \in \mathbb{D}\mathcal{X}$ and a channel C with inputs $\mathcal{X}$ and outputs $\mathcal{Y}$ induce a joint distribution $p(x, y) = \pi(x)C(x, y)$ on $\mathcal{X} \times \mathcal{Y}$, producing joint random variables X, Y with marginal probabilities $p(x) = \sum_y p(x, y)$ and $p(y) = \sum_x p(x, y)$,

---

[4] More precisely, if posterior vulnerability is defined as the expectation of the vulnerability of posterior distributions, the measure respects the data-processing inequality and always yields non-negative leakage iff vulnerability is convex.

and conditional probabilities $p(x|y) = p(x,y)/p(y)$ if $p(y) \neq 0$. For a given y (s.t. $p(y) \neq 0$), the conditional probabilities $p(x|y)$ for each $x \in \mathcal{X}$ form the *posterior distribution* $p_{X|y}$.

A channel C in which $\mathcal{X}$ is a set of secret values and $\mathcal{Y}$ is a set of observable values produced by a system can be used to model computations on secrets. Assuming the attacker has prior knowledge π about the secret value, knows how a channel C works, and can observe the channel's outputs, the effect of the channel is to update the attacker's knowledge from π to a collection of posteriors $p_{X|y}$, each occurring with probability $p(y)$.

Given a vulnerability $\mathbb{V}$, a prior π, and a channel C, the *posterior vulnerability* $\mathbb{V}[\pi, C]$ is the vulnerability of the secret after the attacker has observed the output of the channel C. Formally: $\mathbb{V}[\pi, C] \stackrel{\text{def}}{=} \sum_{y \in \mathcal{Y}} p(y) \mathbb{V}[p_{X|y}]$.

It is known from the literature [5] that the posterior vulnerability is a convex function of π. Namely, for any channel C, any family of distributions $\{\pi_i\}$, and any set of convex coefficients $\{c_i\}$, we have: $\mathbb{V}\left[\sum_i c_i \pi_i, C\right] \leq \sum_i c_i \mathbb{V}[\pi_i, C]$.

The *(information) leakage* of channel C under prior π is a comparison between the vulnerability of the secret before the system was run—called *prior vulnerability*—and the posterior vulnerability of the secret. Leakage reflects by how much the observation of the system's outputs increases the attacker's information about the secret. It can be defined either *additively* ($\mathbb{V}[\pi, C] - \mathbb{V}[\pi]$), or *multiplicatively* ($\mathbb{V}[\pi,C]/\mathbb{V}[\pi]$).

3 An Illustrative Example

We introduce an example which will serve as running example through the paper. Although admittedly contrived, this example is simple and yet produces different leakage measures for all different combinations of visible/invisible choice and simultaneous/sequential games, thus providing a way to compare all different scenarios we are interested in.

Consider that a binary secret must be processed by a program. As usual, a defender wants to protect the secret value, whereas an attacker wants to infer it by observing the system's output. Assume the defender can choose which among two alternative versions of the program to run. Both programs take the secret value x as high input, and a binary low input a whose value is chosen by the attacker. They both return the output in a low variable y.[5] Program 0 returns the binary product of x and a, whereas Program 1 flips a coin with bias $a/3$ (i.e., a coin which returns heads

Program 0

High Input: $x \in \{0, 1\}$
Low Input: $a \in \{0, 1\}$
Output: $y \in \{0, 1\}$
$y = x \cdot a$
return y

Program 1

High Input: $x \in \{0, 1\}$
Low Input: $a \in \{0, 1\}$
Output: $y \in \{0, 1\}$
$c \leftarrow$ flip coin with bias $a/3$
if $c = heads$ $\{y = x\}$
else $\{y = \bar{x}\}$
return y

Fig. 1. Running example.

---

[5] We adopt the usual convention in QIF of referring to secret variables, inputs and outputs in programs as *high*, and to their observable counterparts as *low*.

with probability $a/3$) and returns x if the result is heads, and the complement $\bar{x}$ of x otherwise. The two programs are represented in Fig. 1.

The combined choices of the defender's and of the attacker's determine how the system behaves. Let $\mathcal{D} = \{0,1\}$ represent the set of the defender's choices— i.e., the index of the program to use—, and $\mathcal{A} = \{0,1\}$ represent the set of the attacker's choices—i.e., the value of the low input a. We shall refer to the elements of $\mathcal{D}$ and $\mathcal{A}$ as *actions*. For each possible combination of actions $d \in \mathcal{D}$ and $a \in \mathcal{A}$, we can construct a channel C_{da} modeling how the resulting system behaves. Each channel C_{da} is a function of type $\mathcal{X} \times \mathcal{Y} \to \mathbb{R}$, where $\mathcal{X} = \{0,1\}$ is the set of possible high input values for the system, and $\mathcal{Y} = \{0,1\}$ is the set of possible output values from the system. Intuitively, each channel provides the probability that the system (which was fixed by the defender) produces output $y \in \mathcal{Y}$ given that the high input is $x \in \mathcal{X}$ (and that the low input was fixed by the attacker). The four possible channels are depicted as matrices below.

C_{00}	$y = 0$	$y = 1$
$x = 0$	1	0
$x = 1$	1	0

C_{01}	$y = 0$	$y = 1$
$x = 0$	1	0
$x = 1$	0	1

C_{10}	$y = 0$	$y = 1$
$x = 0$	0	1
$x = 1$	1	0

C_{11}	$y = 0$	$y = 1$
$x = 0$	$1/3$	$2/3$
$x = 1$	$2/3$	$1/3$

Note that channel C_{00} does not leak any information about the input x (i.e., it is *non-interferent*), whereas channels C_{01} and C_{10} completely reveal x. Channel C_{11} is an intermediate case: it leaks some information about x, but not all.

We want to investigate how the defender's and the attacker's choices influence the leakage of the system. For that we can just consider the (simpler) notion of posterior vulnerability, since in order to make the comparison fair we need to assume that the prior is always the same in the various scenarios, and this implies that the leakage is in a one-to-one correspondence with the posterior vulnerability (this happens for both additive and multiplicative leakage).

For this example, assume we are interested in Bayes vulnerability [10,27], defined as $\mathbb{V}(\pi) = \max_x \pi(x)$ for every $\pi \in \mathbb{D}\mathcal{X}$. Assume for simplicity that the prior is the uniform prior π_u. In this case we know from [9] that the posterior Bayes vulnerability of a channel is the sum of the greatest elements

Table 1. Vulnerability of each channel C_{da} in the running example.

$\mathbb{V}$	$a = 0$	$a = 1$
$d = 0$	$1/2$	1
$d = 1$	1	$2/3$

of each column, divided by the total number of inputs. Table 1 provides the Bayes vulnerability $\mathbb{V}_{da} \overset{\text{def}}{=} \mathbb{V}[\pi_u, C_{da}]$ of each channel considered above.

Naturally, the attacker aims at maximizing the vulnerability of the system, while the defender tries to minimize it. The resulting vulnerability will depend on various factors, in particular on whether the two players make their choice *simultaneously* (i.e. without knowing the choice of the opponent) or *sequentially*. Clearly, if the choice of a player who moves first is known by an opponent who moves second, the opponent will be in advantage. In the above example, for instance, if the defender knows the choice a of the attacker, the most convenient choice for him is to set $d = a$, and the vulnerability will be at most $2/3$. Vice versa, if the attacker knows the choice d of the defender, the most convenient choice for him is to set $a \neq d$. The vulnerability in this case will be 1.

Things become more complicated when players make choices simultaneously. None of the pure choices of d and a are the best for the corresponding player, because the vulnerability of the system depends also on the (unknown) choice of the other player. Yet there is a strategy leading to the best possible situation for both players (the *Nash equilibrium*), but it is mixed (i.e., probabilistic), in that the players randomize their choices according to some precise distribution.

Another factor that affects vulnerability is whether or not the defender's choice is known to the attacker at the moment in which he observes the output of the channel. Obviously, this corresponds to whether or not the attacker knows what channel he is observing. Both cases are plausible: naturally the defender has all the interest in keeping his choice (and, hence, the channel used) secret, since then the attack will be less effective (i.e., leakage will be smaller). On the other hand, the attacker may be able to identify the channel used anyway, for instance because the two programs have different running times. We will call these two cases *hidden* and *visible* choice, respectively.

It is possible to model players' strategies, as well as hidden and visible choices, as operations on channels. This means that we can look at the whole system as if it were a single channel, which will turn out to be useful for some proofs of our technical results. Next section is dedicated to the definition of these operators. We will calculate the exact values for our example in Sect. 5.

4   Visible and Hidden Choice Operators on Channels

In this section we define matrices and some basic operations on them. Since channels are a particular kind of matrix, we use these matrix operations to define the operations of visible and hidden choice among channels, and to prove important properties of these channel operations.

4.1   Matrices, and Their Basic Operators

Given two sets $\mathcal{X}$ and $\mathcal{Y}$, a *matrix* is a total function of type $\mathcal{X} \times \mathcal{Y} \to \mathbb{R}$. Two matrices $M_1 : \mathcal{X}_1 \times \mathcal{Y}_1 \to \mathbb{R}$ and $M_2 : \mathcal{X}_2 \times \mathcal{Y}_2 \to \mathbb{R}$ are said to be *compatible* if $\mathcal{X}_1 = \mathcal{X}_2$. If it is also the case that $\mathcal{Y}_1 = \mathcal{Y}_2$, we say that the matrices *have the same type*. The *scalar multiplication* $r \cdot M$ between a scalar r and a matrix M is defined as usual, and so is the *summation* $\left(\sum_{i \in \mathcal{I}} M_i\right)(x, y) = M_{i_1}(x, y) + \ldots + M_{i_n}(x, y)$ of a family $\{M_i\}_{i \in \mathcal{I}}$ of matrices all of a same type.

Given a family $\{M_i\}_{i \in \mathcal{I}}$ of compatible matrices s.t. each M_i has type $\mathcal{X} \times \mathcal{Y}_i \to \mathbb{R}$, their *concatenation* $\Diamond_{i \in \mathcal{I}}$ is the matrix having all columns of every matrix in the family, in such a way that every column is tagged with the matrix it came from. Formally, $\left(\Diamond_{i \in \mathcal{I}} M_i\right)(x, (y, j)) = M_j(x, y)$, if $y \in \mathcal{Y}_j$, and the resulting matrix has type $\mathcal{X} \times (\bigsqcup_{i \in \mathcal{I}} \mathcal{Y}_i) \to \mathbb{R}.$[6] When the family $\{M_i\}$ has only two elements we may use the *binary* version $\diamond$ of the concatenation operator. The following depicts the concatenation of two matrices M_1 and M_2 in tabular form.

M_1	y_1	y_2
x_1	1	2
x_2	3	4

$\diamond$

M_2	y_1	y_2	y_3
x_1	5	6	7
x_2	8	9	10

$=$

$M_1 \diamond M_2$	$(y_1, 1)$	$(y_2, 1)$	$(y_1, 2)$	$(y_2, 2)$	$(y_3, 2)$
x_1	1	2	5	6	7
x_2	3	4	8	9	10

4.2   Channels, and Their Hidden and Visible Choice Operators

A channel is a *stochastic* matrix, i.e., all elements are non-negative, and all rows sum up to 1. Here we will define two operators specific for channels. In the following, for any real value $0 \le p \le 1$, we denote by $\bar{p}$ the value $1 - p$.

Hidden Choice. The first operator models a hidden probabilistic choice among channels. Consider a family $\{C_i\}_{i \in \mathcal{I}}$ of channels of a same type. Let $\mu \in \mathbb{D}\mathcal{I}$ be a probability distribution on the elements of the index set $\mathcal{I}$. Consider an input x is fed to one of the channels in $\{C_i\}_{i \in \mathcal{I}}$, where the channel is randomly picked according to μ. More precisely, an index $i \in \mathcal{I}$ is sampled with probability $\mu(i)$, then the input x is fed to channel C_i, and the output y produced by the channel is then made visible, but not the index i of the channel that was used. Note that we consider hidden choice only among channels of a same type: if the sets of outputs were not identical, the produced output might implicitly reveal which channel was used.

Formally, given a family $\{C_i\}_{i \in \mathcal{I}}$ of channels s.t. each C_i has same type $\mathcal{X} \times \mathcal{Y} \to \mathbb{R}$, the *hidden choice operator* $\sum_{i \leftarrow \mu}$ is defined as $\sum_{i \leftarrow \mu} C_i = \sum_{i \in \mathcal{I}} \mu(i) C_i$.

Proposition 2. *Given a family* $\{C_i\}_{i \in \mathcal{I}}$ *of channels of type* $\mathcal{X} \times \mathcal{Y} \to \mathbb{R}$, *and a distribution* μ *on* $\mathcal{I}$, *the hidden choice* $\sum_{i \leftarrow \mu} C_i$ *is a channel of type* $\mathcal{X} \times \mathcal{Y} \to \mathbb{R}$.

In the particular case in which the family $\{C_i\}$ has only two elements C_{i_1} and C_{i_2}, the distribution μ on indexes is completely determined by a real value $0 \le p \le 1$ s.t. $\mu(i_1) = p$ and $\mu(i_2) = \bar{p}$. In this case we may use the *binary* version $_p\oplus$ of the hidden choice operator: $C_{i_1}\ _p\oplus\ C_{i_2} = p\,C_{i_1} + \bar{p}\,C_{i_2}$. The example below depicts the hidden choice between channels C_1 and C_2, with probability $p = 1/3$.

C_1	y_1	y_2
x_1	$1/2$	$1/2$
x_2	$1/3$	$2/3$

$_{1/3}\oplus$

C_2	y_1	y_2
x_1	$1/3$	$2/3$
x_2	$1/2$	$1/2$

$=$

$C_1\ _{1/3}\oplus\ C_2$	y_1	y_2
x_1	$7/18$	$11/18$
x_2	$4/9$	$5/9$

Visible Choice. The second operator models a visible probabilistic choice among channels. Consider a family $\{C_i\}_{i \in \mathcal{I}}$ of compatible channels. Let $\mu \in \mathbb{D}\mathcal{I}$ be a probability distribution on the elements of the index set $\mathcal{I}$. Consider an

---

[6] $\bigsqcup_{i \in \mathcal{I}} \mathcal{Y}_i = \mathcal{Y}_{i_1} \sqcup \mathcal{Y}_{i_2} \sqcup \ldots \sqcup \mathcal{Y}_{i_n}$ denotes the *disjoint union* $\{(y, i) \mid y \in \mathcal{Y}_i, i \in \mathcal{I}\}$ of the sets $\mathcal{Y}_{i_1}, \mathcal{Y}_{i_2}, \ldots, \mathcal{Y}_{i_n}$.

input x is fed to one of the channels in $\{C_i\}_{i \in \mathcal{I}}$, where the channel is randomly picked according to μ. More precisely, an index $i \in \mathcal{I}$ is sampled with probability $\mu(i)$, then the input x is fed to channel C_i, and the output y produced by the channel is then made visible, along with the index i of the channel that was used. Note that visible choice makes sense only between compatible channels, but it is not required that the output set of each channel be the same.

Formally, given $\{C_i\}_{i \in \mathcal{I}}$ of compatible channels s.t. each C_i has type $\mathcal{X} \times \mathcal{Y}_i \to \mathbb{R}$, and a distribution μ on $\mathcal{I}$, the *visible choice operator* $\lfloor \cdot \rceil_{i \leftarrow \mu}$ is defined as $\lfloor \cdot \rceil_{i \leftarrow \mu} C_i = \diamond_{i \in \mathcal{I}} \, \mu(i) \, C_i$.

Proposition 3. *Given a family $\{C_i\}_{i \in \mathcal{I}}$ of compatible channels s.t. each C_i has type $\mathcal{X} \times \mathcal{Y}_i \to \mathbb{R}$, and a distribution μ on $\mathcal{I}$, the result of the visible choice $\lfloor \cdot \rceil_{i \leftarrow \mu} C_i$ is a channel of type $\mathcal{X} \times (\bigsqcup_{i \in \mathcal{I}} \mathcal{Y}_i) \to \mathbb{R}$.*

In the particular case the family $\{C_i\}$ has only two elements C_{i_1} and C_{i_2}, the distribution μ on indexes is completely determined by a real value $0 \le p \le 1$ s.t. $\mu(i_1) = p$ and $\mu(i_2) = \bar{p}$. In this case we may use the *binary* version $_p\sqcup$ of the visible choice operator: $C_{i_1} \, _p\sqcup \, C_{i_2} = p \, C_{i_1} \diamond \bar{p} \, C_{i_2}$. The following depicts the visible choice between channels C_1 and C_3, with probability $p = 1/3$.

C_1	y_1	y_2
x_1	$1/2$	$1/2$
x_2	$1/3$	$2/3$

$_{1/3}\sqcup$

C_3	y_1	y_3
x_1	$1/3$	$2/3$
x_2	$1/2$	$1/2$

$=$

$C_1 \, _{1/3}\sqcup \, C_3$	$(y_1, 1)$	$(y_2, 1)$	$(y_1, 3)$	$(y_3, 3)$
x_1	$1/6$	$1/6$	$2/9$	$4/9$
x_2	$1/9$	$2/9$	$1/3$	$1/3$

4.3   Properties of Hidden and Visible Choice Operators

We now prove algebraic properties of channel operators. These properties will be useful when we model a (more complex) protocol as the composition of smaller channels via hidden or visible choice.

Whereas the properties of hidden choice hold generally with equality, those of visible choice are subtler. For instance, visible choice is not idempotent, since in general $C \, _p\sqcup \, C \ne C$. (In fact if C has type $\mathcal{X} \times \mathcal{Y} \to \mathbb{R}$, $C \, _p\sqcup \, C$ has type $\mathcal{X} \times (\mathcal{Y} \sqcup \mathcal{Y}) \to \mathbb{R}$.) However, idempotency and other properties involving visible choice hold if we replace the notion of equality with the more relaxed notion of "equivalence" between channels. Intuitively, two channels are equivalent if they have the same input space and yield the same value of vulnerability for every prior and every vulnerability function.

Definition 4 (Equivalence of channels). *Two compatible channels C_1 and C_2 with domain $\mathcal{X}$ are equivalent, denoted by $C_1 \approx C_2$, if for every prior $\pi \in \mathbb{D}\mathcal{X}$ and every posterior vulnerability $\mathbb{V}$ we have $\mathbb{V}[\pi, C_1] = \mathbb{V}[\pi, C_2]$.*

Two equivalent channels are indistinguishable from the point of view of information leakage, and in most cases we can just identify them. Indeed, nowadays there is a tendency to use *abstract channels* [5,23], which capture exactly the important behavior with respect to any form of leakage. In this paper, however, we cannot use abstract channels because the hidden choice operator needs a concrete representation in order to be defined unambiguously.

The first properties we prove regard idempotency of operators, which can be used do simplify the representation of some protocols.

Proposition 5 (Idempotency). *Given a family* $\{C_i\}_{i \in \mathcal{I}}$ *of channels s.t.* $C_i = C$ *for all* $i \in \mathcal{I}$, *and a distribution* μ *on* $\mathcal{I}$, *then: (a)* $\sum_{i \leftarrow \mu} C_i = C$; *and (b)* $\bigsqcup_{i \leftarrow \mu} C_i \approx C$.

The following properties regard the reorganization of operators, and they will be essential in some technical results in which we invert the order in which hidden and visible choice are applied in a protocol.

Proposition 6 ("Reorganization of operators"). *Given a family* $\{C_{ij}\}_{i \in \mathcal{I}, j \in \mathcal{J}}$ *of channels indexed by sets* $\mathcal{I}$ *and* $\mathcal{J}$, *a distribution* μ *on* $\mathcal{I}$, *and a distribution* η *on* $\mathcal{J}$:

(a) $\sum_{i \leftarrow \mu} \sum_{j \leftarrow \eta} C_{ij} = \sum_{\substack{i \leftarrow \mu \\ j \leftarrow \eta}} C_{ij}$, *if all* C_i's *have the same type;*

(b) $\bigsqcup_{i \leftarrow \mu} \bigsqcup_{j \leftarrow \eta} C_{ij} \approx \bigsqcup_{\substack{i \leftarrow \mu \\ j \leftarrow \eta}} C_{ij}$, *if all* C_i's *are compatible; and*

(c) $\sum_{i \leftarrow \mu} \bigsqcup_{j \leftarrow \eta} C_{ij} \approx \bigsqcup_{j \leftarrow \eta} \sum_{i \leftarrow \mu} C_{ij}$, *if, for each* i, *all* C_{ij}'s *have same type* $\mathcal{X} \times \mathcal{Y}_j \to \mathbb{R}$.

4.4   Properties of Vulnerability w.r.t. Channel Operators

We now derive some relevant properties of vulnerability w.r.t. our channel operators, which will be later used to obtain the Nash equilibria in information leakage games with different choice operations.

The first result states that posterior vulnerability is convex w.r.t. hidden choice (this result was already presented in [4]), and linear w.r.t. to visible choice.

Theorem 7. *Let* $\{C_i\}_{i \in \mathcal{I}}$ *be a family of channels, and* μ *be a distribution on* $\mathcal{I}$. *Then, for every distribution* π *on* $\mathcal{X}$, *and every vulnerability* $\mathbb{V}$:

(a) *posterior vulnerability is convex w.r.t. to hidden choice:* $\mathbb{V}\left[\pi, \sum_{i \leftarrow \mu} C_i\right] \leq \sum_{i \in \mathcal{I}} \mu(i) \mathbb{V}[\pi, C_i]$ *if all* C_i's *have the same type.*

(b) *posterior vulnerability is linear w.r.t. to visible choice:* $\mathbb{V}\left[\pi, \bigsqcup_{i \leftarrow \mu} C_i\right] = \sum_{i \in \mathcal{I}} \mu(i) \mathbb{V}[\pi, C_i]$ *if all* C_i's *are compatible.*

The next result is concerned with posterior vulnerability under the composition of channels using both operators.

Corollary 8. *Let* $\{C_{ij}\}_{i \in \mathcal{I}, j \in \mathcal{J}}$ *be a family of channels, all with domain* $\mathcal{X}$ *and with the same type, and let* $\pi \in \mathbb{D}\mathcal{X}$, *and* $\mathbb{V}$ *be any vulnerability. Define* $U : \mathbb{D}\mathcal{I} \times \mathbb{D}\mathcal{J} \to \mathbb{R}$ *as follows:* $U(\mu, \eta) \stackrel{\text{def}}{=} \mathbb{V}\left[\pi, \sum_{i \leftarrow \mu} \bigsqcup_{j \leftarrow \eta} C_{ij}\right]$. *Then* U *is convex on* μ *and linear on* η.

5 Information Leakage Games

In this section we present our framework for reasoning about information leakage, extending the notion of *information leakage games* proposed in [4] from only simultaneous games with hidden choice to both simultaneous and sequential games, with either hidden or visible choice.

In an information leakage game the defender tries to minimize the leakage of information from the system, while the attacker tries to maximize it. In this basic scenario, their goals are just opposite (zero-sum). Both of them can influence the execution and the observable behavior of the system via a specific set of actions. We assume players to be rational (i.e., they are able to figure out what is the best strategy to maximize their expected payoff), and that the set of actions and the payoff function are common knowledge.

Players choose their own strategy, which in general may be mixed (i.e. probabilistic), and choose their action by a random draw according to that strategy. After both players have performed their actions, the system runs and produces some output value which is visible to the attacker and may leak some information about the secret. The amount of leakage constitutes the attacker's gain, and the defender's loss.

To quantify the leakage we model the system as an information-theoretic channel (cf. Sect. 2.2). We recall that leakage is defined as the difference (additive leakage) or the ratio (multiplicative leakage) between posterior and prior vulnerability. Since we are only interested in comparing the leakage of different channels for a given prior, *we will define the payoff just as the posterior vulnerability*, as the value of prior vulnerability will be the same for every channel.

5.1 Defining Information Leakage Games

An *(information) leakage game* consists of: (1) two nonempty sets $\mathcal{D}$, $\mathcal{A}$ of defender's and attacker's actions respectively, (2) a function $C : \mathcal{D} \times \mathcal{A} \rightarrow (\mathcal{X} \times \mathcal{Y} \rightarrow \mathbb{R})$ that associates to each pair of actions $(d, a) \in \mathcal{D} \times \mathcal{A}$ a channel $C_{da} : \mathcal{X} \times \mathcal{Y} \rightarrow \mathbb{R}$, (3) a prior $\pi \in \mathbb{D}\mathcal{X}$ on secrets, and (4) a vulnerability measure $\mathbb{V}$. The payoff function $u : \mathcal{D} \times \mathcal{A} \rightarrow \mathbb{R}$ for pure strategies is defined as $u(d, a) \overset{\text{def}}{=} \mathbb{V}[\pi, C_{da}]$. We have only one payoff function because the game is zero-sum.

Like in traditional game theory, the order of actions and the extent by which a player knows the move performed by the opponent play a critical role in deciding strategies and determining the payoff. In security, however, knowledge of the opponent's move affects the game in yet another way: the effectiveness of the attack, i.e., the amount of leakage, depends crucially on whether or not the attacker knows what channel is being used. It is therefore convenient to distinguish two phases in the leakage game:

Phase 1: Each player determines the most convenient strategy (which in general is mixed) for himself, and draws his action accordingly. One of the players may commit first to his action, and his choice may or may not be revealed to the follower. In general, knowledge of the leader's action may help the follower choose a more advantageous strategy.

Phase 2: The attacker observes the output of the selected channel C_{da} and performs his attack on the secret. In case he knows the defender's action, he is able to determine the exact channel C_{da} being used (since, of course, the attacker knows his own action), and his payoff will be the posterior vulnerability $\mathbb{V}[\pi, C_{da}]$. However, if the attacker does not know exactly which channel has been used, then his payoff will be smaller.

Note that the issues raised in Phase 2 are typical of leakage games; they do not have a correspondence (to the best of our knowledge) in traditional game theory. On the other hand, these issues are central to security, as they reflect the principle of preventing the attacker from inferring the secret by obfuscating the link between secret and observables.

Following the above discussion, we consider various possible scenarios for games, along two lines of classification. First, there are three possible orders for the two players' actions.

Simultaneous: The players choose (draw) their actions in parallel, each without knowing the choice of the other.
Sequential, defender-first: The defender draws an action, and commits to it, before the attacker does.
Sequential, attacker-first: The attacker draws an action, and commits to it, before the defender does.

Note that these sequential games may present imperfect information (i.e., the follower may not know the leader's action).

Second, the visibility of the defender's action during the attack may vary:

Visible choice: The attacker knows the defender's action when he observes the output of the channel, and therefore he knows which channel is being used. Visible choice is modeled by the operator $\lfloor \cdot \rfloor$.
Hidden choice: The attacker does not know the defender's action when he observes the output of the channel, and therefore in general he does not exactly know which channel is used (although in some special cases he may infer it from the output). Hidden choice is modeled by the operator $\sum$.

Note that the distinction between sequential and simultaneous games is orthogonal to that between visible and hidden choice. Sequential and simultaneous games model whether or not, respectively, the follower's choice can be affected by knowledge of the leader's action. This dichotomy captures how knowledge about the other player's actions can *help a player choose his own action*. On the other hand, visible and hidden choice capture whether or not, respectively, the attacker is able to fully determine the channel representing the system, *once defender and attacker's actions have already been fixed*. This dichotomy reflects the different *amounts of information leaked* by the system as viewed by the adversary. For instance, in a simultaneous game neither player can choose his action based on the choice of the

Table 2. Kinds of games we consider. All sequential games have perfect information, except for game V.

		Order of action		
		simultaneous	defender 1st	attacker 1st
Defender's choice	visible $\lfloor \cdot \rfloor$	Game I	Game II	Game III
	hidden $\sum$	Game IV	Game V	Game VI

other. However, depending on whether or not the defender's choice is visible, the adversary will or will not, respectively, be able to completely recover the channel used, which will affect the amount of leakage.

If we consider also the subdivision of sequential games into perfect and imperfect information, there are 10 possible different combinations. Some, however, make little sense. For instance, defender-first sequential game with perfect information (by the attacker) does not combine naturally with hidden choice $\sum$, since that would mean that the attacker knows the action of the defender and choses his strategy accordingly, but forgets it at the moment of the attack. (We assume *perfect recall*, i.e., the players never forget what they have learned.) Yet other combinations are not interesting, such as the attacker-first sequential game with (totally) imperfect information (by the defender), since it coincides with the simultaneous-game case. Note that attacker and defender are not symmetric with respect to hiding/revealing their actions a and d, since the knowledge of a affects the game only in the usual sense of game theory, while the knowledge of d also affects the computation of the payoff (cf. "Phase 2" above).

Table 2 lists the meaningful and interesting combinations. In Game V we assume imperfect information: the attacker does not know the action chosen by the defender. In all the other sequential games we assume that the follower has perfect information. In the remaining of this section, we discuss each game individually, using the example of Sect. 3 as running example.

Game I (simultaneous with visible choice). This simultaneous game can be represented by a tuple $(\mathcal{D}, \mathcal{A}, u)$. As in all games with visible choice $\lfloor \cdot \rfloor$, the expected payoff U of a mixed strategy profile (δ, α) is defined to be the expected value of u, as in traditional game theory: $U(\delta, \alpha) \overset{\text{def}}{=} \mathbb{E}_{\substack{d \leftarrow \delta \\ a \leftarrow \alpha}} u(d, a) = \sum_{\substack{d \in \mathcal{D} \\ a \in \mathcal{A}}} \delta(d)\, \alpha(a)\, u(d, a)$, where we recall that $u(d, a) = \mathbb{V}[\pi, C_{da}]$.

From Theorem 7(b) we derive: $U(\delta, \alpha) = \mathbb{V}\left[\pi, \lfloor \cdot \rfloor_{\substack{d \leftarrow \delta \\ a \leftarrow \alpha}} C_{da}\right]$. Hence the whole system can be equivalently regarded as the channel $\lfloor \cdot \rfloor_{\substack{d \leftarrow \delta \\ a \leftarrow \alpha}} C_{da}$. Still from Theorem 7(b) we can derive that $U(\delta, \alpha)$ is linear in δ and α. Therefore the Nash equilibrium can be computed using the minimax method (cf. Sect. 2.1).

Example 9. *Consider the example of Sect. 3 in the setting of Game I. The Nash equilibrium (δ^*, α^*) can be obtained using the closed formula from Sect. 2.1, and* it is given by $\delta^*(0) = \alpha^*(0) = (2/3-1)/(1/2-1-1+2/3) = 2/5$. *The corresponding payoff is* $U(\delta^*, \alpha^*) = 2/5\,2/5\,1/2 + 2/5\,3/5 + 3/5\,2/5 + 3/5\,3/5\,2/3 = 4/5$.

Game II (defender 1st with visible choice). This defender-first sequential game can be represented by a tuple $(\mathcal{D},\, \mathcal{D} \to \mathcal{A},\, u)$. A mixed strategy profile is of the form (δ, σ_a), with $\delta \in \mathbb{D}\mathcal{D}$ and $\sigma_a \in \mathbb{D}(\mathcal{D} \to \mathcal{A})$, and the corresponding payoff is $U(\delta, \sigma_a) \overset{\text{def}}{=} \mathbb{E}_{\substack{d \leftarrow \delta \\ s_a \leftarrow \sigma_a}} u(d, s_a(d)) = \sum_{\substack{d \in \mathcal{D} \\ s_a : \mathcal{D} \to \mathcal{A}}} \delta(d)\,\sigma_a(s_a)\,u(d, s_a(d))$, where $u(d, s_a(d)) = \mathbb{V}\left[\pi, C_{d s_a(d)}\right]$.

Again, from Theorem 7(b) we derive: $U(\delta, \sigma_a) = \mathbb{V}\left[\pi, \lfloor \cdot \rfloor_{\substack{d \leftarrow \delta \\ s_a \leftarrow \sigma_a}} C_{d s_a(d)}\right]$ and hence the system can be expressed as channel $\lfloor \cdot \rfloor_{\substack{d \leftarrow \delta \\ s_a \leftarrow \sigma_a}} C_{d s_a(d)}$. From the same Theorem we also derive that $U(\delta, \sigma_a)$ is linear in δ and σ_a, so the mutually optimal strategies can be obtained again by solving the minimax problem. In this case, however, the solution is particularly simple, because it is known that there are optimal strategies which are deterministic. Hence it is sufficient for the defender to find the action d which minimizes $\max_a u(d, a)$.

Example 10. *Consider the example of Sect. 3 in the setting of Game II. If the defender chooses 0 then the attacker chooses 1. If the defender chooses 1 then the attacker chooses 0. In both cases, the payoff is 1. The game has therefore two solutions, $(0,1)$ and $(1,0)$.*

Game III (attacker 1st with visible choice). This game is also a sequential game, but with the attacker as the leader. Therefore it can be represented as tuple of the form $(\mathcal{A} \to \mathcal{D},\, \mathcal{A},\, u)$. It is the same as Game II, except that the roles of the attacker and the defender are inverted. In particular, the payoff of a mixed strategy profile $(\sigma_d, \alpha) \in \mathbb{D}(\mathcal{A} \to \mathcal{D}) \times \mathbb{D}\mathcal{A}$ is given by $U(\sigma_d, \alpha) \overset{\text{def}}{=} \mathbb{E}_{\substack{s_d \leftarrow \sigma_d \\ a \leftarrow \alpha}} u(s_d(a), a) = \sum_{\substack{s_d : \mathcal{A} \to \mathcal{D} \\ a \in \mathcal{A}}} \sigma_d(s_d)\,\alpha(a)\,u(s_d(a), a) = \mathbb{V}\left[\pi, \lfloor \cdot \rfloor_{\substack{s_d \leftarrow \sigma_d \\ a \leftarrow \alpha}} C_{s_d(a)a}\right]$, and the whole system can be equivalently regarded as channel $\lfloor \cdot \rfloor_{\substack{s_d \leftarrow \sigma_d \\ a \leftarrow \alpha}} C_{s_d(a)a}$. Obviously, also in this case the minimax problem has a deterministic solution.

In summary, in the sequential case, whether the leader is the defender or the attacker (Games II and III, respectively), the minimax problem has always a deterministic solution [24].

Theorem 11. *In a defender-first sequential game with visible choice, there exist $d \in \mathcal{D}$ and $a \in \mathcal{A}$ such that, for every $\delta \in \mathbb{D}\mathcal{D}$ and $\sigma_a \in \mathbb{D}(\mathcal{D} \to \mathcal{A})$ we have: $U(d, \sigma_a) \leq u(d, a) \leq U(\delta, a)$. Similarly, in an attacker-first sequential game with visible choice, there exist $d \in \mathcal{D}$ and $a \in \mathcal{A}$ such that, for every $\sigma_d \in \mathbb{D}(\mathcal{A} \to \mathcal{D})$ and $\alpha \in \mathbb{D}\mathcal{A}$ we have: $U(d, \alpha) \leq u(d, a) \leq U(\sigma_d, a)$.*

Example 12. *Consider now the example of Sect. 3 in the setting of Game III. If the attacker chooses 0 then the defender chooses 0 and the payoff is $1/2$. If the attacker chooses 1 then the defender chooses 1 and the payoff is $2/3$. The latter case is more convenient for the attacker, hence the solution of the game is the strategy profile $(1,1)$.*

Game IV (simultaneous with hidden choice). This game is a tuple $(\mathcal{D}, \mathcal{A}, u)$. However, *it is not an ordinary game* in the sense that *the payoff a mixed strategy profile cannot be defined by averaging the payoff of the corresponding pure strategies.* More precisely, the payoff of a mixed profile is defined by averaging on the strategy of the attacker, but not on that of the defender. In fact, when hidden choice is used, there is an additional level of uncertainty in the relation between the observables and the secret from the point of view of the attacker, since he is not sure about which channel is producing those observables. A mixed strategy δ for the defender produces a convex combination of channels (the channels associated to the pure strategies) with the same coefficients, and we know from previous sections that the vulnerability is a convex function of the channel, and in general is not linear.

In order to define the payoff of a mixed strategy profile (δ, α), we need therefore to consider the channel that the attacker perceives given his limited knowledge. Let us assume that the action that the attacker draws from α is a. He does not know the action of the defender, but we can assume that he knows his strategy (each player can derive the optimal strategy of the opponent, under the assumption of common knowledge and rational players).

The channel the attacker will see is $\sum_{d \leftarrow \delta} C_{da}$, obtaining a corresponding payoff of $\mathbb{V}[\pi, \sum_{d \leftarrow \delta} C_{da}]$. By averaging on the strategy of the attacker we obtain $U(\delta, \alpha) \overset{\text{def}}{=} \mathbb{E}_{a \leftarrow \alpha} \mathbb{V}[\pi, \sum_{d \leftarrow \delta} C_{da}] = \sum_{a \in \mathcal{A}} \alpha(a) \mathbb{V}[\pi, \sum_{d \leftarrow \delta} C_{da}]$. From Theorem 7(b) we derive: $U(\delta, \alpha) = \mathbb{V}[\pi, \bigsqcup_{a \leftarrow \alpha} \sum_{d \leftarrow \delta} C_{da}]$ and hence the whole system can be equivalently regarded as channel $\bigsqcup_{a \leftarrow \alpha} \sum_{d \leftarrow \delta} C_{da}$. Note that, by Proposition 6(c), the order of the operators is interchangeable, and the system can be equivalently regarded as $\sum_{d \leftarrow \delta} \bigsqcup_{a \leftarrow \alpha} C_{da}$. This shows the robustness of this model.

From Corollary 8 we derive that $U(\delta, \alpha)$ is convex in δ and linear in η, hence we can compute the Nash equilibrium by the minimax method.

Example 13. *Consider now the example of Sect. 3 in the setting of Game IV. For $\delta \in \mathbb{DD}$ and $\alpha \in \mathbb{DA}$, let $p = \delta(0)$ and $q = \alpha(0)$. The system can be represented by the channel $(C_{00\ p} \oplus C_{10})\ {}_q \bigsqcup (C_{01\ p} \oplus C_{11})$ represented below.*

$C_{00\ p} \oplus C_{10}$	$y = 0$	$y = 1$
$x = 0$	p	$\bar{p}$
$x = 1$	1	0

$_q \bigsqcup$

$C_{01\ p} \oplus C_{11}$	$y = 0$	$y = 1$
$x = 0$	$1/3 + 2/3\,p$	$2/3 - 2/3\,p$
$x = 1$	$2/3 - 2/3\,p$	$1/3 + 2/3\,p$

For uniform π, we have $\mathbb{V}[\pi, C_{00\ p} \oplus C_{10}] = 1 - 1/2$; and $\mathbb{V}[\pi, C_{10\ p} \oplus C_{11}]$ is equal to $2/3 - 2/3\,p$ if $p \leq 1/4$, and equal to $1/3 + 2/3\,p$ if $p > 1/4$. Hence the payoff, expressed in terms of p and q, is $U(p,q) = q(1 - 1/2) + \bar{q}(2/3 - 2/3\,p)$ if $p \leq 1/4$, and $U(p,q) = q(1 - 1/2) + \bar{q}(1/3 + 2/3\,p)$ if $p > 1/4$. The Nash equilibrium (p^*, q^*) is given by $p^* = \operatorname{argmin}_p \max_q U(p,q)$ and $q^* = \operatorname{argmax}_q \min_p U(p,q)$, and by solving the above, we obtain $p^* = q^* = 4/7$.

Game V (defender 1st with hidden choice). This is a defender-first sequential game with imperfect information, hence it can be represented as a tuple of the form $(\mathcal{D}, K_a \to \mathcal{A}, u_d, u_a)$, where K_a is a partition of $\mathcal{D}$. Since we are assuming perfect recall, and the attacker does not know anything about the action chosen by the defender in Phase 2, i.e., at the moment of the attack (except the probability distribution determined by his strategy), we must assume that the attacker does not know anything in Phase 1 either. Hence the indistinguishability relation must be total, i.e., $K_a = \{\mathcal{D}\}$. But $\{\mathcal{D}\} \to \mathcal{A}$ is equivalent to $\mathcal{A}$, hence this kind of game is equivalent to Game IV.

It is also a well known fact in Game theory that when in a sequential game the follower does not know the leader's move before making his choice, the game is equivalent to a simultaneous game.[7]

Game VI (attacker 1st with hidden choice). This game is also a sequential game with the attacker as the leader, hence it is a tuple of the form $(\mathcal{A} \to \mathcal{D}, \mathcal{A}, u)$. It is similar to Game III, except that the payoff is convex on the strategy of the defender, instead of linear. The payoff of the mixed strategy profile $(\sigma_d, \alpha) \in \mathbb{D}(\mathcal{A} \to \mathcal{D}) \times \mathbb{D}\mathcal{A}$ is $U(\sigma_d, \alpha) \overset{\text{def}}{=} \mathbb{E}_{a \leftarrow \alpha} \mathbb{V}\left[\pi, \sum_{s_d \leftarrow \sigma_d} C_{s_d(a)a}\right] = \mathbb{V}\left[\pi, \sum_{a \leftarrow \alpha} \bigsqcup_{s_d \leftarrow \sigma_d} C_{s_d(a)a}\right]$, so the whole system can be equivalently regarded as channel $\sum_{a \leftarrow \alpha} \bigsqcup_{s_d \leftarrow \sigma_d} C_{s_d(a)a}$. Also in this case the minimax problem has a deterministic solution, but only for the attacker.

Theorem 14. *In an attacker-first sequential game with hidden choice, there exist $a \in \mathcal{A}$ and $\delta \in \mathbb{D}\mathcal{D}$ such that, for every $\alpha \in \mathbb{D}\mathcal{A}$ and $\sigma_d \in \mathbb{D}(\mathcal{A} \to \mathcal{D})$ we have that $U(\delta, \alpha) \leq U(\delta, a) \leq U(\sigma_d, a)$.*

Example 15. *Consider again the example of Sect. 3, this time in the setting of Game VI. Consider also the calculations made in Example 13, we will use the same results and notation here. In this setting, the attacker is obliged to make its choice first. If he chooses 0, which corresponds to committing to the system $C_{00\ p} \oplus C_{10}$, then the defender will choose $p = 1/4$, which minimizes its vulnerability. If he chooses 1, which corresponds to committing to the system $C_{01\ p} \oplus C_{11}$, the defender will choose $p = 1$, which minimizes its vulnerability of the above channel. In both cases, the leakage is $p = 1/2$, hence both these strategies are solutions to the minimax. Note that in the first case the strategy of the defender is mixed, while that of the attacker is always pure.*

5.2   Comparing the Games

If we look at the various payoffs obtained for the running example in the various games, we obtain the following values (listed in decreasing order): II : 1; I : 4/5; III : 2/3; IV : 4/7; V : 4/7; VI : 1/2.

---

[7] However, one could argue that, since the defender has already committed, the attacker does not need to perform the action corresponding to the Nash equilibrium, any payoff-maximizing solution would be equally good for him.

This order is not accidental: for any vulnerability function, and for any prior, the various games are ordered, with respect to the payoff, as shown in Fig. 2. The relations between II, I, and III, and between IV-V and VI come from the fact that, in any zero-sum sequential game the leader's payoff will be less or equal to his payoff in the corresponding simultaneous game. We think this result is well-known in game theory, but we give the hint of the proof nevertheless, for the sake of clarity.

Fig. 2. Order of games w.r.t. payoff. Games higher in the lattice have larger payoff.

Theorem 16. *It is the case that:*

$$(a) \quad \min_\delta \max_{\sigma_a} \mathbb{V}\left[\pi, \bigsqcup_{\substack{d \leftarrow \delta \\ s_a \leftarrow \sigma_a}} C_{ds_a(d)}\right] \geq \min_\delta \max_\alpha \mathbb{V}\left[\pi, \bigsqcup_{\substack{d \leftarrow \delta \\ a \leftarrow \alpha}} C_{da}\right]$$

$$\geq \max_\alpha \min_{\sigma_d} \mathbb{V}\left[\pi, \bigsqcup_{\substack{s_d \leftarrow \sigma_d \\ a \leftarrow \alpha}} C_{s_d(a)a}\right]$$

$$(b) \quad \min_\delta \max_\alpha \mathbb{V}\left[\pi, \bigsqcup_{a \leftarrow \alpha} \sum_{d \leftarrow \delta} C_{da}\right] \geq \max_\alpha \min_{\sigma_d} \mathbb{V}\left[\pi, \sum_{a \leftarrow \alpha} \bigsqcup_{s_d \leftarrow \sigma_d} C_{s_d(a)a}\right]$$

Proof. We prove the first inequality in (a). Independently of δ, consider the attacker strategy τ_a that assigns probability 1 to the function s_a defined as $s_a(d) = \text{argmax}_a \mathbb{V}[\pi, C_{da}]$. Then we have that

$$\min_\delta \max_{\sigma_a} \mathbb{V}\left[\pi, \bigsqcup_{\substack{d \leftarrow \delta \\ s_a \leftarrow \sigma_a}} C_{ds_a(d)}\right] \geq \min_\delta \mathbb{V}\left[\pi, \bigsqcup_{\substack{d \leftarrow \delta \\ s_a \leftarrow \tau_a}} C_{ds_a(d)}\right]$$

$$\geq \min_\delta \max_\alpha \mathbb{V}\left[\pi, \bigsqcup_{\substack{d \leftarrow \delta \\ a \leftarrow \alpha}} C_{da}\right]$$

Note that the strategy τ_a is optimal for the adversary, so the first of the above inequalities is actually an equality. All other cases can be proved with an analogous reasoning. □

Concerning III and IV-V: these are not related. In the running example the payoff for III is higher than for IV-V, but it is easy to find other cases in which the situation is reversed. For instance, if in the running example we set C_{11} to be the same as C_{00}, the payoff for III will be $1/2$, and that for IV-V will be $2/3$.

Finally, the relation between III and VI comes from the fact that they are both attacker-first sequential games, and the only difference is the way in which the payoff is defined. Then, just observe that in general we have, for every $a \in \mathcal{A}$ and every $\delta \in \mathbb{DD}$: $\mathbb{V}\left[\pi, \sum_{d \leftarrow \delta} C_{da}\right] \leq \mathbb{V}\left[\pi, \bigsqcup_{d \leftarrow \delta} C_{da}\right]$.

The relations in Fig. 2 can be used by the defender as guidelines to better protect the system, if he has some control over the rules of the game. Obviously, for the defender the games lower in the ordering are to be preferred.

6 Case Study: A Safer, Faster Password-Checker

In this section we apply our game-theoretic, compositional approach to show how a defender can mitigate an attacker's typical timing side-channel attack while avoiding the usual burden imposed on the password-checker's efficiency.

Consider the password-checker PWD_{123} of Fig. 3, which performs a bitwise-check of a 3-bit low-input $a = a_1 a_2 a_3$, provided by the attacker, against a 3-bit secret password $x = x_1 x_2 x_3$. The low-input is rejected as soon as it mismatches the secret, and is accepted otherwise.

The attacker can choose low-inputs to try to gain information about the password.

```
Program PWD₁₂₃

High Input: x ∈ {000, 001, ..., 111}
Low Input: a ∈ {000, 001, ..., 111}
Output: y ∈ {T, F}
accept := T
for i = 1, 2, 3 do
    if aᵢ ≠ xᵢ then
        accept := F
        break
    end if
end for
return accept
```

Fig. 3. Password-checker algorithm.

Obviously, in case PWD_{123} accepts the low-input, the attacker learns the password value is $a = x$. Yet, even when the low-input is rejected, there is some leakage of information: from the duration of the execution the attacker can estimate how many iterations have been performed before the low-input was rejected, thus inferring a prefix of the secret password.

To model this scenario, let $\mathcal{X} = \{000, 001, \ldots, 111\}$ be the set of all possible 3-bit passwords, and $\mathcal{Y} = \{(F, 1), (F, 2), (F, 3), (T, 3)\}$ be the set of observables produced by the system. Each observable is an ordered pair whose first element indicates whether the password was accepted (T or F), and the second element indicates the duration of the computation (1, 2, or 3 iterations). For instance, channel $C_{123,101}$ in Fig. 4 models PWD_{123}'s behavior when the attacker provides low-input $a = 101$.

We will adopt as a measure of information *Bayes vulnerability* [27]. The *prior Bayes vulnerability* of a distribution $\pi \in \mathbb{D}\mathcal{X}$ is defined as $V_g[\pi] = \max_{x \in \mathcal{X}} \pi_x$, and represents the probability that the attacker guesses correctly the password in one try. For instance, if the distribution on all possible 3-bit passwords is $\hat{\pi} = (0.0137, 0.0548, 0.2191, 0.4382, 0.0002, 0.0002, 0.0548, 0.2191)$, its prior Bayes vulnerability is $\mathbb{V}[\hat{\pi}] = 0.4382$.

The *posterior Bayes vulnerability* of a prior π and a channel $C : \mathcal{X} \times \mathcal{Y} \to \mathbb{R}$ is defined as $\mathbb{V}[\pi, C] = \sum_{y \in \mathcal{Y}} \max_{x \in \mathcal{X}} \pi_x C(x, y)$, and it represents the probability that the attacker guesses correctly the password in one try, after he observes the output of the channel (i.e., after he has measured the time needed for the checker to accept or reject the low-input). For prior $\hat{\pi}$ above, the posterior Bayes vulnerability of channel $C_{123,101}$ is $\mathbb{V}[\hat{\pi}, C_{123,101}] = 0.6577$ (which represents an increase in Bayes vulnerability of about 50%), and the expected running time for this checker is of 1.2747 iterations.

A way to mitigate this timing side-channel is to make the checker's execution time independent of the secret. Channel $C_{\text{cons},101}$ from Fig. 4 models a checker that does that (by eliminating the **break** command within the loop in PWD_{123})

when the attacker's low-input is $a = 101$. This channel's posterior Bayes vulnerability is $\mathbb{V}[\hat{\pi}, C_{123,101}] = 0.4384$, which brings the multiplicative Bayes leakage down to an increase of only about 0.05%. However, the expected running time goes up to 3 iterations (an increase of about 135% w.r.t. that of $C_{123,101}$).

Seeking some compromise between security and efficiency, assume that the defender can employ password-checkers that perform the bitwise comparison among low-input a and secret password x in different orders. More precisely, there is one version of the checker for every possible order in which the index i ranges in the control of the loop. For instance, while PWD_{123} checks the bits in the order $1, 2, 3$, the alternative algorithm PWD_{231} uses the order $2, 3, 1$.

$C_{123,101}$	$y= (F,1)$	$y= (F,2)$	$y= (F,3)$	$y= (T,3)$
$x=000$	1	0	0	0
$x=001$	1	0	0	0
$x=010$	1	0	0	0
$x=011$	1	0	0	0
$x=100$	0	0	1	0
$x=101$	0	0	0	1
$x=110$	0	1	0	0
$x=111$	0	1	0	0

$C_{cons,101}$	$y= (F,3)$	$y= (T,3)$
$x=000$	1	0
$x=001$	1	0
$x=010$	1	0
$x=011$	1	0
$x=100$	1	0
$x=101$	0	1
$x=110$	1	0
$x=111$	1	0

Fig. 4. Channels C_{da} modeling the password checker for defender's action d and attacker's action a.

To determine a defender's best choice of which versions of the checker to run, we model this problem as game. The attacker's actions $\mathcal{A} = \{000, 001, \ldots, 111\}$ are all possible low-inputs to the checker, and the defender's $\mathcal{D} = \{123, 132, 213, 231, 312, 321\}$ are all orders to perform the comparison. Hence, there is a total of 48 possible channels $C_{ad}: \mathcal{X} \times \mathcal{Y} \to \mathbb{R}$, one for each combination of $d \in \mathcal{D}$, $a \in \mathcal{A}$.

In our framework, the utility of a mixed strategy profile (δ, α) is given by $U(\delta, \alpha) = \mathbb{E}_{a \leftarrow \alpha} \mathbb{V}[\pi, \sum_{d \leftarrow \delta} C_{da}]$. For each pure strategy profile (d, a),

Table 3. Utility for each pure strategy profile.

$U(d,a)$	Attacker's action a							
	000	001	010	011	100	101	110	111
123	0.7257	0.7257	0.9311	0.9311	0.6577	0.6577	0.7122	0.7122
132	0.8900	0.9311	0.8900	0.9311	0.7122	0.7122	0.7122	0.7122
213	0.5068	0.5068	0.9311	0.9311	0.4934	0.4934	0.7668	0.7668
231	0.5068	0.5068	0.7668	0.9311	0.5068	0.5068	0.7668	0.9311
312	0.7257	0.9311	0.7257	0.9311	0.7122	0.8766	0.7122	0.8766
321	0.6712	0.7122	0.7257	0.9311	0.6712	0.7122	0.7257	0.9311

(Defender's action d)

the payoff of the game will be the posterior Bayes vulnerability of the resulting channel C_{da} (since, if we measuring leakage, the prior vulnerability is the same for every channel once the prior is fixed). Table 3 depicts such payoffs. Note that the attacker's and defender's actions substantially affect the effectiveness of the attack: vulnerability ranges between 0.4934 and 0.9311 (and so multiplicative leakage is in the range between an increase of 12% and one of 112%). Using techniques from [4], we can compute the best (mixed) strategy for the defender in this game, which turns out to be $\delta^* = (0.1667, 0.1667, 0.1667, 0.1667, 0.1667, 0.1667)$. This strategy is part of an equilibrium and guarantees that for any choice of the attacker the posterior Bayes vulnerability is at most 0.6573 (so the multiplicative leakage is bounded by 50%, an intermediate value between the minimum of about 12% and the maximum of about 112%). It is interesting to note that the expected running time, for any action of the attacker, is bounded by at most

2.3922 iterations (an increase of only 87% w.r.t. the channel PWD_{123}), which is below the worst possible expected 3 iterations of the constant-time password checker.

7   Related Work

Many studies have applied game theory to analyses of security and privacy in networks [3,7,14], cryptography [15], anonymity [1], location privacy [13], and intrusion detection [30], to cite a few. See [20] for a survey.

In the context of quantitative information flow, most works consider only passive attackers. Boreale and Pampaloni [8] consider adaptive attackers, but not adaptive defenders, and show that in this case the adversary's optimal strategy can be always deterministic. Mardziel et al. [21] propose a model for both adaptive attackers and defenders, but in none of their extensive case-studies the attacker needs a probabilistic strategy to maximize leakage. In this paper we characterize when randomization is necessary, for either attacker or defender, to achieve optimality in our general information leakage games.

Security games have been employed to model and analyze payoffs between interacting agents, especially between a defender and an attacker. Korzhyk et al. [19] theoretically analyze security games and study the relationships between Stackelberg and Nash Equilibria under various forms of imperfect information. Khouzani and Malacaria [18] study leakage properties when perfect secrecy is not achievable due to constraints on the allowable size of the conflating sets, and provide universally optimal strategies for a wide class of entropy measures, and for g-entropies. These works, contrarily to ours, do not consider games with hidden choice, in which optimal strategies differ from traditional game-theory.

Several security games have modeled leakage when the sensitive information are the defender's choices themselves, rather than a system's high input. For instance, Alon et al. [2] propose zero-sum games in which a defender chooses probabilities of secrets and an attacker chooses and learns some of the defender's secrets. Then they present how the leakage on the defender's secrets gives influences on the defender's optimal strategy. More recently, Xu et al. [29] show zero-sum games in which the attacker obtains partial knowledge on the security resources that the defender protects, and provide the defender's optimal strategy under the attacker's such knowledge.

Regarding channel operators, sequential and parallel composition of channels have been studied (e.g., [17]), but we are unaware of any explicit definition and investigation of hidden and visible choice operators. Although Kawamoto et al. [16] implicitly use the hidden choice to model a probabilistic system as the weighted sum of systems, they do not derive the set of algebraic properties we do for this operator, and for its interaction with the visible choice operator.

8   Conclusion and Future Work

In this paper we used protocol composition to model the introduction of noise performed by the defender to prevent leakage of sensitive information. More precisely, we formalized visible and hidden probabilistic choices of different protocols. We then formalized the interplay between defender and adversary in a game-theoretic framework adapted to the specific issues of QIF, where the payoff is information leakage. We considered various kinds of leakage games, depending on whether players act simultaneously or sequentially, and whether the choices of the defender are visible or not to the adversary. We established a hierarchy of these games, and provided methods for finding the optimal strategies (at the points of equilibrium) in the various cases.

As future research, we would like to extend leakage games to the case of repeated observations, i.e., when the attacker can observe the outcomes of the system in successive runs, under the assumption that both attacker and defender may change the channel in each run. We would also like to extend our framework to non zero-sum games, in which the costs of attack and defense are not equivalent, and to analyze differentially-private mechanisms.

Acknowledgments. The authors are thankful to anonymous reviewers for helpful comments. This work was supported by JSPS and Inria under the project LOGIS of the Japan-France AYAME Program, and by the project Epistemic Interactive Concurrency (EPIC) from the STIC AmSud Program. Mário S. Alvim was supported by CNPq, CAPES, and FAPEMIG. Yusuke Kawamoto was supported by JSPS KAKENHI Grant Number JP17K12667.

References

1. Acquisti, A., Dingledine, R., Syverson, P.: On the economics of anonymity. In: Wright, R.N. (ed.) FC 2003. LNCS, vol. 2742, pp. 84–102. Springer, Heidelberg (2003). https://doi.org/10.1007/978-3-540-45126-6_7
2. Alon, N., Emek, Y., Feldman, M., Tennenholtz, M.: Adversarial leakage in games. SIAM J. Discret. Math. **27**(1), 363–385 (2013)
3. Alpcan, T., Buchegger, S.: Security games for vehicular networks. IEEE Trans. Mob. Comput. **10**(2), 280–290 (2011)
4. Alvim, M.S., Chatzikokolakis, K., Kawamoto, Y., Palamidessi, C.: Information leakage games. In: Rass, S., An, B., Kiekintveld, C., Fang, F., Schauer, S. (eds.) GameSec 2017. LNCS, vol. 10575, pp. 437–457. Springer, Cham (2017). https://doi.org/10.1007/978-3-319-68711-7_23
5. Alvim, M.S., Chatzikokolakis, K., McIver, A., Morgan, C., Palamidessi, C., Smith, G.: Axioms for information leakage. In: Proceedings of CSF, pp. 77–92 (2016)
6. Alvim, M.S., Chatzikokolakis, K., Palamidessi, C., Smith, G.: Measuring information leakage using generalized gain functions. In: Proceedings of CSF, pp. 265–279 (2012)
7. Basar, T.: The Gaussian test channel with an intelligent jammer. IEEE Trans. Inf. Theory **29**(1), 152–157 (1983)

8. Boreale, M., Pampaloni, F.: Quantitative information flow under generic leakage functions and adaptive adversaries. Log. Methods Comput. Sci. **11**(4–5), 1–31 (2015)

9. Braun, C., Chatzikokolakis, K., Palamidessi, C.: Quantitative notions of leakage for one-try attacks. In: Proceedings of MFPS. ENTCS, vol. 249, pp. 75–91. Elsevier (2009)

10. Chatzikokolakis, K., Palamidessi, C., Panangaden, P.: On the Bayes risk in information-hiding protocols. J. Comput. Secur. **16**(5), 531–571 (2008)

11. Chaum, D.: The dining cryptographers problem: unconditional sender and recipient untraceability. J. Cryptol. **1**, 65–75 (1988)

12. Dwork, C., McSherry, F., Nissim, K., Smith, A.: Calibrating noise to sensitivity in private data analysis. In: Halevi, S., Rabin, T. (eds.) TCC 2006. LNCS, vol. 3876, pp. 265–284. Springer, Heidelberg (2006). https://doi.org/10.1007/11681878_14

13. Freudiger, J., Manshaei, M.H., Hubaux, J.-P., Parkes, D.C.: On non-cooperative location privacy: a game-theoretic analysis. In: Proceedings of CCS, pp. 324–337 (2009)

14. Grossklags, J., Christin, N., Chuang, J.: Secure or insure? A game-theoretic analysis of information security games. In: Proceedings of WWW, pp. 209–218 (2008)

15. Katz, J.: Bridging game theory and cryptography: recent results and future directions. In: Canetti, R. (ed.) TCC 2008. LNCS, vol. 4948, pp. 251–272. Springer, Heidelberg (2008). https://doi.org/10.1007/978-3-540-78524-8_15

16. Kawamoto, Y., Biondi, F., Legay, A.: Hybrid statistical estimation of mutual information for quantifying information flow. In: Fitzgerald, J., Heitmeyer, C., Gnesi, S., Philippou, A. (eds.) FM 2016. LNCS, vol. 9995, pp. 406–425. Springer, Cham (2016). https://doi.org/10.1007/978-3-319-48989-6_25

17. Kawamoto, Y., Chatzikokolakis, K., Palamidessi, C.: On the compositionality of quantitative information flow. Log. Methods Comput. Sci. **13**(3–11), 1–31 (2017)

18. Khouzani, M.H.R., Malacaria, P.: Relative perfect secrecy: universally optimal strategies and channel design. In: Proceedings of CSF, pp. 61–76 (2016)

19. Korzhyk, D., Yin, Z., Kiekintveld, C., Conitzer, V., Tambe, M.: Stackelberg vs. nash in security games: an extended investigation of interchangeability, equivalence, and uniqueness. J. Artif. Intell. Res. **41**, 297–327 (2011)

20. Manshaei, M.H., Zhu, Q., Alpcan, T., Bacşar, T., Hubaux, J.-P.: Game theory meets network security and privacy. ACM Comput. Surv. **45**(3), 25:1–25:39 (2013)

21. Mardziel, P., Alvim, M.S., Hicks, M.W., Clarkson, M.R.: Quantifying information flow for dynamic secrets. In: Proceedings of S&P, pp. 540–555 (2014)

22. Massey, J.L.: Guessing and entropy. In: Proceedings of the IEEE International Symposium on Information Theory, p. 204. IEEE (1994)

23. McIver, A., Morgan, C., Smith, G., Espinoza, B., Meinicke, L.: Abstract channels and their robust information-leakage ordering. In: Abadi, M., Kremer, S. (eds.) POST 2014. LNCS, vol. 8414, pp. 83–102. Springer, Heidelberg (2014). https://doi.org/10.1007/978-3-642-54792-8_5

24. Osborne, M.J., Rubinstein, A.: A Course in Game Theory. The MIT Press, Cambridge (1994)

25. Rizzo, J., Duong, T.: The CRIME attack (2012)

26. Shannon, C.E.: A mathematical theory of communication. Bell Syst. Tech. J. **27**, 379–423, 625–656 (1948)

27. Smith, G.: On the foundations of quantitative information flow. In: de Alfaro, L. (ed.) FOSSACS 2009. LNCS, vol. 5504, pp. 288–302. Springer, Heidelberg (2009). https://doi.org/10.1007/978-3-642-00596-1_21

28. Sun, Q., Simon, D.R., Wang, Y.-M., Russell, W., Padmanabhan, V.N., Qiu, L.: Statistical identification of encrypted web browsing traffic. In: Proceedings of S&P, pp. 19–30. IEEE (2002)
29. Xu, H., Jiang, A.X., Sinha, A., Rabinovich, Z., Dughmi, S., Tambe, M.: Security games with information leakage: modeling and computation. In: Proceedings of IJCAI, pp. 674–680 (2015)
30. Zhu, Q., Fung, C.J., Boutaba, R., Basar, T.: A game-theoretical approach to incentive design in collaborative intrusion detection networks. In: Proceedings of GAMENETS, pp. 384–392. IEEE (2009)

Equivalence Properties by Typing
in Cryptographic Branching Protocols

Véronique Cortier[1], Niklas Grimm[2], Joseph Lallemand[1(✉)],
and Matteo Maffei[2]

[1] Université de Lorraine, CNRS, Inria, LORIA, Vandœuvre-lès-Nancy, France
joseph.lallemand@loria.fr
[2] TU Wien, Vienna, Austria

Abstract. Recently, many tools have been proposed for automatically
analysing, in symbolic models, equivalence of security protocols. Equivalence is a property needed to state privacy properties or game-based
properties like strong secrecy. Tools for a bounded number of sessions
can decide equivalence but typically suffer from efficiency issues. Tools
for an unbounded number of sessions like Tamarin or ProVerif prove a
stronger notion of equivalence (diff-equivalence) that does not properly
handle protocols with else branches.

Building upon a recent approach, we propose a type system for reasoning about branching protocols and dynamic keys. We prove our type
system to entail equivalence, for all the standard primitives. Our type
system has been implemented and shows a significant speedup compared
to the tools for a bounded number of sessions, and compares similarly
to ProVerif for an unbounded number of sessions. Moreover, we can also
prove security of protocols that require a mix of bounded and unbounded
number of sessions, which ProVerif cannot properly handle.

1 Introduction

Formal methods provide a rigorous and convenient framework for analysing security protocols. In particular, mature push-button analysis tools have emerged
and have been successfully applied to many protocols from the literature in the
context of *trace properties* such as authentication or confidentiality. These tools
employ a variety of analysis techniques, such as model checking (e.g., Avispa [6]
and Scyther [31]), Horn clause resolution (e.g., ProVerif [13]), term rewriting
(e.g., Scyther [31] and Tamarin [38]), and type systems [7,12,16–21,34,36,37].

In the recent years, attention has been given also to equivalence properties,
which are crucial to model privacy properties such as vote privacy [8,33], unlinkability [5], or anonymity [9]. For example, consider an authentication protocol
P_{pass} embedded in a biometric passport. P_{pass} preserves anonymity of passport holders if an attacker cannot distinguish an execution with Alice from an
execution with Bob. This can be expressed by the equivalence $P_{pass}(Alice) \approx_t P_{pass}(Bob)$. Equivalence is also used to express properties closer to cryptographic
games like strong secrecy.

© The Author(s) 2018
L. Bauer and R. Küsters (Eds.): POST 2018, LNCS 10804, pp. 160–187, 2018.
https://doi.org/10.1007/978-3-319-89722-6_7

Two main classes of tools have been developed for equivalence. First, in the case of an unbounded number of sessions (when the protocol is executed arbitrarily many times), equivalence is undecidable. Instead, the tools ProVerif [13,15] and Tamarin [11,38] try to prove a stronger property, namely diff-equivalence, that may be too strong e.g. in the context of voting. Tamarin covers a larger class of protocols but may require some guidance from the user. Maude-NPA [35,40] also proves diff-equivalence but may have non-termination issues. Another class of tools aim at deciding equivalence, for bounded number of sessions. This is the case in particular of SPEC [32], APTE [23], Akiss [22], and SatEquiv [26]. SPEC, APTE, and Akiss suffer from efficiency issues and can typically not handle more than 3–4 sessions. SatEquiv is much more efficient but is limited to symmetric encryption and requires protocols to be well-typed, which often assumes some additional tagging of the protocol.

Our Contribution. Following the approach of [28], we propose a novel technique for proving equivalence properties for a bounded number of sessions as well as an unbounded number of sessions (or a mix of both), based on typing. [28] proposes a first type system that entails trace equivalence $P \approx_t Q$, provided protocols use fixed (long-term) keys, identical in P and Q. In this paper, we target a larger class of protocols, that includes in particular key-exchange protocols and protocols whose security relies on branching on the secret. This is the case e.g. of the private authentication protocol [3], where agent B returns a true answer to A, encrypted with A's public key if A is one of his friends, and sends a decoy message (encrypted with a dummy key) otherwise.

We devise a new type system for reasoning about keys. In particular, we introduce bikeys to cover behaviours where keys in P differ from the keys in Q. We design new typing rules to reason about protocols that may branch differently (in P and Q), depending on the input. Following the approach of [28], our type system collects sent messages into constraints that are required to be consistent. Intuitively, the type system guarantees that any execution of P can be matched by an execution of Q, while consistency imposes that the resulting sequences of messages are indistinguishable for an attacker. We had to entirely revisit the approach of [28] and prove a finer invariant in order to cope with the case where keys are used as variables. Specifically, most of the rules for encryption, signature, and decryption had to be adapted to accommodate the flexible usage of keys. For messages, we had to modify the rules for keys and encryption, in order to encrypt messages with keys of different type (bi-key type), instead of only fixed keys. We show that our type system entails equivalence for the standard notion of trace equivalence [24] and we devise a procedure for proving consistency. This yields an efficient approach for *proving* equivalence of protocols for a bounded and an unbounded number of sessions (or a combination of both).

We implemented a prototype of our type-checker that we evaluate on a set of examples, that includes private authentication, the BAC protocol (of the biometric passport), as well as Helios together with the setup phase. Our tool requires a light type annotation that specifies which keys and names are likely to be secret or public and the form of the messages encrypted by a given key. This can be easily inferred from the structure of the protocol. Our type-checker outperforms even the most efficient existing tools for a bounded number of sessions by two (for examples with few processes) to three (for examples with more processes) orders of magnitude. Note however that these tools *decide* equivalence while our type system is incomplete. In the case of an unbounded number of sessions, on our examples, the performance is comparable to ProVerif, one of the most popular tools. We consider in particular vote privacy in the Helios protocol, in the case of a dishonest ballot board, with no revote (as the protocol is insecure otherwise). ProVerif fails to handle this case as it cannot (faithfully) consider a mix of bounded and unbounded number of sessions. Compared to [28], our analysis includes the setup phase (where voters receive the election key), which could not be considered before.

The technical details and proofs omitted due to space constraints are available in the companion technical report [29].

2   High-Level Description

2.1   Background

Trace equivalence of two processes is a property that guarantees that an attacker observing the execution of either of the two processes cannot decide which one it is. Previous work [28] has shown how trace equivalence can be proved statically using a type system combined with a constraint checking procedure. The type system consists of typing rules of the form $\Gamma \vdash P \sim Q \rightarrow C$, meaning that in an environment Γ two processes P and Q are equivalent if the produced set of constraints C, encoding the attacker observables, is consistent.

The typing environment Γ is a mapping from nonces, keys, and variables to types. Nonces are assigned security labels with a confidentiality and an integrity component, e.g. HL for high confidentiality and low integrity. Key types are of the form $\text{key}^l(T)$ where l is the security label of the key and T is the type of the payload. Key types are crucial to convey typing information from one process to another one. Normally, we cannot make any assumptions about values received from the network – they might possibly originate from the attacker. If we however successfully decrypt a message using a secret symmetric key, we know that the result is of the key's payload type. This is enforced on the sender side, whenever outputting an encryption.

A core assumption of virtually any efficient static analysis for equivalence is uniform execution, meaning that the two processes of interest always take the same branch in a branching statement. For instance, this means that all decryptions must always succeed or fail equally in the two processes. For this reason, previous work introduced a restriction to allow only encryption and decryption with keys whose equality could be statically proved.

2.2   Limitation

There are however protocols that require non-uniform execution for a proof of trace equivalence, e.g., the private authentication protocol [3]. The protocol aims

$\Gamma(k_b, k_b) = \text{key}^{\text{HH}}(\text{HL} * \text{LL})$ initial message uses same key on both sides
$\Gamma(k_a, k) = \text{key}^{\text{HH}}(\text{HL})$ authentication succeeded on the left, failed on the right
$\Gamma(k, k_c) = \text{key}^{\text{HH}}(\text{HL})$ authentication succeeded on the right, failed on the left
$\Gamma(k_a, k_c) = \text{key}^{\text{HH}}(\text{HL})$ authentication succeeded on both sides
$\Gamma(k, k) = \text{key}^{\text{HH}}(\text{HL})$ authentication failed on both sides

Fig. 1. Key types for the private authentication protocol

at authenticating B to A, anonymously w.r.t. other agents. More specifically, agent B may refuse to communicate with agent A but a third agent D should not learn whether B declines communication with A or not. The protocol can be informally described as follows, where $\text{pk}(k)$ denotes the public key associated to key k, and $\text{aenc}(M, \text{pk}(k))$ denotes the asymmetric encryption of message M with this public key.

$A \rightarrow B:$ $\text{aenc}(\langle N_a, \text{pk}(k_a)\rangle, \text{pk}(k_b))$

$B \rightarrow A:$ $\begin{cases} \text{aenc}(\langle N_a, \langle N_b, \text{pk}(k_b)\rangle\rangle, \text{pk}(k_a)) & \text{if } B \text{ accepts } A\text{'s request} \\ \text{aenc}(N_b, \text{pk}(k)) & \text{if } B \text{ declines } A\text{'s request} \end{cases}$

If B declines to communicate with A, he sends a decoy message $\text{aenc}(N_b, \text{pk}(k))$ where $\text{pk}(k)$ is a decoy key (no one knows the private key k).

2.3   Encrypting with Different Keys

Let $P_a(k_a, \text{pk}(k_b))$ model agent A willing to talk with B, and $P_b(k_b, \text{pk}(k_a))$ model agent B willing to talk with A (and declining requests from other agents). We model the protocol as:

$P_a(k_a, pk_b) = \text{new } N_a.\text{out}(\text{aenc}(\langle N_a, \text{pk}(k_a)\rangle, pk_b)). \text{ in}(z)$
$P_b(k_b, pk_a) = \text{new } N_b. \text{ in}(x).$
      $\text{let } y = \text{adec}(x, k_b) \text{ in let } y_1 = \pi_1(y) \text{ in let } y_2 = \pi_2(y) \text{ in}$
            $\text{if } y_2 = pk_a \text{ then}$
                  $\text{out}(\text{aenc}(\langle y_1, \langle N_b, \text{pk}(k_b)\rangle\rangle, pk_a))$
            $\text{else out}(\text{aenc}(N_b, \text{pk}(k)))$

where $\text{adec}(M, k)$ denotes asymmetric decryption of message M with private key k. We model anonymity as the following equivalence, intuitively stating that an attacker should not be able to tell whether B accepts requests from the agent A or C:

$$P_a(k_a, \text{pk}(k_b)) \mid P_b(k_b, \text{pk}(k_a)) \approx_t P_a(k_a, \text{pk}(k_b)) \mid P_b(k_b, \text{pk}(k_c))$$

We now show how we can type the protocol in order to show trace equivalence. The initiator P_a is trivially executing uniformly, since it does not contain any branching operations. We hence focus on typing the responder P_b.

The beginning of the responder protocol can be typed using standard techniques. Then however, we perform the test $y_2 = \text{pk}(k_a)$ on the left side and

$y_2 = \mathsf{pk}(k_c)$ on the right side. Since we cannot statically determine the result of the two equality checks – and thus guarantee uniform execution – we have to typecheck the four possible combinations of **then** and **else** branches. This means we have to typecheck outputs of encryptions that use different keys on the left and the right side.

To deal with this we do not assign types to single keys, but rather to pairs of keys (k, k') – which we call *bikeys* – where k is the key used in the left process and k' is the key used in the right process. The key types used for typing are presented in Fig. 1.

As an example, we consider the combination of the **then** branch on the left with the **else** branch on the right. This combination occurs when A is successfully authenticated on the left side, while being rejected on the right side. We then have to typecheck B's positive answer together with the decoy message: $\Gamma \vdash \mathsf{aenc}(\langle y_1, \langle N_b, \mathsf{pk}(k_b) \rangle \rangle, \mathsf{pk}(k_a)) \sim \mathsf{aenc}(N_h, \mathsf{pk}(k)) : \mathsf{LL}$. For this we need the type for the bikey (k_a, k).

2.4 Decrypting Non-uniformly

When decrypting a ciphertext that was potentially generated using two different keys on the left and the right side, we have to take all possibilities into account. Consider the following extension of the process P_a where agent A decrypts B's message.

$$P_a(k_a, pk_b) = \mathsf{new}\ N_a.\mathsf{out}(\mathsf{aenc}(\langle N_a, \mathsf{pk}(k_a) \rangle, pk_b)).\ \mathsf{in}(z).$$
$$\mathsf{let}\ z' = \mathsf{adec}(z, k_a)\ \mathsf{in}\ \mathsf{out}(1)$$
$$\mathsf{else}\ \mathsf{out}(0)$$

In the decryption, there are the following possible cases:

- The message is a valid encryption supplied by the attacker (using the public key $\mathsf{pk}(k_a)$), so we check the **then** branch on both sides with $\Gamma(z') = \mathsf{LL}$.
- The message is not a valid encryption supplied by the attacker so we check the **else** branch on both sides.
- The message is a valid response from B. The keys used on the left and the right are then one of the four possible combinations $(k_a, k), (k_a, k_c), (k, k_c)$ and (k, k).
  - In the first two cases the decryption will succeed on the left and fail on the right. We hence check the **then** branch on the left with $\Gamma(z') = \mathsf{HL}$ with the **else** branch on the right. If the type $\Gamma(k_a, k)$ were different from $\Gamma(k_a, k_c)$, we would check this combination twice, using the two different payload types.
  - In the remaining two cases the decryption will fail on both sides. We hence would have to check the two **else** branches (which however we already did).

While checking the **then** branch together with the **else** branch, we have to check $\Gamma \vdash 1 \sim 0 : \mathsf{LL}$, which rightly fails, as the protocol does not guarantee trace equivalence.

3   Model

In symbolic models, security protocols are typically modelled as processes of a process algebra, such as the applied pi-calculus [2]. We present here a calculus used in [28] and inspired from the calculus underlying the ProVerif tool [14]. This section is mostly an excerpt of [28], recalled here for the sake of completeness, and illustrated with the private authentication protocol.

3.1   Terms

Messages are modelled as terms. We assume an infinite set of names $\mathcal{N}$ for nonces, further partitioned into the set $\mathcal{FN}$ of free nonces (created by the attacker) and the set $\mathcal{BN}$ of bound nonces (created by the protocol parties), an infinite set of names $\mathcal{K}$ for keys similarly split into $\mathcal{FK}$ and $\mathcal{BK}$, and an infinite set of variables $\mathcal{V}$. Cryptographic primitives are modelled through a *signature* $\mathcal{F}$, that is, a set of function symbols, given with their arity (*i.e.* the number of arguments). Here, we consider the following signature:

$$\mathcal{F}_c = \{\mathsf{pk}, \mathsf{vk}, \mathsf{enc}, \mathsf{aenc}, \mathsf{sign}, \langle \cdot, \cdot \rangle, \mathsf{h}\}$$

that models respectively public and verification key, symmetric and asymmetric encryption, concatenation and hash. The companion primitives (symmetric and asymmetric decryption, signature check, and projections) are represented by the following signature:

$$\mathcal{F}_d = \{\mathsf{dec}, \mathsf{adec}, \mathsf{checksign}, \pi_1, \pi_2\}$$

We also consider a set $\mathcal{C}$ of (public) constants (used as agent names for instance). Given a signature $\mathcal{F}$, a set of names $\mathcal{N}$, and a set of variables $\mathcal{V}$, the set of *terms* $\mathcal{T}(\mathcal{F}, \mathcal{V}, \mathcal{N})$ is the set inductively defined by applying functions to variables in $\mathcal{V}$ and names in $\mathcal{N}$. We denote by names(t) (resp. vars(t)) the set of names (resp. variables) occurring in t. A term is *ground* if it does not contain variables.

We consider the set $\mathcal{T}(\mathcal{F}_c \cup \mathcal{F}_d \cup \mathcal{C}, \mathcal{V}, \mathcal{N} \cup \mathcal{K})$ of *cryptographic terms*, simply called *terms*. *Messages* are terms with constructors from $\mathcal{T}(\mathcal{F}_c \cup \mathcal{C}, \mathcal{V}, \mathcal{N} \cup \mathcal{K})$. We assume the set of variables to be split into two subsets $\mathcal{V} = \mathcal{X} \uplus \mathcal{AX}$ where $\mathcal{X}$ are variables used in processes while $\mathcal{AX}$ are variables used to store messages. An *attacker term* is a term from $\mathcal{T}(\mathcal{F}_c \cup \mathcal{F}_d \cup \mathcal{C}, \mathcal{AX}, \mathcal{FN} \cup \mathcal{FK})$. In particular, an attacker term cannot use nonces and keys created by the protocol's parties.

A *substitution* $\sigma = \{M_1/x_1, \ldots, M_k/x_k\}$ is a mapping from variables $x_1, \ldots, x_k \in \mathcal{V}$ to messages $M_1, \ldots, M_k$. We let dom(σ) = $\{x_1, \ldots, x_k\}$. We say that σ is ground if all messages $M_1, \ldots, M_k$ are ground. We let names(σ) = $\bigcup_{1 \leq i \leq k}$ names(M_i). The application of a substitution σ to a term t is denoted $t\sigma$ and is defined as usual.

The *evaluation* of a term t, denoted $t \downarrow$, corresponds to the bottom-up application of the cryptographic primitives and is recursively defined as follows.

$$
\begin{aligned}
u \downarrow &= u && \text{if } u \in \mathcal{N} \cup \mathcal{V} \cup \mathcal{K} \cup \mathcal{C} \\
\mathsf{pk}(t) \downarrow &= \mathsf{pk}(t \downarrow) && \text{if } t \downarrow \in \mathcal{K} \\
\mathsf{vk}(t) \downarrow &= \mathsf{vk}(t \downarrow) && \text{if } t \downarrow \in \mathcal{K} \\
\mathsf{h}(t) \downarrow &= \mathsf{h}(t \downarrow) && \text{if } t \downarrow \neq \bot \\
\langle t_1, t_2 \rangle \downarrow &= \langle t_1 \downarrow, t_2 \downarrow \rangle && \text{if } t_1 \downarrow \neq \bot \text{ and } t_2 \downarrow \neq \bot \\
\mathsf{enc}(t_1, t_2) \downarrow &= \mathsf{enc}(t_1 \downarrow, t_2 \downarrow) && \text{if } t_1 \downarrow \neq \bot \text{ and } t_2 \downarrow \in \mathcal{K} \\
\mathsf{sign}(t_1, t_2) \downarrow &= \mathsf{sign}(t_1 \downarrow, t_2 \downarrow) && \text{if } t_1 \downarrow \neq \bot \text{ and } t_2 \downarrow \in \mathcal{K} \\
\mathsf{aenc}(t_1, t_2) \downarrow &= \mathsf{aenc}(t_1 \downarrow, t_2 \downarrow) && \text{if } t_1 \downarrow \neq \bot \text{ and } t_2 \downarrow = \mathsf{pk}(k) \\
&&& \text{for some } k \in \mathcal{K}
\end{aligned}
$$

$$
\begin{aligned}
\pi_1(t) \downarrow &= t_1 \text{ if } t \downarrow = \langle t_1, t_2 \rangle \\
\pi_2(t) \downarrow &= t_2 \text{ if } t \downarrow = \langle t_1, t_2 \rangle \\
\mathsf{dec}(t_1, t_2) \downarrow &= t_3 \text{ if } t_1 \downarrow = \mathsf{enc}(t_3, t_4) \text{ and } t_4 = t_2 \downarrow \\
\mathsf{adec}(t_1, t_2) \downarrow &= t_3 \text{ if } t_1 \downarrow = \mathsf{aenc}(t_3, \mathsf{pk}(t_4)) \text{ and } t_4 = t_2 \downarrow \\
\mathsf{checksign}(t_1, t_2) \downarrow &= t_3 \text{ if } t_1 \downarrow = \mathsf{sign}(t_3, t_4) \text{ and } t_2 \downarrow = \mathsf{vk}(t_4) \\
t \downarrow &= \bot \text{ otherwise}
\end{aligned}
$$

Note that the evaluation of term t succeeds only if the underlying keys are atomic and always returns a message or $\bot$. For example we have $\pi_1(\langle a, b \rangle) \downarrow = a$, while $\mathsf{dec}(\mathsf{enc}(a, \langle b, b \rangle), \langle b, b \rangle) \downarrow = \bot$, because the key is non atomic. We write $t =_\downarrow t'$ if $t \downarrow = t' \downarrow$.

Destructors used in processes:

$$
d ::= \mathsf{dec}(x, t) \mid \mathsf{adec}(x, t) \mid \mathsf{checksign}(x, t') \mid \pi_1(x) \mid \pi_2(x)
$$

where $x \in \mathcal{X}, t \in \mathcal{K} \cup \mathcal{X}, t' \in \{\mathsf{vk}(k) | k \in \mathcal{K}\} \cup \mathcal{X}$.

Processes:

$$
\begin{aligned}
P, Q ::= \; & 0 \mid \mathsf{new} \; n.P \mid \mathsf{out}(M).P \mid \mathsf{in}(x).P \mid (P \mid Q) \mid !P \\
& \mid \mathsf{let} \; x = d \; \mathsf{in} \; P \; \mathsf{else} \; Q \mid \mathsf{if} \; M = N \; \mathsf{then} \; P \; \mathsf{else} \; Q
\end{aligned}
$$

where $n \in \mathcal{BN} \cup \mathcal{BK}$, $x \in \mathcal{X}$, and M, N are messages.

Fig. 2. Syntax for processes.

3.2 Processes

Security protocols describe how messages should be exchanged between participants. We model them through a process algebra, whose syntax is displayed in Fig. 2. We identify processes up to α-renaming, *i.e.*, avoiding substitution of bound names and variables, which are defined as usual. Furthermore, we assume that all bound names, keys, and variables in the process are distinct.

A *configuration* of the system is a tuple $(\mathcal{P}; \phi; \sigma)$ where:

- $\mathcal{P}$ is a multiset of processes that represents the current active processes;
- ϕ is a substitution with $\mathrm{dom}(\phi) \subseteq \mathcal{AX}$ and for any $x \in \mathrm{dom}(\phi)$, $\phi(x)$ (also denoted $x\phi$) is a message that only contains variables in $\mathrm{dom}(\sigma)$. ϕ represents the terms that have been sent;
- σ is a ground substitution.

The semantics of processes is given through a transition relation $\xrightarrow{\alpha}$, defined in Fig. 3 (τ denotes a silent action). The relation $\xrightarrow{w}_*$ is defined as the reflexive transitive closure of $\xrightarrow{\alpha}$, where w is the concatenation of all actions. We also write equality up to silent actions $=_\tau$.

Intuitively, process new $n.P$ creates a fresh nonce or key, and behaves like P. Process $\mathrm{out}(M).P$ emits M and behaves like P, provided that the evaluation of M is successful. The corresponding message is stored in the frame ϕ, corresponding to the attacker knowledge. A process may input any message that an attacker can forge (rule IN) from her knowledge ϕ, using a recipe R to compute a new message from ϕ. Note that all names are initially assumed to be secret. Process $P \mid Q$ corresponds to the parallel composition of P and Q. Process let $x = d$ in P else Q behaves like P in which x is replaced by d if d can be successfully evaluated and behaves like Q otherwise. Process if $M = N$ then P else Q behaves like P if M and N correspond to two equal messages and behaves like Q otherwise. The replicated process $!P$ behaves as an unbounded number of copies of P.

A *trace* of a process P is any possible sequence of transitions in the presence of an attacker that may read, forge, and send messages. Formally, the set of traces $\mathrm{trace}(P)$ is defined as follows.

$$\mathrm{trace}(P) = \{(w, \phi, \sigma) | (\{P\}; \emptyset; \emptyset) \xrightarrow{w}_* (\mathcal{P}; \phi; \sigma)\}$$

Example 1. Consider the private authentication protocol (PA) presented in Sect. 2. The process $P_b(k_b, \mathrm{pk}(k_a))$ corresponding to responder B answering a request from A has already been defined in Sect. 2.3. The process $P_a(k_a, \mathrm{pk}(k_b))$ corresponding A willing to talk to B is:

$$P_a(k_a, pk_b) = \text{new } N_a.\mathrm{out}(\mathrm{aenc}(\langle N_a, \mathrm{pk}(k_a)\rangle, pk_b)).\ \mathrm{in}(z)$$

Altogether, a session between A and B is represented by the process:

$$P_a(k_a, \mathrm{pk}(k_b)) \mid P_b(k_b, \mathrm{pk}(k_a))$$

where $k_a, k_b \in \mathcal{BK}$, which models that the attacker initially does not know k_a, k_b.

$$(\{P_1 \mid P_2\} \cup \mathcal{P}; \phi; \sigma) \xrightarrow{\tau} (\{P_1, P_2\} \cup \mathcal{P}; \phi; \sigma) \qquad \text{PAR}$$

$$(\{0\} \cup \mathcal{P}; \phi; \sigma) \xrightarrow{\tau} (\mathcal{P}; \phi; \sigma) \qquad \text{ZERO}$$

$$(\{\text{new } n.P\} \cup \mathcal{P}; \phi; \sigma) \xrightarrow{\tau} (\{P\} \cup \mathcal{P}; \phi; \sigma) \qquad \text{NEW}$$

$$(\{\text{new } k.P\} \cup \mathcal{P}; \phi; \sigma) \xrightarrow{\tau} (\{P\} \cup \mathcal{P}; \phi; \sigma) \qquad \text{NEWKEY}$$

$$(\{\text{out}(t).P\} \cup \mathcal{P}; \phi; \sigma) \xrightarrow{\text{new } ax_n.\text{out}(ax_n)} (\{P\} \cup \mathcal{P}; \phi \cup \{t/ax_n\}; \sigma) \qquad \text{OUT}$$
$$\text{if } t\sigma \text{ is a ground term}, (t\sigma) \downarrow \neq \bot, ax_n \in \mathcal{AX} \text{ and } n = |\phi| + 1$$

$$(\{\text{in}(x).P\} \cup \mathcal{P}; \phi; \sigma) \xrightarrow{\text{in}(R)} (\{P\} \cup \mathcal{P}; \phi; \sigma \cup \{(R\phi\sigma) \downarrow /x\}) \qquad \text{IN}$$
$$\text{if } R \text{ is an attacker term such that } \text{vars}(R) \subseteq \text{dom}(\phi),$$
$$\text{and}(R\phi\sigma) \downarrow \neq \bot$$

$$(\{\text{let } x = d \text{ in } P \text{ else } Q\} \cup \mathcal{P}; \phi; \sigma) \xrightarrow{\tau} (\{P\} \cup \mathcal{P}; \phi; \sigma \cup \{(d\sigma) \downarrow /x\}) \qquad \text{LET-IN}$$
$$\text{if } d\sigma \text{ is ground and } (d\sigma) \downarrow \neq \bot$$

$$(\{\text{let } x = d \text{ in } P \text{ else } Q\} \cup \mathcal{P}; \phi; \sigma) \xrightarrow{\tau} (\{Q\} \cup \mathcal{P}; \phi; \sigma) \qquad \text{LET-ELSE}$$
$$\text{if } d\sigma \text{ is ground and } (d\sigma) \downarrow = \bot, \text{ i.e. } d \text{ fails}$$

$$(\{\text{if } M = N \text{ then } P \text{ else } Q\} \cup \mathcal{P}; \phi; \sigma) \xrightarrow{\tau} (\{P\} \cup \mathcal{P}; \phi; \sigma) \qquad \text{IF-THEN}$$
$$\text{if } M, N \text{ are messages such that } M\sigma, N\sigma \text{ are ground},$$
$$(M\sigma) \downarrow \neq \bot, (N\sigma) \downarrow \neq \bot, \text{ and } M\sigma = N\sigma$$

$$(\{\text{if } M = N \text{ then } P \text{ else } Q\} \cup \mathcal{P}; \phi; \sigma) \xrightarrow{\tau} (\{Q\} \cup \mathcal{P}; \phi; \sigma) \qquad \text{IF-ELSE}$$
$$\text{if } M, N \text{ are messages such that } M\sigma, N\sigma \text{ are ground}$$
$$\text{and } (M\sigma) \downarrow = \bot \text{ or } (N\sigma) \downarrow = \bot \text{ or } M\sigma \neq N\sigma$$

$$(\{!P\} \cup \mathcal{P}; \phi; \sigma) \xrightarrow{\tau} (\{P, !P\} \cup \mathcal{P}; \phi; \sigma) \qquad \text{REPL}$$

Fig. 3. Semantics

An example of a trace describing an "honest" execution, where the attacker does not interfere with the intended run of the protocol, can be written as (tr, ϕ) where

$$tr =_\tau \text{new } x_1.\text{out}(x_1).\text{in}(x_1).\text{new } x_2.\text{out}(x_2).\text{in}(x_2)$$

and

$$\phi = \{x_1 \mapsto \text{aenc}(\langle N_a, \text{pk}(k_a)\rangle, \text{pk}(k_b)), x_2 \mapsto \text{aenc}(\langle N_a, \langle N_b, \text{pk}(k_b)\rangle\rangle, \text{pk}(k_a))\}.$$

The trace tr describes A outputting the first message of the protocol, which is stored in $\phi(x_1)$. The attacker then simply forwards $\phi(x_1)$ to B. B then performs several silent actions (decrypting the message, comparing its content to $\text{pk}(k_a)$), and outputs a response, which is stored in $\phi(x_2)$ and forwarded to A by the attacker.

$$l \quad ::= \quad \text{LL} \mid \text{HL} \mid \text{HH}$$
$$KT ::= \quad \text{key}^l(T) \mid \text{eqkey}^l(T) \mid \text{seskey}^{l,a}(T) \text{ with } a \in \{1, \infty\}$$
$$T \quad ::= \quad l \mid T * T \mid T \vee T \mid [\![\tau_n^{l,a} ; \tau_m^{l',a}]\!] \text{ with } a \in \{1, \infty\}$$
$$\mid KT \mid \text{pkey}(KT) \mid \text{vkey}(KT) \mid (T)_T \mid \{T\}_T$$

Fig. 4. Types for terms

3.3   Equivalence

When processes evolve, sent messages are stored in a substitution ϕ while the values of variables are stored in σ. A *frame* is simply a substitution ψ where $\mathrm{dom}(\psi) \subseteq \mathcal{AX}$. It represents the knowledge of an attacker. In what follows, we will typically consider $\phi\sigma$.

Intuitively, two sequences of messages are indistinguishable to an attacker if he cannot perform any test that could distinguish them. This is typically modelled as static equivalence [2]. Here, we consider of variant of [2] where the attacker is also given the ability to observe when the evaluation of a term fails, as defined for example in [25].

Definition 1 (Static Equivalence). *Two ground frames ϕ and ϕ' are statically equivalent if and only if they have the same domain, and for all attacker terms R, S with variables in $\mathrm{dom}(\phi) = \mathrm{dom}(\phi')$, we have*

$$(R\phi =_\downarrow S\phi) \iff (R\phi' =_\downarrow S\phi')$$

Then two processes P and Q are in equivalence if no matter how the adversary interacts with P, a similar interaction may happen with Q, with equivalent resulting frames.

Definition 2 (Trace Equivalence). *Let P, Q be two processes. We write $P \sqsubseteq_t Q$ if for all $(s, \phi, \sigma) \in \mathrm{trace}(P)$, there exists $(s', \phi', \sigma') \in \mathrm{trace}(Q)$ such that $s =_\tau s'$ and $\phi\sigma$ and $\phi'\sigma'$ are statically equivalent. We say that P and Q are trace equivalent, and we write $P \approx_t Q$, if $P \sqsubseteq_t Q$ and $Q \sqsubseteq_t P$.*

Note that this definition already includes the attacker's behaviour, since processes may input any message forged by the attacker.

Example 2. As explained in Sect. 2, anonymity is modelled as an equivalence property. Intuitively, an attacker should not be able to know which agents are executing the protocol. In the case of protocol PA, presented in Example 1, the anonymity property can be modelled by the following equivalence:

$$P_a(k_a, \mathrm{pk}(k_b)) \mid P_b(k_b, \mathrm{pk}(k_a)) \approx_t P_a(k_a, \mathrm{pk}(k_b)) \mid P_b(k_b, \mathrm{pk}(k_c))$$

4   A Type System for Dynamic Keys

Types. In our type system we give types to pairs of messages – one from the left process and one from the right one. We store the types of nonces, variables, and keys in a typing environment Γ. While we store a type for a single nonce or variable occurring in both processes, we assign a potentially different type to every different combination of keys (k, k') used in the left and right process – so called *bikeys*. This is an important non-standard feature that enables us to type protocols using different encryption and decryption keys.

The types for messages are defined in Fig. 4 and explained below. Selected subtyping rules are given in Fig. 5. We assume three security labels HH, HL and LL,

$$\frac{}{\text{eqkey}^l(T) <: \text{key}^l(T)} \text{ (SEQKEY)} \qquad \frac{}{\text{seskey}^{l,a}(T) <: \text{eqkey}^l(T)} \text{ (SSESKEY)}$$

$$\frac{}{\text{key}^l(T) <: l} \text{ (SKEY)} \qquad \frac{T <: \text{eqkey}^l(T')}{\text{pkey}(T) <: \text{LL}} \text{ (SPUBKEY)} \qquad \frac{T <: \text{eqkey}^l(T')}{\text{vkey}(T) <: \text{LL}} \text{ (SVKEY)}$$

$$\frac{T <: T'}{(T)_{T''} <: (T')_{T''}} \text{ (SENC)} \qquad \frac{T <: T'}{\{T\}_{T''} <: \{T'\}_{T''}} \text{ (SAENC)}$$

Fig. 5. Selected subtyping rules

ranged over by l, whose first (resp. second) component denotes the confidentiality (resp. integrity) level. Intuitively, values of high confidentiality may never be output to the network in plain, and values of high integrity are guaranteed not to originate from the attacker. Pair types $T * T'$ describe the type of their components and the type $T \vee T'$ is given to messages that can have type T or type T'.

The type $\tau_n^{l,a}$ describes nonces and constants of security level l: the label a ranges over $\{\infty, 1\}$, denoting whether the nonce is bound within a replication or not (constants are always typed with $a = 1$). We assume a different identifier n for each constant and restriction in the process. The type $\tau_n^{l,1}$ is populated by a single name, (i.e., n describes a constant or a non-replicated nonce) and $\tau_n^{l,\infty}$ is a special type, that is instantiated to $\tau_{n_j}^{l,1}$ in the jth replication of the process. Type $[\![\tau_n^{l,a} ; \tau_m^{l',a}]\!]$ is a refinement type that restricts the set of possible values of a message to values of type $\tau_n^{l,a}$ on the left and type $\tau_m^{l',a}$ on the right. For a refinement type $[\![\tau_n^{l,a} ; \tau_n^{l,a}]\!]$ with equal types on both sides we write $\tau_n^{l,a}$.

Keys can have three different types ranged over by KT, ordered by a subtyping relation (SEQKEY, SSESKEY): $\text{seskey}^{l,a}(T) <: \text{eqkey}^l(T) <: \text{key}^l(T)$. For all three types, l denotes the security label (SKEY) of the key and T is the type of the payload that can be encrypted or signed with these keys. This allows us to transfer typing information from one process to another one: e.g. when encrypting, we check that the payload type is respected, so that we can be sure to get a value of the payload type upon decryption. The three different types encode different relations between the left and the right component of a bikey (k, k'). While type $\text{key}^l(T)$ can be given to bikeys with different components $k \neq k'$, type $\text{eqkey}^l(T)$ ensures that the keys are equal on both sides in the specific typed instruction. Type $\text{seskey}^{l,a}(T)$ additionally guarantees that the key is always the same on the left and the right throughout the whole process. We allow for dynamic generation of keys of type $\text{seskey}^{l,a}(T)$ and use a label a to denote whether the key is generated under replication or not – just like for nonce types.

For a key of type T, we use types $\text{pkey}(T)$ and $\text{vkey}(T)$ for the corresponding public key and verification key, and types $(T')_T$ and $\{T'\}_T$ for symmetric and asymmetric encryptions of messages of type T' with this key. Public keys and verification keys can be treated as LL if the corresponding keys are equal (SPUBKEY, SVKEY) and subtyping on encryptions is directly induced by subtyping of the payload types (SENC, SAENC) (Fig. 6).

$$\frac{\Gamma(n) = \tau_n^{l,a} \quad \Gamma(m) = \tau_m^{l,a} \quad l \in \{\mathrm{HH}, \mathrm{HL}\}}{\Gamma \vdash n \sim m : l \rightarrow \emptyset} \; (\text{TNONCE}) \qquad \frac{\Gamma(n) = \tau_n^{\mathrm{LL},a}}{\Gamma \vdash n \sim n : \mathrm{LL} \rightarrow \emptyset} \; (\text{TNONCEL})$$

$$\frac{\Gamma(x) = T}{\Gamma \vdash x \sim x : T \rightarrow \emptyset} \; (\text{TVAR}) \qquad \frac{\Gamma \vdash M \sim N : T' \rightarrow c \quad T' <: T}{\Gamma \vdash M \sim N : T \rightarrow c} \; (\text{TSUB})$$

$$\frac{\Gamma \vdash M \sim N : T \rightarrow c \quad \Gamma \vdash M' \sim N' : T' \rightarrow c'}{\Gamma \vdash \langle M, M' \rangle \sim \langle N, N' \rangle : T * T' \rightarrow c \cup c'} \; (\text{TPAIR})$$

$$\frac{M, N \text{ well formed}}{\Gamma \vdash M \sim N : \mathrm{HL} \rightarrow \emptyset} \; (\text{THIGH})$$

$$\frac{\Gamma(k, k') = T}{\Gamma \vdash k \sim k' : T \rightarrow \emptyset} \; (\text{TKEY}) \qquad \frac{k \in \mathrm{keys}(\Gamma) \cup \mathcal{FK}}{\Gamma \vdash \mathrm{pk}(k) \sim \mathrm{pk}(k) : \mathrm{LL} \rightarrow \emptyset} \; (\text{TPUBKEYL})$$

$$\frac{\Gamma \vdash M \sim N : T \rightarrow \emptyset \quad \exists T', l.T <: \mathrm{key}^l(T')}{\Gamma \vdash \mathrm{pk}(M) \sim \mathrm{pk}(N) : \mathrm{pkey}(T) \rightarrow \emptyset} \; (\text{TPUBKEY})$$

$$\frac{\Gamma \vdash M \sim N : T \rightarrow c \quad \Gamma \vdash M' \sim N' : T' \rightarrow c'}{T' = \mathrm{LL} \; \vee \; (\exists T'', T''', l.T' = \mathrm{pkey}(T'') \wedge T'' <: \mathrm{key}^l(T'''))} \qquad \frac{}{\Gamma \vdash \mathrm{aenc}(M, M') \sim \mathrm{aenc}(N, N') : \{T\}_{T'} \rightarrow c \cup c'} \; (\text{TAENC})$$

$$\frac{\Gamma \vdash M \sim N : \{T\}_{\mathrm{pkey}(T')} \rightarrow c \quad T' <: \mathrm{key}^{\mathrm{HH}}(T)}{\Gamma \vdash M \sim N : \mathrm{LL} \rightarrow c \cup \{M \sim N\}} \; (\text{TAENCH})$$

$$\frac{\Gamma \vdash M \sim N : \{\mathrm{LL}\}_T \rightarrow c \quad (T = \mathrm{pkey}(T') \wedge T' <: \mathrm{eqkey}^l(T'')) \text{ or } T = \mathrm{LL}}{\Gamma \vdash M \sim N : \mathrm{LL} \rightarrow c} \; (\text{TAENCL})$$

Fig. 6. Selected rules for messages

Constraints. When typing messages, we generate constraints of the form $(M \sim N)$, meaning that the attacker may see M and N in the left and right process, respectively, and these two messages are thus required to be indistinguishable.

Due to space reasons we only present a few selected rules that are characteristic of the typing of branching protocols. The omitted rules are similar in spirit to the presented ones or are standard rules for equivalence typing [28].

4.1 Typing Messages

The typing judgement for messages is of the form $\Gamma \vdash M \sim N : T \rightarrow c$ which reads as follows: under the environment Γ, M and N are of type T and either this is a high confidentiality type (i.e., M and N are not disclosed to the attacker) or M and N are indistinguishable for the attacker assuming the set of constraints c is consistent.

Confidential nonces can be given their label from the typing environment in rule TNONCE. Since their label prevents them from being released in clear, the attacker cannot observe them and we do not need to add constraints for them. They can however be output in encrypted form and will then appear in the constraints of the encryption. Public nonces (labeled as LL) can be typed if they are equal on both sides (rule TNONCEL). These are standard rules, as well as the rules TVAR, TSUB, TPAIR and THIGH [28].

A non-standard rule that is crucial for the typing of branching protocols is rule TKEY. As the typing environment contains types for bikeys (k, k') this rule allows us to type two potentially different keys with their type from the environment. With the standard rule TPUBKEYL we can only type a public key of the same keys on both sides, while rule TPUBKEY allows us to type different public keys $\text{pk}(M), \text{pk}(N)$, provided we can show that there exists a valid key type for the terms M and N. This highlights another important technical contribution of this work, as compared to existing type systems for equivalence: we do not only support a fixed set of keys, but also allow for the usage of keys in variables, that have been received from the network.

To show that a message is of type $\{T\}_{T'}$ – a message of type T encrypted asymmetrically with a key of type T', we have to show that the corresponding terms have exactly these types in rule TAENC. The generated constraints are simply propagated. In addition we need to show that T' is a valid type for a public key, or LL, which models untrusted keys received from the network. Note, that this rule allows us to encrypt messages with different keys in the two processes. For encryptions with honest keys (label HH) we can use rule TAENC to give type LL to the messages, if we can show that the payload type is respected. In this case we add the entire encryptions to the constraints, since the attacker can check different encryptions for equality, even if he cannot obtain the plaintext. Rule TAENCL allows us to give type LL to encryptions even if we do not respect the payload type, or if the key is corrupted. However, we then have to type the plaintexts with type LL since we cannot guarantee their confidentiality. Additionally, we have to ensure that the same key is used in both processes, because the attacker might possess the corresponding private keys and test which decryption succeeds. Since we already add constraints for giving type LL to the plaintext, we do not need to add any additional constraints.

4.2   Typing Processes

From now on, we assume that processes assign a type to freshly generated nonces and keys. That is, new $n.P$ is now of the form new $n : T. P$. This requires a (very light) type annotation from the user. The typing judgement for processes is of the form $\Gamma \vdash P \sim Q \to C$ and can be interpreted as follows: If two processes P and Q can be typed in Γ and if the generated constraint set C is consistent, then P and Q are trace equivalent. We present selected rules in Fig. 7.

Rule POUT states that we can output messages to the network if we can type them with type LL, i.e., they are indistinguishable to the attacker, provided that the generated set c of constraints is consistent. The constraints of c are then added to all constraints in the constraint set C. We define $C \cup_\forall c' := \{(c \cup c', \Gamma) \mid (c, \Gamma) \in C\}$. This rule, as well as the rules PZERO, PIN, PNEW, PPAR, and PLET, are standard rules [28].

$$\frac{\Gamma \vdash P \sim Q \rightarrow C \qquad \Gamma \vdash M \sim N : \mathsf{LL} \rightarrow c}{\Gamma \vdash \mathsf{out}(M).P \sim \mathsf{out}(N).Q \rightarrow C \cup_\forall c} \text{ (POUT)}$$

$$\frac{\Gamma \vdash \diamond \quad \Gamma \text{ does not contain union types}}{\Gamma \vdash 0 \sim 0 \rightarrow (\emptyset, \Gamma)} \text{ (PZERO)} \qquad \frac{\Gamma, x : \mathsf{LL} \vdash P \sim Q \rightarrow C}{\Gamma \vdash \mathsf{in}(x).P \sim \mathsf{in}(x).Q \rightarrow C} \text{ (PIN)}$$

$$\frac{\Gamma, n : \tau_n^{l,a} \vdash P \sim Q \rightarrow C}{\Gamma \vdash \mathsf{new}\ n : \tau_n^{l,a}.P \sim \mathsf{new}\ n : \tau_n^{l,a}.Q \rightarrow C} \text{ (PNEW)}$$

$$\frac{\Gamma, (k,k) : \mathsf{seskey}^{l,a}(T) \vdash P \sim Q \rightarrow C}{\Gamma \vdash \mathsf{new}\ k : \mathsf{seskey}^{l,a}(T).P \sim \mathsf{new}\ k : \mathsf{seskey}^{l,a}(T).Q \rightarrow C} \text{ (PNEWKEY)}$$

$$\frac{\Gamma \vdash P \sim Q \rightarrow C \qquad \Gamma \vdash P' \sim Q' \rightarrow C'}{\Gamma \vdash P \mid P' \sim Q \mid Q' \rightarrow C \cup_\times C'} \text{ (PPAR)}$$

$$\frac{\Gamma \vdash_d t \sim t' : T \qquad \Gamma, x : T \vdash P \sim Q \rightarrow C \qquad \Gamma \vdash P' \sim Q' \rightarrow C'}{\Gamma \vdash \mathsf{let}\ x = t\ \mathsf{in}\ P\ \mathsf{else}\ P' \sim \mathsf{let}\ x = t'\ \mathsf{in}\ Q\ \mathsf{else}\ Q' \rightarrow C \cup C'} \text{ (PLET)}$$

(PLETADECSAME)

$$\frac{\begin{array}{c} \Gamma(y) = \mathsf{LL} \qquad \Gamma(k,k) <: \mathsf{key}^{\mathsf{HH}}(T) \\ \Gamma, x : T \vdash P \sim Q \rightarrow C \quad \Gamma, x : \mathsf{LL} \vdash P \sim Q \rightarrow C' \quad \Gamma \vdash P' \sim Q' \rightarrow C'' \\ (\forall T'.\forall k' \neq k.\ \Gamma(k,k') <: \mathsf{key}^{\mathsf{HH}}(T') \Rightarrow \Gamma, x : T' \vdash P \sim Q' \rightarrow C_{k'}) \\ (\forall T'.\forall k' \neq k.\ \Gamma(k',k) <: \mathsf{key}^{\mathsf{HH}}(T') \Rightarrow \Gamma, x : T' \vdash P' \sim Q \rightarrow C'_{k'}) \end{array}}{\begin{array}{c} \Gamma \vdash \mathsf{let}\ x = \mathsf{adec}(y,k)\ \mathsf{in}\ P\ \mathsf{else}\ P' \sim \mathsf{let}\ x = \mathsf{adec}(y,k)\ \mathsf{in}\ Q\ \mathsf{else}\ Q' \\ \rightarrow C \cup C' \cup C'' \cup (\bigcup_{k'} C_{k'}) \cup (\bigcup_{k'} C'_{k'}) \end{array}}$$

$$\frac{\begin{array}{c} \Gamma \vdash P \sim Q \rightarrow C_1 \\ \Gamma \vdash P \sim Q' \rightarrow C_2 \quad \Gamma \vdash P' \sim Q \rightarrow C_3 \quad \Gamma \vdash P' \sim Q' \rightarrow C_4 \end{array}}{\begin{array}{c} \Gamma \vdash \mathsf{if}\ M = M'\ \mathsf{then}\ P\ \mathsf{else}\ P' \sim \mathsf{if}\ N = N'\ \mathsf{then}\ Q\ \mathsf{else}\ Q' \\ \rightarrow C_1 \cup C_2 \cup C_3 \cup C_4 \end{array}} \text{ (PIFALL)}$$

Fig. 7. Selected rules for processes

Rule PNEWKEY allows us to generate new session keys at runtime, which models security protocols more faithfully. It also allows us to generate infinitely many keys, by introducing new keys under replication.

Rule PLETADECSAME treats asymmetric decryptions where we use the same fixed honest key (label HH) for decryptions in both processes. Standard type systems for equivalence have a simplifying (and restrictive) invariant that guarantees that encryptions are always performed using the same keys in both processes and hence guarantee that both processes always take the same branch in decryption (compare rule PLET). In our system however, we allow encryptions with potentially different keys, which requires cross-case validation in order to retain soundness. Still, the number of possible combinations of encryption keys is limited by the assignments in the typing environment Γ. To cover all the possibilities, we type the following combinations of continuation processes:

$$\frac{\Gamma(k,k) <: \mathrm{key}^{\mathrm{LL}}(T) \qquad \Gamma(x) = \mathrm{LL}}{\Gamma \vdash_d \mathrm{adec}(x,k) \sim \mathrm{adec}(x,k) : \mathrm{LL}} \text{ (DADECL)}$$

$$\frac{\Gamma(y) = \mathrm{seskey}^{\mathrm{HH},a}(T) \qquad \Gamma(x) = \mathrm{LL}}{\Gamma \vdash_d \mathrm{adec}(x,y) \sim \mathrm{adec}(x,y) : T \vee \mathrm{LL}} \text{ (DADECH')}$$

$$\frac{(\Gamma(y) = \mathrm{seskey}^{\mathrm{LL},a}(T) \vee \Gamma(y) = \mathrm{LL}) \qquad \Gamma(x) = \mathrm{LL}}{\Gamma \vdash_d \mathrm{adec}(x,y) \sim \mathrm{adec}(x,y) : \mathrm{LL}} \text{ (DADECL')}$$

$$\frac{\Gamma(k,k) = \mathrm{seskey}^{l,a}(T') \qquad \Gamma(x) = \{T\}_{\mathrm{pkey}(\mathrm{seskey}^{l,a}(T'))}}{\Gamma \vdash_d \mathrm{adec}(x,k) \sim \mathrm{adec}(x,k) : T} \text{ (DADECT)}$$

$$\frac{\Gamma(y) = \mathrm{seskey}^{l,a}(T') \qquad \Gamma(x) = \{T\}_{\mathrm{pkey}(\mathrm{seskey}^{l,a}(T'))}}{\Gamma \vdash_d \mathrm{adec}(x,y) \sim \mathrm{adec}(x,y) : T} \text{ (DADECT')}$$

Fig. 8. Selected destructor rules

- Both **then** branches: In this case we know that key k was used for encryption on both sides. Because of $\Gamma(k,k) = \mathrm{key}^{\mathrm{HH}}(T)$, we know that in this case the payload type is T and we type the continuation with $\Gamma, x : T$.
  Because the message may also originate from the attacker (who also has access to the public key), we have to type the two **then** branches also with $\Gamma, x : \mathrm{LL}$.
- Both **else** branches: If decryption fails on both sides, we type the two **else** branches without introducing any new variables.
- Left **then**, right **else**: The encryption may have been created with key k on the left side and another key k' on the right side. Hence, for each $k' \neq k$, such that $\Gamma(k,k')$ maps to a key type with label HH and payload type T', we have to typecheck the left **then** branch and the right **else** branch with $\Gamma, x : T'$.
- Left **else**, right **then**: This case is analogous to the previous one.

The generated set of constraints is simply the union of all generated constraints for the subprocesses. Rule PIFALL lets us typecheck any conditional by simply checking the four possible branch combinations. In contrast to the other rules for conditionals that we present in a companion technical report, this rule does not require any other preconditions or checks on the terms M, M', N, N'.

Destructor Rules. The rule PLET requires that a destructor application succeeds or fails equally in the two processes. To ensure this property, it relies on additional rules for destructors. We present selected rules in Fig. 8. Rule DADECL is a standard rule that states that a decryption of a variable of type LL with an untrusted key (label LL) yields a result of type LL. Decryption with a trusted (label HH) session key gives us a value of the key's payload type or type LL in case the encryption was created by the attacker using the public key. Here it is important that the key is of type $\mathrm{seskey}^{\mathrm{HH},a}(T)$, since this guarantees that the key is never used in combination with a different key and hence decryption will always equally succeed or fail in both processes. Rule DADECL' is similar to

$$* = \frac{\langle y_1, \langle N_b, \mathrm{pk}(k_b)\rangle\rangle, N_b \text{ well formed}}{\Gamma \vdash \langle y_1, \langle N_b, \mathrm{pk}(k_b)\rangle\rangle \sim N_b : \mathrm{HL} \rightarrow \emptyset} \text{ THigh}$$

$$\frac{\Gamma(k_a, k) = \mathrm{key}^{\mathrm{HH}}(\mathrm{HL})}{\Gamma \vdash k_a \sim k : \mathrm{key}^{\mathrm{HH}}(\mathrm{HL}) \rightarrow \emptyset} \text{ TKey}$$

$$* \quad \frac{\Gamma \vdash \mathrm{pk}(k_a) \sim \mathrm{pk}(k) : \mathrm{pkey}(\mathrm{key}^{\mathrm{HH}}(\mathrm{HL})) \rightarrow \emptyset}{} \text{ TPubKey}$$

$$\frac{\Gamma \vdash \mathrm{aenc}(\langle y_1, \langle N_b, \mathrm{pk}(k_b)\rangle\rangle, \mathrm{pk}(k_a)) \sim \mathrm{aenc}(N_b, \mathrm{pk}(k)) : \{\mathrm{HL}\}_{\mathrm{pkey}(\mathrm{key}^{\mathrm{HH}}(\mathrm{HL}))} \rightarrow \emptyset}{\Gamma \vdash \mathrm{aenc}(\langle y_1, \langle N_b, \mathrm{pk}(k_b)\rangle\rangle, \mathrm{pk}(k_a)) \sim \mathrm{aenc}(N_b, \mathrm{pk}(k)) : \mathrm{LL} \rightarrow C} \begin{matrix} \text{TAenc} \\ \text{TAencH} \end{matrix}$$

where $C = \{\mathrm{aenc}(\langle y_1, \langle N_b, \mathrm{pk}(k_b)\rangle\rangle, \mathrm{pk}(k_a)) \sim \mathrm{aenc}(N_b, \mathrm{pk}(k))\}$.

Fig. 9. Type derivation for the response to A and the decoy message

rule DAdecL except it uses a variable for decryption instead of a fixed key. Rule DAdecT treats the case in which we know that the variable x is an asymmetric encryption of a specific type. If the type of the key used for decryption matches the key type used for encryption, we know the exact type of the result of a successful decryption. DAdecT' is similar to DAdecT, with a variable as key. In a companion technical report we present similar rules for symmetric decryption and verification of signatures.

4.3 Typing the Private Authentication Protocol

We now show how our type system can be applied to type the Private Authentication protocol presented in Sect. 2.3, by showing the most interesting parts of the derivation. We type the protocol using the initial environment Γ presented in Fig. 1.

We focus on the responder process P_b and start with the asymmetric decryption. As we use the same key k_b in both processes, we apply rule PLetAdec-Same. We have $\Gamma(x) = \mathrm{LL}$ by rule PIn and $\Gamma(k_b, k_b) = \mathrm{key}^{\mathrm{HH}}(\mathrm{HH}, \mathrm{LL})$. We do not have any other entry using key k_b in Γ. We hence typecheck the two **then** branches once with $\Gamma, y : (\mathrm{HH} * \mathrm{LL})$ and once with $\Gamma, y : \mathrm{LL}$, as well as the two **else** branches (which are just 0 in this case).

Typing the let expressions is straightforward using rule PLet. In the conditional we check $y_2 = \mathrm{pk}(k_a)$ in the left process and $y_2 = \mathrm{pk}(k_c)$ in the right process. Since we cannot guarantee which branches are taken or even if the same branch is taken in the two processes, we use rule PIfAll to typecheck all four possible combinations of branches. We now focus on the case where A is successfully authenticated in the left process and is rejected in the right process. We then have to typecheck B's positive answer together with the decoy message: $\Gamma \vdash \mathrm{aenc}(\langle y_1, \langle N_b, \mathrm{pk}(k_b)\rangle\rangle, \mathrm{pk}(k_a)) \sim \mathrm{aenc}(N_c, \mathrm{pk}(k)) : \mathrm{LL}$.

Figure 9 presents the type derivation for this example. We apply rule TAenc to give type LL to the two terms, adding the two encryptions to the constraint set. Using rule TAencH we can show that the encryptions are well-typed with type $\{\mathrm{HL}\}_{\mathrm{pkey}(\mathrm{key}^{\mathrm{HH}}(\mathrm{HL}))}$. The type of the payload is trivially shown with rule THigh.

To type the public key, we use rule TPubKey followed by rule TKey, which looks up the type for the bikey (k_a, k) in the typing environment Γ.

5   Consistency

Our type system collects constraints that intuitively correspond to (symbolic) messages that the attacker may see (or deduce). Therefore, two processes are in trace equivalence only if the collected constraints are in static equivalence for any plausible instantiation.

However, checking static equivalence of symbolic frames for any instantiation corresponding to a real execution may be as hard as checking trace equivalence [24]. Conversely, checking static equivalence for *any* instantiation may be too strong and may prevent proving equivalence of processes. Instead, we use again the typing information gathered by our type system and we consider only instantiations that comply with the type. Actually, we even restrict our attention to instantiations where variables of type LL are only replaced by deducible terms. This last part is a key ingredient for considering processes with dynamic keys. Hence, we define a constraint to be *consistent* if the corresponding two frames are in static equivalence for any instantiation that can be typed and produces constraints that are included in the original constraint.

Formally, we first introduce the following ingredients:

- $\phi_\ell(c)$ and $\phi_r(c)$ denote the frames that are composed of the left and the right terms of the constraints respectively (in the same order).
- ϕ_{LL}^Γ denotes the frame that is composed of all low confidentiality nonces and keys in Γ, as well as all public encryption keys and verification keys in Γ. This intuitively corresponds to the initial knowledge of the attacker.
- Two ground substitutions σ, σ' are well-typed in Γ with constraint c_σ if they preserve the types for variables in Γ, *i.e.*, for all x, $\Gamma \vdash \sigma(x) \sim \sigma'(x) : \Gamma(x) \to c_x$, and $c_\sigma = \bigcup_{x \in \text{dom}(\Gamma)} c_x$.

The instantiation of a constraint is defined as expected. If c is a set of constraints, and σ, σ' are two substitutions, let $[\![c]\!]_{\sigma,\sigma'}$ be the instantiation of c by σ on the left and σ' on the right, that is, $[\![c]\!]_{\sigma,\sigma'} = \{M\sigma \sim N\sigma' \mid M \sim N \in c\}$.

Definition 3 (Consistency). *A set of constraints c is consistent in an environment Γ if for all substitutions σ, σ' well-typed in Γ with a constraint c_σ such that $c_\sigma \subseteq [\![c]\!]_{\sigma,\sigma'}$, the frames $\phi_{LL}^\Gamma \cup \phi_\ell(c)\sigma$ and $\phi_{LL}^\Gamma \cup \phi_r(c)\sigma'$ are statically equivalent. We say that (c, Γ) is consistent if c is consistent in Γ and that a constraint set C is consistent in Γ if each element $(c, \Gamma) \in C$ is consistent.*

Compared to [28], we now require $c_\sigma \subseteq [\![c]\!]_{\sigma,\sigma'}$. This means that instead of considering any (well typed) instantiations, we only consider instantiations that use fragments of the constraints. For example, this now imposes that low variables are instantiated by terms deducible from the constraint. This refinement of consistency provides a tighter definition and is needed for non fixed keys, as explained in the next section.

6   Soundness

In this section, we provide our main results. First, soundness of our type system: whenever two processes can be typed with consistent constraints, then they are in trace equivalence. Then we show how to automatically prove consistency. Finally, we explain how to lift these two first results from finite processes to processes with replication. But first, we discuss why we cannot directly apply the results from [28] developed for processes with long term keys.

6.1   Example

Consider the following example, typical for a key-exchange protocol: Alice receives some key and uses it to encrypt, e.g. a nonce. Here, we consider a semi-honest session, where an honest agent A is receiving a key from a dishonest agent D. Such sessions are typically considered in combination with honest sessions.

$$C \rightarrow A : \mathsf{aenc}(\langle k, C \rangle, \mathsf{pk}(A))$$
$$A \rightarrow C : \mathsf{aenc}(n, k)$$

The process modelling the role of Alice is as follows.

$$P_A = \mathsf{in}(x).\ \mathsf{let}\ x' = \mathsf{adec}(x, k_A)\ \mathsf{in}\ \mathsf{let}\ y = \pi_1(x')\ \mathsf{in}\ \mathsf{let}\ z = \pi_2(x')\ \mathsf{in}$$
$$\mathsf{if}\ z = C\ \mathsf{then}\ \mathsf{new}\ n.\ \mathsf{out}(\mathsf{enc}(n, y))$$

When type-checking $P_A \sim P_A$ (as part as a more general process with honest sessions), we would collect the constraint $\mathsf{enc}(n, y) \sim \mathsf{enc}(n, y)$ where y comes from the adversary and is therefore a low variable (that is, of type LL). The approach of [28] consisted in opening messages as much as possible. In this example, this would yield the constraint $y \sim y$ which typically renders the constraint inconsistent, as exemplified below.

When typechecking the private authentication protocol, we obtain constraints containing $\mathsf{aenc}(\langle y_1, \langle N_b, \mathsf{pk}(k_b) \rangle \rangle, \mathsf{pk}(k_a)) \sim \mathsf{aenc}(N_b, \mathsf{pk}(k))$ (as seen in Fig. 9), where y_1 has type HL. Assume now that the constraint also contains $y \sim y$ for some variable y of type LL and consider the following instantiations of y and y_1: $\sigma(y_1) = \sigma'(y_1) = a$ for some constant a and $\sigma(y) = \sigma'(y) = \mathsf{aenc}(N_b, \mathsf{pk}(k))$. Note that such an instantiation complies with the type since $\Gamma \vdash \sigma(y) \sim \sigma'(y) : \mathsf{LL} \rightarrow c$ for some constraint c. The instantiated constraint would then contain

$$\{\mathsf{aenc}(\langle a, \langle N_b, \mathsf{pk}(k_b) \rangle \rangle, \mathsf{pk}(k_a)) \sim \mathsf{aenc}(N_b, \mathsf{pk}(k)),$$
$$\mathsf{aenc}(N_b, \mathsf{pk}(k)) \sim \mathsf{aenc}(N_b, \mathsf{pk}(k))\}$$

and the corresponding frames are not statically equivalent, which makes the constraint inconsistent for the consistency definition of [28].

Therefore, our first idea consists in proving that we only collect constraints that are saturated w.r.t. deduction: any deducible subterm can already be constructed from the terms of the constraint. Second, we show that for any execution, low variables are instantiated by terms deducible from the constraints.

This guarantees that our new notion of consistency is sound. The two results are reflected in the next section.

6.2   Soundness

Our type system, together with consistency, implies trace equivalence.

Theorem 1 (Typing implies trace equivalence). *For all P, Q, and C, for all Γ containing only keys, if $\Gamma \vdash P \sim Q \to C$ and C is consistent, then $P \approx_t Q$.*

Example 3. We can typecheck PA, that is

$$\Gamma \vdash P_a(k_a, \mathrm{pk}(k_b)) \mid P_b(k_b, \mathrm{pk}(k_a)) \sim P_a(k_a, \mathrm{pk}(k_b)) \mid P_b(k_b, \mathrm{pk}(k_c)) \to C_{PA}$$

where Γ has been defined in Fig. 1 and assuming that nonce N_a of process P_a has been annotated with type $\tau_{N_a}^{\mathrm{HH},1}$ and nonce N_b of P_b has been annotated with type $\tau_{N_b}^{\mathrm{HH},1}$. The constraint set C_{PA} can be proved to be consistent using the procedure presented in the next section. Therefore, we can conclude that

$$P_a(k_a, \mathrm{pk}(k_b)) \mid P_b(k_b, \mathrm{pk}(k_a)) \approx_t P_a(k_a, \mathrm{pk}(k_b)) \mid P_b(k_b, \mathrm{pk}(k_c))$$

which shows anonymity of the private authentication protocol.

The first key ingredient in the proof of Theorem 1 is the fact that any well-typed low term is deducible from the constraint generated when typing it.

Lemma 1 (Low terms are recipes on their constraints). *For all ground messages M, N, for all Γ, c, if $\Gamma \vdash M \sim N : \mathrm{LL} \to c$ then there exists an attacker recipe R without destructors such that $M = R(\phi_\ell(c) \cup \phi_{\mathrm{LL}}^{\Gamma})$ and $N = R(\phi_r(c) \cup \phi_{\mathrm{LL}}^{\Gamma})$.*

The second key ingredient is a finer invariant on protocol executions: for any typable pair of processes P, Q, any execution of P can be mimicked by an execution of Q such that low variables are instantiated by well-typed terms constructible from the constraint.

Lemma 2. *For all processes P, Q, for all ϕ, σ, for all multisets of processes $\mathcal{P}$, constraint sets C, sequences s of actions, for all Γ containing only keys, if $\Gamma \vdash P \sim Q \to C$, C is consistent, and $(\{P\}, \emptyset, \emptyset) \xrightarrow{s}_* (\mathcal{P}, \phi, \sigma)$, then there exist a sequence s' of actions, a multiset $\mathcal{Q}$, a frame ϕ', a substitution σ', an environment Γ', a constraint c such that:*

$- (\{Q\}, \emptyset, \emptyset) \xrightarrow{s'}_* (\mathcal{Q}, \phi', \sigma')$, *with* $s =_\tau s'$
$- \Gamma' \vdash \phi\sigma \sim \phi'\sigma' : \mathrm{LL} \to c$, *and for all* $x \in \mathrm{dom}(\sigma) \cap \mathrm{dom}(\sigma')$, *there exists* c_x *such that* $\Gamma' \vdash \sigma(x) \sim \sigma(x) : \Gamma'(x) \to c_x$ *and* $c_x \subseteq c$.

Note that this finer invariant guarantees that we can restrict our attention to the instantiations considered for defining consistency.

As a by-product, we obtain a finer type system for equivalence, even for processes with long term keys (as in [28]). For example, we can now prove equivalence of processes where some agent signs a low message that comes from the adversary. In such a case, we collect $\mathrm{sign}(x, k) \sim \mathrm{sign}(x, k)$ in the constraint, where x has type LL, which we can now prove to be consistent (depending on how x is used in the rest of the constraint).

6.3   Procedure for Consistency

We devise a procedure check_const(C) for checking consistency of a constraint C, depicted in Fig. 10. Compared to [28], the procedure is actually simplified. Thanks to Lemmas 1 and 2, there is no need to open constraints anymore. The rest is very similar and works as follows:

- First, variables of refined type $[\![\tau_m^{l,1} ; \tau_n^{l',1}]\!]$ are replaced by m on the left-hand-side of the constraint and n on the right-hand-side.
- Second, we check that terms have the same shape (encryption, signature, hash) on the left and on the right and that asymmetric encryption and hashes cannot be reconstructed by the adversary (that is, they contain some fresh nonce).
- The most important step consists in checking that the terms on the left satisfy the same equalities than the ones on the right. Whenever two left terms M and N are unifiable, their corresponding right terms M' and N' should be equal after applying a similar instantiation.

For constraint sets without infinite nonce types, check_const entails consistency.

Theorem 2. *Let C be a set of constraints such that*

$$\forall (c, \Gamma) \in C. \ \forall l, l', m, p. \ \Gamma(x) \neq [\![\tau_m^{l,\infty} ; \tau_p^{l',\infty}]\!].$$

If check_const$(C) =$ true, *then C is consistent.*

Example 4. Continuing Example 3, typechecking the PA protocol yields the set C_{PA} of constraint sets. C_{PA} contains in particular the set

$$\{\text{aenc}(\langle N_a, \text{pk}(k_a) \rangle, \text{pk}(k_b)) \sim \text{aenc}(\langle N_a, \text{pk}(k_a) \rangle, \text{pk}(k_b)),$$
$$\text{aenc}(\langle y_1, \langle N_b, \text{pk}(k_b) \rangle \rangle, \text{pk}(k_a)) \sim \text{aenc}(N_b, \text{pk}(k))\}$$

where variable y_1 has type HL (we also have the same constraint but where y_1 has type LL). The other constraint sets of C_{PA} are similar and correspond to the various cases (else branch of P_a with then branch of P_b, etc.). The procedure check_const returns true since no two terms can be unified, which proves consistency. Similarly, the other constraints generated for PA can be proved to be consistent applying check_const.

6.4   From Finite to Replicated Processes

The previous results apply to processes without replication only. In the spirit of [28], we lift our results to replicated processes. We proceed in two steps.

1. Whenever $\Gamma \vdash P \sim Q \rightarrow C$, we show that:
   $[\Gamma]_1 \cup \cdots \cup [\Gamma]_n \vdash [P]_1 | \ldots | [P]_n \sim [Q]_1 | \ldots | [Q]_n \rightarrow [C]_1 \cup_\times \cdots \cup_\times [C]_n$,
   where $[\Gamma]_i$ is intuitively a copy of Γ, where variables x have been replaced by x_i, and nonces or keys n of infinite type $\tau_n^{l,\infty}$ (or seskey$^{l,\infty}(T)$) have been replaced by n_i. The copies $[P]_i$, $[Q]_i$, and $[C]_i$ are defined similarly.

$\mathbf{step1}_\Gamma(c) := (\llbracket c \rrbracket_{\sigma_F, \sigma'_F}, \Gamma')$, with

$$F := \{x \in \mathrm{dom}(\Gamma) \mid \exists m, n, l, l'.\ \Gamma(x) = \llbracket \tau_m^{l,1} ; \tau_n^{l',1} \rrbracket\}$$

and σ_F, σ'_F defined by

$$\begin{cases} \bullet\ \mathrm{dom}(\sigma_F) = \mathrm{dom}(\sigma'_F) = F \\ \bullet\ \forall x \in F.\ \forall m, n, l, l'.\Gamma(x) = \llbracket \tau_m^{l,1} ; \tau_n^{l',1} \rrbracket \Rightarrow \sigma_F(x) = m\ \wedge\ \sigma'_F(x) = n \end{cases}$$

and Γ' is $\Gamma|_{\mathrm{dom}(\Gamma) \setminus F}$ extended with $\Gamma'(n) = \tau_n^{l,1}$ for all nonce n such that $\tau_n^{l,1}$ occurs in Γ.

$\mathbf{step2}_\Gamma(c) :=$ check that for all $M \sim N \in c$, M and N are both

- $\mathrm{enc}(M', M'')$, $\mathrm{enc}(N', N'')$ where M'', N'' are either
  - keys k, k' where $\exists T.\Gamma(k, k') <: \mathrm{key}^{\mathrm{HH}}(T)$;
  - or a variable x such that $\exists T.\Gamma(x) <: \mathrm{key}^{\mathrm{HH}}(T)$;
- or encryptions $\mathrm{aenc}(M', M'')$, $\mathrm{aenc}(N', N'')$ where
  - M' and N' contain directly under pairs a nonce n such that $\Gamma(n) = \tau_n^{\mathrm{HH},a}$ or a secret key k such that $\exists T, k'.\Gamma(k, k') <: \mathrm{key}^{\mathrm{HH}}(T)$ or $\Gamma(k', k) <: \mathrm{key}^{\mathrm{HH}}(T)$, or a variable x such that $\exists m, n, a.\Gamma(x) = \llbracket \tau_m^{\mathrm{HH},a} ; \tau_n^{\mathrm{HH},a} \rrbracket$, or a variable x such that $\exists T.\Gamma(x) <: \mathrm{key}^{\mathrm{HH}}(T)$;
  - M'' and N'' are either
    * public keys $\mathrm{pk}(k)$, $\mathrm{pk}(k')$ where $\exists T.\Gamma(k, k') <: \mathrm{key}^{\mathrm{HH}}(T)$;
    * or public keys $\mathrm{pk}(x)$, $\mathrm{pk}(x)$ where $\exists T.\Gamma(x) <: \mathrm{key}^{\mathrm{HH}}(T)$;
    * or a variable x such that $\exists T, T'.\Gamma(x) = \mathrm{pkey}(T)$ and $T <: \mathrm{key}^{\mathrm{HH}}(T')$;
- or hashes $\mathrm{h}(M')$, $\mathrm{h}(N')$, where M', N' similarly contain a secret value under pairs;
- or signatures $\mathrm{sign}(M', M'')$, $\mathrm{sign}(N', M'')$ where M'', N'' are either
  - keys k, k' where $\exists T.\Gamma(k, k') <: \mathrm{key}^{\mathrm{HH}}(T)$;
  - or a variable x such that $\exists T.\Gamma(x) <: \mathrm{key}^{\mathrm{HH}}(T)$;

$\mathbf{step3}_\Gamma(c) :=$ If for all $M \sim M'$ and $N \sim N' \in c$ such that M, N are unifiable with a most general unifier μ, and such that

$$\forall x \in \mathrm{dom}(\mu).\exists l, l', m, p.\ (\Gamma(x) = \llbracket \tau_m^{l,\infty} ; \tau_p^{l',\infty} \rrbracket) \Rightarrow (x\mu \in \mathcal{X} \ \vee\ \exists i.\ x\mu = m_i)$$

we have

$$M'\alpha\theta = N'\alpha\theta$$

where

$$\forall x \in \mathrm{dom}(\mu).\forall l, l', m, p, i.(\Gamma(x) = \llbracket \tau_m^{l,\infty} ; \tau_p^{l',\infty} \rrbracket\ \wedge\ \mu(x) = m_i) \Rightarrow \theta(x) = p_i$$

and α is the restriction of μ to $\{x \in \mathrm{dom}(\mu) \mid \Gamma(x) = \mathrm{LL}\ \wedge\ \mu(x) \in \mathcal{N}\}$;
and if the symmetric condition for the case where M', N' are unifiable holds as well, then return true.

$\mathbf{check\_const}(C) :=$ for all $(c, \Gamma) \in C$, let $(c_1, \Gamma_1) := \mathbf{step1}_\Gamma(c)$ and check that $\mathbf{step2}_{\Gamma_1}(c_1) = \mathrm{true}$ and $\mathbf{step3}_{\Gamma_1}(c_1) = \mathrm{true}$.

Fig. 10. Procedure for checking consistency.

2. We cannot directly check consistency of infinitely many constraints of the form $[C]_1 \cup_\times \cdots \cup_\times [C]_n$. Instead, we show that it is sufficient to check consistency of two copies $[C]_1 \cup_\times [C]_2$ only. The reason why we need two copies (and not just one) is to detect when messages from different sessions may become equal.

Formally, we can prove trace equivalence of replicated processes.

Theorem 3. *Consider* P, Q, P', Q', C, C', *such that* P, Q *and* P', Q' *do not share any variable. Consider* Γ, *containing only keys and nonces with finite types.*

Assume that P *and* Q *only bind nonces and keys with infinite nonce types, i.e. using* **new** $m : \tau_m^{l,\infty}$ *and* **new** $k : \mathsf{seskey}^{l,\infty}(T)$ *for some label* l *and type* T; *while* P' *and* Q' *only bind nonces and keys with finite types, i.e. using* **new** $m : \tau_m^{l,1}$ *and* **new** $k : \mathsf{seskey}^{l,1}(T)$.

Let us abbreviate by **new** $\overline{n}$ *the sequence of declarations of each nonce* $m \in \mathrm{dom}(\Gamma)$ *and session key* k *such that* $\Gamma(k,k) = \mathsf{seskey}^{l,1}(T)$ *for some* l, T. *If*

- $\Gamma \vdash P \sim Q \to C$,
- $\Gamma \vdash P' \sim Q' \to C'$,
- $\mathsf{check\_const}([C]_1 \cup_\times [C]_2 \cup_\times [C']_1) = \mathtt{true}$,

then   **new** $\overline{n}.\ ((!P) \mid P') \approx_t$ **new** $\overline{n}.\ ((!Q) \mid Q')$.

Interestingly, Theorem 3 allows to consider a mix of finite and replicated processes.

7 Experimental Results

We implemented our typechecker as well as our procedure for consistency in a prototype tool TypeEq. We adapted the original prototype of [28] to implement additional cases corresponding to the new typing rules. This also required to design new heuristics w.r.t. the order in which typing rules should be applied. Of course, we also had to support for the new bikey types, and for arbitrary terms as keys. This represented a change of about 40% of the code of the software. We ran our experiments on a single Intel Xeon E5-2687Wv3 3.10 GHz core, with 378 GB of RAM (shared with the 19 other cores). Actually, our own prototype does not require a large amount of RAM. However, some of the other tools we consider use more than 64 GB of RAM on some examples (at which point we stopped the experiment). More precise figures about our tool are provided in the table of Fig. 11. The corresponding files can be found at [27].

We tested TypeEq on two symmetric key protocols that include a handshake on the key (Yahalom-Lowe and Needham-Schroeder symmetric key protocols). In both cases, we prove key usability of the exchanged key. Intuitively, we show that an attacker cannot distinguish between two encryptions of public constants: $P.\mathsf{out}(\mathsf{enc}(a,k)) \approx_t P.\mathsf{out}(\mathsf{enc}(b,k))$. We also consider one standard asymmetric key protocol (Needham-Schroeder-Lowe protocol), showing strong secrecy of the exchanged nonce.

Helios [4] is a well known voting protocol. We show ballot privacy, in the presence of a dishonest board, assuming that voters do not revote (otherwise the protocol is subject to a copy attack [39], a variant of [30]). We consider a more precise model than the previous Helios models which assume that voters initially know the election public key. Here, we model the fact that voters actually receive the (signed) freshly generated election public key from the network. The BAC protocol is one of the protocols embedded in the biometric passport [1]. We show anonymity of the passport holder $P(A) \approx_t P(B)$. Actually, the only data that distinguish $P(A)$ from $P(B)$ are the private keys. Therefore we consider an additional step where the passport sends the identity of the agent to the reader, encrypted with the exchanged key. Finally, we consider the private authentication protocol, as described in this paper.

7.1 Bounded Number of Sessions

We first compare TypeEq with the tools for a bounded number of sessions. Namely, we consider Akiss [22], APTE [23] as well as its optimised variant with partial order reduction APTE-POR [10], SPEC [32], and SatEquiv [26]. We step by step increase the number of sessions until we reach a "complete" scenario where each role is instantiated by A talking to B, A talking to C, B talking to A, and B talking to C, where A, B are honest while C is dishonest.

Protocols (# sessions)		Akiss	APTE	APTE-POR	Spec	Sat-Eq	TypeEq	
							Time	Memory
Needham -	3	4.2s	0.39s	0.086s	59.3s	0.14s	0.006s	4.0 MB
Schroeder	6	TO	TO	9m22s	TO	0.53s	0.009s	4.7 MB
(symmetric)	10			SO		3.7s	0.012s	5.0 MB
	14					18s	0.015s	6.9 MB
	3	1.0s	2.9s	0.095s	10s	0.063s	0.006s	3.8 MB
Yahalom -	6	MO	TO	11m20s	MO	0.26s	0.017s	4.9 MB
Lowe	10			SO		3.0s	0.015s	4.9 MB
	14					18s	0.019s	5.0 MB
Needham-	2	0.10s	3.8s	0.06s	28s	x	0.004s	3.1 MB
Schroeder-	4	1m8s	BUG	BUG	TO		0.004s	3.4 MB
Lowe	8	TO					0.007s	4.7 MB
Private	2	0.19s	1.2s	0.034s	x	x	0.004s	3.2 MB
Authentication	4	99m	TO	24.6s			0.013s	4.9 MB
	8	MO		TO			1s	37 MB
Helios	3	MO	BUG	BUG	x	x	0.005s	3.5 MB
	2	4.0s	0.20s	0.032s	x	x	0.004s	2.9 MB
BAC	3	SO	185m	2.6s			0.004s	3.1 MB
	5		TO	107m			0.005s	3.4 MB
	7			TO			0.005s	3.8 MB

TO: Time Out (>12h)   MO: Memory Overflow (>64GB)   SO: Stack Overflow

Fig. 11. Experimental results for the bounded case

This yields 14 sessions for symmetric-key protocols with two agents and one server, and 8 sessions for a protocol with two agents. In some cases, we further increase the number of sessions (replicating identical scenarios) to better compare tools performance. The results of our experiments are reported in Fig. 11. Note that SatEquiv fails to cover several cases because it does not handle asymmetric encryption nor else branches.

7.2 Unbounded Number of Sessions

We then compare TypeEq with Proverif. As shown in Fig. 12, the performances are similar except that ProVerif cannot prove Helios. The reason lies in the fact that Helios is actually subject to a copy attack if voters revote and ProVerif cannot properly handle processes that are executed only once. Similarly, Tamarin cannot properly handle the else branch of Helios (which models that the ballot box rejects duplicated ballots). Tamarin fails to prove that the underlying check either succeeds or fails on both sides.

Protocols	ProVerif	TypeEq
Helios	x	0.005s
Needham-Schroeder (sym)	0.23s	0.016s
Needham-Schroeder-Lowe	0.08s	0.008s
Yahalom-Lowe	0.48s	0.020s
Private Authentication	0.034s	0.008s
BAC	0.038s	0.005s

Fig. 12. Experimental results for an unbounded number of sessions

8   Conclusion and Discussion

We devise a new type system to reason about keys in the context of equivalence properties. Our new type system significantly enhances the preliminary work of [28], covering a larger class of protocols that includes key-exchange protocols, protocols with setup phases, as well as protocols that branch differently depending on the decryption key.

Our type system requires a light type annotation that can be directly inferred from the structure of the messages. As future work, we plan to develop an automatic type inference system. In our case study, the only intricate case is the Helios protocol where the user has to write a refined type that corresponds to an over-approximation of any encrypted message. We plan to explore whether such types could be inferred automatically.

We also plan to study how to add phases to our framework, in order to cover more properties (such as unlinkability). This would require to generalize our type system to account for the fact that the type of a key may depend on the phase in which it is used.

Another limitation of our type system is that it does not address processes with too dissimilar structure. While our type system goes beyond diff-equivalence, e.g. allowing else branches to be matched with then branches, we cannot prove equivalence of processes where traces of P are dynamically mapped to traces of Q, depending on the attacker's behaviour. Such cases occur for example when proving unlinkability of the biometric passport. We plan to explore how to enrich our type system with additional rules that could cover such cases, taking advantage of the modularity of the type system.

Conversely, the fact that our type system discards processes that are in equivalence shows that our type system proves something stronger than trace equivalence. Indeed, processes P and Q have to follow some form of uniformity. We could exploit this to prove stronger properties like oblivious execution, probably further restricting our typing rules, in order to prove e.g. the absence of side-channels of a certain form.

Acknowledgments. This work has been partially supported by the European Research Council (ERC) under the European Union's Horizon 2020 research (grant agreements No. 645865-SPOOC and No. 771527-BROWSEC).

References

1. Machine readable travel document. Technical report 9303. International Civil Aviation Organization (2008)
2. Abadi, M., Fournet, C.: Mobile values, new names, and secure communication. In: 28th ACM SIGPLAN-SIGACT Symposium on Principles of Programming Languages (POPL 2001), pp. 104–115. ACM (2001)
3. Abadi, M., Fournet, C.: Private authentication. Theoret. Comput. Sci. **322**(3), 427–476 (2004)
4. Adida, B.: Helios: web-based open-audit voting. In: 17th Conference on Security Symposium, SS 2008, pp. 335–348 (2008)
5. Arapinis, M., Chothia, T., Ritter, E., Ryan, M.: Analysing unlinkability and anonymity using the applied pi calculus. In: 2nd IEEE Computer Security Foundations Symposium (CSF 2010). IEEE Computer Society Press (2010)
6. Armando, A., et al.: The AVISPA Tool for the automated validation of internet security protocols and applications. In: Etessami, K., Rajamani, S.K. (eds.) CAV 2005. LNCS, vol. 3576, pp. 281–285. Springer, Heidelberg (2005). https://doi.org/10.1007/11513988_27
7. Backes, M., Catalin, H., Maffei, M.: Union, intersection and refinement types and reasoning about type disjointness for secure protocol implementations. J. Comput. Secur. **22**(2), 301–353 (2014)
8. Backes, M., Hritcu, C., Maffei, M.: Automated verification of remote electronic voting protocols in the applied pi-calculus. In: 21st IEEE Computer Security Foundations Symposium, CSF 2008, pp. 195–209. IEEE Computer Society (2008)
9. Backes, M., Maffei, M., Unruh, D.: Zero-knowledge in the applied pi-calculus and automated verification of the direct anonymous attestation protocol. In: IEEE Symposium on Security and Privacy, SP 2008, pp. 202–215. IEEE Computer Society (2008)

10. Baelde, D., Delaune, S., Hirschi, L.: Partial order reduction for security protocols. In: Proceedings of the 26th International Conference on Concurrency Theory (CONCUR 2015). LIPIcs, vol. 42, pp. 497–510. Leibniz-Zentrum für Informatik (2015)
11. Basin, D., Dreier, J., Sasse, R.: Automated symbolic proofs of observational equivalence. In: 22nd ACM SIGSAC Conference on Computer and Communications Security (ACM CCS 2015), pp. 1144–1155. ACM, October 2015
12. Bengtson, J., Bhargavan, K., Fournet, C., Gordon, A.D., Maffeis, S.: Refinement types for secure implementations. ACM Trans. Program. Lang. Syst. 33(2), 8:1–8:45 (2011)
13. Blanchet, B.: An efficient cryptographic protocol verifier based on prolog rules. In: 14th IEEE Computer Security Foundations Workshop (CSFW 2014), pp. 82–96. IEEE Computer Society, June 2001
14. Blanchet, B.: Modeling and verifying security protocols with the applied pi calculus and ProVerif. Found. Trends Priv. Secur. 1(1–2), 1–135 (2016)
15. Blanchet, B., Abadi, M., Fournet, C.: Automated verification of selected equivalences for security protocols. J. Logic Algebraic Program. 75(1), 3–51 (2008)
16. Bugliesi, M., Calzavara, S., Eigner, F., Maffei, M.: Resource-aware authorization policies for statically typed cryptographic protocols. In: 24th IEEE Computer Security Foundations Symposium, CSF 2011, pp. 83–98. IEEE Computer Society (2011)
17. Bugliesi, M., Calzavara, S., Eigner, F., Maffei, M.: Logical foundations of secure resource management in protocol implementations. In: Basin, D., Mitchell, J.C. (eds.) POST 2013. LNCS, vol. 7796, pp. 105–125. Springer, Heidelberg (2013). https://doi.org/10.1007/978-3-642-36830-1_6
18. Bugliesi, M., Calzavara, S., Eigner, F., Maffei, M.: Affine refinement types for secure distributed programming. ACM Trans. Program. Lang. Syst. 37(4), 11:1–11:66 (2015)
19. Bugliesi, M., Focardi, R., Maffei, M.: Authenticity by tagging and typing. In: 2004 ACM Workshop on Formal Methods in Security Engineering, FMSE 2004, pp. 1–12. ACM (2004)
20. Bugliesi, M., Focardi, R., Maffei, M.: Analysis of typed analyses of authentication protocols. In: 18th IEEE Workshop on Computer Security Foundations, CSFW 2005, pp. 112–125. IEEE Computer Society (2005)
21. Bugliesi, M., Focardi, R., Maffei, M.: Dynamic types for authentication. J. Comput. Secur. 15(6), 563–617 (2007)
22. Chadha, R., Ciobâcă, Ş., Kremer, S.: Automated verification of equivalence properties of cryptographic protocols. In: Seidl, H. (ed.) ESOP 2012. LNCS, vol. 7211, pp. 108–127. Springer, Heidelberg (2012). https://doi.org/10.1007/978-3-642-28869-2_6
23. Cheval, V.: APTE: an algorithm for proving trace equivalence. In: Ábrahám, E., Havelund, K. (eds.) TACAS 2014. LNCS, vol. 8413, pp. 587–592. Springer, Heidelberg (2014). https://doi.org/10.1007/978-3-642-54862-8_50
24. Cheval, V., Cortier, V., Delaune, S.: Deciding equivalence-based properties using constraint solving. Theoret. Comput. Sci. 492, 1–39 (2013)
25. Cheval, V., Cortier, V., Plet, A.: Lengths may break privacy – or how to check for equivalences with length. In: Sharygina, N., Veith, H. (eds.) CAV 2013. LNCS, vol. 8044, pp. 708–723. Springer, Heidelberg (2013). https://doi.org/10.1007/978-3-642-39799-8_50
26. Cortier, V., Delaune, S., Dallon, A.: SAT-Equiv: an efficient tool for equivalence properties. In: Proceedings of the 30th IEEE Computer Security Foundations Symposium (CSF 2017). IEEE Computer Society Press, August 2017

27. Cortier, V., Grimm, N., Lallemand, J., Maffei, M.: TypeEq. https://members.loria.fr/JLallemand/files/typing
28. Cortier, V., Grimm, N., Lallemand, J., Maffei, M.: A type system for privacy properties. In: 24th ACM Conference on Computer and Communications Security (CCS 2017), pp. 409–423. ACM (2017)
29. Cortier, V., Grimm, N., Lallemand, J., Maffei, M.: Equivalence properties by typing in cryptographic branching protocols. Research report, Université de Lorraine, CNRS, Inria, LORIA; TU Wien, February 2018. https://hal.archives-ouvertes.fr/hal-01715957
30. Cortier, V., Smyth, B.: Attacking and fixing Helios: an analysis of ballot secrecy. J. Comput. Secur. 21(1), 89–148 (2013)
31. Cremers, C.J.F.: The Scyther tool: verification, falsification, and analysis of security protocols. In: Gupta, A., Malik, S. (eds.) CAV 2008. LNCS, vol. 5123, pp. 414–418. Springer, Heidelberg (2008). https://doi.org/10.1007/978-3-540-70545-1_38
32. Dawson, J., Tiu, A.: Automating open bisimulation checking for the spi-calculus. In: IEEE Computer Security Foundations Symposium (CSF 2010) (2010)
33. Delaune, S., Kremer, S., Ryan, M.D.: Verifying privacy-type properties of electronic voting protocols. J. Comput. Secur. 17(4), 435–487 (2009)
34. Eigner, F., Maffei, M.: Differential privacy by typing in security protocols. In: 26th IEEE Computer Security Foundations Symposium, CSF 2013, pp. 272–286. IEEE Computer Society (2013)
35. Escobar, S., Meadows, C., Meseguer, J.: A rewriting-based inference system for the NRL protocol analyzer and its meta-logical properties. Theoret. Comput. Sci. 367(1–2), 162–202 (2006)
36. Focardi, R., Maffei, M.: Types for security protocols. In: Formal Models and Techniques for Analyzing Security Protocols, Cryptology and Information Security Series, chap. 7, vol. 5, pp. 143–181. IOS Press (2011)
37. Gordon, A.D., Jeffrey, A.: Authenticity by typing for security protocols. J. Comput. Secur. 11(4), 451–519 (2003)
38. Meier, S., Schmidt, B., Cremers, C., Basin, D.: The TAMARIN prover for the symbolic analysis of security protocols. In: Sharygina, N., Veith, H. (eds.) CAV 2013. LNCS, vol. 8044, pp. 696–701. Springer, Heidelberg (2013). https://doi.org/10.1007/978-3-642-39799-8_48
39. Roenne, P.: Private communication (2016)
40. Santiago, S., Escobar, S., Meadows, C., Meseguer, J.: A formal definition of protocol indistinguishability and its verification using Maude-NPA. In: Mauw, S., Jensen, C.D. (eds.) STM 2014. LNCS, vol. 8743, pp. 162–177. Springer, Cham (2014). https://doi.org/10.1007/978-3-319-11851-2_11

Design, Formal Specification and Analysis of Multi-Factor Authentication Solutions with a Single Sign-On Experience

Giada Sciarretta[1,2]([✉])([iD]), Roberto Carbone[1]([iD]), Silvio Ranise[1]([iD]),
and Luca Viganò[3]([iD])

[1] Security & Trust, FBK, Trento, Italy
{giada.sciarretta,carbone,ranise}@fbk.eu
[2] University of Trento, Trento, Italy
[3] King's College London, London, UK
luca.vigano@kcl.ac.uk

Abstract. Over the last few years, there has been an almost exponential increase of the number of mobile applications that deal with sensitive data, such as applications for e-commerce or health. When dealing with sensitive data, classical authentication solutions based on username-password pairs are not enough, and multi-factor authentication solutions that combine two or more authentication elements of different categories are required. Many different such solutions are available, but they usually cover the scenario of a user accessing web applications on their laptops, whereas in this paper we focus on native mobile applications. This changes the exploitable attack surface and thus requires a specific analysis. In this paper, we present the design, the formal specification and the security analysis of a solution that allows users to access different mobile applications through a multi-factor authentication solution providing a Single Sign-On experience. The formal and automated analysis that we performed validates the security goals of the solution we propose.

1 Introduction

Context and Motivations. Over the last few years, there has been an almost exponential increase of the number of *mobile applications* (or *apps*, for short) that deal with sensitive data, ranging from apps for e-commerce, banking and finance to apps for well-being and health. One of the main reasons behind such a success is that mobile apps considerably increase the portability and efficiency of online services. Banking apps allow users not only to check their account balances but also to move money and pay bills or friends [1]. Mobile health apps range from personal health records (PHR) to personal digital assistants using connected devices such as smartwatches and other body-worn devices or implants. As reported in [2], there are nowadays more than 100,000 mobile health apps on the market, a number that is increasing on a weekly basis.

However, also the reports on security and privacy issues in mobile apps are increasing on a weekly basis, bearing concrete witness to the fact that the

© The Author(s) 2018
L. Bauer and R. Küsters (Eds.): POST 2018, LNCS 10804, pp. 188–213, 2018.
https://doi.org/10.1007/978-3-319-89722-6_8

management of sensitive data is often not properly taken into account by the developers of the apps. For example, the studies performed by He et al. [3] on free mobile health apps available on the Google Play store show that the majority of these apps send sensitive data in clear text and store it on third party servers that do not support the required confidentiality measures.

When dealing with sensitive data, classical authentication solutions based on username-password pairs are not enough. The "General Data Protection Regulation" [4] mandates that specific security measures must be implemented, including *multi-factor authentication*, a strong(er) authentication solution that combines two or more authentication elements of different categories (e.g., a password combined with a pin sent to a mobile device, or some biometric data). There are many alternative solutions on the market for providing multi-factor authentication. Examples are FIDO (Fast IDentity Online, https:// fidoalliance.org), which enables mobile devices to act as U2F (Universal 2nd Factor) authentication devices over Bluetooth or NFC, and Mobile Connect (https://mobileconnect.io), which identifies users through their mobile phone numbers.

In addition to the establishment of high-level security for authentication solutions for mobile apps, it is essential to take the usability aspect into consideration. Monitoring apps often require a daily or even hourly use, but understandably users cannot be bothered by a long and complex authentication procedure each time they want to read or update their data, especially on mobile devices where the keyboard is small and sometimes uncomfortable to use. A better usability can be provided by supporting a *Single Sign-On (SSO) experience*, which allows users to access different, federated apps by performing a single login carried out with a selected identity provider (e.g., Facebook or Google). While the authentication session is valid, users can directly access all the apps in the federation, without having to enter their credentials again and again.

Contributions. In this paper, we present the design, the formal specification and the security analysis of a solution that allows users to access different mobile apps through a multi-factor authentication solution providing a SSO experience.

We focus on multi-factor authentication solutions that use *One Time Passwords (OTPs)*, which are passwords that are valid for a short time and can only be used once. We have selected OTP-generation approaches as they are commonly used to provide strong authentication and many alternative solutions (from physical to software tools) are available on the market. For instance, Google Authenticator is a mobile app that generates OTPs [5]. Like Google Authenticator, many of the OTP-generation solutions on the market are applicable only for web solutions and use mobile devices as an additional factor.

However, in the scenario considered in this paper, users are not accessing web apps on their laptops or desktop computers, but instead they are accessing native mobile apps. In relation to SSO and multi-factor authentication, web and mobile environments and channels guarantee different security properties, e.g., in web scenarios identity providers can authenticate service provider apps using shared secrets, but this is not possible for native mobile apps that are unable to keep values secret. This changes the exploitable attack surface and thus requires a specific analysis. To the best of our knowledge, the definition of a multi-factor authentication solution for native apps is still not well specified. Even if there are some solutions currently used, their security analyses have been performed informally or semi-formally at best, and without following a standardized formal procedure. This makes a comparison between the different solutions both complex and potentially misleading.

For the security assumptions and the design of a native SSO solution, our work is based on [6,7]. In this previous work, we presented a solution for native SSO and performed a semi-formal security analysis. In this work, we extend these studies by providing a multi-factor authentication solution and a formal analysis of the identified security goals.

Summarizing, our contributions are four-fold as we have

1. designed a multi-factor authentication solution that uses OTPs as an authenticator factor and provides a SSO experience for native apps;
2. provided a description of the proposed solution detailing the security and trust assumptions;
3. formally defined the security goals of our multi-factor authentication solution;
4. formally analyzed our solution by modeling the flow, assumptions and goals using a formal language (ASLan++) and model-checking the identified security goals with the SATMC tool.

The results of our analysis show that our solution behaves as expected.

Organization. Section 2 provides background on strong authentication solutions and SSO for native mobile apps, and on ASLan++ and SATMC. Section 3 describes the design of the proposed multi-factor authentication solution, discusses the peculiarities of a multi-factor authentication solution compared to a basic username-password authentication, and identifies the corresponding security assumptions and security goals. For concreteness, Sect. 4 describes our solution in the context of mHealth apps, and the solution is then formally analyzed using SATMC. Section 5 discusses related work and Sect. 6 draws conclusions.

2   Background

This section provides the basic notions required to understand the proposed design for a multi-factor authentication solution that supports a SSO experience and its security assessment. In Sect. 2.1, we describe the entities involved in a multi-factor authentication and SSO solution, discuss the different OTP-generation approaches, and identify the functional requirements of a native SSO solution. In Sect. 2.2, we provide useful background for our formal analysis.

2.1   Multi-factor Authentication and Native SSO

The entities involved in a multi-factor native SSO solution are: a *User (User)* that wants to access a native *Service Provider app (SP$_C$)*; an *Identity Provider* *server (IdP$_S$)* that manages the digital identities of the users and provides the multi-factor process; a *User Agent (UA)*, which could be a browser or a native app used to perform the multi-factor process between the SP_C and IdP_S. Optionally, the SP_C app could have a backend server (SP_S).

A multi-factor authentication solution augments the security of the basic username-password authentication by exploiting two or more authentication factors. In [8], it is defined as:

> *"a procedure based on the use of two or more of the following elements — categorised as knowledge, ownership and inherence: i) something only the user knows, e.g., static password, code, personal identification number; ii) something only the user possesses, e.g., token, smart card, mobile phone; iii) something the user is, e.g. biometric characteristic, such as a fingerprint. In addition, the elements selected must be mutually independent [...] at least one of the elements should be non-reusable and non-replicable".*

The more factors are used during the authentication process, the more confidence a service has that the user is correctly identified.

There are many multi-factor techniques on the market. In this paper, we focus on a well-accepted solution that combines a PIN code ("something only the user knows") with the generation of an OTP using a software OTP generator ("something only the user possesses"). When an OTP-generation approach is used, a different password is generated for each authentication request and is valid only once, providing a fresh authentication property. Thus, compromising an old OTP does not have security consequences in the authentication process.

There exist many algorithms for generating OTPs and we can classify them into three main OTP-generation approaches:

- *Time synchronization:* the OTP is generated starting from a shared secret key (called *seed*) and the current time of the operation. IdP_S must validate this value: only OTPs that fall into a short temporal range are accepted.
- *Lamport's algorithm* [9]: the first OTP is generated from a seed value and each successor OTP value is based on the value of its predecessor. For example, if s is a seed value and $F(x)$ is a one-way function, we have the following OTPs: $o_1 = s, o_2 = F(o_1), o_3 = F(o_2), \ldots o_n = F(o_{n-1})$. The last OTP, o_n, is stored on IdP_S. When a *User* wants to login, she sends o_{n-1} to the server, and the server applies the function F and checks that the result corresponds to the stored value. If the two values correspond, IdP_S authenticates *User* and updates the stored value with o_{n-1}. In the next login, *User* will use o_{n-2} and so on. After n logins, *User* has to change the seed value and calculate new OTP values.
- *Challenge/Response:* in the execution of this approach, IdP_S presents a "challenge" (e.g., a random number) and *User* answers with a valid "response", which is an OTP value calculated using a mathematical algorithm starting from the challenge.

Although our solution is parametric in the OTP-generation approach, in Sect. 4, we will detail and analyze the time synchronization approach in the context of a real-world scenario.

Native SSO protocols allow users to access multiple SP_C apps through a single authentication performed with an IdP_S. As identified in [6], the two requirements that we expect for a native SSO solution are: (i) the IdP user credentials can be used to gain access to several SP_C apps—this implies that a *User* does not need to have credentials with a SP_C to access it; (ii) if a *User* has already a login session with an IdP_S, then she can access new SP_C apps without re-entering her IdP credentials—only the *User* consent is required.

2.2 Formal Analysis: ASLan++ and SATMC

The use of formal languages and automatic tools for analyzing security protocols has allowed researchers to uncover a large number of vulnerabilities in protocols that had been thought to be, or even informally proved to be, secure. Famous examples range from protocols such as the Needham-Schroeder Public Key protocol to Kerberos or TLS (see [10] for details). These examples underline how the design of a protocol that requires specific security goals is not a simple task, as its security depends on several assumptions on trust and communication channels (e.g., the federation between the involved parties, and the transport protocol used in the message exchange). Several formal languages have been developed, all sharing the idea to extract from the protocol message flow a description of the entities involved, the exchanged messages and the channel assumptions. Formal protocol specifications are then given in input to automated tools that check the desired security goals of the protocol against realistic threat models.

In this paper, we use ASLan++ [11], the input specification language of the AVANTSSAR Platform [12]. ASLan++ is a high-level formal language that formalizes the interactions between the different protocol roles, where a role represents a sequence of operations (e.g., sending and receiving messages) that must be executed by the entity that plays that role. ASLan++ supports the specification of different channel assumptions and security goals, most notably different variants of authentication and confidentiality. In our analysis, we use SATMC [13], which is one of the model checkers of the AVANTSSAR platform. SATMC uses state-of-the-art SAT Solvers and allows for the specification of security goals written using the Linear Temporal Logic.

3   Description of Our *mID(OTP)* Solution

In this section, we present a mobile identity management solution that augments the security of the native SSO solution proposed in [6] by adding a multi-factor authentication based on the generation of OTPs. We called it *mID(OTP)* to highlight the dual goal that our solution pursued: (i) to establish a multi-factor authentication and (ii) to manage identities for native mobile apps, e.g., providing a SSO service. As we will describe, *mID(OTP)* is parametric on the OTP generation (i.e., it supports different OTP-generation approaches).

In the mobile context, two possible design choices are available: a *UA* could be played either by a browser (external or embedded in the SP_C app) or by a native app. In the design of *mID(OTP)*, we have preferred the latter choice, as a native app can be (easily) extended to support the generation of an authentication factor (e.g., by adding the code for a OTP generator or a library to process the user's fingerprint). In addition, as the *UA* is involved in the authentication phase with the IdP_S, it must be trusted in knowing the user's IdP credentials. Thus, we assume that this native app, called *IDOTP*, is released directly by the IdP_S.

mID(OTP) consists of three phases: *registration*, *activation* and *exploitation*, which we describe in the following subsections.

3.1   Registration and Activation Phases of *mID(OTP)*

The registration phase of *mID(OTP)* is performed by the SP_C developers and corresponds to the exchange of some information about SP_C, such as the package name and logo, together with its certificate fingerprint *key_hash* (i.e., the hash of the certificate of the app). Note that *key_hash* depends on the private key of the SP_C developer and is thus different for apps by different developers. The registration phase can be performed in different ways, e.g., entering the data into an online dashboard or via an email exchange. As a trust relationship between SP_C and IdP_S is established as result of the registration phase, it is important that the IdP_S validates the SP_C data and in some cases (e.g., when user personal or sensitive data are involved) a service-level agreement could be required as well.

The activation phase of *mID(OTP)* is performed by the *User* to configure the native app *IDOTP* on her smartphone. In addition to the procedure described in [6]—user login and release of a token (*token_IdP*) used (from here on) to identify the user session in place of the user credentials—at the end of the activation phase the *IDOTP* is configured to generate OTPs, usually requiring the creation of a PIN code for the future interactions.

Also the activation phase can be performed in different ways. As a multi-factor authentication is configured during this phase, it is essential to provide the *User* with an activation code—exchanged using a secure channel (e.g., after an in-person identification)—that she has to enter during the process.

3.2   Exploitation Phase of *mID(OTP)*

The exploitation phase of *mID(OTP)*, which is shown in Fig. 1, is performed every time the *User* accesses a SP_C that requires the multi-factor authentication and SSO experience offered by *IDOTP*. In Step S1, *User* opens the SP_C app that sends a request to SP_S including a session token *token_sync* (Step S2). SP_S checks the validity of *token_sync*. If *token_sync* has expired, SP_S sends an error message asking for a login to SP_C (Step S3), otherwise Step S7 is executed. If a login form is presented to *User*, she clicks the login button (Step A1) and SP_C sends a login request to *IDOTP* (Step A2). As a consequence, in Step A3 *IDOTP* reads the *key_hash* value of SP_C and in Step A4 sends a request to IdP_S asking the SP_C data. The received *key_hash* is used by IdP_S to validate

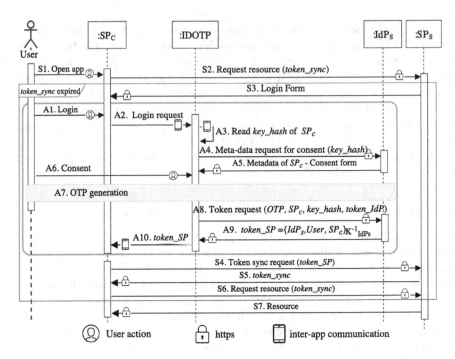

Fig. 1. Exploitation phase of *mID(OTP)*.

the SP_C identity. If SP_C is valid, IdP_S returns to *IDOTP* a consent containing the meta-data of SP_C (Step A5). In Step A6, *User* checks whether SP_C is the app that she wants to access and decides whether to give her consent or not. If *User* agrees, the OTP is generated following one of the approaches described in Sect. 2.1 (Step A7). Then, in Step A8, *IDOTP* sends a token request to IdP_S including the OTP value, *key_hash* and *token_IdP*, which corresponds to the user credentials entered during the activation phase. IdP_S checks the validity of OTP, *key_hash* and *token_IdP*. If they are valid, a token (*token_SP*) for the *SP* app is returned (Step A9). *token_SP* contains the identity of *User*, IdP_S and *SP*, and is digitally signed with $K_{IdP_S}^{-1}$, the private key of IdP_S. In Step A10, *IDOTP* returns *token_SP* to SP_C as result of Step A2. To finalize the authentication, SP_C sends a token request to SP_S with *token_SP* (Step S4). SP_S checks the validity of *token_SP*, and if it is valid, creates and sends to SP_C a token *token_sync* (Step S5). This token will be used by SP_C to synchronize user data in the future interactions, until its expiration. When SP_C needs to synchronize data, sends a request to the SP_S including *token_sync* (Step S6), and SP_S returns the requested resource to SP_C (Step S7).

We have labeled the steps with "S" and "A". The S steps are related to the *SP* (but note that our representation is only an example and each *SP* could support different solutions). The A steps represent the steps related to the authentication solution. As the S steps can vary depending on the choices of the SP developers, in our analysis, we will focus on the A steps. Compared to the protocol flow proposed in [6], we have enhanced its security by adding the generation, exchange and validation of OTPs. For example, the OTP extension protects mainly against a stolen smartphone. Indeed, even if the user's smartphone is stolen, the intruder cannot login as the victim without generating the expected OTP.

3.3   Towards a Formal Specification of Multi-factor Authentication

We now discuss the peculiarities of a multi-factor authentication solution compared to a basic username-password authentication; in doing so, we introduce some concepts that will be the key for the formal analysis.

In a basic username-password authentication, the expected security goal is:

($\mathbf{G1}_A$) *SP* authenticates *User*

Here, *User* is required to provide an authentication factor: either credentials (something only she knows) or a session token (e.g., a cookie stored in her browser) in order to properly complete the authentication process. If this is the case, it is possible to specify a minimum set of security assumptions (e.g., on the behavior of *User* or on the communication channels) that are necessary to guarantee G1$_A$. For example, if the channel used for the login is not https, then an intruder can eavesdrop the *User*'s password and impersonate her in the future. We call these assumptions *strong assumptions* (to distinguish them from the *weak assumptions* that we define later).

A multi-factor authentication solution augments the security of the basic username-password authentication by exploiting two or more authentication factors. By the definition given in Sect. 2.1, we infer that *mID(OTP)* is a two-factor authentication solution using knowledge and ownership elements (factors). We do not consider inherence factors. In addition, instead of considering the independent factors, we introduce the concept of instance-factors.

We call *instance-factor* (*IFactor*) every specific instance of either an ownership factor (*IFactor$_o$*) or a knowledge factor (*IFactor$_k$*). The multi-factor authentication solution *mID(OTP)* that we propose contains three instance-factors:

- the *IFactor$_o$* *token_IdP* that is stored in *IDOTP* and in *IdP$_S$* as a result of the activation phase (used as a session token in place of the user credentials to provide a SSO experience);
- another *IFactor$_k$* that can vary according to the specific OTP generator used, e.g., a PIN known by the user (used to protect the OTP generator);
- an *IFactor$_o$* that is stored in *IDOTP* (and possibly shared with *IdP$_S$*), according to the OTP-generator approach used (e.g., a seed value or a private key).

Note that the *IFactor$_o$* *token_IdP* is present in all instances of our solution, whereas the other two factors may differ depending on the specific solution (and this is the reason why we cannot name them explicitly a priori).

Compared to classic notion of authentication factors, instance-factors can have a dependency. For example, the two *IFactor$_o$* are stored in *IDOTP*. Thus, by breaching the *IDOTP* app both of them are compromised. However, it is important to note that different mitigations can be implemented for the different instance-factors. For example, in our solution, if a *User* realizes that the *IDOTP* has been compromised (e.g., if her smartphone has been stolen), she can invalidate *token_IdP*, thus blocking possible attacks.

We are not aware of any formal definition of the multi-factor authentication property apart from [14]. In [14] they analyzed a two-factor and two-channel authentication solution that combines a classic single-factor solution with the exchange of a second factor using the GSM/3G/4G communication infrastructure of the user's mobile phone. By generalizing the definition in [14] by considering a solution involving n instance-factors, we can define the following security goal:

($G1_{MFA}$) Goal $G1_A$ (i.e., *SP* authenticates *User*) holds even if an intruder knows up to $n - 1$ instance-factors.

Thus, the addition of instance-factors ensures some "redundancy", meaning that even if one of them is compromised there are no attacks.

We call *weak assumption* (*wa*) an assumption that, whenever it is not valid or not implemented properly, causes the disclosure of a non-empty set of instance-factors of the same type, i.e., either $IFactor_o$ or $IFactor_k$. We refer to this set as the *set of instance-factors associated with wa* and denote it by writing $IF(wa)$.[1] For example, if a weak assumption *wa1* states that the intruder cannot read the values typed by *User*, and in the authentication process *User* has to enter her *password* and *PIN*, then $IF(wa1) = \{password, PIN\}$. This definition can be easily extended to a set of weak assumptions WA' as follows: $IF(WA') = \bigcup_{wa_i \in WA'} IF(wa_i)$. We write WA to denote the *set of all the weak assumptions*.

Defining Security Goals. The notions that we just introduced allow us to rephrase the definition of the security goal $G1_{MFA}$ of a multi-factor authentication solution in the following way:

($G1_{MFA}$) Goal $G1_A$ holds under the strong assumptions and under chosen subsets of weak assumptions (WA') such that the set of instance factors associated to $WA \setminus WA'$ does not include all the instance-factors. That is, $|IF(WA \setminus WA')| < n$.

A main characteristic of *mID(OTP)* is the use of OTPs. In $G1_{MFA}$, we considered (among others) the instance-factors linked to the OTP generation. In addition, as reported in Sect. 2, an OTP "should be non-reusable and non-replicable." Indeed, if the OTP is not fresh, then the knowledge of an OTP leads to the same attacks possible when knowing the instance-factors linked to

---

[1] To compromise all instance-factors, at least two weak assumptions must be not valid.

its generation. Thus, it is crucial that the following security goal about the OTP is satisfied:

(G2) The OTP must prove its origin (meaning that IdP_S authenticates $IDOTP$, as $IDOTP$ is the only app that possesses a secret value shared with IdP_S or a private key), and it is non-reusable (i.e., IdP_S accepts only one OTP for a specific operation so as to avoid replay attacks).

3.4 Assumptions

Our solution is based on different security assumptions, which we have classified as *strong* or *weak* assumptions.

Strong Assumptions. We have identified the following assumptions and checked them to be strong assumptions (see Sect. 4.5): *Trust Assumption* that clarifies the trust relationships between the different entities, *Communication Assumptions* that specify the concrete implementation of the communication channels required in *mID(OTP)*, and *Activation Assumption* that identifies the assumptions related to the activation phase of *mID(OTP)*.

Trust Assumption. mID(OTP) is based on the following trust relationship:

(TA) IdP_S is trusted by SP_C.

Communication Assumptions. Communications between the parties are subject to the following assumptions:

(ComA1) The communication between SP_C and $IDOTP$ is carried over an inter-app communication implemented using `StartActivity ForResult()`. This Android method—which allows an app to open another app and get a result back—guarantees that the SP_C app that sends a request to $IDOTP$ at Step A2 in Fig. 1 is the same app that receives the result back from $IDOTP$ at Step A10.

(ComA2) To read the *key_hash* value (Step A3 of Fig. 1), $IDOTP$ uses the Android method `getPackageInfo(client packageName, PackageManager. GET SIGNATURES)`, which extracts the information about the certificate fingerprint included in the package of SP_C.

(ComA3) The communication between $IDOTP$ and IdP_S occurs over a unilateral SSL or TLS channel (henceforth SSL/TLS), established through the exchange of a valid certificate (from IdP_S to $IDOTP$).

Note that even if these assumptions refer to a concrete implementation of the communication channels, in Sect. 4.3 we will provide the formal counterpart abstracting away the implementation details. By doing so, any implementation satisfying the abstract assumptions can be used in place of the implementation mentioned above (e.g., considering a similar solution in the case of iOS), and the results of our security analysis still hold. For example, the main reason to have ComA1 is to avoid the eavesdropping of the identity assertion (*token_SP*) by a malicious app, as in this way an intruder can use it to impersonate the user on another smartphone. An alternative implementation of ComA1 could be obtained by requiring SP_C to insert a fresh value in the token request. In this way, SP_C will accept only the *token_SP* that includes the expected fresh value. Regardless of the design choice, it is crucial that SP_C (and SP_S if it is involved) only accepts tokens that are released for itself for a particular operation.

Activation Assumption. Phishing attacks (e.g., a malicious app that creates a fake login form and steals the user's credentials) are one of the most common types of attack and usually are beyond the scope of an authentication protocol. In our analysis, together with a secure communication, we assume that no phishing is possible during the activation phase:

(**ActivA**) The activation phase is correctly performed by *User*. That is, *User* downloads the correct *IDOTP* (it is not a fake app) and correctly follows the process, and the communication channels used are secure.

Weak Assumptions. We have identified two categories for weak assumptions: *Background Assumptions* that specify the assumptions on the environment (user's smartphone), and *User Behavior Assumptions* that specify which user behaviors are allowed in our model.

Background Assumptions. The environment is subject to these assumptions:

(**BA1**) Integrity and confidentiality of data stored in the device.
(**BA2**) There is no surveillance software (e.g., keylogger) installed on the user's device capable of reading the values that *User* types.

User Behavior Assumptions. To enforce a correct execution of the flow and to investigate the security consequences of a stolen smartphone, in our analysis we take into account the following behavioral rules:

(**UBA1**) *User* enters her $IFactor_k$ only in the correct *IDOTP* app being careful not to be seen by other people.
(**UBA2**) *User* is the only person using the *IDOTP* app that stores the $IFactor_p$ associated to her identity.

4   Formal Specification and Analysis of the mID(OTP) Solution: The mHealth Use-Case

In this section, we describe how the semi-formal description of the *mID(OTP)* solution can be translated into a formal model (in this case, specified in ASLan++). *mID(OTP)* provides a general solution for several application contexts. Instead of presenting at first the general model and then the formalization of a use-case, for brevity and concreteness, here we describe directly the formalization of a real use-case scenario that involves mHealth (mobile health) apps. All the concepts presented apply in general to every solution based on $mID(OTP)$ (apart from a trivial renaming of the entities). Only the steps and instance-factors related to the particular OTP generator used are specific for this use-case.

In Sect. 4.1, we describe the entities and the steps of the OTP-generator approach for this use-case. In Sects. 4.2 and 4.3, we detail the mapping between the assumptions and their formal specification. In Sect. 4.4, we give the formalization of the security goals. In Sect. 4.5, we present the results of our security analysis.

4.1 Description of the TreC Scenario

TreC is an acronym for "Cartella Clinica del Cittadino", i.e., "Citizens' Clinical Record". TreC is a platform developed in the Trentino region (Italy) for managing personal health records (PHRs).[2] In addition to the web platform, which is routinely used by around 80,000 users, TreC is currently designing and implementing a number of native Android applications to support self-management and remote monitoring of chronic conditions. These applications are used in a "living lab" by voluntary chronic patients according to their hospital physicians. Examples are:

– "TreC-Lab: Diario Diabete", a mobile diary that allows patients to record health data, such as the blood glucose level and physical activity, and
– "TreC: Referti", which permits patients to consult their personal health data and medical prescriptions from the smartphone.

In the traditional web scenario, patients access services using their local healthcare system credentials (leveraging a SAML-based SSO [15] solution), but a solution for native SSO was missing. The solution we have proposed will allow patients to access different TreC e-health native mobile apps (and possibly other third-party e-health apps) through a single authentication act. An implementation of the proposed model is currently being tested by TreC users.

In the following, we instantiate the entities described in Sect. 3 with the entities involved in TreC: *Patient* plays the role of *User* who wants to access her PHR on her smartphone. *ADC* ("Autenticazione del Cittadino") is the IdP of the local health care system and plays the role of IdP_S. *OTP-PAT* plays the role of $IDOTP$ and manages the generation of OTPs and the SSO experience for the apps installed on the phone that are part of the federation. $TreC_C$ (TreC client) plays the role of SP_C and is one of the apps that are part of the ADC federation and it is used by *Patient* to read her PHR. $TreC_S$ (TreC server) plays the role of SP_S and manages user health data.

Figure 2 shows the A-steps of the exploitation phase of $mID(OTP)$ for this use-case. Compared to Fig. 1, we have detailed the OTP generation box (steps A7 a–c), and graphically shown the channel properties, which we will explain

---

[2] More information is available at https://trec.trentinosalute.net/.

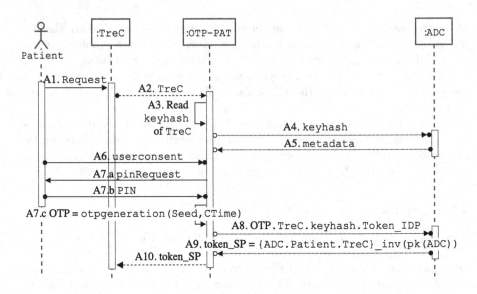

Fig. 2. MSC of the exploitation phase of the TreC scenario.

in Sect. 4.3. Given that $TreC_S$ is not involved in the A-steps, for the sake of brevity, in the rest of the section we refer to $TreC_C$ simply with $TreC$. Steps A7 (a–c) model the behavior of a Time-OTP (TOTP) algorithm [16], which is a time synchronization algorithm that generates OTPs as a function of the time of the execution and a seed (i.e., a shared secret). In general, the TOTP algorithm requires that "the prover and verifier must either share the same secret or the knowledge of a secret transformation to generate a shared secret" [16], without specifying when and how to exchange this secret. In the analyzed use-case, $OTP\text{-}PAT$ obtains the seed value as part of the activation phase, and then stores it encrypted with the PIN code ($\{|seed|\}\_PIN$) selected by $Patient$. Thus, the OTP generation box depicted in Fig. 1 is replaced here with a PIN request (Steps A7.a), the entering of the PIN (Steps A7.b) and the generation of the OTP as a function of the seed—extracted using the PIN as decryption key—and of time (Steps A7.c).

The TreC scenario corresponds to a multi-factor authentication with 3 instance-factors: $token\_IdP$ and $\{|seed|\}\_PIN$ are $IFactor_o$, and PIN is an $IFactor_k$.

In the rest of this section, we present the formalism that we have used to specify this use-case, detailing the initial state and the behavior of the entities, the channels and the security goals. We also describe how we have formalized the assumptions presented in Sect. 3.4. In Table 1, we show each assumption and the corresponding formal specification. In addition, we model what in Sect. 3.3 is indicated as *an assumption not valid or not implemented properly* by removing it from the formal model, as shown in the last column of Table 1.

4.2   Formal Specification of the Initial State and of the Behavior of Entities

Initial States. The initial state of a protocol defines the initial knowledge of the intruder, who is indicated with the letter i, and of all the honest entities that participate in the protocol session, where a protocol session is a particular run of the protocol, played by specific entities, using specific instances of the communication channels and optionally, additional parameters that must be passed as initial knowledge to the different entities. To model the TA assumption, as shown in Table 1, in our analysis we have not considered sessions with i playing the role of *OTP-PAT* and *ADC*.

Regarding the registration phase, we have modeled the data provided by the *TreC* developer as initial knowledge of *ADC*. In general, after the registration phase, IdP_S creates two databases: trustedSPs, containing the relation between the SP_C identities and their *key_hash* values, and metadataDB, containing the relation between the *key_hash* and the information (e.g., name and logo) provided by the SP developers. As shown in Table 1 by the ActivA assumption, we have modeled the data obtained as result of the activation phase (*token_IdP* and data required for generating OTPs) as initial knowledge of *User*, *IDOTP*

Table 1. Mapping between assumptions (Asm(s) for short) and formal specification.

Asm	Formal specification	
	Specification of Asm	Removal of Asm
TA	We do not consider sessions with i playing the role of *ADC*	add sessions with i playing the role of *ADC*
ComA1	link(T20,O2T);	delete link(T20,O2T);
ComA2	authentic_on(T20,TreC); and DB Keyhash	delete authentic_on(T20,TreC);
ComA3	confidential_to(O2A,ADC); weakly_authentic(O2A); weakly_confidential(A2O); authentic_on(A2O,ADC); link(O2A,A2O);	delete confidential_to(O2A,ADC); weakly_authentic(O2A); weakly_confidential(A2O); authentic_on(A2O,ADC); link(O2A,A2O);
ActivA	Data obtained during the activation phase are nonpublic values shared as parameters between *Patient*, *OTP-PAT* and *ADC*	add iknows(pinUser); iknows(token_IDP); iknows({|seed|}_pinUser); in general add all the iknows(*IFactor*); obtained during the activation phase
BA1	"Built-in": i cannot read the internal state of the other entities	add iknows(token_IDP); and iknows({|seed|}_pinUser); in general add all the iknows(*IFactor$_p$*);
BA2	"Built-in": i cannot read the internal state of the other entities	add iknows(pinUser); in general add all the iknows(*IFactor$_k$*);
UBA1	confidential_to(P2O,OTP-PAT);	delete confidential_to(P2O,OTP-PAT);
UBA2	authentic_on(P2O,Patient);	delete authentic_on(P2O,Patient);

and IdP_S. In particular, for the use-case, as result of the activation phase: a *Patient* knows her PIN value (`pinUser`), *OTP-PAT* knows `token_IDP` and `{|seed|}_pinUser`, and *ADC* creates a DB (`usersDB`) with `Patient`, `token_IDP` and `seed` as entry.

To specify that the intruder knows a message m, we use the ASLan++ predicate `iknows(m)`. As shown in Table 1 for ActivA, BA1 and BA2, the removal of an assumption (which we will do to consider different scenarios of the analysis) boils down to adding some `iknows` facts to the initial knowledge of the intruder.

Behavior of Entities. The behavior of the honest entities is specified by the evolution of the system, which consists of a sequence of operations performed by each role. For simplicity, Fig. 3 shows the evolution of the protocol using a process view, which describes the messages exchanged in Fig. 2 for each entity as a set of actions (e.g., receive or send a message and DB access). This formal representation can be translated into various role-based formal languages and input to different state-of-the-art security protocol analyzers. In our analysis, we use ASLan++ and SATMC (see [11] for more details on language and tool).

The translation of the process view into ASLan++ is quite straightforward. The complete ASLan++ specification can be found at https://st.fbk.eu/publications/POST-2018. Here, for lack of space, we provide only an example by considering Steps 1 and 2 of Fig. 2, which involve the entities *Patient*, *TreC* and *OTP-PAT*. Focusing on *TreC*, this exchange of messages in ASLan++ corresponds to

```
Patient -Ch_P2T-> Actor: Request;  % Step 1
Actor -Ch_T2O-> OTP-PAT: Actor;    % Step 2
```

where `Actor` is the keyword used in ASLan++ to represent the entity taken into consideration, in our example *TreC*.

In our analysis, we have considered the behavior of a Dolev-Yao intruder [17], who can overhear and modify messages using his initial knowledge and the knowledge obtained from the traffic—this behavior is built-in in the SATMC tool. An operation that is not allowed to i is the reading of the internal state of another entity, where an internal state is a list of expressions known by the corresponding entity. Thus, as highlighted in Table 1, BA1 and BA2 are built-in in the tool.

4.3 Formal Specification of Channels

For a detailed definition of the properties of channels between two protocol entities A and B we point the reader to [18,19]. In a nutshell, consider a message M sent on a channel $A2B$ from A to B. $A2B$ is *authentic* if B can rely on the fact that only A could have sent M. $A2B$ is *confidential* if A can rely on the fact that only B can receive M. $A2B$ is *weakly authentic* if the channel input is exclusively accessible to a single, but yet unknown, sender, and $A2B$ is *weakly confidential* if the channel output is exclusively accessible to a single, yet unknown, receiver. A *link* between two channels $A2B$ and $B2A$ means that the entity sending messages

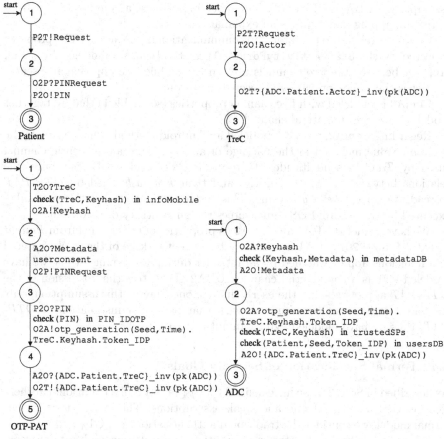

Fig. 3. Protocol view.

Legend:

- P, T, O, and *A* stands for `Patient`, `TreC`, `OTP-PAT`, and ADC respectively, and P2T, P2O, O2P, O2T, O2A, T2O, A2O are their unidirectional channels.
- *Ch* ! *M* means that message *M* is sent over channel *Ch*.
- *Ch* ? *M* means that a message, says *M*, is received over channel *Ch* and a variable *X* is set to *M*.
- *M1* . *M2* is the concatenation of messages *M1* and *M2*.
- *check(X,Y,...,Z)* in *DB* means that *(X,Y,...,Z)* must be in *DB*, otherwise the protocol stops.
- *M*_inv (pk (ADC)) means that message *M* is digitally signed with the private key of ADC.

over the *A2B* is the same entity that receives messages from *B2A*. We have represented these properties graphically in Fig. 2 as follows: $A \bullet\!\!\to B$, $A \circ\!\!\to B$, $A \to\!\!\bullet B$, $A \to\!\!\circ B$ mean authentic, weak authentic, confidential and weak confidential channel, respectively; moreover, we indicate a link property between two channels with the same trace for the corresponding arrows.

As shown in Table 1, we have modeled as channel properties the tree communication assumptions (ComA1, ComA2 and ComA3) and the two user behavior assumptions (UBA1 and UBA2). The modeling of these assumption is far from a trivial mapping and requires an explanation.

ComA1 is related to the inter-app communication in the mobile. The property expected by the `StartActivityForResult` method can be modeled by a link property between the two channels used in the mobile: the app that has sent a request is the same app that will receive the result.

ComA3 is modeled with five channel properties (see Table 1) that all together model a TLS/SSL unilateral channel.

Regarding ComA2, we have modeled an Android method, which extracts the *key_hash* value included in the package of an app, using an authentic channel (used by *TreC* to send its identity to *OTP-PAT*) and a DB containing the relations between the SP_C identities and their *key_hash*, used by *OTP-PAT* to read the correct *key_hash* value. This is due to the fact that this method— executed by the Android OS—guarantees the authenticity of its output.

We have modeled UBA1 and UBA2 as properties of the channel from *Patient* to *OTP-PAT* (P20). UBA1 is necessary to prevent leakage of the *PIN*—entered in a malicious app or watched by an intruder during the typing—thus, we have modeled P20 as a confidential channel. UBA2 guarantees the possession of the *OTP-PAT* app installed in the user's smartphone. Having this assumption, only the valid *Patient* can communicate with that particular installation of *OTP-PAT*, thus we have modeled P20 as an authentic channel.

4.4   Formal Specification of Security Goals

As described in Sect. 3.3, we have defined $G1_{MFA}$ in terms of a traditional authentication goal and the strong and weak assumptions. This means that, in the formal model, we consider the traditional authentication goal $G1_A$ and we check whether it holds under the strong assumptions and different (sub)sets of weak-assumptions. The property must hold if the intruder is not able to compromise all the instance-factors. $G1_A$ requires that a message is transmitted in an authenticated and fresh manner, thus allowing *TreC* to authenticate *Patient* and offering replay-protection at the same time. For the definition of authentication we refer to [20]: whenever the entity B completes a run of the protocol apparently with the entity A, then A has previously been running the protocol apparently with B, and the two entities agree on a message M. In ASLan++, this corresponds to specifying the goal

($G1_A$) SP_authn_U_on_Request: (_) *Patient* *->> *TreC*;

where *->> indicates authenticity, directedness (i.e., the only (honest) receiver of a message is the intended one [11]) and freshness. In addition, following the definition in [20], associated goal labels are used to specify which values of M the goal is referring to, namely, the Request value in State 1 of the *Patient* process (in Fig. 3) and the corresponding value in the last state of the *TreC* process (State 3 in Fig. 3).

Similarly, the OTP properties are checked by means of the goal

(G2) IDP_authn_UA_on_OTP: (_) *OTP-PAT* *->> *ADC*;

with the associated goal labels specifying for M the values otp_generation (Seed,Time) in States 3 of both the *OTP-PAT* and the *ADC* processes in Fig. 3, where we have modeled Seed as a constant value shared between *OTP-PAT* and *ADC*, and Time as a session parameter (cf. [16]) shared between *OTP-PAT* and *ADC*. Thus, *ADC* will accept only one OTP value for each session, enforcing the property (informally described in Sect. 3.3) that OTP is non-reusable.

4.5   Results of the Security Analysis

We are now ready to discuss the results of the security assessment that we have performed on the mHealth use-case. Our focus is determining whether the concurrent execution of a finite number of protocol sessions enjoys the expected security goals in spite of the intruder. To this aim, we have mechanically analyzed the formal model of our use-case using SATMC, a state-of-the-art model checker for security protocols. SATMC carries out an iterative deepening strategy on k. Initially k is set to 0, and then it is incremented till an attack is found (if any) or k_{max} is reached. If this is the case, no attack traces of length up to k_{max} exist, where the length of the trace is computed by taking into account the parallel execution of non-conflicting actions (actions executed in parallel are considered as a single step). The trace includes the actions performed by attacker and honest participants, where most of the actions of the attacker are executed in parallel (and counted as a single step) with the ones of honest participants. We set k_{max} to 1.5 times the length of the longest trace of the protocol when only honest entities participate. As a rule of thumb, with this choice we are reasonably confident that no attack is possible with greater values of k_{max}. In our analysis, the length of the longest trace of the protocol when only honest entities participate is 19, and thus we have set $k_{max} = 30$. We have considered several scenarios including (at most) three parallel sessions in which the intruder either does not play any role or plays the role of SP_C (the *TreC* app in the use-case). In each session, we used different instances of the channels. The complete set of specifications can be found at the companion website.

In Sect. 3.4, in relation to the security goal $G1_{MFA}$ (and consequently to $G1_A$), we have described a list of strong and weak assumptions that we have

Table 2. Analyses performed for $G1_A$.

Analysis	Strong Asm(s)	Weak Asm(s)	Atk
1	all −1	all	Yes
2	all	all −1	No
3	all	all −m $(1 < m \leq 4)$	*

added to the model to constrain the intruder's abilities. Table 2 summarizes the security analyses that we have performed to check this goal.

Regarding the strong assumptions (TA, ComA1, ComA2, ComA3 and ActivA), we have performed the following analyses:

Analysis 1: We have checked that by removing only one of the five strong assumptions from the model we have a violation of $G1_A$ (i.e., there is an attack). For this analysis, we have thus performed 5 executions of SATMC removing one strong assumption at a time. To provide an example of an attack, Fig. 4 shows the attack trace deriving from removing ComA2. In this attack, i can impersonate trec simply because the channel used to exchange its identity is not authentic; thus, i can pretend to be another app. Note that, for the sake of clarity, this figure (and, similarly, the other figures shown in this section) represents only the significant steps of the attack traces found by the SATMC tool.[3]

Regarding the weak assumptions (BA1, BA2, UBA1, and UBA2), we have performed the following analyses that are detailed in Table 3:

Analysis 2: We have checked that by removing only one of the four weak assumptions from the model, SATMC does not find any attack on the solution (i.e., the intruder is not able to impersonate the user). Indeed, as shown in Table 3, by removing only one weak assumption, the intruder obtains only 1 or 2 instance-factors.

Analysis 3: We have checked that by removing specific subsets of weak assumptions it is possible to compromise all the instance-factors, causing a violation of $G1_A$. In Table 2, the star (*) denotes that the result

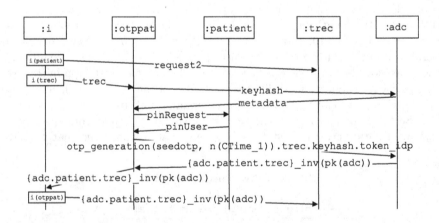

Fig. 4. Attack trace without the strong assumption ComA2.

---

[3] The original charts can be examined on the companion website https://st.fbk.eu/publications/POST-2018.

Table 3. Results for G1$_A$ (Analyses 2 and 3).

Removed weak Asm(s)	Compromised factors			Atk
	PIN	{seed}_PIN	token_IdP	
BA1	×	✓	✓	No
BA2	✓	×	×	No
UBA1	✓	×	×	No
UBA2	×	✓	✓	No
(UBA1 ∨ BA2) ∧ BA1	✓	✓	✓	Yes
(UBA1 ∨ BA2) ∧ UBA2	✓	✓	✓	Yes

can be "yes" or "no" depending on the chosen subset of weak assumptions. The subsets shown in Table 3 violate G1$_A$ and result in different attack traces. Figure 5 shows the attack trace deriving from removing UBA1 and UBA2 (e.g., a proximity intruder that watches the *PIN* entered by *Patient* and then steals the smartphone). In the attack, i initiates a session of the protocol with trec pretending to be patient (indicated as i(patient)). By entering the PIN code (pinUser) when requested by otppat, i is able to impersonate the patient and obtaining the requested resource (resources1). Figure 6 shows the attack trace deriving from removing both BA1 and BA2 (e.g., a hacker that steals the *PIN* typed by *Patient* using a keylogger and reads *token_IdP* and {|*seed*|}_*PIN* exploiting a malware installed on the smartphone). In this case, i is able to generate an OTP and sends a token request to adc.

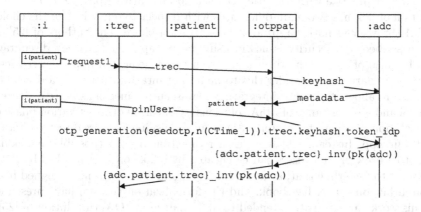

Fig. 5. Attack trace obtained removing UBA1 and UBA2.

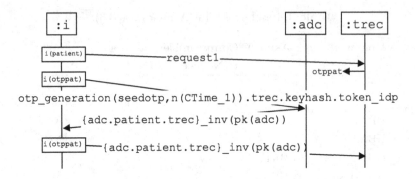

Fig. 6. Attack trace obtained removing BA1 and BA2.

As expected, when checking the solution w.r.t. the security goal G2—which embodies the OTP properties—under all the (weak and strong) assumptions, SATMC does not find any attack.

5 Related Work

OAuth 2.0 [21] and OpenID Connect [22] have been designed for light-RESTful API services, and are considered the de-facto standards for managing authentication and authorization. These protocols are well-accepted in the web scenario, but they provide only partial support for mobile apps (frequent use of the expression "out of scope"). This could lead to the implementation of insecure solutions. An in-depth analysis of OAuth in the mobile environment—underlining possible security problems and vulnerabilities—is available in [23,24].

Given the lack of specifications, the OAuth Working Group has released in 2017 a best practice with the title "OAuth 2.0 for Native Apps" [25]. The specification of [25] has two main differences with respect to our solution: the choice of UA (browser vs native app) and the activation phase. The authors of [25] do not described any security issues in using native apps as UA; they discourage this because of the overhead on users to install a dedicated app. Nevertheless, in some scenarios, we consider this to be an advantage rather than a drawback because it allows for easily integrating new security mechanisms (e.g., access control and a wider range of MFA solutions). Concerning the activation phase of our solution, it allows for better mitigation of phishing as users directly interact with our app. Instead, [25] requires a redirection from a (possible malicious) SP_C to a browser, thus users can be cheated by a fake browser invoked by SP_C. We want to underline that, as described in [7], our solution is not designed from scratch but on top of Facebook; and the formalization that we have presented in this work can be easily extended to also analyze the OAuth solution of [25].

Much research has been carried out to discover vulnerabilities in different implementations of OAuth 2.0 and OpenID Connect in web and mobile scenarios. For instance, Sun et al. [26] analyzed hundreds of OAuth apps focusing on classical web attacks such as Cross-Site Scripting (XSS) and Cross-Site Request Forgery (CSRF). Other studies, such as [27,28], analyzed the implementations of multi-party web apps via browser-related messages. In the context of mobile apps, a similar work is described in [29], where Yang et al. discovered an incorrect use of OAuth that permits an intruder to login as a victim without the victim's awareness. To evaluate the impact of this attack, they have shown that more than 40% of 600 top-ranked apps were vulnerable.

Although these techniques are useful for the analysis of a specific implementation (as they are able to discover serious security flaws), it is important to perform a comprehensive security analysis of the standard itself. In the context of web apps, Fett et al. [30] performed a formal analysis of the OAuth protocol using an expressive web model (defined in [31]) that describes the interaction between browsers and servers in a real-world set-up. This formal analysis revealed two unknown attacks on OAuth that violate the authorization and authentication properties. A similar analysis is performed for OpenID Connect in [32]. Two other examples of formalizations of OAuth are [33], where the different OAuth flows are modeled in the Applied Pi calculus and verified using ProVerif extended with WebSpi (a library that models web users, apps and intruders), and [34], where OAuth is modeled in Alloy.

In our analysis (cf. Sect. 4) we used ASLan++ and SATMC. In the past, SATMC has revealed severe security flaws in the SAML 2.0 protocol [15] and in the variant implemented by Google [18]; by exploiting these flaws a dishonest service provider could impersonate a user at another service provider. Moreover, Yan et al. [35] used ASLan++ and SATMC to analyze four security properties of OAuth: confidentiality, authentication, authorization, and consistency.

The aforementioned formal analyses, however, focus on the web app scenario, whereas in this paper we deal with native apps. In [36], Ye et al. used Proverif to analyze the security of a SSO implementation for Android. They applied their approach to the implementation of the Facebook Login and identified a vulnerability that exploits super user (SU) permissions. In contrast, our analysis assumes that the user smartphone cannot be rooted. Indeed, if a malicious app is able to obtain a SU permission, then it can set for itself the permission to access all the data stored in the smartphone, compromising all the user data and the tokens of the other apps installed on the rooted smartphone.

YubiKey NEO [37] is one of the most attractive mobile identity management products on the market. It is a token device that supports OTPs and the FIDO Alliance Universal 2nd Factor (U2F) protocol, and, by integrating an NFC (Near Field Communication) technology, it can be used to provide a second-factor also in the mobile context. Compared to this product, our solution provides a multi-factor authentication solution for native mobile apps without requiring an additional device.

6   Conclusions

We have presented the design of *mID(OTP)*, a multi-factor authentication solution for native mobile apps that includes an OTP exchange and provides a

SSO experience. In addition to the protocol flow, we have detailed the security assumptions and defined two security goals: $G1_{MFA}$ related to a multi-factor authentication solution and G2 that identifies the properties of a OTP. To perform a security analysis of $mID(OTP)$, we have detailed the OTP-generation approach in the context of a real use-case scenario (TreC). We have formally modeled the flow, assumptions and goals of TreC using a formal language (ASLan++) and checked the identified security goals using a model-checker (SATMC).

The solution we have presented, as well as the formal specification and analysis that we have given, can be generalized quite straightforwardly to other use-cases, which we are currently doing. As future work, we also plan to extend the analysis to other authentication factors, such as biometric traits. In addition, we started exploring an alternative formalization of multi-factor authentication protocols that decomposes the protocol and models the authentication property as a composition of two goals: one related to basic authentication (involving $User$, UA, SP_C and IdP_S) and one related only to the generation and validation of the OTP (without involving SP_C). In this way, a proper separation is kept between the multi-factor authentication performed with IdP_S and the basic authentication plus SSO experience offered to SP_C. As a preliminary analysis, we can affirm that the two different definitions of goals lead to similar attack traces.

Acknowledgements. This work has partially been supported by the Health & Wellbeing high-impact initiative (HII-H&WB) of FBK, the TreC (Cartella del Cittadino) project of the Azienda Provinciale per i Servizi Sanitari, and the activity "API Assistant" of the action line Digital Infrastructure of the EIT Digital.

References

1. BBA – British Bankers' Association: An app-etite for banking (2017). https://www.bba.org.uk/wp-content/uploads/2017/06/WWBN-IV.pdf
2. European Commission: mHealth (2016). https://ec.europa.eu/digital-single-market/en/mhealth
3. He, D., Naveed, M., Gunter, C.A., Nahrstedt, K.: Security Concerns in Android mHealth App (2014). https://www.ncbi.nlm.nih.gov/pmc/articles/PMC4419898/
4. European Commission: Regulation EU 2016/679 on the protection of natural persons with regard to the processing of personal data and on the free movement of such data, and repealing Directive 95/46/EC (General Data Protection Regulation). http://www.eugdpr.org
5. Google: Google Authenticator. https://support.google.com/accounts/answer/1066447?hl=en
6. Sciarretta, G., Carbone, R., Ranise, S., Armando, A.: Anatomy of the Facebook solution for mobile single sign-on: security assessment and improvements. J. Comput. Secur. (COSE 2017) **F71**, 71–86 (2017). https://doi.org/10.1016/j.cose.2017.04.011
7. Sciarretta, G., Armando, A., Carbone, R., Ranise, S.: Security of mobile single sign-on: a rational reconstruction of Facebook login solution. In: Proceedings of the 13th International Joint Conference on e-Business and Telecommunications (ICETE 2016). SECRYPT, vol. 4, pp. 147–158 (2016)

8. ECB - European Central Bank: Final guidelines on the security of Internet payments (2014). https://www.eba.europa.eu/documents/10180/934179/EBA-GL-2014-12+%28Guidelines+on+the+security+of+internet+payments%29.pdf/f27bf266-580a-4ad0-aaec-59ce52286af0

9. Lamport, L.: Password authentication with insecure communication communications. Commun. ACM **24**(11), 770–772 (1981)

10. Coulouris, G., Dollimore, J., Kindberg, T.: Distributed Systems: Concepts and Design, 4th edn. Addison-Wesley, Boston (2005)

11. AVANTSSAR Project: Deliverable D2.3 (update) ASLan++ specification and tutorial. http://www.avantssar.eu/pdf/deliverables/avantssar-d2-3_update.pdf (2008)

12. Armando, A., et al.: The AVANTSSAR platform for the automated validation of trust and security of service-oriented architectures. In: Flanagan, C., König, B. (eds.) TACAS 2012. LNCS, vol. 7214, pp. 267–282. Springer, Heidelberg (2012). https://doi.org/10.1007/978-3-642-28756-5_19

13. Armando, A., Carbone, R., Compagna, L.: SATMC: a SAT-based model checker for security protocols, business processes, and security APIs. STTT **18**(2), 187–204 (2016)

14. Armando, A., Carbone, R., Zanetti, L.: Formal modeling and automatic security analysis of two-factor and two-channel authentication protocols. In: Lopez, J., Huang, X., Sandhu, R. (eds.) NSS 2013. LNCS, vol. 7873, pp. 728–734. Springer, Heidelberg (2013). https://doi.org/10.1007/978-3-642-38631-2_63

15. OASIS: SAML V2.0 technical overview (2005). https://docs.oasis-open.org/security/saml/v2.0/saml-core-2.0-os.pdf

16. IETF: TOTP: Time-Based One-Time Password Algorithm (2011). https://tools.ietf.org/html/rfc6238

17. Dolev, D., Yao, A.: On the security of public-key protocols. IEEE Trans. Inf. Theor. **29**(2), 198–208 (1983)

18. Armando, A., Carbone, R., Compagna, L., Cuéllar, J., Tobarra, L.: Formal analysis of SAML 2.0 web browser single sign-on: breaking the SAML-based single sign-on for Google Apps. In: Proceedings of the 6th ACM Workshop on Formal Methods in Security Engineering (FMSE), pp. 1–10 (2008)

19. Mödersheim, S., Viganò, L.: Secure pseudonymous channels. In: Backes, M., Ning, P. (eds.) ESORICS 2009. LNCS, vol. 5789, pp. 337–354. Springer, Heidelberg (2009). https://doi.org/10.1007/978-3-642-04444-1_21

20. Lowe, G.: A hierarchy of authentication specifications. In: Proceedings of the 10th IEEE Workshop on Computer Security Foundations (1997)

21. IETF: The OAuth 2.0 Authorization Framework (2012). http://tools.ietf.org/html/rfc6749

22. OIDF: OpenID Connect Core 1.0 (2014). http://openid.net/specs/openid-connect-core-1_0.html

23. Chen, E., Pei, Y., Chen, S., Tian, Y., Kotcher, R., Tague, P.: OAuth demystified for mobile application developers. In: Proceedings of the ACM Conference on Computer and Communications Security (CCS) (2014)

24. Shehab, M., Mohsen, F.: Towards enhancing the security of OAuth implementations in smart phones. In: IEEE International Conference on Mobile Services (MS), pp. 39–46 (2014)

25. OAuth Working Group: OAuth 2.0 for Native Apps (2016). https://tools.ietf.org/html/rfc8252

26. Sun, S., Beznosov, K.: The devil is in the (implementation) details: an empirical analysis of OAuth SSO systems. In: Proceedings of the ACM Conference on Computer and Communications Security (CCS 2012) (2012)
27. Wang, R., Chen, S., Wang, X.: Signing me onto your accounts through Facebook and Google: a traffic-guided security study of commercially deployed single-sign-on web services. In: Proceedings of the IEEE Symposium on Security and Privacy (S&P), pp. 365–379 (2012)
28. Sudhodanan, A., Armando, A., Carbone, R., Compagna, L.: Attack patterns for black-box security testing of multi-party web applications. In: Proceedings of the 23rd Annual Network and Distributed System Security Symposium (NDSS) (2016)
29. Yang, R., Lau, W.C., Liu, T.: Signing into one billion mobile app accounts effortlessly with OAuth2.0. In: Black Hat Europe (2016)
30. Fett, D., Küsters, R., Schmitz, G.: A comprehensive formal security analysis of OAuth 2.0. In: Proceedings of the 23rd ACM SIGSAC Conference on Computer and Communications Security (CCS), pp. 1204–1215. ACM (2016)
31. Fett, D., Küsters, R., Schmitz, G.: An expressive model for the web infrastructure: definition and application to the BrowserID SSO system. In: Proceedings of the 35th IEEE Symposium on Security and Privacy (S&P), pp. 673–688. IEEE Computer Society (2014)
32. Fett, D., Küsters, R., Schmitz, G.: The web SSO standard OpenID connect: in-depth formal security analysis and security guidelines. In: Proceedings of the 30th Computer Security Foundations Symposium (CSF). IEEE Computer Society (2017)
33. Bansal, C., Bhargavan, K., Maffeis, S.: Discovering concrete attacks on website authorization by formal analysis. In: Proceedings of 25th IEEE Computer Security Foundations Symposium (CSF 2012), pp. 247–262 (2012)
34. Pai, S., Sharma, Y., Kumar, S., Pai, R.M., Singh, S.: Formal verification of OAuth 2.0 using alloy framework. In: Proceedings of the IEEE International Conference on Communication Systems and Network Technologies (CSNT), pp. 655–659 (2011)
35. Yan, H., Fang, H., Kuka, C., Zhu, H.: Verification for OAuth using ASLan++. In: Proceedings of 16th IEEE International Symposium on High Assurance Systems Engineering HASE, pp. 76–84 (2015)
36. Ye, Q., Bai, G., Wang, K., Dong, J.S.: Formal analysis of a single sign-on protocol implementation for Android. In: Proceedings of the 20th ICECCS, pp. 90–99 (2015)
37. Yubico: YubiKey NEO. https://www.yubico.com/products/yubikey-hardware/yubikey-neo

Smart Contracts and Privacy

SoK: Unraveling Bitcoin Smart Contracts

Nicola Atzei[1], Massimo Bartoletti[1](✉), Tiziana Cimoli[1],
Stefano Lande[1], and Roberto Zunino[2]

[1] Università degli Studi di Cagliari, Cagliari, Italy
bart@unica.it
[2] Università degli Studi di Trento, Trento, Italy

Abstract. Albeit the primary usage of Bitcoin is to exchange currency, its blockchain and consensus mechanism can also be exploited to securely execute some forms of *smart contracts*. These are agreements among mutually distrusting parties, which can be automatically enforced without resorting to a trusted intermediary. Over the last few years a variety of smart contracts for Bitcoin have been proposed, both by the academic community and by that of developers. However, the heterogeneity in their treatment, the informal (often incomplete or imprecise) descriptions, and the use of poorly documented Bitcoin features, pose obstacles to the research. In this paper we present a comprehensive survey of smart contracts on Bitcoin, in a uniform framework. Our treatment is based on a new formal specification language for smart contracts, which also helps us to highlight some subtleties in existing informal descriptions, making a step towards automatic verification. We discuss some obstacles to the diffusion of smart contracts on Bitcoin, and we identify the most promising open research challenges.

1 Introduction

The term "smart contract" was conceived in [43] to describe agreements between two or more parties, that can be automatically enforced without a trusted intermediary. Fallen into oblivion for several years, the idea of smart contract has been resurrected with the recent surge of distributed ledger technologies, led by Ethereum (http://www.ethereum.org/) and Hyperledger (https://www.hyperledger.org/). In such incarnations, smart contracts are rendered as computer programs. Users can request the execution of contracts by sending suitable *transactions* to the nodes of a peer-to-peer network. These nodes collectively maintain the history of all transactions in a public, append-only data structure, called *blockchain*. The sequence of transactions on the blockchain determines the state of each contract, and, accordingly, the assets of each user.

A crucial feature of smart contracts is that their correct execution does *not* rely on a trusted authority: rather, the nodes which process transactions are assumed to be mutually untrusted. Potential conflicts in the execution of contracts are resolved through a *consensus* protocol, whose nature depends on the

L. Bauer and R. Küsters (Eds.): POST 2018, LNCS 10804, pp. 217–242, 2018.
https://doi.org/10.1007/978-3-319-89722-6_9

specific platform (e.g., it is based on "proof-of-work" in Ethereum). Ideally, contracts execute correctly whenever the adversary does not control the majority of some resource (e.g., computational power for "proof-of-work" consensus).

The absence of a trusted intermediary, combined with the possibility of transferring money given by blockchain-based cryptocurrencies, creates a fertile ground for the development of smart contracts. For instance, a smart contract may promise to pay a reward to anyone who provides some value that satisfies a given public predicate. This generalises cryptographic puzzles, like breaking a cipher, inverting a hash function, etc.

Since smart contracts handle the ownership of valuable assets, attackers may be tempted to exploit vulnerabilities in their implementation to steal or tamper with these assets. Although analysis tools [17,30,34] may improve the security of contracts, so far they have not been able to completely prevent attacks. For instance, a series of vulnerabilities in Ethereum contracts [10] have been exploited, causing money losses in the order of hundreds of millions of dollars [3–5].

Using domain-specific languages (possibly, not Turing-complete) could help to overcome these security issues, by reducing the distance between contract specification and implementation. For instance, despite the discouraging limitations of its scripting language, Bitcoin has been shown to support a variety of smart contracts. Lotteries [6,14,16,36], gambling games [32], contingent payments [13,24,35], and other kinds of fair multi-party computations [8,31] are some examples of the capabilities of Bitcoin as a smart contracts platform.

Unlike Ethereum, where contracts can be expressed as computer programs with a well-defined semantics, Bitcoin contracts are usually realised as cryptographic protocols, where participants send/receive messages, verify signatures, and put/search transactions on the blockchain. The informal (often incomplete or imprecise) narration of these protocols, together with the use of poorly documented features of Bitcoin (e.g., segregated witnesses, scripts, signature modifiers, temporal constraints), and the overall heterogeneity in their treatment, pose serious obstacles to the research on smart contracts in Bitcoin.

Contributions. This paper is, at the best of our knowledge, the first systematic survey of smart contracts on Bitcoin. In order to obtain a uniform and precise treatment, we exploit a new formal model of contracts. Our model is based on a process calculus with primitives to construct Bitcoin transactions, to put them on the blockchain, and to search the blockchain for transactions matching given patterns. Our calculus allows us to give smart contracts a precise operational semantics, which describes the interactions of the (possibly dishonest) participants involved in the execution of a contract.

We exploit our model to systematically formalise a large portion of the contracts proposed so far both by researchers and Bitcoin developers. In many cases, we find that specifying a contract with the intended security properties is significantly more complex than expected after reading the informal descriptions of the contract. Usually, such informal descriptions focus on the case where all participants are honest, neglecting the cases where one needs to compensate for some unexpected behaviour of the dishonest environment.

Overall, our work aims at building a bridge between research communities: from that of cryptography, where smart contracts have been investigated first, to those of programming languages and formal methods, where smart contracts could be expressed using proper linguistic models, supporting advanced analysis and verification techniques. We outline some promising research perspectives on smart contracts, both in Bitcoin and in other cryptocurrencies, where the synergy between the two communities could have a strong impact in future research.

2   Background on Bitcoin Transactions

In this section we give a minimalistic introduction to Bitcoin [21,38], focussing on the crucial notion of transaction. To this purpose, we rely on the model of Bitcoin transactions in [11]. Here, instead of repeating the formal machinery of [11], we introduce the needed concepts through a series of examples. We will however follow the same notation of [11], and point to the formal definitions therein, to allow the reader to make precise the intuitions provided in this paper.

Bitcoin is a decentralised infrastructure to securely transfer currency (the *bitcoins*, ฿) between users. Transfers of bitcoins are represented as *transactions*, and the history of all transactions is stored in a public, append-only, distributed data structure called *blockchain*. Each user can create an arbitrary number of pseudonyms through which sending and receiving bitcoins. The balance of a user is not explicitly stored within the blockchain, but it is determined by the amount of unspent bitcoins directed to the pseudonyms under her control, through one or more transactions. The logic used for linking inputs to outputs is specified by programmable functions, called *scripts*.

Hereafter we will abstract from a few technical details of Bitcoin, e.g. the fact that transactions are grouped into blocks, and that each transaction must pay a fee to the "miner" who appends it to the blockchain. We refer to [11] for a discussion on the differences between the formal model and the actual Bitcoin.

2.1   Transactions

In their simplest form, Bitcoin transactions allow to transfer bitcoins from one participant to another one. The only exception are the so-called *coinbase* transactions, which can generate fresh bitcoins. Following [11], we assume that there exists a single coinbase transaction, the first one in the blockchain. We represent this transaction, say T_0, as follows:

T_0
in: ⊥
wit: ⊥
out: $(\lambda x.\, x < 51, 1$฿$)$

The transaction T_0 has three fields. The fields in and wit are set to ⊥, meaning that T_0 does not point backwards to any other transaction (since T_0 is the first one on the blockchain). The field out contains a pair. The first element of the pair, $\lambda x.\, x < 51$, is a *script*, that given as input a value x, checks if $x < 51$

(this is just for didactical purposes: we will introduce more useful scripts in a while). The second element of the pair, 1$, is the amount of currency that can be transferred to other transactions.

Now, assume that participant A wants to *redeem* 1$ from T_0, and transfer that amount under her control. To do this, A has to append to the blockchain a new transaction, e.g.:

T_A
in: T_0
wit: 42
out: $(\lambda x.\text{versig}_{k_A}(x), 1\text{\$})$

The field in points to the transaction T_0 in the blockchain. To be able to redeem from there 1$, A must provide a *witness* which makes the script within $T_0.\text{out}$ evaluate to true. In this case the witness is 42, hence the redeem succeeds, and T_0 is considered *spent*. The script within $T_A.\text{out}$ is the most commonly used one in Bitcoin: it verifies the signature x with A's public key. The message against which the signature is verified is the transaction[1] which attempts to redeem T_A.

Now, to transfer 1$ to another participant B, A can append to the blockchain the following transaction:

T_B
in: T_A
wit: $sig_{k_A}(T_B)$
out: $(\lambda x.\text{versig}_{k_B}(x), 1\text{\$})$

where the witness $sig_{k_A}(T_B)$ is A's signature on T_B (but for the wit field itself).

The ones shown above represent just the simplest cases of transactions. More in general, a Bitcoin transaction can collect bitcoins from many inputs, and split them between one or more outputs; further, it can use more complex scripts, and specify time constraints on when it can be appended to the blockchain.

Following [11], hereafter we represent transactions as tuples of the form (in, wit, out, absLock, relLock), where:

- in contains the list of *inputs*. An input (T, i) refers to the i-th output of transaction T.
- wit contains the list of *witnesses*, of the same length as the list of inputs. For each input (T, i) in the in list, the witness at the same index must make the i-th output script of T evaluate to true.
- out contains the list of *outputs*. Each index refers to a pair $(\lambda z.e, v)$, where the first component is a script, and the second is a currency value.
- absLock and relLock indicate absolute and relative time constraint on when the transaction can be added to the blockchain.

In transaction fields, we represent a list $\ell_1 \cdots \ell_n$ as $1 \mapsto \ell_1, \ldots, n \mapsto \ell_n$, or just as ℓ_1 when $n = 1$. We denote with $\widetilde{T}_A^v$ the *canonical* transaction, i.e. the transaction with a single output of the form $(\lambda\varsigma.\text{versig}_{k_A}(\varsigma), v\text{\$})$, and with all the other fields empty (denoted with $\bot$).

---

[1] Actually, the signature is not computed on the whole redeeming transaction, but only on a part of it, as shown in Sect. 2.3.

T_1	T_2	T_3
in: $\cdots$	in: $1 \mapsto (T_1, 1)$	in: $1 \mapsto (T_1, 2)$ $2 \mapsto (T_2, 1)$
wit: $\cdots$	wit: $1 \mapsto \sigma_1$	wit: $1 \mapsto \sigma_2, \sigma_2'$ $2 \mapsto \sigma_3$
out: $1 \mapsto (\lambda x.\text{versig}_k(x), v_1 \text{\BitcoinB})$	out: $1 \mapsto (\lambda x.e_2, v_1 \text{\BitcoinB})$	out: $1 \mapsto (\lambda x.e_3, (v_1 + v_2)\text{\BitcoinB})$
$\quad 2 \mapsto (\lambda x, x'.e_1, v_2 \text{\BitcoinB})$	relLock: $1 \mapsto t$	absLock: t'

Fig. 1. Three Bitcoin transactions.

Example 1. Consider the transactions in Fig. 1. In T_1 there are two outputs: the first one transfers $v_1 \text{\BitcoinB}$ to any transaction T' which provides as witness a signature of T' with key k; the second output can transfer $v_2 \text{\BitcoinB}$ to a transaction whose witness satisfies the script e_1. The transaction T_2 tries to redeem $v_1 \text{\BitcoinB}$ from the output at index 1 of T_1, by providing the witness σ_1. Since $T_2.\text{relLock}(1) = t$, then T_2 can be appended only after at least t time units have passed since the transaction in $T_2.\text{in}(1)$ (i.e., T_1) appeared on the blockchain. In T_3, the input 1 refers to the output 2 of T_1, and the input 2 refers to the output 1 of T_2. The witness σ_2 and σ_2' are used to evaluate $T_1.\text{out}(2)$, replacing the occurrences of x and x' in e_1. Similarly, σ_3 is used to evaluate $T_2.\text{out}(1)$, replacing the occurrences of x in e_2. The transaction T_3 can be put on the blockchain only after time t'. $\square$

2.2 Scripts

In Bitcoin, scripts are small programs written in a non-Turing equivalent language. Whoever provides a witness that makes the script evaluate to "true", can redeem the bitcoins retained in the associated (unspent) output. In the abstract model, scripts are terms of the form $\lambda z.e$, where z is a sequence of variables occurring in e, and e is an expression with the following syntax:

$$e ::= x \mid k \mid e + e \mid e - e \mid e = e \mid e < e \mid \text{if } e \text{ then } e \text{ else } e \mid$$
$$|e| \mid H(e) \mid \text{versig}_k(e) \mid \text{absAfter } t : e \mid \text{relAfter } t : e$$

Besides variables x, constants k, and basic arithmetic/logical operators, the other expression are peculiar: $|e|$ denotes the size, in bytes, of the evaluation of e; $H(e)$ evaluates to the hash of e; $\text{versig}_k(e)$ evaluates to true iff the sequence of signatures e (say, of length m) is verified by using m out of the n keys in k. For instance, the script $\lambda x.\text{versig}_k(x)$ is satisfied if x is a signature on the redeeming transaction, verified with the key k. The expressions $\text{absAfter } t : e$ and $\text{relAfter } t : e$ define absolute and relative time constraints: they evaluate as e if the constraints are satisfied, otherwise they evaluate to false.

In Fig. 2 we recap from [11] the semantics of script expressions. The function $[\![\cdot]\!]_{T,i,\rho}$ takes three parameters: T is the redeeming transaction, i is the index of the redeeming witness, and ρ is a map from variables to values. We use $\perp$ to represent the "failure" of the evaluation, H for a public hash function, and $size(n)$ for the size (in bytes) of an integer n. The function $\text{ver}_k(\sigma, T, i)$ verifies

$$[\![x]\!]_{\mathsf{T},i,\rho} = \rho(x) \qquad [\![k]\!]_{\mathsf{T},i,\rho} = k \qquad [\![e \circ e']\!]_{\mathsf{T},i,\rho} = [\![e]\!]_{\mathsf{T},i,\rho} \circ_\perp [\![e']\!]_{\mathsf{T},i,\rho} \ (\circ \in \{+,-,=,<\})$$

$$[\![\text{if } e_0 \text{ then } e_1 \text{ else } e_2]\!]_{\mathsf{T},i,\rho} = \textit{if } [\![e_0]\!]_{\mathsf{T},i,\rho} \textit{ then } [\![e_1]\!]_{\mathsf{T},i,\rho} \textit{ else } [\![e_2]\!]_{\mathsf{T},i,\rho}$$

$$[\![|e|]\!]_{\mathsf{T},i,\rho} = \textit{size}([\![e]\!]_{\mathsf{T},i,\rho}) \ [\![\mathsf{H}(e)]\!]_{\mathsf{T},i,\rho} = H([\![e]\!]_{\mathsf{T},i,\rho}) \ [\![\mathsf{versig}_k(e)]\!]_{\mathsf{T},i,\rho} = \textit{ver}_k([\![e]\!]_{\mathsf{T},i,\rho}, \mathsf{T}, i)$$

$$[\![\mathsf{absAfter}\ t : e]\!]_{\mathsf{T},i,\rho} = \textit{if } \mathsf{T}.\mathsf{absLock} \geq t \textit{ then } [\![e]\!]_{\mathsf{T},i,\rho} \textit{ else } \perp$$

$$[\![\mathsf{relAfter}\ t : e]\!]_{\mathsf{T},i,\rho} = \textit{if } \mathsf{T}.\mathsf{relLock}(i) \geq t \textit{ then } [\![e]\!]_{\mathsf{T},i,\rho} \textit{ else } \perp$$

Fig. 2. Semantics of script expressions.

a sequence of signatures σ against a sequence of keys k (see Sect. 2.3) All the semantic operators used in Fig. 2 are *strict*, i.e. they evaluate to $\perp$ if some of their operands is $\perp$. We use syntactic sugar for expressions, e.g. *false* denotes $1 = 0$, *true* denotes $1 = 1$, while e and e' denotes if e then e' else *false*.

Example 2. Recall the transactions in Fig. 1. Let e_1 (the script expression within $\mathsf{T}_1.\mathsf{out}(2)$) be defined as $e_1 = \mathsf{absAfter}\ t' : \mathsf{versig}_k(x)$ and $\mathsf{H}(x') = h$, for h and t' constants such that $\mathsf{T}_3.\mathsf{absLock} \geq t'$. Further, let σ_2 and σ_2' (the witnesses within $\mathsf{T}_3.\mathsf{wit}(1)$) be respectively $\mathsf{sig}_k(\mathsf{T}_3)$ and s, where $\mathsf{sig}_k(\mathsf{T}_3)$ is the signature of T_3 (excluding its witnesses) with key k, and s is a preimage of h, i.e. $h = H(s)$. Let $\rho = \{x \mapsto \mathsf{sig}_k(\mathsf{T}_3), x' \mapsto s\}$. To redeem $\mathsf{T}_1.\mathsf{out}(2)$ with the witness $\mathsf{T}_3.\mathsf{wit}(1)$, the script expression is evaluated as follows:

$$[\![\mathsf{absAfter}\ t' : \mathsf{versig}_k(x) \text{ and } \mathsf{H}(x') = h]\!]_{\mathsf{T}_3,1,\rho}$$
$$= [\![\mathsf{versig}_k(x) \text{ and } \mathsf{H}(x') = h]\!]_{\mathsf{T}_3,1,\rho} \qquad\qquad \text{as } \mathsf{T}_3.\mathsf{absLock} \geq t'$$
$$= [\![\mathsf{versig}_k(x)]\!]_{\mathsf{T}_3,1,\rho} \ \wedge \ [\![\mathsf{H}(x') = h]\!]_{\mathsf{T}_3,1,\rho}$$
$$= \textit{ver}_k(\rho(x), \mathsf{T}_3, 1) \ \wedge \ ([\![\mathsf{H}(x')]\!]_{\mathsf{T}_3,1,\rho} = [\![h]\!]_{\mathsf{T}_3,1,\rho})$$
$$= \textit{ver}_k(\mathsf{sig}_k(\mathsf{T}_3), \mathsf{T}_3, 1) \ \wedge \ (H(\rho(x')) = h) \qquad \text{as } \rho(x) = \mathsf{sig}_k(\mathsf{T}_3)$$
$$= \textit{true} \qquad\qquad\qquad\qquad\qquad\qquad\qquad\qquad \text{as } \rho(x') = s \qquad \square$$

2.3   Transaction Signatures

The signatures verified with versig never apply to the whole transaction: the content of wit field is never signed, while the other fields can be excluded from the signature according to some predefined patterns. To sign parts of a transaction, we first erase the fields which we want to neglect in the signature. Technically, we set these fields to the "null" value $\perp$ using a *transaction substitution*.

A transaction substitution $\{\mathsf{f} \mapsto d\}$ replaces the content of field f with d. If the field is indexed (i.e., all fields but absLock), we denote with $\{\mathsf{f}(i) \mapsto d\}$ the substitution of the i-th item in field f, and with $\{\mathsf{f}(\neq i) \mapsto d\}$ the substitution of all the items of field f *but* the i-th. For instance, to set *all* the elements of the wit field of T to $\perp$, we write $\mathsf{T}\{\mathsf{wit} \mapsto \perp\}$, and to additionally set the second input to $\perp$ we write $\mathsf{T}\{\mathsf{wit} \mapsto \perp\}\{\mathsf{in}(2) \mapsto \perp\}$.

In Bitcoin, there exists a fixed set of transaction substitutions. We represent them as *signature modifiers*, i.e. transaction substitutions which set to $\perp$ the fields which will not be signed. Signatures never apply to the whole transaction: modifiers always discard the content of the wit, while they can keep all the inputs or only one, and all the outputs, or only one, or none. Modifiers also take a parameter i, which is instantiated to the index of the witness where the signature will be included. Below we only present two signature modifiers, since the others are not commonly used in Bitcoin smart contracts.

The modifier aa_i only sets the first witness to i, and the other witnesses to $\bot$ (so, all inputs and all outputs are signed). This ensures that a signature computed for being included in the witness at index i can not be used in any witness with index $j \neq i$:

$$aa_i(\mathsf{T}) = \mathsf{T}\{\mathsf{wit}(1) \mapsto i\}\{\mathsf{wit}(\neq 1) \mapsto \bot\}$$

The modifier sa_i removes the witnesses, and all the inputs but the one at index i (so, a single input and all outputs are signed). Differently from aa_i, this modifier discards the index i, so the signature can be included in any witness:

$$sa_i(\mathsf{T}) = aa_1(\mathsf{T}\{\mathsf{wit} \mapsto \bot\}\{\mathsf{in}(1) \mapsto \mathsf{T}.\mathsf{in}(i)\}\{\mathsf{in}(\neq 1) \mapsto \bot\}$$
$$\{\mathsf{relLock}(1) \mapsto \mathsf{T}.\mathsf{relLock}(i)\}\{\mathsf{relLock}(\neq 1) \mapsto \bot\})$$

Signatures carry information about which parts of the transaction are signed: formally, they are pairs $\sigma = (w, \mu)$, where μ is the modifier, and w is the signature on the transaction T modified with μ. We denote such signature as $\mathsf{sig}_k^{\mu,i}(\mathsf{T})$, where k is a key, and i is the index used by μ, if any. Verification of a signature σ for index i is denoted by $\mathsf{ver}_k(\sigma, \mathsf{T}, i)$. Formally:

$$\mathsf{sig}_k^{\mu,i}(\mathsf{T}) = (sig_k(\mu_i(\mathsf{T})), \mu) \qquad \mathsf{ver}_k(\sigma, \mathsf{T}, i) = ver_k(w, \mu_i(\mathsf{T})) \text{ if } \sigma = (w, \mu)$$

where sig and ver are, respectively, the signing function and the verification function of a digital signature scheme.

Multi-signature verification $\mathsf{ver}_k(\boldsymbol{\sigma}, \mathsf{T}, i)$ extends verification to the case where $\boldsymbol{\sigma}$ is a sequence of signatures and $\boldsymbol{k}$ is a sequence of keys. Intuitively, if $|\boldsymbol{\sigma}| = m$ and $|\boldsymbol{k}| = n$, it implements a m-of-n multi-signature scheme, evaluating to true if all the m signatures match (some of) the keys in $\boldsymbol{k}$. The actual definition also takes into account the order of signatures, as formalised in Definition 6 of [11].

2.4 Blockchain and Consistency

Abstracting away from the fact that the actual Bitcoin blockchain is formed by blocks of transactions, here we represent a blockchain $\mathbf{B}$ as a sequence of pairs (T_i, t_i), where t_i is the time when T_i has been appended, and the values t_i are increasing. We say that the j-th output of the transaction T_i in the blockchain is *spent* (or, for brevity, that (T_i, j) is spent) if there exists some transaction $\mathsf{T}_{i'}$ in the blockchain (with $i' > i$) and some j' such that $\mathsf{T}_{i'}.\mathsf{in}(j') = (\mathsf{T}_i, j)$.

We now describe when a pair (T, t) can be appended to $\mathbf{B} = (\mathsf{T}_0, t_0) \cdots (\mathsf{T}_n, t_n)$. Following [11], we say that T is a *consistent update* of $\mathbf{B}$ at time t, in symbols $\mathbf{B} \rhd (\mathsf{T}, t)$, when the following conditions hold:

1. for each input i of T, if $T.in(i) = (T', j)$ then:
   (a) T' corresponds to one of the transactions in **B**;
   (b) (T', j) is *unspent* in **B**;
   (c) the witness $T.wit(i)$ makes the script in $T'.out(j)$ evaluate to true;
2. the time constraints absLock and relLock in T are satisfied at time $t \geq t_n$;
3. the sum of the amounts of the inputs of T is greater or equal[2] to the sum of the amount of its outputs.

We assume that each transaction T_i in the blockchain is a consistent update of the sequence of past transactions $T_0 \cdots T_{i-1}$. The consistency of the blockchain is actually ensured by the Bitcoin consensus protocol.

Example 3. Recall the transactions in Fig. 1. Assume a blockchain **B** whose last pair is (T_1, t_1) and $t_1 \geq t'$, while T_2 and T_3 are not in **B**.

We verify that (T_2, t_2) is a consistent update of **B**, assuming $t_2 = t_1 + t$ and that σ_1 is the signature of T_2 with (the private part of) key k. The only input of T_2 is $(T_1, 1)$. Conditions 1a and 1b are satisfied, since $(T_1, 1)$ is unspent in **B**. Condition 1c holds because $\mathsf{versig}_k(\sigma_1)$ evaluates to true. Condition 2 holds: indeed the relative timelock in T_2 is satisfied because $t_2 - t_1 \geq t$. Condition 3 holds because the amount of the input of T_2, i.e. $v_1 \mathcal{B}$, is equal to the amount of its output. Note instead that (T_3, t_2) would *not* be a consistent update of **B**, since it violates condition 1a on the second input.

Now, let $\mathbf{B}' = \mathbf{B}(T_2, t_2)$. We verify that (T_3, t_3) is a consistent update of $\mathbf{B}'$, assuming $t_3 \geq t_2$, e_1 as in Example 2, and $e_2 = \mathsf{versig}_{k'}(x)$. Further, let $\sigma_2 = \mathsf{sig}_k(T_3)$, let $\sigma_2' = s$, and $\sigma_3 = \mathsf{sig}_{k'}(T_3)$. Conditions 1a and 1b hold, because T_1 and T_2 are in $\mathbf{B}'$, and the referred outputs are unspent. Condition 1c holds because the output scripts $T_1.out(2)$ and $T_2.out(1)$ against σ_2, σ_2' and σ_3 evaluate to true. Condition 2 is satisfied at $t_3 \geq t_2 \geq t_1 \geq t'$. Finally, condition 3 holds because the amount $(v_1 + v_2)\mathcal{B}$ in $T_3.out(1)$ is equal to the sum of the amounts in $T_1.out(2)$ and $T_2.out(1)$.   □

3   Modelling Bitcoin Contracts

In this section we introduce a formal model of the behavior of the participants in a contract, building upon the model of Bitcoin transactions in [11].

We start by formalising a simple language of expressions, which represent both the messages sent over the network, and the values used in internal computations made by the participants. Hereafter, we assume a set Var of *variables*, and we define the set Val of *values* comprising constants $k \in \mathbb{Z}$, signatures σ, scripts $\lambda z.e$, transactions T, and currency values v.

---

[2] The difference between the amount of inputs and that of outputs is the *fee* paid to the miner who publishes the transaction.

$$\llbracket \nu \rrbracket = \nu \qquad \llbracket \mathsf{sig}_k^{\mu,i}(T) \rrbracket = \mathsf{sig}_k^{\mu,i}(\llbracket T \rrbracket) \qquad \llbracket \mathsf{versig}_k(\boldsymbol{E}, \mathsf{T}, i) \rrbracket = \mathsf{ver}_k(\llbracket \boldsymbol{E} \rrbracket, \llbracket T \rrbracket, i)$$

$$\llbracket T\{\mathsf{f}(i) \mapsto \boldsymbol{E}\} \rrbracket = \llbracket T \rrbracket \{\mathsf{f}(i) \mapsto \llbracket \boldsymbol{E} \rrbracket\} \qquad \llbracket (E, E') \rrbracket = (\llbracket E \rrbracket, \llbracket E' \rrbracket)$$

$$\llbracket E \circ E' \rrbracket = \llbracket E \rrbracket \circ \llbracket E' \rrbracket \quad \text{for } \circ \in \{ \text{ and}, \text{ or}, +, \dots \} \qquad \llbracket \text{not } E \rrbracket = \neg \llbracket E \rrbracket$$

$$\llbracket \boldsymbol{E} \rrbracket = \llbracket E_1 \rrbracket \cdots \llbracket E_n \rrbracket \quad \text{if } \boldsymbol{E} = E_1 \cdots E_n$$

Fig. 3. Semantics of contract expressions.

Definition 1 (Contract expressions). *We define contract expressions through the following syntax:*

$$
\begin{aligned}
E, T ::= \; &\nu & &\textit{value } (\nu \in \mathsf{Val}) \\
\mid \; &x & &\textit{variable } (x \in \mathsf{Var}) \\
\mid \; &\mathsf{sig}_k^{\mu,i}(T) & &\textit{signature } (\mu \textit{ signature modifier}) \\
\mid \; &\mathsf{versig}_k(\boldsymbol{E}, \mathsf{T}, i) & &\textit{(multi) signature verification} \\
\mid \; &T\{\mathsf{f}(i) \mapsto \boldsymbol{E}\} & &\textit{transaction field update} \\
\mid \; &(E, E) & &\textit{pair} \\
\mid \; &E \text{ and } E \mid E \text{ or } E \mid \text{not } E & &\textit{logical expressions} \\
\mid \; &E + E \mid \cdots & &\textit{arithmetic expressions}
\end{aligned}
$$

where $\boldsymbol{E}$ denotes a finite sequence of expressions (i.e., $\boldsymbol{E} = E_1 \cdots E_n$). We define the function $\llbracket \cdot \rrbracket$ from (variable-free) contract expressions to values in Fig. 3. As a notational shorthand, we omit the index i in sig (resp. versig) when the signed (resp. verified) transactions have a single input.

Intuitively, when T evaluates to a transaction T, the expression $T\{\mathsf{f}(i) \mapsto \boldsymbol{E}\}$ represents the transaction obtained from T by substituting the field $\mathsf{f}(i)$ with the sequence of values obtained by evaluating $\boldsymbol{E}$. For instance, $\mathsf{T}\{\mathsf{wit}(1) \mapsto \sigma\}$ denotes the transaction obtained from T by replacing the witness at index 1 with the signature σ. Further, $\mathsf{sig}_k^{\mu,i}(T)$ evaluates to the signature of the transaction represented by T, and $\mathsf{versig}_k(\boldsymbol{E}, \mathsf{T}, i)$ represents the m-of-n multi-signature verification of the transaction represented by T. Both for the signing and verification, the parameter i represents the index where the signature will be used. We assume a simple type system (not specified here) that rules out ill-formed expressions, like e.g. $k\{\mathsf{wit}(1) \mapsto \mathsf{T}\}$.

We formalise the behaviour of a participant as an *endpoint protocol*, i.e. a process where the participant can perform the following actions: (i) send/receive messages to/from other participants; (ii) put a transaction on the ledger; (iii) wait until some transactions appear on the blockchain; (iv) do some internal computation. Note that the last kind of operation allows a participant to craft a transaction before putting it on the blockchain, e.g. setting the wit field to her signature, and later on adding the signature received from another participant.

Definition 2 (Endpoint protocols). *Assume a set of* participants *(named* A, B, C, . . . *). We define* prefixes *π, and* protocols *P, Q, R, . . . as follows:*

$$\pi ::= \mathsf{A}\,!\,\boldsymbol{E} \qquad\qquad send\ messages\ to\ \mathsf{A}$$

$$|\ \mathsf{A}\,?\,\boldsymbol{x} \qquad\qquad receive\ messages\ from\ \mathsf{A}$$

$$|\ \mathsf{put}\ T \qquad\qquad append\ transaction\ T\ to\ the\ blockchain$$

$$|\ \mathsf{ask}\ \boldsymbol{T}\ \mathsf{as}\ \boldsymbol{x} \qquad wait\ until\ all\ transactions\ in\ \boldsymbol{T}\ are\ on\ the\ blockchain$$

$$|\ \mathsf{check}\ \boldsymbol{E} \qquad\qquad test\ condition$$

$$P ::= \textstyle\sum_{i \in I} \pi_i\,.\,P_i \quad guarded\ choice\ (I\ finite\ set)$$

$$|\ P\ |\ P \qquad\qquad parallel\ composition$$

$$|\ \mathsf{X}(\boldsymbol{E}) \qquad\qquad named\ process$$

We assume that each name X *has a unique defining equation* $\mathsf{X}(\boldsymbol{x}) = P$ *where the free variables in P are included in* $\boldsymbol{x}$*. We use the following syntactic sugar:*

- $\tau \triangleq \mathsf{check}\ true$, *the* internal action*;*
- $0 \triangleq \sum_\emptyset P$, *the* terminated *protocol (as usual, we omit trailing 0s);*
- *if* E *then* P *else* $Q \triangleq \mathsf{check}\ E\ .\ P + \mathsf{check}\ \mathsf{not}\ E\ .\ Q;$
- $\pi_1.Q_1 + P \triangleq \sum_{i \in I \cup \{1\}} \pi_i.Q_i$, *provided that* $P = \sum_{i \in I} \pi_i.Q_i$ *and* $1 \notin I;$
- *let* $x = E$ *in* $P \triangleq P\{E/x\}$, *i.e.* P *where* x *is replaced by* E.

The behaviour of protocols is defined in terms of a LTS between *systems*, i.e. the parallel composition of the protocols of all participants, and the blockchain.

Definition 3 (Semantics of protocols). *A* system *S is a term of the form* $\mathsf{A}_1[P_1] \mid \cdots \mid \mathsf{A}_n[P_n] \mid (\mathbf{B}, t)$, *where (i) all the* A_i *are distinct; (ii) there exists a single component* $(\mathbf{B}, t)$, *representing the current state of the blockchain* $\mathbf{B}$, *and the current time t; (iii) systems are up-to commutativity and associativity of* |. *We define the relation* $\rightarrow$ *between systems in Fig. 4, where* $match_{\mathbf{B}}(\mathsf{T})$ *is the set of all the transactions in* $\mathbf{B}$ *that are equal to* T, *except for the witnesses. When writing* $S \mid S'$ *we intend that the conditions above are respected.*

Intuitively, a guarded choice $\sum_i \pi_i.P_i$ can behave as one of the branches P_i. A parallel composition $P \mid Q$ executes concurrently P and Q. All the rules (except the last two) specify how a protocol $(\pi.P + Q) \mid R$ evolves within a system. Rule [Com] models a message exchange between A and B: participant A sends messages $\boldsymbol{E}$, which are received by B on variables $\boldsymbol{x}$. Communication is synchronous, i.e. A is blocked until B is ready to receive. Rule [Check] allows the branch P of a sum to proceed if the condition represented by E is true. Rule [Put] allows A to append a transaction to the blockchain, provided that the update is consistent. Rule [Ask] allows the branch P of a sum to proceed only when the blockchain contains some transactions $\mathsf{T}'_1 \cdots \mathsf{T}'_n$ obtained by instantiating some $\bot$ fields in $\boldsymbol{T}$ (see Sect. 2). This form of pattern matching is crucial because the value of some fields (e.g., wit), may not be known at the time the protocol is written. When the ask prefix unblocks, the variables $\boldsymbol{x}$ in P are bound to

$$\mathsf{A}[\mathsf{B}\,!\,\boldsymbol{E}.\,P + R \mid Q] \mid \mathsf{B}[\mathsf{A}\,?\,\boldsymbol{x}.\,P' + R' \mid Q'] \mid S \to \mathsf{A}[P \mid Q] \mid \mathsf{B}[P'\{[\![\boldsymbol{E}]\!]/\boldsymbol{x}\} \mid Q'] \mid S \quad [\text{Com}]$$

$$\frac{[\![E]\!] = true}{\mathsf{A}[\mathsf{check}\ E\,.\,P + R \mid Q] \mid S \to \mathsf{A}[P \mid Q] \mid S}\ [\text{Check}]$$

$$\frac{[\![T]\!] = \mathsf{T} \qquad \mathsf{B} \rhd (\mathsf{T},t)}{\mathsf{A}[\mathsf{put}\ T.\,P + R \mid Q] \mid S \mid (\mathsf{B},t) \to \mathsf{A}[P \mid Q] \mid S \mid (\mathsf{B}(\mathsf{T},t),t)}\ [\text{Put}]$$

$$\frac{[\![\boldsymbol{T}]\!] = \mathsf{T}_1 \cdots \mathsf{T}_n \quad \forall i \in 1..n : match_\mathsf{B}(\mathsf{T}_i) = \mathsf{T}'_i \neq \bot}{\mathsf{A}[\mathsf{ask}\ \boldsymbol{T}\ \mathsf{as}\ \boldsymbol{x}.\,P + R \mid Q] \mid S \mid (\mathsf{B},t) \to \mathsf{A}[P\{^{\mathsf{T}'_1 \cdots \mathsf{T}'_n}/\boldsymbol{x}\} \mid Q] \mid S \mid (\mathsf{B},t)}\ [\text{Ask}]$$

$$\frac{X(\boldsymbol{x}) = P \quad \mathsf{A}[P\{[\![\boldsymbol{E}]\!]/\boldsymbol{x}\} \mid Q] \mid S \to S'}{\mathsf{A}[X(\boldsymbol{E}) \mid Q] \mid S \to S'}\ [\text{Def}] \qquad\qquad \frac{t' > 0}{S \mid (\mathsf{B},t) \xrightarrow{t'} S' \mid (\mathsf{B},t+t')}\ [\text{Delay}]$$

Fig. 4. Semantics of endpoint protocols.

T	T'_A	T'_B
in: $(\mathsf{T}_\mathsf{A}, 1)$	in: $(\mathsf{T}, 1)$	in: $(\mathsf{T}, 1)$
wit: $\bot$	wit: $\bot$	wit: $\bot$
out: $(\lambda\varsigma\varsigma'.\mathsf{versig}_{k_\mathsf{A} k_\mathsf{B}}(\varsigma\varsigma'), 1\overset{.}{\mathsf{B}})$	out: $(\lambda\varsigma.\mathsf{versig}_{k_\mathsf{A}}(\varsigma), 1\overset{.}{\mathsf{B}})$	out: $(\lambda\varsigma.\mathsf{versig}_{k_\mathsf{B}}(\varsigma), 1\overset{.}{\mathsf{B}})$

Fig. 5. Transactions of the naïve escrow contract.

$\mathsf{T}'_1 \cdots \mathsf{T}'_n$, so making it possible to inspect their actual fields. Rule [Def] allows a named process $X(\boldsymbol{E})$ to evolve as P, assuming a defining equation $X(\boldsymbol{x}) = P$. The variables $\boldsymbol{x}$ in P are substituted with the results of the evaluation of $\boldsymbol{E}$. Such defining equations can be used to specify recursive behaviours. Finally, rule [Delay] allows time to pass[3].

Example 4 (Naïve escrow). A buyer A wants to buy an item from the seller B, but they do not trust each other. So, they would like to use a contract to ensure that B will get paid if and only if A gets her item. In a naïve attempt to realise this, they use the transactions in Fig. 5, where we assume that $(\mathsf{T}_\mathsf{A}, 1)$ used in T.in, is a transaction output redeemable by A through her key k_A. The transaction T makes A deposit $1\overset{.}{\mathsf{B}}$, which can be redeemed by a transaction carrying the signatures of both A and B. The transactions T'_A and T'_B redeem T, transferring the money to A or B, respectively.

The protocols of A and B are, respectively, P_A and Q_B:

$$P_\mathsf{A} = \mathsf{put}\ \mathsf{T}\{\mathsf{wit} \mapsto \mathsf{sig}^{aa}_{k_\mathsf{A}}(\mathsf{T})\}.\,P'$$

$$P' = \tau.\mathsf{B}\,!\,\mathsf{sig}^{aa}_{k_\mathsf{A}}(\mathsf{T}'_\mathsf{B}) + \tau.\mathsf{B}\,?\,x.\,\mathsf{put}\ \mathsf{T}'_\mathsf{A}\{\mathsf{wit} \mapsto \mathsf{sig}^{aa}_{k_\mathsf{A}}(\mathsf{T}'_\mathsf{A})\,x\}$$

$$Q_\mathsf{B} = \mathsf{ask}\ \mathsf{T}.\,\big(\tau.\mathsf{A}\,?\,x.\,\mathsf{put}\ \mathsf{T}'_\mathsf{B}\{\mathsf{wit} \mapsto x\ \mathsf{sig}^{aa}_{k_\mathsf{B}}(\mathsf{T}'_\mathsf{B})\} + \tau.\mathsf{A}\,!\,\mathsf{sig}^{aa}_{k_\mathsf{B}}(\mathsf{T}'_\mathsf{A})\big)$$

---

[3] To keep our presentation simple, we have not included time-constraining operators in endpoint protocols. In case one needs a finer-grained control of time, well-known techniques [39] exist to extend a process algebra like ours with these operators.

First, A adds her signature to T, and puts it on the blockchain. Then, she internally chooses whether to unblock the deposit for B or to request a refund. In the first case, A sends $\mathsf{sig}_{k_A}^{aa}(\mathsf{T}'_B)$ to B. In the second case, she waits to receive the signature $\mathsf{sig}_{k_B}^{aa}(\mathsf{T}'_A)$ from B (saving it in the variable x); afterwards, she puts T'_A on the blockchain (after setting wit) to redeem the deposit. The seller B waits to see T on the blockchain. Then, he chooses either to receive the signature $\mathsf{sig}_{k_A}^{aa}(\mathsf{T}'_B)$ from A (and then redeem the payment by putting T'_B on the blockchain), or to refund A, by sending his signature $\mathsf{sig}_{k_B}^{aa}(\mathsf{T}'_A)$.

This contract is not secure if either A or B are dishonest. On the one hand, a dishonest A can prevent B from redeeming the deposit, even if she had already received the item (to do that, it suffices not to send her signature, taking the rightmost branch in P'). On the other hand, a dishonest B can just avoid to send the item and the signature (taking the leftmost branch in Q_B): in this way, the deposit gets frozen. For instance, let $S = \mathsf{A}[P_A] \mid \mathsf{B}[Q_B] \mid (\mathbf{B}, t)$, where $\mathbf{B}$ contains T_A unredeemed. The scenario where A has never received the item, while B dishonestly attempts to receive the payment, is modelled as follows:

$$S \to \mathsf{A}[P'] \mid \mathsf{B}[Q_B] \mid (\mathbf{B}(\mathsf{T}, t), t)$$
$$\to \mathsf{A}[P'] \mid \mathsf{B}[\tau.\mathsf{A}\,?\,x.\,\mathsf{put}\,\mathsf{T}'_B\,\{\mathsf{wit} \mapsto x\,\mathsf{sig}_{k_B}^{aa}(\mathsf{T}'_B)\} \;+\; \tau.\mathsf{A}\,!\,\mathsf{sig}_{k_B}^{aa}(\mathsf{T}'_A)] \mid \cdots$$
$$\to \mathsf{A}[\mathsf{B}\,?\,x.\,\mathsf{put}\,\mathsf{T}'_A\,\{\mathsf{wit} \mapsto \mathsf{sig}_{k_A}^{aa}(\mathsf{T}'_A)\,x\}] \mid \mathsf{B}[\mathsf{A}\,?\,x.\,\mathsf{put}\,\mathsf{T}'_B\,\{\mathsf{wit} \mapsto x\,\mathsf{sig}_{k_B}^{aa}(\mathsf{T}'_B)\}] \mid \cdots$$

At this point the computation is stuck, because both A and B are waiting a message from the other participant. We will show in Sect. 4.3 how to design a secure escrow contract, with the intermediation of a trusted arbiter.

4   A Survey of Smart Contracts on Bitcoin

We now present a comprehensive survey of smart contracts on Bitcoin, comprising those published in the academic literature, and those found online. To this aim we exploit the model of computation introduced in Sect. 3. Remarkably, all the following contracts can be implemented by only using so-called *standard* transactions[4], e.g. via the compilation technique in [11]. This is crucial, because non-standard transactions are currently discarded by the Bitcoin network.

4.1   Oracle

In many concrete scenarios one would like to make the execution of a contract depend on some real-world events, e.g. results of football matches for a betting contract, or feeds of flight delays for an insurance contract. However, the evaluation of Bitcoin scripts can not depend on the environment, so in these scenarios one has to resort to a trusted third-party, or *oracle* [2,19], who notifies real-world events by providing signatures on certain transactions.

For example, assume that A wants to transfer $v\mathcal{B}$ to B only if a certain event, notified by an oracle O, happens. To do that, A puts on the blockchain

---

[4] https://bitcoin.org/en/developer-guide#standard-transactions.

T
in: $(T_A, 1)$
wit: $sig_{k_A}^{aa}(T)$
out: $(\lambda \varsigma \varsigma'.versig_{k_B k_O}(\varsigma \varsigma'), v\cancel{B})$

T'_B
in: $(T, 1)$
wit: $\bot$
out: $(\lambda \varsigma.versig_{k_B}(\varsigma), v\cancel{B})$

Fig. 6. Transactions of a contract relying on an oracle.

the transaction T in Fig. 6, which can be redeemed by a transactions carrying the signatures of both B and O. Further, A instructs the oracle to provide his signature to B upon the occurrence of the expected event.

We model the behaviour of B as the following protocol:

$$P_B = O\,?\,x.\,put\ T'_B\{wit \mapsto sig_{k_B}^{aa}(T'_B)\,x\}$$

Here, B waits to receive the signature $sig_{k_O}^{aa}(T'_B)$ from O, then he puts T'_B on the blockchain (after setting its wit) to redeem T. In practice, oracles like the one needed in this contract are available as services in the Bitcoin ecosystem[5].

Notice that, in case the event certified by the oracle never happens, the $v\cancel{B}$ within T are frozen forever. To avoid this situation, one can add a time constraint to the output script of T, e.g. as in the transaction T_{bond} in Fig. 10.

4.2   Crowdfunding

Assume that the curator C of a crowdfunding campaign wants to fund a venture V by collecting $v\cancel{B}$ from a set $\{A_i\}_{i \in I}$ of investors. The investors want to be guaranteed that either the required amount $v\cancel{B}$ is reached, or they will be able to redeem their funds. To this purpose, C can employ the following contract. She starts with a canonical transaction $\widetilde{T}_V^v$ (with empty in field) which has a single output of $v\cancel{B}$ to be redeemed by V. Intuitively, each A_i can invest money in the campaign by "filling in" the in field of the $\widetilde{T}_V^v$ with a transaction output under their control. To do this, A_i sends to C a transaction output (T_i, j_i), together with the signature σ_i required to redeem it. We denote with $val(T_i, j_i)$ the value of such output. Notice that, since the signature σ_i has been made on $\widetilde{T}_V^v$, the only valid output is the one of $v\cancel{B}$ to be redeemed by V. Upon the reception of the message from A_i, C updates $\widetilde{T}_V^v$: the provided output is appended to the in field, and the signature is added to the corresponding wit field. If all the outputs (T_i, j_i) are distinct (and not redeemed) and the signatures are valid, when $\sum_i val(T_i, j_i) \geq v$ the filled transaction $\widetilde{T}_V^v$ can be put on the blockchain. If C collects $v' > v\cancel{B}$, the difference $v' - v$ goes to the miners as transaction fee.

The endpoint protocol of the curator is defined as $X(\widetilde{T}_V^v, 1, 0)$, where:

$$X(x, n, d) = \text{if } d < v \text{ then } P \text{ else put } x$$
$$P = \sum_i A_i\,?\,(y, j, \sigma).\,X(x\{in(n) \mapsto (y, j)\}\{wit(n) \mapsto \sigma\}, n+1, d + val(y, j))$$

---

[5] For instance, https://www.oraclize.it and https://www.smartcontract.com/.

T	$T'_{AB}(z)$
in: $(T_A, 1)$ wit: $\bot$ out: $(\lambda\varsigma\varsigma'.\text{versig}_{k_A k_B k_C}(\varsigma\varsigma'), 1\dot{B})$	in: $(T, 1)$ wit: $\bot$ out: $1 \mapsto (\lambda\varsigma.\text{versig}_{k_A}(\varsigma), z\dot{B}), 2 \mapsto (\lambda\varsigma.\text{versig}_{k_B}(\varsigma), (1-z)\dot{B})$

Fig. 7. Transactions of the escrow contract.

while the protocol of each investor A_i is the following:

$$P_{A_i} = C\,!\,(T_i, j_i, \text{sig}_{k_{A_i}}^{sa,1}(\widetilde{T}_V^v\{\text{in}(1) \mapsto (T_i, j_i)\}))$$

Note that the transactions sent by investors are not known *a priori*, so they cannot just create the final transaction and sign it. Instead, to allow C to complete the transaction $\widetilde{T}_V^v$ without invalidating the signatures, they compute them using the modifier sa_1. In this way, only a single input is signed, and when verifying the corresponding signature, the others are neglected.

4.3 Escrow

In Example 4 we have discussed a naïve escrow contract, which is secure only if both the buyer A and the seller B are honest (so making the contract pointless). Rather, one would like to guarantee that, even if either A or B (or both) are dishonest, exactly one them will be able to redeem the money: in case they disagree, a trusted participant C, who plays the role of arbiter, will decide who gets the money (possibly splitting the initial deposit in two parts) [1,19].

The output script of the transaction T in Fig. 7 is a *2-of-3* multi-signature schema. This means that T can be redeemed either with the signatures A and B (in case they agree), or with the signature of C (with key k_C) and the signature of A or that of B (in case they disagree). The transaction $T'_{AB}(z)$ in Fig. 7 allows the arbiter to issue a *partial* refund of $z\dot{B}$ to A, and of $(1-z)\dot{B}$ to B. Instead, to issue a full refund to either A or B, the arbiter signs, respectively, the transactions $T'_A = \widetilde{T}_A^{1B}\{\text{in}(1) \mapsto (T, 1)\}$ or $T'_B = \widetilde{T}_B^{1B}\{\text{in}(1) \mapsto (T, 1)\}$ (not shown in the figure). The protocols of A and B are similar to those in Example 4, except for the part where they ask C for an arbitration:

$$P_A = \text{put } T\{\text{wit} \mapsto \text{sig}_{k_A}^{aa}(T)\}.\,(\tau.B\,!\,\text{sig}_{k_A}^{aa}(T'_B) + \tau.P')$$

$$P' = \big(B\,?\,x.\,(\text{put } T'_A\{\text{wit} \mapsto \text{sig}_{k_A}^{aa}(T'_A)\,x\} + P'')\big) + P''$$

$$P'' = C\,?\,(z, x).\big(\text{check } z = 1\,.\,\text{put } T'_A\{\text{wit} \mapsto \text{sig}_{k_A}^{aa}(T'_A)\,x\}$$

$$+ \text{check } 0 < z < 1\,.\,\big(\text{put } T'_{AB}(z)\{\text{wit} \mapsto \text{sig}_{k_A}^{aa}(T'_{AB}(z))\,x\} + \tau.0\big)$$

$$+ \text{check } z = 0\,.\,0\big)$$

In the summation within P_A, participant A internally chooses whether to send her signature to B (so allowing B to redeem $1\dot{B}$ via T'_B), or to proceed with P'. There, A waits to receive either B's signature (which allows A to redeem $1\dot{B}$

T_{AB}	T_{BC}
in: (T_A, v_C) wit: $\bot$ out: $(\lambda \varsigma \varsigma'.\text{versig}_{k_A k_B}(\varsigma \varsigma'), (v_B + v_C) \cancel{B})$	in: $(T_{AB}, 1)$ wit: $\bot$ out: $1 \mapsto (\lambda \varsigma.\text{versig}_{k_B}(\varsigma), v_B \cancel{B}), 2 \mapsto (\lambda \varsigma.\text{versig}_{k_C}(\varsigma), v_C \cancel{B})$

Fig. 8. Transactions of the intermediated payment contract.

by putting T'_A on the blockchain), or a response from the arbiter, in the process P''. The three cases in the summation of check in P'' correspond, respectively, to the case where A gets a full refund ($z = 1$), a partial refund ($0 < z < 1$), or no refund at all ($z = 0$).

The protocol for B is dual to that of A:

$$Q_B = \text{ask } T.\left(\tau.A\,!\,\text{sig}_{k_B}^{aa}(T'_A) + \tau.Q'\right)$$

$$Q' = \left(A\,?\,x.\left(\text{put } T'_B\{\text{wit} \mapsto x\,\text{sig}_{k_B}^{aa}(T'_B)\} + Q''\right)\right) + Q''$$

$$Q'' = C\,?\,(z,x).\left(\text{check } z = 0\,.\,\text{put } T'_B\{\text{wit} \mapsto \text{sig}_{k_B}^{aa}(T'_B)\,x\}\right.$$
$$+ \,\text{check } 0 < z < 1\,.\,\left(\text{put } T'_{AB}(z)\{\text{wit} \mapsto \text{sig}_{k_B}^{aa}(T'_{AB}(z))\,x\} + \tau.0\right)$$
$$\left. + \,\text{check } z = 1\,.\,0\right)$$

If an arbitration is requested, C internally decides (through the τ actions) who between A and B can redeem the deposit in T, by sending its signature to one of the two participants, or decide for a partial refund of z and $1 - z$ bitcoins, respectively, to A and B, by sending its signature on T'_{AB} to both participants:

$$R_C = \text{ask } T.\left(\tau.A\,!\,(1, \text{sig}_{k_C}^{aa}(T'_A)) + \tau.B\,!\,(1, \text{sig}_{k_C}^{aa}(T'_B)) + \tau.R_{AB}\right)$$

$$R_{AB} = \sum_{0<z<1} \tau.\left(A\,!\,(z, \text{sig}_{k_C}^{aa}(T'_{AB}(z))) \mid B\,!\,(z, \text{sig}_{k_C}^{aa}(T'_{AB}(z)))\right)$$

Note that, in the unlikely case where both A and B choose to send their signature to the other participant, the $1\cancel{B}$ deposit becomes "frozen". In a more concrete version of this contract, a participant could keep listening for the signature, and attempt to redeem the deposit when (unexpectedly) receiving it.

4.4 Intermediated Payment

Assume that A wants to send an indirect payment of $v_C \cancel{B}$ to C, routing it through an intermediary B who retains a fee of $v_B < v_C$ bitcoins. Since A does not trust B, she wants to use a contract to guarantee that: (i) if B is honest, then $v_C \cancel{B}$ are transferred to C; (ii) if B is *not* honest, then A does not lose money. The contract uses the transactions in Fig. 8: T_{AB} transfers $(v_B + v_C)\cancel{B}$ from A to B, and T_{BC} splits the amount to B ($v_B \cancel{B}$) and to C ($v_C \cancel{B}$). We assume that $(T_A, 1)$ is a transaction output redeemable by A. The behaviour of A is as follows:

$$P_A = (B\,?\,x.\,\text{if versig}_{k_B}(x, T_{BC}) \text{ then } P' \text{ else } 0) + \tau$$

$$P' = \text{put } T_{AB}\{\text{wit} \mapsto \text{sig}_{k_A}^{aa}(T_{AB})\}.\,\text{put } T_{BC}\{\text{wit} \mapsto \text{sig}_{k_A}^{aa}(T_{BC})\,x\}$$

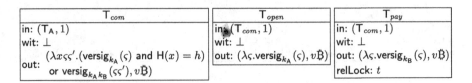

Fig. 9. Transactions of the timed commitment.

Here, A receives from B his signature on T_{BC}, which makes it possible to pay C later on. The τ branch and the else branch ensure that A will correctly terminate also if B is dishonest (i.e., B does not send anything, or he sends an invalid signature). If A receives a valid signature, she puts T_{AB} on the blockchain, adding her signature to the wit field. Then, she also appends T_{BC}, adding to the wit field her signature and B's one. Since A takes care of publishing both transactions, the behaviour of B consists just in sending his signature on T_{BC}. Therefore, B's protocol can just be modelled as $Q_B = A \, ! \, \mathsf{sig}_{k_B}^{aa}(\mathsf{T}_{BC})$.

This contract relies on SegWit. In Bitcoin without SegWit, the identifier of T_{AB} is affected by the instantiation of the wit field. So, when T_{AB} is put on the blockchain, the input in T_{BC} (which was computed before) does not point to it.

4.5   Timed Commitment

Assume that A wants to choose a secret s, and reveal it after some time—while guaranteeing that the revealed value corresponds to the chosen secret (or paying a penalty otherwise). This can be obtained through a *timed commitment* [20], a protocol with applications e.g. in gambling games [25,28,42], where the secret contains the player move, and the delay in the revelation of the secret is intended to prevent other players from altering the outcome of the game. Here we formalise the version of the timed commitment protocol presented in [8].

Intuitively, A starts by exposing the hash of the secret, i.e. $h = H(s)$, and at the same time depositing some amount $v\cancel{B}$ in a transaction. The participant B has the guarantee that after t time units, he will either know the secret s, or he will be able to redeem $v\cancel{B}$.

The transactions of the protocol are shown in Fig. 9, where we assume that $(\mathsf{T}_A, 1)$ is a transaction output redeemable by A. The behaviour of A is modelled as the following protocol:

$$P_A \;=\; \mathsf{put}\;\mathsf{T}_{com}\{\mathsf{wit} \mapsto \mathsf{sig}_{k_A}^{aa}(\mathsf{T}_{com})\}.\,B\,!\,\mathsf{sig}_{k_A}^{aa}(\mathsf{T}_{pay}).\,P'$$

$$P' \;=\; \tau\,.\,\mathsf{put}\;\mathsf{T}_{open}\{\mathsf{wit} \mapsto s\;\mathsf{sig}_{k_A}^{aa}(\mathsf{T}_{open})\perp\} \;+\; \tau$$

Participant A starts by putting the transaction T_{com} on the blockchain. Note that within this transaction A is committing the hash of the chosen secret: indeed, h is encoded within the output script $\mathsf{T}_{com}.\mathsf{out}$. Then, A sends to B her signature on T_{pay}. Note that this transaction can be redeemed by B only when t time units have passed since T_{com} has been published on the blockchain, because

T_{bond}	$T_{pay}(v)$	T_{ref}
in: $(T_A, 1)$	in: $(T_{bond}, 1)$	in: $(T_{bond}, 1)$
wit: $\bot$	wit: $\bot$	wit: $\bot$
out: $(\lambda\varsigma\varsigma'.\text{versig}_{k_A\,k_B}(\varsigma\varsigma'))$ or	out: $1 \mapsto (\lambda\varsigma.\text{versig}_{k_A}(\varsigma), (k-v)\dot{B})$	out: $(\lambda\varsigma.\text{versig}_{k_A}(\varsigma), v\dot{B})$
relAfter t : $\text{versig}_{k_A}(\varsigma), k\dot{B})$	$2 \mapsto (\lambda\varsigma.\text{versig}_{k_C}(\varsigma), v\dot{B})$	relLock: t

Fig. 10. Transactions of the micropayment channel contract.

of the relative timelock declared in T_{pay}.relLock. After sending her signature on T_{pay}, A internally chooses whether to reveal the secret, or do nothing (via the τ actions). In the first case, A must put the transaction T_{open} on the blockchain. Since it redeems T_{com}, she needs to write in T_{open}.wit both the secret s and her signature, so making the former public.

A possible behaviour of the receiver B is the following:

$$Q_B = \left(A\,?\,x.\,\text{if versig}_{k_A}(x, T_{pay}) \text{ then } Q \text{ else } 0\right) + \tau$$
$$Q = \text{put } T_{pay}\{\text{wit} \mapsto \bot\;x\;\text{sig}_{k_B}^{aa}(T_{pay})\} + \text{ask } T_{open} \text{ as } o.\,Q'(get_{secret}(o))$$

In this protocol, B first receives from A (and saves in x) her signature on the transaction T_{pay}. Then, B checks if the signature is valid: if not, he aborts the protocol. Even if the signature is valid, B cannot put T_{pay} on the blockchain and redeem the deposit immediately, since the transaction has a timelock t. Note that B cannot change the timelock: indeed, doing so would invalidate A's signature on T_{pay}. If, after t time units, A has not published T_{open} yet, B can proceed to put T_{pay} on the blockchain, writing A's and his own signatures in the witness. Otherwise, B retrieves T_{open} from the blockchain, from which he can obtain the secret, and use it in Q'.

A variant of this contract, which implements the timeout in T_{com}.out, and does not require the signature exchange, is used in Sect. 4.7.

4.6 Micropayment Channels

Assume that A wants to make a series of micropayments to B, e.g. a small fraction of $\dot{B}$ every few minutes. Doing so with one transaction per payment would result in conspicuous fees[6], so A and B use a micropayment channel contract [29]. A starts by depositing $k\dot{B}$; then, she signs a transaction that pays $v\dot{B}$ to B and $(k-v)\dot{B}$ back to herself, and she sends that transaction to B. Participant B can choose to publish that transaction immediately and redeem its payment, or to wait in case A sends another transaction with increased value. A can stop sending signatures at any time. If B redeems, then A can get back the remaining amount. If B does not cooperate, A can redeem all the amount after a timeout.

The protocol of A is the following (the transactions are in Fig. 10). A publishes the transaction T_{bond}, depositing $k\dot{B}$ that can be spent with her signature and that of B, or with her signature alone, after time t. A can redeem the deposit by

---

[6] https://bitinfocharts.com/comparison/bitcoin-transactionfees.html.

publishing the transaction T_{ref}. To pay for the service, A sends to B the amount v she is paying, and her signature on $\mathsf{T}_{pay}(v)$. Then, she can decide to increase v and recur, or to terminate.

$$P_A = \text{put } \mathsf{T}_{bond}\{\text{wit} \mapsto \mathsf{sig}_{k_A}^{aa}(\mathsf{T}_{bond})\}.(P(1) \mid \text{put } \mathsf{T}_{ref}\{\text{wit} \mapsto \mathsf{sig}_{k_A}^{aa}(\mathsf{T}_{ref})\})$$
$$P(v) = \mathsf{B}\,!\,(v, \mathsf{sig}_{k_A}^{aa}(\mathsf{T}_{pay}(v))).(\tau + \tau.P(v+1))$$

The participant B waits for T_{bond} to appear on the blockchain, then receives the first value v and A's signature σ. Then, B checks if σ is valid, otherwise he aborts the protocol. At this point, B waits for another pair (v', σ'), or, after a timeout, he redeems $v\mathring{\mathsf{B}}$ using $\mathsf{T}_{pay}(v)$.

$$Q_B = \text{ask } \mathsf{T}_{bond}.\mathsf{A}\,?\,(v,\sigma).\text{if } \mathsf{versig}_{k_A}(\sigma, \mathsf{T}_{pay}(v)) \text{ then } P'(v,\sigma) \text{ else } \tau$$
$$P'(v,\sigma) = \tau.P_{pay}(v,\sigma) \; +$$
$$\mathsf{A}\,?\,(v',\sigma').\text{if } v' > v \text{ and } \mathsf{versig}_{k_A}(\sigma', \mathsf{T}_{pay}(v')) \text{ then } P'(v',\sigma') \text{ else } P'(v,\sigma)$$
$$P_{pay}(v,\sigma) = \text{put } \mathsf{T}_{pay}(v)\{\text{wit} \mapsto \sigma\,\mathsf{sig}_{k_B}^{aa}(\mathsf{T}_{pay}(v))\}$$

Note that Q_B should redeem T_{pay} before the timeout expires, which is not modelled in Q_B. This could be obtained by enriching the calculus with time-constraining operators (see Footnote 3).

4.7   Fair Lotteries

A multiparty lottery is a protocol where N players put their bets in a pot, and a winner—uniformly chosen among the players—redeems the whole pot. Various contracts for multiparty lotteries on Bitcoin have been proposed in [8,9,12,14,16,36]. These contracts enjoy a *fairness* property, which roughly guarantees that: (i) each honest player will have (on average) a non-negative payoff, even in the presence of adversaries; (ii) when all the players are honest, the protocol behaves as an ideal lottery: one player wins the whole pot (with probability $1/N$), while all the others lose their bets (with probability $N-1/N$).

Here we illustrate the lottery in [8], for $N = 2$. Consider two players A and B who want to bet $1\mathring{\mathsf{B}}$ each. Their protocol is composed of two phases. The first phase is a timed commitment (as in Sect. 4.5): each player chooses a secret (s_A and s_B) and commits its hash ($h_A = H(s_A)$ and $h_B = H(s_B)$). In doing that, both players put a deposit of $2\mathring{\mathsf{B}}$ on the ledger, which is used to compensate the other player in case one chooses not to reveal the secret later on. In the second phase, the two bets are put on the ledger. After that, the players reveal their secrets, and redeem their deposits. Then, the secrets are used to compute the winner of the lottery in a fair manner. Finally, the winner redeems the bets.

The transactions needed for this lottery are displayed in Fig. 11 (we only show A's transactions, as those of B are similar). The transactions for the commitment phase ($\mathsf{T}_{com}, \mathsf{T}_{open}, \mathsf{T}_{pay}$) are similar to those in Sect. 4.5: they only differ in the script of $\mathsf{T}_{com}.\mathsf{out}$, which now also checks that the length of the secret is either 128 or 129. This check forces the players to choose their secret so that it has one

$T_{Acom}(h_A)$
in: $(T_{Adep}, 1)$
wit: $\bot$
out: $(\lambda x \varsigma.(\text{versig}_{k_A}(\varsigma) \text{ and } H(x) = h_A$ and $(\|x\| = 128 \text{ or } \|x\| = 129))$ or $\text{absAfter } t : \text{versig}_{k_B}(\varsigma), 2\dot{B})$

$T_{lottery}(h_A, h_B)$
in: $1 \mapsto (T_{Abet}, 1), 2 \mapsto (T_{Bbet}, 1)$
wit: $\bot$
out: $(\lambda \varsigma x y. H(x) = h_A \text{ and } H(y) = h_B$ and $(\|x\| = 128 \text{ or } \|x\| = 129) \text{ and } (\|y\| = 128 \text{ or } \|y\| = 129)$ and if $\|x\| = \|y\|$ then $\text{versig}_{k_A}(\varsigma)$ else $\text{versig}_{k_B}(\varsigma), 2\dot{B})$

$T_{Aopen}(h_A)$
in: $(T_{Acom}(h_A), 1)$
wit: $\bot$
out: $(\lambda \varsigma. \text{versig}_{k_A}(\varsigma), 2\dot{B})$

$T_{Apay}(h_A)$
in: $(T_{Acom}(h_A), 1)$
wit: $\bot$
out: $(\lambda \varsigma. \text{versig}_{k_B}(\varsigma), 2\dot{B})$
absLock: t

$T_{Awin}(h_A, h_B)$
in: $(T_{lottery}(h_A, h_B), 1)$
wit: $\bot$
out: $(\lambda \varsigma. \text{versig}_{k_A}(\varsigma), 2\dot{B})$

Fig. 11. Transactions of the fair lottery with deposit.

of these lengths, and reveal it (using T_{open}) before the absLock deadline, since otherwise they will lose their deposits (enabling T_{pay}).

The bets are put using $T_{lottery}$, whose output script computes the winner using the secrets, which can then be revealed. For this, the secret lengths are compared: if equal, A wins, otherwise B wins. In this way, the lottery is equivalent to a coin toss. Note that, if a malicious player chooses a secret having another length than 128 or 129, the $T_{lottery}$ transaction will become stuck, but its opponent will be compensated using the deposit.

The endpoint protocol P_A of player A follows (the one for B is similar):

$$P_A = \text{put } T_{Acom}\{\text{wit} \mapsto \text{sig}_{k_A}^{aa}(T_{Acom})\}. \left(\text{ask } T_{Bcom} \text{ as } y. P' + \tau.P_{open}\right)$$

$$P' = \text{let } h_B = \text{get}_{hash}(y) \text{ in if } h_B \neq h_A \text{ then } P_{pay} \mid P'' \text{ else } P_{pay} \mid P_{open}$$

$$P'' = B ? x. P''' + \tau.P_{open}$$

$$P''' = \text{let } \sigma = \text{sig}_{k_A}^{aa,1}(T_{lottery}(h_A, h_B)) \text{ in}$$
$$\left(\text{put } T_{lottery}(h_A, h_B)\{\text{wit}(1) \mapsto \sigma\}\{\text{wit}(2) \mapsto x\}. \left(P_{open} \mid P_{win}\right)\right) + \tau.P_{open}$$

$$P_{pay} = \text{put } T_{Bpay}\{\text{wit} \mapsto \bot \ \text{sig}_{k_A}^{aa}(T_{Bpay})\}$$

$$P_{open} = \text{put } T_{Aopen}\{\text{wit} \mapsto s_A \ \text{sig}_{k_A}^{aa}(T_{Aopen})\}$$

$$P_{win} = \text{ask } T_{Bopen} \text{ as } z. P'_{win}$$

$$P'_{win} = \text{put } T_{Awin}(h_A, h_B)\{\text{wit} \mapsto \text{sig}_{k_A}^{aa}(T_{Awin}(h_A, h_B)) \ s_A \ \text{get}_{secret}(z)\}$$

Player A starts by putting T_{Acom} on the blockchain, then she waits for B doing the same. If B does not cooperate, A can safely abort the protocol taking its $\tau.P_{open}$ branch, so redeeming her deposit with T_{Aopen} (as usual, here with τ we are modelling a timeout). If B commits his secret, A executes P', extracting the hash h_B of B's secret, and checking whether it is distinct from h_A. If the hashes are found to be equal, A aborts the protocol using P_{open}. Otherwise, A runs $P'' \mid P_{pay}$. The P_{pay} component attempts to redeem B's deposit, as soon as the absLock deadline of T_{Bpay} expires, forcing B to timely reveal his secret. Instead, P'' proceeds with the lottery, asking B for his signature of $T_{lottery}$. If B does not sign, A aborts using P_{open}. Then, A runs P''', finally putting the bets

$T_{cp}(h)$	$T_{open}(h)$	$T_{refund}(h)$
in: $(T_A, 1)$ wit: $\bot$ out: $(\lambda x \varsigma.(\text{versig}_{k_B}(\varsigma) \text{ and } H(x) = h)$ or relAfter t : $\text{versig}_{k_A}(\varsigma), v\tilde{B})$	in: $(T_{cp}(h), 1)$ wit: $\bot$ out: $(\lambda \varsigma.\text{versig}_{k_B}(\varsigma), v\tilde{B})$	in: $(T_{cp}(h), 1)$ wit: $\bot$ out: $(\lambda \varsigma.\text{versig}_{k_A}(\varsigma), v\tilde{B})$ relLock: t

Fig. 12. Transactions of the contingent payment.

($T_{lottery}$) on the ledger. If this is not possible (e.g., because one of the T_{bet} is already spent), A aborts using P_{open}. After $T_{lottery}$ is on the ledger, A reveals her secret and redeems her deposit with P_{open}. In parallel, with P_{win} she waits for the secret of B to be revealed, and then attempts to redeem the pot ($T_{A\,win}$).

The fairness of this lottery has been established in [8]. This protocol can be generalised to $N > 2$ players [8,9] but in this case the deposit grows quadratically with N. The works [14,36] have proposed fair multiparty lotteries that require, respectively, zero and constant (≥ 0) deposit. More precisely, [36] devises two variants of the protocol: the first one only relies on SegWit, but requires each player to statically sign $O(2^N)$ transactions; the second variant reduces the number of signatures to $O(N^2)$, at the cost of introducing a custom opcode. Also the protocol in [14] assumes an extension of Bitcoin, i.e. the malleability of in fields, to obtain an ideal fair lottery with $O(N)$ signatures per player (see Sect. 5).

4.8   Contingent Payments

Assume a participant A who wants to pay $v\tilde{B}$ to receive a value s which makes a public predicate p true, where $p(s)$ can be verified efficiently. A seller B who knows such s is willing to reveal it to A, but only under the guarantee that he will be paid $v\tilde{B}$. Similarly, the buyer wants to pay only if guaranteed to obtain s.

A naïve attempt to implement this contract in Bitcoin is the following: A creates a transaction T such that $T.\text{out}(\varsigma, x)$ evaluates to true if and only if $p(x)$ holds and ς is a signature of B. Hence, B can redeem $v\tilde{B}$ from T by revealing s. In practice, though, this approach is arguably useful, since it requires coding p in the Bitcoin scripting language, whose expressiveness is quite limited.

More general contingent payment contracts can be obtained by exploiting zero-knowledge proofs [13,24,35]. In this setting, the seller generates a fresh key k, and sends to the buyer the encryption $e_s = E_k(s)$, together with the hash $h_k = H(k)$, and a zero-knowledge proof guaranteeing that such messages have the intended form. After verifying this proof, A is sure that B knows a preimage k' of h_k (by collision resistance, $k' = k$) such that $D_{k'}(e_s)$ satisfies the predicate p, and so she can buy the preimage k of h_k with the naïve protocol, so obtaining the solution s by decrypting e_s with k.

The transactions implementing this contract are displayed in Fig. 12. The relAfter clause in T_{cp} allows A to redeem $v\cancel{B}$ if no solution is provided by the deadline t. The behaviour of the buyer A can be modelled as follows:

$$P_A = B\,?\,(e_s, h_k, z).\,P\,+\,\tau$$

$$P = \text{if } verify(e_s, h_k, z) \text{ then put } T_{cp}(h_k)\{\text{wit} \mapsto \text{sig}_{k_A}^{aa}(T_{cp}(h_k))\}.\,P' \text{ else } 0$$

$$P' = \text{ask } T_{open}(h_k) \text{ as } x.\,P''(D_{get_k(x)}(e_s))\,+$$
$$\text{put } T_{refund}(h_k)\{\text{wit} \mapsto \bot \text{ sig}_{k_A}^{aa}(T_{refund}(h_k))\})$$

Upon receiving e_s, h_k and the proof z[7] the buyer verifies z. If the verification succeeds, A puts $T_{cp}(h_k)$ on the blockchain. Then, she waits for T_{open}, from which she can retrieve the key k, and so use the solution $D_{get_k(x)}(e_s)$ in P''. In this way, B can redeem $v\cancel{B}$. If B does not put T_{open}, after t time units A can get her deposit back through T_{refund}. The protocol of B is simple, so it is omitted.

5   Research Challenges and Perspectives

Extensions to Bitcoin. The formal model of smart contracts we have proposed is based on the current mechanisms of Bitcoin; indeed, this makes it possible to translate endpoint protocols into actual implementations interacting with the Bitcoin blockchain. However, constraining smart contracts to perfectly adhere to Bitcoin greatly reduces their expressiveness. Indeed, the Bitcoin scripting language features a very limited set of operations[8], and over the years many useful (and apparently harmless) opcodes have been disabled without a clear understanding of their alleged insecurity[9]. This is the case e.g., of bitwise logic operators, shift operators, integer multiplication, division and modulus.

For this reason some developers proposed to re-enable some disabled opcodes[10], and some works in the literature proposed extensions to the Bitcoin scripting language so to enhance the expressiveness of smart contracts.

A possible extension is *covenants* [37], a mechanism that allows an output script to constrain the structure of the redeeming transaction. This is obtained through a new opcode, called CHECKOUTPUTVERIFY, which checks if a given out of the redeeming transaction matches a specific pattern. Covenants are also studied in [41], where they are implemented using the opcode CAT (currently disabled) and a new opcode CHECKSIGFROMSTACK which verifies a signature against an arbitrary bitstring on the stack. In both works, covenants can also be recursive, e.g. a covenant can check if the redeeming transaction contains itself. Using recursive covenants allows to implement a state machine through a sequence of transactions that store its state.

---

[7] For simplicity, here we model the zero-knowledge proof as a single message. More concretely, it should be modelled as a sub-protocol.

[8] https://en.bitcoin.it/wiki/Script.

[9] https://en.bitcoin.it/wiki/Common_Vulnerabilities_and_Exposures#CVE-2010-5141.

[10] https://lists.linuxfoundation.org/pipermail/bitcoin-dev/2017-May/014356.html.

Secure cash distribution with penalties [8,16,32] is a cryptographic primitive which allows a set of participants to make a deposit, and then provide inputs to a function whose evaluation determines how the deposits are distributed among the participants. This primitive guarantees that dishonest participants (who, e.g., abort the protocol after learning the value of the function) will pay a penalty to the honest participants. This primitive does not seem to be directly implementable in Bitcoin, but it becomes so by extending the scripting language with the opcode CHECKSIGFROMSTACK discussed above. Secure cash distribution with penalties can be instantiated to a variety of smart contracts, e.g. lotteries [8] poker [32], and contingent payments. The latter smart contract can also be obtained through the opcode CHECKKEYPAIRVERIFY in [24], which checks if the two top elements of the stack are a valid key pair.

Another new opcode, called MULTIINPUT [36] consumes from the stack a signature σ and a sequence of in values $(T_1, j_1) \cdots (T_n, j_n)$, with the following two effects: (i) it verifies the signature σ against the redeeming transaction T, neglecting T.in; (ii) it requires T.in to be equal to some of the T_i. Exploiting this opcode, [36] devise a fair N-party lottery which requires zero deposit, and $O(N^2)$ off-chain signed transaction. The first one of these effects can be alternatively obtained by extending, instead of the scripting language, the signature modifiers. More specifically, [14] introduces a new signature modifier, which can set to $\perp$ *all* the inputs of a transaction (i.e., no input is signed). In this way they obtain a fair multi-party lottery with similar properties to the one in [36].

Another way improve the expressiveness of smart contracts is to replace the Bitcoin scripting language, e.g. with the one in [40]. This would also allow to establish bounds on the computational resources needed to run scripts.

Unfortunately, none of the proposed extensions has been yet included in the main branch of the Bitcoin Core client, and nothing suggests that they will be considered in the near future. Indeed, the development of Bitcoin is extremely conservative, as any change to its protocol requires an overwhelming consensus of the miners. So far, new opcodes can only be empirically assessed through the Elements alpha project[11], a testnet for experimenting new Bitcoin features. A significant research challenge would be that of formally proving that new opcodes do not introduce vulnerabilities, exploitable e.g. by Denial-of-Service attacks. For instance, unconstrained uses of the opcode CAT may cause an exponential space blow-up in the verification of transactions.

Formal Methods for Bitcoin Smart Contracts. As witnessed in Sect. 4, designing secure smart contracts on Bitcoin is an error-prone task, similarly to designing secure cryptographic protocols. The reason lies in the fact that, to devise a secure contract, a designer has to anticipate any possible (mis-)behaviour of the other participants. The side effect is that endpoint protocols may be quite convoluted, as they must include compensations at all the points where something can go wrong. Therefore, tools to automate the analysis and verification of smart contracts may be of great help.

---

[11] https://elementsproject.org/elements/opcodes/.

Recent works [7] propose to verify Bitcoin smart contracts by modelling the behaviour of participants as timed automata, and then using UPPAAL [15] to check properties against an attacker. This approach correctly captures the time constraints within the contracts. The downside is that encoding this UPPAAL model into an actual implementation with Bitcoin transactions is a complex task. Indeed, a designer without a deep knowledge of Bitcoin technicalities is likely to produce an UPPAAL model that can *not* be encoded in Bitcoin. A relevant research challenge is to study specification languages for Bitcoin contracts (like e.g. the one in Sect. 3), and techniques to *automatically* encode them in a model that can be verified by a model checker.

Remarkably, the verification of security properties of smart contracts requires to deal with non-trivial aspects, like temporal constraints and probabilities. This is the case, e.g., for the verification of fairness of lotteries (like e.g. the one discussed in Sect. 4.7); a further problem is that fairness must hold against any adversarial strategy. It is not clear whether in this case it is sufficient to consider a "most powerful" adversary, like e.g. in the symbolic Dolev-Yao model. In case a contract is not secure against arbitrary (PTIME) adversaries, one would like to verify that, at least, it is secure against *rational* ones [27], which is a relevant research issue. Additional issues arise when considering more concrete models of the Bitcoin blockchain, respect to the one in Sect. 2. This would require to model *forks*, i.e. the possibility that a recent transaction is removed from the blockchain. This could happen with rational (but dishonest) miners [33].

DSLs for Smart Contracts. As witnessed in Sect. 4, modelling Bitcoin smart contracts is complex and error-prone. A possible way to address this complexity is to devise high-level domain-specific languages (DSLs) for contracts, to be compiled in low-level protocols (e.g., the ones in Sect. 3). Indeed, the recent proliferation of non-Turing complete DSLs for smart contracts [18,22,26] suggests that this is an emerging research direction.

A first proposal of an high-level language implemented on top of Bitcoin is Typecoin [23]. This language allows to model the updates of a state machine as affine logic propositions. Users can "run" this machine by putting transactions on the Bitcoin blockchain. The security of the blockchain guarantees that only the legit updates of the machine can be triggered by users. A downside of this approach is that liveness is guaranteed only by assuming cooperation among the participants, i.e., a dishonest participant can make the others unable to complete an execution. Note instead that the smart contracts in Sect. 4 allow honest participants to terminate, regardless of the behaviours of the environment. In some cases, e.g. in the lottery in Sect. 4.7, abandoning the contract may even result in penalties (i.e., loss of the deposit paid upfront to stipulate the contract).

Acknowledgments. This work is partially supported by Aut. Reg. of Sardinia project P.I.A. 2013 "NOMAD". Stefano Lande gratefully acknowledges Sardinia Regional Government for the financial support of his PhD scholarship (P.O.R. Sardegna F.S.E. Operational Programme of the Autonomous Region of Sardinia, European Social Fund 2014–2020).

References

1. Bitcoin developer guide - escrow and arbitration. https://goo.gl/8XL5Fn
2. Bitcoin wiki - contracts - using external state. https://en.bitcoin.it/wiki/Contract#Example_4:_Using_external_state
3. Understanding the DAO attack, June 2016. http://www.coindesk.com/understanding-dao-hack-journalists/
4. Parity Wallet security alert, July 2017. https://paritytech.io/blog/security-alert.html
5. A Postmortem on the Parity Multi-Sig library self-destruct, November 2017. https://goo.gl/Kw3gXi
6. Andrychowicz, M., Dziembowski, S., Malinowski, D., Mazurek, L.: Fair two-party computations via Bitcoin deposits. In: Böhme, R., Brenner, M., Moore, T., Smith, M. (eds.) FC 2014. LNCS, vol. 8438, pp. 105–121. Springer, Heidelberg (2014). https://doi.org/10.1007/978-3-662-44774-1_8
7. Andrychowicz, M., Dziembowski, S., Malinowski, D., Mazurek, L.: Modeling Bitcoin contracts by timed automata. In: Legay, A., Bozga, M. (eds.) FORMATS 2014. LNCS, vol. 8711, pp. 7–22. Springer, Cham (2014). https://doi.org/10.1007/978-3-319-10512-3_2
8. Andrychowicz, M., Dziembowski, S., Malinowski, D., Mazurek, L.: Secure multiparty computations on Bitcoin. In: IEEE Symposium on Security and Privacy, pp. 443–458 (2014)
9. Andrychowicz, M., Dziembowski, S., Malinowski, D., Mazurek, L.: Secure multiparty computations on Bitcoin. Commun. ACM 59(4), 76–84 (2016)
10. Atzei, N., Bartoletti, M., Cimoli, T.: A survey of attacks on ethereum smart contracts (SoK). In: Maffei, M., Ryan, M. (eds.) POST 2017. LNCS, vol. 10204, pp. 164–186. Springer, Heidelberg (2017). https://doi.org/10.1007/978-3-662-54455-6_8
11. Atzei, N., Bartoletti, M., Lande, S., Zunino, R.: A formal model of Bitcoin transactions. In: Financial Cryptography and Data Security. LNCS, Springer (2018)
12. Back, A., Bentov, I.: Note on fair coin toss via Bitcoin (2013). http://www.cs.technion.ac.il/~idddo/cointossBitcoin.pdf
13. Banasik, W., Dziembowski, S., Malinowski, D.: Efficient zero-knowledge contingent payments in cryptocurrencies without scripts. In: Askoxylakis, I., Ioannidis, S., Katsikas, S., Meadows, C. (eds.) ESORICS 2016, Part II. LNCS, vol. 9879, pp. 261–280. Springer, Cham (2016). https://doi.org/10.1007/978-3-319-45741-3_14
14. Bartoletti, M., Zunino, R.: Constant-deposit multiparty lotteries on Bitcoin. In: Brenner, M., Rohloff, K., Bonneau, J., Miller, A., Ryan, P.Y.A., Teague, V., Bracciali, A., Sala, M., Pintore, F., Jakobsson, M. (eds.) FC 2017. LNCS, vol. 10323, pp. 231–247. Springer, Cham (2017). https://doi.org/10.1007/978-3-319-70278-0_15
15. Behrmann, G., David, A., Larsen, K.G.: A tutorial on UPPAAL. In: Bernardo, M., Corradini, F. (eds.) SFM-RT 2004. LNCS, vol. 3185, pp. 200–236. Springer, Heidelberg (2004). https://doi.org/10.1007/978-3-540-30080-9_7
16. Bentov, I., Kumaresan, R.: How to use Bitcoin to design fair protocols. In: Garay, J.A., Gennaro, R. (eds.) CRYPTO 2014, Part II. LNCS, vol. 8617, pp. 421–439. Springer, Heidelberg (2014). https://doi.org/10.1007/978-3-662-44381-1_24
17. Bhargavan, K., Delignat-Lavaud, A., Fournet, C., Gollamudi, A., Gonthier, G., Kobeissi, N., Rastogi, A., Sibut-Pinote, T., Swamy, N., Zanella-Beguelin, S.: Formal verification of smart contracts. In: PLAS (2016)

18. Biryukov, A., Khovratovich, D., Tikhomirov, S.: Findel: secure derivative contracts for ethereum. In: Brenner, M., Rohloff, K., Bonneau, J., Miller, A., Ryan, P.Y.A., Teague, V., Bracciali, A., Sala, M., Pintore, F., Jakobsson, M. (eds.) FC 2017. LNCS, vol. 10323, pp. 453–467. Springer, Cham (2017). https://doi.org/10.1007/978-3-319-70278-0_28

19. BitFury group: Smart contracts on Bitcoin blockchain (2015). http://bitfury.com/content/5-white-papers-research/contracts-1.1.1.pdf

20. Boneh, D., Naor, M.: Timed commitments. In: Bellare, M. (ed.) CRYPTO 2000. LNCS, vol. 1880, pp. 236–254. Springer, Heidelberg (2000). https://doi.org/10.1007/3-540-44598-6_15

21. Bonneau, J., Miller, A., Clark, J., Narayanan, A., Kroll, J.A., Felten, E.W.: SoK: research perspectives and challenges for Bitcoin and cryptocurrencies. In: IEEE S & P, pp. 104–121 (2015)

22. Brown, R.G., Carlyle, J., Grigg, I., Hearn, M.: Corda: an introduction (2016). http://r3cev.com/s/corda-introductory-whitepaper-final.pdf

23. Crary, K., Sullivan, M.J.: Peer-to-peer affine commitment using Bitcoin. In: ACM Conference on Programming Language Design and Implementation, pp. 479–488 (2015)

24. Delgado-Segura, S. et al.: A fair protocol for data trading based on Bitcoin transactions. In: Future Generation Computer Systems (2017, in press). http://dx.doi.org/10.1016/j.future.2017.08.021

25. Delmolino, K., Arnett, M., Kosba, A., Miller, A., Shi, E.: Step by step towards creating a safe smart contract: lessons and insights from a cryptocurrency lab. In: Clark, J., Meiklejohn, S., Ryan, P.Y.A., Wallach, D., Brenner, M., Rohloff, K. (eds.) FC 2016. LNCS, vol. 9604, pp. 79–94. Springer, Heidelberg (2016). https://doi.org/10.1007/978-3-662-53357-4_6

26. Frantz, C.K., Nowostawski, M.: From institutions to code: towards automated generation of smart contracts. In: eCAS Workshop (2016)

27. Garay, J.A., Katz, J., Maurer, U., Tackmann, B., Zikas, V.: Rational protocol design: cryptography against incentive-driven adversaries. In: FOCS, pp. 648–657 (2013)

28. Goldschlag, D.M., Stubblebine, S.G., Syverson, P.F.: Temporarily hidden bit commitment and lottery applications. Int. J. Inf. Secur. 9(1), 33–50 (2010)

29. Hearn, M.: Rapidly-adjusted (micro) payments to a pre-determined party (2013). https://bitcointalk.org

30. Hirai, Y.: Defining the ethereum virtual machine for interactive theorem provers. In: Brenner, M., Rohloff, K., Bonneau, J., Miller, A., Ryan, P.Y.A., Teague, V., Bracciali, A., Sala, M., Pintore, F., Jakobsson, M. (eds.) FC 2017. LNCS, vol. 10323, pp. 520–535. Springer, Cham (2017). https://doi.org/10.1007/978-3-319-70278-0_33

31. Kumaresan, R., Bentov, I.: How to use Bitcoin to incentivize correct computations. In: ACM CCS, pp. 30–41 (2014)

32. Kumaresan, R., Moran, T., Bentov, I.: How to use Bitcoin to play decentralized poker. In: ACM CCS, pp. 195–206 (2015)

33. Liao, K., Katz, J.: Incentivizing blockchain forks via whale transactions. In: Brenner, M., Rohloff, K., Bonneau, J., Miller, A., Ryan, P.Y.A., Teague, V., Bracciali, A., Sala, M., Pintore, F., Jakobsson, M. (eds.) FC 2017. LNCS, vol. 10323, pp. 264–279. Springer, Cham (2017). https://doi.org/10.1007/978-3-319-70278-0_17

34. Luu, L., Chu, D.H., Olickel, H., Saxena, P., Hobor, A.: Making smart contracts smarter. In: ACM CCS (2016). http://eprint.iacr.org/2016/633

35. Maxwell, G.: The first successful zero-knowledge contingent payment (2016). https://bitcoincore.org/en/2016/02/26/zero-knowledge-contingent-payments-announcement/
36. Miller, A., Bentov, I.: Zero-collateral lotteries in Bitcoin and Ethereum. In: EuroS&P Workshops, pp. 4–13 (2017)
37. Möser, M., Eyal, I., Gün Sirer, E.: Bitcoin covenants. In: Clark, J., Meiklejohn, S., Ryan, P.Y.A., Wallach, D., Brenner, M., Rohloff, K. (eds.) FC 2016. LNCS, vol. 9604, pp. 126–141. Springer, Heidelberg (2016). https://doi.org/10.1007/978-3-662-53357-4_9
38. Nakamoto, S.: Bitcoin: a peer-to-peer electronic cash system (2008). https://bitcoin.org/bitcoin.pdf
39. Nicollin, X., Sifakis, J.: An overview and synthesis on timed process algebras. In: Larsen, K.G., Skou, A. (eds.) CAV 1991. LNCS, vol. 575, pp. 376–398. Springer, Heidelberg (1992). https://doi.org/10.1007/3-540-55179-4_36
40. O'Connor, R.: Simplicity: a new language for blockchains. In: PLAS (2017). http://arxiv.org/abs/1711.03028
41. O'Connor, R., Piekarska, M.: Enhancing Bitcoin transactions with covenants. In: Brenner, M., Rohloff, K., Bonneau, J., Miller, A., Ryan, P.Y.A., Teague, V., Bracciali, A., Sala, M., Pintore, F., Jakobsson, M. (eds.) FC 2017. LNCS, vol. 10323, pp. 191–198. Springer, Cham (2017). https://doi.org/10.1007/978-3-319-70278-0_12
42. Syverson, P.F.: Weakly secret bit commitment: applications to lotteries and fair exchange. In: IEEE CSFW, pp. 2–13 (1998)
43. Szabo, N.: Formalizing and securing relationships on public networks. First Monday 2(9) (1997). http://firstmonday.org/htbin/cgiwrap/bin/ojs/index.php/fm/article/view/548

A Semantic Framework for the Security Analysis of Ethereum Smart Contracts

Ilya Grishchenko, Matteo Maffei, and Clara Schneidewind[✉]

TU Wien, Vienna, Austria
{ilya.grishchenko,matteo.maffei,clara.schneidewind}@tuwien.ac.at

Abstract. Smart contracts are programs running on cryptocurrency (e.g., Ethereum) blockchains, whose popularity stem from the possibility to perform financial transactions, such as payments and auctions, in a distributed environment without need for any trusted third party. Given their financial nature, bugs or vulnerabilities in these programs may lead to catastrophic consequences, as witnessed by recent attacks. Unfortunately, programming smart contracts is a delicate task that requires strong expertise: Ethereum smart contracts are written in Solidity, a dedicated language resembling JavaScript, and shipped over the blockchain in the EVM bytecode format. In order to rigorously verify the security of smart contracts, it is of paramount importance to formalize their semantics as well as the security properties of interest, in particular at the level of the bytecode being executed.

In this paper, we present the first complete small-step semantics of EVM bytecode, which we formalize in the F* proof assistant, obtaining executable code that we successfully validate against the official Ethereum test suite. Furthermore, we formally define for the first time a number of central security properties for smart contracts, such as call integrity, atomicity, and independence from miner controlled parameters. This formalization relies on a combination of hyper- and safety properties. Along this work, we identified various mistakes and imprecisions in existing semantics and verification tools for Ethereum smart contracts, thereby demonstrating once more the importance of rigorous semantic foundations for the design of security verification techniques.

1 Introduction

One of the determining factors for the growing interest in blockchain technologies is the groundbreaking promise of secure distributed computations even in absence of trusted third parties. Building on a distributed ledger that keeps track of previous transactions and the state of each account, whose functionality and security is ensured by a delicate combination of incentives and cryptography, software developers can implement sophisticated distributed, transactions-based computations by leveraging the scripting language offered by the underlying cryptocurrency. While many of these cryptocurrencies have an intentionally limited scripting language (e.g., Bitcoin [1]), Ethereum was designed from the

© The Author(s) 2018
L. Bauer and R. Küsters (Eds.): POST 2018, LNCS 10804, pp. 243–269, 2018.
https://doi.org/10.1007/978-3-319-89722-6_10

ground up with a quasi Turing-complete language[1]. Ethereum programs, called *smart contracts*, have thus found a variety of appealing use cases, such as financial contracts [2], auctions [3], elections [4], data management systems [5], trading platforms [6,7], permission management [8] and verifiable cloud computing [9], just to mention a few. Given their financial nature, bugs and vulnerabilities in smart contracts may lead to catastrophic consequences. For instance, the infamous DAO vulnerability [10] recently led to a 60M$ financial loss and similar vulnerabilities occur on a regular basis [11,12]. Furthermore, many smart contracts in the wild are intentionally fraudulent, as highlighted in a recent survey [13].

A rigorous security analysis of smart contracts is thus crucial for the trust of the society in blockchain technologies and their widespread deployment. Unfortunately, this task is a quite challenging for various reasons. First, Ethereum smart contracts are developed in an ad-hoc language, called Solidity, which resembles JavaScript but features specific transaction-oriented mechanisms and a number of non-standard semantic behaviours, as further described in this paper. Second, smart contracts are uploaded on the blockchain in the form of Ethereum Virtual Machine (EVM) bytecode, a stack-based low-level code featuring dynamic code creation and invocation and, in general, very little static information, which makes it extremely difficult to analyze.

Related Work. Recognizing the importance of solid semantic foundations for smart contracts, the Ethereum foundation published a yellow paper [14] to describe the intended behaviour of smart contracts. This semantics, however, exhibits several under-specifications and does not follow any standard approach for the specification of program semantics, thereby hindering program verification. In order to provide a more precise characterization, Hirai formalizes the EVM semantics in the proof assistant Isabelle/HOL and uses it for manually proving safety properties for concrete programs [15]. This semantics, however, constitutes just a sound over-approximation of the original semantics [14]. More specifically, once a contract performs a call that is not a self-call, it is assumed that arbitrary code gets executed and consequently arbitrary changes to the account's state and to the global state can be performed. Consequently, this semantics can not serve as a general-purpose basis for static analysis techniques that might not rely on the same over-approximation.

In a concurrent, unpublished work, Hildebrandt et al. [16] define the EVM semantics in the $\mathbb{K}$ framework [17] – a language independent verification framework based on reachability logics. The authors leverage the power of the $\mathbb{K}$ framework in order to automatically derive analysis tools for the specified semantics, presenting as an example a gas analysis tool, a semantic debugger, and a program verifier based on reachability logics. The underlying semantics relies on non-standard local rewriting rules on the system configuration. Since parts of the execution are treated in separation such as the exception behavior and the gas calculations, one small-step consists of several rewriting steps, which makes

---

[1] While the language itself is Turing complete, computations are associated with a bounded computational budget (called gas), which gets consumed by each instruction thereby enforcing termination.

this semantics harder to use as a basis for new static analysis techniques. This is relevant whenever the static analysis tools derivable by the 𝕂 framework are not sufficient for the desired purposes: for instance, their analysis requires the user to manually specify loop invariants, which is hardly doable for EVM bytecode and clearly does not scale to large programs. Furthermore, all these works concentrate on the semantics of EVM bytecode but do not study security properties for smart contracts.

Sergey and Hobor [18] compare smart contracts on the blockchain with concurrent objects using shared memory and use this analogy to explain typical problems that arise when programming smart contracts in terms of concepts known from concurrency theory. They encourage the application of state-of-the art verification techniques for concurrent programs to smart contracts, but do not describe any specific analysis method applied to smart contracts themselves. Mavridou and Laszka [19] define a high-level semantics for smart contracts that is based on finite state machines and aims at simplifying the development of smart contracts. They provide a translation of their state machine specification language to Solidity, a higher-order language for writing Ethereum smart contracts, and present design patterns that should help users to improve the security of their contracts. The translation to Solidity is not backed up by a correctness proof and the design patterns are not claimed to provide any security guarantees.

Bhargavan et al. [20] introduce a framework to analyze Ethereum contracts by translation into F*, a functional programming language aimed at program verification and equipped with an interactive proof assistant. The translation supports only a fragment of the EVM bytecode and does not come with a justifying semantic argument.

Luu et al. have recently presented Oyente [21], a state-of-the-art static analysis tool for EVM bytecode that relies on symbolic execution. Oyente comes with a semantics of a simplified fragment of the EVM bytecode and, in particular, misses several important commands related to contract calls and contract creation. Furthermore, it is affected by a major bug related to calls as well as several other minor ones which we discovered while formalizing our semantics, which is inspired by theirs. Oyente supports a variety of security properties, such as transaction order dependency, timestamp dependency, and reentrancy, but the security definitions are rather syntactic and described informally. As we show in this paper, the lack of solid semantic foundations causes several sources of unsoundness in Oyente.

Our Contributions. This work lays the semantic foundations for Ethereum smart contracts. Specifically, we introduce

- The first complete small-step semantics for EVM bytecode;
- A formalization in F* of a large fragment of our semantics, which can serve as a foundation for verification techniques based on encoding into this language [20] as well as machine-checked proofs for other analysis techniques (e.g., [21]). By compiling F* in OCaml, we could successfully validate our semantics against the official Ethereum test suite;

- The first formal definitions of crucial security properties for smart contracts, such as call integrity, for which we devise a dedicated proof technique, atomicity, and independence from miner controlled parameters. Interestingly enough, the formalization of these properties requires hyper-properties, while existing static analysis techniques for smart contracts rely on reachability properties and syntactic conditions;
- A collection of examples showing how the syntactic conditions employed in current analysis techniques are imprecise and, in several cases, unsound, thereby further motivating the need for solid semantic foundations and rigorous security definitions for smart contracts.

The complete semantics as well as the formalization in F* are publicly available [22].

Outline. The remainder of this paper is organized as follows. Section 2 briefly overviews the Ethereum architecture, Sect. 3 introduces the Ethereum semantics and our formalization in F*, Sect. 4 formally defines various security properties for Ethereum smart contracts, and Sect. 5 concludes highlighting interesting research directions.

2   Background on Ethereum

Ethereum. Ethereum is a cryptographic currency system built on top of a blockchain. Similar to Bitcoin, network participants publish transactions to the network that are then grouped into blocks by distinct nodes (the so called *miners*) and appended to the blockchain using a proof of work (PoW) consensus mechanism. The state of the system – that we will also refer to as *global state* – consists of the state of the different accounts populating it. An account can either be an external account (belonging to a user of the system) that carries information on its current balance or it can be a contract account that additionally obtains persistent storage and the contract's code. The account's balances are given in the subunit *wei* of the virtual currency *Ether*.[2]

Transactions can alter the state of the system by either creating new contract accounts or by calling an existing account. Calls to external accounts can only transfer Ether to this account, but calls to contract accounts additionally execute the code associated to the contract. The contract execution might alter the storage of the account or might again perform transactions – in this case we talk about *internal transactions*.

The execution model underlying the execution of contract code is described by a virtual state machine, the *Ethereum Virtual Machine* (EVM). This is *quasi Turing complete* as the otherwise Turing complete execution is restricted by the upfront defined resource *gas* that effectively limits the number of execution steps. The originator of the transaction can specify the maximal gas that should be spent for the contract execution and also determines the gas prize

---

[2] One Ether is equivalent to 10^{18} wei.

(the amount of wei to pay for a unit of gas). Upfront, the originator pays for the gas limit according to the gas prize and in case of successful contract execution that did not spend the whole amount of gas dedicated to it, the originator gets reimbursed with gas that is left. The remaining wei paid for the used gas are given as a fee to a beneficiary address specified by the miner.

EVM Bytecode. The code of contracts is written in *EVM bytecode* – an Assembler like bytecode language. As the core of the EVM is a stack-based machine, the set of instructions in EVM bytecode consists mainly of standard instructions for stack operations, arithmetics, jumps and local memory access. The classical set of instructions is enriched with an opcode for the SHA3 hash and several opcodes for accessing the environment that the contract was called in. In addition, there are opcodes for accessing and modifying the storage of the account currently running the code and distinct opcodes for performing internal call and create transactions. Another instruction particular to the blockchain setting is the SELFDESTRUCT code that deletes the currently executed contract - but only after the successful execution of the external transaction.

Gas and Exceptions. The execution of each instruction consumes a positive amount of gas. There is a gas limit set by the sender of the transaction. Exceeding the gas limit results in an exception that reverts the effects of the current transaction on the global state. In the case of nested transactions, the occurrence of an exception only reverts its own effects, but not those of the calling transaction. Instead, the failure of an internal transaction is only indicated by writing zero to the caller's stack.

Solidity. In practice, most Ethereum smart contracts are not written in EVM bytecode directly, but in the high-level language Solidity which is developed by the Ethereum Foundation [23]. For understanding the typical problems that arise when writing smart contracts, it is important to consider the design of this high-level language.

Solidity is a so called "contract-oriented" programming language that uses the concept of class from object-oriented languages for the representation of contracts. Similar to classes in object-oriented programming, contracts specify fields and methods for contract instances. Fields can be seen as persistent storage of a contract (instance) and contract methods can by default be invoked by any internal or external transaction. For interacting with another contract one either needs to create a new instance of this contract (in which case a new contract account with the functionality described in the contract class is created) or one can directly make transactions to a known contract address holding a contract of the required shape. The syntax of Solidity resembles JavaScript, enriched with additional primitives accounting for the distributed setting of Ethereum. In particular, Solidity provides primitives for accessing the transaction and the block information, like msg.sender for accessing the address of the account invoking the method or msg.value for accessing the amount of *wei* transferred by the transaction that invoked the method.

Solidity shows some particularities when it comes to transferring money to another contract especially using the provided low level functions `send` and `call`. A value transfer initiated using these functions is finally translated to an internal call transaction which implies that calling a contract might also execute code and in particular it can fail because the available gas is not sufficient for executing the code. In addition – as in the EVM – these kinds of calls do not enable exception propagation, so that the caller manually needs to checks for the return result. Another special feature of Solidity is that it allows for defining so called *fallback functions* for contracts that get executed when a call via the `send` function was performed or (using the `call` function) an address is called that however does not properly specifies the concrete function of the contract to be called.

3   Small-Step Semantics

We introduce a small-step semantics covering the full EVM bytecode, inspired by the one presented by Luu et al. [21], which we substantially revise in order to handle the missing instructions, in particular contract calls and call creation. In addition, while formalizing our semantics, we found a major flaw related to calls and several minor ones (cf. Sect. 3.7), which we fixed and reported to the authors. Due to space constraints, we refer the interested reader to the full version of the paper [22] for a formal account of the semantic rules and present below the most significant ones.

3.1   Preliminaries

In the following, we will use $\mathbb{B}$ to denote the set $\{0, 1\}$ of bits and accordingly $\mathbb{B}^x$ for sets of bitstrings of size x. We further let $\mathbb{N}_x$ denote the set of non-negative integers representable by x bits and allow for implicit conversion between those two representations. In addition, we will use the notation $[X]$ (resp. $\mathcal{L}(X)$) for arrays (resp. lists) of elements from the set X. We use standard notations for operations on arrays and lists.

3.2   Global State

As mentioned before, the global state is a (partial) mapping from account addresses (that are bitstrings of size 160) to accounts. In the case that an account does not exist, we assume it to map to $\bot$. Accounts, irrespectively of their type, are tuples of the form $(n, b, stor, code)$, with $n \in \mathbb{N}_{256}$ being the account's nonce that is incremented with every other account that the account creates, $b \in \mathbb{N}_{256}$ being the account's balance in *wei*, $stor \in \mathbb{B}^{256} \to \mathbb{B}^{256}$ being the accounts persistent storage that is represented as a mapping from 256-bit words to 256-bit words and finally $code \in [\mathbb{B}^8]$ being the contract that is an array of bytes. In contrast to contract accounts, external accounts have the empty bytearray as code. As only the execution of code in the context of the account can access and modify the account's storage, the fact that formally external accounts have persistent storage does not have any effect. In the following, we will denote the set of addresses with $\mathcal{A}$ and the set of global states with Σ and we will assume that $\sigma \in \Sigma$.

3.3   Small-Step Relation

In order to define the small-step semantics, we give a small-step relation $\Gamma \vDash S \rightarrow S'$ that specifies how a call stack $S \in \mathbb{S}$ representing the state of the execution evolves within one step under the transaction environment $\Gamma \in \mathcal{T}_{env}$.

In Fig. 1 we give a full grammar for call stacks and transaction environments:

$$
\begin{array}{rll}
\text{Call stacks } \mathbb{S} & \ni S & := EXC :: S_{plain} \mid HALT(\sigma, d, g, \eta) :: S_{plain} \mid S_{plain} \\
\text{Plain call stacks } \mathbb{S}_{plain} & \ni S_{plain} & := (\mu, \iota, \sigma, \eta) :: S_{plain} \\
\text{Machine states } M & \ni \mu & := (gas, pc, m, i, s) \\
\text{Execution environments } I & \ni \iota & := (actor, input, sender, value, code) \\
\text{Global states } \Sigma & \ni \sigma & \\
\text{Account states } A & \ni acc & := (n, b, code, stor) \mid \bot \\
\text{Transaction effects } N & \ni \eta & := (b, L, S_\dagger) \\
\text{Transaction environments } \mathcal{T}_{env} & \ni \Gamma & := (o, prize, H)
\end{array}
$$

Notations: $d \in [\mathbb{B}^8]$, $g \in \mathbb{N}_{256}$, $\eta \in N$, $o \in \mathcal{A}$, $prize \in \mathbb{N}_{256}$, $H \in \mathcal{H}$
$gas \in \mathbb{N}_{256}$, $pc \in \mathbb{N}_{256}$, $m \in \mathbb{B}^{256}, \rightarrow \mathbb{B}^8$ $i \in \mathbb{N}_{256}$, $s \in \mathcal{L}(\mathbb{B}^{256})$
$sender \in \mathcal{A}$ $input \in [\mathbb{B}^8]$ $sender \in \mathcal{A}$ $value \in \mathbb{N}_{256}$ $code \in [\mathbb{B}^8]$
$b \in \mathbb{N}_{256}$ $L \in \mathcal{L}(Ev_{log})$ $S_\dagger \subseteq \mathcal{A}$ $\Sigma = \mathcal{A} \rightarrow \mathcal{A}$

Fig. 1. Grammar for call stacks and transaction environments

Transaction Environments. The transaction environment represents the static information of the block that the transaction is executed in and the immutable parameters given to the transaction as the gas prize or the gas limit. More specifically, the transaction environment $\Gamma \in \mathcal{T}_{env} = \mathcal{A} \times \mathbb{N}_{256} \times \mathcal{H}$ is a tuple of the form $(o, prize, H)$ with $o \in \mathcal{A}$ being the address of the account that made the transaction, $prize \in \mathbb{N}_{256}$ denoting amount of wei that needs to paid for a unit of gas in this transaction and $H \in \mathcal{H}$ being the header of the block that the transaction is part of. We do not specify the format of block headers here, but just assume a set $\mathcal{H}$ of block headers.

Callstacks. A call stack S is a stack of execution states which represents the state of the execution within one internal transaction. We give a formal definition of the set of possible callstacks $\mathbb{S}$ as follows:

$$
\begin{aligned}
\mathbb{S} := \{ & EXC :: S_{plain},\ HALT(\sigma, gas, d, \eta) :: S_{plain},\ S_{plain} \\
& \mid \sigma \in \Sigma,\ gas \in \mathbb{N},\ d \in [\mathbb{B}^8],\ \eta \in N,\ S_{plain} \in \mathcal{L}(M \times I \times \Sigma \times N) \}
\end{aligned}
$$

Syntactically, a call stack is a stack of regular execution states of the form $(\mu, \iota, \sigma, \eta)$ that can optionally be topped with a halting state $HALT(\sigma, gas, d, \eta)$

or an exception state EXC. We summarize these three types of states as execution states $\mathcal{S}$. Semantically, halting states indicate regular halting of an internal transaction, exception states indicate exceptional halting, and regular execution states describe the state of internal transactions in progress. Halting and exception states can only occur as top elements of the call stack as they represent terminated internal transactions. Exception states of the form EXC do not carry any information as in the case of an exception all effects of the terminated internal transaction are reverted and the caller state therefore stays unaffected, except for the gas. Halting states instead are of the form $HALT(\sigma, gas, d, \eta)$ specifying the global state σ the execution halted in, the gas $gas \in \mathbb{N}_{256}$ remaining from the execution, the return data $d \in [\mathbb{B}^8]$ and the additional transaction effects $\eta \in N$ of the internal transaction. The additional transaction effects carry information that are accumulated during execution, but do not influence the small-step execution itself. Formally, the additional transaction effects are a triple of the form $(b, L, S_\dagger) \in N = \mathbb{N}_{256} \times \mathcal{L}(Ev_{log}) \times \mathcal{P}(\mathcal{A})$ with $b \in \mathbb{N}_{256}$ being the refund balance that is increased by account storage operations and will finally be paid to the transaction's beneficiary, $L \in \mathcal{L}(Ev_{log})$ being the sequence of log events that the bytecode execution invoked during execution and $S_\dagger \subseteq \mathcal{A}$ being the so called suicide set – the set of account addresses that executed the SELFDESTRUCT command and therefore registered their account for deletion. The information held by the halting state is carried over to the calling state.

The state of a non-terminated internal transaction is described by a regular execution state of the form $(\mu, \iota, \sigma, \eta)$. The state is determined by the current global state σ of the system as well as the execution environment $\iota \in I$ that specifies the parameters of the current transaction (including inputs and the code to be executed), the local state $\mu \in M$ of the stack machine, and the transaction effects $\eta \in N$ collected during execution so far.

Execution Environment. The execution environment ι of an internal transaction specifies the static parameters of the transaction. It is a tuple of the form $(actor, input, sender, value, code) \in I = \mathcal{A} \times [\mathbb{B}^8] \times \mathcal{A} \times \mathbb{N}_{256} \times [\mathbb{B}^8]$ with the following components:

- $actor \in \mathcal{A}$ is the address of the account currently executing;
- $input \in [\mathbb{B}^8]$ is the data given as an input to the internal transaction;
- $sender \in \mathcal{A}$ is the address of the account that initiated the internal transaction;
- $value \in \mathbb{N}_{256}$ is the value transferred by the internal transaction;
- $code \in [\mathbb{B}^8]$ is the code currently executed.

This information is determined at the beginning of an internal transaction execution and it can be accessed, but not altered during the execution.

Machine State. The local machine state μ represents the state of the underlying state machine used for execution and is a tuple of the form (gas, pc, m, i, s) where

- $gas \in N_{256}$ is the current amount of gas still available for execution;
- $pc \in N_{256}$ is the current program counter;
- $m \in \mathbb{B}^{256} \rightarrow \mathbb{B}^8$ is a mapping from 256-bit words to bytes that represents the local memory;
- $i \in N_{256}$ is the current number of active words in memory;
- $s \in \mathcal{L}(\mathbb{B}^{256})$ is the local 256-bit word stack of the stack machine.

The execution of each internal transaction starts in a fresh machine state, with an empty stack, memory initialized to all zeros, and program counter and active words in memory set to zero. Only the gas is instantiated with the gas value available for the execution.

3.4   Small-Step Rules

In the following, we will present a selection of interesting small-step rules in order to illustrate the most important features of the semantics.

For demonstrating the overall design of the semantics, we start with the example of the arithmetic expression ADD performing addition of two values on the machine stack. Note that as the word size of the stack machine is 256, all arithmetic operations are performed modulo 2^{256}.

$$\frac{\iota.code\,[\mu.\mathsf{pc}] = \mathsf{ADD}}{\mu.\mathsf{s} = a :: b :: s \qquad \mu.\mathsf{gas} \geq 3 \qquad \mu' = \mu[\mathsf{s} \rightarrow (a+b) :: s][\mathsf{pc} \mathrel{+}= 1][\mathsf{gas} \mathrel{-}= 3]}{\Gamma \vDash (\mu, \iota, \sigma, \eta) :: S \rightarrow (\mu', \iota, \sigma, \eta) :: S}$$

$$\frac{\iota.code\,[\mu.\mathsf{pc}] = \mathsf{ADD} \qquad (|\mu.\mathsf{s}| < 2 \vee \mu.\mathsf{gas} < 3)}{\Gamma \vDash (\mu, \iota, \sigma, \eta) :: S \rightarrow EXC :: S}$$

We use a dot notation, in order to access components of the different state parameters. We name the components with the variable names introduced for these components in the last section written in sans-serif-style. In addition, we use the usual notation for updating components: $t[\mathsf{c} \rightarrow v]$ denotes that the component c of tuple t is updated with value v. For expressing incremental updates in a simpler way, we additionally use the notation $t[\mathsf{c} \mathrel{+}= v]$ to denote that the (numerical) component of c is incremented by v and similarly $t[\mathsf{c} \mathrel{-}= v]$ for decrementing a component c of t.

The execution of the arithmetic instruction ADD only performs local changes in the machine state affecting the local stack, the program counter, and the gas budget. For deciding upon the correct instruction to execute, the currently executed code (that is part of the execution environment) is accessed at the position of the current program counter. The cost of an ADD instruction is constantly three units of gas that get subtracted from the gas budget in the machine state. As every other instruction, ADD can fail due to lacking gas or due to underflows on the machine stack. In this case, the exception state is entered and the execution of the current internal transaction is terminated. For better readability, we use here the slightly sloppy $\vee$ notation for combining the two error cases in one inference rule.

A more interesting example of a semantic rule is the one of the CALL instruction that initiates an internal call transaction. In the case of calling, several corner cases need to be treated which results in several inference rules for this case. Here, we only present one rule for illustrating the main functionality. More precisely, we present the case in that the account that should be called exists, the call stack limit of 1024 is not reached yet, and the account initiating the transaction has a sufficiently large balance for sending the specified amount of wei to the called account.

$$\frac{\begin{array}{c} \iota.code\,[\mu.\mathsf{pc}] = \mathsf{CALL} \qquad \mu.\mathsf{s} = g :: to :: va :: io :: is :: oo :: os :: s \\ \sigma(to) \neq \bot \qquad |A| + 1 < 1024 \qquad \sigma(\iota.\mathsf{actor}).\mathsf{b} \geq va \qquad aw = M\,(M\,(\mu.\mathsf{i}, io, is), oo, os) \\ c_{call} = C_{gascap}\,(va, 1, g, \mu.\mathsf{gas}) \qquad c = C_{base}\,(va, 1) + C_{mem}\,(\mu.\mathsf{i}, aw) + c_{call} \\ \mu.\mathsf{gas} \geq c \qquad \sigma' = \sigma\langle to \to \sigma(to)[\mathsf{b}\ += va]\rangle\langle\iota.\mathsf{actor} \to \sigma(\iota.\mathsf{actor})[\mathsf{b}\ -= va]\rangle \\ d = \mu.\mathsf{m}\,[io, io + is - 1] \qquad \mu' = (c_{call}, 0, \lambda x.\,0, 0, \epsilon) \\ \iota' = \iota[\mathsf{sender} \to \iota.\mathsf{actor}][\mathsf{actor} \to to][\mathsf{value} \to va][\mathsf{input} \to d][\mathsf{code} \to \sigma(to).\mathsf{code}] \end{array}}{\Gamma \vDash (\mu, \iota, \sigma, \eta) :: S \to (\mu', \iota', \sigma', \eta) :: (\mu, \iota, \sigma, \eta) :: S}$$

For performing a call, the parameters to this call need to be specified on the machine stack. These are the amount of gas g that should be given as budget to the call, the recipient to of the call and the amount va of wei to be transferred with the call. In addition, the caller needs to specify the input data that should be given to the transaction and the place in memory where the return data of the call should be written after successful execution. To this end, the remaining arguments specify the offset and size of the memory fragment that input data should be read from (determined by io and is) and return data should be written to (determined by oo and os).

Calculating the cost in terms of gas for the execution is quite complicated in the case of CALL as it is influenced by several factors including the arguments given to the call and the current machine state. First of all, the gas that should be given to the call (here denoted by c_{call}) needs to be determined. This value is not necessarily equal to the value g specified on the stack, but also depends on the value va transferred by the call and the currently available gas. In addition, as the memory needs to be accessed for reading the input value and writing the return value, the number of active words in memory might be increased. This effect is captured by the memory extension function M. As accessing additional words in memory costs gas, this cost needs to be taken into account in the overall cost. The costs resulting from an increase in the number of active words is calculated by the function C_{mem}. Finally, there is also a base cost charged for the call that depends on the value va. As the cost also depends on the specific case for calling that is considered, the cost calculation functions receive a flag (here 1) as arguments. These technical details are spelled out in the full version [22].

The call itself then has several effects: First, it transfers the balance from the executing state ($actor$ in the execution environment) to the recipient (to). To this end, the global state is updated. Here we use a special notation for the functional update on the global state using $\langle\rangle$ instead of $[]$. Second, for initializing the execution of the initiated internal transaction, a new regular execution state is placed on top of the execution stack. The internal transaction starts in a fresh machine state at program counter zero. This means that the initial memory is initialized to all zeros and consequently the number of active words in memory is zero as well and additionally the initial stack is empty. The gas budget given to the internal transaction is c_{call} calculated before. The transaction environment of the new call records the call parameters. This includes the sender that is the currently executing account *actor*, the new active account that is now the called account *to* as well as the value *va* sent and the input data given to the call. To this end the input data is extracted from the memory using the offset *io* and the size *is*. We use an interval notation here to denote that a part of the memory is extracted. Finally, the code in the execution environment of the new internal transaction is the code of the called account.

Note that the execution state of the caller stays completely unaffected at this stage of the execution. This is a conscious design decision in order to simplify the expression of security properties and to make the semantics more suitable to abstractions.

Besides CALL there are two different instructions for initiating internal call transactions that implement slight variations of the simple CALL instruction. These variations are called CALLCODE and DELEGATECALL, which both allow for executing another's account code in the context of the caller. The difference is that in the case of CALLCODE a new internal transaction is started and the currently executed account is registered as the sender of this transaction while in the case of DELEGATECALL an existing call is really forwarded in the sense that the sender and the value of the initiating transaction are propagated to the new internal transaction.

Analogously to the instructions for initiating internal call transactions, there is also one instruction CREATE that allows for the creation of a new account. The semantics of this instruction is similar to the one of CALL, with the exception that a fresh account is created, which gets the specified transferred value, and that the input provided to this internal transaction, which is again specified in the local memory, is interpreted as the initialization code to be executed in order to produce the newly created account's code as output. In contrast to the call transaction, a create transaction does not await a return value, but only an indication of success or failure.

For discussing how to return from an internal transaction, we show the rule for returning from a successful internal call transaction.

$$\frac{\begin{array}{c} \iota.code\,[\mu.\mathsf{pc}] = \mathsf{CALL} \qquad \mu.\mathsf{s} = g :: to :: va :: io :: is :: oo :: os :: s \\ flag = \sigma(to) = \bot\,?\,0 : 1 \qquad aw = M\,(M\,(\mu.\mathsf{i}, io, is), oo, os) \\ c_{call} = C_{gascap}\,(va, flag, g, \mu.\mathsf{gas}) \qquad c = C_{base}\,(va, flag) + C_{mem}\,(\mu.\mathsf{i}, aw) + c_{call} \\ \mu' = \mu[\mathsf{i} \to aw][\mathsf{s} \to 1 :: s][\mathsf{pc}\,+\!= 1][\mathsf{gas}\,+\!= gas - c][\mathsf{m} \to \mu.\mathsf{m}[[oo, oo + s - 1] \to d]] \end{array}}{\Gamma \vDash HALT(\sigma', gas, d, \eta') :: (\mu, \iota, \sigma, \eta) :: S \; \to \; (\mu', \iota, \sigma', \eta') :: S}$$

Leaving the caller state unchanged at the point of calling has the negative side effect that the cost calculation needs to be redone at this point in order to determine the new gas value of the caller state. But besides this, the rule is straightforward: the program counter is incremented as usual and the number of active words in memory is adjusted as memory accesses for reading the input and return data have been made. The gas is decreased, meaning that the overall amount of gas c allocated for the execution is subtracted. However, as this cost already includes the gas budget given to the internal transaction, the gas gas that is left after the execution is refunded again. In addition, the return data d is written to the local memory of the caller at the place specified by oo and os. Finally, the value one is written to the caller's stack in order to indicate the success of the internal call transaction. As the execution was successful, as indicated by the halting state, the global state and the transaction effects of the callee are adopted by the caller.

EVM bytecode offers several instructions for explicitly halting (internal) transaction execution. Besides the standard instructions STOP and RETURN, there is the SELFDESTRUCT instruction that is very particular to the blockchain setting. The STOP instruction causes regular halting of the internal transaction without returning data to the caller. In contrast, the RETURN instruction allows one to specify the memory fragment containing the return data that will be handed to the caller.

Finally, the SELFDESTRUCT instruction halts the execution and lists the currently execution account for later deletion. More precisely, this means that this account will be deleted when finalizing the external transaction, but its behavior during the ongoing small-step execution is not affected. Additionally, the whole balance of the deleted account is transferred to some beneficiary specified on the machine stack.

We show the small-step rules depicting the main functionality of SELFDESTRUCT. As for CALL, capturing the whole functionality of SELFDESTRUCT would require to consider several corner cases. Here we consider the case where the beneficiary exists, the stack does not underflow and the available amount of gas is sufficient.

$$
\frac{
\begin{array}{c}
\omega_{\mu,\iota} = \mathsf{SELFDESTRUCT} \qquad \mu.\mathsf{s} = a_{ben} :: s \\
a = a_{ben} \mod 2^{160} \qquad \sigma(a) \neq \bot \qquad \mu.\mathsf{gas} \geq 5000 \qquad g = \mu.\mathsf{gas} - 5000 \\
\sigma' = \sigma\langle \iota.\mathsf{actor} \to \sigma(\iota.\mathsf{actor})[\mathsf{balance} \to 0]\rangle\langle a \to \sigma(a)[\mathsf{balance} \mathrel{+}= \sigma.(\iota.\mathsf{actor}).\mathsf{balance}]\rangle \\
r = (\iota.\mathsf{actor} \in \Gamma.S_\dagger)\,?\,0 : 24000 \qquad \eta' = \eta[S_\dagger \to \eta.S_\dagger \cup \{\iota.\mathsf{actor}\}][\mathsf{balance} \mathrel{+}= r]
\end{array}
}{
\Gamma \vDash (\mu, \iota, \sigma, \eta) :: S \;\to\; HALT(\sigma', g, \epsilon, \eta') :: S
}
$$

The SELFDESTRUCT command takes one argument a_{ben} from the stack specifying the address of the beneficiary that should get the balance of the account that is destructed. If all preconditions are satisfied, the balance of the executing account ($\iota.\mathsf{actor}$) is transferred to the beneficiary address and the current internal transaction execution enters a halting state. Additionally, the transaction effects are extended by adding $\iota.\mathsf{actor}$ to the suicide set and by possibly increasing the refund balance. The refund balance is only increased in case that $\iota.\mathsf{actor}$ is not already scheduled for deletion. The halting state captures the global state σ after the money transfer, the remaining gas g after executing the SELFDESTRUCT and the updated transaction effects η'. As no return data is handed to the caller, the empty bytearray ϵ is specified as return data in the halting state.

Note that SELFDESTRUCT deletes the currently executing account ι.actor which is not necessarily the same account as the one owning the code ι.code. This might be due a previous execution of DELEGATECALL or CALLCODE.

3.5 Transaction Execution

The outcome of an external transaction execution does not only consist of the result of the EVM bytecode execution. Before executing the bytecode, the transaction environment and the execution environment are determined from the transaction information and the block header. In the following we assume $\mathcal{T}$ to denote the set of transactions. An (external) transaction $T \in \mathcal{T}$, similar to the internal transactions, specifies a gas limit, a recipient and a value to be transferred. In addition, it also contains the originator and the gas prize that will be recorded in the transaction environment. Finally, it specifies an input to the transaction and the transaction type that can either be a call or a create transaction. The transaction type determines whether the input will be interpreted as input data to a call transaction or as initialization code for a create transaction. In addition to the transaction of the environment initialization, some initial changes on the global state and validity checks are performed. For the sake of presentation we assume in the following a function $initialize(\cdot, \cdot, \cdot) \in \mathcal{T} \times \mathcal{H} \times \Sigma \rightarrow (\mathcal{T}_{env} \times \mathcal{S}) \cup \{\bot\}$ performing the initialization phase and returning a transaction environment and initial execution state in the case of a valid transaction and $\bot$ otherwise. Similarly, we assume a function $finalize(\cdot, \cdot, \cdot) \in T \times \mathcal{S} \times N \times \Sigma$ that given the final global state of the execution, the accumulated transaction effects and the transaction, computes the final effects on the global state. These include for example the deletion of the contracts from the suicide set and the payout to the beneficiary of the transaction.

Formally we can define the execution of a transaction $T \in \mathcal{T}$ in a block with header $H \in \mathcal{H}$ as follows:

$$\frac{(\Gamma, s) = initialize(T, H, \sigma) \quad \Gamma \vDash s :: \epsilon \rightarrow^* s' :: \epsilon \quad final(s') \quad \sigma' = finalize(s', \eta', T)}{\sigma \xrightarrow{T,H} \sigma'}$$

where $\rightarrow^*$ denotes the reflexive and transitive closure of the small-step relation and the predicate $final(\cdot)$ characterizes a state that cannot be further reduced using the small-step relation.

3.6 Formalization in F*

We provide a formalization of a large fragment of our small-step semantics in the proof assistant F* [24]. At the time of writing, we are formalizing the remaining part, which only consists of straightforward local operations, such as bitwise operators and opcodes to write code to (resp. read code from) the memory.

F* is an ML-dialect that is optimized for program verification and allows for performing manual proofs as well as automated proofs leveraging the power of SMT solvers.

Our formalization strictly follows the small-step semantics as presented in this paper. The core functionality is implemented by the function step that describes how an execution stack evolves within one execution state. To this end it has two possible outcomes: either it performs an execution step and returns the new callstack or – in the case that a final configuration is reached (which is a stack containing only one element that is either a halting or an exception state) – it reports the final state. In order to provide a total function for the step relation, we needed to introduce a third execution outcome that signalizes that a problem occurred due to an inconsistent state. When running the semantics from a valid initial configuration this result, however, should never be produced. For running the semantics, the function execution is defined that subsequently performs execution steps using step until reaching the final state and reports it.

The current implementation encompasses approximately thousand lines of code. Since F* code can be compiled into OCaml, we validate our semantics against the official EVM test suite [25]. Our semantics passes 304 out of 624 tests, failing only in those involving any of the missing functionalities.

We make the formalization in F* publicly available [22] in order to facilitate the design of static analysis techniques for EVM bytecode as well as their soundness proofs.

3.7 Comparison with the Semantics by Luu et al. [21]

The small-step semantics defined by Luu et al. [21] encompasses only a variation of a subset of EVM bytecode instructions (called EtherLite) and assumes a heavily simplified execution configuration. The instructions covered span simple stack operations for pushing and popping values, conditional branches, binary operations, instructions for accessing and altering local memory and account storage, as well as as the ones for calling, returning and destructing the account. Essential instructions as CREATE and those for accessing the transaction and block information are omitted. The authors represent a configuration as a tuple of a call stack of activation records and the global state. An activation record contains the code to be executed, the program counter, the local memory and the machine stack. The global state is modelled as mapping from addresses to accounts, with the latter consisting of code, balance and persistent storage.

The overall abstraction contains a conceptual flaw, as not including the global state in the activation records of the call stack does not allow for modelling that, in the case of an exception in the execution of the callee, the global state is rolled back to the one of the caller at the point of calling. In addition, the model cannot be easily extended with further instructions – such as further call instructions or instructions accessing the environment – without major changes in the abstraction as a lot of information, e.g., the one captured in our small-step semantics in the transaction and the execution environment, are missing.

4 Security Definitions

In the following, we introduce the semantic characterization of the most significant security properties for smart contracts, motivating them with typical vulnerabilities recurring in the wild.

For selecting those properties, we inspected the classification of bugs performed in [13,21]. To our knowledge, these are the only works published so far that aim at systematically summarizing bugs in Ethereum smart contracts.

For the presented bugs, we synthesized the semantic security properties that were violated. In this process we realized that some bugs share the same underlying property violation and that other bugs can not be captured by such generic properties – either because they are of a purely syntactic nature or because they constitute a derivation from a desired behavior that is particular to a specific contract.

Preliminary Notations. Formally, we represent a contract as a tuple of the form $(a, code)$ where $a \in \mathcal{A}$ denotes the address of the contract and $code \in [\mathbb{B}]$ denotes the contract's code. We denote the set of contracts by $\mathcal{C}$ and assume functions $address\,(\cdot)$ and $code\,(\cdot)$ that extract the contract address and code respectively.

As we will argue about contracts being called in an arbitrary setting, we additionally introduce the notion of *reachable configuration*. Intuitively, a pair (Γ, S) of a transaction environment Γ and a call stack S is reachable if there exists a state s such that S, s are the result of $initialize\,(T, H, \sigma)$, for some transaction T, block header H, a global state σ, and S is reachable from s.

Definition 1 (Reachable Configuration). *The pair* $(\Gamma, A) \in \mathcal{T}_{env} \times \mathcal{S}$ *is a reachable configuration if for some transaction* $T \in \mathcal{T}$, *some block header* $H \in \mathcal{H}$ *and some global state* $\sigma \in \mathcal{A} \to \mathbb{A}$ *of the blockchain it holds that*

$$(\Gamma, s) = initialize\,(T, H, \sigma) \wedge \Gamma \vDash s :: \epsilon \to^* S$$

In order to give concise security definitions, we further introduce, and assume throughout the paper, an annotation to the small step semantics in order to highlight the contract c that is currently executed. In the case of initialization code being executed, we use $\bot$. Specifically, we let

$$\mathbb{S}_n := \{EXC_c :: S_{plain}, \; HALT(\sigma, gas, \eta, d)_c :: S_{plain}, \; S_{plain}$$

$$| \; \sigma \in \Sigma, \; gas \in \mathbb{N}, \; d \in [\mathbb{B}^8], \; \eta \in N, \; S_{plain} \in \mathcal{L}((M \times I \times \Sigma \times N) \times \mathcal{C})\}$$

where $c \in \mathcal{C} \cup \{\bot\} = \mathcal{C}_\bot$.

Next, we introduce the notion of execution trace for smart contract execution. Intuitively, a trace is a sequence of actions. In our setting, the actions to be recorded are composed of an opcode, the address of the executing contract, and a sequence of arguments to the opcode. We denote the set of actions with Act. Accordingly, every small step produces a trace consisting of a single action. Again, we lift the resulting trace semantics to multiple execution steps that then produce sequences of actions $\pi \in \mathcal{L}(Act)$. We only report the trace semantics definition for the CALL case here, referring to the full version of the paper for the details [22].

$$\frac{\iota.code\,[\mu.\mathsf{pc}] = \mathsf{CALL} \qquad \mu.\mathsf{s} = g :: to :: va :: io :: is :: oo :: os :: s \quad \cdots \quad \mu' = \cdots \quad \iota' = \cdots \quad \sigma' = \cdots}{\Gamma \vDash (\mu,\iota,\sigma)_c :: S \xrightarrow{\mathsf{CALL}_c\,(g,to,io,is,oo,os)} (\mu',\iota',\sigma')_{to} :: (\mu,\iota,\sigma)_c :: S}$$

We will write $\pi \downarrow_{\mathsf{calls}_c}$ to denote the projection of π to calls performed by contract c, i.e., actions of the form $\mathsf{CALL}_c(g, to, va, io, is, oo, os)$, $\mathsf{CREATE}_c(va, io, is)$, $\mathsf{CALLCODE}_c(g, to, va, io, is, oo, os)$, and $\mathsf{DELEGATECALL}_c(g, to, io, is, oo, os)$.

4.1 Call Integrity

Dependency on Attacker Code. One of the most famous bugs of Ethereum's history is the so called DAO bug that led to a loss of 60 million dollars in June 2016 [10]. This bug is in the literature classified as reentrancy bug [13,21] as the affected contract was drained out of money by subsequently reentering it and performing transactions to the attacker on behalf of the contract. More generally, the problem of this contract was that malicious code was able to affect the outgoing money flows of the contract. The cause of such bugs mostly roots in the developer's misunderstanding of the semantics of Solidity's call primitives. In general, calling a contract can invoke two kinds of actions: Transferring Ether to the contract's account or Executing (parts of) a contracts code. In particular, the call construct invokes the called contract's fallback function when no particular function of the contract is specified (2). Consequently, the developer may expect an atomic value transfer where potentially another contract's code is executed. For illustrating how to exploit this sort of bug, we consider the following contracts:

```
1  contract Bob{
2      bool sent = false;
3      function ping( address c){
4          if (!sent) { c.call.value(2)();
5                      sent = true; }}}
```

```
1  contract Mallory{
2      function (){
3          Bob(msg.sender).ping(this);}}
```

The function ping of contract Bob sends an amount of 2 *wei* to the address specified in the argument. However, this should only be possible once, which is potentially ensured by the sent variable that is set after the successful money transfer. Instead, it turns out that invoking the call.value function on a contract's address invokes the contract's fallback function as well.

Given a second contract Mallory, it is possible to transfer more money than the intended 2 *wei* to the account of Mallory. By invoking Bob's function ping with the address of Mallory's account, 2 *wei* are transferred to Mallory's account and additionally the fallback function of Mallory is invoked. As the fallback function again calls the ping function with Mallory's address another 2 *wei* are transferred before the variable sent of contract Bob was set. This looping goes on until all gas of the initial call is consumed or the callstack limit is reached. In this case, only the last transfer of *wei* is reverted and the effects of all former calls stay in place. Consequently the intended restriction on contract Bob's `ping` function (namely to only transfer 2 *wei* once) is circumvented.

Call Integrity. In order to protect from this class of bugs, it is crucial to secure the code against being reentered before regaining control over the control flow. From a security perspective, the fundamental problem is that the contract behaviour depends on untrusted code, even though this was not intended by the developer. We capture this intuition through a hyperproperty, which we name *call integrity*. The idea is that no matter how the attacker can schedule c (callstacks S and S' in the definition), the calls of c (traces π, π') cannot be controlled by the attacker, even if c hands over the control to the attacker.

Definition 2 (Call Integrity). *A contract $c \in C$ satisfies call integrity for a set of addresses $\mathcal{A}_C \subseteq \mathcal{A}$ if for all reachable configurations $(\Gamma, s_c :: S), (\Gamma, s'_c :: S')$ with s, s' differing only in the code with address in $\mathcal{A}_C$, it holds that for all t, t'*

$$\Gamma \vDash s_c :: S \xrightarrow{\pi}{}^* t_c :: S \wedge final(t_c) \wedge \Gamma \vDash s'_c :: S' \xrightarrow{\pi'}{}^* t'_c :: S' \wedge final(t'_c)$$
$$\implies \pi \downarrow_{calls_c} = \pi' \downarrow_{calls_c}$$

4.2   Proof Technique for Call Integrity

We now establish a proof technique for call integrity, based on local properties that are arguably easier to verify and that we show to imply call integrity. As a first observation, we identify the different ways in which external contracts can influence the execution of a smart contract c and introduce corresponding security properties:

Code Dependency. The contract c might access (information on) the untrusted contracts code via the EXTCODECOPY or the EXTCODESIZE instructions and make his behaviour depend on those values;

Effect Dependency. The contract c might call the untrusted contract and might depend on its execution effects and return value;

Re-entrancy. The contract c might call the untrusted contract, with the latter influencing the behaviour of the former by performing changes to the global state itself or "on behalf" of c by reentering it and thereby potentially decreasing the balance of c.

The first two of these properties can be seen as value dependencies and therefore can be formalized as hyperproperties. The first property says that the calls performed by a contract should not be affected by the effects on the execution state produced by adversarial contracts. Technically, we consider a contract c calling an adversarial contract c' (captured as $\Gamma \vDash s_c :: S \to s''_{c'} :: s_c :: S$ in the premise), which we let terminate in two arbitrary states s', t': we require that c's continuation code performs the same calls in both states.

Definition 3 ($\mathcal{A}_C$-effect Independence). *A contract $c \in \mathcal{C}$ is $\mathcal{A}_C$-effect independent of for a set of addresses $\mathcal{A}_C \subseteq \mathcal{A}$ if for all reachable configurations $(\Gamma, s_c :: S)$ such that $\Gamma \vDash s_c :: S \rightarrow s''_{c'} :: s_c :: S$ for some s'' and address $(c') \in \mathcal{A}_C$, it holds that for all final states s', t' whose global state might differ in all components but the code from the global state of s,*

$$\Gamma_{init} \vDash s'_{c'} :: s_c :: S \xrightarrow{\pi}^{*} s''_c :: S \wedge \mathit{final}(s'')$$

$$\wedge\ \Gamma_{init} \vDash t'_{c'} :: s_c :: S \xrightarrow{\pi'}^{*} t''_c :: S \wedge \mathit{final}(t'')$$

$$\implies \pi \downarrow_{calls_c} = \pi' \downarrow_{calls_c}$$

The second property says that the calls of a contract should not be affected by the code read from the blockchain (e.g., the code does not branch on code read from the blockchain). To this end we introduce the notation $\Gamma \vdash s :: S \xrightarrow{\pi}_{f}^{*} s' :: S$ to denote that the local small-step execution of state s on stack S under Γ results in several steps in state s' producing trace π given that in the local execution steps of EXTCODECOPY and EXTCODESIZE, which are the operations used to access the code on the global state, the code returned by these functions is determined by the partial function $f \in \mathcal{A} \twoheadrightarrow [\mathbb{B}]$ as opposed to the global state. In other words, we consider in the premise a contract c reading two different codes from the blockchain and terminating in both runs (captured as $\Gamma \vdash s_c :: S \xrightarrow{\pi}_{f}^{*}$ $s'_c :: S$ and $\Gamma \vdash s_c :: S \xrightarrow{\pi'}_{f'}^{*} s''_c :: S$), and we require that c performs the same calls in both runs.

Definition 4 ($\mathcal{A}_C$-code Independence). *A contract $c \in \mathcal{C}$ is $\mathcal{A}_C$-code independent for a set of addresses $\mathcal{A}_C \subseteq \mathcal{A}$ if for all reachable configurations $(\Gamma, s_c :: S)$ it holds for all local code updates $f, f' \in \mathcal{A} \twoheadrightarrow [\mathbb{B}]$ on $\mathcal{A}_C$ that*

$$\Gamma \vdash s_c :: S \xrightarrow{\pi}_{f}^{*} s'_c :: S \wedge \mathit{final}(s') \wedge \Gamma \vdash s_c :: S \xrightarrow{\pi'}_{f'}^{*} s''_c :: S \wedge \mathit{final}(s'')$$

$$\implies \pi \downarrow_{calls_c} = \pi' \downarrow_{calls_c}$$

Both these independence properties can be overapproximated by static analysis techniques based on program dependence graphs [26], as done by Joana to verify non-interference in Java [27]. The idea is to traverse the dependence graph in order to detect dependencies between the sensitive sources, in our case the data controlled by the adversary and returned to the contract, and the observable sinks, in our case the local contract calls.

The last property constitutes a safety property. Specifically, single-entrancy states that it cannot happen that when reentering the contract c another call is performed before returning (i.e., after reentrancy, which we capture in the call stack as two distinct states with the same running contract c, the call stack cannot further increase).

Definition 5 (Single-entrancy). *A contract $c \in C$ is single-entrant if for all reachable configurations $(\Gamma, s_c :: S)$, it holds for all s', s'', S' that*

$$\Gamma \vDash s_c :: S \rightarrow^* s'_c :: S' + + s_c :: S$$
$$\implies \neg \exists s'' \in \mathcal{S}, c' \in \mathcal{C}_{\bot}. \Gamma \vDash s'_c :: S' + + s_c :: S \rightarrow^* s''_{c'} :: s'_c :: S' + + s_c :: S$$

This safety property can be easily overapproximated by syntactic conditions, as for instance done in the Oyente analyzer [21].

Finally, the next theorem proves the soundness of our proof technique, i.e., the two independence properties and the single-entrancy property together entail call integrity.

Theorem 1. *Let $c \in C$ be a contract and $\mathcal{A}_C \subseteq \mathcal{A}$ be a set of untrusted addresses. If c is $\mathcal{A}_C$-local independent, c is $\mathcal{A}_C$-effect independent, and c is single-entrant then c provides call integrity for $\mathcal{A}_C$.*

Proof Sketch. Let $(\Gamma, s_c :: S), (\Gamma, s'_c :: S')$ be reachable configurations such that s, s' differ only in the code with address in $\mathcal{A}_C$. We now compare the two small-step runs of those configurations. Due to $\mathcal{A}_C$-code independence, the execution until the first call to an address $a \in \mathcal{A}_C$ produces the same partial trace until the call to a. Indeed, we can express the runs under different address mappings through the code update from the $\mathcal{A}_C$-code independence property, as long as no call to one of the updated addresses is performed. When a first call to $a \in \mathcal{A}_C$ is performed, we know due to single-entrancy that the following call cannot produce any partial execution trace for any of the runs as this would imply that contract c is reentered and a call out of the contract is performed. Due to $\mathcal{A}_C$-code independence and $\mathcal{A}_C$-effect independence , the traces after returning must coincide till the next call to an address in $\mathcal{A}_C$. This argument can be iteratively applied until reaching the final state of the execution of c.

4.3   Atomicity

Exception Handling. As discussed in Sect. 2, the way exceptions are propagated varies with the way contracts are called. In particular, in the case of `call` and `send`, exceptions are not propagated, but a manual check for the successful completion of the called function's execution is required. This behavior reflects the way exceptions are reported during bytecode execution: Instead of propagating up through the call stack, the callee reports the exception to the caller by writing zero to the stack. In the context of Ethereum, the issue of exception handling is particularly delicate as due to the gas restriction, it might always happen that a call fails simply because it ran out of gas. Intuitively, a user would expect a contract not to depend on the concrete gas value that is given to it, with the exception that a contract might always fail completely (and consequently does not perform any changes on the global state). Such a behavior would prevent contracts from entering an inconsistent state as the one presented in the following excerpt of a simple banking contract:

```
1  contract SimpleBank{mapping( address => uint) balances;
2    function withdraw(){ msg.sender.send(balances[msg.sender]));
3      balances[msg.sender] = 0;}}
```

The contract keeps a record of the user balances and provides a function that allows a user to withdraw its own balance – which results in an update of the record. A developer might not expect that the send might fail, but as it is on the bytecode level represented by a CALL instruction, additional to the Ether transfer, code might be executed that runs out of gas. As a consequence, the contract would end up in a state where the money was not transferred (as all effects of the call are reverted in case of an exception), but still the internal balance record of the contract was updated and consequently the money cannot be withdrawn by the owner anymore.

Inspired by such situations where an inconsistent state is entered by a contract due to mishandled gas exceptions, we introduce the notion of *atomicity* of a contract. Intuitively, atomicity requires that the effects of the execution on the global state do not depend on the amount of gas available – except when an exception is triggered, in which case the overall execution should have no effect at all. The last condition is captured by requiring that the final global state is the same as the initial one for at least one of the two executions (intuitively, the one causing the exception).

Definition 6. *A contract $c \in C$ satisfies atomicity if for all reachable configurations (Γ, S') such that $\Gamma \vDash S' \to s_c :: S$, it holds for all gas values $g, g' \in \mathbb{N}_{256}$ that*

$$\Gamma \vDash s_c[\mu.gas \to g] :: S \to^* s'_c :: S \wedge final(s')$$
$$\wedge \ \Gamma \vDash s_c[\mu.gas \to g'] :: S \to^* s''_c :: S \wedge final(s'')$$
$$\implies s'.\sigma = s''.\sigma \vee s.\sigma = s'.\sigma \vee s.\sigma = s''.\sigma$$

4.4   Independence of Miner Controlled Parameters

Another particularity of the distributed blockchain environment is that users while performing transactions cannot make assumptions on large parts of the context their transaction will be executed in. A part of this is due to the asynchronous nature of the system: it can always be that another transaction that alters the context was performed first. Actually, the situation is even more delicate as transactions are not processed in a first-come-first-serve manner, but miners have a big influence on the execution context of transactions. They can decide upon the order of the transactions in a block (and also sneak their own transactions in first) and in addition they can even control some parameters as the block timestamp within a certain range. Consequently, contracts whose (outgoing) money flows depend either on miner controlled block information or on state information (as the state of their storage or their balance) that might be changed by other transactions are prone to manipulations by miners. A typical example adduced in the literature is the use of block timestamps as source of randomness [13,21]. In a classical lottery implementation that randomly pays out to one of the participants and uses the block timestamp as source of randomness, a malicious miner can easily influence the result in his favor by selecting a beneficial timestamp.

We capture the absence of the miner's influence by two definitions, one saying that the outgoing Ether flows of a contract should not be influenced by components of the transaction environment that can be (within a certain range) set by miners and the other one saying that the Ether flows should not depend on those parts of the contract state that might have been influenced by previously executed transactions. The first definition rules out what is in the literature often described as timestamp dependency [13,21].

First, we define *independence of* (parts of) *the transaction environment.* To this end, we assume $\mathcal{C}_\Gamma$ to be the set of components of the transaction environment and write $\Gamma =_{/c_\Gamma} \Gamma'$ to denote that the transaction environments Γ, Γ' are equal up to component c_Γ.

Definition 7 (Independence of the Transaction Environment). *A contract $c \in \mathcal{C}$ is independent of a subset $I \subseteq \mathcal{C}_\Gamma$ of components of the transaction environment if for all $c_\Gamma \in I$ and all reachable configurations $(\Gamma, s_c :: S)$ it holds for all Γ' that*

$$c_\Gamma(\Gamma) \neq c_\Gamma(\Gamma') \wedge \Gamma =_{/c_\Gamma} \Gamma'$$

$$\wedge \, \Gamma \vDash s_c :: S \xrightarrow{\pi}{}^* s'_c :: S \, \wedge \, \mathit{final}(s') \, \wedge \, \Gamma' \vDash s_c :: S \xrightarrow{\pi'}{}^* s''_c :: S \, \wedge \, \mathit{final}(s'')$$

$$\implies \pi \downarrow_{\mathit{calls}_c} = \pi' \downarrow_{\mathit{calls}_c}$$

Next, we define the notion of *independence of the account state.* Formally, we capture this property by requiring that the outgoing Ether flows of the contract under consideration should not be affected by those parameters of the contract that might have been changed by previous executions which are the balance, the account's nonce, and the account's persistent storage.

Definition 8 (Independence of Mutable Account State). *A contract $c \in \mathcal{C}$ is independent of the account state if for all reachable configurations $(\Gamma, s_c :: S), (\Gamma, s_c :: S')$ with s, s' differing only in the nonce, balance and storage for address(c), it holds that*

$$\Gamma \vDash s_c :: S \xrightarrow{\pi}{}^* s'_c :: S \, \wedge \, \mathit{final}(s'_c) \, \wedge \, \Gamma \vDash s_c :: S' \xrightarrow{\pi'}{}^* s''_c :: S \, \wedge \, \mathit{final}(s''_c)$$

$$\implies \pi \downarrow_{\mathit{calls}_c} = \pi' \downarrow_{\mathit{calls}_c}$$

As far the other independence properties, both these properties can be statically verified using program dependence graphs.

4.5   Classification of Bugs

The previously presented security definitions are motivated by the bugs that
were observed in real Ethereum smart contracts and studied in [13,21]. Table 1
gives an overview on the bugs from the literature that are ruled out by our
security properties.

Table 1. Bugs from [13,21] ruled out by the security properties

Security property	Bug
Call integrity	Reentrancy [13,21]
	Call to the unknown [13]
Atomicity	Mishandled exceptions [13,21]
Independence of mutable account state	Transaction order dependency [21]
	Unpredictable state [13]
Independence of transaction environment	Timestamp dependancy [21]
	Time constraints [13]
	Generating randomness [13]

Our security properties do not cover all bugs described by Atzei et al. [13],
as some of the bugs do not constitute violations of general security properties,
i.e., properties that are not specific to the particular contract implementation.
There are two classes of bugs that we do not consider: The first class deals
with the occurrence of unexpected exceptions (such as the Gasless Send and
the Call stack Limit bug) and the second class encompasses bugs caused by
the Solidity semantics deviating from the programmer's intuitions (such as the
Keeping Secrets, Type Cast and Exception Disorders bugs).

The first class of bugs encompasses runtime exceptions that are hard to
predict for the developer and that are consequently not handled correctly. Of
course, it would be possible to formalize the absence of those particular kinds
of exceptions as simple reachability properties using the small-step semantics.
Still, such properties would not give any insight about the security of a contract:
the fact that a particular exception occurs can be unproblematic in the case
that proper exception handling is in place. In general, the notion of a correct
exception handling highly depends on the specific contract's intended behavior.
For the special case of out-of-gas exceptions, we could introduce the notion of
atomicity in order to capture a generic goal of proper exception handling. But
such a notion is not necessarily sufficient for characterizing reasonable ways of
dealing with other kinds of runtime exceptions.

The second class of bugs are introduced on the Solidity level and are similarly
hard to account for by using generic security properties. Even though these
bugs might all originate from similar idiosyncrasies of the Solidity semantics,
the impact of the bugs on the contract's semantics might deviate a lot. This

might result in violations of the security properties discussed before, but also in violating the contract's functional correctness. Consequently, catching those bugs might require the introduction of contract-specific correctness properties.

Finally, Atzei et al. [13] discuss the Ether Lost in Transfer bug. This bug is introduced by sending Ether to addresses that do not belong to any contract or user, so called orphan addresses. We could easily formalize a reachability property stating that no valid contract execution should ever send Ether to such an address. We omit such a definition here as it is quite straightforward and at the same time it is not a property that directly affects the security of an individual contract: Sending Ether to such an orphan address might have negative impacts on the overall system as money is effectively lost. For the specific contract sending this money, this bug can be seen as a corner case of sending Ether to an unintended address which rather constitutes a correctness violation.

4.6   Discussion

As previously discussed, we are not aware of any prior formal security definitions of smart contracts. Nevertheless, we compared our definitions with the verification conditions used in Oyente [21]. Our investigation shows that the verification conditions adopted in this tool are neither sound nor complete.

For detecting mishandled exceptions, it is checked whether each CALL instruction in the contract code is directly followed by the ISZERO instruction that checks whether the top element of the stack is zero. Unfortunately, Oyente (although stated in the paper) does not implement this check, so that we needed to manually inspect the bytecodes for determining the outcomes of the syntactic check. As shown in Fig. 2a a check for the caller returning zero does not necessarily imply a proper exception handling and therefore atomicity of the contract. This excerpt of a simple banking contract that keeps track of the users' balances and allows users to withdraw their balances using the function withdraw checks for the success of the performed call, but still does not react accordingly. It only makes sure that the number of successes is updated consistently, but does not perform the update on the user's balance record according to the call outcome.

On the other hand, not performing the desired check does not imply the absence of atomicity as illustrated in Fig. 2b. Writing the outcome in some variable before checking it, satisfies the negative pattern, but still correct exception handling is performed. For detecting timestamp dependency, Oyente checks whether the contract has a symbolic execution path with the timestamp (that is represented as own symbolic variable) being included in one of its constraints. This definition however, does not capture the case shown in Fig. 2c.

This contract is clearly timestamp dependent as whether or not the function pay pays out some money to the sender depends on the timestamp set when creating the contract. A malicious miner could consequently manipulate the block timestamp for a transaction that creates such a contract in a way that money is paid out and then subsequently query it for draining it out. This is however, not captured by the characterization of the property in Oyente as they only capture the local execution paths of the contract.

```
1  contract SimpleBank{                          1  contract SimpleBank{
2    mapping( address => uint) bal;              2    mapping( address => uint) bal;
3    uint successes;                             4    function withdraw(){
4    function withdraw(){                        4      bool b =
5      if (msg.sender.send(bal[msg.sender]))     5        msg.sender.send(bal[msg.sender]);
6      { successes++; }                          6      if (b) bal[msg.sender] = 0;}}
7    bal[msg.sender] = 0;}}
```

(a)   (b)

```
1  contract Test{                                1  contract Test {
2    uint time = block.timestamp;                2    function pay (){
3    function pay (){                             3      if (block.timestamp % 2 == 1 ||
4      if (time % 2 == 1){                        4      block.timestamp % 2 == 0){
5        msg.sender.send(100);}}}                 5        msg.sender.send(100);}}}
```

(c)   (d)

```
                                                 1  contract Bob{
1  contract Fund{                                2    bool sent = false;
2    mapping( address => uint) shares;           3    function ping( address c){
3    function withdraw(){                         4      if (!sent) {
4      if (msg.sender.send(shares[msg.sender]))   5        sent = true;
5      shares[msg.sender] = 0;}}                  6        c.call.value(2)();}}}
```

(e)   (f)

Fig. 2. (a) Exception handling: false negative (b) Exception handling: false positive
(c) Timestamp dependency: false negative (d) Timestamp dependency: false positive
(e) Reentrancy: false negative (f) Reentrancy: false positive

On the other hand, using the block timestamp in path constraints does not imply a dependency as can easily be seen by the example in Fig. 2d.

For the transaction order dependency and the reentrancy property, we were unfortunately not able to reconcile the property characterization provided in the paper with the implementation of Oyente.

For checking reentrancy according to the paper, it should be checked whether the constraints on the path leading to a CALL instruction can still be satisfied after performing the updates on the path (e.g. changing the storage). If so, the contract is flagged as reentrant. According to our understanding, this approach should not flag contracts that correctly guard their calls as reentrant. Still, by the version of Oyente provided with the paper the contract in Fig. 2f is tagged as reentrant.

There exists an updated version of Oyente [28] that is able to precisely tag this contract as not reentrant, but we could not find any concrete information on the criteria used for checking this property. Still, we found out that the underlying characterization can not be sufficient for detecting reentrancy as the contract in Fig. 2e is classified not to exhibit a reentrancy vulnerability even though it should as the send command also executes the recipient's callback function (even though with limited gas). The example is taken from the Solidity documentation [23] where it is listed as negative example. For transaction order dependency, Oyente should check whether execution traces exhibiting different Ether flows exists. But it turned out that not even a simple example of a transaction dependent contract can be detected by any of the versions of Oyente.

5 Conclusions

We presented the first complete small-step semantics of EVM bytecode and formalized a large fragment thereof in the F* proof assistant, successfully validating it against the official Ethereum test suite. We further defined for the first time a number of salient security properties for smart contracts, relying on a combination of hyper- and safety properties. Our framework is available to the academic community in order to facilitate future research on rigorous security analysis of smart contracts.

In particular, this work opens up a number of interesting research directions. First, it would be interesting to formalize in F* the semantics of Solidity code and a compiler from Solidity into EVM, formally proving its soundness against our semantics. This would allow us to provide software developers with a tool to verify the security of their code, from which they could obtain bytecode that is secure by construction. Second, we intend to design an efficient static analysis technique for EVM bytecode and to formally prove its soundness against our semantics.

Acknowledgments. This work has been partially supported by the European Research Council (ERC) under the European Union's Horizon 2020 research (grant agreement No 771527-BROWSEC), by Netidee through the project EtherTrust (grant agreement 2158), and by the Austrian Research Promotion Agency through the Bridge-1 project PR4DLT (grant agreement 13808694).

References

1. Nakamoto, S.: Bitcoin: a peer-to-peer electronic cash system (2008). http://bitcoin. org/bitcoin.pdf
2. Biryukov, A., Khovratovich, D., Tikhomirov, S.: Findel: secure derivative contracts for Ethereum. In: Brenner, M., Rohloff, K., Bonneau, J., Miller, A., Ryan, P.Y.A., Teague, V., Bracciali, A., Sala, M., Pintore, F., Jakobsson, M. (eds.) FC 2017. LNCS, vol. 10323, pp. 453–467. Springer, Cham (2017). https://doi. org/10.1007/978-3-319-70278-0_28. http://orbilu.uni.lu/bitstream/10993/30975/ 1/Findel_2017-03-08-CR.pdf
3. Hahn, A., Singh, R., Liu, C.C., Chen, S.: Smart contract-based campus demonstration of decentralized transactive energy auctions. In: 2017 IEEE Power and Energy Society Innovative Smart Grid Technologies Conference (ISGT), pp. 1–5. IEEE (2017)
4. McCorry, P., Shahandashti, S.F., Hao, F.: A smart contract for boardroom voting with maximum voter privacy. In: Kiayias, A. (ed.) FC 2017. LNCS, vol. 10322, pp. 357–375. Springer, Cham (2017). https://doi.org/10.1007/978-3-319-70972-7_20
5. Adhikari, C.: Secure framework for healthcare data management using Ethereum-based blockchain technology (2017)

6. Notheisen, B., Gödde, M., Weinhardt, C.: Trading stocks on blocks-engineering decentralized markets. In: Maedche, A., vom Brocke, J., Hevner, A. (eds.) DESRIST 2017. LNCS, vol. 10243, pp. 474–478. Springer, Cham (2017). https://doi.org/10.1007/978-3-319-59144-5_34

7. Mathieu, F., Mathee, R.: Blocktix: decentralized event hosting and ticket distribution network (2017). https://blocktix.io/public/doc/blocktix-wp-draft.pdf

8. Azaria, A., Ekblaw, A., Vieira, T., Lippman, A.: MedRec: using blockchain for medical data access and permission management. In: International Conference on Open and Big Data (OBD), pp. 25–30. IEEE (2016)

9. Dong, C., Wang, Y., Aldweesh, A., McCorry, P., van Moorsel, A.: Betrayal, distrust, and rationality: smart counter-collusion contracts for verifiable cloud computing (2017)

10. The DAO smart contract (2016). http://etherscan.io/address/0xbb9bc244d798123 fde783fcc1c72d3bb8c189413#code

11. The parity wallet breach (2017). https://www.coindesk.com/30-million-ether-reported-stolen-parity-wallet-breach/

12. The parity wallet vulnerability (2017). https://paritytech.io/blog/security-alert.html

13. Atzei, N., Bartoletti, M., Cimoli, T.: A survey of attacks on Ethereum smart contracts (SoK). In: Maffei, M., Ryan, M. (eds.) POST 2017. LNCS, vol. 10204, pp. 164–186. Springer, Heidelberg (2017). https://doi.org/10.1007/978-3-662-54455-6_8

14. Wood, G.: Ethereum: a secure decentralised generalised transaction ledger. Ethereum Project Yellow Paper **151** (2014). https://ethereum.github.io/yellowpaper/paper.pdf

15. Hirai, Y.: Defining the Ethereum virtual machine for interactive theorem provers. In: Brenner, M., Rohloff, K., Bonneau, J., Miller, A., Ryan, P.Y.A., Teague, V., Bracciali, A., Sala, M., Pintore, F., Jakobsson, M. (eds.) FC 2017. LNCS, vol. 10323, pp. 520–535. Springer, Cham (2017). https://doi.org/10.1007/978-3-319-70278-0_33

16. Hildenbrandt, E., Saxena, M., Zhu, X., Rodrigues, N., Daian, P., Guth, D., Rosu, G.: KEVM: a complete semantics of the Ethereum virtual machine. http://hdl.handle.net/2142/97207

17. Stefǎnescu, A., Park, D., Yuwen, S., Li, Y., Roşu, G.: Semantics-based program verifiers for all languages. In: Proceedings of the 2016 ACM SIGPLAN International Conference on Object-Oriented Programming, Systems, Languages, and Applications, pp. 74–91. ACM (2016)

18. Sergey, I., Hobor, A.: A concurrent perspective on smart contracts. arXiv preprint arXiv:1702.05511 (2017)

19. Mavridou, A., Laszka, A.: Designing secure ethereum smart contracts: a finite state machine based approach. http://aronlaszka.com/papers/mavridou2018designing.pdf

20. Bhargavan, K., Delignat-Lavaud, A., Fournet, C., Gollamudi, A., Gonthier, G., Kobeissi, N., Kulatova, N., Rastogi, A., Sibut-Pinote, T., Swamy, N., Zanella-Béguelin, S.: Formal verification of smart contracts: short paper. In: Proceedings of the 2016 ACM Workshop on Programming Languages and Analysis for Security, pp. 91–96. ACM (2016)

21. Luu, L., Chu, D.H., Olickel, H., Saxena, P., Hobor, A.: Making smart contracts smarter. In: Proceedings of the 2016 ACM SIGSAC Conference on Computer and Communications Security, pp. 254–269. ACM (2016)

22. Grishchenko, I., Maffei, M., Schneidewind, C.: A semantic framework for the security analysis of Ethereum smart contracts. Technical report (2018). https://secpriv.tuwien.ac.at/tools/ethsemantics
23. Solidity documentation. http://solidity.readthedocs.io/en/develop/
24. F*. https://fstar-lang.org
25. Consensus test suite. https://github.com/ethereum/tests
26. Hammer, C., Snelting, G.: Flow-sensitive, context-sensitive, and object-sensitive information flow control based on program dependence graphs. Int. J. Inf. Secur. 8(6), 399–422 (2009)
27. Snelting, G., Giffhorn, D., Graf, J., Hammer, C., Hecker, M., Mohr, M., Wasserrab, D.: Checking probabilistic noninterference using JOANA. IT - Inf. Technol. 56, 280–287 (2014)
28. Luu, L., Chu, D.H., Olickel, H., Saxena, P., Hobor, A.: An analysis tool for smart contracts. https://github.com/melonproject/oyente

Tool Demonstration: FSolidM for Designing Secure Ethereum Smart Contracts

Anastasia Mavridou[1] and Aron Laszka[2(✉)]

[1] Vanderbilt University, Nashville, USA
[2] University of Houston, Houston, USA
alaszka@uh.edu

Abstract. Blockchain-based distributed computing platforms enable the trusted execution of computation—defined in the form of *smart contracts*—without trusted agents. Smart contracts are envisioned to have a variety of applications, ranging from financial to IoT asset tracking. Unfortunately, the development of smart contracts has proven to be extremely error prone. In practice, contracts are riddled with security vulnerabilities comprising a critical issue since bugs are by design non-fixable and contracts may handle financial assets of significant value. To facilitate the development of secure smart contracts, we have created the *FSolidM* framework, which allows developers to define contracts as finite state machines (FSMs) with rigorous and clear semantics. FSolidM provides an easy-to-use graphical editor for specifying FSMs, a code generator for creating Ethereum smart contracts, and a set of plugins that developers may add to their FSMs to enhance security and functionality.

Keywords: Smart contract · Security · Finite state machine
Ethereum · Solidity · Automatic code generation · Design patterns

1 Introduction

In recent years, blockchains have seen wide adoption. For instance, the market capitalization of Bitcoin, the leading blockchain-based cryptocurrency, has grown from $15 billion to more than $100 billion in 2017. The goal of the first generation of blockchains was only to provide cryptocurrencies and payment systems. In contrast, more recent blockchains, such as Ethereum, strive to provide distributed computing platforms [1,2]. Blockchain-based distributed computing platforms enable the trusted execution of general purpose computation, implemented in the form of *smart contracts*, without any trusted parties. Blockchains and smart contracts are envisioned to have a variety of applications, ranging from finance to IoT asset tracking [3]. As a result, they are embraced by an increasing number of organizations and companies, including major IT and financial firms, such as Cisco, IBM, Wells Fargo, and J.P. Morgan [4].

© The Author(s) 2018
L. Bauer and R. Küsters (Eds.): POST 2018, LNCS 10804, pp. 270–277, 2018.
https://doi.org/10.1007/978-3-319-89722-6_11

However, the development of smart contracts has proven to be extremely error prone in practice. Recently, an automated analysis of a large sample of smart contracts from the Ethereum blockchain found that more than 43% of contracts have security issues [5]. These issues often result in security vulnerabilities, which may be exploited by cyber-criminals to steal cryptocurrencies and other digital assets. For instance, in 2016, $50 million worth of cryptocurrencies were stolen in the infamous "The DAO" attack, which exploited a combination of smart-contract vulnerabilities [6]. In addition to theft, malicious attackers may also be able to cause damage by leading a smart contract into a deadlock, which prevents account holders from spending or withdrawing their own assets.

The prevalence of smart-contract vulnerabilities poses a severe problem in practice due to multiple reasons. First, smart contracts handle assets of significant financial value: at the time of writing, contracts deployed on the Ethereum blockchain together hold more than $6 billion worth of cryptocurrency. Second, it is *by design* impossible to fix bugs in a contract (or change its functionality in any way) once the contract has been deployed. Third, due to the "code is law" principle [7], it is also *by design* impossible to remove a faulty or malicious transaction from the blockchain, which means that it is often impossible to recover from a security incident.[1]

Previous work focused on alleviating security issues in *existing* smart contracts by providing tools for verifying correctness [7] and for identifying common vulnerabilities [5]. In contrast, we take a different approach by developing a framework, called *FSolidM* [9], which helps developers to create smart contracts that are secure by design. The main features of our framework are as follows.

Formal Model: One of the key factors contributing to the prevalence of security issues is the semantic gap between the developers' assumptions about the underlying execution semantics and the actual semantics of smart contracts [5]. To close this semantic gap, FSolidM is based on a simple, formal, finite-state machine (FSM) based model for smart contracts, which we introduced in [9]. The model was designed to support Ethereum smart contracts, but it could easily be extended to other platforms.

Graphical Editor: To further decrease the semantic gap and facilitate development, FSolidM provides an easy-to-use graphical editor that enables developers to design smart contracts as FSMs.

Code Generator: FSolidM provides a tool for translating FSMs into Solidity, the most widely used high-level language for developing Ethereum contracts. Solidity code can be translated into Ethereum Virtual Machine bytecode, which can be deployed and executed on the platform.

Plugins: FSolidM enables extending the functionality of FSM based smart contract using plugins. As part of our framework, we provide a set of plugins that address common security issues and implement common design patterns, which

---

[1] It is possible to remove a transaction or hard fork the blockchain if the stakeholders reach a consensus; however, this undermines the trustworthiness of the platform [8].

Table 1. Common smart-contract vulnerabilities and design patterns

Type	Common name	FSolidM plugin
Vulnerabilities	Reentrancy [5, 10]	Locking
	Transaction ordering [5, 10]	Transition counter
Patterns	Time constraint [11]	Timed transitions
	Authorization [11]	Access control

were identified by prior work [5, 10, 11]. In Table 1, we list these vulnerabilities and patterns with the corresponding plugins.

Open Source: FSolidM is open-source and available online (see Sect. 3).

The advantages of our framework, which helps developers to create secure contracts instead of trying to fix existing ones, are threefold. First, we decrease the semantic gap and eliminate the issues arising from it by providing a formal model and an easy-to-use graphical editor. Second, since the process is rooted in rigorous semantics, our framework may be connected to formal analysis tools [12, 13]. Third, the code generator and plugins enable developers to implement smart contracts with minimal amount of error-prone manual coding.

The rest of this paper is organized as follows. In Sect. 2, we present blind auction as a motivating example, which we implement as an FSM-based smart contract. In Sect. 3, we describe our FSolidM tool and its built-in plugins. Finally, in Sect. 4, we offer concluding remarks and outline future work.

2   Defining Smart Contracts as FSMs

Consider as an example a blind auction (similar to the one presented in [14]), in which a bidder does not send her actual bid but only a hash of it (i.e., a blinded bid). A bidder is required to make a deposit—which does not need to be equal to her actual bid—to prevent her from not paying after she has won the auction. A deposit is considered valid if its value is higher than or equal to the actual bid. A blind auction has four main *states*:

1. `AcceptingBlindedBids`: blinded bids and deposits may be submitted;
2. `RevealingBids`: bidders may reveal their bids (i.e., they can send their actual bids and the contract checks if the hash value is the same as the one submitted in the previous state and if they made sufficient deposit);
3. `Finished`: the highest bid wins the auction; bidders can withdraw their deposits except for the winner, who can withdraw only the difference between her deposit and bid;
4. `Canceled`: bidders can retract bids and withdraw their deposits.

Since smart contracts have *states* (e.g., `AcceptingBlindedBids`) and provide functions that allow other entities (e.g., contracts or users) to invoke *actions* that change the current state of a contract, they can be naturally represented as

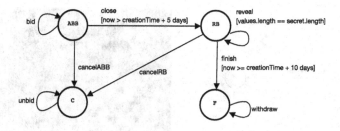

Fig. 1. Example FSM for blinded auctions.

FSMs [15]. An FSM has a finite set of states and a finite set of transitions between these states. A transition forces a contract to take a set of actions if the associated conditions, i.e., the *guards* of the transition, are satisfied. Since such states and transitions have intuitive meaning for developers, representing contracts as FSMs provides an adequate level of abstraction for behavior reasoning.

Figure 1 presents the blind auction example in the form of an FSM. For simplicity, we have abbreviated AcceptingBlindedBids, RevealingBids, Finished, and Canceled to ABB, RB, F, and C, respectively. ABB is the initial state of the FSM. Each transition (e.g., bid, reveal, cancel) is associated to a set of actions that a user can perform during the blind auction. For instance, a bidder can execute the bid transition at the ABB state to send a blind bid and a deposit value. Similarly, a user can execute the close transition, which signals the end of the bidding period, if the associated guard now >= creationTime + 5 days evaluates to true. To differentiate transition names from guards, we use square brackets for the latter. A bidder can reveal her bids by executing the reveal transition. The finish transition signals the completion of the auction, while the cancelABB and cancelRB transitions signal the cancellation of the auction. Finally, the unbid and withdraw transitions can be executed by the bidders to withdraw their deposits. For ease of presentation, we omit from Fig. 1 the actions that correspond to each transition. For instance, during the execution of the withdraw transition, the following action is performed amount = pendingReturns[msg.sender].

3   The FSolidM Tool

FSolidM is an open-source[2], web-based tool that is built on top of WebGME [16]. FSolidM enables collaboration between multiple users during the development of smart contracts. Changes in FSolidM are committed and versioned, which enables branching, merging, and viewing the history of a contract. We present the FSolidM tool in more detail in [17].

To generate the Solidity code of a smart contract using FSolidM, a user must follow three steps: (1) specify the smart contract in the form of the FSM by using the dedicated graphical editor of FSolidM; (2) specify attributes of the smart

---

[2] https://github.com/anmavrid/smart-contracts.

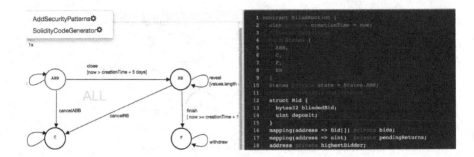

Fig. 2. The FSolidM model and code editors.

contract such as variable definition, statements, etc. in the `Property Editor` or in the dedicated Solidity code editor of FSolidM; (3) optionally apply security patterns and functionality extensions, and finally, generate the Solidity code. Figure 2 shows the graphical and code editors of the tool (for steps 1 and 2) and the list of services (i.e., `AddSecurityPatterns` and `SolidityCodeGenerator` for step 3) that are provided by FSolidM. We have integrated a Solidity parser[3] to check the syntax of the Solidity code that is given as input by the users.

Notice that in Fig. 2, parts of the code shown in the code editor are darker (lines 1–10) than other parts (lines 12–15). The darker lines of code include code that was generated from the FSM model defined in the graphical editor and are locked—cannot be altered in the code editor. The non-dark parts indicate code that was directly specified in the code editor.

FSolidM provides mechanisms for checking if the FSM is correctly specified (e.g., whether an initial state exists or not). FSolidM notifies developers of errors and provides links to the erroneous nodes of the model (e.g., a transition or a guard). Through the `SolidityCodeEditor` service, FSolidM provides an FSM-to-Solidity code generator. Additionally, through the `AddSecurityPatterns` service, FSolidM enables developers to enhance the functionality and security of contracts conveniently by adding plugins to them. Our framework provides four built-in plugins: locking, transition counter, timed transitions, and access control. Plugins can be simply added with a "click," as shown in Fig. 3.

Locking: When an Ethereum contract calls a function of another contract, the caller has to wait for the call to finish. This allows the callee—who may be malicious—to exploit the intermediate state of the caller, e.g., by invoking a function of the caller. This re-entrancy issue is one of the most well-known vulnerabilities, which was also exploited in the infamous "The DAO" attack.

To prevent re-entrancy, we provide a security plugin for locking the smart contract. Locking eliminates re-entrancy vulnerabilities in a "foolproof" manner: functions within the contract cannot be nested within each other in any way.

---

[3] https://github.com/ConsenSys/solidity-parser.

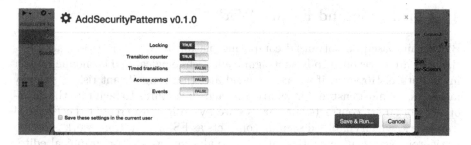

Fig. 3. Running the `AddSecurityPatterns`.

Transition Counter: If multiple functions calls are invoked around the same time, then the order in which these calls are executed on the Ethereum blockchain may be unpredictable. Hence, when a user invokes a function, she may be unable to predict what the state and the values stored within a contract will be when the function is actually executed. This issue has been referred to as "transaction-ordering dependence" [5] and "unpredictable state" [10], and it can lead to various security vulnerabilities.

We provide a plugin that prevents unpredictable-state vulnerabilities by enforcing a strict ordering on function call executions. The plugin expects a transition number in every function as a parameter and ensures that the number is incremented by one for each function execution. As a result, when a user invokes a function with the next transition number in sequence, she can be sure that the function is executed before any other state changes can take place.

Automatic Timed Transitions: We provide a plugin for implementing time-constraint patterns. We extend our language with timed transitions, which are similar to non-timed transitions, but (1) their guards and assignments do not use input or output data and (2) they include a number specifying transition time.

We implement timed transitions as a modifier that is applied to every function, and which ensures that timed transitions are executed automatically if their time and data guards are satisfied. Writing such modifiers manually could lead to vulnerabilities. For example, a developer might forget to add a modifier to a function, which enables malicious users to invoke functions without the contract progressing to the correct state (e.g., place bids in an auction even though the auction should have already been closed due to a time limit).

Access Control: In many contracts, access to certain transitions (i.e., functions) needs to be controlled and restricted. For example, any user can participate in a typical blind auction by submitting a bid, but only the creator should be able to cancel the auction. To facilitate the enforcement of such constraints, we provide a plugin that (1) manages a list of administrators at runtime (identified by their addresses) and (2) enables developers to forbid non-administrators from accessing certain functions.

4   Conclusion and Future Work

Blockchain-based decentralized computing platforms with smart-contract functionality are envisioned to have a significant technological and economic impact in the future. However, if we are to avoid an equally significant risk of security incidents, we must ensure that smart contracts are secure. To facilitate the development of smart contracts that are secure by design, we created the FSolidM framework, which enables designing contracts as FSMs. Our framework is rooted in rigorous yet clear semantics, and it provides an easy-to-use graphical editor and code generator. We also implemented a set of plugins that developers can use to enhance the security or functionality of their contracts. In the future, we plan to integrate model checkers and compositional verification tools into our framework [12,13] to enable the verification of security and safety properties.

References

1. Underwood, S.: Blockchain beyond bitcoin. Commun. ACM **59**(11), 15–17 (2016)
2. Wood, G.: Ethereum: a secure decentralised generalised transaction ledger. Technical report EIP-150, Ethereum Project - Yellow Paper, April 2014
3. Christidis, K., Devetsikiotis, M.: Blockchains and smart contracts for the internet of things. IEEE Access **4**, 2292–2303 (2016)
4. Vukolić, M.: Rethinking permissioned blockchains. In: Proceedings of ACM Workshop on Blockchain, Cryptocurrencies and Contracts, pp. 3–7. ACM (2017)
5. Luu, L., Chu, D.H., Olickel, H., Saxena, P., Hobor, A.: Making smart contracts smarter. In: Proceedings of 23rd ACM SIGSAC Conference on Computer and Communications Security (CCS), pp. 254–269. ACM, October 2016
6. Finley, K.: A $50 million hack just showed that the DAO was all too human, June 2016. Wired https://www.wired.com/2016/06/50-million-hack-just-showed-dao-human/
7. Bhargavan, K., Delignat-Lavaud, A., Fournet, C., Gollamudi, A., Gonthier, G., Kobeissi, N., Rastogi, A., Sibut-Pinote, T., Swamy, N., Zanella-Béguelin, S.: Short paper: formal verification of smart contracts. In: Proceedings of 11th ACM Workshop on Programming Languages and Analysis for Security (PLAS), in Conjunction with ACM CCS 2016, pp. 91–96, October 2016
8. Leising, M.: The Ether thief, June 2017. Bloomberg Markets https://www.bloomberg.com/features/2017-the-ether-thief/
9. Mavridou, A., Laszka, A.: Designing secure Ethereum smart contracts: a finite state machine based approach. In: Proceedings of 22nd International Conference on Financial Cryptography and Data Security (FC), February 2018
10. Atzei, N., Bartoletti, M., Cimoli, T.: A survey of attacks on Ethereum smart contracts (SoK). In: Maffei, M., Ryan, M. (eds.) POST 2017. LNCS, vol. 10204, pp. 164–186. Springer, Heidelberg (2017). https://doi.org/10.1007/978-3-662-54455-6_8
11. Bartoletti, M., Pompianu, L.: An empirical analysis of smart contracts: platforms, applications, and design patterns. In: Brenner, M., Rohloff, K., Bonneau, J., Miller, A., Ryan, P.Y.A., Teague, V., Bracciali, A., Sala, M., Pintore, F., Jakobsson, M. (eds.) FC 2017. LNCS, vol. 10323, pp. 494–509. Springer, Cham (2017). https://doi.org/10.1007/978-3-319-70278-0_31

12. Bensalem, S., Bozga, M., Nguyen, T.-H., Sifakis, J.: D-Finder: a tool for compositional deadlock detection and verification. In: Bouajjani, A., Maler, O. (eds.) CAV 2009. LNCS, vol. 5643, pp. 614–619. Springer, Heidelberg (2009). https://doi.org/10.1007/978-3-642-02658-4_45

13. Cavada, R., Cimatti, A., Dorigatti, M., Griggio, A., Mariotti, A., Micheli, A., Mover, S., Roveri, M., Tonetta, S.: The NUXMV symbolic model checker. In: Biere, A., Bloem, R. (eds.) CAV 2014. LNCS, vol. 8559, pp. 334–342. Springer, Cham (2014). https://doi.org/10.1007/978-3-319-08867-9_22

14. Solidity by example: blind auction. http://solidity.readthedocs.io/en/develop/solidity-by-example.html. Accessed 9 May 2017

15. Solidity specification: common patterns. http://solidity.readthedocs.io/en/develop/common-patterns.html. Accessed 9 May 2017

16. Maróti, M., Kecskés, T., Kereskényi, R., Broll, B., Völgyesi, P., Jurácz, L., Levendovszky, T., Lédeczi, Á.: Next generation (meta) modeling: web-and cloud-based collaborative tool infrastructure. In: Proceedings of MPM@ MoDELS, pp. 41–60 (2014)

17. Mavridou, A., Laszka, A.: Tool demonstration: FSolidM for designing secure Ethereum smart contracts. arXiv:1802.09949 [cs.CR] (2018)

UniTraX: Protecting Data Privacy
with Discoverable Biases

Reinhard Munz[1][(✉)], Fabienne Eigner[2], Matteo Maffei[3], Paul Francis[1],
and Deepak Garg[1]

[1] MPI-SWS, Kaiserslautern and Saarbrücken, Germany
{munz,francis,dg}@mpi-sws.org
[2] CISPA, Saarland University, Saarbrücken, Germany
eigner@cs.uni-saarland.de
[3] TU Wien, Vienna, Austria
matteo.maffei@tuwien.ac.at

Abstract. An ongoing challenge with differentially private database systems is that of maximizing system utility while staying within a certain privacy budget. One approach is to maintain per-user budgets instead of a single global budget, and to silently drop users whose budget is depleted. This, however, can lead to very misleading analyses because the system cannot provide the analyst any information about which users have been dropped.

This paper presents UniTraX, the first differentially private system that allows per-user budgets while providing the analyst information about the budget state. The key insight behind UniTraX is that it tracks budget not only for actual records in the system, but at all points in the domain of the database, including points that could exist but do not. UniTraX can safely report the budget state because the analyst does not know if the state refers to actual records or not. We prove that UniTraX is differentially private. UniTraX is compatible with existing differentially private analyses and our implementation on top of PINQ shows only moderate runtime overheads on a realistic workload.

1 Introduction

Differential Privacy (DP) is a model of anonymity that measures privacy loss resulting from queries made to a database [6]. A bound on privacy loss can be enforced by preventing queries after a privacy budget has been exceeded. An ongoing challenge with DP systems is that of maximizing system utility while staying within a privacy budget, where system utility is measured in terms of both number of queries and amount of distortion (noise) in query answers.

A simple but common approach to DP budgets is to maintain a single global budget. With this approach, all queries draw from the budget regardless of how many user records are used to answer a given query. In systems where users can specify their own individual budgets, the global budget is effectively the *minimum* of user budgets.

© The Author(s) 2018
L. Bauer and R. Küsters (Eds.): POST 2018, LNCS 10804, pp. 278–299, 2018.
https://doi.org/10.1007/978-3-319-89722-6_12

An alternative approach is to maintain per-user budgets. The idea here is that a given query draws only from the budgets of users whose records contribute to the answer. This can substantially improve system utility. An analysis that for instance targets smokers in a medical dataset would not reduce the budgets of non-smokers. Furthermore, per-user budgets maximize utility in systems where users specify their individual budgets because low-budget users do not constrain the queries that are made over only high-budget users.

In spite of the tremendous potential for increasing the utility of DP systems, we are aware of only a single system, ProPer [10], that tracks per-user budgets.[1] This is because of a fundamental difficulty with per-user budget systems. Namely, the system cannot report on the remaining budget of individual users without revealing private information. If budgets were made *public* in this way, then an analyst could trivially obtain information about users just by observing which users' budgets changed in response to a query.

Because of this, ProPer keeps user budgets *private*: it silently drops the record of a user from the dataset when the user's budget is depleted. This creates a serious usability problem for the analyst. Suppose there are two analysts, Alice and Bob. Alice wishes to learn about smokers, Bob wishes to learn about lung-cancer patients. Suppose Alice makes a set of queries about smokers, and as a result many smokers' budgets are depleted and these smokers' records are dropped from the dataset. Afterwards Bob asks the question: "What fraction of lung cancer patients are smokers?". Because many smokers have been dropped from the dataset, and non-smokers have not, Bob's answer is incorrect. Worse, Bob has no way of knowing whether the answer is incorrect, or how incorrect it is. Bob's answer is effectively useless. We call this *unknown dataset bias*.

To address this problem, this paper presents UniTraX, a DP system that allows for the benefits of keeping per-user budgets without the disadvantage of unknown dataset bias. The key insight of UniTraX is in how it tracks budget. Rather than *privately* tracking individual users' remaining budget, UniTraX *publicly* tracks the budget consumed by prior queries over regions of the data parameter space. In addition, UniTraX adds each user's initial budget to the dataset, making it a queryable parameter.

For example, assume a query asks for the count of users between the ages of 10 and 20. ProPer would *privately* deduct the appropriate amount from the individual remaining budget of *all users* in that age range. By contrast, UniTraX *publicly* records that a certain amount of budget was consumed for the *age range 10–20*. Because the consumed budget is public, the analyst can calculate how much initial budget any given point in the data parameter space would need in order to still have enough remaining budget for some specific query the analyst may wish to make. Because initial budgets are also a queryable parameter, the analyst can then explicitly *exclude* from the query any points whose initial budget is too small. This allows the analyst to control which points are included in answers and therefore avoid unknown dataset bias. (See Sect. 2 for a detailed example.)

---

[1] Other DP systems also permit per-user or per-field *initial* budgets [1,15]. However, these systems do not track the *consumption* of budget on a per-user basis.

		budget attribution	
		global	per-user
consumed budget	private		ProPer
visibility	public	DP reference	UniTraX

Fig. 1. System comparison

Internally, UniTraX utilizes the same calculation of required initial budget to reject any query that covers points without sufficient budget. Critically, such a rejection does not leak any private information as it solely depends on public budget consumption data and query parameters. In fact, the decision to reject a query does not even look at the actual data.

A significant practical concern is that tracking budgets across the entire parameter space, which will usually be substantially larger than the number of actual records in the database, can be quite expensive. To understand this cost, we built a prototype implementation of UniTraX on top of PINQ [17]. By carefully clubbing budgets over contiguous regions of the parameter space, we obtain average overheads of less than 80% over a no-privacy baseline on a realistic workload.

The contributions of this paper are threefold:

1. A system model and design that maintains the advantages of per-user privacy budgets, while avoiding the problems due to unknown dataset bias.
2. A theoretical framework and proof that the design provides DP.
3. An implementation and evaluation showing that the system is able to efficiently track budgets with average overheads of less than 80%.

In Sect. 2 we compare different system models for DP and provide an example to illustrate the effect of unknown dataset bias. We introduce the design of UniTraX in Sect. 3 and detail the theoretical framework and the proof of DP in Sect. 4. Our implementation and its evaluation are presented in Sects. 5 and 6. We discuss related work in Sect. 7 and conclude in Sect. 8.

2 System Comparison

To better understand the differences and advantages of UniTraX, we start with overviews of UniTraX and two prior system models, the classic DP "reference" model with a global budget, and ProPer with private per-user budgets. We use a simple running example to illustrate the differences. Figure 1 contrasts the public, per-user budget model of UniTraX with DP reference and ProPer.

For the example we assume that two analysts Alice and Bob want to analyze a dataset of patient records. These records contain a variety of fields among which is one that indicates whether a patient is a smoker, and one that indicates whether the patient suffers from lung cancer. We assume that Alice is interested in smokers and wants to run various queries over different fields of smokers while Bob is interested in the fraction of lung cancer patients that are smokers. We assume that Alice does her analysis first, followed by Bob.

Regarding the setting of each patient's (user's) initial budget, we consider two cases: (1) all initial budgets are the same (uniform initial budgets), and (2) each budget is set by the user (non-uniform initial budgets). In the case of UniTraX, the initial budget is just another field in each record.

DP Reference. The DP reference mechanism uses a publicly visible global budget. In the case of uniform initial budgets, the global budget is set as the system default. In the case of non-uniform initial budgets, the global budget is set to the lowest initial budget among all users.

The reference mechanism counts every query against this single global budget. First, Alice runs her queries against smokers. Since each query decrements from the global budget, this budget may well be depleted before Bob can even start. At this point no information about non-smokers will have left the system. Still, the system has to reject all further queries.

ProPer. ProPer tracks one budget per user but must keep it private. Users whose budgets are depleted are silently dropped from the dataset and not considered for any further queries. Nevertheless, each user's full budget can be used.

Staying in our example, Alice's queries use no budget of non-smokers under this tracking mechanism. Once Alice has finished her queries, Bob starts his analysis. Bob wishes to make two queries, one counting the number of smokers with lung cancer, and one counting the number of non-smokers with lung cancer. Bob may look at Alice's queries, and observe that she focused on smokers, and therefore know that there is a danger that his answers will be biased against smokers. In the general case, however, he cannot be sure if his answers are biased or not.

In the case of uniform budgets, if Alice requested histograms, then she would have consumed the smokers' budgets uniformly and depleted either all or none of the smokers' budgets. If Bob gets an answer that, keeping in mind the noise, is significantly larger than zero, then Bob's confidence that his answer is non-biased may be high. If on the other hand Alice focused some of her queries on specific ranges (e.g., certain age groups), or if budgets are non-uniform, then Bob knows that the answer for smokers with lung cancer may be missing users, while the answer for non-smokers with lung cancer will not. He may therefore have unknown dataset bias, and cannot confidently carry out his analysis.

Our System (UniTraX). UniTraX tracks public budgets that are computable from the history of previous queries. UniTraX is able to tell an analyst how much budget has been consumed by previous queries for any subspace of the parameter space. For example, the analyst may request how much budget has been consumed in the subspace defined by "age$\geq$10 AND age<20 AND gender=male AND smoker=1".

UniTraX tracks budget consumption over regions of the parameter space. For example, if a query selects records over the subspace "age$\geq$10 AND age<20", then UniTraX records (publicly) that a certain amount of budget has been consumed from this region of the parameter space. Initial budgets are an additional

dimension of the parameter space in UniTraX. In particular, the initial budget
of an actual record in the database is stored in a field in the record. By comparing the (public) consumed budget of any point in the parameter space to
the initial budget of that point, UniTraX can determine publicly whether that
point's budget has been fully consumed or not. This allows UniTraX to reject a
query safely: If, after the query, the consumed budget of any point selected by
the query will exceed that point's initial budget, then the query is immediately
rejected. This decision does not require looking at the actual data, and reveals
no private information.

Critically, public consumed budgets combined with the ability to filter queries
based on users' initial budgets allows analysts to control and eliminate unknown
dataset bias. Returning to our example, when Bob is ready to start his analysis,
he queries UniTraX to determine the consumed budgets for "smoker=1 AND
disease=lungCancer", and "smoker=0 AND disease=lungCancer". Because no
queries have been made for non-smokers, the consumed budget of the latter
query's region would be zero. Suppose that UniTraX indicates that the consumed
budget for the region "smoker=1 AND disease=lungCancer" is 50, and that
Bob's two queries will further consume a budget of 10 each. Because the two
groups are disjoint, Bob knows that any user with an initial budget of 60 or
higher has enough remaining budget for his queries. (If the two queries were not
known to have disjoint user populations, then Bob would need to filter for initial
budgets of 70 or higher.)

Bob generates the following two queries:

- "count WHERE smoker=1 AND disease=lungCancer AND initBudget$\geq$60",
- "count WHERE smoker=0 AND disease=lungCancer AND initBudget$\geq$60".

In doing so, Bob is assured that no users are excluded from either query, and
avoids unknown dataset bias.[2]

So far, we have described how Bob may query only points with sufficient
remaining budget. However, when this is not the case, UniTraX is able to simply
reject Bob's queries. In fact, UniTraX can even inform him about which points
are out of budget without leaking private information. Privacy is protected by
the fact that Bob does not know whether these points exist in the dataset or
not. UniTraX's rejection does not reveal this information to Bob as it solely
depends on public consumed budgets and query parameters. Using the returned
information, Bob is able to debug his analysis and retry.

UniTraX not only allows analysts to debug their analyses but is fully compatible with existing DP systems. Any analysis that successfully executes over a
dataset protected by a global budget system requires only a simple initialization

---

[2] Note that if users select their own initial budgets, and there is some correlation
between user attributes and initial budgets, then there may still be a specific bias in
the data. For instance if smokers tend to choose high budgets and non-smokers tend
to choose low budgets, then Bob's queries would be biased towards smokers. This
problem appears fundamental to any system that allows individual user budgets.

to run on the same dataset protected by UniTraX (see Sect. 5 for PINQ-based analyses). Thus, analysts can easily adapt to UniTraX and exploit the increased utility of per-user budgets.

3 Design Overview

Threat Model. UniTraX uses the standard threat model for DP. The goal is to prevent malicious analysts from discovering whether a specific record (user) exists in the queried database (dataset). We assume, as usual, that analysts are limited to the interface offered by UniTraX and that they do not have direct access to the database. We make no assumptions about the background or auxiliary knowledge of the analysts. Analysts may collude with each other offline.

Goals. We designed UniTraX with the following goals in mind.

Privacy: Users should be able to set privacy preferences (budgets) for their records individually. These preferences must be respected across queries.

Utility: Querying a parameter subspace should not affect the usability of records in a disjoint subspace.

Bias Discovery: The system should allow the analyst to discover when there may be a bias in query answers because privacy budgets of some parts of the parameter space have been depleted by past queries.

Efficiency: The overhead of the system should be moderate.

In the following we describe the design of UniTraX, explaining how it attains the first three goals above. The fourth goal, efficiency, is justified by the experimental evaluation in Sect. 6.

Design Overview. For simplicity, we assume that the entire database is organized as a single table with a fixed schema. The schema includes a designated column for the initial privacy budget of each record. UniTraX is agnostic to how this initial budget is chosen—it may be a default value common to all records or it may be determined individually for each record by the person who owns the record. Higher values of initial budget indicate less privacy concerns for that record. Records may be added to the database or removed from it at any time.

The set of all possible records constitutes the *parameter space*.[3] We use the term *point* for any point in the parameter space; a point may or may not exist in the actual database under consideration. We use the terms *actual record* and *record* for the points that actually exist in the database under consideration.

Like most DP systems, UniTraX supports statistical or aggregate queries. The query model is similar to that of PINQ [17]. An analyst performs a query in two steps. First, the analyst *selects* a subspace of the parameter space using a SQL SELECT-like syntax. For example, the analyst may select the subspace "age≥10 AND age<20 AND gender=male AND smoker=1". Next, the analyst

---

[3] The parameter space is also sometimes called the "domain" of the database.

runs an aggregate query like count, sum or average on this selected subspace. To protect privacy, UniTraX adds random noise to the result of the query. The amount of noise added is determined by a privacy parameter, ε, that the analyst provides with the query. For lower values of ε, the result is more noisy, but the reduction of privacy budget is less (thus leaving more budget for future queries).

The novel aspect of UniTraX is how it tracks budgets. When an aggregate query with privacy parameter ε is made on a selected subspace S, UniTraX simply records that budget ε has been consumed from subspace S. The *remaining budget* of any point in the parameter space is the point's initial budget (from the point's designated initial budget field) minus the ε's of all past queries that ran on subspaces containing the point.

The consumed budgets of all subspaces are *public*—analysts can ask for them at any time. This allows analysts to determine which subspaces have been heavily queried in the past and, hence, become aware of possible data biases. Moreover, analysts may select only subspaces with sufficient remaining budgets in subsequent queries, thus increasing their confidence in analysis outcomes, as illustrated in Sect. 2.

To respect privacy budgets, it is imperative that a query with privacy parameter ε does not execute on any points whose remaining budget is less than ε. This is enforced by query rejection, where a query is executed only if all points in the selected subspace have remaining budget at least ε. Note that this check is made on not only actual records but all points in the selected subspace. If any such point does not have sufficient remaining budget, the query is rejected and an error is returned to the analyst (who may then select a smaller subspace with higher initial budgets and retry the query). Whether a query is executed or rejected depends only on the consumption history, which is public, so rejecting the query provides no additional information to the analyst.

Initial Budgets. UniTraX is agnostic to the method used to determine initial budgets of actual records and supports any scheme for setting initial budgets on actual records. The simplest scheme would assign the same, fixed initial budget to every actual record. A more complex scheme may allow users to choose from a small fixed set of initial budgets for each record they provide, while the most complex scheme may let users freely choose any initial budget for every record.

4   Formal Description and Differential Privacy

In this section, we describe UniTraX using a formal model. We specify the differential privacy property that we expect UniTraX to satisfy and formally prove that the property is indeed satisfied. Our formalization is directly based on ProPer's formalization [10], which we find both elegant and natural.

4.1   Formal Model of UniTraX

Database. We treat the database as a table with n columns of arbitrary types $\mathcal{C}_1, \ldots, \mathcal{C}_n$ and an initial budget column—a non-negative real number. The type of each record, also called the parameter space, is $\mathcal{R} = \mathcal{C}_1 \times \ldots \times \mathcal{C}_n \times \mathcal{C}_B$, where $\mathcal{C}_B = \mathbb{R}^{\geq 0}$ is the type of the initial budget column. At any point of time, the state of the database is a set E of records from the parameter space ($E \in 2^{\mathcal{R}}$).

UniTraX. UniTraX acts as a reference monitor between the database and the analyst. Its internal state consist of two components: (1) the consumption history H and (2) the select table T.

1. UniTraX tracks the budget consumed by past queries on every subspace of the parameter space. Formally, this is equivalent to storing a map from points in the parameter space to non-negative real numbers. We call this map the *consumption history*, denoted H. H has the type $\mathcal{H} = \mathcal{R} \to \mathbb{R}^{\geq 0}$. Intuitively, $H(r)$ is the amount of budget consumed by past queries that ran on subspaces containing the point r of the parameter space.

2. To run an aggregate query in UniTraX, the analyst must first select a subspace of the parameter space. To support selection of records that have at least a stipulated *remaining budget*, UniTraX allows selected subspaces to also span the consumption history. Consequently, a selected subspace is a subset of $\mathcal{R} \times \mathbb{R}^{\geq 0}$ (points extended with their *consumed* budgets). We represent such subspaces via logical predicates *sspace* of type $\mathcal{P} = \mathcal{R} \times \mathbb{R}^{\geq 0} \to \{\text{true, false}\}$. For the analyst's convenience, UniTraX allows storing a list of selected subspaces, indexed by *subspace variables* drawn from a set SVar. UniTraX stores the association between subspace variables and subspaces in a *select table, T*, of type $\text{SVar} \to \mathcal{P}$.

Analyst. We model an adaptive analyst, who queries UniTraX based on an internal program and previously received answers. Formally, the analyst is a (possibly infinite) state machine with states denoted by P and its decorated variants, and state transitions defined by the relation $P \xrightarrow{a} P'$. Here a, b denote *interactions* between the analyst and UniTraX. Allowed interactions are summarized in Fig. 2. Note that interactions consist of either an instruction to, or an observable output from UniTraX, or both. In detail, the interactions are:

- $sv := sspace$ represents the instruction to UniTraX to associate the subspace variable sv with the subspace *sspace*, which must be in $\mathcal{P}$. This models the selection of a subspace (for use in later aggregation queries).
- $Q_{\varepsilon}(sv)?n$ models the instruction to UniTraX to run the aggregation query Q with privacy parameter ε on the subspace previously mapped to variable sv. The interaction also includes the noised result n of the query. If some point in subspace sv has remaining budget less than ε, the output n is 'reject'.
- update represents an output from UniTraX to the analyst indicating that the database has been updated. The output does not specify which records were added or deleted (else the analyst could trivially break DP).
- read?H models reading the entire current consumption history by the analyst. H is the history returned by UniTraX.

a, b	$::=$	$sv := sspace$	select subspace $sspace$ and name it sv
		$Q_\varepsilon(sv)?n$	run aggregation query Q on sv, observe output n
		update	database update
		read?H	read consumption history, result is H

Fig. 2. Allowed interactions between analyst and UniTraX

We make no assumptions about the analyst (i.e., its state machine). It may select any subspace, run any aggregation query, and read the consumption history at any time. However, for technical reasons we assume (like ProPer) that the analyst is internally deterministic and deadlock-free, meaning that it branches only on observable output from the database and that it can always make progress.[4] Our assumptions are formalized by the following condition: If $P \xrightarrow{a} P'$ and $P \xrightarrow{b} P''$, then

1. if $a = b$ then $P' = P''$
2. if $a = (sv := sspace)$ then $a = b$
3. if $a = Q_\varepsilon(sv)?n$ then $b = Q_\varepsilon(sv)?n'$ for some n' and for all n'' there exists P''' with $P \xrightarrow{Q_\varepsilon(sv)?n''} P'''$
4. if $a = $ read?H then $b = $ read?H' for some H' and for all H'' there exists P''' with $P \xrightarrow{\text{read}?H''} P'''$

Configuration. A configuration $\mathbb{C} = (P, E, H, T)$ represents the state of the complete system. It includes the state of the analyst (P), the database of actual records (E) and the internal state of UniTraX (consumption history H and select table T).

Execution Semantics. We model the evolution of the system using transitions $\mathbb{C} \xrightarrow{\alpha}_p \mathbb{C}'$. Here, $\alpha \in$ Act denotes an *action label* describing an operation within the system and p is a transition probability (real number between 0 and 1). The transition $\mathbb{C} \xrightarrow{\alpha}_p \mathbb{C}'$ reads as follows: If, in configuration $\mathbb{C}$, the operation α happens, then, with probability p, the configuration changes to $\mathbb{C}'$. α may be any one of:

- τ: analyst selects a subspace
- $n \in$ Val: query by analyst that returns result n
- reject: query by analyst that is rejected
- $R_{in} : R_{del}$: database update that adds records R_{in} and removes records R_{del}
- H: analyst reads consumption history H

The transition system $\mathbb{C} \xrightarrow{\alpha}_p \mathbb{C}'$ is defined by the five rules shown in Fig. 3. These rules model the system's behavior as follows.

(UPDATE) Models a database update by adding some record set R_{in} and removing some record set R_{del} from the database E. This transition returns to the analyst the observable output 'update' (first premise).

---

[4] These restrictions do not affect the analyst's attack capabilities.

UPDATE

$$\frac{P \xrightarrow{\text{update}} P' \qquad R_{in}, R_{del} \subseteq \mathcal{R}}{(P, E, H, T) \xrightarrow{R_{in}:R_{del}}_1 (P', (E \cup R_{in}) \setminus R_{del}, H, T)}$$

SELECT

$$\frac{P \xrightarrow{sv := sspace} P' \qquad sspace \in \mathcal{P}}{(P, E, H, T) \xrightarrow{\tau}_1 (P', E, H, T[sv := sspace])}$$

READ-HISTORY

$$\frac{P \xrightarrow{\text{read}?H} P'}{(P, E, H, T) \xrightarrow{H}_1 (P', E, H, T)}$$

QUERY

$$\frac{P \xrightarrow{Q_\varepsilon(sv)?n} P' \qquad sspace := T(sv) \in \mathcal{P}}{\forall r \in \mathcal{R}.sspace(r, H(r)) \Rightarrow H(r) + \varepsilon \le r.c_B \qquad p = \text{Prob}[Q_\varepsilon(E|_{sspace,H}) = n]}{(P, E, H, T) \xrightarrow{n}_p (P', E, H', T)}$$

$$\text{where } H'(r) := \begin{cases} H(r) + \varepsilon & \text{if } sspace(r, H(r)) \\ H(r) & \text{otherwise} \end{cases}$$

$$\text{and } E|_{sspace,H} \stackrel{\text{def}}{=} \{r \in E \mid sspace(r, H(r))\}$$

REJECT

$$\frac{P \xrightarrow{Q_\varepsilon(sv)?\,\text{reject}} P'}{sspace := T(sv) \in \mathcal{P} \qquad \exists r \in \mathcal{R}.sspace(r, H(r)) \wedge H(r) + \varepsilon > r.c_B}{(P, E, H, T) \xrightarrow{\text{reject}}_1 (P', E, H, T)}$$

Fig. 3. Semantics of UniTraX

(SELECT) Represents the analyst's selection of subspace *sspace*, naming it *sv*.

(READ-HISTORY) Denotes the analyst reading the current consumption history H. This rule forces our privacy proofs to internally show that the consumption history is indeed public.

(QUERY) Models the successful execution of aggregation query Q on subspace *sspace* identified by *sv* with privacy parameter ε. The execution requires all points in *sspace* to have a remaining budget of at least ε. A point r is in *sspace* if $sspace(r, H(r)) = \text{true}$. (In the rule, $r.c_B$ is short-hand for the initial budget column of point r.) As a consequence of the query, two things happen. First, the consumption history of all points in the subspace is increased by ε, to record that a query with privacy parameter ε has run on the subspace. Second, the answer to query Q executed over those records that are both in the subspace and actually exist in the database E (selected by the operation $E|_{sspace,H}$) is returned to the analyst after adding differentially private noise for the parameter ε. The transition's probability p is equal to the probability of getting the specific noised answer for the query (the noised answer is denoted n in the rule).

(REJECT) Represents UniTraX's rejection of query Q due to some point in the query's selected subspace not having sufficient remaining budget. The analyst observes a special response 'reject' (first premise).

With the notable exception of (QUERY), all rules are deterministic—they happen with probability 1 (the p in $\xrightarrow{\alpha}_p$ is 1).

Trace Semantics. The relation $\mathbb{C} \xrightarrow{\alpha}_p \mathbb{C}'$ describes a single step of system evolution. We lift this definition to multiple steps. A *trace* σ is a (possibly empty) finite sequence of labels $\alpha_1, \ldots, \alpha_n$. We write $\mathbb{C} \xRightarrow{\sigma}_q \mathbb{C}'$ to signify that configuration $\mathbb{C}$ evolves in multiple steps to configuration $\mathbb{C}'$ with probability q. The individual steps of the evolution have labels in σ. Formally, we have:

$$\frac{}{\mathbb{C} \xRightarrow{[]}_1 \mathbb{C}} \qquad \frac{\mathbb{C} \xrightarrow{\alpha}_p \mathbb{C}' \qquad \mathbb{C}' \xRightarrow{\sigma}_q \mathbb{C}''}{\mathbb{C} \xRightarrow{\alpha\sigma}_{p \cdot q} \mathbb{C}''}$$

We abbreviate $\mathbb{C} \xRightarrow{\sigma}_q \mathbb{C}'$ to $\mathbb{C} \xRightarrow{\sigma}_q$ when $\mathbb{C}'$ is irrelevant.

Note that from the transition semantics (Fig. 3) it follows that a trace σ records all updates to the database and all observations of the analyst (the latter is comprised of all responses from UniTraX to the analyst).

Extension to Silent Record Dropping. Up to this point, our design rejects a query whose selected subspace includes at least one point with insufficient remaining budget. This protects user privacy and prevents unknown dataset bias. However, in some cases, an analyst might prefer the risk of unknown dataset bias over modifying their existing programs to handle query rejections. This might be the case, for instance, if the analyst already knows by other means that the percentage of records with insufficient budget will be negligible. In this case, it would be preferable to *automatically drop records* with insufficient budget during query execution, as in ProPer. It turns out that we can provide silent record dropping without weakening the privacy guarantee. In the following paragraph, we detail a simple extension of UniTraX that allows the analyst to specify *for each query individually* whether the system should silently drop records with insufficient remaining budgets instead of rejecting the query.

In order to enable silent record dropping, we introduce an extended query interaction $Q_\varepsilon^{\mathrm{drop}}(sv)?n$ for the analyst's program. Unlike the previously described interaction, $Q_\varepsilon(sv)?n$, this interaction cannot fail (be rejected). The semantics of $Q_\varepsilon^{\mathrm{drop}}(sv)?n$ is defined by the new rule (QUERY-DROP) shown in Fig. 4. The query executes on those records in database E that (1) are in subspace $sspace$, and (b) have remaining budget at least ε. These records are selected by $E\|_{sspace, H, \varepsilon}$. As a consequence of the query, two things happen. First, the consumption history of all points in the parameter space satisfying (1) and (2) is increased by ε. Second, the answer of the query is returned to the analyst with probability p, which is determined by the same method used in (QUERY).

4.2   Privacy Property and Its Formalization

UniTraX respects the initial privacy budget of every record added to the database in the sense of differential privacy. Before explaining this property formally, we recap the standard notion of differential privacy due to Dwork et al. [6].

QUERY-DROP

$$\dfrac{P \xrightarrow{Q_\varepsilon^{\mathrm{drop}}(sv)?n} P' \qquad sspace := T(sv) \in \mathcal{P} \qquad p = \mathrm{Prob}[Q_\varepsilon^{\mathrm{drop}}(E\|_{sspace,H,\varepsilon}) = n]}{(P,E,H,T) \xrightarrow{\ n\ }_p (P',E,H',T)}$$

$$\text{where } H'(r) := \begin{cases} H(r) + \varepsilon & \text{if } sspace(r,H(r)) \wedge H(r) + \varepsilon \le r.c_B \\ H(r) & \text{otherwise} \end{cases}$$

$$\text{and } E\|_{sspace,H,\varepsilon} \overset{\mathrm{def}}{=} \{r \in E \mid sspace(r,H(r)) \wedge H(r) + \varepsilon \le r.c_B\}$$

Fig. 4. Semantics extension for silent record dropping

Standard Differential Privacy. Let Q be a randomized algorithm on a database that produces a value in the set V. For example, the algorithm may compute a noisy count of the number of entries in the database. We say that Q is ε-differentially private if for any two databases D, D' that differ in one record and for any $V' \subseteq V$,

$$\left| \ln\left(\frac{Pr\,[Q(D) \in V']}{Pr\,[Q(D') \in V']} \right) \right| \le \varepsilon.$$

In words, the definition says that for two databases that differ in only one record, the probabilities that the analyst running Q makes a specific observation are very similar. This means that any individual record does not significantly affect the probability of observing any particular outcome. Hence, the analyst cannot infer (with high confidence) whether any specific record exists in the database.

If the analyst runs n queries that are ε_1-, ..., ε_n-differentially private, then the total *loss* of privacy is defined as $\varepsilon_1 + ... + \varepsilon_n$. Typically, a maximum *privacy budget* is set when the analyst is given access to the database and after each ε-differentially private query, ε is subtracted from this budget. Once the budget becomes zero, no further queries are allowed. In this mode of use, DP guarantees that for any two possible databases D, D' that differ in at most one record, for any sequence of queries $\boldsymbol{Q}$, and for any sequence of observations $\boldsymbol{o}$,

$$\left| \ln\left(\frac{Pr\,[\boldsymbol{Q} \text{ results in } \boldsymbol{o} \text{ on } D]}{Pr\,[\boldsymbol{Q} \text{ results in } \boldsymbol{o} \text{ on } D']} \right) \right| \le \eta,$$

where η is the privacy budget.

Our Privacy Property. We use the same privacy property as ProPer. This privacy property generalizes differential privacy described above by accounting for dynamic addition and deletion of records and, importantly, allowing all new records to carry their own initial budgets. Informally, our privacy property is the following. Consider two possible traces σ_0 and σ_1 that can result from the same starting configuration. Suppose that σ_0 and σ_1 differ *only* in the updates made to the database and are otherwise identical. Let p_0 and p_1 be the respective probabilities of the traces. Then, $\left|\ln\left(\frac{p_0}{p_1}\right)\right| \le \eta$, where η is the sum of the initial budgets of all records in which the database updates differ between σ_0 and σ_1.

$$dist(\sigma, \sigma') \stackrel{\text{def}}{=} \begin{cases} \bigcup_{i \in [1,n]} dist(\alpha_i, \alpha'_i) & \text{if } \sigma = \alpha_1, \ldots, \alpha_n \text{ and } \sigma' = \alpha'_1, \ldots, \alpha'_n \\ (R_{in} \Delta R'_{in}) \cup (R_{del} \Delta R'_{del}) & \text{if } \sigma = R_{in} : R_{del} \text{ and } \sigma' = R'_{in} : R'_{del} \\ \emptyset & \text{if } \sigma = \sigma' \end{cases}$$

Fig. 5. Trace distance

Why is this a meaningful privacy property? We remarked earlier that a trace records all observations that the analyst (adversary) makes. Consequently, by insisting that the traces agree everywhere except on database updates, we are saying that the two traces agree on the analyst's observations. Hence, if an analyst makes a sequence of observations under database updates from σ_0 with probability p_0, then the probability that the analyst makes the *same* observations under database updates from σ_1 is very close to p_0. In fact, the log of the ratio of the two probabilities is bounded by the sum of the initial budgets of the records in which the updates differ. This is a natural generalization of DP's per-database budgets to per-record budgets.

To formalize this property, we define a partial function $dist(\sigma, \sigma')$ that returns the set of records in which database updates in σ and σ' differ if σ and σ' agree pointwise on all labels other than database updates. If σ and σ' differ at a label other than database update then $dist(\sigma, \sigma')$ is undefined. The formal definition is shown in Fig. 5.

Definition 1 (Privacy). *We say that UniTraX preserves privacy if whenever* $\mathbb{C} \stackrel{\sigma_0}{\Longrightarrow}_{p_0}$ *and* $\mathbb{C} \stackrel{\sigma_1}{\Longrightarrow}_{p_1}$ *and* $dist(\sigma_0, \sigma_1) = R$, *then* $\left| \ln\left(\frac{p_0}{p_1}\right) \right| \leq \sum_{r \in R} r.c_B$.

Our main result is that UniTraX is private in the sense of the above definition.

Theorem 1 (Privacy of UniTraX). *UniTraX preserves privacy in the sense of Definition 1.*

We prove this theorem by first proving a strong invariant of configurations that takes into account how UniTraX tracks the consumption history. The entire proof is in our technical report [19].

5   Implementation

We have implemented UniTraX on top of PINQ, an earlier framework for enforcing differential privacy with a global budget for the database [17]. We briefly review relevant details of PINQ before explaining our implementation.

PINQ Review. PINQ adds differential privacy to LINQ, a general-purpose database query framework. LINQ defines *Queryable* objects, abstractions over data sources, e.g., a database table. The Queryable object may be *transformed* by a SQL SELECT-like operation to obtain another Queryable object representing selected records from the table. One may run an aggregate query on this second object to obtain a specific value.

Building on LINQ, PINQ maintains a global privacy budget for the entire database. This budget is set when a Queryable object is initialized. Subsequently, differentially-private noise is added to every aggregation query on every object derived from this Queryable object and the global budget is appropriately reduced.

UniTraX Implementation. Our implementation currently supports only query execution with rejection. The main addition to PINQ is tracking of consumption budgets over subspaces. *In principle*, we must store the consumption budget for every point in the parameter space. *In practice*, queries tend to select contiguous ranges, so at any point of time, the parameter space splits into contiguous subspaces, each with a uniform consumption budget. Accordingly, our implementation tries to cluster contiguous subspaces with identical consumption and represents them efficiently.

Our interface defines a new object type, UQueryable, which represents a subspace. Like Queryable, this object can be transformed via SQL SELECT-like operations to derive other, smaller UQueryable objects. To run an analysis on a subspace, the analyst invokes a special function, GetAsPINQ, to convert a UQueryable object representing the subspace into a PINQ object representing the same subspace. This special function also takes as an argument a budget, which the analysis will eventually consume. The function first checks that this budget is larger than the remaining budget of all points in the subspace. If not, the function fails. Otherwise, this budget is immediately added to the consumption budget of the subspace and a fresh PINQ object initialized with this budget is returned. Subsequently, the analyst can run any queries on the PINQ object and PINQ's existing framework enforces the allocated budget.

We also provide a new interface to the analyst to ask for the maximum budget consumed in a given subspace.

Typical Analysis Workflow. We briefly describe the steps an analyst must follow to run an analysis on our implementation. Assume that the analyst wants to analyze records within a specific subspace with a set of queries that require a certain amount of budget to run successfully. Further assume that the analysis needs to run on a stipulated minimum number of user records for its results to be meaningful. The analyst would perform the following steps:

1. Obtain the initial UQueryable object representing the entire database.
2. Select the desired subspace obtaining another UQueryable object.
3. Obtain the maximum budget consumed on the second object.
4. Add the budget required for the analysis and a budget for a noisy count to the just-obtained maximum budget.
5. Select the subspace that has at least the just-calculated sum of budgets available, obtaining yet another UQueryable object.
6. Obtain a PINQ object from the last UQueryable object with the PINQ budget set to the budget of the count.
7. Perform a (noisy) count on the PINQ object. If it is too low, stop here.

8. Otherwise, obtain another PINQ object, this time with the budget required for the analysis.
9. Perform the analysis on the second PINQ object. All records in the PINQ object have enough budget for the full analysis.

Data Stream Analysis. UniTraX can be directly used for analysis on streams of data since its design and privacy proof already take record addition and deletion into account. To allow analysts to use the full budget of newly arriving records, we assume records to be timestamped on arrival; this timestamp is another column in our parameter space. At any time, all active analyses use points with timestamps in a specific window of time only. When the budgets of points in the window run out, the window is shifted to newer timestamps. Records with timestamps in the old window can be discarded. All analyses share the budgets of points in the active time window.

6   Preliminary Evaluation

This section presents a preliminary evaluation of the performance of our implementation of UniTraX. It is preliminary in that (1) it uses only one dataset (the New York City taxi ride dataset [18,21]), and (2) we carry out only one "analysis session". The session consists of queries that perform the basic statistical operations of count, average, and median.

Objective. Of primary interest to us is the increase in end-to-end latency experienced by the analyst (time from query submission to answer reception) as compared to both PINQ (reference DP) and LINQ (baseline that provides no privacy). Additionally, we want to understand the overhead of storing UniTraX's budget consumption history data structure.

In absolute terms, these overheads are a function of the access pattern on the parameter space. The exact column names, the data in them or the precise queries do not matter for this. Nonetheless, we briefly describe the dataset we use and the queries we run. The queries are deliberately chosen to be simple since long-running, complex queries will mask UniTraX's relative overheads.

Dataset. We use all taxi rides of New York City reported for January 2013 ($\approx$14M records). We modify these records to only contain numerical data and add an additional initial budget for each. For the purpose of our measurements all budgets are chosen high enough so that no budgets expire.

Analysis Session. Our session is roughly patterned off of the analysis of the same dataset described in [12]. The session consists of 1213 queries split into three groups. The first group covers the entire geographic area, and consists of six histograms for different columns. The subsequent groups focus on a 16 $\times$ 16 grid of squares in Manhattan. The second group of queries counts the number of rides in each square, and takes averages over two different columns for squares that have more than 5000 rides with sufficient budget. The third group counts rides again and takes the median of one column for squares that have more than 1000 rides with sufficient budget.

Experimental Setups. We run the session over each of the following three setups:

1. Directly on LINQ using the LINQ-to-SQL interface (no privacy protection).
2. Through a PINQ object (DP protection with a global budget).
3. With UniTraX.

All numbers presented in this section are averages of five runs of the session.

Hardware. All experiments run on two identical commodity Dell PowerEdge M620 blade systems. Each is equipped with dual Intel Xeon E5-2667 v2 8-core CPUs with Hyperthreading (total of 32 hardware threads per machine) and 256 GB of main memory. Both systems are connected to the same top-of-rack switch with two bonded 1 Gbit/s connections each.

Software. We use Microsoft Windows Server 2016 on both systems. The first system runs both UniTraX as well as the client query program. Microsoft Visual Studio Community 2015 is the only additional software installed for these tasks. The second system runs Microsoft SQL Server 2016 Developer Edition as the remote database server. To optimize database performance we put data and index files of our database onto a RAM-disk, create indexes that fit our queries, and make the database read-only.

Absolute and Relative Latency Overheads. Figure 6 presents absolute end-to-end latencies for the three experimental setups: direct, only PINQ, and UniTraX. A random 5% sample of the 1213 queries is shown, sorted on the x-axis by increasing latency with respect to the direct experiment. Overheads are moderate. As expected, UniTraX is usually slower than PINQ, which is slower than direct query execution without any privacy protection. In 3.2% of the cases, UniTraX outperforms direct and PINQ. We verified that in these cases the database server chose to do a sequential table scan for direct and PINQ but a parallel and thus faster index scan for UniTraX. We were unable to force parallel execution for direct and PINQ.

Figure 7 presents a CDF for all 1213 queries in terms of the overhead of UniTraX relative to direct and PINQ respectively. We observe that in half of the cases, UniTraX is 1.5x slower than PINQ and 2x slower than the direct case. At the 99th-percentile UniTraX is 2.5x slower than PINQ and 3.5x slower than the direct case. The figure includes a tail between 0 and 1, indicating that UniTraX is sometimes faster than PINQ or the direct case. As explained before, this behavior is due to the database choosing sub-optimal query plans for PINQ and the direct case. On average, UniTraX is 1.3x slower than PINQ and 1.8x slower than the direct case. In summary, latency overheads introduced by UniTraX are moderate.

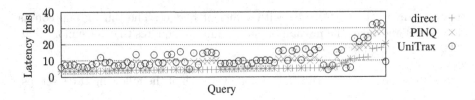

Fig. 6. End-to-end latencies of a 5% sample of the 1213 queries ordered according to latencies of direct. The trend in the order of performance is evident. UniTraX is slower than PINQ, which is slower than direct. Where UniTraX outperforms the others, the database chose a better query plan for UniTraX's queries.

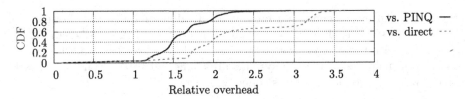

Fig. 7. CDF of relative overheads incurred by UniTraX across all 1213 queries. At the 99th-percentile UniTraX is 2.5x slower than PINQ and 3.5x slower than the direct case. The initial tail of inverse overhead before 1 consists of 3.2% of queries where the database chooses sub-optimal query plans for PINQ and the direct case.

Size of Budget Tracking State. Figure 8 shows the number of subspaces tracked by UniTraX at the beginning of each query. Numbers are again ordered according to query latencies in the direct case (see Fig. 6). These numbers do not change across different runs. The two curves represent two analyst query strategies, one with and one without *re-balancing*. These two curves illustrate that the analyst can dramatically affect the size of the budget tracking state based on how queries are formulated.

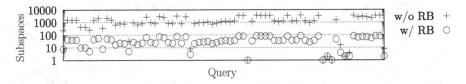

Fig. 8. Number of subspaces UniTraX tracks throughout the execution of the queries shown in Fig. 6. Reported numbers are obtained at the beginning of each query and do not change across different runs. The different curves represent two different analyst query strategies, one where the analyst only requests data of interest (w/o RB), and one where the analyst requests extra data in order to improve UniTraX's re-balancing (w/ RB). This shows that analysts can substantially reduce the overhead of UniTraX through careful selection of query parameters.

In the "without re-balancing" strategy (w/o RB), the analyst queries data only within a range of interest. For instance, suppose that the analyst is interested in a histogram of fares between $0 and $100. The analyst may request ten $10 bars. As long as each bar consumes the same budget, UniTraX will optimize tracking state and merge the subspaces of these 10 bars into a single subspace. The range above the histogram (above $100), however, cannot be merged. As a result, UniTraX stores two subspaces for the fare column. The same happens with other columns, with the result that there is a combinatoric explosion in the number of subspaces because of the combinations of the columns' multiple subspaces.

In the "with re-balancing" strategy (w/ RB), the analyst instead queries data that covers the full range of a column, even though the analyst may not be interested in all of that range, or may even know that no data exists in some subrange (e.g., no taxi pickups over water). As a result, UniTraX is able to merge more subspaces, even those of different columns. At the cost of budget, this reduces the number of subspaces substantially, in this case by more than an order of magnitude. Re-balancing thus allows analysts to trade-off overheads against budget savings.

7   Related Work

Due to its age, the area of privacy-preserving data analytics has amassed a vast amount of work. The related work section of [16] provides a good overview of early work in this space. Around ten years ago Dwork et al. introduced differential privacy or DP [6], which quickly developed into a standard for private data analytics research (see [7,8]). In this section, we focus on research that investigates heterogeneous or personalized budgets, tracking of personalized budgets, private analytics on dynamic data sets, and PINQ, the system our implementation is based on.

Alaggan et al. [1] propose heterogeneous differential privacy (HDP) to deal with user-specific privacy preferences. They allow users to provide a separate *privacy weight* for each individual data field, a granularity finer than that supported by UniTraX. However, the total privacy budget is a global parameter. When computing a statistical result over the dataset, HDP perturbs each accessed data value individually according to its weight and the global privacy budget. UniTraX can be extended to support per field rather than per record budgets at the cost of additional runtime latency. Further, UniTraX allows analysts to query parts of a dataset without consuming the privacy budget of other parts. UniTraX also supports a greater set of analytic functions, e.g., *median*. HDP does not provide these capabilities. Queries can only run over the whole dataset and, as privacy weights are secret, the exact amount of answer perturbation remains unknown to the analyst.

Jorgensen et al.'s personalized differential privacy (PDP) is a different approach to the same problem [15]. In contrast to UniTraX, PDP trusts analysts and assumes that per-user budgets are public. It tracks the budget globally but

manages to avoid being limited to the most restrictive user's budget by allowing the analyst to sample the dataset prior to generating any statistical output.
Depending on the sampling parameters the analyst is able to use more than the
smallest user budget for a query (but on a subset of records). PDP only supports
querying the entire dataset at once. Nevertheless, we believe that a combination
of PDP and UniTraX could be useful, in particular to allow analysts to make
high budget queries on low budget records. The combination could also do away
with PDP's assumption that analysts be trusted.

In place of personalized privacy protection, Nissim et al. [20] and earlier
research projects [5,14] provide users different monetary compensation based
on their individual privacy preferences. It is unclear whether these models can
be combined with UniTraX as they do not provide any personalized privacy
protection. Users with a higher valuation receive a higher compensation but
suffer the same privacy loss as other users.

Despite allowing users to specify individual privacy preferences, all the above
systems track budget globally and do not allow analysts to selectively query
records and consume budget only from the queried records. To the best of our
knowledge, ProPer [10] is the only system that allows this. We compared exten-
sively to ProPer in Sect. 2. Our formal model in Sect. 4 is also based on ProPer's
formal model. Google's RAPPOR [11] likewise provides differential privacy guarantees based on user-provided parameters, but the system model is significantly
different from ours and the privacy guarantee holds only when certain cross-
query correlations do not occur. In contrast, we (and ProPer) need no such
assumptions.

Differential privacy is being increasingly applied to dynamic datasets rather
than static databases. Since the first consideration of such scenarios in 2010 [9],
numerous systems have emerged [2–4,13,22,23] that aggregate dynamic data
streams rather than static datasets in a privacy-preserving manner. UniTraX and
ProPer can be immediately used for dynamic data streams since their designs
and privacy proofs already take record addition and deletion into account.

As explained in Sect. 5, our UniTraX implementation is based on the Privacy Integrated Queries (PINQ) [17] platform, which offers privacy-preserving
data analysis capabilities. PINQ, in turn, is based on the Language Integrated
Queries (LINQ) framework, a well-integrated declarative extension of the .NET
platform. LINQ provides a unified object-oriented data access and query interface, allowing analysts data access independent of how the data is provided and
where the answer is finally computed. Data providers can be switched without
changing code and can be, e.g., local files, remote SQL servers, or even mas-
sive parallel cluster systems like DryadLINQ [24]. PINQ provides a thin DP
wrapper over LINQ. For all queries, it ensures that sufficient budget is available
and that returned answers are appropriately noised. The maximum budget must
be provided during object initialization. Our implementation uses PINQ in an
unconventional way—we initialize a new PINQ object prior to every data analysis, and use PINQ to enforce a stipulated budget. Additionally, we track budget
consumption on subspaces of the parameter space across queries.

8   Conclusion and Future Work

This paper presented UniTraX, the first differentially private system that supports per-record privacy budgets, tells the analyst where (in the parameter space) budgets have been used in the past, and allows the analyst to query only those points that still have sufficient budget for the analyst's task. UniTraX attains this by tracking budget consumption not on actual records in the database, but on points in the parameter space. As a result, information about budget consumption reveals nothing about actual records to the analyst.

We have also presented a formal model of UniTraX and a formal proof that UniTraX respects differential privacy for all records. Our prototype implementation incurs moderate overheads on a realistic workload.

There are several directions for future work. First, our implementation is not very optimized and there is scope for reducing overheads even further. Second, UniTraX can be extended to track budgets at even finer granularity, e.g., a budget for every field. Third, one could investigate how queries can be optimized to reduce budget consumption.

References

1. Allagan, M., Gambs, S., Kermarrec, A.M.: Heterogeneous differential privacy. J. Priv. Confidentiality **7**(2), 127–158 (2016). Article 6, http://repository.cmu.edu/jpc/vol7/iss2/6/
2. Chan, T.-H.H., Li, M., Shi, E., Xu, W.: Differentially private continual monitoring of heavy hitters from distributed streams. In: Fischer-Hübner, S., Wright, M. (eds.) PETS 2012. LNCS, vol. 7384, pp. 140–159. Springer, Heidelberg (2012). https://doi.org/10.1007/978-3-642-31680-7_8
3. Chan, T.-H.H., Shi, E., Song, D.: Private and continual release of statistics. ACM Trans. Inf. Syst. Secur. (TISSEC) **14**(3), 26:1–26:24 (2011). https://doi.org/10.1145/2043621.2043626
4. Chan, T.-H.H., Shi, E., Song, D.: Privacy-preserving stream aggregation with fault tolerance. In: Keromytis, A.D. (ed.) FC 2012. LNCS, vol. 7397, pp. 200–214. Springer, Heidelberg (2012). https://doi.org/10.1007/978-3-642-32946-3_15
5. Dandekar, P., Fawaz, N., Ioannidis, S.: Privacy auctions for recommender systems. In: Goldberg, P.W. (ed.) WINE 2012. LNCS, vol. 7695, pp. 309–322. Springer, Heidelberg (2012). https://doi.org/10.1007/978-3-642-35311-6_23
6. Dwork, C.: Differential privacy. In: Bugliesi, M., Preneel, B., Sassone, V., Wegener, I. (eds.) ICALP 2006, Part II. LNCS, vol. 4052, pp. 1–12. Springer, Heidelberg (2006). https://doi.org/10.1007/11787006_1
7. Dwork, C.: Differential privacy: a survey of results. In: Agrawal, M., Du, D., Duan, Z., Li, A. (eds.) TAMC 2008. LNCS, vol. 4978, pp. 1–19. Springer, Heidelberg (2008). https://doi.org/10.1007/978-3-540-79228-4_1
8. Dwork, C.: A firm foundation for private data analysis. Commun. ACM (CACM) **54**(1), 86–95 (2011). https://doi.org/10.1145/1866739.1866758
9. Dwork, C., Naor, M., Pitassi, T., Rothblum, G.N.: Differential privacy under continual observation. In: Mitzenmacher, M., Schulman, L.J. (eds.) Proceedings of the 42nd ACM Symposium on Theory of Computing (STOC 2010), pp. 715–724. ACM, New York (2010). https://doi.org/10.1145/1806689.1806787

10. Ebadi, H., Sands, D., Schneider, G.: Differential privacy: now it's getting personal. In: Rajamani, S.K., Walker, D. (eds.) Proceedings of the 42nd Annual ACM SIGPLAN-SIGACT Symposium on Principles of Programming Languages (POPL 2015), pp. 69–81. ACM, New York (2015). https://doi.org/10.1145/2676726. 2677005

11. Erlingsson, Ú., Pihur, V., Korolova, A.: RAPPOR: randomized aggregatable privacy-preserving ordinal response. In: Ahn, G., Yung, M., Li, N. (eds.) Proceedings of the 2014 ACM SIGSAC Conference on Computer and Communications Security (CCS 2014), pp. 1054–1067. ACM, New York (2014). https://doi.org/10. 1145/2660267.2660348

12. Espín Noboa, L., Lemmerich, F., Singer, P., Strohmaier, M.: Discovering and characterizing mobility patterns in urban spaces: a study of Manhattan taxi data. In: Bourdeau, J., Hendler, J., Nkambou, R., Horrocks, I., Zhao, B.Y. (eds.) Proceedings of the 25th International Conference Companion on World Wide Web (WWW 2016 Companion), pp. 537–542. International World Wide Web Conferences Steering Committee, Republic and Canton of Geneva, Switzerland (2016). https://doi. org/10.1145/2872518.2890468

13. Friedman, A., Sharfman, I., Keren, D., Schuster, A.: Privacy-preserving distributed stream monitoring. In: Proceedings of the 21st Annual Symposium on Network and Distributed System Security (NDSS 2014). ISOC (2014). https://doi.org/10. 14722/ndss.2014.23128

14. Ghosh, A., Roth, A.: Selling privacy at auction. In: Shoham, Y., Chen, Y., Roughgarden, T. (eds.) Proceedings of the 12th ACM Conference on Electronic Commerce (EC 2011), pp. 199–208. ACM, New York (2011). https://doi.org/10.1145/ 1993574.1993605

15. Jorgensen, Z., Yu, T., Cormode, G.: Conservative or liberal? Personalized differential privacy. In: Gehrke, J., Lehner, W., Shim, K., Cha, S.K., Lohman, G.M. (eds.) Proceedings of the 31st IEEE International Conference on Data Engineering (ICDE 2015), pp. 1023–1034. IEEE (2015). https://doi.org/10.1109/ICDE.2015. 7113353

16. Machanavajjhala, A., Kifer, D., Gehrke, J., Venkitasubramaniam, M.: l-diversity: privacy beyond k-anonymity. ACM Trans. Knowl. Discov. Data (TKDD) 1(1) (2007). Article 3, https://doi.org/10.1145/1217299.1217302

17. McSherry, F.: Privacy integrated queries: an extensible platform for privacy-preserving data analysis. In: Çetintemel, U., Zdonik, S.B., Kossmann, D., Tatbul, N. (eds.) Proceedings of the ACM SIGMOD International Conference on Management of Data (SIGMOD 2009), pp. 19–30. ACM, New York (2009). https://doi. org/10.1145/1559845.1559850

18. Monroy-Hernández, A.: NYC taxi trips, June 2014. http://www.andresmh.com/ nyctaxitrips/

19. Munz, R., Eigner, F., Maffei, M., Francis, P., Garg, D.: UniTraX: protecting data privacy with discoverable biases. Technical report MPI-SWS-2018-001, Max Planck Institute for Software Systems (MPI-SWS), Kaiserslautern and Saarbrücken, Germany, February 2018. https://www.mpi-sws.org/tr/2018-001.pdf

20. Nissim, K., Vadhan, S.P., Xiao, D.: Redrawing the boundaries on purchasing data from privacy-sensitive individuals. In: Naor, M. (ed.) Proceedings of the 5th Conference on Innovations in Theoretical Computer Science (ITCS 2014), pp. 411–422. ACM, New York (2014). https://doi.org/10.1145/2554797.2554835

21. NYC Taxi & Limousine Commission: TLC trip record data, May 2017. http:// www.nyc.gov/html/tlc/html/about/trip_record_data.shtml

22. Rastogi, V., Nath, S.: Differentially private aggregation of distributed time-series with transformation and encryption. In: Elmagarmid, A.K., Agrawal, D. (eds.) Proceedings of the ACM SIGMOD International Conference on Management of Data (SIGMOD 2010), pp. 735–746. ACM, New York (2010). https://doi.org/10.1145/1807167.1807247
23. Shi, E., Chan, T.-H.H., Rieffel, E.G., Chow, R., Song, D.: Privacy-preserving aggregation of time-series data. In: Proceedings of the Symposium on Network and Distributed System Security (NDSS 2011). ISOC (2011). https://www.isoc.org/isoc/conferences/ndss/11/pdf/9_3.pdf
24. Yu, Y., Isard, M., Fetterly, D., Budiu, M., Erlingsson, Ú., Gunda, P.K., Currey, J.: DryadLINQ: a system for general-purpose distributed data-parallel computing using a high-level language. In: Draves, R., van Renesse, R. (eds.) Proceedings of the 8th USENIX Symposium on Operating Systems Design and Implementation (OSDI 2008), pp. 1–14. USENIX (2008). https://www.usenix.org/event/osdi08/tech/full_papers/yu_y/yu_y.pdf

Firewalls and Attack-Defense Trees

Transcompiling Firewalls

Chiara Bodei[1], Pierpaolo Degano[1], Riccardo Focardi[2], Letterio Galletta[1,3P (✉)],
and Mauro Tempesta[2]

[1] Università di Pisa, Pisa, Italy
galletta@di.unipi.it
[2] Università Ca' Foscari, Venice, Italy
[3] IMT School for Advanced Studies, Lucca, Italy

Abstract. Porting a policy from a firewall system to another is a difficult and error prone task. Indeed, network administrators have to know in
detail the policy meaning, as well as the internals of the firewall systems
and of their languages. Equally difficult is policy maintenance and refactoring, e.g., removing useless or redundant rules. In this paper, we present
a transcompiling pipeline that automatically tackles both problems: it
can be used to port a policy into an equivalent one, when the target firewall language is different from the source one; when the two languages
coincide, transcompiling supports policy maintenance and refactoring.
Our transcompiler and its correctness are based on a formal intermediate firewall language that we endow with a formal semantics.

1 Introduction

Firewalls are one of the standard mechanisms for protecting computer networks.
Configuring and maintaining them is very difficult also for expert system administrators since firewall policy languages are varied and usually rather complex,
they account for low-level system and network details and support non trivial
control flow constructs. Additional difficulties come from the way in which packets are processed by the network stack of the operating system and further issues
are due to Network Address Translation (NAT), the mechanism for translating
addresses and performing port redirection while packets traverse the firewall.

A configuration is typically composed of a large number of rules and it is often
hard to figure out the overall firewall behavior. Also, firewall rules interact with
each other, e.g., some shadow others making them redundant or preventing them
to be triggered. Often administrators resort to policy *refactoring* to solve these
issues and to obtain minimal and clean configurations. Software Defined Network
(SDN) paradigm has recently been proposed for programming the network as a
whole at a high level, making network and firewall configuration simpler and less

Work partially supported by CINI Cybersecurity National Laboratory within the
project FilieraSicura: Securing the Supply Chain of Domestic Critical Infrastructures from Cyber Attacks (www.filierasicura.it) funded by CISCO Systems Inc. and
Leonardo SpA.

© The Author(s) 2018
L. Bauer and R. Küsters (Eds.): POST 2018, LNCS 10804, pp. 303–324, 2018.
https://doi.org/10.1007/978-3-319-89722-6_13

error prone. However, network administrators have still to face the *porting* of firewall configurations from a variety of legacy devices into this new paradigm.

Both policy refactoring and porting are demanding operations because they require system administrators to have a deep knowledge about the policy meaning, as well as the internals of the firewall systems and of their languages. To automatically solve these problems we propose here a transcompiling pipeline composed of the following stages:

1. decompile the policy in the source language into an intermediate language;
2. extract the meaning of the policy as a set of non overlapping declarative rules describing the accepted packets and their translations in logical terms;
3. compile the declarative rules into the target language.

Another key contribution of this paper is to formalize this pipeline and to prove that it preserves the meaning of the original policy (Theorems 1, 2 and 3). The core of our proposal is the intermediate language IFCL (Sect. 4), which offers all the typical features of firewall languages such as NAT, jumps, invocations to rulesets and stateful packet filtering. This language unveils the bipartite structure common to real firewall languages: the rulesets determining the destiny of packets and the control flow in which the rules are applied. The relevant aspects of IFCL are its independence from specific firewall systems and their languages, and its formal semantics (Sect. 5). Remarkably, stage 1 provides real languages, which usually have no formal semantics, with the one inherited by the decompilation to IFCL. In this way the meaning of a policy is formally defined, so allowing algorithmic manipulations that yield the rules of stage 2 (Sect. 6). These rules represent minimal configurations in a declarative way, covering all accepted packets and their transformations, with neither overlapping nor shadowing rules. These two stages are implemented in a tool appearing in a companion paper [1] and surveyed below, in the section on related work. The translation algorithm of stage 3 (Sect. 7) distributes the rules determined in the previous stage on the relevant points of the firewall where it decides the destiny of packets.

To show our transcompilation at work, we consider **iptables** [2] and **pf** [3] (Sect. 2), since they have very different packet processing schemes making policy porting hard. In particular, we apply the stages of our pipeline to port a policy from **iptables** to **pf** (Sect. 3). For brevity, we do not include an example of refactoring, which occurs when the source and the target languages coincide.

Related Work. Formal methods have been used to model firewalls and access control, e.g., [4–6]. Below we restrict our attention to language-based approaches.

Transcompilation is a well-established technique to address the problem of code refactoring, automatic parallelization and porting legacy code to a new programming language. Recently, this technique has been largely used in the field of web programming to implement high level languages into JavaScript, see e.g., [7,8]. We tackle transcompilation in the area of firewall languages to support porting and refactoring of policies.

To the best of our knowledge, the literature has no approaches to mechanically porting firewall policies, while it has some to refactoring. The proposal in [9] is similar to ours, in that it "cleans" rulesets, then analyzes them by an automatic tool. It uses a formal semantics of `iptables` (without NAT) and a semantics-preserving ruleset simplification. The tool FIREMAN [10] detects inconsistencies and inefficiencies of firewall policies (without NAT). The Margrave policy analyzer [11] analyzes IOS firewalls, and is extensible to other languages. However the analysis focuses on finding specific problems in policies rather then synthesizing a high-level policy specification. Another tool for discovering anomalies is Fang [12,13], which also synthesizes an abstract policy. Our approach differs from the above proposals mainly because *at the same time* it (i) is language-independent; (ii) defines a formal semantics of firewall behavior; (iii) gives a declarative, concise and neat representation of such a behavior; (iv) supports NAT; (v) generates policies in a target language.

Among the papers that formalize the semantics of firewall languages, we mention [14,15] that specify abstract filtering policies to be then compiled into the actual firewall systems. More generally, NetKat [16] proposes linguistic constructs for programming a network as a whole within the SDN paradigm. All these approaches propose their own high level language with a formal semantics, and then compile it to a specific target language (cf. our stage 3). Instead, IFCL intermediates between real source and target languages. It thus takes from real languages actions both for filtering/rewriting packets (notably NAT and MARK) and for controlling the inspection flow, widely used in practice.

Our companion paper [1] describes the design of an automated tool and its application to real cases. The tool implements the first two stages of our pipeline and supports system administrators in the verification of some properties of a given firewall policy. In particular, the user can ask queries to check implication, equivalence and difference of policies, and reachability among hosts. The tool uses the same syntax of Sect. 4 but only sketches how to obtain the declarative representation of a given policy, while here we fully formalize the process and prove it correct (Sect. 6.2). In detail, the present paper partially overlaps with [1] on Sect. 4, where the language is presented, and on Sect. 6.2, where the logical characterization is introduced. Besides the technical details and theorems, which support the semantics and the correctness of the whole approach missing in [1], here we also address the issue of compiling the declarative firewall representation to a target language, enabling transcompilation (cf. Sects. 3 and 7).

2 Background

Usually, system administrators classify networks into security domains. Through firewalls they monitor the traffic and enforce a predetermined set of access control policies (*packet filtering*), possibly performing some network address translation.

Firewalls are implemented either as proprietary, special devices, or as software tools running on general purpose operating systems. Independently of their actual implementations, they are usually characterized by a set of rules that determine which packets reach the different subnetworks and hosts, and how they are modified or translated. We briefly review `iptables` [2] and `pf` [3] that are two of the most used firewall tools in Linux and Unix.

iptables. It is the default in Linux distributions, and operates on top of Netfilter, the standard framework for packets processing of the Linux kernel [2]. This tool is based on the notions of *tables* and *chains*. Intuitively, a table is a collection of ordered lists of policy rules called chains. The most commonly used tables are: `filter` for packet filtering; `nat` for network address translation; `mangle` for packet alteration. There are five built-in chains that are inspected at specific moments of the packet life cycle [17]: `PreRouting`, when the packet reaches the host; `Forward`, when the packet is routed through the host; `PostRouting`, right before the packet leaves the host; `Input`, when the packet is routed to the host; `Output`, when the packet is generated by the host. Moreover, users can define additional chains, besides the built-in ones.

Each rule specifies a condition and a target. If the packet matches the condition then it is processed according to the specified target. The most common targets are: ACCEPT and DROP, to accept and discard packets; DNAT/SNAT, to perform destination/source NAT; MARK to mark a packet with a numeric identifier which can be used in the conditions of other rules, even placed in different chains; RETURN, to stop examining the current chain and resume the processing of a previous chain. When the target is a user-defined chain, two "jumping" modes are available: *call* and *goto*. They differ when a RETURN is executed or the end of the chain is reached: the evaluation resumes from the rule following the last matched call. Built-in chains have a user-configurable default policy (ACCEPT or DROP): if the evaluation reaches the end of a built-in chain without matches, its default policy is applied.

pf. This is the standard firewall of OpenBSD [3] and is included in macOS since version 10.7. Similarly to `iptables`, each rule consists of a predicate which is used to select packets and an action that specifies how to process the packets satisfying the predicate. The most frequently used actions are `pass` and `block` to accept and reject packets, `rdr` and `nat` to perform destination and source NAT. Packet marking is supported also by `pf`: if a rule containing the `tag` keyword is applied, the packet is marked with the specified identifier and then processed according to the rule's action.

Differently from other firewalls, the action taken on a packet is determined by the *last matched rule*, unless otherwise specified. `pf` has a single ruleset that is inspected both when the packet enters and exits the host. When a packet enters the host, DNAT rules are examined first and filtering is performed after the address translation. Similarly when a packet leaves the host: first its source address is translated by the relevant SNAT rules, and then the resulting packet is possibly filtered. Notice also that packets belonging to established connections are accepted by default, thus bypassing the filters.

3   Porting a Policy: An Example

Consider the simple, yet realistic network of Fig. 1, where the IP addresses 10.0.0.0/8 identify the private LAN; 54.230.203.0/24 identify servers and production machines in the demilitarized zone DMZ that also hosts the HTTPS server

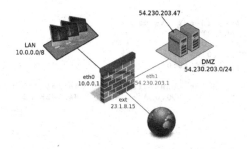

Fig. 1. A network.

Table 1. Declarative representation of the configuration in Fig. 2.

Src IP	Src Port	SNAT IP	SNAT Port	DNAT IP	DNAT Port	Dest IP	Dest Port	Prot	State
*	*	-	-	-	-	{54.230.203.47}	443	tcp	NEW
10.0.0.0/8	*	-	-	-	-	54.230.203.0/24	*	*	NEW

10.0.0.0/8	*	23.1.8.15	-	-	-	* \ {
						10.0.0.0/8
						54.230.203.0/24
						127.0.0.0/8
						}
							80
							443
								tcp	NEW

*	*	*	*	*	*	*	*	*	ESTABLISHED

with address 54.230.203.47. The firewall has three interfaces: eth0 connected to the LAN with IP 10.0.0.1, eth1 connected to the DMZ with IP 54.230.203.1 and ext connected to the Internet with public IP 23.1.8.15.

The iptables configuration in Fig. 2 enforces the following policy on the traffic: (i) hosts from the Internet can connect to the HTTPS server; (ii) LAN hosts can freely connect to any host in the DMZ; (iii) LAN hosts can connect to the Internet over HTTP and HTTPS (with source NAT). Now, suppose the system administrator has to migrate the firewall configuration of Fig. 2 from iptables to pf. Performing this porting by hand is complex and error prone because the administrator has to write the pf configuration from scratch and test that it is equivalent to the original one. Furthermore, this requires a deep understanding of the policy meaning, as well as of both iptables and pf and of their configuration languages. We apply below the stages of our pipeline to solve this problem, guaranteeing by construction that the firewall semantics is preserved. The next sections detail the following intuitive description.

First we extract the meaning of the iptables configuration represented by a table, in our case Table 1 (stages 1 and 2). For instance, its second row says that the packets of a new connection with source address in the range 10.0.0.0/8 (i.e., from the LAN) can reach the hosts in the range 54.230.203.0/24 (the DMZ), with no NAT, regardless of the protocol and the port. The last row says that packets of an already established connection are always allowed. Note that each row in the table declaratively describes a set of packets accepted by the firewall, and their network translation. Actually, Table 1 is a clean, *refactored* policy automatically generated by the tool of [1]. Indeed, each row is disjoint from the others, so they need not to be ordered and none of the typical firewall anomalies arises, like

```
1    *nat
2    # ACCEPT policy in nat chains
3    :PREROUTING ACCEPT [0:0]
4    :INPUT ACCEPT [0:0]
5    :OUTPUT ACCEPT [0:0]
6    :POSTROUTING ACCEPT [0:0]
7
8    #(iii) Apply SNAT on connections from the LAN towards the Internet
9    -A POSTROUTING -s 10.0.0.0/8 -o ext -j MASQUERADE
10
11   COMMIT
12
13   *filter
14   # DROP policy in filtering chains
15   :INPUT DROP [0:0]
16   :FORWARD DROP [0:0]
17   :OUTPUT DROP [0:0]
18
19   # Allow established packets
20   -A FORWARD -m state --state ESTABLISHED -j ACCEPT
21   #(ii) LAN hosts can connect to DMZ
22   -A FORWARD -s 10.0.0.0/8 -d 54.230.203.0/24 -j ACCEPT
23   #(iii) LAN hosts can connect to the Internet over HTTP/HTTPS
24   -A FORWARD -s 10.0.0.0/8 -o ext -p tcp --dport 80 -j ACCEPT
25   -A FORWARD -s 10.0.0.0/8 -o ext -p tcp --dport 443 -j ACCEPT
26   #(i) Any host can connect to the HTTPS server in the DMZ
27   -A FORWARD -d 54.230.203.47 -p tcp --dport 443 -j ACCEPT
28
29   COMMIT
```

Fig. 2. Firewall configuration in `iptables`.

```
1   nat proto tcp from 10.0.0.0/8 to {!10.0.0.0/8, !54.230.203.0/24, !127.0.0.0/8}
2     port {80, 443} tag T1 -> 23.1.8.15
3
4   block all
5   pass proto tcp from any to 54.230.203.47 port 443
6   pass from 10.0.0.0/8 to 54.230.203.0/24
7   pass tagged T1
```

Fig. 3. The policy in Fig. 2 ported in `pf`.

shadowing, rule overlapping, etc. According to stage 3, we compile the refactored policy in `pf`, in two steps. First, the rows are translated in a sequence of IFCL rules that are then compiled in `pf`. The result is in Fig. 3 and was computed with a proof-of-concept extension of [1] based on the theory presented in Sect. 7.

4   The Intermediate Firewall Configuration Language

We now present our intermediate firewall configuration language (IFCL). It is parametric w.r.t. the notion of state and the steps performed to elaborate packets. For generality, we do not detail the format of network packets. In the following we only use $sa(p)$ and $da(p)$ to denote the source and destination addresses of a given packet p; additionally, $tag(p)$ returns the tag m associated with p. An address a consists of an IP address $ip(a)$ and possibly a port $port(a)$. An *address range* n is a pair consisting of a set of IP addresses and a set of ports, denoted $IP(n):port(n)$. An address a is in the range n (written $a \in n$) if $ip(a) \in ip(n)$

and $port(a) \in port(n)$, when $port(a)$ is defined, e.g., for ICMP packets we only check if the IP address is in the range.

Firewalls modify packets, e.g., through network address translations. We write $p[da \mapsto a]$ and $p[sa \mapsto a]$ to denote a packet identical to p, except for the destination address da and source address sa, which is equal to a, respectively. Similarly, $p[tag \mapsto m]$ denotes the packet with a modified tag m.

Here we consider *stateful* firewalls that keep track of the state s of network connections and use this information to process a packet. Any existing network connection can be described by several protocol-specific properties, e.g., source and destination addresses or ports, and by the translations to apply. In this way, filtering and translation decisions are not only based on administrator-defined rules, but also on the information built by previous packets belonging to the same connection. We omit a precise definition of a state, but we assume that it tracks at least the source and destination ranges, NAT operations and the state of the connection, i.e., established or not. When receiving a packet p one may check whether it matches the state s or not. We left unspecified the match between a packet and the state because it depends on the actual shape of the state. When the match succeeds, we write $p \vdash_s \alpha$, where α describes the actions to be carried on p; otherwise we write $p \nvdash_s$.

A firewall rule is made of two parts: a predicate ϕ expressing criteria over packets, and an action t, called *target*, defining the "destiny" of matching packets. Here we consider a core set of actions included in most of the real firewalls. These actions not only determine whether or not a packet passes across the firewall, but also control the flow in which the rules are applied. They are the following:

ACCEPT	a packet passes
DROP	a packet is discarded
CALL(R)	invoke the ruleset R (see below)
GOTO(R)	jump to the ruleset R
RETURN	exit from the current ruleset
NAT(n_d, n_s)	network translation
MARK(m)	marking with tag m
CHECK-STATE(X)	examine the state

The targets CALL(_) and RETURN implement a procedure-like behavior; GOTO(_) is similar to unconditional jumps. In the NAT action n_d and n_s are address ranges used to translate the destination and source address of a packet, respectively; in the following we use the symbol $\star$ to denote an identity translation, e.g., $n : \star$ means that the address is translated according to n, whereas the port is kept unchanged. The MARK action marks a packet with a tag m. The argument $X \in \{\leftarrow, \rightarrow, \leftrightarrow\}$ of the CHECK-STATE action denotes the fields of the packets that are rewritten according to the information from the state. More precisely, $\rightarrow$ rewrites the destination address, $\leftarrow$ the source one and $\leftrightarrow$ both. Formally:

Definition 1 (Firewall rule). *A firewall rule r is a pair (ϕ, t) where ϕ is a logical formula over a packet, and t is the target action of the rule.*

A packet p matches a rule r with target t whenever ϕ holds.

Definition 2 (Rule match). *Given a rule $r = (\phi, t)$ we say that p matches r with target t, denoted $p \models_r t$, iff $\phi(p)$. We write $p \not\models_r$ when p does not match r.*

We can now define how a packet is processed given a possibly empty list of rules (denoted with ϵ), hereafter called *ruleset*. Similarly to real implementations of firewalls, we inspect the rules in the list, one after the other, until we find a matching one, which establishes the destiny (or target) of the packet. For sanity, we assume that no GOTO(R) and CALL(R) occur in the ruleset R, so avoiding self-loops. We also assume that rulesets may have a default target denoted by $t_d \in \{\text{ACCEPT}, \text{DROP}\}$, which accepts or drops according to the will of the system administrator.

Definition 3 (Ruleset match). *Given a ruleset $R = [r_1, \ldots, r_n]$, we say that p matches the i-th rule with target t, denoted $p \models_R (t, i)$, iff*

$$i \leq n \, . \, r_i = (\phi, t) \wedge p \models_{r_i} t \wedge \forall j < i \, . \, p \not\models_{r_j} .$$

We also write $p \not\models_R$ if p matches no rules in R, formally if $\forall r \in R \, . \, p \not\models_r$. Afterwords, we will omit the index i when immaterial, and we simply write $p \models_R t$.

In our model we do not explicitly specify the steps performed by the kernel of the operating system to process a single packet passing through the host. We represent this algorithm through a *control diagram*, i.e., a graph where nodes represent different processing steps and the arcs determine the sequence of steps. The arcs are labeled with a predicate describing the requirements a packet has to meet in order to pass to the next processing phase. Therefore, they are not finite state auomata. We assume that control diagrams are deterministic, i.e., that every pair of arcs leaving the same node has mutually exclusive predicates. For generality, we let these predicates abstract, since they depend on the specific firewall.

Definition 4 (Control diagram). *Let Ψ be a set of predicates over packets. A control diagram $\mathcal{C}$ is a tuple (Q, A, q_i, q_f), where*

- *Q is the set of nodes;*
- *$A \subseteq Q \times \Psi \times Q$ is the set of arcs, such that whenever $(q, \psi, q'), (q, \psi', q'') \in A$ and $q' \neq q''$ then $\neg(\psi \wedge \psi')$;*
- *$q_i, q_f \in Q$ are special nodes denoting the start and the end of elaboration.*

The firewall filters and possibly translates a given packet by traversing a control diagram accordingly to the following transition function.

Definition 5 (Transition function). *Let (Q, A, q_i, q_f) be a control diagram and let p be a packet. The transition function $\delta \colon Q \times Packet \mapsto Q$ is defined as*

$$\delta(q, p) = q' \quad iff \quad \exists (q, \psi, q') \in A. \ \psi(p) \ holds.$$

We can now define a firewall in IFCL.

Definition 6 (Firewall). *A firewall $\mathcal{F}$ is a triple $(\mathcal{C}, \rho, c)$, where $\mathcal{C}$ is a control diagram; ρ is a set of rulesets; and $c \colon Q \mapsto \rho$ is the correspondence mapping from the nodes of $\mathcal{C}$ to the actual rulesets.*

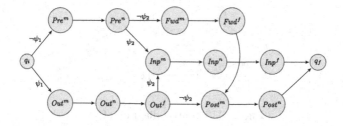

Fig. 4. The control diagram of `iptables`

4.1 Decompiling Two Real Languages into IFCL

Here we encode the two *de facto* standard Unix firewalls `iptables` and `pf` as triples $(\mathcal{C}, \rho, c)$ of our framework (stage 1). An immediate fallout is a formal semantics for both `iptables` and `pf` defined in terms of that of IFCL (see Sect. 5).

Modelling `iptables`. Let $\mathcal{L}$ be the set of local addresses of a host; and let ψ_1 and ψ_2 predicates over packets defined as follows:

$$\psi_1(p) = sa(p) \in \mathcal{L} \qquad \psi_2(p) = da(p) \in \mathcal{L}.$$

Figure 4 shows the control diagram $\mathcal{C}$ of `iptables`, where unlabeled arcs carry the label *"true."* It also implicitly defines the transition function according to Definition 5. In `iptables` there are twelve built-in chains, each of which correspond to a single ruleset. So we can define the set $\rho_p \subseteq \rho$ of primitive rulesets as the one made of R_{INP}^{man}, R_{INP}^{nat}, R_{INP}^{fil}, R_{OUT}^{man}, R_{OUT}^{nat}, R_{OUT}^{fil}, R_{PRE}^{man}, R_{PRE}^{nat}, R_{FOR}^{man}, R_{FOR}^{fil}, R_{POST}^{man} and R_{POST}^{nat}, where the superscript represents the chain name and the subscript the table name. Note that the set $\rho \setminus \rho_p$ contains the user-defined chains.

The mapping function $c\colon Q \mapsto \rho$ is defined as follows:

$$
\begin{aligned}
c(q_i) &= R & c(q_f) &= R & c(Pre^m) &= R_{\text{PRE}}^{man} \\
c(Pre^n) &= R_{\text{PRE}}^{nat} & c(Inp^m) &= R_{\text{INP}}^{man} & c(Fwd^f) &= R_{\text{FOR}}^{fil} \\
c(Inp^n) &= R_{\text{INP}}^{nat} & c(Inp^f) &= R_{\text{INP}}^{fil} & c(Out^m) &= R_{\text{OUT}}^{man} \\
c(Out^n) &= R_{\text{OUT}}^{nat} & c(Out^f) &= R_{\text{OUT}}^{fil} & c(Fwd^m) &= R_{\text{FOR}}^{man} \\
c(Fwd^f) &= R_{\text{FOR}}^{fil} & c(Post^m) &= R_{\text{POST}}^{man} & c(Post^n) &= R_{\text{POST}}^{nat}
\end{aligned}
$$

where R is an empty ruleset with ACCEPT as default policy.

Finally, note that the action CALL(_) implements the built in target JUMP(_).

Modelling `pf`. Differently from `iptables`, `pf` has a single ruleset and the rule applied to a packet is the last one matched, apart from the case of the so-called `quick` rules: as soon as one of these rules matches the packet, its action is applied and the remaining part of the ruleset is skipped.

Figure 5 shows the control diagram $\mathcal{C}_{pf}$ for `pf` that also defines the transition function. The nodes Inp^n and Inp^f represent the procedure executed when an

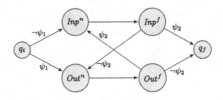

Fig. 5. The control diagram of pf

IP packet reaches the host from the net. Dually, Out^n and Out^f are for when the packet leaves the host. The predicates ψ_1 and ψ_2 are those defined for iptables. Given the pf ruleset R_{pf} we include the following rulesets in ρ_{pf}:

- R_{dnat} contains the rule $(state == 1, \text{CHECK-STATE}(\rightarrow))$ as the first one, followed by all the rules rdr of R_{pf};
- R_{snat} contains the rule $(state == 1, \text{CHECK-STATE}(\leftarrow))$ as the first one, followed by all the rules nat of R_{pf};
- R_{finp} contains the rule $(state == 1, \text{ACCEPT})$ followed by all the quick filtering rules of R_{pf} without modifier out, and finally the rule $(true, \text{GOTO}(R_{finpr}))$;
- R_{finpr} contains all the no quick filtering rules of R_{pf} without modifier out, in reverse order;
- R_{fout} contains the rule $(state == 1, \text{ACCEPT})$ followed by all the quick filtering rules of R_{pf} without modifier in, and $(true, \text{GOTO}(R_{foutr}))$ as last rule;
- R_{foutr} includes all the no quick filtering rules of R_{pf} without modifier in in reverse order.

Given the ruleset R with the only rule for ACCEPT as default policy, the mapping function c_{pf} is defined as follows:

$$c_{pf}(q_i) = R \qquad c_{pf}(Inp^n) = R_{dnat} \qquad c_{pf}(Out^n) = R_{snat}$$
$$c_{pf}(q_f) = R \qquad c_{pf}(Inp^f) = R_{finp} \qquad c_{pf}(Out^f) = R_{fout}$$

5   Formal Semantics

Now, we formally define the semantics of a firewall through two transition systems operating in a master-slave fashion. The master has a labeled transition relation of the form $s \xrightarrow{p,p'} s'$. The intuition is that the state s of a firewall changes to s' when a new packet p reaches the host and becomes p'.

The configurations of the slave transition system are triples (q, s, p) where: (i) $q \in Q$ is a control diagram node; (ii) s is the state of the firewall; (iv) p is the packet. A transition $(q, s, p) \rightarrow (q', s, p')$ describes how a firewall in a state s deals with a packet p and possibly transforms it in p', according to the control diagram $\mathcal{C}$. Recall that the state records established connections and other kinds of information that are updated after the transition.

In the slave transition relation, we use the following predicate, which describes an algorithm that runs a ruleset R on a packet p in the state s

$$p, s \models_R^S (t, p')$$

This predicate searches for a rule in R matching the packet p through $p \models_R (t, i)$. If it finds a match with target t, t is applied to p to obtain a new packet p'.

Recall that actions CALL(R), RETURN and GOTO(R) are similar to procedure calls, returns and jumps in imperative programming languages. To correctly deal with them, our predicate $p, s \models_R^S (t, p')$ uses a stack S to implement a behavior similar to the one of procedure calls. We will denote with ϵ the empty stack and with $\cdot$ the concatenation of elements on the stack. This stack is also used to detect and prevent loops in ruleset invocation, as it is the case in real firewalls.

In the stack S we overline a ruleset R to indicate that it was pushed by a GOTO(.) action and it has to be skipped when returning. Indeed, we use the following pop^* function in the semantics of the RETURN action:

$$pop^*(\epsilon) = \epsilon \qquad pop^*(R \cdot S) = (R, S) \qquad pop^*(\overline{R} \cdot S) = pop^*(S)$$

In case there is a non-overlined ruleset on the top of S, it behaves as a standard pop operation; otherwise it extracts the first non-overlined ruleset. When S is empty, we assume that pop^* returns ϵ to signal the error.

Furthermore, in the definition of $p, s \models_R^S (t, p')$ we use the notation R_k to indicate the ruleset $[r_k, ..., r_n]$ ($k \in [1, n]$) resulting from dropping the first $k - 1$ rules from the given ruleset $R = [r_1, ..., r_n]$.

We also assume the function $establ$ that, taken an action α from the state, a packet p and the fields $X \in \{\leftarrow, \rightarrow, \leftrightarrow\}$ to rewrite, returns a possibly changed packet p', e.g., in case of an established connection. Also this function depends on the specific firewall we are modeling, and so it is left unspecified.

Finally, we assume as given a function $nat(p, s, d_n, s_n)$ that returns the packet p translated under the corresponding NAT operation in the state s. The argument d_n is used to modify the destination range of p, i.e., destination NAT (DNAT), while s_n is used to modify the source range, i.e., source NAT (DNAT). Recall that a range of the form $\star : \star$ is interpreted as the identity translation, whereas one of the form $a : \star$ modifies only the address. Also this function is left abstract.

Table 2 shows the rules defining $p, s \models_R^S (t, p')$. The first inference rule deals with the case when the packet p matches a rule that says ACCEPT or DROP; in this case the ruleset execution stops returning the found action and leaving p unmodified. When a packet p matches a rule with action CHECK-STATE, we query the state s: if p belongs to an established connection, we return ACCEPT and a p' obtained rewriting p. If p belongs to no existent connection the packet is matched against the remaining rules in the ruleset. When a packet p matches a NAT rule, we return ACCEPT and the packet resulting by the invocation of the function nat. There are two cases if a packet p matches a GOTO(.). If the ruleset R' is not already in the stack, we push the current ruleset R onto the stack overlined to record that this ruleset dictated a GOTO(.). Otherwise, if R' is in the stack, we detect a loop and discard p. The case when a packet p matches a rule with action CALL(.) is similar,

Table 2. The predicate $p, s \models_R^S (t, p')$.

$$(1) \quad \frac{p \models_R (t, i) \quad t \in \{\text{ACCEPT}, \text{DROP}\}}{p, s \models_R^S (t, p)}$$

$$(2) \quad \frac{p \models_R (\text{CHECK-STATE}(X), i) \quad p \vdash_s \alpha \quad p' = establ(\alpha, X, p)}{p, s \models_R^S (\text{ACCEPT}, p')}$$

$$(3) \quad \frac{p \models_R (\text{CHECK-STATE}(X), i) \quad p \not\vdash_s \quad p, s \models_{R_{i+1}}^S (t, p')}{p, s \models_R^S (t, p')}$$

$$(4) \quad \frac{p \models_R (\text{NAT}(d_n, s_n), i)}{p, s \models_R^S (\text{ACCEPT}, nat(p, s, d_n, s_n))}$$

$$(5) \quad \frac{p \models_R (\text{GOTO}(R'), i) \quad R' \notin S \quad p, s \models_{R'}^{\overline{R}, S} (t, p')}{p, s \models_R^S (t, p')}$$

$$(6) \quad \frac{p \models_R (\text{GOTO}(R'), i) \quad R' \in S}{p, s \models_R^S (\text{DROP}, p)}$$

$$(7) \quad \frac{p \models_R (\text{CALL}(R'), i) \quad R' \notin S \quad p, s \models_{R'}^{R_{i+1} \cdot S} (t, p')}{p, s \models_R^S (t, p')}$$

$$(8) \quad \frac{p \models_R (\text{CALL}(R'), i) \quad R' \in S}{p, s \models_R^S (\text{DROP}, p)}$$

$$(9) \quad \frac{p \models_R (\text{RETURN}, i) \quad pop^*(S) = (R', S') \quad p, s \models_{R'}^{S'} (t, p')}{p, s \models_R^S (t, p')}$$

$$(10) \quad \frac{p \models_R (\text{RETURN}, i) \quad pop^*(S) = \epsilon}{p, s \models_R^S (t_d, p)}$$

$$(11) \quad \frac{p \not\models_R \quad S \neq \epsilon \quad pop^*(S) = (R', S') \quad p, s \models_{R'}^{S'} (t, p')}{p, s \models_R^S (t, p')}$$

$$(12) \quad \frac{p \not\models_R \quad (S = \epsilon \vee pop^*(S) = \epsilon)}{p, s \models_R^S (t_d, p)}$$

$$(13) \quad \frac{p \models_R (\text{MARK}(m), i) \quad p[tag \mapsto m], s \models_{R_{i+1}}^S (t, p')}{p, s \models_R^S (t, p')}$$

except that the ruleset pushed on the stack is not overlined. When a packet p matches a rule with action RETURN, we pop the stack and match p against the top of the stack. Finally, when no rule matches, an implicit return occurs: we continue from the top of the stack, if non empty. The MARK rule simply changes the tag of the matching packet to the value m. If none of the above applies, we return the default action t_d of the current ruleset.

We can now define the slave transition relation as follows.

$$\frac{c(q) = R \quad p, s \models_R^\epsilon (\text{ACCEPT}, p') \quad \delta(q, p') = q'}{(q, s, p) \to (q', s, p')}$$

The rule describes how we process the packet p when the firewall is in the elaboration step represented by the node q with a state s. We match p against the ruleset R associated with q and if p is accepted as p', we continue considering the next step of the firewall execution represented by the node q'.

Finally, we define the master transition relation that transforms states and packets as follows (as usual, below $\to^+$ stands for the transitive closure of $\to$):

$$\frac{(q_i, s, p) \to^+ (q_f, s, p')}{s \xrightarrow{p, p'} s \uplus (p, p')}$$

This rule says that when the firewall is in the state s and receives a packet p, it elaborates p starting from the initial node q_i of its control diagram. If this elaboration succeeds, i.e., it reaches the node q_f accepts p as p', we update the state s by storing information about p, its translation p' and the connection they belong to, through the function $\uplus$, left unspecified for the sake of generality.

Example 1. Suppose to have the user-defined chains below

Chain C_B	Chain u_1	Chain u_2
(ϕ_1, DROP)	$(\phi_{11}, \text{ACCEPT})$	$(\phi_{21}, \text{ACCEPT})$
$(\phi_2, \text{CALL}(u_1))$	$(\phi_{12}, \text{CALL}(u_2))$	$(\phi_{22}, \text{RETURN})$
(ϕ_3, ACCEPT)	(ϕ_{13}, DROP)	(ϕ_{23}, DROP)

and that the condition $\neg\phi_1 \wedge \phi_2 \wedge \phi_{11}$ holds for a packet p. Then, the semantic rules (a), (b) and (c) are applied in order:

$$(a) \quad \frac{p \models_{C_B} (\text{CALL}(u_1), i) \quad u_1 \notin S \quad p, s \models_{u_1}^{C_{B_3} \cdot \epsilon} (\text{ACCEPT}, p)}{p, s \models_{C_B}^{\epsilon} (\text{ACCEPT}, p)}$$

$$(b) \quad \frac{p \models_{u_1} (\text{ACCEPT}, 1)}{p, s \models_{u_1}^{C_{B_3} \cdot \epsilon} (\text{ACCEPT}, p)} \qquad (c) \quad \frac{c(q) = C_B \quad p, s \models_{C_B}^{\epsilon} (\text{ACCEPT}, p) \quad \delta(q, p) = q'}{(q, s, p) \rightarrow (q', s, p)}$$

6 From Operational to Declarative Descriptions

We now extract the meaning of a firewall written in our intermediate language by transforming it in a declarative, logical presentation that preserves the semantics (stage 2). This transformation is done in three steps: (i) generate an unfolded firewall with a single ruleset for each node of the control diagram; (ii) transform the unfolded firewall in a first-order formula; (iii) determine a model for the obtained formula, through a SAT solver (the procedure for this step is described in [1] and is omitted here). The correctness of stage 2 follows from Theorem 1, which guarantees that the unfolded firewall is semantically equivalent to the original one, and from Theorem 2, which ensures that the derived formula characterizes exactly the accepted packets and their translations.

6.1 Unfolding Chains

Our intermediate language can deal with involved control flows, by using the targets GOTO(_), CALL(_) and RETURN (see Example 1). The following unfolding operation $[\![\_]\!]$ rewrites a ruleset into an equivalent one with no control flow rules.

Hereafter, let $r; R$ be a non empty ruleset consisting of a rule r followed by a possibly empty ruleset R; and let $R_1 @ R_2$ be the concatenation of R_1 and R_2. The unfolding of a ruleset R is defined as follows:

$$[\![R]\!] = [\![R]\!]_{\{R\}}^{true}$$

$$[\![\epsilon]\!]_I^f = \epsilon$$

$$[\![(\phi, t); R]\!]_I^f = (f \wedge \phi, t); [\![R]\!]_I^f \quad \text{if } t \notin \{\text{GOTO}(R'), \text{CALL}(R'), \text{RETURN}\}$$

$$[\![(\phi, \text{RETURN}); R]\!]_I^f = [\![R]\!]_I^{f \wedge \neg\phi}$$

$$[\![(\phi, \text{CALL}(R')); R]\!]_I^f = \begin{cases} [\![R']\!]_{I \cup \{R'\}}^{f \wedge \phi} @ [\![R]\!]_I^f & \text{if } R' \notin I \\ (f \wedge \phi, \text{DROP}); [\![R]\!]_I^f & \text{otherwise} \end{cases}$$

316 C. Bodei et al.

$$[\![(\phi, \text{GOTO}(\text{R'})); R]\!]_I^f = \begin{cases} [\![R']\!]_{I \cup \{R'\}}^{f \wedge \phi} @ [\![R]\!]_I^{f \wedge \neg \phi} & \text{if } R' \notin I \\ (f \wedge \phi, \text{DROP}); [\![R]\!]_I^{f \wedge \neg \phi} & \text{otherwise} \end{cases}$$

The auxiliary procedure $[\![R]\!]_I^f$ recursively inspects the ruleset R. The formula f accumulates conjuncts of the predicate ϕ; the set I records the rulesets traversed by the procedure and helps detecting loops. If a rule does not affect control flow, we just substitute the conjunction $f \wedge \phi$ for ϕ, and continue to analyze the rest of the ruleset with the recursive call $[\![R]\!]_I^f$.

In the case of a return rule (ϕ, RETURN) we generate no new rule, and we continue to recursively analyze the rest of the ruleset, by updating f with the negation of ϕ. For the rule $(\phi, \text{CALL}(\text{R'}))$ we have two cases: if the callee ruleset R' is not in I, we replace the rule with the unfolding of R' with $f \wedge \phi$ as predicate, and append $\{R'\}$ to the traversed rulesets. If R' is already in I, i.e., we have a loop, we replace the rule with a DROP, with $f \wedge \phi$ as predicate. In both cases, we continue unfolding the rest of the ruleset. We deal with the rule $(\phi, \text{GOTO}(\text{R'}))$ as the previous one, except that the rest of the ruleset has $f \wedge \neg \phi$ as predicate.

Example 2. Back to Example 1, unfolding the chain C_B gives the following rules:

$$\begin{aligned} [\![C_B]\!] = \ & (\phi_1, \text{DROP}); \\ & (\phi_2 \wedge \phi_{11}, \text{ACCEPT}); \\ & (\phi_2 \wedge \phi_{12} \wedge \phi_{21}, \text{ACCEPT}); \\ & (\phi_2 \wedge \phi_{12} \wedge \neg\phi_{22} \wedge \phi_{23}, \text{DROP}); \\ & (\phi_2 \wedge \phi_{13}, \text{DROP}); \\ & (\phi_3, \text{ACCEPT}); \\ & \epsilon \end{aligned}$$

We just illustrate the first three steps:

$$\begin{aligned} [\![C_B]\!] &= [\![(\phi_1, \text{DROP}); C_{B2}]\!]_{\{C_B\}}^{true} = (\phi_1, \text{DROP}); [\![(\phi_2, \text{CALL}(u_1)); C_{B3}]\!]_{\{C_B\}}^{true} \\ &= [\![u_1]\!]_{\{C_B\} \cup \{u_1\}}^{true \wedge \phi_2} @ [\![C_{B3}]\!]_{\{C_B\}}^{true} \end{aligned}$$

Note that our transformation does not change the set of accepted packets, e.g., all packets satisfying $\neg\phi_1 \wedge \phi_2 \wedge \phi_{11}$ are still accepted by the unfolded ruleset.

An unfolded firewall is obtained by repeatedly rewriting the rulesets associated with the nodes of its control diagram, using the procedure above. Formally,

Definition 7 (Unfolded firewall). *Given a firewall $\mathcal{F} = (\mathcal{C}, \rho, c)$, its unfolded version $[\![\mathcal{F}]\!]$ is $(\mathcal{C}, \rho', c')$ where $\forall q \in \mathcal{C}. c'(q) = [\![c(q)]\!]$ and $\rho' = \{[\![c(q)]\!] \mid q \in \mathcal{C}\}$.*

We now prove that a firewall $\mathcal{F}$ and its unfolded version $[\![\mathcal{F}]\!]$ are semantically equivalent, i.e., they perform the same action over a given packet p in a state s, and reach the same state s'. Formally, the following theorem holds:

Table 3. Translation of rulesets into logical predicates.

$$P_\epsilon(p, \tilde{p}) = dp(R) \wedge p = \tilde{p}$$

$$P_{r;R}(p, \tilde{p}) = (\phi(p) \wedge p = \tilde{p}) \vee (\neg\phi(p) \wedge P_R(p, \tilde{p})) \qquad \text{if } r = (\phi, \text{ACCEPT})$$

$$P_{r;R}(p, \tilde{p}) = \neg\phi(p) \wedge P_R(p, \tilde{p}) \qquad \text{if } r = (\phi, \text{DROP})$$

$$P_{r;R}(p, \tilde{p}) = (\phi(p) \wedge \tilde{p} \in tr(p, d_n, s_n, \leftrightarrow)) \vee (\neg\phi(p) \wedge P_R(p, \tilde{p})) \qquad \text{if } r = (\phi, \text{NAT}(d_n, s_n))$$

$$P_{r;R}(p, \tilde{p}) = (\phi(p) \wedge \tilde{p} \in tr(p, *:*, *:*, X)) \vee (\neg\phi(p) \wedge P_R(p, \tilde{p})) \qquad \text{if } r = (\phi, \text{CHECK-STATE}(X))$$

$$P_{r;R}(p, \tilde{p}) = (\phi(p) \wedge P_R(p[tag \mapsto m], \tilde{p})) \vee (\neg\phi(p) \wedge P_R(p, \tilde{p})) \qquad \text{if } r = (\phi, \text{MARK}(m))$$

Theorem 1 (Correctness of unfolding). *Let $\mathcal{F} = (\mathcal{C}, \rho, c)$ be a firewall and $[\![\mathcal{F}]\!]$ its unfolding. Let $s \xrightarrow{p, p'}_X s'$ be a step of the master transition system performed by the firewall $X \in \{\mathcal{F}, [\![\mathcal{F}]\!]\}$. Then, it holds*

$$s \xrightarrow{p, p'}_{\mathcal{F}} s' \iff s \xrightarrow{p, p'}_{[\![\mathcal{F}]\!]} s'.$$

6.2 Logical Characterization of Firewalls

We construct a logical predicate that characterizes all the packets accepted by an unfolded ruleset, together with the relevant translations.

To deal with NAT, we define an auxiliary function tr that computes the set of packets resulting from all possible translations of a given packet p. The parameter $X \in \{\leftarrow, \rightarrow, \leftrightarrow\}$ specifies if the translation applies to source, destination or both addresses, respectively, similarly to CHECK-STATE(X).

$$tr(p, d_n, s_n, \leftrightarrow) \triangleq \{p[da \mapsto a_d, sa \mapsto a_s] \mid a_d \in d_n, a_s \in s_n\}$$

$$tr(p, d_n, s_n, \rightarrow) \triangleq \{p[da \mapsto a_d] \mid a_d \in d_n\}$$

$$tr(p, d_n, s_n, \leftarrow) \triangleq \{p[sa \mapsto a_s] \mid a_s \in s_n\}$$

Furthermore, we model the default policy of a ruleset R with the predicate dp, true when the policy is ACCEPT, false otherwise.

Given an unfolded ruleset R, we build the predicate $P_R(p, \tilde{p})$ that holds when the packet p is accepted as $\tilde{p}$ by R. Its definition is in Table 3 that induces on the rules in R. Intuitively, the empty ruleset applies the default policy $dp(R)$ and does not transform the packet, encoded by the constraint $p = \tilde{p}$. The rule (ϕ, ACCEPT) considers two cases: when $\phi(p)$ holds and the packet is accepted as it is; when instead $\neg\phi(p)$ holds, p is accepted as $\tilde{p}$ only if the continuation R accepts it. The rule (ϕ, DROP) accepts p only if the continuation does and $\phi(p)$ does not hold. The rule $(\phi, \text{NAT}(d_n, s_n))$ is like an (ϕ, ACCEPT): the difference is when $\phi(p)$ holds, and it gives $\tilde{p}$ by applying to p the NAT translations $tr(p, d_n, s_n, \leftrightarrow)$. Finally, $(\phi, \text{CHECK-STATE}(X))$ is like a NAT that applies all possible translations of kind X (written as $tr(p, *:*, *:*, X)$). The idea is that, since we abstract away from the actual established connections, we over-approximate the state by considering any possible translations. At run-time, only the connections corresponding to the actual state will be possible. The rule $(\phi, \text{MARK}(m))$ is like a NAT, but when $\phi(p)$ holds it requires that the continuation accepts p tagged by m as $\tilde{p}$.

Example 3. The predicate of the unfolded ruleset in Example 2 when $dp(C_B) = F$ is

$$
\begin{aligned}
P_{[C_B]}\,(p,\tilde{p}) = \neg\phi_1 \wedge (\\
(\phi_2 \wedge \phi_{11} \wedge p = \tilde{p}) \vee (\neg(\phi_2 \wedge \phi_{11}) \wedge (\\
(\phi_2 \wedge \phi_{12} \wedge \phi_{21} \wedge p = \tilde{p}) \vee (\neg(\phi_2 \wedge \phi_{12} \wedge \phi_{21}) \wedge (\\
\neg(\phi_2 \wedge \phi_{12} \wedge \neg\phi_{22} \wedge \phi_{23}) \wedge (\\
\neg(\phi_2 \wedge \phi_{13}) \wedge (\\
(\phi_3 \wedge p = \tilde{p}) \vee (\neg\phi_3 \wedge (\\
F \wedge p = \tilde{p})))))))))
\end{aligned}
$$

Note that if $\neg\phi_1 \wedge \phi_2 \wedge \phi_{11}$ holds then the formula trivially holds and therefore the formula accepts the packet as the semantics does.

As a further example, consider the case in which $\phi_2, \phi_{12}, \phi_{22}, \phi_{23}, \phi_3$ hold for a packet p, while all the other ϕ's does not. Then, p is accepted as it is: the rule (ϕ_{23}, DROP) is not evaluated since ϕ_{22} holds and the RETURN is performed (cf. Example 1). Indeed, the predicate $P_{[C_B]}(p, p)$ evaluates to:

$$T \wedge (F \vee (T \wedge (F \vee (T \wedge (T \wedge (T \wedge (T \vee (F \wedge F))))))))) = T$$

Instead, if ϕ_{13} holds too, the packet is rejected as expected:

$$T \wedge (F \vee (T \wedge (F \vee (T \wedge (T \wedge (F \wedge (T \vee (F \wedge F))))))))) = F$$

The predicate in Table 3 is semantically correct, because if a packet p is accepted by a ruleset R as p', then $P_R(p, p')$ holds, and vice versa. Formally,

Lemma 1. *Given a ruleset R we have that*

1. $\forall p, s.\ p, s \models^\epsilon_R (\text{ACCEPT}, p') \implies P_R(p, p');$ *and*
2. $\forall p, p'.\ P_R(p, p') \implies \exists s.p, s \models^\epsilon_R (\text{ACCEPT}, p')$

We eventually define the predicate associated with a whole firewall as follows.

Definition 8. *Let $\mathcal{F} = (\mathcal{C}, \rho, c)$ be a firewall with control diagram $\mathcal{C} = (Q, A, q_i, q_f)$. The predicate associated with $\mathcal{F}$ is defined as*

$$\mathcal{P}_{\mathcal{F}}(p, \tilde{p}) \triangleq \mathcal{P}^\emptyset_{q_i}(p, \tilde{p}) \qquad \text{where}$$

$$\mathcal{P}^I_{q_f}(p, \tilde{p}) \triangleq p = \tilde{p} \qquad \mathcal{P}^I_q(p, \tilde{p}) \triangleq \exists p'.P_{c(q)}(p, p') \wedge \left(\bigvee_{\substack{(q,\psi,q') \in A \\ q' \notin I}} \psi(p') \wedge \mathcal{P}^{I \cup \{q\}}_{q'}(p', \tilde{p}) \right)$$

for all $q \in Q$ such that $q \neq q_f$, and where $P_{c(q)}$ is the predicate constructed from the ruleset associated with the node q of the control diagram.

Intuitively, in the final node q_f we accept p as it is. In all the other nodes, p is accepted as $\tilde{p}$ if and only if there is a path starting from p in the control diagram that obtains $\tilde{p}$ through intermediate transformations. More precisely, we look for an intermediate packet p', provided that (i) p is accepted as p' by the ruleset $c(q)$ of node q; (ii) p' satisfies one of the predicates ψ labeling the branches of the control diagram; and (iii) p' is accepted as $\tilde{p}$ in the reached node q'. Note that we ignore paths with loops, because firewalls have mechanisms to detect and discard a packet when its elaboration loops. To this aim, our predicate uses the set I for recording the nodes already traversed.

We conclude this section by establishing the correspondence between the logical formulation and the operational semantics of a firewall. Formally, $\mathcal{F}$ accepts the packet p as $\tilde{p}$ if the predicate $\mathcal{P}_{\mathcal{F}}(p, \tilde{p})$ is satisfied, and vice versa:

Theorem 2 (Correctness of the logical characterization). *Given a firewall* $\mathcal{F} = (\mathcal{C}, \rho, c)$ *and its corresponding predicate* $\mathcal{P}_{\mathcal{F}}$ *we have that*

1. $s \xrightarrow{p,p'} s \uplus (p, p') \implies \mathcal{P}_{\mathcal{F}}(p, p')$
2. $\forall p, p'. \ \mathcal{P}_{\mathcal{F}}(p, p') \implies \exists s. s \xrightarrow{p,p'} s \uplus (p, p')$

Recall that the logical characterization abstracts away the notion of state, and thus $\mathcal{P}_{\mathcal{F}}(p, p')$ holds if and only if there exists a state s in which p is accepted as p'. In particular, if the predicate holds for a packet p that belongs to an established connection, p will be accepted only if the relevant state is reached at runtime. This is the usual interpretation of firewall rules for established connections.

7 Policy Generation

The declarative specification extracted from a firewall policy (cf. Table 1) can be mapped to a firewall $\mathcal{F}_S$ whose control diagram has just one node. The ruleset R_S associated with this node only contains ACCEPT and NAT rules, each corresponding to a line of the declarative specification. In Sect. 3 we showed that each line is disjoint from the others. Hence, the ordering of rules in R_S is irrelevant.

Here we compile $\mathcal{F}_S$ into an equivalent firewall $\mathcal{F}_C$. First, we introduce an algorithm that computes the basic rulesets of $\mathcal{F}_C$. Then, we map these rulesets to the nodes of the control diagram of a real system. Finally, we prove the correctness of the compilation.

For simplicity, we produce a firewall that automatically accepts all the packets that belong to established connections with the appropriate translations. We claim this is not a limitation, since it is the default behavior of some real firewall systems (e.g., pf) and it is quite odd to drop packets, once the initial connection has been established. Moreover, this is consistent with the over-approximation on the firewall state done in Sect. 6.2.

Algorithm 1. Generation of the rulesets R_{dnat}, R_{fil}, R_{snat}, R_{mark} from R_S

1: $R_{dnat} = R_{fil} = R_{snat} = R_{mark} = \epsilon$
2: **for** r in R_S **do**
3:     **if** $r = (\phi, \text{ACCEPT})$ **then**
4:         add r to R_{fil}
5:     **else if** $r = (\phi, \text{NAT}(d_n, s_n))$ **then**
6:         generate fresh tag m
7:         add $(\phi \wedge tag(p) = \bullet, \text{MARK}(m))$ to R_{mark}
8:         add $(tag(p) = m, \text{NAT}(d_n, \star))$ to R_{dnat}
9:         add $(tag(p) = m, \text{NAT}(\star, s_n))$ to R_{snat}
10:     **end if**
11: **end for**
12: add $(tag(p) \neq \bullet, \text{ACCEPT})$ and $(true, \text{DROP})$ to R_{fil}
13: prepend R_{mark} to R_{dnat}, R_{fil} and R_{snat}

7.1 Compiling a Firewall Specification

Our algorithm takes as input the ruleset R_S derived from a synthesized specification and yields the rulesets R_{fil}, R_{dnat}, R_{snat} (with default ACCEPT policy) containing filtering, DNAT and SNAT rules. This separation reflects that all the real systems we have analyzed impose constraints on where NAT rules can be placed, e.g., in `iptables`, DNAT is allowed only in rulesets R_{PRE}^{nat} and R_{OUT}^{nat}, while SNAT only in R_{INP}^{nat} and R_{POST}^{nat}.

Intuitively, Algorithm 1 produces rules that assign different tags to packets that must be processed by different NAT rules (lines 6 and 7). Each NAT rule is split in a DNAT (line 8) and an SNAT (line 9), where the predicate ϕ becomes a check on the tag of the packet. Filtering rules are left unchanged (line 4). Packets subject to NAT are accepted in R_{fil} while the others are dropped (line 12). We prepend R_{mark} to all rulesets making sure that packets are always marked, independently of which ruleset will be processed first (line 13). We use $\bullet$ to denote the empty tag used when a packet has never been tagged.

Recall that the @ operator combines rulesets in sequence. Note that R_{fil} drops by default and shadows any ruleset appended to it. In practice, the only interesting rulesets are $\mathcal{R} = \{R_\epsilon, R_{fil}, R_{dnat}, R_{snat}, R_{dnat} @ R_{fil}, R_{snat} @ R_{fil}\}$ where R_ϵ is the empty ruleset with default ACCEPT policy. Since here we do not discuss `ipfw` [18] and other firewalls with a minimal control diagram, we neither use $R_{dnat} @ R_{fil}$ nor $R_{snat} @ R_{fil}$.

We now introduce the notion of *compiled firewall*.

Definition 9 (Compiled firewall). *A firewall* $\mathcal{F}_C = (\mathcal{C}, \rho, c)$ *with control diagram* $\mathcal{C} = (Q, A, q_i, q_f)$ *is a compiled firewall if*

- $c(q_i) = c(q_f) = R_\epsilon$
- $c(q) \in \mathcal{R}$ *for every* $q \in Q \setminus \{q_i, q_f\}$
- *every path* π *from* q_i *to* q_f *in the control diagram* $\mathcal{C}$ *traverses a node* q *such that* $c(q) \in \{R_{fil}, R_{dnat} @ R_{fil}, R_{snat} @ R_{fil}\}$

Intuitively, the above definition requires that only rulesets in $\mathcal{R}$ are associated with the nodes in the control diagram and that all paths pass at least one through a node with the filtering ruleset.

Example 4. Now we map the rulesets to the nodes of the control diagrams of the real systems presented in Sect. 4.1. For iptables we have:

$$c(Pre^n) = R_{dnat} \quad c(Out^n) = R_{dnat} \quad c(Inp^n) = R_{snat} \quad c(Post^n) = R_{snat}$$
$$c(Fwd^f) = R_{fil} \qquad c(Inp^f) = R_{fil} \qquad c(Out^f) = R_{fil}$$

while the remaining nodes get the empty ruleset R_ϵ. For pf we have:

$$c(Inp^n) = R_{dnat} \qquad c(Out^n) = R_{snat} \qquad c(Inp^f) = R_{fil} \qquad c(Out^f) = R_{fil}$$

7.2 Correctness of the Compiled Firewall

We start by showing that a compiled firewall $\mathcal{F}_C$ accepts the same packets as $\mathcal{F}_S$, possibly with a different translation.

Lemma 2. *Let $\mathcal{F}_C$ be a compiled firewall. Given a packet p, we have that*

$$\exists p'. \, \mathcal{P}_{\mathcal{F}_S}(p, p') \Leftrightarrow \exists p''. \, \mathcal{P}_{\mathcal{F}_C}(p, p'').$$

Let be $\mathcal{T} = \{id, dnat, snat, nat\}$ the set of translations possibly applied to a packet while it traverses a firewall. The first, id, represents the identity, $dnat$ and $snat$ are for DNAT and SNAT, while nat represents both DNAT and SNAT. Also, let $(\mathcal{T}, <)$ be the partial order such that $id < dnat$, $id < snat$, $dnat < nat$ and $snat < nat$. Finally, given a packet p and a firewall $\mathcal{F}$, let $\pi_{\mathcal{F}}(p)$ be the path in the control diagram of $\mathcal{F}$ along which p is processed. Note that there exists a unique path for each packet because the control diagram is deterministic.

The following function computes the *translation capability* of a path π, i.e., which translations can be performed on packets processed along π.

Definition 10 (Translation capability). *Let $\pi = \langle q_1, \dots, q_n \rangle$ be a path on the control diagram of a compiled firewall $\mathcal{F} = (\mathcal{C}, \rho, c)$. The translation capability of π is*

$$tc(\pi) = \text{lub} \left(\bigcup_{q_i \in \pi} \gamma(c(q_i)) \right)$$

where lub is the least upper bound of a set $T \subseteq \mathcal{T}$ w.r.t. $<$ and γ is defined as

$$\gamma(R) = \{id\} \text{ for } R \in \{R_\epsilon, R_{fil}\}$$
$$\gamma(R_t) = \{t\} \text{ for } t \in \{dnat, snat\}$$
$$\gamma(R_1 \, @ \, R_2) = \gamma(R_1) \cup \gamma(R_2)$$

We write $p \approx p'$ to denote that $p' = p[tag \mapsto m]$ for some marking m. In addition, let t_β be a function that, given a packet p and its translation p', computes a packet p'' where only the translation $\beta \in \mathcal{T}$ is applied to p, defined as:

$$t_{id}(p, p') = p \qquad\qquad t_{dnat}(p, p') = p[da \mapsto da(p')]$$
$$t_{nat}(p, p') = p' \qquad\qquad t_{snat}(p, p') = p[sa \mapsto sa(p')]$$

The following theorem describes the relationship between a compiled firewall $\mathcal{F}_C$ and the firewall $\mathcal{F}_S$. Intuitively, $\mathcal{F}_S$ accepts a packet p as p' if and only if $\mathcal{F}_C$ accepts a packet p as p'' where p' and p'' only differ on marking and NAT. More specifically, p'' is derived from p by applying all the translations available on the path $\pi_{\mathcal{F}_C}(p)$ in the control diagram of $\mathcal{F}_C$, along which p is processed.

Theorem 3. *Let p, p' be two packets such that p is accepted by both $\mathcal{F}_S$ and $\mathcal{F}_C$. Moreover, let $p'' \approx t_\beta(p, p')$ where $\beta = tc(\pi_{\mathcal{F}_C}(p))$. We have that*

$$\mathcal{P}_{\mathcal{F}_S}(p, p') \Leftrightarrow \mathcal{P}_{\mathcal{F}_C}(p, p'').$$

Example 5. Consider again Example 4. Any path π in `iptables` has $tc(\pi) = nat$, which implies $p' \approx p''$, i.e., $\mathcal{F}_C$ behaves exactly as $\mathcal{F}_S$. Interestingly, paths $\pi_1 = \langle q_i, Inp^n, Inp^f, q_o \rangle$ and $\pi_2 = \langle q_i, Out^n, Out^f, q_o \rangle$ in `pf` have $tc(\pi)$ equal to *dnat* and *snat*, respectively. In fact, `pf` cannot perform *snat* and *dnat* on packets directed to and generated from the host, respectively.

8   Conclusions

We have proposed a transcompiling pipeline for firewall languages, made of three stages. Its core is IFCL, an intermediate language equipped here with a formal semantics. It has the typical actions of real configuration languages, and it keeps them apart from the way the firewall applies them, represented by a control diagram. In stage 1, a real firewall policy language can be encoded in IFCL by simply instantiating the state and the control diagram. As a by-product, we give a formal semantics to the source language, which usually has none. In stage 2, we have built a logical predicate that describes the flow of packets accepted by the firewall together with their possible translations. From that, we have synthesized a declarative firewall specification, in the form of a table that succinctly represents the firewall behavior. This table is the basis for supporting policy analysis, like policy implication and comparison, as described in our companion paper [1]. The declarative specification is the input of stage 3, which compiles it to a real target language. To illustrate, we have applied these stages on two among the most used firewall systems in Linux and Unix: `iptables` and `pf`. We have selected these two systems because they exhibit very different packet processing schemes, making the porting of configurations very challenging. All the stages above have been proved to preserve the semantics of the original policy, so guaranteeing that our transcompilation is correct. As a matter of fact, we have proposed a way to mechanically implement policy refactoring, when the source and the target languages coincide. This is because the declarative specification has no anomalies, e.g., rule overlapping or shadowing, so helping the system administrator also in policy maintenance. At the same time, we have put forward a manner to mechanically port policies from one firewall system to another, when their languages differ. We point out that, even though [1] intuitively presents and implements the first two stages of our transcompiling pipeline, the overlap with this paper is only on Sects. 4 and 6.2. Indeed, the theory, the semantics, the compilation of stage 3 and the proofs of the correctness of the whole transcompilation are original material.

As a future work, we intend to further experiment on our proposal by encoding more languages, e.g., from specialized firewall devices, like commercial Cisco IOS, or within the SDN paradigm. We plan to include a (more refined) policy generator of stage 3 in the existing tool [1] that implements the stages 1 and 2, and can deal with configurations made of hundreds of rules. Also testing and improving the performance of our transcompiler, as well as providing it with a friendly interface would make it more appealing to network administrators. For example, readability can be improved by automatically grouping rules and by adding comments that explain the meaning of refactored configurations. Finally, it would be very interesting to extend our approach to deal with networks with more than one firewall. The idea would be to combine the synthesized specifications based on network topology and routing.

References

1. Bodei, C., Degano, P., Focardi, R., Galletta, L., Tempesta, M., Veronese, L.: Language-independent synthesis of firewall policies. In: Proceedings of the 3rd IEEE European Symposium on Security and Privacy (2018)
2. The Netfilter Project. https://www.netfilter.org/
3. Packet Filter (PF). https://www.openbsd.org/faq/pf/
4. Cuppens, F., Cuppens-Boulahia, N., Sans, T., Miège, A.: A formal approach to specify and deploy a network security policy. In: Dimitrakos, T., Martinelli, F. (eds.) Formal Aspects in Security and Trust. IFIP, vol. 173, pp. 203–218. Springer, Boston, MA (2005). https://doi.org/10.1007/0-387-24098-5_15
5. Gouda, M., Liu, A.: Structured firewall design. Comput. Netw. **51**(4), 1106–1120 (2007)
6. Foley, S.N., Neville, U.: A firewall algebra for openstack. In: 2015 IEEE Conference on Communications and Network Security, CNS 2015, pp. 541–549 (2015)
7. Babel: The compiler for writing next generation JavaScript. https://babeljs.io
8. Runtime converter. http://www.runtimeconverter.com
9. Diekmann, C., Michaelis, J., Haslbeck, M.P.L., Carle, G.: Verified iptables firewall analysis. In: Proceedings of the 15th IFIP Networking Conference, Vienna, Austria, 17–19 May 2016, pp. 252–260 (2016)
10. Yuan, L., Mai, J., Su, Z., Chen, H., Chuah, C., Mohapatra, P.: FIREMAN: a toolkit for firewall modeling and analysis. In: IEEE Symposium on Security and Privacy (S&P 2006), May 2006, Berkeley, California, USA, pp. 199–213 (2006)
11. Nelson, T., Barratt, C., Dougherty, D.J., Fisler, K., Krishnamurthi, S.: The Margrave tool for firewall analysis. In: Uncovering the Secrets of System Administration: Proceedings of the 24th Large Installation System Administration Conference, LISA 2010, San Jose, CA, USA, 7–12 November 2010 (2010)

12. Mayer, A.J., Wool, A., Ziskind, E.: Fang: a firewall analysis engine. In: 2000 IEEE Symposium on Security and Privacy, Berkeley, California, USA, 14–17 May 2000, pp. 177–187 (2000)
13. Mayer, A.J., Wool, A., Ziskind, E.: Offline firewall analysis. Int. J. Inf. Secur. 5(3), 125–144 (2006)
14. Adão, P., Bozzato, C., Rossi, G.D., Focardi, R., Luccio, F.L.: Mignis: a semantic based tool for firewall configuration. In: IEEE 27th Computer Security Foundations Symposium, CSF 2014, pp. 351–365 (2014)
15. Bartal, Y., Mayer, A.J., Nissim, K., Wool, A.: Firmato: a novel firewall management toolkit. ACM Trans. Comput. Syst. 22(4), 381–420 (2004)
16. Anderson, C.J., Foster, N., Guha, A., Jeannin, J.B., Kozen, D., Schlesinger, C., Walker, D.: NetKAT: semantic foundations for networks. In: Proceedings of the 41st ACM SIGPLAN-SIGACT Symposium on Principles of Programming Languages (POPL 2014). ACM (2014)
17. The Netfilter Project: Traversing of tables and chains. http://www.iptables.info/en/structure-of-iptables.html
18. The IPFW Firewall. https://www.freebsd.org/doc/handbook/firewalls-ipfw.html

On Quantitative Analysis
of Attack–Defense Trees with Repeated
Labels

Barbara Kordy[(✉)] and Wojciech Wideł

Univ Rennes, INSA Rennes, CNRS, IRISA, Rennes, France
{barbara.kordy,wojciech.widel}@irisa.fr

Abstract. Ensuring security of complex systems is a difficult task that
requires utilization of numerous tools originating from various domains.
Among those tools we find *attack–defense trees*, a simple yet practical
model for analysis of scenarios involving two competing parties. Enhancing the well-established model of attack trees, attack–defense trees are
trees with labeled nodes, offering an intuitive representation of possible
ways in which an attacker can harm a system, and means of countering
the attacks that are available to the defender. The growing palette of
methods for quantitative analysis of attack–defense trees provides security experts with tools for determining the most threatening attacks
and the best ways of securing the system against those attacks. Unfortunately, many of those methods might fail or provide the user with
distorted results if the underlying attack–defense tree contains multiple
nodes bearing the same label. We address this issue by studying conditions ensuring that the standard bottom-up evaluation method for quantifying attack–defense trees yields meaningful results in the presence of
repeated labels. For the case when those conditions are not satisfied, we
devise an alternative approach for quantification of attacks.

1 Introduction

Beginning with 19th century chemistry and a groundbreaking work of Cayley,
who used them for the purposes of enumeration of isomers, trees – connected
acyclic graphs – have a long history of application to various domains. Those
include safety analysis of systems using the model of *fault trees* [10], developed
in 1960s, and security analysis with the assistance of the *attack trees*, which
the fault trees inspired. Attack trees were introduced by Schneier in [26], for
the purpose of analyzing security of systems and organizations. Seemingly simple, attack trees offer a compromise between expressiveness and usability, which
not only makes them applicable for industrial purposes [23], but also puts them
at the core of many more complex models and languages [11,24]. An extensive overview and comparison of attack tree-based graphical models for security
can be found in [20]. A survey focusing on scalability, complexity analysis and
practical usability of such models has recently been provided in [12].

© The Author(s) 2018
L. Bauer and R. Küsters (Eds.): POST 2018, LNCS 10804, pp. 325–346, 2018.
https://doi.org/10.1007/978-3-319-89722-6_14

Attack–defense trees [18] are one of the most well-studied extensions of attack trees, with new methods of their analysis developed yearly [2,3,8,21]. Attack–defense trees enhance attack trees with nodes labeled with goals of a defender, thus enabling modeling of interactions between the two competing actors. They have been used to evaluate the security of real-life systems, such as ATMs [7], RFID managed warehouses [4] and cyber-physical systems [16]. Both the theoretical developments and the practical studies have proven that attack–defense trees offer a promising methodology for security evaluation, but they also highlighted room for improvements. The objective of the current paper is to address the problem of quantitative analysis of attack–defense trees with repeated labels.

Related Work. It is well-know that the analysis of an attack–defense tree becomes more difficult if the tree contains repeated labels. This difficulty is sometimes recognized, e.g., in [2,21], where authors explicitly assume lack of repeated labels in order for their methods to be valid. In some works the problem is avoided (or overlooked) by interpretation of repeated labels as distinct instances of the same goal, thus, *de facto* as distinct goals (e.g., [8,13,18,22]), or by distinguishing between the repetitions occurring in specific subtrees of a tree, as in [3]. Recently, Bossuat and Kordy have established a classification of repeated labels in attack–defense trees, depending on whether the corresponding nodes represent exactly the same instance or different instances of a goal [5]. They point out that, if the meaning of repeated labels is not properly specified, then the fast, bottom-up method for identifying attacks that optimize an attribute (e.g., *minimal cost, probability of success*, etc.), as used in [15,18,22], might yield tainted results.

Repeated labels are also problematic in other tree-based models, for instance fault trees. Whereas some methods for qualitative analysis of fault trees with repeated basic events (or generally, shared subtrees) have been developed [6, 27], their quantification might rely on approximate methods. For example, the probability of a system failure can be evaluated using rare event approximation approach (see [10], Chap. XI), while a simple bottom-up procedure gives an exact result in fault trees with no shared subtrees [1]. This last observation is consistent with the results previously obtained for attack–defense trees (see Theorems 2–4 in [2]).

Contribution. The contribution of this work is threefold. First, we determine sufficient conditions ensuring that the standard quantitative bottom-up analysis of attack–defense trees with repeated labels is valid. Second, we prove that some of these conditions are in fact necessary for the analysis to be compatible with a selected semantics for attack–defense trees. Finally, for the case when these conditions are not satisfied, we propose a novel, alternative method of evaluation of attributes that takes the presence of repeated labels into account.

Paper Structure. The model of attack–defense trees is introduced in detail in the next section. In Sect. 3, the attributes and exisiting methods for their evaluation are explained. In Sect. 4, we present our main results on quantification of attack–defense trees with repeated labels. We give proofs of these results in Sect. 5, and conclude in Sect. 6.

2   Attack–Defense Trees

Attack–defense trees are rooted trees with labeled nodes that allow for an intuitive graphical representation of scenarios involving two competing actors, usually called *attacker* and *defender*. Nodes of a tree are labeled with goals of the actors, with the label of the root of the tree being the main goal of the modeled scenario. The actor whose goal is represented by the root is called *proponent* and the other one is called *opponent*. The aim of the proponent is to achieve the root goal, whereas the opponent tries to make this impossible.

In order for an actor to *achieve* some particular goal g, they might need to achieve other goals. In such a case the node labeled with g is a *refined node*. The basic model of attack–defense trees (as introduced in [18]) admits two types of refinements: the goal of a *conjunctively refined node* (an AND node) is achieved if the goals of all its child nodes are achieved, and the goal of a *disjunctively refined node* (an OR node) is achieved if at least one of the goals of its children is achieved. If a node is not refined, then it represents a goal that is considered to be directly achievable, for instance by executing a simple action. Such a goal is called a *basic action*. Hence, in order to achieve goals of refined nodes, the actors execute (some of) their basic actions. What distinguishes attack–defense trees model from attack trees is the possibility of the goals of the actors to be *countered* by goals of their adversary, which themselves can be again countered, and so on. To represent the countering of a goal, the symbol C will be used. A goal g is *countered* by a goal g' (denoted $C(g, g')$) if achieving g' by one of the actors makes achieving g impossible for the other actor.

It is not rare that in an attack–defense tree, whether generated by hand or in a semi–automatic way [14,25,28] some nodes bear the same label. In such a case, there are two ways of interpreting them:

1. either the nodes represent the same single instance of the goal – e.g., cutting the power off in a building can be done once and has multiple consequences, thus a number of refined nodes might have a node labeled cutPowerOff among their child nodes, but all these nodes will represent exactly the same action of cutting the power off;
2. or else each of the nodes is treated as a distinct instance of the goal. For instance, while performing an attack, the attacker might need to pass through a door twice – once to enter and second time to leave a building. Since these actions refer to the same door and the same attacker, the corresponding nodes will, in most cases, hold the same label goThroughDoor. However, it is clear that they represent two different instances of the same goal.

In this work we assume the first of these ways of interpretation. In particular, following [5], we call a basic action that serves as a label for at least two nodes a *clone* or a *cloned basic action*, and interpret them as the same instance of a goal. Nodes representing distinct instances of the same goal or distinct goals are assumed in this work to have different labels.

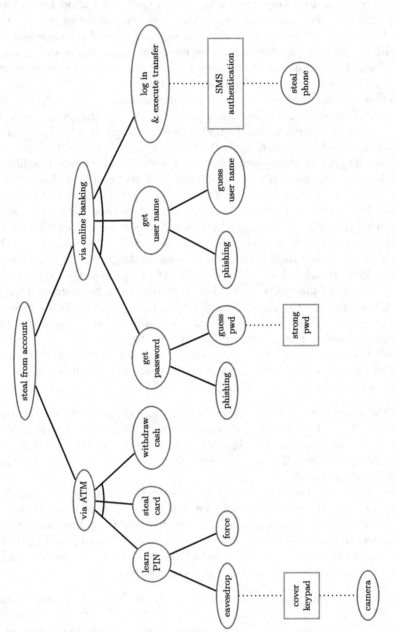

Fig. 1. Attack–defense tree for stealing money from a bank account

An example of attack–defense tree[1] is represented in Fig. 1. In this tree, the proponent is the attacker and the opponent is the defender. According to the attack–defense trees' convention, nodes representing goals of the attacker are depicted using red circles, and those of the defender using green rectangles. Children of an AND node are joined by an arc, and countermeasures are attached to nodes they are supposed to counter via dotted edges.

Example 1. In the attack–defense scenario represented by the attack–defense tree from Fig. 1, the proponent wants to steal money from the opponent's account. To achieve this goal, they can use physical means, i.e., force the opponent to reveal their PIN, steal the opponent's card and then withdraw money from an ATM. One way of learning the PIN would be to eavesdrop on the victim when they enter the PIN. This could be prevented by covering the keypad with hand. Covering the keypad fails if the proponent monitors the keypad with a hidden micro–camera installed at an appropriate spot. Another way of getting the PIN would be to force the opponent to reveal it.

Instead of attacking from a physical angle, the proponent can steal money by exploiting online banking services. In order to do so, they need to learn the opponent's user name and password. Both of these goals can be achieved by creating a fake bank website and using phishing techniques for tricking the opponent into entering their credentials. The proponent could also try to guess what the password and the user name are. Using very strong password would counter such guessing attack. Once the proponent obtains the credentials, they use them for logging into the online banking services and execute a transfer. Transfer dispositions might be additionally secured with two-factor authentication using mobile phone text messages. This security measure could be countered by the proponent by stealing the opponent's phone.

Note that even though there are two nodes labeled with `phishing` in the tree, they actually represent the same instance of the same action. The proponent does not need to perform two different phishing attacks to get the password and the user name—setting up one phishing website and sending one phishing e-mail will suffice for the proponent to get both credentials. Thus, the two nodes labeled `phishing` are clones.

Let us now introduce a formal notation for attack–defense trees, which we will use throughout this paper. Such notation is necessary to formally define the meaning of attack–defense trees in terms of formal semantics and to specify the algorithms for their quantitative analysis.

We use symbols p and o to distinguish between the proponent and the opponent. By $\mathbb{B}^p$ and $\mathbb{B}^o$ we denote the sets of labels representing basic actions of the proponent and of the opponent, respectively. We assume that $\mathbb{B}^p \cap \mathbb{B}^o = \emptyset$, and we set $\mathbb{B} = \mathbb{B}^p \cup \mathbb{B}^o$. For $s \in \{p, o\}$, the symbol $\bar{s}$ stands for the other actor, i.e., $\bar{p} = o$ and $\bar{o} = p$. We denote the elements of $\mathbb{B}^s$ with b^s, for $s \in \{p, o\}$. Attack–defense trees can be seen as terms generated by the following grammar, where OR^s and AND^s are unranked refinement operators, i.e., they may take an arbitrary number of arguments, and C^s is a binary counter operator.

---

[1] The example is based on one of exemplary trees provided by ADTool [9].

$$T^{\mathrm{s}}: \mathtt{b}^{\mathrm{s}} \mid \mathtt{OR}^{\mathrm{s}}(T^{\mathrm{s}}, \ldots, T^{\mathrm{s}}) \mid \mathtt{AND}^{\mathrm{s}}(T^{\mathrm{s}}, \ldots, T^{\mathrm{s}}) \mid \mathtt{C}^{\mathrm{s}}(T^{\mathrm{s}}, T^{\bar{\mathrm{s}}}) \qquad (1)$$

Example 2. Consider the tree from Fig. 1. The term corresponding to the subtree rooted in the via ATM node is

$$\mathtt{AND}^{\mathrm{P}}\Big(\mathtt{OR}^{\mathrm{P}}\Big(\mathtt{C}^{\mathrm{P}}(\mathtt{eavesdrop}, \mathtt{C}^{\mathrm{o}}(\mathtt{coverKey}, \mathtt{camera})), \mathtt{force}\Big), \mathtt{stealCard},$$

$$\mathtt{withdrawCash}\Big),$$

where the labels of basic actions have been shortened for better readability.

We denote the set of trees generated by grammar (1) with $\mathbb{T}$.

In order to analyze possible attacks in an attack–defense tree, in particular, determine cheapest ones, or the ones that require the least amount of time to execute, one needs to decide what is considered to be an attack. This can be achieved with the help of semantics that provide formal interpretations for attack–defense trees. Several semantics for attack–defense trees have been proposed in [18]. Below, we recall two ways of interpreting attack–defense trees and the notions of attack they entail.

Definition 1. *The propositional semantics for attack–defense trees is a function $\mathcal{P}$ that assigns to each attack–defense tree a propositional formula, in a recursive way, as follows*

$$\mathcal{P}(\mathtt{b}) = x_{\mathtt{b}}, \qquad\qquad \mathcal{P}(\mathtt{OR}^{\mathrm{s}}(T_1^{\mathrm{s}}, \ldots, T_k^{\mathrm{s}})) = \mathcal{P}(T_1^{\mathrm{s}}) \vee \cdots \vee \mathcal{P}(T_k^{\mathrm{s}}),$$
$$\mathcal{P}(\mathtt{C}^{\mathrm{s}}(T_1^{\mathrm{s}}, T_2^{\bar{\mathrm{s}}})) = \mathcal{P}(T_1^{\mathrm{s}}) \wedge \neg\mathcal{P}(T_2^{\bar{\mathrm{s}}}), \ \mathcal{P}(\mathtt{AND}^{\mathrm{s}}(T_1^{\mathrm{s}}, \ldots, T_k^{\mathrm{s}})) = \mathcal{P}(T_1^{\mathrm{s}}) \wedge \cdots \wedge \mathcal{P}(T_k^{\mathrm{s}}),$$

where $\mathtt{b} \in \mathbb{B}$, and $x_{\mathtt{b}}$ is the corresponding propositional variable. Two attack–defense trees are equivalent wrt $\mathcal{P}$ if their interpretations are equivalent propositional formulæ.

Definition 1 formalizes one of the most intuitive and widely used ways of interpreting attack–defense trees, where every basic action is assigned a propositional variable indicating whether or not the action is satisfiable. In the light of the propositional semantics, an attack in an attack–defense tree T is any assignment of values to the propositional variables, such that the formula $\mathcal{P}(T)$ evaluates to true. We note that this natural approach is often used without invoking the propositional semantics explicitly (e.g., in [2] or [8]). Observe also that due to the idempotency of the logical operators $\vee$ and $\wedge$, and the fact that every basic action is assigned a single variable, when the propositional semantics is used, cloned actions are indeed treated as the same instance of the same action. In particular, this implies that the trees $\mathtt{AND}^{\mathrm{P}}(\mathtt{b}, \mathtt{OR}^{\mathrm{P}}(\mathtt{b}, \mathtt{b}'))$ and $\mathtt{b}$ are equivalent under the propositional interpretation. Such approach might not always be desirable, especially when we do not only want to know *whether* attacks are possible, but actually *how* they can be achieved. To accommodate this point of view, the set semantics has recently been introduced in [5]. We briefly recall its construction below.

In the sequel, we set

$$S \odot Z = \{(P_S \cup P_Z, O_S \cup O_Z) | (P_S, O_S) \in S, \ (P_Z, O_Z) \in Z\}, \qquad (2)$$

for $S, Z \subseteq \mathbb{B}^p \times \mathbb{B}^o$. Furthermore, for a set X we denote its power set with $\wp(X)$.

Definition 2. *The set semantics for attack–defense trees is a function $\mathcal{S} \colon \mathbb{T} \to \wp(\wp(\mathbb{B}^p) \times \wp(\mathbb{B}^o))$ that assigns to each attack–defense tree a set of pairs of sets of labels, as follows*

$$\mathcal{S}(\mathtt{b}^p) = \{(\{\mathtt{b}^p\}, \emptyset)\}, \qquad\qquad \mathcal{S}(\mathtt{b}^o) = \{(\emptyset, \{\mathtt{b}^o\})\},$$

$$\mathcal{S}(\mathtt{OR}^p(T_1^p, \ldots, T_k^p)) = \bigcup_{i=1}^{k} \mathcal{S}(T_i^p), \quad \mathcal{S}(\mathtt{OR}^o(T_1^o, \ldots, T_k^o)) = \bigodot_{i=1}^{k} \mathcal{S}(T_i^o),$$

$$\mathcal{S}(\mathtt{AND}^p(T_1^p, \ldots, T_k^p)) = \bigodot_{i=1}^{k} \mathcal{S}(T_i^p), \mathcal{S}(\mathtt{AND}^o(T_1^o, \ldots, T_k^o)) = \bigcup_{i=1}^{k} \mathcal{S}(T_i^o),$$

$$\mathcal{S}(\mathtt{C}^p(T_1^p, T_2^o)) = \mathcal{S}(T_1^p) \odot \mathcal{S}(T_2^o), \quad \mathcal{S}(\mathtt{C}^o(T_1^o, T_2^p)) = \mathcal{S}(T_1^o) \cup \mathcal{S}(T_2^p).$$

Two trees T_1 and T_2 are equivalent wrt the set semantics, denoted $T_1 \equiv_S T_2$, if and only if the two sets $\mathcal{S}(T_1)$ and $\mathcal{S}(T_2)$ are equal.

The meaning of a pair (P, O) belonging to $\mathcal{S}(T)$ is that if the proponent executes all actions from P and the opponent does not execute any of the actions from O, then the root goal of the tree T is achieved. In particular, if $(P, \emptyset) \in \mathcal{S}(T)$, then the opponent cannot prevent the proponent from achieving the root goal when they execute all actions from P.

Example 3. The set semantics of the tree in Fig. 1 is the following

$$\mathcal{S}(T) = \{(\{\mathtt{force}, \mathtt{stealCard}, \mathtt{withdrawCash}\}, \emptyset),$$
$$(\{\mathtt{camera}, \mathtt{eavesdrop}, \mathtt{stealCard}, \mathtt{withdrawCash}\}, \emptyset),$$
$$(\{\mathtt{eavesdrop}, \mathtt{stealCard}, \mathtt{withdrawCash}\}, \{\mathtt{coverKey}\}),$$
$$(\{\mathtt{phish}, \mathtt{logIn\&execTrans}\}, \{\mathtt{SMS}\}),$$
$$(\{\mathtt{phish}, \mathtt{guessUN}, \mathtt{logIn\&execTrans}\}, \{\mathtt{SMS}\}),$$
$$(\{\mathtt{phish}, \mathtt{guessPwd}, \mathtt{logIn\&execTrans}\}, \{\mathtt{strongPWD}, \mathtt{SMS}\}),$$
$$(\{\mathtt{guessUN}, \mathtt{guessPwd}, \mathtt{logIn\&execTrans}\}, \{\mathtt{strongPWD}, \mathtt{SMS}\}),$$
$$(\{\mathtt{phish}, \mathtt{stealPhone}, \mathtt{logIn\&execTrans}\}, \emptyset),$$
$$(\{\mathtt{phish}, \mathtt{guessUN}, \mathtt{stealPhone}, \mathtt{logIn\&execTrans}\}, \emptyset),$$
$$(\{\mathtt{phish}, \mathtt{guessPwd}, \mathtt{stealPhone}, \mathtt{logIn\&execTrans}\}, \{\mathtt{strongPWD}\}),$$
$$(\{\mathtt{guessUN}, \mathtt{guessPwd}, \mathtt{stealPhone}, \mathtt{logIn\&execTrans}\}, \{\mathtt{strongPWD}\})\}.$$

Throughout the rest of the paper, by an *attack in an attack–defense tree T* we mean an element of its set semantics $\mathcal{S}(T)$.

Grammar (1) ensures that attack–defense trees are well-typed with respect to the two players, i.e., p and o. However, not every well-typed tree is necessarily well-formed wrt the labels used. In particular, it should be ensured that the usage of repeated labels is consistent throughout the whole tree. For instance, if the action `coverKey`, of covering an ATM's keypad with a hand, can be countered by monitoring with a camera, this countermeasure should also be attached to every other node labeled `coverKey`. Similarly, if execution of the action `logIn&execTrans` contributes to the achievement of the proponent's goal of stealing money via the online banking services, this information should be kept in every subtree rooted in a node labeled `via online banking`. Thus, to ensure that the results of the methods developed further in the paper indeed reflect the intended aspects of a modeled scenario, in the following we assume that subtrees of an attack–defense tree that are rooted in identically labeled nodes are equivalent wrt the set semantics.

3   Quantitative Analysis Using Attributes

Among methods for quantitative analysis of scenarios modeled with attack–defense trees are so called *attributes*, introduced intuitively by Schneier in [26] and formalized for attack trees in [15,22], and for attack–defense trees in [18]. Attributes represent quantitative aspects of the modeled scenario, such as a *minimal cost* of executing an attack or *maximal damage* caused by an attack. Numerous methods to evaluate the value of an attribute on attack–defense trees exist [2,8], and the most often used approach is based on so called bottom-up evaluation [18]. The idea behind the bottom-up evaluation is to assign attribute values to the basic actions and to propagate them up to the root of the tree using appropriate operations on the intermediate nodes. The notions of attribute and bottom-up evaluation are formalized using attribute domains.

Definition 3. *An attribute domain for an attribute α on attack–defense trees is a tuple*

$$A_\alpha = (D_\alpha, \text{OR}_\alpha^{\text{p}}, \text{AND}_\alpha^{\text{p}}, \text{OR}_\alpha^{\text{o}}, \text{AND}_\alpha^{\text{o}}, \text{C}_\alpha^{\text{p}}, \text{C}_\alpha^{\text{o}}),$$

where D_α is a set, and for $\text{s} \in \{\text{p}, \text{o}\}$, $\text{OP} \in \{\text{OR}, \text{AND}\}$,

1. *$\text{OP}_\alpha^{\text{s}}$ is an unranked function on D_α,*
2. *$\text{C}_\alpha^{\text{s}}$ is a binary function on D_α.*

Let $A_\alpha = (D_\alpha, \text{OR}_\alpha^{\text{p}}, \text{AND}_\alpha^{\text{p}}, \text{OR}_\alpha^{\text{o}}, \text{AND}_\alpha^{\text{o}}, \text{C}_\alpha^{\text{p}}, \text{C}_\alpha^{\text{o}})$ be an attribute domain. A function $\beta_\alpha \colon \mathbb{B} \to D_\alpha$ that assigns values from the set D_α to basic actions of attack–defense trees is called a *basic assignment* for attribute α.

Definition 4. *Let $A_\alpha = (D_\alpha, \text{OR}_\alpha^{\text{p}}, \text{AND}_\alpha^{\text{p}}, \text{OR}_\alpha^{\text{o}}, \text{AND}_\alpha^{\text{o}}, \text{C}_\alpha^{\text{p}}, \text{C}_\alpha^{\text{o}})$ be an attribute domain, T be an attack–defense tree, and β_α be a basic assignment for attribute α. The value of attribute α for T obtained via the bottom–up procedure, denoted $\alpha_B(T, \beta_\alpha)$, is defined recursively as*

$$\alpha_B(T, \beta_\alpha) = \begin{cases} \beta_\alpha(\text{b}) & \text{if } T = \text{b}, \text{b} \in \mathbb{B}, \\ \text{OP}_\alpha^{\text{s}}(\alpha_B(T_1^{\text{s}}, \beta_\alpha), \ldots, \alpha_B(T_n^{\text{s}}, \beta_\alpha)) & \text{if } T = \text{OP}^{\text{s}}(T_1^{\text{s}}, \ldots, T_n^{\text{s}}), \\ \text{C}_\alpha^{\text{s}}(\alpha_B(T_1^{\text{s}}, \beta_\alpha), \alpha_B(T_2^{\bar{\text{s}}}, \beta_\alpha)) & \text{if } T = \text{C}^{\text{s}}(T_1^{\text{s}}, T_2^{\bar{\text{s}}}), \end{cases}$$

where $\text{s} \in \{\text{p}, \text{o}\}$, $\text{OP} \in \{\text{OR}, \text{AND}\}$. (In the notation $\alpha_B(T, \beta_\alpha)$, the index B refers to the "bottom-up" computation.)

An extensive overview of attribute domains and their classification can be found in [19]. The article [4] contains a case study and guidelines for practical application of the bottom-up procedure. Numerous examples of attributes for attack trees and attack trees extended with additional sequential refinement have been given in [13,15]. We gather some relevant attribute domains for attack–defense trees in Table 1.

Table 1. Selected attribute domains for attack–defense trees

Attribute	D_α	OR_α^p	AND_α^p	OR_α^o	AND_α^o	C_α^p	C_α^o	$\beta_\alpha(b^o)$
min. attack cost	$\mathbb{R}_{\geq 0} \cup \{+\infty\}$	min	+	+	min	+	min	$+\infty$
max. damage	$\mathbb{R}_{\geq 0} \cup \{-\infty\}$	max	+	+	max	+	max	$-\infty$
min. skill level	$\mathbb{N} \cup \{0, +\infty\}$	min	max	max	min	max	min	$+\infty$
min. nb of experts	$\mathbb{N} \cup \{0, +\infty\}$	min	+	+	min	+	min	$+\infty$
satisfiability for p	$\{0,1\}$	$\vee$	$\wedge$	$\wedge$	$\vee$	$\wedge$	$\vee$	0

Example 4 illustrates the bottom-up procedure on the tree from Fig. 1.

Example 4. Consider the tree T given in Fig. 1, and let α be the *minimal attack cost* attribute (see Table 1 for its attribute domain). We fix the basic assignment β_{cost} to be as follows:

basic action b	$\beta_{\text{cost}}(b)$	basic action b	$\beta_{\text{cost}}(b)$
stealCard	60	force	100
camera	75	withdrawCash	10
phish	70	eavesdrop	20
guessPwd	120	guessUN	120
logIn&execTrans	10	stealPhone	60

Furthermore, for every basic action b of the opponent, we set $\beta_{\text{cost}}(b) = +\infty$. The bottom-up computation of the *minimal cost* on T gives

$$\text{cost}_B(T, \beta_{\text{cost}}) = 165.$$

This value corresponds to monitoring with the camera, eavesdropping on the victim to learn their PIN, stealing the card, and withdrawing money.

As already noticed in [22], the value of an attribute for a tree can also be evaluated directly on its semantic. For our purposes we define this evaluation as follows.

Definition 5. *Let $(D_\alpha, OR_\alpha^p, AND_\alpha^p, OR_\alpha^o, AND_\alpha^o, C_\alpha^p, C_\alpha^o)$ be an attribute domain and let T be an attack–defense tree with a basic assignment β_α. The value of the attribute α for T evaluated on the set semantics, denoted $\alpha_S(T, \beta_\alpha)$, is defined as*

$$\alpha_\mathcal{S}(T, \beta_\alpha) = (\text{OR}^\text{P}_\alpha)_{(P,O)\in\mathcal{S}(T)}\left(\text{C}^\text{P}_\alpha\big((\text{AND}^\text{P}_\alpha)_{b\in P}\beta_\alpha(b), (\text{OR}^\text{O}_\alpha)_{b\in O}\beta_\alpha(b)\big)\right).$$

(In the notation $\alpha_\mathcal{S}(T, \beta_\alpha)$, the index $\mathcal{S}$ refers to the computation on the "set semantics".)

Example 5. Consider again the tree from Fig. 1 and the basic assignment for the *minimal cost* attribute given in Example 4. The cost of all elements of the set semantics for T are as follows

$(\{\texttt{force}, \texttt{stealCard}, \texttt{withdrawCash}\}, \emptyset)$,	170
$(\{\texttt{camera}, \texttt{eavesdrop}, \texttt{stealCard}, \texttt{withdrawCash}\}, \emptyset)$,	165
$(\{\texttt{eavesdrop}, \texttt{stealCard}, \texttt{withdrawCash}\}, \{\texttt{coverKey}\})$	$+\infty$
$(\{\texttt{phish}, \texttt{logIn\&execTrans}\}, \{\texttt{SMS}\})$,	$+\infty$
$(\{\texttt{phish}, \texttt{guessUN}, \texttt{logIn\&execTrans}\}, \{\texttt{SMS}\})$,	$+\infty$
$(\{\texttt{phish}, \texttt{guessPwd}, \texttt{logIn\&execTrans}\}, \{\texttt{strongPWD}, \texttt{SMS}\})$,	$+\infty$
$(\{\texttt{guessUN}, \texttt{guessPwd}, \texttt{logIn\&execTrans}\}, \{\texttt{strongPWD}, \texttt{SMS}\})$,	$+\infty$
$(\{\texttt{phish}, \texttt{stealPhone}, \texttt{logIn\&execTrans}\}, \emptyset)$,	140
$(\{\texttt{phish}, \texttt{guessUN}, \texttt{stealPhone}, \texttt{logIn\&execTrans}\}, \emptyset)$,	260
$(\{\texttt{phish}, \texttt{guessPwd}, \texttt{stealPhone}, \texttt{logIn\&execTrans}\}, \{\texttt{strongPWD}\})$,	$+\infty$
$(\{\texttt{guessUN}, \texttt{guessPwd}, \texttt{stealPhone}, \texttt{logIn\&execTrans}\}, \{\texttt{strongPWD}\})$	$+\infty$.

The evaluation of the *minimal cost* attribute on the set semantics for T gives

$$\alpha_\mathcal{S}(T, \beta_{\text{cost}}) = \min\{170, 165, +\infty, 140, 260\} = 140,$$

which corresponds to performing the phishing attack to get the user name and their password, stealing the phone, and logging into the online bank application to execute the transfer.

Notice that the values obtained for the same tree in Examples 4 and 5 are different, despite the fact that the same basic assignment and the same attribute domain have been used. This is due to the fact that the tree from Fig. 1 contains cloned nodes which the standard bottom-up evaluation cannot handle properly. In the next section, we provide conditions and develop a method for a proper evaluation of attributes on attack–defense trees with cloned nodes.

4   Quantification On Attack–Defense Trees with Clones

Depending on what is considered to be an attack in an attack–defense tree, different semantics can be used. Note that a semantics for attack–defense trees naturally introduces an equivalence relation in $\mathbb{T}$. It is thus of great importance to select a method of quantitative analysis that is consistent with a chosen semantics, i.e., a method that for any two trees equivalent wrt the employed semantics returns the same result. This issue was recognized by the authors of [22] for attack trees, and addressed, in the case of attack–defense trees in [18], with the notion of compatibility between an attribute domain and a semantics. Below, we adapt the definition of compatibility from [18] to the bottom-up computation.

Definition 6. *Let* $A_\alpha = (D_\alpha, \text{OR}_\alpha^p, \text{AND}_\alpha^p, \text{OR}_\alpha^o, \text{AND}_\alpha^o, \text{C}_\alpha^p, \text{C}_\alpha^o)$ *be an attribute domain. The bottom-up procedure, defined in Definition 4, is compatible with a semantics* $\equiv$ *for attack–defense trees, if for every two trees* T_1, T_2 *satisfying* $T_1 \equiv T_2$, *the equality* $\alpha_B(T_1, \beta_\alpha) = \alpha_B(T_2, \beta_\alpha)$ *holds for any basic assignment* β_α.

For instance, it is well-known that the bottom-up computation of the *minimal cost* using the domain from Table 1 is not compatible with the propositional semantics. Indeed, consider the trees $T_1 = \text{OR}^p(\text{b}, \text{AND}(\text{b}', \text{b}''))$ and $T_2 = \text{AND}^p(\text{OR}^p(\text{b}, \text{b}'), (\text{b}, \text{b}''))$ whose corresponding propositional formulæ are equivalent. However, for the basic assignment $\beta_{\text{cost}}(\text{b}) = 3$, $\beta_{\text{cost}}(\text{b}') = 4$, $\beta_{\text{cost}}(\text{b}'') = 1$ the values $\alpha_B(T_1, \beta_\alpha) = 3$ and $\alpha_B(T_2, \beta_\alpha) = 4$ are different. Similarly, the bottom-up computation of the *minimal cost* attribute is not compatible with the set semantics. This can be shown by considering trees $T_3 = \text{AND}^p(\text{b}, \text{b})$ and $T_4 = \text{b}$ and will further be discussed in Corollary 1.

This notion of compatibility defined in Definition 6 can be generalized to any computation on attack–defense trees.

Definition 7. *Let* $\mathcal{D}$ *be a set and let* f *be a function on* $\mathbb{T} \times \mathcal{D}$. *We say that* f *is compatible with a semantics* $\equiv$ *for attack–defense trees, if for every two trees* T_1, T_2 *satisfying* $T_1 \equiv T_2$ *the equality* $f(T_1, d) = f(T_2, d)$ *holds for any* $d \in \mathcal{D}$.

To illustrate the difference between the compatibility notions defined in Definitions 6 and 7, one can consider the method for computing the so called *attacker's expected outcome*, proposed by Jürgenson and Willemson in [17]. Since this method is not based on an attribute domain, it cannot be simulated using the bottom-up evaluation. However, the authors show that the outcome of their computations is independent from the Boolean representation of an attack tree. This means that the method proposed in [17] is compatible with the propositional semantics for attack trees.

Remark 1. Consider an attribute domain $A_\alpha = (D_\alpha, \oplus, \otimes, \otimes, \oplus, \otimes, \oplus)$ with $\oplus$ and $\otimes$ being binary, associative, and commutative operations on $D_\alpha{}^2$. Under these assumptions, for a tree T and a basic assignment β_α, we have

$$\alpha_S(T, \beta_\alpha) = \bigoplus_{(P,O) \in \mathcal{S}(T)} \left(\otimes \left(\bigotimes_{\text{b} \in P} \beta_\alpha(\text{b}), \bigotimes_{\text{b} \in O} \beta_\alpha(\text{b}) \right) \right)$$

$$= \bigoplus_{(P,O) \in \mathcal{S}(T)} \bigotimes_{\text{b} \in P \cup O} \beta_\alpha(\text{b}).$$

---

[2] Note that a binary and associative operation can be modeled with an unranked operator.

Since for any two trees T_1 and T_2 that are equivalent wrt the set semantics the expressions $\alpha_S(T_1, \beta_\alpha)$ and $\alpha_S(T_2, \beta_\alpha)$ differ only in the order of the terms, they yield the same (numerical) result. In other words, under the above assumptions, the computation α_S is compatible with the set semantics.

As it has been observed in [18,19], there is a wide class of attribute domains of the form $(D_\alpha, \oplus, \otimes, \otimes, \oplus, \otimes, \oplus)$, where $(D_\alpha, \oplus, \otimes)$ constitutes a commutative idempotent semiring. Recall that an algebraic structure $(R, \oplus, \otimes)$ is a commutative idempotent semiring if $\oplus$ is an idempotent operation, both operations $\oplus$ and $\otimes$ are associative and commutative, their neutral elements, denoted here by $e_\oplus$ and $e_\otimes$, belong to R, operation $\otimes$ distributes over $\oplus$, and the absorbing element of $\otimes$, denoted $a_\otimes$, is equal to $e_\oplus$.

Remark 2. In order for the computations performed using the bottom-up evaluation to be consistent with the intuition, the basic actions of the opponent are assigned a specific value. In the case of an attribute domain $(D_\alpha, \oplus, \otimes, \otimes, \oplus, \otimes, \oplus)$ based on a commutative idempotent semiring $(D_\alpha, \oplus, \otimes)$ this value is equal to $a_\otimes$. One of the consequences of this choice is that if for every attack $(P, O) \in \mathcal{S}(T)$ the set O is not empty, then $\alpha_S(T, \beta_\alpha) = a_\otimes = e_\oplus$, indicating the fact that the proponent cannot achieve the root goal if the opponent executes all of their actions present in the tree. Note that this is closely related to the choice of the functions $C_\alpha^P = \otimes$ and $C_\alpha^O = \oplus$.

Example 6. For instance, in the case of the *minimal cost* attribute domain (cf. Table 1), which is based on the idempotent commutative semiring $(\mathbb{R}_{\geq 0} \cup \{+\infty\}, \min, +)$, the basic actions of the opponent are originally assigned $+\infty$, which is both a neutral element for the min operation, and the absorbing element for the addition. This implies that, if on a certain path, there is an opponent's action which is not countered by the proponent, the corresponding branch will result in the value $+\infty$, which models that it is impossible (since too costly) for the proponent. This is due to the fact that $C_{\text{cost}}^P = +$. However, if the opponent's action is countered by the proponent's action, the corresponding branch will yield a real value different from $+\infty$, because the min operator, used for C_{cost}^O, will be applied between a real number assigned to the proponent's counter and the $+\infty$.

The first contribution of this work is presented in Theorem 1. It establishes a relation between the evaluation of attributes via the bottom-up procedure and their evaluation on the set semantics. Its proof is postponed to Sect. 5.

Theorem 1. *Let T be an attack–defense tree generated by grammar (1) and let $A_\alpha = (D_\alpha, \oplus, \otimes, \otimes, \oplus, \otimes, \oplus)$ be an attribute domain such that the operations $\oplus$ and $\otimes$ are associative and commutative, $\oplus$ is idempotent, and $\otimes$ distributes over $\oplus$. If*

- *there are no repeated labels in T, or*
- *the operator $\otimes$ is idempotent,*

then the equality $\alpha_B(T, \beta_\alpha) = \alpha_S(T, \beta_\alpha)$ holds for any basic assignment β_α.

Note that the assumptions of Theorem 1 are satisfied by any commutative idempotent semiring, thus the same result also holds for attributes whose attribute domains are based on commutative idempotent semirings. Furthermore, one can compare the assumption on the lack of repeated labels in Theorem 1 with the linearity of an attack–defense tree, considered in [2]. The authors of [2] have proven that under this strong assumption, the evaluation method that they have developed for multi-parameter attributes coincides with their bottom-up evaluation.

Remark 3. Consider again the attribute domain specified in Theorem 1. Suppose that the operation $\otimes$ is not idempotent. Then there exists $d \in D_\alpha$, such that $d \otimes d \neq d$. In consequence, for $\beta_\alpha(\mathsf{b}) = d$ and the trees $T_1 = \mathsf{b}$ and $T_2 = \mathrm{AND}^\mathrm{P}(\mathsf{b}, \mathsf{b})$ that are equivalent wrt to the set semantics, we have $\alpha_B(T_1, \beta_\alpha) \neq \alpha_B(T_2, \beta_\alpha)$. This shows that if the operation $\otimes$ is not idempotent, then the bottom-up evaluation based on the attribute domain satisfying the remaining assumptions of Theorem 1 is not compatible with the set semantics.

Theorem 1 and Remarks 1 and 3 immediately yield the following corollary.

Corollary 1. *Let $A_\alpha = (D_\alpha, \oplus, \otimes, \otimes, \oplus, \otimes, \oplus)$ be an attribute domain such that the operations $\oplus$ and $\otimes$ are associative and commutative, $\oplus$ is idempotent, and $\otimes$ distributes over $\oplus$. The bottom-up procedure based on A_α is compatible with the set semantics if and only if the operation $\otimes$ is idempotent.*

We can also notice that if the assumptions from Corollary 1 are satisfied but the operation $\otimes$ is not idempotent, then the bottom-up procedure is compatible with the so called multiset semantics (introduced for attack trees in [22] and attack–defense trees in [18]) which uses pairs of multisets instead of pairs of sets.

Some of the domains based on idempotent semirings have a specific property that we encapsulate in the notion of *non-increasing* domain.

Definition 8. *Let A_α be an attribute domain. We say that A_α is non-increasing if $A_\alpha = (D_\alpha, \oplus, \otimes, \otimes, \oplus, \otimes, \oplus)$, $(D_\alpha, \oplus, \otimes)$ is a commutative idempotent semiring, and for every $d, c \in D_\alpha$, the inequality $d \otimes c \preceq d$ holds, where $\preceq$ stands for the canonical partial order on D_α, i.e., the order defined by $d \preceq c$ if and only if $d \oplus c = c$.*

Example 7. From the attribute domains presented in Table 1 all but one are non-increasing. The only one which is not non-increasing is the *maximal damage* domain.

Note that in order to be able to evaluate the value of an attribute on the set semantics $\mathcal{S}(T)$, one needs to construct the semantics itself. This task might be computationally expensive, since, in the worst case, the number of elements of $\mathcal{S}(T)$ is exponential in the number of nodes of T. In contrast, the complexity of the bottom-up procedure is linear in the number of nodes of the underlying tree (if the operations performed on the intermediate nodes are linear in the number of arguments). Thus, it is desirable to ensure that $\alpha_B(T, \beta_\alpha) = \alpha_\mathcal{S}(T, \beta_\alpha)$.

338   B. Kordy and W. Wideł

By Theorem 1, this equality holds in a wide class of attributes, provided that there are no clones in T. If T contains clones, then the two methods might return different values (as illustrated in Remark 3).

To deal with this issue, we present our second contribution of this work. In Algorithm 1, we propose a method of evaluating the value of attributes having non-increasing domains on attack–defense trees, that takes the repetition of labels into account. The algorithm relies on the following notion of *necessary clones*.

Definition 9. *Let* b *be a cloned basic action of the proponent in an attack–defense tree* T. *If* b *is present in every attack of the form* $(P, \emptyset) \in \mathcal{S}(T)$, *then* b *is a necessary clone; otherwise it is an optional clone.*

It is easy to see that the tree from Fig. 1 does not contain any necessary clones. Indeed, this tree contains only one clone – phish – however, there exists the attack $(\{\texttt{force}, \texttt{stealCard}, \texttt{withdrawCash}\}, \emptyset)$ which does not make use of the corresponding phishing action.

The sets of all necessary and optional clones in a tree T are denoted with $\mathcal{C}_N(T)$ and $\mathcal{C}_O(T)$, respectively. When there is no danger of ambiguity, we use $\mathcal{C}_N$ and $\mathcal{C}_O$ instead of $\mathcal{C}_N(T)$ and $\mathcal{C}_O(T)$. The idea behind Algorithm 1 is to first recognize the set $\mathcal{C}_N$ of necessary clones and temporarily ensure that the values of the attribute assigned to them do not influence the result of the bottom–up procedure. Then the values of the optional clones are also temporarily modified, and the corresponding bottom-up evaluations are performed. Only then the result is adjusted in such a way that the original values of the necessary clones are taken into account. Before explaining Algorithm 1 in detail, we provide a simple method for determining whether a cloned basic action of the proponent is a necessary clone in the following lemma.

Lemma 1. *Let* T *be an attack–defense tree generated by grammar* (1) *and* $a \in \mathbb{B}^P$ *be a cloned action of the proponent in* T. *Let* α *be the minimal skill level attribute (cf. Table 1) with the following basic assignment, for* $b \in \mathbb{B}$

$$\beta_{\mathrm{skill}}(\mathtt{b}) = \begin{cases} 0 & \textit{if } \mathtt{b} \neq \mathtt{a} \textit{ and } \mathtt{b} \in \mathbb{B}^P, \\ 1 & \textit{if } \mathtt{b} = \mathtt{a}, \\ +\infty & \textit{otherwise.} \end{cases}$$

Then, a *is a necessary clone in* T *if and only if* $\mathrm{skill}_B(T, \beta_{\mathrm{skill}}) = 1$.

Proof. Observe that under the given basic assignment the value of $\mathrm{skill}_S(T, \beta_{\mathrm{skill}})$ is equal to 1 if and only if a is a necessary clone. Since max is an idempotent operation, $\mathrm{skill}_B(T, \beta_{\mathrm{skill}}) = \mathrm{skill}_S(T, \beta_{\mathrm{skill}})$, by Theorem 1. The lemma follows. □

We now explain our algorithm for evaluating attributes on attack–defense trees with repeated labels. Algorithm 1 takes as input an attack–defense tree T generated by grammar (1), an attribute domain A_α, and a basic assignment β_α for the attribute. Once the sets of necessary and the optional clones have been determined, new basic assignments are created. Under each of these assignments β'_α, the necessary clones receive value $e_\otimes$ (in line 3). Intuitively, this ensures two things. First, that when the bottom–up procedure with the assignment β'_α is performed (in line 8), the value selected at the nodes corresponding to a choice made by the proponent (e.g., at the $\mathtt{OR}^\mathrm{P}$ nodes) is likely to be the one corresponding to a subset of actions of some optimal attack (i.e., a subset containing a necessary clone). The second outcome is that in the final result of the algorithm, the values of β_α assigned to the necessary clones are taken into account exactly once (line 11).

Algorithm 1. Evaluation of attributes in attack–defense tree with clones

---

Input: Attack–defense tree T, attribute domain $(D_\alpha, \oplus, \otimes, \otimes, \oplus, \otimes, \oplus)$, $\beta_\alpha : \mathbb{B} \to D_\alpha$
Output: $\alpha_\mathcal{A}(T, \beta_\alpha)$

1: $\alpha_\mathcal{A}(T, \beta_\alpha) \leftarrow e_\otimes$
2: initialize $\mathcal{C}_N$, $\mathcal{C}_O$
3: $\beta'_\alpha(\mathbf{b}) \leftarrow e_\otimes$ for every $\mathbf{b} \in \mathcal{C}_N$
4: $\beta'_\alpha(\mathbf{b}) \leftarrow \beta_\alpha(\mathbf{b})$ for every $\mathbf{b} \in \mathbb{B} \setminus (\mathcal{C}_N \cup \mathcal{C}_O)$
5: **for** every subset $\mathcal{C} \subseteq \mathcal{C}_O$ **do**
6:     $\beta'_\alpha(\mathbf{b}) \leftarrow a_\otimes$ for every $\mathbf{b} \in \mathcal{C}$
7:     $\beta'_\alpha(\mathbf{b}) \leftarrow e_\otimes$ for every $\mathbf{b} \in \mathcal{C}_O \setminus \mathcal{C}$
8:     $r^c \leftarrow \alpha_B(T, \beta'_\alpha) \otimes \bigotimes_{\mathbf{b} \in \mathcal{C}_O \setminus \mathcal{C}} \beta_\alpha(\mathbf{b})$
9:     $\alpha_\mathcal{A}(T, \beta_\alpha) \leftarrow \alpha_\mathcal{A}(T, \beta_\alpha) \oplus r^c$
10: **end for**
11: $\alpha_\mathcal{A}(T, \beta_\alpha) \leftarrow \alpha_\mathcal{A}(T, \beta_\alpha) \otimes \bigotimes_{\mathbf{b} \in \mathcal{C}_N} \beta_\alpha(\mathbf{b})$
12: **return** $\alpha_\mathcal{A}(T, \beta_\alpha)$

In lines 6–7, an assignment β'_α is created for every subset $\mathcal{C}$ of the set of optional clones $\mathcal{C}_O$. The clones from $\mathcal{C}$ are assigned $a_\otimes$, which intuitively ensures that they are ignored by the bottom–up procedure, and the remaining optional clones are assigned $e_\otimes$ (again, to ensure that their values under β_α will eventually be counted exactly once). The result of computations performed in the **for** loop is multiplied (in the sense of performing operation $\otimes$) in line 11 by the product of values assigned to the necessary clones. (Note that the index $\mathcal{A}$ in the notation $\alpha_\mathcal{A}(T, \beta_\alpha)$ refers to the evaluation using Algorithm 1.)

Example 8. We illustrate Algorithm 1 on the tree T from Fig. 1 and the *minimal cost* attribute domain. Consider the basic assignment of cost given in Example 4. Observe that $\mathcal{C}_N = \emptyset$ and $\mathcal{C}_O = \{\mathtt{phish}\}$.

The sets $\mathcal{C}$ considered in the **for** loop, their influence on the assignment of cost, and their corresponding results r^c are the following

$$\mathcal{C} = \emptyset, \qquad \beta'_{cost}(\mathtt{phish}) = 0, \qquad r^c = 140,$$
$$\mathcal{C} = \{\mathtt{phish}\}, \qquad \beta'_{cost}(\mathtt{phish}) = +\infty, \qquad r^c = 165.$$

The value of $\mathrm{cost}_{\mathcal{A}}(T, \beta_{\mathrm{cost}})$ after the **for** loop is $\min\{140, 165\}$. Since $\mathcal{C}_N = \emptyset$, the algorithm returns $\mathrm{cost}_{\mathcal{A}}(T, \beta_{\mathrm{cost}}) = 140$. This value corresponds to the cost of the attack $(\{\texttt{phish}, \texttt{logIn\&execTrans}, \texttt{stealPhone}\}, \emptyset)$, which is indeed the cheapest attack in the tree under the given basic assignment, as already illustrated in Example 5. Notice furthermore, that $\mathrm{cost}_{\mathcal{A}}(T, \beta_{\mathrm{cost}}) = \alpha_{\mathcal{S}}(T, \beta_{\mathrm{cost}})$ (cf. Example 5).

Now we turn our attention to complexity of Algorithm 1. Let k be the number of distinct clones of the proponent in T. Furthermore, let n be the number of nodes in T. We assume that the complexity of operations $\oplus$ and $\otimes$ is linear in the number of arguments, which is a reasonable assumption in the view of the existing attribute domains (cf. Table 1). This implies that the result of a single bottom up-procedure in T is obtained in time $\mathcal{O}(n)$. Thus, from the operations performed in lines 1–4, the most complex one is the initialization of the sets $\mathcal{C}_N$ and $\mathcal{C}_O$, the time complexity of which is in $\mathcal{O}(kn)$ (by Lemma 1). Since the **for** loop from line 5 iterates over all of the subsets of the optional clones, and the operations inside the loop are linear in n, the overall time complexity of Algorithm 1 is in $\mathcal{O}(n2^k)$.

In Theorem 2 we give sufficient conditions for the result $\alpha_{\mathcal{A}}(T, \beta_{\alpha})$ of Algorithm 1 to be equal to the result $\alpha_{\mathcal{S}}(T, \beta_{\alpha})$ of evaluation on the set semantics. Its proof is presented in Sect. 5.

Theorem 2. *Let T be an attack–defense tree generated by grammar (1) and A_{α} be a non–increasing attribute domain. Then the equality $\alpha_{\mathcal{A}}(T, \beta_{\alpha}) = \alpha_{\mathcal{S}}(T, \beta_{\alpha})$ holds for every basic assignment $\beta_{\alpha} \colon \mathbb{B} \to D_{\alpha}$ satisfying $\beta_{\alpha}|_{\mathbb{B}^{\circ}} \equiv \mathtt{a}_{\otimes}$.*

Remark 1 and Theorem 2 imply the following corollary.

Corollary 2. *Let $A_{\alpha} = (D_{\alpha}, \oplus, \otimes, \otimes, \oplus, \otimes, \oplus)$ be a non–increasing attribute domain and let $\beta := \{\beta_{\alpha} \colon \mathbb{B} \to D_{\alpha} \text{ st } \beta_{\alpha}|_{\mathbb{B}^{\circ}} \equiv \mathtt{a}_{\otimes}\}$. Then, the evaluation procedure $\alpha_{\mathcal{A}} \colon \mathbb{T} \times \beta \to D_{\alpha}$ specified by Algorithm 1 is compatible with the set semantics (in the sense of Definition 7).*

5   Proofs of Theorems 1 and 2

Throughout this section it is assumed that T is an attack–defense tree generated by grammar (1) and $A_{\alpha} = (D_{\alpha}, \oplus, \otimes, \otimes, \oplus, \otimes, \oplus)$ is an attribute domain with the operations $\oplus$ and $\otimes$ that are associative and commutative, $\oplus$ is idempotent, and $\otimes$ distributes over $\oplus$. We begin with examining parallels between attribute domains of this type and the set semantics.

Since the operation $\otimes$ distributes over $\oplus$, the result of the bottom–up procedure for any basic assignment β_{α} of α can be represented as

$$\alpha_B(T, \beta_{\alpha}) = (\beta_{\alpha}(\mathbf{b}_1^1) \otimes \beta_{\alpha}(\mathbf{b}_2^1) \otimes \ldots \otimes \beta_{\alpha}(\mathbf{b}_{k_1}^1)) \oplus$$

$$\cdots$$

$$\oplus (\beta_{\alpha}(\mathbf{b}_1^i) \otimes \beta_{\alpha}(\mathbf{b}_2^i) \otimes \ldots \otimes \beta_{\alpha}(\mathbf{b}_{k_i}^i)) \oplus \quad (3)$$

$$\cdots$$

$$\oplus (\beta_{\alpha}(\mathbf{b}_1^n) \otimes \beta_{\alpha}(\mathbf{b}_2^n) \otimes \ldots \otimes \beta_{\alpha}(\mathbf{b}_{k_n}^n)).$$

Observe that with the set $D_{\mathcal{S}} = \wp(\wp(\mathbb{B}^p) \times \wp(\mathbb{B}^o))$ and the operation $\odot$ defined by equality (2), the algebraic structure $(D_{\mathcal{S}}, \cup, \odot)$ constitutes a commutative idempotent semiring. Consider the attribute domain $A_{\mathcal{S}} = (D_{\mathcal{S}}, \cup, \odot, \odot, \cup, \odot, \cup)$ and the basic assignment

$$\beta_{\mathcal{S}}(b) = \begin{cases} \{(\{b\}, \emptyset)\} & \text{if } b \in \mathbb{B}^p, \\ \{(\emptyset, \{b\})\} & \text{otherwise.} \end{cases}$$

Clearly, $\mathcal{S}(T) = \mathcal{S}_B(T, \beta_{\mathcal{S}})$. By the previous observations $\mathcal{S}_B(T, \beta_{\mathcal{S}})$ can be represented as

$$\mathcal{S}_B(T, \beta_{\mathcal{S}}) = (\beta_{\mathcal{S}}(b_1^1) \odot \beta_{\mathcal{S}}(b_2^1) \odot \cdots \odot \beta_{\mathcal{S}}(b_{k_1}^1)) \cup$$

$$\cdots$$

$$\cup (\beta_{\mathcal{S}}(b_1^i) \odot \beta_{\mathcal{S}}(b_2^i) \odot \cdots \odot \beta_{\mathcal{S}}(b_{k_i}^i)) \cup \qquad (4)$$

$$\cdots$$

$$\cup (\beta_{\mathcal{S}}(b_1^n) \odot \beta_{\mathcal{S}}(b_2^n) \odot \cdots \odot \beta_{\mathcal{S}}(b_{k_n}^n)).$$

We chose the representations (3) and (4) in such a way that for $i \in \{1, \ldots, n\}$ and $j \in \{1, \ldots, k_i\}$ the basic action b_j^i in (3) is the same as b_j^i in (4), which is possible due to the commutativity of the operations.

From definitions of the basic assignment $\beta_{\mathcal{S}}$ and the operation $\odot$ it follows that for every $i \in \{1, \ldots, n\}$ the ith term

$$\beta_{\mathcal{S}}(b_1^i) \odot \beta_{\mathcal{S}}(b_2^i) \odot \cdots \odot \beta_{\mathcal{S}}(b_{k_i}^i)$$

of representation (4) is a set consisting of exactly one pair of sets. Let us denote this term with $\{(P_i, O_i)\}$. Observe that since $\mathcal{S}(T) = \mathcal{S}_B(T, \beta_{\mathcal{S}})$, we have $(P_i, O_i) \in \mathcal{S}(T)$ for every i, and, conversely, for every $(P, O) \in \mathcal{S}(T)$ there exists at least one i such that $(P, O) = (P_i, O_i)$.

Finally, we denote the ith term of representation (3) with α_i. Now we are ready to prove Theorem 1.

Proof of Theorem 1. If there are no repeated labels in T or the operator $\otimes$ is idempotent, then for $i \in \{1, \ldots, n\}$ it holds that $\alpha_i = \bigotimes_{b \in P_i \cup O_i} \beta_\alpha(b)$. Together with the idempotency of $\oplus$ this implies that

$$\alpha_B(T, \beta_\alpha) = \bigoplus_{i=1}^{n} \alpha_i = \bigoplus_{(P,O) \in \mathcal{S}(T)} \bigotimes_{b \in P \cup O} \beta_\alpha(b).$$

$\square$

We finish this section by providing the proof of Theorem 2.

Proof of Theorem 2. Consider a result r^c of the bottom–up procedure obtained in the line 8 of Algorithm 1 for a set $\mathcal{C} \subseteq \mathcal{C}_O$ of optional clones. Using representation (3), it can be written as

$$r^c = \alpha_B(T, \beta'_\alpha) \otimes \bigotimes_{b \in \mathcal{C}_O \setminus \mathcal{C}} \beta_\alpha(b)$$

$$= \left(\beta'_\alpha(b_1^1) \otimes \beta'_\alpha(b_2^1) \otimes \dots \otimes \beta'_\alpha(b_{k_1}^1)\right) \otimes \bigotimes_{b \in \mathcal{C}_O \setminus \mathcal{C}} \beta_\alpha(b) \oplus$$

$$\dots$$

$$\oplus \left(\beta'_\alpha(b_1^i) \otimes \beta'_\alpha(b_2^i) \otimes \dots \otimes \beta'_\alpha(b_{k_i}^i)\right) \otimes \bigotimes_{b \in \mathcal{C}_O \setminus \mathcal{C}} \beta_\alpha(b) \oplus$$

$$\dots$$

$$\oplus \left(\beta'_\alpha(b_1^n) \otimes \beta'_\alpha(b_2^n) \otimes \dots \otimes \beta'_\alpha(b_{k_n}^n)\right) \otimes \bigotimes_{b \in \mathcal{C}_O \setminus \mathcal{C}} \beta_\alpha(b).$$

Let us denote the ith term of the above expression with r_i^c. Observe that the result of Algorithm 1 is

$$\alpha_{\mathcal{A}}(T, \beta_\alpha) = \left[\bigoplus_{\mathcal{C} \subseteq \mathcal{C}_O} r^c\right] \otimes \bigotimes_{b \in \mathcal{C}_N} \beta_\alpha(b) = \left(\bigoplus_{i=1}^n \left[\bigoplus_{\mathcal{C} \subseteq \mathcal{C}_O} r_i^c\right]\right) \otimes \bigotimes_{b \in \mathcal{C}_N} \beta_\alpha(b).$$

Due to the values assigned to the optional clones in the **for** loop, the inner expression can be expanded as follows.

$$\bigoplus_{\mathcal{C} \subseteq \mathcal{C}_O} r_i^c = \left[\bigoplus_{\substack{\mathcal{C} \subseteq \mathcal{C}_O \\ \mathcal{C} \cap (P_i \cup O_i) \neq \emptyset}} [a_\otimes \otimes \bigotimes_{b \in \mathcal{C}_O \setminus \mathcal{C}} \beta_\alpha(b)]\right]$$

$$\oplus \bigoplus_{\substack{\mathcal{C} \subseteq \mathcal{C}_O \\ \mathcal{C} \cap (P_i \cup O_i) = \emptyset}} \left[\bigotimes_{\substack{b \in P_i \cup O_i \\ b \notin \mathcal{C}_N \cup \mathcal{C}_O}} \beta_\alpha(b) \otimes \bigotimes_{\substack{b \in P_i \cup O_i \\ b \in \mathcal{C}_N \cup \mathcal{C}_O \setminus \mathcal{C}}} e_\otimes \otimes \bigotimes_{b \in \mathcal{C}_O \setminus \mathcal{C}} \beta_\alpha(b)\right]$$

$$= \bigoplus_{\substack{\mathcal{C} \subseteq \mathcal{C}_O \\ \mathcal{C} \cap (P_i \cup O_i) = \emptyset}} \left[\bigotimes_{\substack{b \in P_i \cup O_i \\ b \notin \mathcal{C}_N}} \beta_\alpha(b) \otimes \bigotimes_{\substack{b \notin P_i \cup O_i \\ b \in \mathcal{C}_O \setminus \mathcal{C}}} \beta_\alpha(b)\right]$$

Since the attribute domain is non–increasing, the last "sum" is absorbed by the term corresponding to the set $\mathcal{C}$ satisfying $\mathcal{C}_O \setminus \mathcal{C} = (P_i \cup O_i) \cap \mathcal{C}_O$, namely, the term $\bigotimes_{\substack{b \in P_i \cup O_i \\ b \notin \mathcal{C}_N}} \beta_\alpha(b)$. Thus,

$$\alpha_{\mathcal{A}}(T, \beta_{\alpha}) = \left(\bigoplus_{i=1}^{n} \left[\bigotimes_{\substack{b \in P_i \cup O_i \\ b \notin \mathcal{C}_N}} \beta_{\alpha}(b) \right] \right) \otimes \bigotimes_{b \in \mathcal{C}_N} \beta_{\alpha}(b)$$

$$= \bigoplus_{i=1}^{n} \bigotimes_{b \in P_i \cup O_i} \beta_{\alpha}(b) = \bigoplus_{(P,O) \in \mathcal{S}(T)} \bigotimes_{b \in P \cup O} \beta_{\alpha}(b),$$

where the second equality follows from definition of necessary clones and the fact that $\beta_{\alpha}|_{\mathbb{B}^{\circ}} \equiv a_{\otimes}$, and the last one holds by the idempotency of $\oplus$. The proof is complete.   □

6 Conclusion

The goal of the work presented in this paper was to tackle the issue of quantitative analysis of attack–defense trees in which a basic action can appear multiple times. We have presented conditions ensuring that in this setting the classical, fast bottom-up procedure for attributes evaluation yields valid result. For a subclass of attributes, we have identified necessary and sufficient condition for compatibility of the bottom-up evaluation with the set semantics. A constructive method of evaluation of attributes belonging to a wide and important subclass of attributes, that takes the presence of repeated labels into account, has been presented.

This work addresses only the tip of the iceberg of a much larger problem which is the analysis and quantification of attack–defense trees with dependent actions. The notion of clones captures the strongest type of dependency between goals, namely where the nodes bearing the same label represent exactly the same instance of the same goal. It is thus obvious that the attribute values for the clones should only be considered once in the attribute computations. However, in practice, weaker dependencies between goals may also be present. For instance, when the attacker has access to a computer with sufficient computation power, the attack consisting in guessing a password becomes de facto the brute force attack and can be performed within a reasonable time, for most of the passwords used in practice. In contrast, if this attack is performed manually, it will, most probably, take much longer to succeed. Similarly, if the attacker knows the victim, guessing their password manually will, in most cases, be faster compared to the situation when the attacker is a stranger to the victim. Of course, this problem can be solved by relabeling the nodes and using differently named goals for the two situations. However, this solution is not in line with the practical usage of attack(–defense) trees whose construction often relies on preexisting libraries of attack patterns where the nodes are already labeled and the labels are as simple as possible. We are currently working on improving the standard bottom-up evaluation procedure for attributes (in the spirit of Algorithm 1) to accommodate such weakly dependent nodes.

Furthermore, it would be interesting to try to generalize Algorithm 1 for the approaches proposed in the past for the restricted class of attack–defense trees without repeated labels. Such approaches include for instance multi-objective optimization defined in [2] and a method for selecting the most suitable set of countermeasures, based on integer linear programing, developed in [21].

Acknowledgments. We would like to thank Angèle Bossuat for fruitful discussions on the interpretation of repeated labels in attack–defense trees and on possible approaches to the problem of quantification in the presence of clones.

References

1. Ruijters, E., Stoelinga, M.: Fault tree analysis: a survey of the state-of-the-art in modeling, analysis and tools. Comput. Sci. Rev. **15–16**, 29–62 (2015)
2. Aslanyan, Z., Nielson, F.: Pareto efficient solutions of attack-defence trees. In: Focardi, R., Myers, A. (eds.) POST 2015. LNCS, vol. 9036, pp. 95–114. Springer, Heidelberg (2015). https://doi.org/10.1007/978-3-662-46666-7_6
3. Aslanyan, Z., Nielson, F., Parker, D.: Quantitative verification and synthesis of attack-defence scenarios. In: CSF, pp. 105–119. IEEE Computer Society (2016)
4. Bagnato, A., Kordy, B., Meland, P.H., Schweitzer, P.: Attribute decoration of attack-defense trees. IJSSE **3**(2), 1–35 (2012)
5. Bossuat, A., Kordy, B.: Evil twins: handling repetitions in attack–defense trees – a survival guide. In: Liu, P., Mauw, S., Stølen, K. (eds.) GraMSec 2017. LNCS, vol. 10744, pp. 17–37. Springer, Cham (2018). https://doi.org/10.1007/978-3-319-74860-3_2
6. Codetta-Raiteri, D.: BDD based analysis of parametric fault trees. In: Proceedings of the RAMS 2006, Annual Reliability and Maintainability Symposium, RAMS 2006, pp. 442–449. IEEE Computer Society, Washington, DC (2006)
7. Fraile, M., Ford, M., Gadyatskaya, O., Kumar, R., Stoelinga, M., Trujillo-Rasua, R.: Using attack-defense trees to analyze threats and countermeasures in an ATM: a case study. In: Horkoff, J., Jeusfeld, M.A., Persson, A. (eds.) PoEM 2016. LNBIP, vol. 267, pp. 326–334. Springer, Cham (2016). https://doi.org/10.1007/978-3-319-48393-1_24
8. Gadyatskaya, O., Hansen, R.R., Larsen, K.G., Legay, A., Olesen, M.C., Poulsen, D.B.: Modelling attack-defense trees using timed automata. In: Fränzle, M., Markey, N. (eds.) FORMATS 2016. LNCS, vol. 9884, pp. 35–50. Springer, Cham (2016). https://doi.org/10.1007/978-3-319-44878-7_3
9. Gadyatskaya, O., Jhawar, R., Kordy, P., Lounis, K., Mauw, S., Trujillo-Rasua, R.: Attack trees for practical security assessment: ranking of attack scenarios with ADTool 2.0. In: Agha, G., Van Houdt, B. (eds.) QEST 2016. LNCS, vol. 9826, pp. 159–162. Springer, Cham (2016). https://doi.org/10.1007/978-3-319-43425-4_10
10. Haasl, D.F., Roberts, N.H., Veselay, W.E., Goldberg, F.F.: Fault tree handbook. Technical report, Systems and Reliability Research, Office of Nuclear Regulatory Research, U.S. Nuclear Regulatory Comission (1981)
11. Hermanns, H., Krämer, J., Krčál, J., Stoelinga, M.: The value of attack-defence diagrams. In: Piessens, F., Viganò, L. (eds.) POST 2016. LNCS, vol. 9635, pp. 163–185. Springer, Heidelberg (2016). https://doi.org/10.1007/978-3-662-49635-0_9
12. Hong, J.B., Kim, D.S., Chung, C.J., Huang, D.: A survey on the usability and practical applications of graphical security models. Comput. Sci. Rev. **26**, 1–16 (2017)

13. Horne, R., Mauw, S., Tiu, A.: Semantics for specialising attack trees based on linear logic. Fundam. Inform. **153**(1–2), 57–86 (2017)
14. Ivanova, M.G., Probst, C.W., Hansen, R.R., Kammüller, F.: Transforming graphical system models to graphical attack models. In: Mauw, S., Kordy, B., Jajodia, S. (eds.) GraMSec 2015. LNCS, vol. 9390, pp. 82–96. Springer, Cham (2016). https://doi.org/10.1007/978-3-319-29968-6_6
15. Jhawar, R., Kordy, B., Mauw, S., Radomirović, S., Trujillo-Rasua, R.: Attack trees with sequential conjunction. In: Federrath, H., Gollmann, D. (eds.) SEC 2015. IFIP AICT, vol. 455, pp. 339–353. Springer, Cham (2015). https://doi.org/10.1007/978-3-319-18467-8_23
16. Ji, X., Yu, H., Fan, G., Fu, W.: Attack-defense trees based cyber security analysis for CPSs. In: SNPD, pp. 693–698. IEEE Computer Society (2016)
17. Jürgenson, A., Willemson, J.: Computing exact outcomes of multi-parameter attack trees. In: Meersman, R., Tari, Z. (eds.) OTM 2008, Part II. LNCS, vol. 5332, pp. 1036–1051. Springer, Heidelberg (2008). https://doi.org/10.1007/978-3-540-88873-4_8
18. Kordy, B., Mauw, S., Radomirovic, S., Schweitzer, P.: Attack-defense trees. J. Log. Comput. **24**(1), 55–87 (2014)
19. Kordy, B., Mauw, S., Schweitzer, P.: Quantitative questions on attack–defense trees. In: Kwon, T., Lee, M.-K., Kwon, D. (eds.) ICISC 2012. LNCS, vol. 7839, pp. 49–64. Springer, Heidelberg (2013). https://doi.org/10.1007/978-3-642-37682-5_5
20. Kordy, B., Piètre-Cambacédès, L., Schweitzer, P.: Dag-based attack and defense modeling: Don't miss the forest for the attack trees. Comput. Sci. Rev. **13–14**, 1–38 (2014)
21. Kordy, B., Wideł, W.: How well can I secure my system? In: Polikarpova, N., Schneider, S. (eds.) IFM 2017. LNCS, vol. 10510, pp. 332–347. Springer, Cham (2017). https://doi.org/10.1007/978-3-319-66845-1_22
22. Mauw, S., Oostdijk, M.: Foundations of attack trees. In: Won, D.H., Kim, S. (eds.) ICISC 2005. LNCS, vol. 3935, pp. 186–198. Springer, Heidelberg (2006). https://doi.org/10.1007/11734727_17
23. National Electric Sector Cybersecurity Organization Resource (NESCOR): Analysis of selected electric sector high risk failure scenarios, version 2.0 (2015). http://smartgrid.epri.com/doc/NESCOR
24. Paja, E., Dalpiaz, F., Giorgini, P.: The socio-technical security requirements modelling language for secure composite services. In: Brucker, A.D., Dalpiaz, F., Giorgini, P., Meland, P.H., Rios, E. (eds.) Secure Service Composition. LNCS, vol. 8900. Springer, Cham (2014). https://doi.org/10.1007/978-3-319-13518-2_5
25. Pinchinat, S., Acher, M., Vojtisek, D.: ATSyRa: an integrated environment for synthesizing attack trees – (Tool Paper). In: Mauw, S., Kordy, B., Jajodia, S. (eds.) GraMSec 2015. LNCS, vol. 9390, pp. 97–101. Springer, Cham (2016). https://doi.org/10.1007/978-3-319-29968-6_7
26. Schneier, B.: Attack trees. Dr Dobb's J. Softw. Tools **24**, 21–29 (1999)
27. Stecher, K.: Evaluation of large fault-trees with repeated events using an efficient bottom-up algorithm. IEEE Trans. Reliab. **35**, 51–58 (1986)
28. Vigo, R., Nielson, F., Nielson, H.R.: Automated generation of attack trees. In: IEEE 27th Computer Security Foundations Symposium, CSF 2014, Vienna, Austria, 19–22 July 2014, pp. 337–350 (2014)

Author Index

Printed in the United States
By Bookmasters